THE SICILY CAMPAIGN

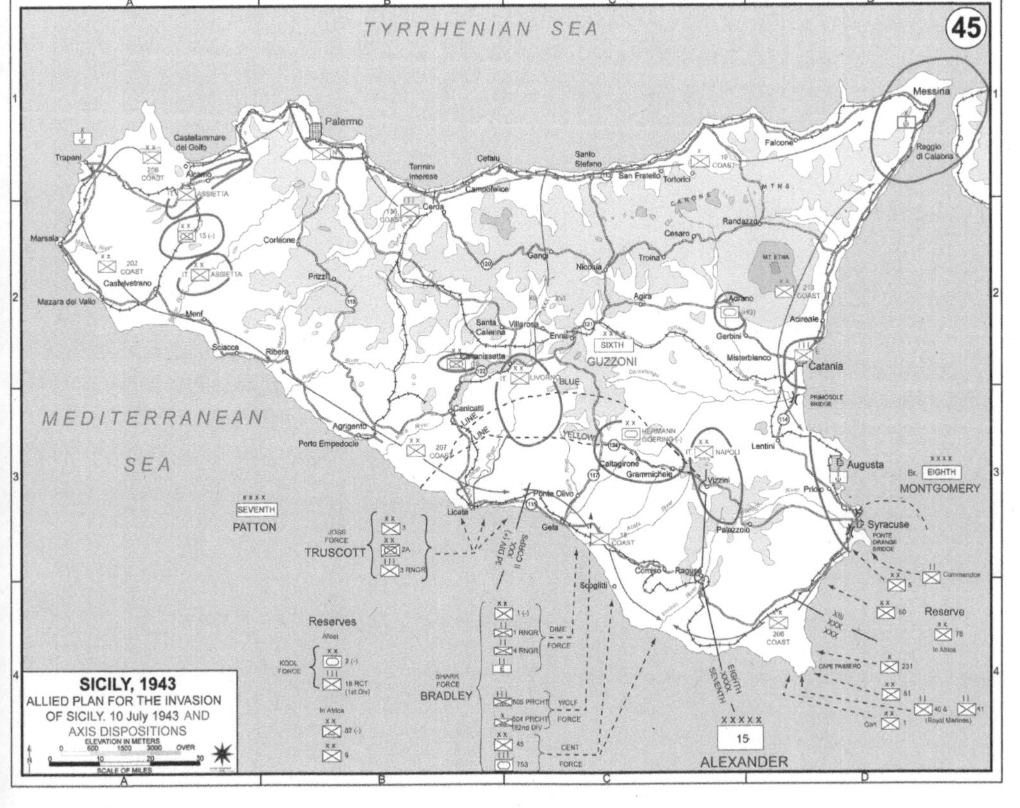

THE SICILY CAMPAIGN

From North Africa to Messina

WILLIAM F. BUCKINGHAM &
DUDLEY GILES

AMBERLEY

Bill Buckingham passed away in 2021 of Covid-related symptoms. I am indebted to Dudley Giles and all at Amberley Publishing for their perseverance in getting Bill's final book completed. Bill was a remarkable man, knowledgeable, passionate and meticulous about Military History. He was sometimes criticised for having too much detail in his books but that was the man he was. He would much rather explain things fully than leave things unsaid.

His other great passion was scootering. He was able to combine many research trips to Europe with Vespa Scooter events on the continent. These trips were planned to the last detail, much like his historical research.

This book is dedicated to all who knew Bill, through his love of Military History, his work within University of Glasgow and his many scootering friends, especially Mark and Kay, whom Bill loved.

Aileen Buckingham, 2025

First published 2025

Amberley Publishing
The Hill, Stroud
Gloucestershire, GL5 4EP

www.amberley-books.com

British Library Cataloguing in Publication Data.
A catalogue record for this book is available from the British Library.

ISBN 978 1 4456 9414 6 (hardback)
ISBN 978 1 4456 9415 3 (ebook)

1 2 3 4 5 6 7 8 9 10

Typesetting by SJmagic DESIGN SERVICES, India.
Printed in the UK.

Appointed GPSR EU Representative:
Easy Access System Europe Oü, 16879218
Address: Mustamäe tee 50, 10621, Tallinn, Estonia
Contact Details: gpsr.requests@easproject.com, +358 40 500 3575

Contents

Introduction

Over the Strait onto the European Mainland

Operation BAYTOWN and the Allied Invasion of Italy, September 1943

Operation BAYTOWN, the initial Allied invasion of mainland Italy across the Strait of Messina, took place in the early morning of Friday 3 September 1943. Major Peter Pettit Royal Artillery (RA), second-in-command of 17 Medium Regiment RA from the 78th Division recorded that the night of 2-3 September was 'dark but starry' when he joined Regimental commander Lieutenant-Colonel Tom Thomas on the coast road overlooking the Strait near the unit's Observation Post (OP) shortly before the supporting artillery programme commenced.[1] The latter was a spectacular large-scale affair, in part to mark the third anniversary of Britain's declaration of war on Germany and also in part, according to one source, as an ego-massaging 'self-indulgent extravaganza' for the benefit of then-General Sir Bernard Law Montgomery.[2] Be that as it may, the programme involved pre-planned fire on beach and coastal defences and artillery positions covering the landing beaches by 630 British field and medium guns drawn largely from XXX Corps and the 5th Army Group RA under the control of the former's Commander Royal Artillery (CRA), Brigadier M. E. Dennis, reinforced with a number of captured enemy heavy pieces manned by personnel from 11th Honourable Artillery Company (HAC).[3] This host was augmented by US Army artillery units and naval gunfire support from Royal Navy (RN) cruisers HMS *Mauritius*, *Orion* and *Uganda*, the monitors HMS *Abercrombie*, *Erebus* and *Roberts*, five RN destroyers, two gunboats and fourteen landing craft adapted to carry rockets and a variety of guns; one source also refers to the battleships HMS *Nelson*, *Rodney*, *Valiant* and *Warspite* being involved, although this may refer to the capital ships' bombardment of coastal artillery positions between Pellaro and Melito on the southern tip of the Calabrian peninsula in the latter half of August 1943, codenamed SLEDGEHAMMER, rather than the immediate pre-landing programme.[4]

The idea of a landing on the toe of Italy actually pre-dated the invasion of Sicily on 9 July 1943. A number of options for possible implementation once Sicily had been secured were mooted in May 1943 and discussed at the Algiers Conference at the end of that month, leading to Allied Forces HQ (AFHQ), the joint British-US command headed by Lieutenant-General Dwight D. Eisenhower, drawing up plans to cover future eventualities. These included plans to secure Sardinia and Corsica, codenamed Operations BRIMSTONE and FIREBRAND respectively, to extend Allied air coverage in case the operational and political conditions were not conducive for a rapid follow-on invasion of the southern Italian mainland, along with three schemes for landings on the latter if the conditions were conducive. Operation BUTTRESS involved a landing by the British X Corps in the vicinity of Gioia Tauro twenty miles or so east of the Strait of Messina on the north side of the Calabrian peninsula, Operation GOBLET was to be a landing by the British V Corps at Crotone on the south side of the peninsula on the eastern tip of the Gulf of Taranto, while the third scheme was for a landing near Taranto proper by the US 5th Army, codenamed Operation MUSKET; BUTTRESS was originally scheduled to commence a month after Sicily had been secured and GOBLET a month after that. In the event MUSKET was discarded in a revamp of AFHQ planning announced on 3 June 1943, although planning for it was revived by Eisenhower on 17 July as an alternative to Operation GANGWAY, the codename for a reinforcing landing in the vicinity of Naples that subsequently became Operation AVALANCHE, the landings at Salerno.[5] The final decision on the options was taken at a conference held by Eisenhower at Carthage on 16 August 1943, as the fighting in Sicily was winding down to a conclusion. The operations against Corsica and Sardinia were cancelled as surplus to requirements as was Operation MUSKET in favour of AVALANCHE, Operation GOBLET was retained as a contingency measure although it too was eventually cancelled on 4 September and BUTTRESS was cancelled in favour of Operation BAYTOWN, a crossing of the Strait of Messina between Reggio Calabria and Villa San Giovanni.[6]

Crossing the Strait of Messina onto the Italian mainland had long been viewed by the British as a 'natural extension' of the Sicilian campaign; as General The Hon. Sir Harold Alexander put it to Winston Churchill at a meeting on 22 July 1943 '...We are prepared to jump a bridgehead on to the mainland at the first opportunity.'[7] The US side of the Allied Force was more pragmatic however, not least because of the paucity of ground forces and more importantly landing craft available to carry out multiple landings. This reality became more pressing as the German withdrawal from Sicily and looming Italian surrender made Operation AVALANCHE an increasingly attractive prospect, and the latter began to take first-call on what resources were available from at least the beginning of August 1943. Thus at a meeting on 7 August Eisenhower had made clear that any move into Calabria should not rely on 'consuming too many of...[the]...scanty number of landing craft' or on the availability of Lieutenant-General Sir Richard McCreery's British X Corps because that formation was required for AVALANCHE.[8]

Despite Montgomery's vociferous insistence that he should have first call on McCreery's formation, Eisenhower's prioritisation was upheld at a subsequent meeting six days later which agreed that every effort was to be made to mount AVALANCHE and was finally confirmed at the Carthage conference on 16 August that, as we have seen, discarded the Corsica and Sardinia operations and cancelled Operations MUSKET & BUTTRESS. The latter was replaced by Operation BAYTOWN, which was on a much smaller scale employing just a reinforced brigade with four battalions rather than an entire corps.[9]

Montgomery was already dissatisfied that Lieutenant-General Mark Clark and the US 5th Army had been assigned to carry out AVALANCHE rather than his more experienced 8th Army and he did not react well to the downgrading of BAYTOWN.[10] On 19 August, just three days after the scaling down was confirmed and two days after General Alexander's 15th Army Group HQ assumed responsibility for AVALANCHE and BAYTOWN, Montgomery complained to Alexander that he '...had been given no clear object for the operation but assume the object to be to secure the Straits [of Messina] for the Navy and to act as a diversion for Avalanche'; in response Alexander clarified that Montgomery's task was '...to secure a bridgehead on the toe of Italy to enable our Naval forces to operate through the Straits of Messina. In the event of the enemy withdrawing from the "Toe" you will follow him up with such force as you can make available, bearing in mind that the greater the extent to which you can engage enemy forces in the southern toe of Italy the more assistance you will be giving to Avalanche.'[11] On the not unreasonable grounds that a reinforced brigade was insufficient for such a task Montgomery then reportedly pressured Alexander into allowing him to expand BAYTOWN back to a corps-sized operation, in part by playing up the prospect of 'massive German counterattacks and the prospects of a landing that would be defeated'.[12] The re-jigged Operation was to employ Lieutenant-General Miles Dempsey's XIII Corps, which appears to have been Montgomery's original intent, given that the Corps' two divisions had been warned off for the Messina crossing and Corps HQ withdrawn from the Sicily fighting in readiness on 6, 12 and 13 August respectively. Be that as it may, Montgomery considered the expansion gave him the wherewithal to 'crack about' in the Calabrian peninsula as directed.[13]

As a subsidiary operation the date for launching BAYTOWN was dictated by the need to shuttle landing craft back for the AVALANCHE landing and the moon and tide conditions at Salerno, which were favourable on 8-9 September 1943 and then again on 21 September; the former was selected as it was assumed that German reinforcements would be in place in the Naples area by the latter.[14] Eisenhower therefore ordered BAYTOWN to be launched on the night of 30-31 August but Montgomery demurred, claiming that he could not launch until the night of 4-5 September because the naval gunfire support would not be available until that date and cited Admiral Sir Andrew Cunningham, commander of Allied Naval Forces in the Mediterranean, in support of his claim; it is unclear if this was actually the case, given that Cunningham was reportedly '...furious at having his name taken in vain'.[15] Whether or not, a compromise was reached and the launch date for BAYTOWN was finally fixed for the night of 3-4 September. The landing was preceded by a considerable air effort intended to support both BAYTOWN and the subsequent landing at Salerno, conducted in part from newly constructed airfields in the area of Milazzo and Messina in Sicily's north-eastern tip.[16] The effort overall involved 1,500 Allied aircraft including 350 heavy bombers, 650 medium and light bombers, 160 fighter-bombers and 352 fighters; the latter figure included 110 carrier-based Supermarine Seafires and thirty-two night-fighters.[17] The objective of neutralising airfields across southern Italy was largely complete by 18 August and thereafter attention turned to interdicting railway links across the length of Italy as far north as Bologna. The BAYTOWN portion involved severing the rail lines running into the Calabrian peninsula and communications generally in that area, tasked to the Northwest African Tactical Air Force (NATAF). A force of seventy light bombers attacked the road and rail junctions in the vicinity of Nicastro at the head of the peninsula on Saturday 28 August and again the following day for example, while Allied fighter-bombers ranged freely, strafing road and rail traffic across Calabria, with particular attention being paid to the area around the proposed landing area near Reggio Calabria from around 26 August. In total, Mediterranean Air Command launched in excess of 13,300 sorties in the fifteen-day period between 17 August and 2 September, equating to 832 sorties every twenty-four hours, 3,800 of which were directed against road and rail communications; in the twelve days between 21 August and 3 September almost 4,000 tons of bombs were dropped on marshalling yard and airfield targets. The effort cost approximately 180 Allied aircraft in exchange for eighty-five German machines, five of which were likely downed by Allied anti-aircraft fire.[18]

The rugged nature of the Calabrian coast narrowed the landing site options but the planners selected an area of beach stretching three and a half miles north from the outskirts of Reggio Calabria where aerial reconnaissance had earlier spotted enemy lighters unloading during the Axis withdrawal across the Strait of Messina.[19] The landing area was bounded by dry riverbeds, the *Fiumare di Gallico* to the north and the *Fiumare dell'Annunziata* to the south in the outskirts of Reggio Calabria proper; a third, walled dry watercourse, the *Torrente Torbido*, bisected the centre of the landing frontage and divided it into two shallow bays. These were backed by a narrow stretch of cultivated ground, *Strada* 18 and the coast railway line, the latter perched atop a twenty-foot-high embankment with several underpasses for the intertwined roadway. The northern bay was allotted to Major-General Gerard Bucknall's 5th Division, with Brigadier A. D. Ward's 17th Brigade on the left tasked to advance north up *Strada* 18 to Villa San Giovanni, the terminus of the rail ferry from Messina and Brigadier Lorne M. Campbell's 13th Brigade on the right tasked to advance inland up the road toward San Stefano, eighteen miles from the coast. The southern bay, codenamed FOX, was subdivided by Major-General Guy Simonds' 1st Canadian Division into AMBER and GREEN Beaches to the north and south respectively, for collective use by Brigadier M. H. S. Penhale's Canadian 3rd Brigade. The West Nova Scotia Regiment was tasked to land at AMBER Beach and secure Point 305 approximately a mile inland, the site of two coastal defence forts overlooking the landing area equipped with four Italian 280mm howitzers and half a dozen smaller calibre pieces. GREEN Beach was to be secured by the Carleton & York Regiment which was peel off to the south and secure Reggio Calabria before pushing south along *Strada* 106 to occupy the airfield south of the city and the village of Gallina, just over two miles inland.[20] BAYTOWN was allotted a total of 268 landing craft to accomplish, which were then to return to the Sicilian side of the Strait to lift the Canadian 1st and British 15th Brigades. The independent 231st Brigade Group, 40 (RM) Commando, No. 3 Commando and the Special Reconnaissance Squadron were on standby to carry out supporting landings if required, while 154th Brigade from the 51st Highland Division was slated to take over from the assault force once all XIII Corps' initial objectives had been achieved.[21]

Zero Hour for BAYTOWN was set for 04:30 on the morning of Friday 3 September 1943, although the Canadian contingent did not make landfall until 04:50 due to confusion during the final marshalling for the run-in to the beach; navigation across the Strait of Messina was aided by illumination from searchlights on the Sicilian shore and automatic anti-aircraft guns firing strings of red tracer ammunition to mark the crossing boundaries. The pre-landing bombardment from 630 assorted Allied artillery pieces and 120 naval guns commenced an hour earlier at 03:30, augmented with 792 5-inch rockets launched 1,000 yards out from the beach by a number of specially configured Landing Craft Assault (LCA) vessels travelling with the assault wave.[22] In the event the beaches lacked the expected mines and barbed wire and the landing was unopposed and 1st Canadian Division HQ was informed of 'Success at Fox Green Amber at 05:26 hrs'. The absence of resistance allowed the Canadian 3rd Brigade's reserve to be landed immediately while the assault wave took over the follow-on wave's missions. As a result Point 305 was secured within two hours of the initial landing as the Italian garrisons had fled, which was perhaps fortunate, given the bombardment had made little impression on the coastal defence forts. Reggio Calabria and the nearby airfield were secured by 08:10 and Gallina shortly before midday, with the most serious resistance being encountered by 3rd Brigade HQ while setting up in the city's zoological gardens where an escaped puma reportedly 'took a fancy' to Brigadier Penhale. The day cost the 1st Canadian Division a total of nine wounded, none of them from the assault wave, in exchange for three German and 3,000 Italian prisoners.[23] The 5th Division enjoyed similar success, as did the post-assault build up. An Airfield Construction Group had the Reggio Calabria airfield ready to handle fighter aircraft by dusk on D-Day, and by the same time on D Plus One the stores and equipment landing effort was a day and a half ahead of schedule, using the 268 landing craft and 312 DUKW amphibious trucks, the latter divided between the two divisions and the central beach control.[24] Thereafter the Canadians pushed on up the mountainous middle of the Calabrian Peninsula paralleled by the 5th Division moving along the coast to the north, meeting resistance from the occasional rearguard and a series of blown bridges and other obstacles for the RE and RCE elements to deal with. In the early morning of 8 September 231st Brigade, supported by 40 (RM) Commando and No. 3 Commando, carried out another landing near Pizzo, just over sixty miles along the north Calabrian coast from Reggio Calabria, in an effort to block the German withdrawal that sparked a day-long fight with elements of *26 Panzer Division* which cost 231st Brigade around 200 casualties before the German force broke contact and continued to move north.[25] On the following day, Thursday 9 September, the AVALANCHE landings at Salerno began along with a simultaneous sea landing by the British 1st Airborne Division at Taranto, codenamed Operation SLAPSTICK.

Although it is frequently overshadowed by Operation AVALANCHE, Operation BAYTOWN's five-day push up the Calabrian peninsula marked the beginning of the nineteen-month fight for the Italian mainland. Via piercing a series of German defensive lines, the controversial Battle of Monte Cassino, a further landing at Anzio, the liberation of Rome and prolonged fighting in difficult weather and terrain, that fight ended on 2 May 1945 with Allied forces approaching the Italian Alpine frontiers. The invasion of mainland Italy thus also effectively marked the point where the campaign in Sicily came fully to a close; but before moving on to examine that campaign in detail it might be enlightening to provide background context by examining the events that made the Sicilian invasion a justifiable and necessary proposition.

1

Establishing a Presence

Operation TORCH and the Invasion of French North Africa, 8-11 November 1942

The precursor to the invasion of Sicily in July 1943 was the expulsion of German and Italian forces from North Africa, a process which began eight months earlier. Following their victory at Gazala in June 1942, *Generalfeldmarschall* Erwin Rommel's *Panzerarmee Afrika* had advanced east along the Libyan coast, captured the port of Tobruk and pushed on 250 miles into Egypt to the coastal town and railway stop at El Alamein, just seventy miles short of the major port and British naval base at Alexandria where General Claude Auchinleck's Eighth Army (hereafter 8th) had erected a blocking line across the forty-mile wide strip from the Mediterranean coast to the largely impassable Qattara Depression. There the German advance was halted via the First Battle of El Alamein and the Battle of Alam el Halfa in July and August 1942 respectively, after which Rommel, with the assistance of his more numerous Italian allies, set about erecting a formidable defensive zone of his own fronted by extensive minefields while the 8th Army was rebuilt in readiness for a counter-stroke.[1] What was to become known as the Second Battle of El Alamein was carried out under the auspices of Lieutenant-General Sir Bernard Law Montgomery, who was appointed commander of the 8th Army on 13 August 1942 following Auchinleck's replacement by General Sir Harold Alexander as Commander-in-Chief Middle East Command at the beginning of the month. Command of the 8th Army had originally been allotted to Lieutenant-General William Gott, but he was killed along with sixteen other passengers when the Bristol Bombay transport in which he was returning to Cairo from the front was shot down and the wreck repeatedly strafed by German fighters on 7 August; Montgomery was brought in from the UK as a replacement at the instigation of Chief of the Imperial General Staff General Sir Alan Brooke.[2]

Montgomery's scheme to evict Axis forces from Egypt became known as the Second Battle of El Alamein and was preceded by an intensive deception effort codenamed Operation BERTRAM and Operation BRAGANZA, a diversionary attack on the Italian *Folgore* Parachute Division near the Deir el Munassib depression at the southern extremity of the Axis line.[3] The subsequent main effort was a two-stage affair beginning with Operation LIGHTFOOT, which was intended to breach the extensive Axis minefields and push the fighting back into the defensive zone where the Axis defenders could be worn down via a process dubbed 'crumbling' and their mobile reserves drawn into the fight.[4] With this achieved, the second phase, codenamed SUPERCHARGE, was to be launched at the junction between the *Deutsches Afrika Korps* (*DAK*) and the less well equipped Italian forces occupying the southern portion of the Axis line with the intention of forcing the Axis force to fight in the open and in the process eroding its stocks of fuel and supplies, cutting its supply lines and destroying its armour.[5]

Operation LIGHTFOOT began on the night of 23-24 October 1942 after an intense preparatory artillery barrage and SUPERCHARGE followed after a week of intense fighting on the night of 1-2 November. By 3 November the Allied attack was exerting such pressure that Rommel issued a preliminary withdrawal order, but this was countermanded by *Führer* Adolf Hitler via one of the grandiloquent statements that were to become increasingly common as the war tilted against Germany; Rommel was thus ordered to '...stand fast, yield not a yard of ground and [to] throw every gun and every man into the battle'.[6] Despite this the pressure finally became too much during the morning of 4 November. While elements of the British 1st Armoured Division fought German armoured units around Tel el Aqaqir at the northern end of the attack frontage,[7] elements of the British 7th and 10th Armoured Divisions and the 2nd New Zealand Division found their way through the Axis line at the south-west corner of the salient created by SUPERCHARGE. British armour swiftly cut the main Axis supply line, known as the Rahman Track, overran the *DAK* battle headquarters complete with its commander *Generalleutnant* Wilhelm *Ritter* von Thoma and began pushing north and west into the Axis rear areas. Facing the imminent encirclement and destruction of his renamed *Deutsch-Italienische Panzerarmee*, Rommel appealed to Hitler to rescind his no retreat order and when the *Führer* reluctantly agreed in the late afternoon Rommel immediately ordered a general withdrawal at 17:30 along the coast road to Fuka, almost fifty miles west of the fighting front. Anxious to avoid giving their provenly resilient foes the opportunity to regroup, the British took up the pursuit at dawn on 5 November and while this failed to completely encircle them it obliged the retiring Axis forces to merely pause at Fuka before continuing to withdraw a further fifty miles to Mersa Matruh where the fuel-starved remnants of *21 Panzer Division* fought a successful delaying action on 6 November. This was followed by a series of similar actions along the North African coast at Sollum and Halfaya on 11 November, just west of Tobruk on 13 November, near Derna on 15 November and the Allied capture of the port of Benghazi five days after that on 20 November 1942. The pace of the Allied advance then slackened in the by now traditional manner of the Desert War as Axis resistance stiffened and the supply lines from Egypt lengthened and it took just under four weeks, from 25 November to 13 December 1942, to overcome Axis defences near El Agheila and a similar period ending on 16 January 1943 to deal with a more extensive blocking position west of Buerat el Hsun.[8] Thus was the *Deutsch-Italienische Panzerarmee* harried west out of Egypt, across the breadth of Libya and halfway into Tunisia before finally coming to a stop behind the Mareth Line, a belt of fixed defences erected by the French in the latter half of the 1930s to defend against incursions from then Italian-controlled Libya, in February 1943 after a three-month, thousand-mile retreat from El Alamein.

The second thread in the chain of events came from the west in the shape of Operation TORCH, the Anglo-US invasion of Vichy-controlled French North Africa, commanded by US Lieutenant-General Dwight D. Eisenhower. The roots of TORCH stretched back almost a year and grew out of optimistic schemes to capitalise on the success of Operation CRUSADER in November and December 1941, which pushed Rommel's *Panzergruppe Afrika* west to El Agheila on the Gulf of Sirte and lifted the 244-day siege of the port of Tobruk in the process. Operation ACROBAT was an immediate continuation of the British advance to Tripoli while Operation GYMNAST envisaged landing 55,000 men on the Algerian coast with the co-operation of the Vichy French authorities and while the former was rendered superfluous by a rapid Axis recovery, the latter became the preferred British method of getting the US involved in the fight against the Axis following the First Washington or ARCADIA Conference held in December 1941-January 1942; the Conference fixed the policy of dealing with Germany first beginning with an operation against French North Africa as a way for US ground forces to become directly involved in the conflict and to alleviate the ongoing pressure against the British in the Western Desert and Libya. GYMNAST was therefore expanded into an Anglo-US effort in January 1942, which envisaged landing three British and three US divisions in French Morocco and Algeria by April 1942, but disagreements over scale led to it morphing into Operation SUPER GYMNAST. The timetable proved unrealistic however, and planning was suspended in April 1942 as US preferences shifted toward engaging the Germans in North-West Europe via Operations SLEDGEHAMMER and ROUNDUP.

The former was a scheme to use British troops to capture the port of Cherbourg and establish a foothold in the Cotentin Peninsula in Normandy in the autumn of 1942, which would be held through the winter to provide a springboard for the latter, which was to be launched in the spring of 1943. The 1942 discussions highlighted a fundamental difference between the two Allies with the British considering the Americans to be overly optimistic, having not faced the Germans on a land battlefield, while the Americans thought the British were wary of engaging the Germans due to the numerous defeats they had suffered at their hands since 1940. This dichotomy was to dog Anglo-US relations to the Normandy invasion and beyond, although at the time Prime Minister Winston Churchill and President Franklin Roosevelt worked together to smooth over the differences between their respective militaries and politicians. In the event a combination of the arguably justified British obduracy, a shortage of aircraft, shipping and landing craft and the need to alleviate pressure on the Soviet Union led to the Second Washington Conference in June 1942 authorising a continuation of planning for ROUNDUP and a last-ditch attempt to sell SLEDGEHAMMER to the British the following month. When this failed, ROUNDUP was postponed until 1944, SLEDGEHAMMER was cancelled, attention switched back to an operation in French North Africa as a compromise and SUPER GYMNAST planning was reactivated under the new codename of Operation TORCH on 25 July 1942, for execution by October 1942.[9]

Lieutenant-General Eisenhower was appointed to command Operation TORCH as Commander-in-Chief, Allied Expeditionary Force on 6 August 1942, with US Major-General Mark W. Clark serving as his deputy and US Brigadier-General Walter Bedell Smith as Chief-of-Staff. The top command slots were allotted to US officers in part because the US Army was supplying the bulk of the troops and in part to create the impression that TORCH was a solely US operation in the hope that Vichy French forces would be less willing to engage US troops than their erstwhile British allies, especially after the Royal Navy's attack on the French fleet at Mers El Kébir in July 1940. To this end the landings were not to be preceded by any preparatory bombardment, all US vehicles were emblazoned with large Stars and Stripes flags and US assault troops wore similarly marked brassards. Below this level Eisenhower made a conscious effort to amalgamate and balance the make-up of his HQ integrating land, air and sea commanders into overall General Staff sections and generally proceeding '...as though all its members belonged to a single nation'; the exception was in administration where the vastly different systems required parallel British and US sections overseen by British Major-General H. M. Gale who was appointed Chief Administrative Officer to co-ordinate the respective administrative staffs and operational logistics.[10] Eisenhower issued his overall outline for TORCH seven days after assuming command, on 13 August. This defined his mission as gaining complete control of North Africa by establishing firm bases from which to extend control over the entirety of French Morocco, Algeria and Tunisia along with Spanish Morocco if necessary, the ultimate aim being the '...complete annihilation of Axis forces now opposing the British forces in the Western Desert and intensification of air and sea operations against the Axis on the European Continent'.[11] To achieve this mission the Allied Expeditionary Force deployed a predominantly US force consisting of two US armoured divisions and four US infantry divisions and a number of supporting units augmented with two British Commandos and a single infantry division totalling approximately 65,000 men.[12] Moving this force involved 370 merchant and 300 warships, the latter drawn predominantly from the Royal Navy;[13] the landing at Oran involved the battleship *Rodney*, the aircraft carrier *Furious*, two auxiliary carriers, two cruisers, an anti-aircraft cruiser, thirteen destroyers, thirty-six smaller vessels including ten motor launches and two submarines, for example.[14] The Vichy French forces facing the Allied invasion were numerically superior overall, totalling approximately 120,000 men,

50,000 of whom were stationed in Algeria, 55,000 in Morocco and 15,000 in Tunisia but lacked weapons, ammunition, modern equipment and training, backed by around 500 largely obsolete aircraft.

The most serious Vichy French threat to the Allied invasion was naval. The battleships *Jean Bart* and *Richelieu* were based in French Morocco along with four cruisers, seven destroyers and eight submarines and while in the Mediterranean Algeria and Tunisia hosted some destroyers, submarines and smaller vessels, the main French fleet based at Toulon boasted an additional six battleships, nine cruisers, twenty-eight destroyers and thirty-five submarines.[15]

The TORCH invasion involved simultaneous landings near Casablanca on the Atlantic coast of French Morocco and at Algiers and Oran in Algeria in the Mediterranean, each of which was to be carried out by a specific Task Force; it is worth examining the landings in a little detail for comparison with the invasion of Sicily seven months later. The Moroccan landing was to be carried out by the Western Task Force, an all-American effort sailing directly from the Continental US made up of 105 vessels commanded by Rear-Admiral Henry Kent Hewitt USN. This host included three battleships, seven cruisers, an aircraft carrier, four escort carriers, thirty-eight destroyers and eight minesweepers escorting eight transports and between twenty-eight and thirty-one assorted transports.[16] The latter were carrying just under 34,000 men from the 2nd Armored Division, the 3rd and 9th Infantry Divisions, a number of Tank and Tank Destroyer Battalions and support units, all under the overall command of Major-General George S. Patton Jr.[17] The Task Force was divided into three separate Forces, each tasked to carry out individual landings. Force Y, the largest, was tasked to land at Fedala, fifteen miles north of Casablanca, codenamed BRUSHWOOD.[18] Force Z was tasked to carry out GOALPOST at Port Lyautey, eighty miles north of Casablanca while Force X was to carry out BLACKSTONE at the port of Safi, 145 miles south of Casablanca, to secure facilities to allow the unloading of the 2nd Armored Division's tanks from some or all of the twenty-three Combat Loader vessels with the Western Task Force.[19] All three landings were scheduled to commence by 05:00 local time on Sunday 8 November 1942.[20]

Whatever element of surprise existed was fatally compromised by the pro-Allied *Général de Division* Antoine Béthouart, who ordered the defence forces to stand down on 7 November before trying to persuade the senior military and naval commanders in Morocco to join him in a coup against the Vichy regime. After some deliberation the latter declined Béthouart's offer and he and his confederates were arrested in readiness to be tried for treason, and the defence forces were re-activated just in time to face the incoming US invasion force.[21] In addition to or perhaps as a result of this, the Allied assumption that the Vichy French forces would not resist a US landing proved to be misplaced, and all the landings came under fire from the French defences. At Safi the invasion force vessels came under fire from 75mm, 130mm and 155mm guns emplaced around the port for example, while at Fedala bad weather delayed the run in until after full daylight. The French response at the latter included fire from four 380mm guns on the partially completed battleship *Jean Bart* moored at Casablanca, fifteen miles down the coast to the south, until it was silenced by a combination of counter-fire from the battleship USS *Massachusetts* and attacks by Douglas Dauntless dive-bombers from the aircraft carrier USS *Ranger*. The latter's Grumman Wildcat fighters also had some success strafing the French airfield at Cazes near Casablanca, but US air superiority did not prevent a number of French destroyers led by the *Milan* sallying forth from Casablanca and taking on their US equivalents at 08:27 and again at 09:35, followed by the French cruiser *Primauguet* at c.10:15. All the French vessels were damaged in the fight, the *Milan* so badly its burning wreck had to be beached while the *Primauguet* sought shelter against a jetty near the Casablanca harbour entrance where it was sunk by repeated attacks from Dauntless dive-bombers. Counter-battery fire from the US warships was constrained by strict orders to avoid damaging vital French infrastructure. Attempts to hit a battery of 100mm guns close to an oil tank farm at Fedala led to some US shells missing their intended target and striking the Hotel Miramar in the town overlooking the harbour.[22]

The northerly landing at Port Lyautey was intended to secure the nearby airfield located inside a loop in the River Sebou for rapid use by US aircraft, which in turn necessitated seizure of the seaside village of Mehdia and the Kasba fortress dominating the river mouth.[23] Marshalling problems led to H Hour being put back thirty minutes to 04:30 on 8 November and one Battalion Landing Team (BLT) was put ashore almost 3,000 yards from its assigned landing beach with the second wave arriving before the first, while another was landed five miles astray. Thus the landing force was still fighting to maintain footholds at 11:00 when it should have been moving off to secure its objectives, and French counter-attacks near Mehdia at 14:00 and 15:30, the latter by French tanks, delayed things further by obliging a short US withdrawal. When the fighting resumed on 9 November the US force rebuffed another French attack employing a number of tanks at or shortly after 06:00 and went on to gain the upper hand through the course of the day and fighting into the night. The airfield was secured by 08:00 on 10 November and P40 fighters from the escort carrier USS *Chenango* were landing there by 10:30, although the delivery of aviation fuel and ammunition by the SS *Contessa* was delayed when the freighter ran aground in the river mouth at 16:20. A French relief column from Meknès was driven off during the morning by gunfire from the USS *Texas*, the Kasba fort surrendered at some point during the day and the French area commander, *Général de Brigade* Maurice-Noël Mathenet, sought terms at 22:30. Operation GOALPOST officially ended at 04:00 on 11 November 1942 at a cost of seventy-nine US killed; French casualties are unclear.[24]

Matters proceeded more smoothly to the south at Safi, although loading difficulties again forced a thirty-minute delay to H Hour. Despite this, all the initial waves reached shore in roughly the correct locations between 05:00 and 05:30 in the face of light resistance and although in some instances it took over an hour from the initial landing before some units were on the move for their objectives, Safi was reported secure by 15:30. One unexpected complication arose from the native Arab population who were 'disdainfully unafraid' of small-arms and artillery fire and gathered in large crowds to watch the action, frequently negating efforts by the US troops to move and emplace tactically in the process; they also engaged in prolific pilfering from supplies being unloaded on the beach to the extent that tons of ammunition and rations were subsequently recovered from native fishing vessels and the US authorities were obliged to co-operate with their French opposite numbers to curb the Arab penchant for random sniping. Nonetheless, by nightfall on 8 November the beachhead had been extended 5,000 yards inland, all the roads were secured and around 300 French prisoners taken in exchange for three US dead and twenty-five wounded; it is unclear if the former figure includes one unfortunate who was drowned while boarding a landing craft from the transport *Lyon*. The move toward Casablanca commenced early in the morning of Monday 9 November and led to a protracted clash with French forces in the late afternoon at Bou Guedra, fifteen miles east of Safi, that continued the following day. By 11 November when hostilities in French Morocco ceased, the BLACKSTONE force had pushed up the coast past Mazagan to Azemmour, just under a hundred miles from Safi and fifty miles short of Casablanca.[25]

The main 8 November landing at Fedala was intended to deliver the US 3rd Infantry Division with a variety of supporting units including a tank battalion from the 67th Armored Regiment onto beaches in the adjacent Bay of Fedala, with the initial landing force carried aboard the transports USS *Charles Carroll*, USS *Joseph T. Dickman*, USS *Leonard Wood* and USS *Thomas Jefferson*. The landing force's initial objectives were to secure Fedala and the cape overlooking it, with priority on neutralising French artillery positions and securing road and rail crossings over the River Mellah flowing into the port from the west; reinforcements were then to establish a perimeter five miles or so around the port, occupying high ground to the south and a lodgement on the east bank of the River Nefifikh as a block to French troops from Rabat. In the event the landing went more awry than those at Port Lyautey and Safi. Again, the scheduled 04:00 H Hour was delayed, initially by thirty and eventually by forty-five minutes, in this instance due to unloading delays and an unexpectedly strong current disrupting the landing ship's formation, with some vessels being pushed up to 10,000 yards from their designated location. It is unclear if the weather was worse at Fedala than the other landing points as the landing force reportedly moved to their landing station through 'intermittent rain squalls', but the BRUSHWOOD landings went especially awry. Twenty-one of the thirty-one landing craft launched by the USS *Leonard Wood* were lost in the surf, the USS *Charles Carroll* lost eighteen craft from a total of twenty-five in the first wave and a further five in the second, leaving just two vessels operating thereafter, while the USS *Thomas Jefferson* lost sixteen out of thirty-three landing craft with a further six damaged; the exception was the USS *Joseph T. Dickman*, which lost only two landing craft in the first wave and two more subsequently.

The surf appears to have been especially fierce in the open stretch of the Bay of Fedala, given that the USS *Joseph T. Dickman* delivered its passengers onto BLUE Beaches 2 and 3 which were on sheltered inlets at the eastern end of the landing area. The problem was compounded by landing during an ebb tide, which left many landing craft beached until the tide turned, frequently due to tardy disembarkation by personnel or vehicles or unloading of materiel. The loss, temporary or otherwise, of so many landing craft impacted adversely on the post-assault build up and by extension upon the subsequent advance on Casablanca fifteen miles down the coast.[26]

Despite all this, Fedala was under US control by 06:00 and the forward element of Force BRUSHWOOD's HQ under Deputy Commander Brigadier-General William. W. Eagles went ashore two hours later; Force Commander Major-General Jonathan W. Anderson followed at 09:45 under ineffectual French shelling. The overall land commander of the Western Task Force, Major-General George S. Patton, was also scheduled to go ashore at Fedala from the cruiser USS *Augusta* at 08:00, but his departure was delayed by the vessel delivering fire missions in support of the landings, with the muzzle blast from the *Augusta's* rear turret reportedly destroying the landing craft suspended on davits in readiness to take him ashore. Matters were then further delayed by the cruiser taking evasive action to avoid attacks by French bombers, providing anti-aircraft cover for the transports and confronting the French warships that ventured out of Casablanca harbour. Patton finally landed at Fedala at 13:20 and after inspecting the town and port took up residence for the night in the shell-damaged Hotel Miramar as a base from which to monitor Force BRUSHWOOD's operations; Western Task Force HQ was established in the same location the following day.[27] The fifteen-mile advance to Casablanca commenced at 07:00 the following day, Monday 9 November and made good progress in the face of light resistance and strafing from Vichy French aircraft; a Vichy French ground reconnaissance along the Rabat-Casablanca highway was rebuffed later in the morning and in the early afternoon US Navy aircraft in turn dispersed a force of around thirty Vichy French armoured vehicles massed around a road junction east of Fedala. However, Major-General Anderson was obliged to temporarily halt the US advance at some point in the late afternoon or early evening to allow transport, communications equipment and heavy weapons to catch up; one artillery battery had only a single Jeep to move its guns and equipment for example, and the 15th Regimental Landing Group was reliant on just five Jeeps for all its transport needs until 18:00. The problem appears to have been a combination of the landing craft losses the previous day exacerbated by poor performance by the Army shore parties; Patton described the unloading effort as a 'mess' and returned to the beach before first light on 9 November to impose some order in person, remaining there until the afternoon.

Anderson was able to resume the advance at midnight and by first light on Tuesday 10 November the elements of Force BRUSHWOOD moving along the coast road from Fedala had reached the outskirts of Casablanca; the other element was tasked to move further inland and secure an area of high ground straddling the Casablanca-Marrakech road to attack the city from the south. The initial plan was to mount a co-ordinated attack on Casablanca at 07:00 but this was delayed, initially when the inland element ran across a Vichy French defence outpost around a crossroads eight miles south-east of the city during its approach march and again when the coastal element attempted to move up to the start line for the 07:00 attack and came into contact with the Vichy French defence line around Casablanca. Clearing the outpost and breaking into the eastern section of the Casablanca defence line consumed the remainder of the day, although both elements had reached the attack start line by 17:00 where they remained for the night as the coordinated assault was rescheduled for 07:30 the following morning; the day had seen the heaviest fighting of the invasion to date, which cost Force BRUSHWOOD thirty-six dead and 113 wounded.[28] In the event the attack was rendered unnecessary after a delegation from the senior French commander in Morocco, *Général d'Armée* Auguste Noguès, arrived at Fedala at around 02:00 on 11 November to discuss the termination of hostilities, although some of Force BRUSHWOOD's units had already commenced the pre-attack bombardment before the resultant postponement order was received. After receiving direct orders from *Général d'Armée* Noguès the commander of the Casablanca garrison, *Général de Brigade* Raymond Desré, surrendered shortly before midday and formal negotiations in the afternoon between *Général d'Armée* Noguès and Major-General Patton at the latter's Western Task Force in the Hotel Miramar in Fedala resulted in an armistice that brought the fighting in Morocco to a close.[29] French casualties are unclear but the four days of fighting cost the Western Task Force a total of 337 killed, 637 wounded, 122 missing and seventy-one taken prisoner.[30]

The main landings in the Mediterranean at Algiers and Oran were to take place in a much less permissive environment due to the presence of German and Italian air and naval forces, and the Royal Navy's (RN) Gibraltar-based Force H was designated to act as a covering force for both landings. Originally formed in 1940, Force H was commanded by Vice-Admiral Sir Edward Syfret from his flagship HMS *Duke of York* and consisted of two other battleships, HMS *Renown* and HMS *Rodney*, the cruisers HMS *Argonaut*, *Bermuda* and *Sirius* and the aircraft carriers HMS *Formidable*, *Furious* and *Victorious* supported by seventeen destroyers and two tankers.[31] The landing effort involved 370 assorted transport ships, with six advance convoys carrying fuel, ammunition and supplies being despatched to Gibraltar from British ports beginning on 2 October 1942, followed by two convoys carrying the assault forces in eighty assorted transport vessels sailing from the Clyde and Loch Ewe in Scotland on 22 and 26 October. The slower lead convoy carrying tanks, vehicles, heavy equipment and stores divided into two increments for the individual landings passed through the Straits of Gibraltar during the night of 5-6 November, while the faster second troop-carrying convoy passed through in the afternoon of Saturday 6 November; the passage was tied into a timetable that reorganised the convoys into the precise order for the landings, scheduled to take place between 19:30 on 5 November and 04:00 on 7 November.[32] The arrival of the advance convoys and associated activities in Gibraltar were detected by *Luftwaffe* reconnaissance flights and reported by Axis agents but while the Italians considered Allied landings in French North Africa to be a possibility, as late as 25 October *Oberkommando der Wehrmacht* (*OKW*) considered the activity to be preparations for another Malta convoy like Operation PEDESTAL, which had fought through to the besieged island in the first half of August 1942.

While landings in the Mediterranean were acknowledged as a possibility, French North Africa was not considered a likely target as Hitler and *OKW* were convinced that any such Allied action would drive the Vichy French into an alliance with the Axis, and German misconceptions were reinforced by only a handful of landing craft and just two troop transports being identified at Gibraltar as late as 4 November.[33] Two days later, as the Allied Assault convoys were en route to their landing areas, *Oberkommando der Kriegsmarine* (*OKM*) finally reoriented its forecast of another Malta convoy to admit that Allied landings were a possibility at 'Tripoli-Bengasi [sic], Sicily, Sardinia, the Italian mainland, and in the last place French North Africa'.[34] As the British Official History put it, 'The Allies had...kept their real intentions secret [and as a result] Hitler...took no precautionary measures in North Africa and dissuaded the Italians from taking any.'[35]

The force tasked to carry out the westernmost landing at Oran, numbering ninety-two assorted vessels and dubbed the Centre Task Force, was commanded by Commodore Thomas Troubridge RN from the HQ ship HMS *Largs*, a converted French cargo ship seized in Gibraltar after the French surrender in 1940. The designated elements of the two equipment and troop carrying convoys were incorporated into the columns assigned to specific landing areas during the afternoon of Saturday 7 November and the entire Force continued to steam eastward on a course for Malta as a deception measure. As in Morocco, the Oran landings were an all-US operation and the plan entailed three separate landings, two of which were relatively small subsidiary affairs. Colonel Paul M. Robinett's Task Force GREEN from the US 1st Armored Division's Combat Command B was assigned Landing Area X at Bou Zadjar, approximately thirty miles west of Oran, with the immediate objective of securing the airfield at Lourmel eight miles inland, while the 26th Regimental Combat Team (RCT) from the US 1st Infantry Division was assigned Landing Area Y sixteen miles west of Oran at Les Andalouses, tasked to secure fortified Vichy artillery positions to the south-east and further east overlooking the naval base at Mers El Kébir. The third and main landing at Landing Area Z involved putting the US 1st Ranger Battalion, Combat Command B's Task Force RED and the US 1st Infantry Division's 16th and 18th RCTs ashore near Arzew at the base of the Cape Carbon, around twenty-two miles east of Oran.[36] The Rangers were to make two separate landings to seize an artillery fort on the tip of Cape Carbon and gun batteries protecting Arzew harbour, the 18th RCT was tasked to secure Arzew harbour before advancing on Oran, the 16th RCT was to secure a beachhead for tanks and heavy equipment to be unloaded before also moving on Oran, while Task Force RED was tasked to move rapidly west to capture the airfields at La Sénia and Tafaraoui, approximately seven and twenty-two miles south of the Oran respectively.[37] The attackers were facing twelve Vichy French fortified coastal artillery positions sited to protect Oran and a further two at Arzew, mounting weapons ranging from 75mm to 240mm calibre protected by numerous anti-aircraft guns manned by an estimated 4,000 naval personnel. Oran was garrisoned by *Général de Division* Robert Boissau's *Division d'Oran* with an estimated strength of just over 10,000 men in and in and around the city, which was expected to expand to approximately 18,000 within twenty-four hours when outlying units were called in. This force was backed by almost a hundred assorted combat aircraft located on half a dozen airfields and a number of Vichy French navy vessels in Oran harbour and the adjacent naval base at Mers el Kébir; these included a number of submarines, the destroyers *Epervier*, *Tornade*, *Tramontane* and *Typhon* and the minesweeping sloop *La Surprise*.[38]

The vessels assigned to Landing Areas X and Y peeled off from the Centre Task Force convoy at 18:15 on 7 November and sailed south for just over two hours to a rendezvous with HM Submarine *Unshaken* which was acting as a beacon sixteen miles off the Algerian coast.[39] The fourteen vessels tasked for the landing at Bou Zadjar then continued south led by a minesweeper toward their launch point off Landing Area X; the eight vessels carrying the 2,257-strong landing force included the SS *Batory* acting as HQ ship and the *Bachaquero*, a Maracaibo tanker converted into a prototype tank landing ship.[40] At least one of the troop transports broadcast the Army Notre Dame football game from Yankee Stadium over the vessel's public address system during the run in.[41] All went well until the ships approached the planned launch point around five miles out when they ran into a six-vessel Vichy French convoy moving across their course, which caused some transports to overtake the minesweeper; it was thus decided to launch the landing craft earlier and further out than planned. Despite an unexpected westward current and one landing craft catching fire and illuminating the run-in, the first craft reached the beach at 01:30 on Sunday 8 November, only thirty minutes or so behind schedule. Additional delay was incurred when the bay proved too shallow for the thirteen Landing Craft Mechanized (LCM) carrying light vehicles; using bulldozers to refloat them caused damage to screws and rudders and reduced the total of serviceable vessels to three. The *Bachaquero* also ran aground 120 yards short of the beach, and while the 16th Armored Engineer Battalion's effort to span the gap with a pontoon bridge proved initially unsuccessful, a motorised reconnaissance platoon managed to get its vehicles ashore and over the soft sand to set off for Lourmel just after 06:00 and by 08:15 the *Bachaquero's* M3 Light Tanks were also ashore, allowing the remainder of Task Force GREEN to move off at around 09:00.

Despite ongoing communication difficulties, the airfield and adjacent village at Lourmel were secured by 11:30 and the Task Force moved on to its secondary objectives in the afternoon. Commanded from the infantry landing ship HMS *Glengyle* the five vessels carrying the approximately 5,262-strong 26th RCT to Les Andalouses had an uneventful passage to the launch point six miles off Landing Area Y and began lowering and loading its forty-five assorted landing craft at 23:20. The run in began twenty-five minutes later and landing craft began to land at 01:16, sixteen minutes past the designated H-Hour. The delay was due to an unexpected sandbank running parallel with the shore with a five-foot deep channel between it and the beach that drowned a number of light vehicles and guns unloaded on the sandbank. Despite this, 2,670 men and thirty-three vehicles were ashore by 05:00 and two battalions were soon on the move to secure Cape Falcon, the town of Ain El Turk and two Vichy French gun batteries overlooking Mers el Kébir ten miles to the east. The US presence at Landing Area Y also provoked more response from the Vichy French. The destroyer HMS *Brilliant* sank the Vichy French sloop *La Surprise* at 07:15 after a half-hour fight, three armoured cars were knocked out by 37mm anti-tank guns at 08:00 while probing the US defences and the landing area came under fire from Fort de Santon at Mers el Kébir at 09:00. The Fort scored several hits on the MV *Llangibby Castle* from 09:17 and another on the SS *Monarch of Bermuda* at 10:50 before being temporarily silenced by counter fire from the battleship HMS *Rodney*; both transport vessels were successfully moved out of range to continue unloading.[42]

The bulk of the Centre Task Force, consisting of thirty-five assorted transport vessels commanded from the troopship HMS *Reina del Pacifico* and escorted by twenty-eight Royal Navy warships including the cruiser HMS *Jamaica*, turned south-east after the X & Y Forces had peeled off. After rendezvousing with beacon vessel HM Submarine *Ursula* five and a half miles off Cape Carbon on schedule at 21:30, the Force steamed on to its launch point for Landing Area Z six miles off Arzew, arriving at 23:15. From there the troop transport HMS *Royal Ulsterman* and infantry landing ship HMS *Ulster Monarch*, escorted by the anti-aircraft cruiser HMS *Delhi*, delivered four companies from the 1st Ranger Battalion commanded by Battalion commander Lieutenant-Colonel William O. Darby to the north-east face of Cape Falcon. The Rangers then scaled the cliffs, moved stealthily over a mile of steep and rocky terrain before launching an assault on the Fort du Nord that overran and secured the Fort's main battery of 105mm guns, which were then prepared for demolition; Lieutenant-Colonel Darby signalled success with a green flare at 04:00.[43] The remaining two companies of Rangers were delivered onto the breakwater at the east side of Arzew harbour from the infantry landing ship HMS *Royal Scotsman* from where they secured the harbour by 02:00 after killing two sentries and finding the garrison asleep. They then secured the northern portion of Arzew and Fort de la Pointe on high ground to the north-east overlooking the approaches to the port, before linking up with Lieutenant-Colonel Darby's force at around 04:00. The main Force Z landing was on a three-mile stretch of beach running south-east from Arzew. The first wave of the 7,092-strong 18th RCT began to land on the northern section, codenamed Z GREEN, at 01:20, twenty minutes behind schedule due to landing craft waves becoming intermixed during the five-mile run in to the beach. The 1st Battalion immediately began moving to secure St. Cloud on high ground eight miles inland, knocking out five Vichy French armoured cars at Renan en route, while the 3rd Battalion moved north into Arzew to secure the town and relieve the Rangers; a fight beginning at 04:00 netted sixty-two prisoners and thirteen fully armed and fuelled seaplanes and the town was secured by mid-morning. Matters ran smoothly on the centre and eastern sections of the Landing Area, codenamed Z WHITE Beach and Z RED Beach respectively. The 5,608 strong 16th RCT came ashore on schedule at 01:00, with the 3rd Battalion advancing inland to clear the villages of Damesme and St. Leu just behind Z WHITE before moving on Fleurus, twelve miles inland while the 1st Battalion cleared Z RED before moving east to secure the flank of the Landing Area, sparking a fight with Vichy French forces at La Macta at around midday; the town was captured with the assistance of gunfire support from the destroyer HMS *Farndale* and a blocking line was established east of the town by 14:00; the remainder of the RCT came ashore at 10:00 and was despatched to Fleurus.

The two converted Maracaibo tankers HMS *Misoa* and HMS *Tasajera* beached themselves at Z RED Beach at around 04:00, began unloading two hours later and by 07:59 had put their cargo of tanks and armoured vehicles from Combat Command B's Task Force RED ashore; the remainder of the 4,772-strong Task Force was delivered into Arzew harbour and onto Z RED by the infantry landing ship HMS *Derbyshire* and MV *Durban Castle*. While the bulk of Task Force RED and Combat Command B HQ assembled at St. Leu, a flying column commanded by Lieutenant-Colonel John K. Waters was despatched south-west at 08:35 tasked to secure the airfield thirty miles away at Tafaraoui. Travelling via the village of St. Barbe du Tlélat, the flying column reached the airfield at just after 11:00.[44] The column's passage was eased by Allied air support from the aircraft carrier HMS *Furious* and the escort carriers HMS *Biter* and HMS *Dasher*, which concentrated Vichy attention on defending its airfields rather than attacking the landing forces; all the Fleet Air Arm (FAA) aircraft involved had their roundel markings temporarily replaced with the US white star insignia in another attempt to persuade the Vichy forces that the invasion was an-all US affair. Eight Fairey Albacore bombers from FAA No. 822 Squadron aboard the former attacked the airfield at La Sénia shortly after dawn, damaging or destroying seventy fully fuelled and armed Vichy French aircraft on the ground for the loss of a single Albacore and a Sea Hurricane escort. A subsequent strafing attack on Tafaraoui by Supermarine Seafires from FAA No.801 Squadron also from HMS *Furious* destroyed three Vichy aircraft on the ground and shot down a defending Dewoitine D520 fighter, the first air-to-air kill by a Seafire.[45] After blocking the surrounding roads Lieutenant-Colonel Waters' flying column quickly overran the airfield with a two-pronged attack from the east and south that netted 300 prisoners and a newly arrived munitions train from Oran, although artillery fire, intermittent air attacks and fears of a Vichy counter-attack from the south deterred a continuation of the advance northward to secure the airfield at La Sénia. Nonetheless, Tafaraoui airfield was declared open to receive Allied aircraft at 12:15 and at 16:30 twenty-four Spitfires from USAAF 308th and 309th Fighter Squadrons arrived from Gibraltar although the final flight of four was attacked by a similar number of Vichy D520 fighters as they came in to land; one Spitfire and three Vichy machines were shot down in the resulting melee.[46]

The Oran landings included two additional subsidiary operations. The first was a seaborne *coup-de-main* attack on Oran harbour to prevent Vichy forces scuttling ships to deny access or sabotaging port infrastructure. Commanded by Captain Frederick Peters RN, the scheme was codenamed Operation RESERVIST and involved 393 men from the 3rd Battalion, 6th Armored Infantry Regiment, six US Marines, a USN detachment of twenty-six and a fifty-two-strong RN party carried aboard HMS *Hartland* and HMS *Walney*, former US Coast Guard cutters on loan to the RN as anti-submarine sloops, accompanied by two motor launches.[47] The original intent was to launch RESERVIST at the same time the landings at X, Y and Z Landing areas commenced but it was then decided to hold back until 02:45, presumably to gauge Vichy reactions to the other landings. The little assault convoy, led by Captain Peters aboard HMS *Walney*, thus sailed directly into a fully alerted defence and a resultant massacre. A smokescreen laid by one of the launches failed to prevent the *Walney* being picked out by a searchlight and targeted by artillery and small-arms fire as it approached the two-hundred-yard floating boom blocking the harbour entrance, despite flying a large Stars and Stripes flag and broadcasting friendly assurances in French via loudhailer. Followed by the *Hartland* Captain Peters then circled for a second attempt at the boom, receiving a redundant message from HMS *Largs* informing him that the main landings had gone ahead with no resistance and to avoid starting a fight unless necessary in the process, before successfully breaching the boom and entering the harbour at 03:10. Vichy fire then switched to the trailing HMS *Hartland* and the *Walney* was able to launch three canoes to secure nearby objectives before almost being rammed head on by the Vichy minesweeping sloop *La Surprise*, which raked the RN vessel with gunfire as it passed, killing and wounding many on board including everyone on the bridge apart from Captain Peters, disabled her engines and set her on fire. The crippled vessel was then caught in crossfire from Vichy submarines and the destroyer *Epervier* as it drifted to the western end of the harbour where it was abandoned and sank, possibly after an explosion.

After hitting a jetty near the entrance in the smoke, HMS *Hartland* also entered the harbour only to be comprehensively shot up by the destroyer *Typhon* that caused numerous casualties including a temporarily blinded commander, Lieutenant-Commander Godfrey Billot RNR, destroyed the vessel's steering and started several fires. The stricken vessel came to a stop in the middle of the harbour where the survivors were evacuated at around 04:00 by the two accompanying launches, which successfully withdrew out to sea; the unfortunate *Hartland* continued to burn and reportedly blew up after daylight.[48] The ship losses were reflected among their passengers who suffered losses in excess of ninety per cent. RN losses totalled 113 dead and eighty-six wounded, the detachment from the 6th Armored Infantry Regiment was virtually wiped out with 189 men killed, including the 3rd Battalion's commander Lieutenant-Colonel George F. Marshall, with 157 wounded, while the USN detachment lost an additional five dead and seven wounded. The number of men captured is unclear but presumably included forty-seven men that landed unscathed and the bulk of the wounded included Captain Peters, all of whom were freed when Oran surrendered to US Forces on 9 November 1942.[49] Ironically, having survived the sinking of the *Walney* Captain Peters was lost off Plymouth Sound aboard a missing aircraft on 11 November; he was posthumously awarded the Victoria Cross and the US Distinguished Service Cross for his actions at Oran.

The second subsidiary operation involved insertion by air rather than sea, which was not only the first parachute operation carried out by the newly created US Airborne force, but also the first Allied use of Airborne Forces in support of a conventional operation. Although the equally new British Airborne Forces had preceded this with two parachute operations, those were small-scale raiding operations: Operation COLOSSUS targeted an aqueduct at Tragino in southern Italy on 11 February 1941 and Operation BITING was mounted to secure equipment from a German radar station at Bruneval on the French Channel coast on the night of 27-28 February 1942.[50] The idea of including an airborne operation in Operation TORCH originated in September 1942 with US Major-General Mark W. Clark, Deputy Commander-in-Chief of the Allied Expeditionary Force, and was intended to secure the Vichy airfields at La Sénia and Tafaraoui south of Oran to prevent Vichy air attacks upon the invasion fleet and to provide a rapid-use base for Allied aircraft. The operation was planned by Clark's Airborne Advisor, then Major William P. Yarborough, one of the original US parachute cadre and involved creating a Paratroop Task Force by amalgamating Lieutenant-Colonel Kerwin Malone's 60th Troop Carrier Group with Lieutenant-Colonel Edson D. Raff's 2nd Battalion 509th Parachute Infantry Regiment, formerly the 2nd Battalion 503rd Parachute Infantry Regiment, under the overall command of Colonel William C. Bentley; both units had been deployed to the UK in June 1942 in preparation for the projected SLEDGEHAMMER and ROUNDUP landings in France in late 1942 and early 1943.[51] On Clark's orders Major Yarborough drew up two variations of his schemes. Influenced by covert negotiations with the Vichy leader, 'Plan Peace' envisaged airlanding Lieutenant-Colonel Raff's unit at La Sénia where it was to stand-by for future operations while 'Plan War' involved a night parachute assault on Tafaraoui airfield tasked to destroy the Vichy fighter aircraft stationed there before detaching a company to move north and perform the same tasks at La Sénia. Both plan variations involved the Paratroop Task Force flying 1,250 miles from the UK out into the Bay of Biscay, south-east across Spain and across the Mediterranean to the objective, guided for the final leg by signals from the anti-aircraft ship HMS *Alynbank* stationed off Cape Figalo just west of Landing Area X, and a EUREKA homing beacon smuggled into Algeria by Lieutenant Norman Hapgood from the US Army Signal Corps.[52]

Lieutenant-Colonel Raff and the 2nd Battalion, 509th Parachute Infantry Regiment moved by train to airfields in Cornwall on 3 November 1942 and the operation was launched four days later on Saturday 7 November after 16:25 instructions to proceed under Plan Peace. A total of 531 paratroopers were lifted in thirty-nine C-47 transport aircraft arranged into four flights. Two flights, totalling nineteen machines and including one flown by Colonel Bentley carrying Lieutenant-Colonel Raff, flew from RAF Saint Eval and the remaining two flights, totalling twenty machines, took off from RAF Predannack. After forming up a mile off Portreath at 22:00 under the protection of RAF Beaufighters and Spitfires the formation set course in rain and fog for the Scilly Isles, fifty-two miles to the west.[53] Cloud interfered with celestial navigation and formation keeping was further degraded by navigation light failure on some aircraft, exacerbated by turbulent headwinds as the formation crossed the mountainous Spanish coast at 10,000 feet. As a result the formation broke up into a stream of groups and individual aircraft that passed close to Madrid and came under Spanish anti-aircraft fire on reaching the Mediterranean, which was wreathed in solid cloud. There was no contact with the beacon ship HMS *Alynbank* because the vessel was transmitting on a different frequency and the C-47s were thus unable to receive the code phrase 'Play Ball' signifying a switch to Plan War due to fears of Vichy resistance, and the smuggled EUREKA beacon had been closed down because Plan Peace rendered it superfluous. As a result Colonel Bentley's C-47s, all of which were running low on fuel, reached the North African coast at a number of widely scattered points apart from one which landed at Gibraltar after becoming lost over Spain. Two machines put down at Fez in French Morocco and were promptly made Prisoners of War while three landed in Spanish Morocco where a fourth also dropped its stick of paratroopers; all were interned by the Spanish authorities but subsequently released after three months of diplomatic negotiation, minus their weapons, equipment and the C-47s.

Of the remainder, the first two C-47s came under anti-aircraft fire as they attempted to land at La Sénia which provided the first inkling that Plan Peace had been superseded; both then landed safely to the east after running out of fuel with crews and passengers being taken prisoner. A larger group of twenty-one machines put down together at the western end of the Sebkra d'Oran, a thirty-mile-long dry salt lake south-west of Oran after receiving the same reception at La Sénia. They were spotted by another group of six more C-47s including Colonel Bentley's, which dropped their sticks on spotting a number of tanks approaching the landed aircraft from the north; Lieutenant-Colonel Raff broke two ribs on landing but perhaps fortunately the tanks proved to be US vehicles from Task Force GREEN moving inland from the Bou Zadjar landings. Next was Major Yarborough leading two machines picked up en route, one of which had taken off from Spanish Morocco hotly pursued by Spanish cavalry, who on landing persuaded Raff to seek medical assistance rather than personally leading his men east toward Tafaraoui, but an attempt to shuttle eighty paratroopers forward in three

C-47s with insufficient fuel resulted in all three machines being forced down half way and comprehensively shot up by two Vichy D520 fighters, killing seven paratroopers and wounding twenty more. Major Yarborough and the survivors reached the US held airfield at Tafaraoui early in the morning of Tuesday 10 November after a fifteen-mile night march where they were joined by Lieutenant-Colonel Raff and the rest of the 509th Parachute Infantry Battalion in the afternoon, travelling in a number of commandeered civilian vehicles. The US Army's first operational parachute jump thus ended with the bulk of the men from the 2nd Battalion, 509th Parachute Infantry Regiment on one of their objectives, albeit later and travelling by different means than originally envisaged.[54]

The main TORCH landing at Algiers, 250 miles to the west of Oran, also involved a harbour *coup-de-main* attack to secure the port infrastructure and prevent the scuttling of ships. Codenamed Operation TERMINAL, the attack was commanded by Captain Henry Fancourt RN and involved the destroyers HMS *Broke* and HMS *Malcolm* carrying a seventy-seven-strong RN/Army landing party and 652 men from the 3rd Battalion, 135th Infantry Regiment from the US 34th Infantry Division, commanded by Lieutenant-Colonel Edwin T. Swenson. Captain Fancourt's force was released at 01:30 or 01:40 on Sunday 8 November, half an hour or more after the main landings had begun, and the two destroyers were thus again confronted with aggressive and fully alert harbour defences as at Oran, again, despite displaying US flags. On approaching Algiers' harbour entrance at 03:45 the *Broke*, with the *Malcolm* trailing a mile astern, was unable to visually identify the harbour entrance due to a combination of the Vichy blackout of the city and dazzle from numerous searchlights and muzzle flashes and was obliged to go around repeatedly. On the third approach at 04:05 hits from Vichy guns knocked out three of HMS *Malcolm*'s four boilers, started a fire, killed ten men and wounded a further twenty-five from the US landing force and four of the crew; with her speed reduced to four knots the destroyer was forced to withdraw from the action, listing badly to starboard.

HMS *Broke* succeeded in piercing the harbour boom on her fourth attempt and despite sustaining hits from Vichy shore batteries succeeded in delivering her half of the landing force, including Lieutenant-Colonel Swenson, onto a nearby jetty at 05:20, from where they secured a nearby power station and fuel tank complex before being pinned down by small-arms fire. The plan was for the *Broke* to remain alongside the jetty but from 08:00 Vichy gunfire obliged the destroyer to relocate twice before several hits from an unlocated field piece at around 09:20 made withdrawal the only option. Only sixty of the landing party were able to reboard on the recall signal before the *Broke* set off across the harbour at 09:40 under smoke and covering fire from the destroyer HMS *Zetland,* but Vichy shore batteries scored several more hits on the hapless destroyer in the process. In all, the action cost the crew of HMS *Broke* seven dead and eighteen wounded with a further two men dying of wounds subsequently. The *Zetland* evacuated the damaged vessel's passengers and took her under tow, but HMS *Broke* sank two days later en route for repair after colliding with her towing vessel. The party from the 135th Infantry Regiment maintained a stalemate with their Vichy opponents despite a shortage of ammunition until the arrival of Vichy armoured cars and tanks in the late morning, which obliged Lieutenant-Colonel Swenson to surrender at 12:30, although their captors then neglected to sabotage the port facilities, which were subsequently secured intact. The action cost the US unit fifteen dead and thirty-three wounded, but the remainder were liberated from Vichy captivity forty-eight hours later.[55]

The Fast Assault Section of the Eastern Task Force, commanded by Vice-Admiral Sir Harold Burrough RN in the HQ ship HMS *Bulolo*, was tasked to carry out the main Algiers landing supported by fifty-five ships including the aircraft carrier HMS *Argus*, escort carrier HMS *Avenger*, the cruisers HMS *Charybdis*, HMS *Scylla* and HMS *Sheffield* and thirteen destroyers.[56] The plan was again to maintain a course toward Malta through the daylight hours of Saturday 7 November and the first naval casualty of Operation TORCH was sustained early in this deception measure. At 05:35 the assault transport USS *Thomas Stone*, carrying the 2nd Battalion 39th Infantry Regiment, was struck by a torpedo that damaged her screw and rudder so badly she had to drop out of the convoy protected by the frigate HMS *Spey*; the source of the attack is unclear, with different sources referring to the submarine *U-205* or a bomber from *Kampfgeschwader* 26. The 2nd Battalion commander, Major Walter M. Oakes, persuaded the assault transport's captain to load around 700 men into the vessel's twenty-four landing craft and embark on the 150-mile journey to Algiers at dusk escorted by HMS *Spey*, although the landing craft engines proved unequal to the task and the infantrymen had to be crowded aboard the frigate, which arrived at the landing area at 21:00 and unloaded its human cargo in Algiers on the morning of 9 November. The *Thomas Stone* was found drifting by the destroyers HMS *Velox* and HMS *Wishart*, which, with the assistance of the tug *St. Day*, delivered the assault transport and the remainder of her passengers and equipment into Algiers harbour on 11 November. The remainder of 7 November appears to have passed uneventfully apart from a *Luftwaffe* attack on the covering force during the afternoon during which a near miss on the destroyer HMS *Panther* killed three of her crew, injured ten more and caused structural damage so severe she was obliged to return to Gibraltar for repair.[57]

The assault force continued to steam eastward until an hour after sunset at18:00, when it changed course to the south and divided into three columns. Like Oran, Algiers was located on the east face of a headland, in this instance Cape Caxine and the assault was also again spread over three separate landing areas. The most westerly, codenamed APPLES, utilised two beaches between Castiglione and Zéralda, around twenty-five miles west of Algiers while the centre area, codenamed BEER, utilised a beach on the western face of Cape Caxine in the bay between Sidi Ferruch and Rass Acrata and another on the northern aspect of the Cape at Pointe Pescade. The most easterly, codenamed CHARLIE, was on the east side of the Bay of Algiers and spread over beaches running six miles east from Cape Matifou to Surcouf. At 19:00 one of the columns broke away and angled south-east heading for the CHARLIE Landing Area. The two remaining columns maintained station and course until 21:30 to a point just over twenty miles from the Algerian coast. There, one veered off to the east for BEER while the third continued almost due south for APPLES.

In contrast to the operations at Morocco and Oran, the Algiers landings were an Anglo-US effort and the 7,230 strong APPLES assault force was British, consisting of the 11th Infantry Brigade Group and B Squadron, 56th Reconnaissance Regiment drawn from Major-General Vyvyan Evelegh's 78th Division; the latter's 36th Infantry Brigade Group was employed as a floating reserve. The assault force was carried aboard the infantry landing ships HMS *Karanja*, HMS *Viceroy of India* and the Dutch MV *Marnix van Sint Aldegonde*, escorted by eleven RN vessels including the anti-aircraft ship HMS *Pozarica* and the sloops HMS *Enchantress* and HMS *Stork*. The column sailed south under a new moon to rendezvous seven miles offshore with beacon vessel HM Submarine *Shakespeare*, which, after transferring pilots to guide the landing craft onto APPLES GREEN & APPLES WHITE Beaches, moved closer inshore to drop off a Combined Operations Piloting Party (COPP) in a collapsible canoe tasked to mark the western extremity of GREEN Beach with a flashing navigation light.[58] Loading the first wave of forty-five landing craft began at c.22:45 and set off at 23:50 and made landfall precisely on schedule at 01:00 in the morning of Sunday 8 November despite unexpected westerly currents. No resistance was encountered and the Brigade's three battalions rapidly secured a beachhead despite unexpected cliffs and heavier than anticipated surf conditions on APPLES WHITE Beach; Brigadier Edward Cass and 11th Brigade HQ came ashore at 02:30 and the Brigade was ashore in its entirety by the late morning. The Brigade was tasked to secure the right flank of the BEER Landing Area by capturing two bridges and the town of Zéralda to the east of APPLES WHITE Beach, securing a ridge centred on the town of Koléa three miles inland from the beaches and blocking the coast road west of APPLES GREEN Beach at Castiglione; all this was achieved before first light, with the town lights and music from a dancehall guiding A Company, 1st Battalion East Surrey Regiment to the latter.[59] A party from the 2nd Battalion Lancashire Fusiliers was despatched twelve miles inland to the airfield at Blida, but on arrival at 09:30 found Lieutenant-Colonel Thomas Trevor and three Troops from No. 1 Commando in a stalemate with the Vichy garrison, having pushed on with French assistance after securing their objective at the BEER Landing Area in the early hours. The situation was resolved by Lieutenant B. H. C. Nation from the aircraft carrier HMS *Victorious* who landed his flight of three Grumman Martlet fighters and secured a written agreement to allow Allied aircraft to land at the airfield. The remainder of the 2nd Lancashire Fusiliers arrived in the late afternoon accompanied by a light anti-aircraft unit and by the end of the day 11th Brigade had also pushed the 5th Battalion Northamptonshire Regiment east to Bir Touta, half way to Algiers, as well as maintaining a perimeter around the APPLES beachhead.[60]

The BEER assault force, consisting of 1,065 men from Nos. 1 and 6 Commandos and the 4,355-strong US 168th RCT, were carried aboard five infantry landing ships commanded by Captain R. J. Shaw RN aboard the infantry landing ship HMS *Keren*, escorted by seventeen RN warships including the anti-aircraft ship HMS *Palomares*, the destroyer HMS *Wilton*, the Polish destroyer ORP *Blyskawica* and three minesweepers. After rendezvousing with HM Submarine *P48*, which again transferred pilots before moving in to deliver two COPPs tasked to provide navigation lights, the column divided into three. HM Troopship *Awatea* carrying No. 6 Commando angled east for the BEER RED Beach at the north of Cape Caxine, the *Keren* and Polish MS *Sobieski* carrying elements of the 168th RCT headed south and east for BEER WHITE Beach and the infantry landing ships HMS *Otranto* and HMS *Winchester Castle* carrying part of No. 1 Commando and the remainder of the 168th RCT ran parallel to the south to the adjacent BEER GREEN Beach. The landings commenced on schedule at 01:00 and Lieutenant-Colonel Trevor's No. 1 Commando, wearing US uniforms in an effort to placate Vichy hostility, had secured Fort de Sidi Ferruch by 03:00 without a fight with the pre-arranged assistance of *Colonel* Louis Baril from the garrison at Koléa; Baril's advice also subsequently despatched Lieutenant-Colonel Trevor to the airfield at Blida in transport provided by the French intelligence officer. Matters ran less smoothly for No. 6 Commando on BEER RED Beach, which was actually four separate landing points where delays in marshalling landing craft from other vessels were exacerbated by a pilot going astray and inexperienced crews on the *Awatea* and the landing craft. Many of the latter were brand new and many suffered engine failures while others leaked badly including that carrying No. 6 Commando's commander, Lieutenant-Colonel Iain MacAlpine, which barely made it to shore. Six landing craft attempted to land inside Algiers harbour, presumably after drifting east from the designated beach, and four were promptly sunk by fire from a Vichy strongpoint; the survivors were taken prisoner and the dead included No. 6 Commando's deputy commander, Major Alexander Ronald. The first wave therefore landed two hours behind schedule at 03:00, the landing was not complete for a further three hours and the Commandos did not reach their primary objective, Fort Duperré overlooking Algiers harbour from the north, until well after full daylight at some point after 08:00. The Fort garrison ignored entreaties in French and held out until 13:30 before surrendering; it is unclear if this was prompted by bombing from nine FAA Albacores or the threat of naval bombardment.

Matters went even more awry for the 168th RCT's 1st and 2nd Battalions, which were slated to land at BEER GREEN and BEER WHITE Beach respectively at 01:00. Elements of both Battalions ended up not only on the wrong beach but scattered all along the coast with the 1st Battalion being the most badly affected. By 01:30 only half of Lieutenant-Colonel Edward J. Doyle's men had arrived at BEER GREEN with some elements landing as far away as APPLES WHITE Beach seven miles or more to the south-west while nine landing craft from Lieutenant-Colonel Dewey H. Baer's 2nd Battalion were delivered onto BEER GREEN. The 168th RCT's commander, Colonel John W. O'Daniel did not reach BEER WHITE until 07:00 after a fifteen mile detour to the APPLES sector, just thirty minutes before his 3rd Battalion began to land, and matters were exacerbated further by a combination of heavy swell and soft sand that closed BEER GREEN and much of BEER WHITE. As a result the 168th RCT did not begin to move on its objective, high ground overlooking Algiers from the west, until 08:30 and by the end of the day had become embroiled in a fight with Vichy forces in the suburb of Lambiridi and the nearby Fort l'Empereur.[61]

The third increment of the Eastern Task Force's Fast Assault Section was assigned to the CHARLIE Landing Area, running east from Cape Matifou on the eastern mouth of the Bay of Algiers. Unlike the other increments it was commanded by a US officer, Captain Campbell D. Edgar USN and the assault force, consisting of Colonel Benjamin F. Caffey 5,688-strong 39th RCT and 312 men from No. 1 Commando commanded by Major Kenneth Trevor, were all carried aboard five USN assault transports, the USS *Almaack*, USS *Exceller*, USS *Leedstown*, USS *Samuel Chase* and USS *Thomas Stone*. RN involvement was restricted to the escort of eleven vessels which included the anti-aircraft ship HMS *Tynwald*, the destroyers HMS *Cowdray* and HMS *Zetland* and four minesweepers. Captain Edgar's force sailed south-east until 22:30, when it rendezvoused with HM Submarine *Unrivalled* around seven miles offshore, which again transferred pilots before moving closer inshore to deliver a COPP team to provide a navigation marker. As we have seen, the early-morning torpedoing had removed the USS *Thomas Stone* and 2nd Battalion 39th RCT from the landing line-up and the landing plan had to be rejigged to accommodate the absence. The USS *Leedstown* was to deliver the detachment from No. 1 Commando onto the most easterly CHARLIE GREEN Beach as originally planned, tasked to deal with several objectives on or near Cape Matifou including Fort d'Estrées and the Batterie du Lazaret. The Commandos were to be followed by Major Farrar O. Griggs' 3rd Battalion 39th RCT which was also aboard the *Leedstown*; originally slated to land later as Regimental reserve, the 3rd Battalion was now tasked to advance west along the coast road and secure the village of Fort de l'Eau, the town of Maison Carrée and a small airfield on the outskirts of Algiers. Lieutenant-Colonel A. H. Rosenfeld's 1st Battalion 39th RCT was to land as planned on the central CHARLIE BLUE Beach from the USS *Samuel Chase*, tasked to secure the ten-mile distant airfield at Maison Blanche by dawn while the 39th RCT's HQ, vehicles and other service and support elements were to land from the *Almaack* and *Exceller* on CHARLIE RED Beach as it had the best vehicle exits.

In the event the No. 1 Commando contingent was late leaving the *Leedstown* and then ran into a fogbank, all of which put their landing two hours or more behind schedule. In the meantime and possibly prompted by a US radio news broadcast prematurely celebrating the successful landings at Algiers, Vichy searchlights on Cape Matifou illuminated the landing force and the Batterie du Lazaret fired several shells at the *Cowdray* and *Zetland*.

The destroyers' return fire destroyed the lights and temporarily silenced the Batterie although it and Fort d'Estrées subsequently refused to yield to Major Trevor and his Commandos, who were obliged to call in fire from the Zetland at 10:40 and, when this failed to make the necessary impression, a further bombardment from the cruiser HMS *Bermuda* was requested at 14:40, backed by bombing from Albacores from HMS *Formidable*. No. 1 Commando attacked again at 16:00 supported by a single 105mm self-propelled howitzer and the Batterie surrendered an hour later, yielding fifty Vichy prisoners, but a subsequent attack on Fort d'Estrées at 17:30 was rebuffed and the attackers withdrew for the night at 20:00.

The other CHARLIE landings enjoyed mixed fortunes. The 39th RCT's 1st Battalion reached Maison Blanche airfield at 06:15 after an all-night march with token resistance from some Vichy tanks encountered en route, and Lieutenant-Colonel Rosenfeld had successfully negotiated the airfield's surrender by 08:30. After being delayed by thick fog eighteen Hawker Hurricane fighters from RAF No. 43 Squadron landed there at 10:35; it is unclear if No. 43 Squadron flew direct from Gibraltar or were embarked on one of the aircraft carriers supporting TORCH. The 3rd Battalion 39th RCT was less successful, running into resistance from Vichy infantry at Fort de l'Eau after covering just six miles or so from the beach; the advance was then stymied altogether by the appearance of three Vichy tanks which shot up some of the US transport and threatened the US unit's flank, obliging it to go onto the defensive. Neither did matters proceed smoothly at the CHARLIE beaches, where deteriorating weather and a consequent high swell were exacerbated by crew inexperience; some landing craft set down on the wrong beaches; slow unloading caused an increasing backlog at the surf line and a number of craft were swamped while trying to get in.[62] Matters were compounded by a dusk attack by thirteen Junkers 88 bombers from *Kampfgeschwader* 26 at 16:30. One of the attackers was shot down by the corvette HMS *Samphire* but the destroyer HMS *Cowdray* was struck a glancing blow by a bomb that then exploded under her hull. The detonation killed five of her crew, wounded a dozen more and caused disabling damage to a boiler room; after being taken under tow by the minesweeper HMS *Algerine*, the *Cowdray* was beached the following day, Tuesday 10 November 1942.[63] The other victim of the attack was USS *Leedstown*, which was struck by a torpedo that destroyed her rudder and flooded her after section, while a subsequent near miss from a bomb caused further damage. *Leedstown* sank in the afternoon of the following day, after being torpedoed again by the *U-331*; the attacks killed fifty-nine of the *Leedstown's* crew. Her captain, Lieutenant-Commander Duncan Cook USNR, and the remaining 103 members of her crew were taken off by the *Samphire*.[64]

By midnight on Sunday 8 November 1942 most of the TORCH landing force was ashore at Algeria. At Oran the fighting continued through Monday 9 November. On the west of the city the 26th RCT had pushed eastward from Landing Area Y at les Andalouses to the coast at Ain El Turk, overrunning the Vichy gun batteries battery at Fermé Combier and Fermé St. Marie on the heights south of Oran but were then held back by shelling from other guns on Cape Falcon and stubborn resistance from the Vichy infantry protecting Fort de Santon overlooking the Mers El Kébir naval base. To the east of Oran, Vichy infantry attacked the 1st Battalion 16th RCT protecting the east flank of Landing Area Z at La Macta after encircling the US unit during the night. The seemingly serious situation prompted the despatch of reinforcements from the 19th Combat Engineer Regiment and armoured vehicles from Task Force RED along with bombing by Albacores from HMS *Furious* in the early afternoon while the cruiser HMS *Jamaica* moved in ready to provide fire support; but the 1st Battalion rectified the situation on its own, driving the Vichy attackers back and consolidating its positions with the aid of reinforcements.

A more serious threat developed south of Oran with the appearance of a column of Vichy tanks and motorised infantry at St. Lucien, just after the Task Force RED column that had captured the airfield the previous day began to move north to secure the airfield at La Sénia. The 1st Armored Regiment's Company A, reinforced with a platoon from the 6th Armored Infantry Regiment, was thus ordered to continue to La Sénia while the remainder of the column returned to Tafraoui to meet the new threat. They arrived in the afternoon to find it occupied by Lieutenant-Colonel John Todd and a detachment from Task Force GREEN, which had arrived at the airfield just after dawn following a night march from Landing Area X at Bou Zadjar along the north of the Sebkra d'Oran dry salt lake. The airfield had been secured at 10:00 without a fight along with 159 prisoners and sixty aircraft, but the latter were subsequently destroyed by Vichy artillery firing from positions near Valmy, two miles to the south-east; on being reinforced Lieutenant-Colonel Todd attacked the Vichy guns, destroying three 75mm pieces and driving off their crews before retiring to the airfield.

In the meantime Task Force RED successfully drove off the Vichy armoured column at St. Lucien in the early afternoon. Covered by a platoon of 75mm tank destroyers, Captain William R. Tuck's Company B, 1st Armored Regiment closed on the Vichy force, knocking out or disabling fourteen French tanks and forcing the remainder to retire for the loss of a single M3 Light Tank and a half-track before occupying St. Lucien until relieved by elements of the 6th Armored Infantry Regiment at nightfall. To the north, the 18th RCT had advanced to within five miles of Oran, encircling a Vichy force at St. Cloud on the way. By dawn on 10 November Oran was fully encircled by US units, the battleship HMS *Rodney* and the cruisers *Aurora* and *Jamaica* had been brought closer inshore to provide gunfire support if required and FAA aircraft were on standby to dive bomb the recalcitrant Fort de Santon to the west. While Vichy resistance continued to the east and west, Task Forces GREEN and RED each despatched armoured columns from the south which entered the city unopposed at 10:15, commanded by Lieutenant-Colonel Todd and Lieutenant-Colonel John Waters respectively. The former was tasked to secure the Oran harbour installations and nearby garrison HQ where he found garrison commander *Général de Division* Boissau and a representative of the senior Vichy naval commander *Vice-Amiral* André Rioult. The French officers issued a cease-fire order at 12:15 on Tuesday 10 November and fifteen minutes later began formal surrender negotiations with the arrival of a delegation led by Major-General Lloyd R. Fredendall, commander of the Centre Task Force, aboard Lieutenant-Colonel Waters' tank. The cease-fire order did not bring hostilities to an end, however. To the west of the city fighting at Fort de Santon continued until 13:30 when the 26th RCT was obliged to order the *Rodney* to cease firing on the Fort to permit the garrison to surrender, while to the east the 1st Battalion 18th RCT was in the process of negotiating the surrender of the Vichy force holding St. Cloud when the order came through.[65] Thereafter hostilities ceased in Oran, apart from sporadic sniping that went on for several days, and the Centre Task Force became the only TORCH force to secure its objectives solely through military action. The three days of fighting cost the US 1st Armored Division 191 dead, 105 wounded and nine missing, although the bulk of these casualties were sustained by the 3rd Battalion 6th Armored Infantry Regiment in the ill-fated *coup-de-main* attack on Oran harbour, while the US 1st Infantry Division lost eighty-five killed, 221 wounded and seven missing. Vichy losses are unclear but included a reported 165 dead.[66]

Matters developed more rapidly and less bloodily at Algiers. The Allies had made extended covert contact with anti-Vichy elements in French North Africa prior to TORCH with regard to installing *Général de Corps d'Armée* Henri Giraud as an anti-Vichy leader in Algeria, most notably with *Général de Division* Charles Mast, the commander of the Algiers Division. Consequently, on the eve of the Eastern Task Force's landings near Algiers Mast ordered Vichy troops in the area to assist the invaders before going out to BEER GREEN Beach to advise US troops, and was also involved in *Colonel* Louis Baril's assistance to No. 1 Commando in moving on the airfield at Blida cited above. In Algiers proper, civilian elements secured key parts of the city's infrastructure including the telephone exchange, the army and police HQs, the governor's residence and the radio station by 01:30 on Sunday 8 November 1942, in readiness for *Général de Corps d'Armée* Giraud's arrival from Gibraltar scheduled for 07:00; the latter's failure to appear led to the insurgents being steadily pushed out of their footholds by pro-Vichy forces as the morning wore on. At the same time US Envoy Robert Murphy visited *Général de Corps d'Armée* Alphonse Juin, the Army commander in chief in French North Africa, at his HQ at Lambiridi in the western outskirts of the city; Murphy warned Juin of the impending invasion and appealed for him to co-operate with the Allies in liberating France and to accept Giraud's leadership. Juin was in turn able to summon the overall commander of the Vichy Armed Forces, *Amiral de France* Jean Darlan, who happened to be visiting his terminally ill son; interestingly, Darlan's presence in Algiers appears to have gone unnoticed by British and US intelligence.

After hearing Murphy out, Darlan and Juin travelled to the nearby Fort l'Empereur to clarify the situation, from where Juin set about wresting control of the local garrison and city infrastructure back from *Général de Division*

Mast's loyalists. By the late afternoon it was clear that the Allies were ashore in force and Darlan authorised Juin to negotiate terms for Algiers and its garrison with Major-General Charles S. Ryder, the commander of the Eastern Assault Force, at 16:00. Two hours and forty minutes later the commanders reached a verbal agreement to cease hostilities forthwith and hand Algiers over to US control with effect from 20:00; full details of an armistice were to be worked out the following day.[67]

Thus by Tuesday 10 November the Mediterranean portion of the TORCH landing force was firmly ashore in Algeria despite the vagaries of inexperience, weather and tidal conditions, aided by successful deception measures and variable Vichy resistance. The amphibious phase had culminated in the securing of Algiers and Oran through a combination of military action and political intervention and the stage was therefore set for the next phase of the invasion, moving eastward to confront the Axis forces occupying Tunisia.

2

Airborne Testing Ground

The Initial Move East toward Tunisia, November–December 1942

The aim of confronting the German and Italian forces in Tunisia was integral to the planning for Operation TORCH, which initially envisaged rapidly securing Bizerte and Tunis, just under 500 miles east of Algiers; the TORCH landings were limited to the latter because it was felt landings further east would be vulnerable to attack from Axis aircraft based in Sardinia and Sicily. Consequently, as soon as the situation at Algiers had been stabilised the Eastern Task Force was renamed the British 1st Army headed by Lieutenant-General Kenneth Anderson, who arrived in Algiers to assume command in the evening of Monday 9 November. A hastily revised move east, codenamed Operation PERPETUAL II in some accounts, began just twenty-four hours later with the more realistic objectives of securing the ports of Bougie and Djidjelli and an airfield near the latter, 110 and 150 miles along the coast from Algiers respectively.[1] Nine assorted transport ships commanded by Captain Norman Dickinson DSC RN from the infantry landing ship HMS *Karanja* thus sailed from Algiers in two increments in the late afternoon and evening of Tuesday 10 November. The assault landing was tasked to Brigadier Arthur Kent-Lemon's 36th Infantry Brigade Group, which had served as floating reserve for the Algiers landing at Area X, carried in the infantry landing ships HMS *Cathay* and MV *Marnix van Sint Aldegonde* using landing-craft from the *Karanja*; the group was also accompanied by the destroyers HMS *Bicester* and HMS *Wilton* escorting HM Troopship *Awatea* carrying an RAF Servicing Commando equipped with fuel, ammunition and other stores destined for Djidjelli airfield. The assault force was escorted by sixteen Royal Navy (RN) warships including the monitor HMS *Roberts*, the anti-aircraft ship HMS *Tynwald*, the destroyers ORP *Blyskawica* and HMS *Bramham*, the corvettes HMS *Penstemon* and HMS *Samphire*, two frigates, two minesweepers and three trawlers.[2] The landing force was also covered by an additional larger force codenamed Force O commanded by Rear-Admiral C. H. J. Harcourt from the cruiser HMS *Sheffield*, which included the aircraft carrier HMS *Argus* tasked to provide air cover for the landing.

The landing force arrived off Bougie at 04:45 on Wednesday 11 November and the first wave of landing craft carrying the 6th Battalion Royal West Kent Regiment set off from the MV *Marnix van Sint Aldegonde* and HMS *Cathay* at 05:30 and 06:00 respectively. The craft were heading for DUFF WHITE Beach, which had been selected because it was outside the range of Vichy shore batteries protecting the port, and began to land through heavy surf at 06:15. The landing was unopposed as fears of Vichy hostility proved unfounded and after negotiations with the local Vichy commanders Bougie harbour was opened to allow three transports to unload while the *Cathay*, *Marnix van Sint Aldegonde*, *Karanja* and *Awatea* continued to offload outside in the bay; the latter had returned to Bougie to unload its RAF Servicing Commando and stores at 06:40, after finding the surf at Djidjelli too high for safe landing. The plan had been to secure and quickly turn the airfield at Djidjelli into a forward base for use by RAF fighters because Bougie was a hundred miles or more from the airfield at Maison Blanche near Algiers and thus on the edge of the aircraft's operational range; the round trip only allowed aircraft to remain over the landing area for around twenty minutes.[3] As Djidjelli was over forty miles from Bougie, seizing the airfield rapidly was not an option, although it was secured on 12 November and Allied fighters from Eastern Air Command landed there on the same day but had to wait twenty-four hours for fuel supplies to arrive. The failure to seize Djidjelli airfield as planned on 11 November thus created a gap in the air cover for the transports unloading in Bougie harbour and bay, although the fact was concealed initially by the presence of fighters from HMS *Argus* but this was only intended to be a temporary provision for the initial stages of the landing. Unloading at Bougie therefore continued without interruption until 11:40, when Rear-Admiral Harcourt ordered Force O and the *Argus* to withdraw west as planned, which effectively left the landing without air cover from around midday on 11 November. The thirty-six hours that followed confirmed both the wisdom of restricting the TORCH landings to Algiers, and the severity of the threat posed by Axis aircraft based in Sardinia and Sicily.[4]

The first attack, by five Italian SM79 torpedo bombers at 13:45, was unsuccessful but the second at around 16:40 by approximately thirty Junkers 88s backed by a number of Heinkel 111 torpedo bombers hit three vessels, two of them fatally. The *Awatea* had set course for Algiers at 16:25 after unloading the RAF Servicing Commando and was hit by four bombs that flooded her engine room and started a fire in No. 2 Hold that rapidly burned out of control; 300 men were taken off by the corvette *Penstemon* and a further three lifeboat loads were picked up by the destroyer *Bicester* and the minesweeping trawler HMS *Mull* before the *Awatea* sank at 23:00. The *Cathay*, with 1,200 troops still on board, suffered several near misses and was struck by a single bomb that penetrated into the galley without detonating; the remaining passengers and 284 crewmen were evacuated by employing every landing craft at the Landing Area before the vessel was abandoned at 19:00. The bomb, apparently fitted with a delayed timer fuse, detonated at around 22:00 and the *Cathay* caught fire just over an hour later and rapidly burned out of control, obliging the nearby *Karanja* and *Marnix van Sint Aldegonde* to weigh anchor as the stricken vessel was carrying depth charges; an explosion blew off her stern at 07:00 the following morning and the *Cathay* sank three hours later. The third vessel hit on 11 November was the monitor HMS *Roberts*, which was struck by two bombs that caused a fire and some bilge flooding on the starboard side; the damage was so severe that the monitor was subsequently despatched to the UK for repair.

The Axis attacks continued through Thursday 12 November, and not exclusively from the air. At 05:15 the anti-aircraft ship HMS *Tynwald* was hit by two torpedoes from the Italian submarine *Argo* shortly after getting underway; the torpedoes killed ten of her crew and the remainder were taken off by boats from the *Roberts* and the corvette HMS *Samphire*. The *Tynwald* sank shortly thereafter. The air attacks resumed at 05:40 with an attack by Junkers 88s using low cloud for cover that scored at least two hits on HMS *Karanja*, starting an oil fire amidships that spread rapidly through the vessel. A number of survivors from the *Cathay* reportedly lowered lifeboats without authorisation, although the vessel's crew abandoned ship in good order at 08:30, bringing some 20mm Oerlikon guns and ammunition with them. Another attack by 30 Junkers 88s at 10:00 lost two aircraft in exchange for a near miss on the Polish destroyer *Blyskawica* and another attack at 12:40 by six torpedo bombers failed to score any hits and also lost two machines, one to a Spitfire from Maison Blanche and another to anti-aircraft fire from the newly arrived fleet tanker RFA *Dewdale*. Two high-level bombing attacks in the hour after 13:30 scored another near miss on the *Blyskawica* that obliged her to depart for Algiers at 16:00 and the final dusk attack at 16:55 was a co-ordinated effort targeting the *Dewdale*, beginning with dive bombing attacks by Junkers 88s followed by two waves of torpedo bombers. The *Dewdale* was unscathed but the destroyer HMS *Wilton* was hit by a single bomb that passed clean through the ship without exploding.[5]

Despite all this, the 36th Infantry Brigade Group was firmly ashore at Bougie and was able to despatch the 8th Battalion Argyll & Sutherland Highlanders to secure the town of Sétif and its airfield, sixty-five miles to the south, later on 12 November.[6] The next move up the coast ran parallel to this, with the seizure of the port of Bône and an adjacent airfield, 150 miles east of Bougie and just fifty miles from the Tunisian border early the same day.[7] The airfield was to be secured by two companies from the unforgettably named Lieutenant-Colonel Geoffrey Pine-Coffin's 3rd Parachute Battalion from the 1st Parachute Brigade and was the first British parachute operation in direct support of conventional operations. The path to its execution was less than straightforward, however.

The 1st Parachute Brigade was formed in September 1941 under then Brigadier Richard Gale who later commanded the British 6th Airborne Division for the Normandy invasion, and came under the auspices of 1st Airborne Division HQ commanded by acting Major-General Frederick Browning DSO the following month; it should be noted that the latter formation was actually an administrative formation at that time set up to fight the Airborne corner in Whitehall, and Browning was selected to head it because he was a consummately skilled political operator rather than for any operational leanings or expertise. As then Lieutenant-Colonel Ernest Down, one of the early pioneers of the British Airborne Force diplomatically put it long after the event, all military enterprises have a political aspect and Browning was ideally suited for such a role because he had the power of the Brigade of Guards and the Monarchy behind him.[8] Be that as it may, the 1st Parachute Brigade was built around the original British parachute cadre set up on Churchill's orders in June 1940 which was by this time known as the 11th Special Air Service (SAS) Battalion. Gale was advised to disband this collection of freebooting raiders due to its not totally undeserved reputation for poor discipline but he was so impressed by Lieutenant-Colonel Down's work in turning it into a conventional parachute infantry unit he simply renamed it the 1st Parachute Battalion, which was augmented with two additional battalions made up of volunteers drawn from across all Army Home Commands, along with a HQ element and a Royal Engineers and Signals contingents.[9]

The 1st Parachute Brigade moved into barracks at Bulford on Salisbury Plain in March 1942 where Brigadier Gale and then Brigadier Edwin Flavell, who was promoted when Gale moved to a post at the War Office in April 1942, implemented a rigorous programme of training and exercises which included working extensively with Lieutenant-Colonel Edson D. Raff's single-battalion 509th Parachute Infantry Regiment after its arrival in the UK in June for the projected SLEDGEHAMMER and ROUNDUP landings in France.[10] This gave the British paratroopers access to Douglas C-47 transports from Lieutenant-Colonel Kerwin Malone's 60th Troop Carrier Group, the generous capacity and large side door of which were a revelation in comparison with the scant and motley collection of unsuitable converted RAF bombers grudgingly provided by the Air Ministry hitherto; the Armstrong-Whitworth Whitley's narrow fuselage precluded seats and obliged passengers to move on all fours for example, and the exit through a circular hole in the floor virtually guaranteed passengers travelling aft of the aperture would strike their faces on the coaming when the slipstream swung their legs back on exit, a phenomenon jocularly referred to as 'ringing the bell'.[11]

Jumping from the spacious and comfortable C-47 proved to be not altogether risk free, however. On 29 June 1942 the 1st Parachute Battalion sent a company to RAF Netheravon where the USAAF had provided three C-47s for the British paratroopers to acquaint themselves with the type and make familiarisation jumps and Private Thomas Newton was killed after his canopy snagged on a C-47 tail wheel. The subsequent investigation revealed that while the existing static-line strop on the British X-Type parachute was sufficiently long for exiting the improvised exits on the various converted RAF bombers, it was too short for C-47 door jumps because it deployed the canopy too close to the aircraft. It was swiftly replaced with a longer item that was to become a vital operational necessity within weeks.[12]

In addition to being a skilled political operator, Browning was also an opportunistic and ruthless empire builder; despite his Division HQ being supposedly a non-operational entity by October 1942 he had expanded its establishment to two parachute brigades with another in the pipeline, a glider-borne airlanding brigade, a pathfinder company and numerous service and support elements including Royal Artillery anti-tank and Royal Engineer units and a light tank squadron.[13] When he learned that the 509th Parachute Infantry Regiment was to participate in Operation TORCH, Browning immediately seized the chance to get his expanding airborne fiefdom into the action, lobbying Commander-in-Chief Home Forces, General Sir Bernard Paget Commander Home Forces and the War Office to get the 1st Parachute Brigade included in the upcoming invasion. The Brigade was duly added to the TORCH invasion force commanded by US Lieutenant-General Eisenhower and the Anglo-US Allied Forces HQ (AFHQ), which in turn allotted it General Anderson's British 1st Army for specific operations while retaining overall control of Brigadier Flavell's formation as a strategic asset. The inclusion brought two problems. First, the 1st Parachute Brigade was not fully manned or equipped to its War Establishment, and deployment therefore necessitated stripping parachute qualified personnel and other resources from the still forming 2nd Parachute Brigade and other 1st Airborne Division units.

Second, and fully in keeping with its attitude to the Airborne Force from its inception, the Air Ministry claimed to be unable to provide any RAF aircraft to carry the Brigade in its upcoming deployment to the Mediterranean.[14] This potentially fatal stumbling block was removed by the USAAF, which not only undertook to provide airlift in North Africa but also to provide aircraft for training jumps in the UK prior to deployment, although the latter again proved problematic. As part of the pre-deployment work up C-47s dropped 250 men from the 2nd Parachute Battalion on 9 October during which at least three men were killed in parachuting accidents. A bad exit caused Lieutenant Peter Street's parachute to snag on his C-47's tailplane, swinging him back to collide with another man in the stick as he exited the door, resulting in both men becoming hopelessly entangled. Another man was killed when his static-line strop was somehow violently twisted and became detached from the parachute pack, meaning the canopy was unable to deploy from its pack; according to one source a fourth man's parachute failed to deploy properly, a phenomenon known as a 'Roman Candle'.[15] All further training on the C-47 was suspended for an investigation and as a result many of the 1st Parachute Brigade deployed to North Africa without having jumped from the aircraft that would shortly be carrying them into battle. USAAF C-47s also transported a portion of the Brigade from the UK to North Africa, although Colonel Tracey K. Dorsett's 64th Troop Carrier Group could only provide thirty-three machines piloted by recently recruited civilian airline pilots for the task.[16] The bulk of the 1st Parachute Brigade therefore moved under sealed orders to Greenock and embarked on the troopship RMS *Arundel Castle* on Thursday 29 October 1942 for the ten-day voyage to North Africa.[17]

The 3rd Parachute Battalion was selected to travel to North Africa by air but there was only sufficient capacity to carry two of the Battalion's three rifle companies, so B and C Companies, commanded by Majors David Dobie and

Stephen Hall respectively, were selected by cutting a deck of cards, leaving Major Stephen Terrell's A Company to travel by sea; the two Rifle Companies were accompanied by Lieutenant-Colonel Pine-Coffin and a small HQ group, the Battalion 3-inch Mortar Platoon, Captain Antony Hewitt and Lieutenant Trevor Livesey with two sticks from C Troop 1st Parachute Squadron RE and No. 3 Section from the 16th Parachute Field Ambulance RAMC commanded by Captain John Keesey.[18] After some confusion over loading schedules and payload due to the C-47s being fitted with auxiliary fuel tanks, the 3rd Parachute Battalion moved to RAF Hurn near Bournemouth on 5 November, but persistent fog obliged a last-minute shift to RAF Saint Eval in Cornwall on 10 November via a special train and RAF trucks that delivered the paratroopers to the waiting C-47s just thirty minutes before take-off. After some last-minute rejigging of loads and passengers because two machines remained at Hurn with engine problems, thirty-one C-47s took off for Gibraltar at 23:30 on Tuesday 10 November, arriving there at dawn the following day.[19] Lieutenant-Colonel Pine-Coffin's orders were to refuel at Gibraltar and proceed to Maison Blanche where he was to prepare to secure airfields at Djidjelli or Bizerte dependent on the situation, but in the meantime Lieutenant-General Anderson had decided securing the airfield at Bône as a forward operating base was more important. Colonel Pine-Coffin was therefore informed that he was to leave Gibraltar combat loaded and ready to jump. This meant redoing the loading schedule for every aircraft, a task that took the entire day and into the night using searchlights for illumination, but the reloaded C-47s took off for Maison Blanche at 04:30 in the morning of Wednesday 11 November. One machine force landed in the sea but all aboard were rescued by a passing ship apart from Captain John Crichton, who was drowned assisting one of his men; the rescue ship was New York-bound and it took two months for the stick to rejoin their Battalion. The rest of the C-47s reached Maison Blanche unscathed apart from one which overflew Algiers harbour despite explicit orders not to do so and was hit by presumably Allied anti-aircraft fire that wounded one paratrooper and punctured a main wheel.

After landing at Maison Blanche at 08:00 Lieutenant-Colonel Pine-Coffin and a liaison officer from 1st Airborne Division HQ, Major Sir Richard Des Vœux, visited the HQ ship HMS *Bulolo*. There Lieutenant-General Anderson ordered Colonel Pine-Coffin to seize an airfield seven miles south of the port of Bône the following day, and added a warning that German airborne troops were likely about to move on the same target.[20] After a day of preparation the paratroopers were briefed at 16:30 for a daylight drop early the next morning, as the recently recruited USAAF pilots were not trained in night dropping techniques – and at the pilot briefing at 20:00 Colonel Dorsett discovered they had no drop training at all; he was obliged to run a crash course in the standard red/green light dropping technique, which was interrupted by a German bombing attack on the airfield. Despite this twenty-nine C-47s carrying between 312 and 360 men from the 3rd Parachute Battalion lifted off from Maison Blanche at dawn on Thursday 12 November to carry out the first large-scale British parachute operation in history. After a premature stand-by when Colonel Dorsett mistook the port of Bougie for Bône, the drop commenced on schedule at 08:30 with all the parachutists landing on or adjacent to the undefended airfield, although a number of containers landed up to a mile astray.[21] The drop came in the nick of time as it was witnessed by an approaching formation of Junkers 52 transports likely carrying men from *Fallschirmjäger* Regiment 5, which had arrived in Tunisia the previous day; on seeing the British parachutes the formation returned to Tunis.[22] Although the airfield was undefended it was not secured without cost. One paratrooper, possibly Sergeant Joseph Godfrey, was killed by an accidental discharge from his Sten Gun during the descent and thirteen men were injured in landing accidents caused by a combination of thin desert air and carrying heavier loads of equipment and ammunition than in training; one officer lay in a coma for several days repeatedly requesting more turbot from an imaginary waiter. Matters were complicated by the local Arab population, which immediately set about stealing whatever they could lay hands on, with silk parachute canopies being especially coveted.[23]

The 3rd Parachute Battalion landing was to be relieved by a seaborne landing force tasked to secure the port of Bône by the simple expedient of sailing the destroyers HMS *Lamerton* and HMS *Wheatland* into the harbour at dawn. The destroyers steamed the 150 miles or so from Bougie through the night of 11-12 November carrying Lieutenant-Colonel Iain MacAlpine's No. 6 Commando reinforced with party of US Army Rangers and a RN party of three cipher officers and twenty-six signal Ratings commanded by Commodore Philip Baker and Paymaster Sub-Lieutenant Gordon 'Mick' Stoke DSC; Commodore Baker had been designated Naval Officer in Charge (NOIC) for Bône and Sub-Lieutenant Stoke his Secretary.[24] Aged just twenty-one, Stoke had joined the RN at the outbreak of war and served as a Cadet aboard the cruiser HMS *Glasgow* until she was dry-docked at Alexandria following an Italian torpedo bomber attack at Suda Bay, Crete on 3 December 1940. *Glasgow's* commander, Captain Harold Hickling, was given command of the newly formed Inshore Squadron tasked to support the British land advance into Cyrenaica on 6 January 1941 and selected now-Midshipman Stoke as his sole staff officer. After being involved in the British advance along the Cyrenaican coast through via Sollum, Bardia and as far west as Benghazi, Stoke was stationed at Admiralty House in Tobruk throughout the siege of the port and was awarded the Distinguished Service Cross and a Mention in Dispatches in the process. By the time of TORCH, Stoke was still serving on the Inshore Squadron staff, now commanded by Captain Albert Poland DSO & Bar under whose authority he was despatched to Bône.[25]

The *Lamerton* and *Wheatland* steamed into the harbour at Bône just after dawn on Thursday 12 November with the Commandos and all hands on deck singing the *Marseillaise* in an effort to placate the French garrison whose reaction, while not overtly hostile, was reportedly 'polite but not cordial'.[26] Be that as it may, Lieutenant-Colonel MacAlpine and No. 6 Commando were on the move to the airfield as soon as the harbour was secured, where they linked up with Lieutenant-Colonel Pine-Coffin and the 3rd Parachute Battalion contingent; according to Saunders the Commandos were approaching the airfield when the drop took place and on arrival set about helping themselves to fruit from the orange groves adjacent to the airfield.[27] By the end of the day the paratroopers and Commandos had been joined by Spitfires from RAF No. 81 Squadron and the 3rd Parachute Battalion remained dug in for three days before being withdrawn on 17 November to rejoin the rest of the 1st Parachute Brigade at Maison Blanche.[28] Matters developed in a less benign manner back at Bône, where the departure of No. 6 Commando left Commodore Baker, Sub-Lieutenant Stoke and the RN party alone to defend the port with 'three revolvers, some rifles and…ingenuity'. Stoke himself was soon working twenty-hour days while simultaneously serving as Secretary and Staff Officer to NOIC Baker, Port Gunnery Officer and Port Signals Officer, operating from a building close to the main quay where he remained until May 1943.[29] He was then posted to the shore base HMS *Hasdrubal* at Bizerte with the commander of the North African Inshore Squadron from January 1943, Commodore Geoffrey Oliver DSO, to assist with the planning for HUSKY and was subsequently involved in the planning and execution of Operation AVALANCHE, the landings at Salerno in September 1943. The first tanker carrying 1,100 tons of petrol berthed at Bône on 17 December, just five days after the arrival of the RN party and by 8 January 1943 a total of 86,000 tons of assorted cargo including 3586 tons in a single twenty-four-hour period had been offloaded there, along with 4,491 vehicles and 31,085 troops. Bône thus became a key supply conduit for the Allied forces fighting in northern Tunisia virtually as soon as the RN party stepped ashore and their work was complicated further by constant Axis bombing beginning on 12 December. That month saw a total of twenty-one daylight raids averaging four machines per attack and forty-seven night raids, rising to thirty-three daylight raids averaging fifteen aircraft and fifteen night attacks across January 1943; by mid-February anti-aircraft fire from RN vessels and latterly land-based guns and night-fighters had reportedly accounted for 111 Axis aircraft shot down, twenty-four of them at night and a further eighty-six damaged.[30] Unsurprisingly, a contemporary account referred to Bône as 'a little Malta on its own', and Sub-Lieutenant Stoke was awarded the MBE for leading a party to move a burning vessel from the dockside during a heavy bombing attack on the night of 4-5 December 1942.[31]

The 3rd Parachute Battalion's drop at Bône was the first in a series of parachute operations ordered by British 1st Army in the immediate aftermath of Operation TORCH, with the next two being intended to seize a hub on a major route into Tunisia and secure the southern flank of the projected Allied line of advance to the east respectively; both were scheduled for Sunday 15 November. The flank mission, which involved capturing two airfields just over a hundred miles south of Bône, was allotted to Lieutenant-Colonel Raff's 509th Parachute Infantry Regiment fresh from its somewhat disjointed participation in the landings at Oran; the unit had moved to billets at Maison Blanche on 13 November and came under operational control of the 1st Parachute Brigade the same day. Raff received a personal briefing from Lieutenant-General Anderson aboard the *Bulolo* on 12 November also attended by Major-General Mark W. Clark, Deputy Commander-in-Chief of the Allied Expeditionary Force. The briefing tasked him to secure the small airfield at Tébessa, just over 300 miles south-east of Maison Blanche on the Tunisian border, although the objective was subsequently changed to a larger airfield at Youks les Bains ten miles to the north-west; Tébessa was downgraded to secondary post-jump objective. The briefing also included warnings about the possibility of German parachute troops pursuing the same objective and ended with Raff being given 25,000 Francs to pay for intelligence from the local population. As only twenty-two C-47s were available, the jump was restricted to 350 men and Colonel Raff selected Companies D and E, commanded by Captains William J. Morrow and John Berry respectively, augmented with elements from HQ Company, two teams from 1st Parachute Brigade Signals Section with No. 65 wireless sets and a totally untrained journalist named John H. Thompson.[32] The C-47s took off from Maison Blanche at 07:30 on 15 November and after following a circuitous route along the coast to Djidjelli where they were joined by an escort of eight RAF Hurricane fighters, successfully delivered their passengers onto Youks les Bains airfield. The jump was unopposed but the Battalion suffered fifteen jump injuries including Captain Berry with a badly broken left leg, and within a short time Company D was digging in to defend the airfield while Company E moved off for Tébessa, which was also secured without incident apart from shooting up a Junkers 88 that mistakenly attempted to land there after Captain Berry's men had taken up residence. Back at Youks les Bains, Colonel Raff secured a large amount of aviation fuel and was alarmed to discover that his drop zone had been overlooked by well dug in, heavily armed but fortunately friendly troops from the 3e *Régiment de Zouaves*; an unofficial exchange between Raff and the French commander, a *Colonel* Berges, led to the 509th Parachute Regiment wearing the French unit insignia as an honorary badge to this day. Once relieved, Raff remained at Youks les Bains and took to leading his men on ever deeper forays into Tunisia, on one occasion penetrating ninety miles to Sidi Bou Zid, where they captured two hundred Axis prisoners; the increasing risk of being cut off during these forays eventually obliged Major-General Clark to order Raff to rein in his activities.[33]

The RMS *Arundel Castle* arrived at Algiers on 12 November and the seaborne portion of the 1st Parachute Brigade disembarked the following evening after spending two days anchored and under air attack in the Bay of Algiers, moving to billets at Maison Blanche airfield and the nearby towns of Maison Carrée and Rouiba, five miles to the west and east respectively. The RAF No. 1 Mobile Parachute Servicing Unit attached to Brigade HQ commanded by a Flight-Lieutenant Hare requisitioned a convenient cinema as a parachute packing and drying facility and immediately set about servicing the more than 3,000 parachutes that had been transported to

North Africa from the UK packed in bundles of twelve inside balloon-fabric lined packing cases; the packing cases were recycled as parachute packing tables.[34] The Brigade's other personnel spent until 16:30 on 14 November unloading and moving the Brigade's equipment from the *Arundel Castle* to their billets, working through the night under blackout conditions utilising a few commandeered trucks. While this work was underway Lieutenant-Colonel James Hill's 1st Parachute Battalion was slated for a jump the following day and Hill requested a postponement as there was insufficient time to complete gathering and preparing equipment and allow his men some rest. When this not unreasonable request was refused by 1st Army HQ he detached a hundred-strong rear party from the upcoming operation under Battalion second-in-command Major Alastair Pearson and set them to finishing the preparation and packing while the rest of the unit slept.[35] The work was completed at 05:00, just two or two and a half hours before take-off depending on the source.[36] The 1st Parachute Battalion was tasked to drop at Souk-el Arba, sixty-four miles south-east of Bône and twenty miles inside Tunisia, to ascertain if the small airfield there was suitable for use as a forward fighter base, secure the road junction at Beja thirty miles to the north-east, persuade the French military units there to come over to the Allied cause and 'harry the enemy wherever they found him'.[37] This was a tall order for a single battalion with no firm intelligence, maps or transport and it raises the suspicion that 1st Army HQ and Lieutenant-General Anderson in particular viewed the 1st Parachute Brigade as an expendable reconnaissance asset rather than an expensively trained and hard to replace specialist formation, a suspicion that was to be strongly reinforced by Anderson's subsequent behaviour.

Be that as it may, Lieutenant-Colonel Hill's force consisted of his R and S Companies, a detachment from the 1st Parachute Squadron RE led by Captain Patrick Geary and Lieutenant David Wright's No.1 Section and Lieutenant Charles Robb's No. 1 Surgical Team from 16th Parachute Field Ambulance, numbering approximately 425 men. The force took off at 07:00 on the morning of Sunday 15 September aboard thirty-two C-47s from the 64th Troop Carrier Group, possibly the same aircraft that had dropped the 3rd Parachute Battalion at Bône three days earlier given that one source refers to the aircrew lacking parachute dropping experience.[38] The transports were escorted by four USAAF Lockheed Lightning fighters which drove off two German fighters but the flight then ran into increasingly thick cloud on the approach to the Tunisian border that eventually led to the mission being abandoned; all thirty-two aircraft landed safely back at Maison Blanche at 11:00.

Lieutenant-General Anderson was reportedly 'furious at the battalion's return and...did nothing to conceal his dislike of paratroops, of which he knew little' and he retaliated by forbidding Colonel Hill from returning to Maison Blanche if weather prevented a second attempt to drop at Souk-el Arba the following day. He was instead instructed to pick a suitable landing area as close as possible to the objective and then advance in 'an easterly direction to make contact with the enemy'.[39] In the event the landing force took off again at 11:00 on 16 November, this time accompanied by a rested Major Pearson and a number of men from the rear party who scrambled aboard the C-47s carrying parachutes and personal weapons as the machines taxied along the perimeter track to the runway.[40] This time the weather co-operated and the drop went in at Souk-el Arba unopposed at approximately 13:45, although again not without cost. Private Walter Webster was throttled to death during his descent after a rigging line somehow encircled his neck, liaison officer Major Des Vœux broke his leg and three more men were wounded in another accidental discharge from a Sten Gun. On a lighter note the commander of S Company, Major Peter Cleasby-Thompson, burst his water bottle on landing and initially thought the wetness was blood rather than his water ration. Lieutenant-Colonel Hill immediately commandeered a number of charcoal gas powered vehicles from the locals and set off for Beja leaving a small party under Major Pearson to gather up the parachutes and jump equipment and bury the unfortunate Private Webster with full military honours; to Pearson's dismay the entire population of Souk-el Arba solemnly turned out for the funeral and he ended up shaking hands 3,000 times in line with French burial etiquette.

The bulk of the Battalion reached Beja at around 18:00 in torrential rain where Lieutenant-Colonel Hill set about winning over the commander of the local French garrison through a mixture of diplomacy and bluff, the latter by marching the well spread-out Battalion through Beja twice, wearing different head dress to create the impression of greater numbers. The deal was clinched the following day when S Company successfully ambushed a column of German light armour at Sidi Nsir, twenty-eight miles to the north-east, destroying four armoured vehicles in return for two wounded and returned to Beja with a captured scout car and a number of prisoners. This was no mean feat given that the paratroopers only anti-armour weapons were Hawkins anti-tank mines and Gammon bombs and the exploit won Major Cleasby Thompson and Lieutenant Phillip Mellor the Military Cross; Company Sergeant-Major Samuel Steadman, who was wounded in the face and thigh, and Sergeant Ryan were awarded the Military Medal.[41]

Colonel Hill then led a thirty-mile foray to the east to Medjez el Bab and secured local French co-operation to protect the bridge over the River Medjerda there before running a programme of aggressive patrolling from Beja that ultimately proved to be his personal undoing. On the night of 23-24 November, Hill led R and S Companies accompanied by a party of approximately nineteen Sappers from the 1st Parachute Squadron RE under Captain Patrick Geary to attack an enemy tank laager atop a hill at Gué, nine miles north-east of Beja. A stealthy approach went initially according to plan with Lieutenant-Colonel Hill and his Adjutant Captain Miles Whitelock accompanying the Sapper party in circling the laager to lay mines across lines of escape while the attack force waited under Major Pearson. This ended at 02:45 when a series of three explosions reportedly caused by a Sapper accidentally dropping a sandbag containing pre-primed Hawkins Mines that set off the devices in two more sandbags, killed Captain Geary and eighteen of his men but left Hill and Whitelock unscathed.[42] The attack force immediately launched themselves up the slope in the teeth of automatic fire with Hill and Whitelock in the lead. Hill reportedly induced the crew of one Italian tank to surrender by firing his pistol into a vision port and the crew of a second by the simple expedient of banging on the armour with a stout stick he habitually carried and demanding their surrender, but a third tank was crewed by Germans who emerged 'firing and throwing grenades'. Lieutenant-Colonel Hill was shot three times in the chest and Captain Whitelock was badly wounded in the arms, head and legs by grenade shrapnel; both men were rushed back by motorcycle combination and then train to Beja, the latter being strafed by German fighters en route. There they were saved by prompt action from Lieutenant Robb and his No. 1 Surgical Team at the civilian hospital in the town which had been taken over by the 16th Parachute Field Ambulance contingent; Lieutenant Robb was still performing surgery despite suffering a fractured tibia from a bomb blast, and had also donated his own blood when plasma supplies ran short.[43] Lieutenant-Colonel Hill was awarded the Distinguished Service Order for his part in the action.[44]

The attack force withdrew from the hilltop laager leaving the Axis casualties to be tended by their own side. The latter's numbers are unclear but the 1st Parachute Battalion lost at least five dead in addition to Captain Geary's party including Captain John Stewart, one of the original No. 2 Commando parachute volunteers.[45] Command of the Battalion devolved to Major Pearson who moved north-east toward Mateur in support of the ground advance from Bône by Major-General Vyvyan Evelegh's 78th Division, which had begun on 15 November. The Battalion was relieved by and came under command of a mixed column codenamed BLADE Force on 26 November and remained in the line for just over two weeks, fighting a successful major defensive action alongside the 2nd Battalion Lancashire Fusiliers and tanks from the 17th/21st Lancers at a hilltop location dubbed Coxen's Farm on 1 December. The 1st Parachute Battalion was finally withdrawn to Maison Blanche eleven days later, on 12 December. [46]

All this and subsequent parachute operations ordered by 1st Army HQ leave no doubt that Lieutenant-General Anderson not only viewed the 1st Parachute Battalion as a disposable reconnaissance asset, but one seemingly to be deployed on a whim. At 10:00 on 17 November Brigadier Flavell was ordered to despatch the 1st Parachute Battalion's T Company rear party to Enfidaville, forty miles south of Tunis on the east Tunisian coast and about as far behind Axis lines as it was possible to get. The Company was to take sufficient light arms and rations to be self-sufficient for ten days and tasked to interdict traffic on the Tripoli-Tunis road using 'guerrilla tactics'; perhaps fortunately for T Company, the mission was cancelled at 13:00 after strenuous objections from Brigadier Flavell that the projected force was simply insufficient for the task. Even then, it appears to have been briefly passed thereafter to Lieutenant-Colonel John Frost's 2nd Parachute Battalion before being cancelled again after an aerial reconnaissance the following day, although

Frost's Battalion remained firmly in the frame for the next British parachute operation thereafter.[47] On 18 November Frost was ordered to prepare to drop at Kairouan airfield and the port of Sousse, thirty miles to the east, to deny the enemy use of those facilities; the operation was to be a two-stage affair due to a shortage of C-47s, the first departing at 11:00 on 19 November and the second on the following day, 20 November. The operation was postponed for twenty-four hours at 23:00 on 18 November and then for a minimum of another three days at 14:30 on 19 November, after which it appears to have been quietly abandoned.

On 22 November, 1st Army HQ gave the 1st and 3rd Parachute Battalions – the latter having returned from Bône three days earlier – three days' notice to stand-by for missions and on 27 November 1st Parachute Brigade HQ received a warning order for an unspecified operation with effect from dawn the following day. Lieutenant-Colonel Frost's Battalion was selected, likely in part because it was becoming restive at being kept out of the action; Frost referred to his men drinking and routinely fighting with their US and French counterparts as an outlet for their pent-up energy.[48] At 15:00 the same day the 2nd Parachute Battalion was detailed to drop at Pont du Fahs, 370 miles east of Maison Blanche, to destroy aircraft and stores at the airfields there and at Depienne and Oudna, around twenty miles south of Tunis, in support of a general Allied advance toward Tunis and Bizerte. At 22:30 this mission was postponed until Sunday 29 November, and in the interim the airfield at Pont du Fahs was evacuated by the Axis and secured by elements of the British 78th Division, which reported that Depienne airfield had also been abandoned and the runway ploughed up. The 2nd Parachute Battalion was therefore ordered to drop at Depienne and make its way across the thirteen miles or so to the remaining objective at Oudna, after which it was to link up with the advancing 78th Division at St. Cyprien, fourteen miles north-west of Oudna. The new information did not arrive until shortly before take-off, obliging a re-brief of the C-47 pilots and Frost to embark on his modified mission with no background information, aerial photography or maps of the drop area; instead he was to travel in the lead aircraft and select a suitable landing zone and jump after a low fly over.[49]

The precise number of men in the lift is unclear, but the 2nd Parachute Battalion appears to have been lifted in its entirety, accompanied by B Troop from the 1st Parachute Squadron RE and Lieutenant J. C. McGavin's No. 2 Section from the 16th Parachute Field Ambulance, all carried in forty-four C-47s from the US 62nd and 64th Troop Carrier Groups. The aircraft from the latter Group were reportedly the same machines that had carried the 1st Parachute Battalion to Souk-el Arba thirteen days earlier; all arrived at Maison Blanche from their base at Blida early in the morning of Monday 29 November.[50] Take off appears to have been scheduled to begin at 11:30 but this was delayed due to confusion in mating sticks of paratroopers and their containers to specific aircraft, as the C-47s had not been parked as expected, and the loading process was complicated yet further by thick mud resulting from heavy overnight rain that prevented the trucks carrying the weapons and equipment containers from reaching the flight line, obliging the paratroopers to offload and manhandle the heavy and unwieldy burdens to the aircraft. Take-off commenced at 12:30 and all the machines were aloft by 12:45 bar one bogged in the mud, although some sticks may have been shifted from other bogged machines at the last minute; Frost's memoir refers to a 'medical stick' almost being run down by a taxiing C-47 as they hurriedly moved to another aircraft while take-offs were underway.[51] Apart from some airsickness due to 'bad and bumpy weather', the flight to Depienne was uneventful, likely due to a strong escort of RAF Spitfires, Hurricanes and USAAF Lightnings, and the drop commenced at 14:50 onto an area of plough land selected by Lieutenant-Colonel Frost. The landing was unopposed but six men were injured in landing accidents and Sapper Harry Craighan was killed when his parachute failed to develop properly; a number of containers were also lost due to parachute failure or the aircraft racks failing to release.[52] At 16:00 the paratroopers were joined briefly by three armoured cars from 56 Reconnaissance Regiment which patrolled northward before returning at 17:00 to report a German roadblock seven miles away on the route to Oudna.

In the meantime parachutes and other jump equipment had been gathered up and cached on the drop zone for later collection as per Brigade standing orders, the jump casualties had been moved to the local school in the care of friendly French locals who informed the new arrivals that the Germans had withdrawn three days ago and B Company rounded up a number of mule carts to carry the Battalion's heavy equipment. After resting until around midnight the Battalion column, less a platoon from C Company detailed to guard the equipment and jump casualties, moved off and marched through the night over rugged terrain until 04:30 on Tuesday 30 November when Frost decided to allow the men to sleep until dawn, although bitter cold largely negated the benefit. Moving off again at 07:15 the column was on high ground at Prise de l'Eau overlooking Oudna from the south by 11:00 and by 14:30 the landing ground had been secured by A Company along with the adjacent Oudna village and railway station after a skirmish with German troops. The landing ground proved to be completely devoid of *Luftwaffe* stores or aircraft apart from a single wrecked and abandoned Junkers 87 and four large haystacks. The 2nd Parachute Battalion's mission was thus negated at a stroke.[53]

It was at this point that matters began to go seriously awry for Frost and his men. At 15:30 A and C Companies came under fire from three to five tanks and possibly four armoured cars depending on the source, located in Roman ruins on the Battalion's right flank. When the German vehicles began moving closer they were kept at bay by a stalking party armed with Gammon bombs organised and led by Lieutenant Kenneth Morrison, who was killed in the process. At the same time the remainder of the Battalion came under repeated strafing attacks, initially from German fighters and at 17:30 by six Junkers 87 dive-bombers, although one source refers to the dive-bombers merely attempting to land before being warned off by flares fired by German troops in the vicinity.[54] The effectiveness of the air attacks was nullified by a combination of the paratrooper's camouflaged Denison smocks and face veils, although the commandeered mule carts and heavy equipment were badly shot up; the surviving carts were used to move the wounded back to the Advanced Dressing Station (ADS) set up by Lieutenant McGavin in an Arab farm building on the high ground. Deciding that his mission had been fulfilled by default and that the landing ground position was too exposed to defend against German armour, Lieutenant-Colonel Frost broke contact at dusk and withdrew south by the light of the burning haystacks to two more defensible adjacent hilltops at Prise de l'Eau to await relief, deploying A and B Companies on the peaks with C Company to the south in reserve. The ground proved too rocky for the paratroopers to dig in and the Battalion spent another freezing night fruitlessly trying to contact 1st Army HQ via radio and listening to the sounds of battle from Tebourba, twenty-five miles to the north-west. The 78th Division had been engaged in a push to take Bizerte and Tunis since 26 November, the effort coming to an abrupt halt in the face of co-ordinated German counter-attacks that almost cut off 11th Infantry Brigade, decimating the 2nd Battalion The Hampshire Regiment in the process, and pushed the British advance back west of Tebourba in four days of intense fighting. Although Frost and his men had no way of knowing, the German counter-attacks also stalled their scheduled relief and the 2nd Parachute Battalion was in the process of being abandoned fifty miles behind German lines.

Lieutenant-Colonel Frost's intention was to remain in place until midday on Tuesday 1 December but at 10:00 a German column of two tanks, two armoured cars and trucks carrying infantry approached the Battalion position from Oudna. The column was halted by an inconclusive defensive ambush and withdrew after a bombardment from Frost's 3-inch mortars. The Battalion location was then strafed repeatedly from the air before a second group of German vehicles approached C Company's positions on from the south displaying yellow Allied recognition panels taken from the platoon left at Depienne, which had been captured. The ruse allowed the vehicles to close up to C Company's perimeter and capture an NCO who was then sent back with a demand for surrender, but they again withdrew when the demand was rejected and the paratroopers attempted to attack the interlopers with Gammon bombs. Frost then relocated just over a mile or so to the south-west into a Battalion perimeter on the slopes of the Djebel Sidi bou Hadjeba, which allowed greater scope for breaking contact again at dusk and fortuitously contained a well; unfortunately, the move also meant severing contact with Lieutenant McGavin's ADS, which was treating in excess of a hundred casualties by then.[55] There the Battalion came under renewed and sustained attack at 15:00 from the north, east and south that killed the commander of B Company, Major Herbert Cleaver, and almost wiped out C Company; the dead included Major Philip Teichman, Lieutenant The Hon. Henry Cecil and Corporal Sydney Duncan.

The situation was saved by *Luftwaffe* aircraft mistakenly strafing their own troops and reportedly knocking out some armoured vehicles; this stalled the German attack which faded away with the onset of dusk. By this point ammunition was running low – Frost noted that ammunition expenditure had been heavier than training in the UK had anticipated – and the 2nd Parachute Battalion was faced with imminent destruction by a resumption of the German attack the following day.[56] Frost therefore decided to break contact after dark and withdraw toward Massicault, around twenty miles to the north-west, in the hope of meeting up with Allied ground forces. The Official History suggests that Frost's decision was prompted by a radio message from 1st Army at some point in the morning informing him that the projected British advance toward Tunis had been postponed, meaning the paratroopers had been left to their fate.[57] However, Frost's account makes no mention of any such message, although it does refer repeatedly to being unable to make contact with 1st Army up to the point when the radios were abandoned before moving to the Djebel Sidi bou Hadjeba because all the batteries had been discharged, along with the Battalion's by then ammunitionless 3-inch mortars.[58] The Official History claim thus looks suspiciously like an *ex post facto* attempt to divert attention away from the fact that Frost and his men had been effectively left to their fate.

Be that as it may, Frost decided to exfiltrate in Company groups rather than in a large Battalion column, although the severely depleted C Company failed to arrive at the designated departure point as arranged; according to Cole the Company had been surrounded and was overwhelmed in place.[59] The wounded from the Djebel Sidi bou Hadjeba fighting, who had been gathered in by Battalion Medical Officer Major Ronald Gordon with the assistance of an 'old and battered mule', were also left behind along with a platoon from B Company led by Lieutenant Patrick Playford, tasked to protect Lieutenant McGavin's ADS after searching the battlefield for any additional wounded. The Battalion successfully broke contact aided by an initially moonless night and there followed an epic two-day withdrawal across thirty miles or more of rugged terrain that involved fighting another delaying action in the late afternoon and evening of Wednesday 2 December when the Germans closed up on a farm where the Battalion had reassembled and holed up for the daylight hours before breaking contact again after dark. This time the move was north-west toward Medjez el Bab, the only location Frost felt certain remained in Allied hands, and the 2nd Parachute Battalion's lead elements arrived there at 16:00 on Thursday 4 December after briefly mistaking patrolling US M3 half-tacks for German vehicles.[60] At this point the Battalion's strength had been reduced to approximately 200 all ranks, less than half of its War Establishment of 556 men, and had suffered 260 casualties since 29 November including at least thirty-five dead, although around fifty stragglers rejoined the Battalion before it was finally withdrawn to Souk el Khemis in Algeria to join the remainder of the 1st Parachute Brigade on 11 November 1942.[61] The 2nd Parachute Battalion was thus practically destroyed in pursuit of a needless mission for which there was no real justification, and the same can be said for the earlier missions carried out by the 1st and 3rd Parachute Battalions. The former's mission to Souk-el Arba was equally nebulous and while the latter's jerry-rigged drop at Bône was successful it could just as easily been achieved by conventional forces, given that the objective was only five miles from Bône harbour from where the paratroopers were rapidly joined by No. 6 Commando.

At least some of this capriciously speculative deployment was likely due to the novelty of the airborne technique, but that does not excuse the subsequent employment of the 1st Parachute Brigade in the conventional infantry role for almost five continuous months. From 11 December 1943, Brigadier Flavell's formation was responsible for a section of the line at Beja in the 78th Division sector and led severe fighting to secure the Djebel Alliliga and Djebel Mansour in the Bou Arada sector under *Général de Corps d'Armée* Maurice Mathenet's 19th *Corps*, took part in heavy defensive fighting under 6th Armoured Division and an *ad hoc* force dubbed 'Y' Division, returned to the Beja sector under control of the 46th Division and then took part in attacks alongside 36th and 138th Infantry Brigades before finally being relieved by the US 39th Regimental Combat Team (RCT) and moving back to Bou Farik, fifteen miles south-west of Algiers, on 18 April 1943.[62] In conjunction with the earlier parachute operations and connected activity these deployments, which extended across every sector of the British front in Tunisia, cost the 1st Parachute Brigade 1,700 casualties, including at least 202 killed during the Brigade's employment in the conventional infantry role between 12 December 1942 and 18 April 1943.[63] At least seventy-five per cent of the already understrength Brigade thus became casualties of some kind during the deployment to North Africa, which also effectively wiped out the carefully selected and expensively trained original British volunteer parachute cadre, as 1st Army HQ saw the 1st Parachute Brigade as a disposable reconnaissance asset and a convenient unprotected source of additional manpower, largely because there was no high ranking officer in theatre to fight Brigadier Flavell's corner to prevent such misuse. As the British Official History of Airborne Forces put it in its lessons learned summary 'It was evident that it was most uneconomical and inefficient to employ a parachute brigade in ground operations... A senior commander or adviser at Army or Supreme Headquarters was required to look after its interest there'.[64]

To be fair, the 1st Parachute Brigade was not alone in feeling the effects of Lieutenant-General Anderson's command style. When General Sir Harold Alexander was appointed to command all the Allied armies in Tunisia, dubbed the 18th Army Group, on 19 February 1943 he reported an overall lack of policy and campaign plan as a result of 'no firm direction or centralized control from above'; he also later claimed to have been 'frankly shocked at [the] whole situation' as he found it in a subsequent report to CIGS Field Marshal Sir Alan Brooke and Prime Minister Churchill.[65] Be that as it may, culpability for placing the 1st Parachute Brigade in such an invidious position lay higher up the chain of command, for there was little if any justification for despatching the 1st Parachute Brigade to North Africa. The still-forming

2nd Parachute Brigade's training and operational progress was hindered by stripping it of parachute qualified personnel to bring the 1st Parachute Brigade up to something approaching its War Establishment. For its part the 1st Parachute Brigade gained little if anything from the experience apart from allegedly earning the nickname 'Red Devils' from their German opponents, appropriating the phrase 'Waho Mohammed' from the Arab locals as a battle cry, an extensive and arguably unnecessary casualty list, and combat experience for the portion of the Brigade that survived, although the value of the latter is also arguable; the 3rd and 5th Parachute Brigades performed to an exemplary standard in Normandy without any combat experience, for example.

The responsibility lay with Major-General Browning whose lobbying to have part of his still-forming Airborne fiefdom involved in TORCH was driven not so much by the desire to advertise and expand the new technique but by his inveterate proclivity for self-promotion, and the deleterious and in some instances literally fatal consequences of this propensity were to bear a full crop of poisoned fruit at Arnhem just under two years later. All that lay in the future and in the meantime there was the matter of clearing Axis forces from Tunisia, and more particularly the German reinforcements that had begun to arrive in the country within twenty-four hours of the TORCH landings.

3

To Become Masters of the North African Shore

The Winter Fighting in Tunisia, November 1942 to May 1943

The TORCH landings in Algeria on 8 November 1942 elicited a swift reaction from Hitler, who immediately ordered *Generalfeldmarschall* Albert Kesselring at *Oberbefehlshaber Süd* (*OB Süd*), the senior German command in the Mediterranean, to set about establishing an air and sea bridgehead into the north of Tunisia as a conduit for reinforcements and materiel. The effort began with II *Fliegerkorps*, which had been moving into the Mediterranean theatre from the Eastern Front since October in response to Allied air and sea activity at Gibraltar; approximately forty *Luftwaffe* aircraft arrived at El Aouina airfield at Tunis on 9 November following 'negotiations' between the Vichy authorities and two *Luftwaffe* officers, a *Hauptmann* Behlau and a *Hauptmann* Schürmeyer, the previous day.[1] By 10 November *Luftwaffe* strength in Tunisia had increased to 445 machines under command of *Oberst* Martin Harlinghausen, the newly created *Fliegerführer Tunesien*; RAF reconnaissance the same day revealed the presence of twenty Macchi C202 fighters from the *Regia Aeronautica* at El Aouina along with twenty-four Junkers 87 dive-bombers, three Heinkel 111 twin-engine bombers and twenty-three Messerschmitt 109 fighters. By 15 November the number of fighters had grown to eighty-one including the first increment of fourteen Focke-Wulf 190 fighter-bombers from the ground-attack unit *Schlachtgeschwader 2*.[2] The RAF reconnaissance also revealed the presence of forty-two Junkers 52, two Junkers 90 and three giant Messerschmitt transports with a payload of around ten tons, although it is unclear if the latter were the 321 glider version or the powered 323 version.

These machines were part of a parallel expansion of the *Luftwaffe* transport fleet in Tunisia over the month from the beginning of October 1942 that increased the number of machines from 205 to 673 and carried out the initial stages of the German reinforcement effort. On 12 November, 500 men including elements of *Fallschirmjäger Regiment* 5 and seventy-four tons of stores were flown in, followed by a further six hundred the following day. Within three days the airlift total had risen to 3,000 men and 170 tons of petrol and by the end of the month had risen to 15,273 men and 581 tonnes of supplies.[3] In December 1942, the airlift system was given its own distinct commander, *Generalleutnant* Ulrich Bucholz, who was appointed *Lufttransportführer Mittelmeer* and the system was streamlined to reduce the number of airfields involved apart from temporary emergency dispersals. At the other end of the chain a dedicated HQ was set up in Rome with staffs controlling airfields in Calabria and Sicily from satellite HQs located at Capodichino on the outskirts of Naples and Trapani on the eastern tip of Sicily. The airlift effort continued until 11 May 1943 with the Junkers 52 fleet capable of carrying 1.8 tonnes apiece providing the bulk of the lift, employing an average of 200 machines per day. This brought in a daily total of 585 tonnes per day during the initial maximum effort, although this tailed off to less than 190 tonnes from April 1943 as Allied fighters began to extract an increasing toll on the slow and vulnerable transports. The flights consisted of formations of eighty to 120 aircraft, dubbed *pulks* (throngs) flying at just 150 feet above the sea to avoid Allied radar. Sicily-based aircraft made two round trips per day starting in the early morning and late evening while formations making the longer run from Naples were escorted for the final 140 miles across the Sicilian Strait by fighters also based on the island. These and Tunisian-based fighters provided cover for the shorter flights and loading, unloading and return journeys and although the Allied air forces became more adept at detecting and attacking the vulnerable transport formations with the aid of ULTRA intelligence, the escorts managed to extend the effectiveness of the airlift until 26 April 1943; on that date *Oberkommando der Luftwaffe* (*OKL*) finally restricted resupply flights to Tunisia to the hours of darkness on direct orders from *Reichsmarschall* Göring, which 'greatly reduced the scale of Axis air deliveries'.[4]

Extensive though the *Luftwaffe* airlift was, the bulk of personnel, heavy equipment and supplies for the Axis build up in northern Tunisia were brought in by sea, with the first increment arriving on the same day the airlift commenced. In the evening of 12 November two Italian transports docked in Bizerte carrying seventeen tanks, fifty-five trucks, four artillery pieces and 340 men along with forty tons of munitions and 101 tonnes of fuel; by the end of the month the total delivered had increased to 159 tanks and armoured cars, 1,097 assorted vehicles, 127 artillery pieces, 1,867 personnel and 12,549 tonnes of supplies.[5] The sea lift employed a pool of Italian and German merchant ships with a total capacity of around 150,000 tonnes augmented with a further 100,000 tons of Vichy shipping, fourteen submarines, and a total of twenty large-capacity ferries belonging to the *Heer* and *Kriegsmarine* from late December.[6] Most ships were channelled into Tunis and Bizerte due to the road and rail network emanating from those ports, with smaller craft using the shallower ports at Sousse and Sfax, although access into Bizerte, Tunis and Sfax was partially blocked by sunken wrecks. Unloading was problematic as the cargo vessels were not generally equipped with heavy lifting equipment, the powered cranes at Bizerte and Tunis had been damaged or destroyed by Allied bombing and attempts to procure replacements from Marseille and Toulon failed when the vessels carrying them were sunk en route. This made unloading tanks and vehicles especially problematic and it took an entire day to unload 1,500 tonnes of cargo by hand, thus leaving the vessels exposed to Allied air attack for prolonged periods. The actual unloading was eventually carried out by members of the *Reichsarbeitsdienst* and dock workers drafted in from Hamburg after local Arab and Italian labour proved unequal to the task.[7] Nonetheless, between November 1942 and January 1943 the combined air and sea lift brought 81,222 German and 30,735 Italian troops into Tunisia along with 100,594 tonnes of materiel.[8]

The air and sea lift allowed the Germans to assemble a formidable force to oppose the TORCH landing force in northern Tunisia in short order. First to arrive on 12 November was *Oberstleutnant* Walter Koch's understrength *Fallschirmjäger Regiment 5*, which secured El Aouina and other airfields and the city of Tunis along with the lead elements of *Panzer Abteilung 190* that arrived at Bizerte in the evening; both units had been previously earmarked as reinforcements for formations in *Generalfeldmarschall* Erwin Rommel's *Deutsch-Italienische Panzerarmee* in Libya. On 20 November, lead elements of *Fallschirm Pionier Regiment Barenthin*, a composite parachute unit commanded by *Oberst* Walther Barenthin also arrived in Bizerte followed three days later by the first increment of *Major* Hans-Georg Lueder's Tiger I-equipped *schwere Panzer Abteilung 501* landing at Tunis. On 27 November *Panzer Regiment 7* from *10 Panzer Division* also began unloading at Tunis, although the passage had not been uneventful as the vessels carrying Nos. 5 & 8 *Kompanien* were sunk en route with the loss of thirty-three assorted tanks; *Division* commander *Generalleutnant* Wolfgang Fischer had arrived in Tunisia two days earlier on 25 November and was promptly appointed *Militärbefehlshaber* of Bizerte, with instructions to pay particular attention to the loyalty of the Vichy troops in and around the port.[9] The second complete German formation assigned to Tunisia was *Oberst* and subsequently *Generalmajor* Friedrich Weber's *334 Infanterie Division*, which began to arrive at Bizerte at the end of December 1942 and was fully present by 15 January 1943. A *Luftwaffe* formation, *Generalmajor* Joseph Schmid's still forming *Hermann Göring Division*, was also slated for Tunisia with the lead elements arriving in November 1942; additional elements of the formation did not arrive until February 1943 and the initial deployment fought under the title *Kampfgruppe* Schmid. *Comando Supremo* in Rome were also swift in despatching units to Tunisia beginning with *1ª Superga Divisione*, a mountain formation commanded by *Generale di Divisione* Dante Lorenzelli, which began disembarking at Bizerte on 11 or 12 November. The *Superga* was followed by *Generale di Brigata* Giovanni Imperiali's *50ª Brigata Speciale*, the *10° Reggimento Bersaglieri* and elements of a marine unit, the *Reggimento San Marco*; the Italian deployment to Tunisia eventually totalled 47,000 men, 2,700 assorted vehicles and 148 artillery pieces.[10]

The deployment of these disparate units and formations to Tunisia also necessitated the creation of new and dedicated command arrangements. *Heer Oberst* Hans-Wolfgang Lederer arrived in Tunis to take command of what was initially dubbed *Kampfgruppe Tunesien* on 11 November and, finding *Oberst* Harlinghausen had matters there in hand, moved his HQ to Bizerte, the principal gateway for the Axis sealift, two days later. There he opted to restrict his activities to protecting the port, not least due to the small size of his force in comparison with around 3,000 Vichy troops in the vicinity, and while his inactivity was reportedly sanctioned by *OB Süd* it does not appear to have gone down well with *Generalfeldmarschall* Kesselring or his soon-to-arrive superior.[11] *General der Panzertruppe* Walther Nehring had been wounded at the Battle of Alam el Halfa in August 1942 and following convalesence in Germany was in Rome on 12 November, en route to rejoin the *Deutsch-Italienische Panzerarmee* in Libya. At that point he was summoned by Kesselring who appointed him head of the newly created *90 Korps* to replace *Oberst* Lederer, whose performance was deemed unsatisfactory, and tasked him to take overall control of the Tunisian bridgehead and expand it westward far enough to permit manoeuvre and preferably as far as the Tunisia-Algeria border. Nehring flew out to Tunisia on a personal reconnaissance on 14 November, returned to Tunis on 16 November after an update from Kesselring and established *90 Korps* HQ in the former US consulate in Tunis on 17 November accompanied by a single officer and with no staff, communications equipment or transport; the latter two shortfalls were reportedly initially overcome by using the insecure local telephone system and French taxi hire.[12] He began his tenure by dividing the bridgehead into two separate parts centred on Bizerte and Tunis, commanded by officers directly responsible to *90 Korps*.

At Bizerte *Oberst* Lederer was replaced by an *Oberstleutnant* Stolz with effect from 16 November, before being replaced in turn by *Oberst* Friedrich *Freiherr* von Broich who established the *Division von Broich* on 18 November as an *ad hoc* umbrella HQ for a number of units including *Fallschirm Pionier Regiment Barenthin*, *Fallschirm Pionier Regiment 11*, the *10° Reggimento Bersaglieri* and, from the end of December, *10 Panzer Division*.[13] Von Broich was replaced by *Generalleutnant* Hasso von Manteuffel with effect from 7 February 1943 and the formation was redesignated *Division von Manteuffel* at that time. Events followed a similar pattern at Tunis, where *Oberst* Harlinghausen was relieved to return to his role as *Fliegerführer Tunesien* by *Oberstleutnant* Koch from *Fallschirmjäger Regiment 5*; according to one source Koch was subsequently replaced by *Generale* Lorenzelli.[14] However, and perhaps ironically given the context of his elevation to *90 Korps* command, Kesselring also reportedly found Nehring's performance lacking during a visit to Tunis on 28 November 1942, although this dissatisfaction may also have been due to Nehring expressing forthright and pessimistic views on the future prospects of Axis operations in Tunisia.[15] Nehring was replaced on Hitler's direct order by *Generaloberst* Hans-Jürgen von Arnim fresh from commanding *39 Panzer Korps* on the Eastern Front; von Arnim arrived in Tunis via Rome on 9 December accompanied by his new deputy commander *Generalleutnant* Heinz Ziegler to confront an unsuspecting Nehring, who would be moved on to another Korps command in Russia; *90 Korps* was renamed *5 Panzerarmee* from that date.[16]

Nehring began his tenure by probing westwards from Bizerte and Tunis while erecting defensive perimeters to protect the ports, which resulted in the first contacts between the newly arrived German forces and the British 1st Army feeling its way east from the TORCH landing along two axes. On the northern axis a composite force from British 36th Infantry Brigade built round the 6th Battalion Royal West Kent Regiment was set in to protect a road junction at a road junction near Djebel Abiod, just under fifty miles south-west of Bizerte. *Kampfgruppe* Witzig, built around *Major* Rudolf Witzig's *Fallschirm Pionier Bataillon 11* and a *kompanie* from *Panzer Abteilung 190* moving west from Mateur reached the Djebel Abiod junction at 14:30 on Tuesday 17 November, sparking an inconclusive two-day fight; the German armoured patrol ambushed by the 1st Parachute Battalion near Sidi Nsir on the same day was also part of the German probing effort from Bizerte toward Bédja.[17] The main probing effort from Tunis was spearheaded by *Hauptmann* Wilhelm Knoche's *3 Bataillon*, *Fallschirmjäger Regiment 5* and reached Medjez el Bab, thirty-three miles west of Tunis, on 17 November.

After unsuccessfully negotiating for access to the bridge over the River Medjerda in the town and a wider Vichy withdrawal for two days with *Général de Division* Georges Barré, the senior Vichy commander in Tunisia, the Germans attacked at 09:15 on Thursday 19 November. The Vichy forces rebuffed two German attacks over the course of a day's heavy fighting but were then obliged to cede control of the bridge after dark and then Medjez el Bab altogether before midnight; the withdrawal included Lieutenant-Colonel Hill's 1st Parachute Battalion, which pulled back twelve miles to the north-west to a point near Oued Zarga on the road to Bédja.[18] Nehring also extended and linked the individual bridgeheads at Bizerte and Tunis into a larger whole across this period, in part to better facilitate defence of the ports and also to protect the lines of communication running south from the bridgehead to Rommel's *Deutsch-Italienische Panzerarmee* in Libya. To that end, small forces of German troops which were rapidly reinforced by more numerous Italian units also secured the ports of Sousse, Sfax and Gabès, seventy-two, 148 and 200 miles south of Tunis respectively, on 17 and 18 November while screening units were also despatched west from Gabès toward Gafsa and Tébessa to forestall any Allied moves to cut the route into Libya. In addition, by rejigging and redeploying his forces on the outer edge of the bridgehead, Nehring also managed to find sufficient strength to create an inner defensive line to protect Tunis.[19]

Nehring's consolidation again serendipitously coincided with the next stage of the Allied move eastwards. On 24 November 1st Army HQ instructed Major-General Evelegh's 78th Division to move up to a line running south-east from Mateur to Tebourba in readiness for a rapid move on Bizerte and Tunis, and 78th Division HQ issued orders the following day. The plan envisaged a three-pronged advance with 36th Infantry Brigade moving along the coast road toward Mateur, specifically to secure a road junction and nearby river bridge on the Bizerte-Mateur road north of the latter, while BLADE Force and 11th Infantry Brigade moved along parallel routes to converge upon Tebourba. 36th Infantry Brigade moved off from Djebel Abiod twenty-four hours behind schedule on the night of 25-26 November and after two days cautious and unopposed advance the Brigade's lead element, the 8th Battalion Argyll & Sutherland Highlanders, was ambushed by *Kampfgruppe* Witzig on 28 November in a defile between the Djebel Azag and Djebel Adjred just west of Djefna, nine miles short of its objective. The initial clash killed thirty men, wounded fifty more, knocked out ten vehicles and prompted a hasty withdrawal that left eighty-six men to be taken prisoner.[20] A subsequent attack aimed at clearing the road by taking the two hills on the night of 29-30 November by the 6th Battalion Royal West Kent's and Lieutenant-Colonel Iain MacAlpine's newly arrived No. 6 Commando was also rebuffed, costing the already understrength Commando eighty killed, wounded and missing, after which 36th Brigade withdrew eleven miles to Sedjenane.[21]

Lieutenant-Colonel Thomas Trevor's No. 1 Commando, which was also attached to 36th Infantry Brigade and contained a large proportion of US Army Rangers, suffered similarly high casualties in a simultaneous amphibious equivalent of the 2nd Parachute Battalion's drop at Depienne. Tasked to interfere with the Axis flank and rear communications in support of the ground advance under the unsubtle codename Operation BIZERTE, the Commando sailed from Tabarka at dusk on 30 November and landed approximately fifteen miles west of Bizerte at 03:15 on Tuesday 1 December. After three days of occupying road junctions, observing the airfield at Sidi Ahmed and playing a deadly game of hide-and-seek with German patrols and pro-Axis Arabs, a growing shortage of food obliged the Commando to withdraw overland to Sedjenane, where the last elements arrived on 5 December. The operation was another example of highly trained specialist troops being despatched on a mission based on wishful thinking, and it cost a total of 134 killed wounded and missing, seventy-four of them US Army Rangers.[22]

The two southern prongs of the advance toward Tebourba, just twenty miles or so from Tunis, made better progress but also sparked an even more severe response from the Germans. On the very southern edge of the advance 11 Infantry Brigade was tasked to secure Medjez el Bab and advance north-west along the River Medjerda toward Tebourba, but retaking the town took longer than expected. *Hauptmann* Knoche's *3 Bataillon, Fallschirmjäger Regiment 5*, reinforced with tanks from *Panzer Abteilung 190*, an Italian anti-tank company and two 88mm guns, rebuffed attacks by the 2nd Battalion Lancashire Fusiliers and 5th Battalion Northamptonshire Regiment before withdrawing after dark on 25 November, leaving the near-deserted town to be taken by a tank and infantry attack at midday the following day. The follow-up advance was delayed by *Luftwaffe* aircraft covering *Hauptmann* Knoche's withdrawal after daybreak and eleven USAAF P-38 fighters repeatedly strafing elements of the US 701st Tank Destroyer Battalion attached to the Brigade, killing five men, wounding sixteen and damaging a number of guns and vehicles. Despite this, the 1st Battalion East Surrey Regiment reached Tebourba at midnight and secured the town before first light the following day, Friday 27 November.[23] Colonel Richard Hull's BLADE Force, built around approximately 100 Crusader and M3 Light tanks from the 17th/21st Lancers and the US 1st Battalion, 1st Armored Regiment backed with reconnaissance, infantry and artillery elements, was tasked to move parallel and to the north of 11th Brigade.[24] Moving off from its concentration area near Beja at 07:00 on 25 November, the column covered the eighteen miles to a junction on the Sidi Nsir road where a screening force moved on toward Sidi Nsir while Lieutenant-Colonel John K. Waters Battalion from the 1st Armored Regiment was despatched east to penetrate the Chouigui Pass, approach Tebourba from the north and reconnoitre bridges across the River Medjerda at El Bathan and Djedeida, three miles south and five miles east of the town respectively.[25]

Lieutenant-Colonel Waters' tanks proceeded to pin down a reinforced *kompanie* from *Fallschirm Pionier Regiment 11* west of the Pass, overran an outpost guarding the eastern exit, endured a strafing from *Luftwaffe* aircraft, bypassed Tebourba to destroy the German security detachment in El Bathan and attacked the recently re-occupied airfield at Djedeida, shooting up the buildings, fuel and supplies and destroying up to twenty *Luftwaffe* aircraft on the ground, possibly the same machines that had strafed the Battalion earlier. The US tanks then withdrew west at dusk to an overnight position near Chouigui village. The day's exploits cost the US unit two dead, one M3 Light tank missing and a number of others damaged, while news of the action and an erroneous report that Allied tanks were within ten miles of Tunis caused some alarm at *90 Korps* HQ. Early the following morning, Thursday 26 November, Lieutenant-Colonel Waters moved his tanks back to positions covering the Pass just before a German force including a *kompanie* from *Panzer Abteilung 190* approached en route to reinforce Tebourba. The resulting battle was the first clash of the war between US and German tanks and drew in the 17th/21st Lancers in an unsuccessful effort to cut the enemy line of retreat before the German force withdrew at dusk. The action cost the latter two *Panzer* IIIs and six *Panzer* IVs in return for six M3 Light tanks and a number of US casualties including company commander Major Carl Siglin, who was killed.[26]

As we have seen 11th Brigade followed up on the 1st Armored Regiment's raid by occupying Tebourba in the early hours of 27 November but a subsequent probe east toward Djedeida was blocked followed by a midday counter-attack by the newly formed *Kampfgruppe* Lueder, which included tanks from *Panzer Abteilung 190* and three Tiger Is from *schwere Panzer Abteilung 501*, the first employment of the new heavy tank against the Western Allies.[27] This disjointed the Allied advance and set the scene for a larger counter-attack by *Generalleutnant* Fischer from *10 Panzer Division* with a force that included *Kampfgruppe* Hudel built around tanks from his recently arrived *Panzer Regiment 7*, *Kampfgruppe* Lueder and *Kampfgruppe* Koch consisting of *Fallschirmjäger Regiment 5* reinforced with elements from *Panzerjäger Abteilung 90*.[28] Beginning at 07:45 on Tuesday 1 December the German attack initially pushed the Allied force back six miles along the River Medjerda in three days of bitter fighting to the point between the Djebel el Ahmera, dubbed 'Longstop Hill', and Djebel Bou Aoukaz on the north and south banks of the river respectively, and then a further seven miles or so back to a point just east of Medjez el Bab by 10 December. After building up reinforcements and supplies the 78th Division attacked again on 22 December as the opening move in a thrust by Major-General Charles Keightley's 6th Armoured Division intended to reach Tunis via Tebourba but was blocked at Longstop Hill by a German force holding onto the adjacent Djebel el Rhaa to the north-east, which proved too well entrenched to overcome. The problem was compounded by torrential rain that fell uninterrupted for three full days and Major-General Evelegh's men finally withdrew in the afternoon of 25 December after a German counter-attack drove them back off Longstop Hill. By 26 December, the Allied force was back on its start line just east of Medjez el Bab, having lost almost 21,000 casualties; the see-saw fight for the Djebel el Ahmera and Djebel el Rhaa cost the 2nd Battalion Coldstream Guards 178 casualties and the US 1st Battalion 18th Infantry Regiment 356 men killed, wounded and missing.[29] The rebuff at Longstop Hill marked the end of the first Allied attempt to take Tunis and the fighting in northern Tunisia then settled down into positional warfare as both sides sought to build up their forces and supplies.

While all this was going on the Allies were making better progress against Rommel's *Deutsch-Italienische Panzerarmee* in Libya. Having successfully broken contact after the defeat at El Alamein, Rommel paused on the coast road between El Agheila and Marsa el Brega on the south-eastern edge of the Gulf of Sirte on 23 November, allowing the British to liberate Cyrenaica and the ports of Tobruk and Benghazi on 13 and 20 November respectively; over 9,000 tons of Axis equipment and supplies were captured at the former, the latter was not as badly sabotaged as expected and 408 *Luftwaffe* and 111 *Regia Aeronautica* aircraft in varying states of repair were captured on airfields across the area, the loss of which seriously diminished Axis aerial reconnaissance capabilities.[30]

Rommel's foremost preoccupation at this stage was to avoid being pinned down by another stand and fight order from Hitler. The latter was also the preferred option of his Italian superiors, keen to hang onto their Libyan colonial territory, while for his part Rommel favoured a withdrawal into Tunisia to create a firm base for future offensive operations. On 28 November Rommel therefore journeyed to Hitler's HQ near Rastenburg in East Prussia and while the *Führer* declined to support Rommel's withdrawal request, he was preoccupied with events on the Eastern Front and left responsibility for deciding the matter with *Duce* Benito Mussolini and his *Comando Supremo*. Rommel was able to persuade the Italians to authorise a 220-mile withdrawal to Buerat el Hsun, in time to avoid encirclement at El Agheila from 12 December, although the action cost the *Deutsch-Italienische Panzerarmee* eighteen tanks, twenty-five artillery pieces and 450 prisoners.[31] The Axis formation regrouped at Buerat el Hsun from 17 December leaving the pursuing 8th Army to liberate Sirte on Christmas Day, and on 31 December Mussolini personally authorised Rommel to carry out a gradual withdraw to Mareth in Tunisia spread over six weeks, which commenced on 2 January 1943. Adherence to this timetable was aided initially by a combination of the perennial North African logistical difficulties, which in this instance obliged the British and Commonwealth force to truck all its supplies around 400 miles from Tobruk and Benghazi, and newly promoted General Montgomery's penchant for assembling overwhelmingly superior force before initiating operations. This created a three-week pause before the 8th Army resumed the offensive on 15 January, which pushed the bulk of Rommel's force back to a line fifty miles east of Tunis in four days. At that point Rommel despatched an officer to establish a HQ in Sfax to regulate logistics traffic and ordered a withdrawal to the Mareth Line that night, abandoning Tripoli after demolishing the port facilities and leaving the Libyan capital to be liberated by the 8th Army during the night of 22-23 January. Lead elements of the *Deutsch-Italienische Panzerarmee* began to arrive at the Mareth Line, 200 miles to the west, the same day, followed by the Axis formation's rearguard on 15 February, while the 8th Army pursued as far as Medenine, twenty-five miles south of Mareth, before pausing to regroup.

The arrival of Rommel's formation at the Mareth Line consolidated the Axis position in Tunisia with *5 Panzerarmee* holding back the British 1st Army in the Atlas Mountains to the east in the northern part of Tunisia while the *Deutsch-Italienische Panzerarmee* blocked access into the country from the south along the narrow strip between the Mediterranean and the Matmata Hills and extensive Chott el Djerid salt lake to the north. Despite all its constituent units being at around half strength after the tribulations in Egypt and Libya, this nonetheless brought 30,000 German and 48,000 Italian combat troops into the Tunisian theatre along with 129 tanks and a large number of armoured troop carriers, guns and trucks. This brought the overall Axis strength up to approximately 100,000 men, 74,000 German and 26,000 Italian personnel.[32] The arrival of the *Deutsch-Italienische Panzerarmee* also prompted another Axis command reorganisation. On 23 January 1943, Mussolini appointed *Generale d'Armata* Giovanni Messe to command the newly created *1a Armata Italiana*, which assumed control of the *Deutsch-Italienische Panzerarmee* on arrival in Tunisia, and three days later *Comando Supremo* in Rome assumed direct operational control of *5 Panzerarmee*; both formations subsequently became subordinate to Rommel's *Heeresgruppe Afrika* when that HQ was created in Tunisia on 23 February. The *Luftwaffe* also reorganised its command structure into a single entity to control the 298 machines gathered in Tunisia. *Generalmajor* Hans Seidemann was appointed to command the newly created *Fliegerkorps Tunis* from a central HQ near Sfax, controlling *Fliegerführer 2* and *Fliegerführer 3* HQs at Tunis and Gabès respectively. The Italians maintained a parallel but separate command structure for the approximately 100 *Regia Aeronautica* machines based in Tunisia, dubbed *5° Squadra* and commanded by *Generale di Brigata* Giuseppe Gaeta from 15 February; this also had two subsidiary HQs, *Settore Aeronautico Nord* and *Settore Aeronautico Sud,* tasked to co-operate with their German counterparts.[33]

This consolidation did not equate to maintaining a defensive posture, as Axis forces mounted four substantial attacks between 14 February and 6 March 1943, starting with a two-stage offensive intended to neutralise gains by the US II Corps near Faïd, sixty-six miles west of Sfax, which threatened communications between Tunis and the *Deutsch-Italienische Panzerarmee*; Rommel had correctly assumed that supply difficulties would handicap the 8th Army's offensive capabilities until the harbour at Tripoli had been repaired and reopened. The first phase was *Unternehmen Frühlingswind* (Operation Spring Breeze) carried out by elements of *5 Panzerarmee* commanded by *Generalleutnant* Heinz Ziegler, specifically four *kampfgruppen* drawn from *10 Panzer Division* and *21 Panzer Division* fielding a total of 140 tanks; *21 Panzer Division* had been detached from the *Deutsch-Italienische Panzerarmee* on arrival in Tunisia to act as a theatre reserve. The Germans attacked at 04:00 on Sunday 14 February and in three days of intense fighting encircled and captured Sidi Bou Zid and pushed on twenty-five miles to Sbeitla, at the end of three passes running north through the eastern spine of the Atlas Mountains toward Tébessa, prompting a major Allied withdrawal on 17 February.[34] According to the US Official History the battle cost the two Combat Commands of the US 1st Armored Division a total of 886 killed, wounded and missing, ninety-two tanks, 130 vehicles, eighteen 105mm guns and a dozen 155mm howitzers, along with an additional 1,025 killed wounded and missing from the attached 168th RCT from the US 34th Infantry Division.[35]

The second stage was codenamed *Unternehmen Morgenluft* (Operation Morning Air), better known as the Battle of the Kasserine Pass, a three-pronged attack launched by the *Deutsch-Italienische Panzerarmee* in the early hours of Friday 19 February; the attack was intended to fully eliminate the potential Allied threat to communications with southern Tunisia and threaten the southern flank of the British 1st Army. On the right, two *kampfgruppen* from *21 Panzer Division* pushed up the pass from Sbeitla toward Sbiba, twenty-five miles to the north but were stopped just short of the town on the following day by elements of the British 6th Armoured Division and US 1st and 34th Infantry Divisions. In the centre *kampfgruppen* from *10 Panzer Division* and *Kampfgruppe* von Broich accompanied by Rommel in person pushed north up the pass from Kasserine toward Thala but the German advance was slowed by a small British all-arms group dubbed GORE Force and elements of the US 26th RCT fighting a series of delaying actions and then it was stopped at a blocking position just south of Thala in the evening of 21 February; resumption of the attack was stymied by elements of the US 9th Infantry

Division, newly arrived from Morocco. On the right *Kampfgruppe Deutsches Afrika Korps* (*DAK*) and the Italian *131ª Divisione Corazzata 'Centauro'* also attacked north from Kasserine and after overrunning an ad hoc Franco-US force tasked to defend the Pass they branched north-west along the River Hatab toward Haida and Tébessa. The attackers then ran into a blocking position manned by the 1st Armored Division's Combat Command B and the 16th RCT from the US 1st Infantry Division near the Djebel el Hamra, twenty miles short of Tébessa, in the afternoon of 21 February; a renewed attack the following morning failed to breach the block and a US counter-attack in the afternoon pushed back the Axis units and netted 400 prisoners. At this point Rommel decided *Morgenluft* had failed and in the evening of 23 February all Axis units were ordered back to their start lines. Allied units reoccupied the Kasserine Pass the following day, followed by Sbeitla and Sidi Bou Zid shortly thereafter.

The third attack was another two-stage operation launched just days after the failure at Kasserine on the *5 Panzerarmee* front in northern Tunisia. Conceived by the latter's commander *Generaloberst* von Arnim, *Unternehmen Ausladung* (Operation Disembarkation) tasked the recently redesignated *Division von Manteuffel*, formerly *Division von Broich*, to act as the northern shoulder of the overall attack by taking Sedjenane and pushing west eleven miles to the road junction at Djebel Abiod. The attack commenced in the morning of Friday 26 February and *Fallschirm Pionier Regiment Barenthin* and the *10° Reggimento Bersaglieri* initially made good progress against the French Colonial troops holding the northern sector of the Allied line, but were brought up short of Sedjenane and then held back by a stubborn five-day defence of the town by 139th Infantry Brigade reinforced with No. 1 Commando. This continued until the defenders withdrew to Djebel Abiod on 4 March, by which time *Division von Manteuffel* lacked the strength to properly follow up and *Ausladung* faded away.

The second and main stage, codenamed *Unternehmen Ochsenkopf* (Operation Oxhead), was commanded by *Generalmajor* Friedrich Weber from a specially created *Korpsgruppe* Weber HQ and envisaged an advance along three axes intended to capture the Allied supply hub at Beja via Sidi Nsir, secure Medjez el Bab via a pincer movement and take Teboursouk to the south-west. The southern axis south of the River Medjerda was alloted to *Kampfgruppe* Schmid, made up of reinforced elements of the *Hermann Göring Division* deployed to Tunisia, was effectively blocked by 11th Brigade and elements of the ad hoc British Y Division and elements were subsequently redeployed to the centre axis. The latter was allotted to *Kampfgruppen* Audorff and Eder, the former tasked to attack and secure Medjez el Bab frontally while the latter looped north and west toward Toukabeur to take Medjez from the rear; *Kampfgruppe* Audorff attacked on 25 February but was stopped short of Medjez el Bab by elements of Y Division. *Kampfgruppe* Eder's flanking move did not commence until 28 February and was slowed short of its objective by French Colonial troops and then abandoned.

The main weight of *Ochsenkopf* was focussed on the Sidi Nsir axis tasked to *Kampfgruppe* Lang, which fielded seventy-seven tanks including around fourteen Tiger Is from *schwere Panzer Abteilung 501* and fifteen tanks on loan from *21 Panzer Division*, supported by *panzergrenadiers* from *10 Panzer Division*. The attack began at 07:15 on 26 February and quickly secured Sidi Nsir, but a spirited defence by infantry and artillery from the British 46th Division dug in nearby prevented further progress until nightfall. The delay allowed the defenders to summon reinforcements including Churchill tanks from the North Irish Horse, which blocked repeated German attacks toward Beja over the next three days before withdrawing toward Sidi Nsir on 2 March. The fight cost the Germans twenty-two tanks destroyed including at least eight Tiger Is, many of which were disabled by mines and then demolished by their crews, a further forty-nine disabled, 2,800 killed, wounded and missing and a further 2,200 prisoners; British losses included 1,800 casualties and sixteen tanks.[36]

The final German attack, codenamed *Unternehmen Capri* (Operation Capri), was a spoiling operation against the regrouping 8th Army near Medenine in the south. Launched from the western end of the Mareth Line and undertaken principally by *15 & 21 Panzer* and *90 Leichte Afrika Divisions*, *Capri* was launched on Saturday 6 March 1943 and commanded by Rommel in person. The 8th Army was handicapped by much of its armour still being en route from Benghazi but forewarned by ULTRA intelligence gleaned from decrypted German signals General Montgomery was able to hurriedly draw in reinforcements and focus anti-tank defences on the precise German axes of attack. Unable to make the anticipated progress and needing to husband his forces to man the Mareth Line, Rommel called the operation off at 20:30 the same day, after losing ninety-four German and Italian dead, 510 wounded and between forty-one and fifty-six tanks in return for six British tanks and fifty-one prisoners.[37]

The series of Axis attacks between 14 February and 6 March 1943 thus ultimately achieved little apart from expending men, tanks and arguably more importantly, supplies of fuel, food and munitions, although to be fair the isolated nature of the Axis position made sitting in place while the Allies expanded their forces an equally self-defeating strategy, especially given that the Axis logistic position had always been tenuous at best. The early January 1943 estimate by *OB Süd* that 60,000 tonnes per month would be required to sustain the Tunisian bridgehead proved to be somewhat optimistic, given that the supply input in January and February 1943 amounted to 35,505 and 32,966 tonnes respectively, sufficient only to provision the troops and replace expended materiel. By the beginning of March 1943 *Heeresgruppe Afrika* had raised its monthly minimum requirement to between 69,000 and 86,000 tonnes, later increased to 140,000 tonnes, while *Comando Supremo* calculated it would only be possible to bring in a maximum of between 70,000 to 82,000 tonnes; in the event even the latter proved to be optimistic, as only 29,267 tonnes were brought in during March, dropping to just over 23,000 tonnes the following month.[38] Unsurprisingly, the Allies paid particular attention to severing the vulnerable Axis supply chain, starting with the air bridge.

Launched on 5 April 1943 and running until the end of the month, Operation FLAX was conceived by the commander of the US 15th Air Force, Major-General James Doolittle, and involved an intensive programme of air raids on Axis airfields in Tunisia and Sicily by B-25 Medium and B-17 Heavy bombers intended to catch Axis transports and their escorting fighters on the ground, in tandem with increasingly effective fighter sweeps to intercept the *pulke* of low-flying transports over the Sicilian Strait. P-38s from the US 12th Air Force reportedly brought down around a dozen Junkers 52 transports on the first day of the operation and a further fifty on 10 and 11 April, while Spitfires from RAF No. 92 Squadron shot down eight Italian SM 82 tri-motor transports from a formation of eighteen on 16 April. In the early evening of 18 April, twelve Spitfires from RAF No. 92 Squadron and forty-eight P-40s from the US 57th Fighter Group happened upon a *pulk* of around a hundred Junkers 52 transports flying at low level for Sicily carrying personnel from *Heeresgruppe Afrika*. In an action later dubbed the *Palmsonntag Massaker* (Palm Sunday Massacre) the Allied fighters reportedly downed between thirty-eight and fifty-eight of the *Luftwaffe* transports, although the latter figure might include thirty-five damaged machines that crash landed on making landfall on Sicily. The following day Spitfires and Kittyhawks from No. 7 (SAAF) Wing downed sixteen Tunisia-bound SM 82s, many in flames leading to speculation they were carrying fuel, and on 22 April downed up to seventeen giant Messerschmitt 323s from a formation of twenty.[39]

The effort to block the aerial route into Tunisia ran in parallel with long-standing anti-shipping operations that had been underway for several months and which overall made a more significant impact on Axis capabilities than the more spectacular effort to cut the Axis air link; thirteen of the ninety-seven vessels employed in November were sunk for example, and the following month a further twenty-six ships were lost with nine more damaged from the 127 employed. In late December 1942, thirteen *Regia Marina* destroyers carrying 300-350 men per trip were employed as a short-term expedient, but the redeployment weakened the *Regia Marina's* already patchy and failing anti-submarine capabilities and a repeat use at the end of April 1943 was rapidly discontinued when the destroyers attracted 'fierce [Allied] air attacks'.[40] The last Axis vessel to successfully access the Tunisian coast was the 4,200-ton converted liner *Belluno*, which docked at Tunis in the morning of 4 May. Allied attacks continued to sink Axis supply vessels virtually to the moment *Heeresgruppe Afrika* finally surrendered. Royal Navy destroyers sank the 3,566-ton merchant ship *Campo Basso* on the night of 5 May followed by the *Kriegsmarine* transport vessels *Kriegstransport* (*KT*) *5* and *KT 21* on 9 May and HM Submarine *Unrivalled* sank the freighter *Santa Mariana Salina* the same day; US B-24 bombers sank the *SS San Antonio* en route to Bizerte with 5,600 tons of supplies on 5 May, while other Allied aircraft damaged the *Belluno* so badly she had to be scuttled on 7 May; they then sank the transport *KT 9* two days later.[41] In April 1943, the resupply effort cost the Axis twenty-nine cargo ships and 15,516 tons of supplies, and twenty-four cargo ships and 6,943 tons of supplies the following month.[42] From 8 May the Allied interdiction effort switched from blocking the inward flow of materiel and supplies to preventing personnel from being evacuated from Tunisia to Sicily with the inception of Operation RETRIBUTION by the Commander Allied Naval Forces in the Mediterranean, Admiral Sir Andrew Cunningham; Cunningham's launch signal instructed his forces to 'Sink, burn and destroy. Let nothing pass.' Allied aircraft were responsible for dealing with Axis vessels up to five miles from the Tunisian coast while surface forces dealt with matters outside the five-mile limit. Up to a dozen Allied destroyers were thus on permanent patrol off the northern tip of Tunisia during daylight from 9 May, while lighter craft carried the blockade closer inshore during the hours of darkness. Around 800 Axis personnel were captured trying to escape in a variety of small craft; the total killed or drowned by the blockade is unclear.[43]

As had been the case throughout the Desert War, the Axis forces, and especially the Germans, had worked logistical miracles, but the severing of the supply line from mainland Italy and Sicily effectively sealed the fate of *Heeresgruppe Afrika*, who acknowledged that 'shortage of fuel paralysed all except local tactics' as early as 23 April 1943, three weeks before the Axis surrender in Tunisia, although the reality took longer to sink in elsewhere. *Generalfeldmarschall* Kesselring issued an optimistic if qualified assessment of *Heeresgruppe Afrika's* prospects to *Oberkommando der Wehrmacht* (*OKW*) the same day and assured Mussolini that the Tunisian situation was 'not desperate' eleven days later for example, while the facts from Tunisia were apparently omitted from situation reports destined for Hitler until 7 May; at that point the *Führer* presciently opined that the situation was 'pretty hopeless'.[44]

Fully overcoming *Heeresgruppe Afrika* required more than just cutting it off from supplies and reinforcement, however, and needed offensive action to dislodge the Axis forces from their positions and either destroy them or induce their surrender. In the south of the country the process was a two-stage affair executed by Montgomery's 8th Army, beginning with Operation PUGILIST.[45] Launched on 19 March 1943 this involved a frontal attack on the Mareth Line defences with a simultaneous move to outflank the landward end of the Line following a route scouted by the Long Range Desert Group (LRDG) in January; this ran up the west side of the Matmata Hills before veering east toward the Tebaga Gap running between the Djebel Tabaga and Djebel Metab to the north and south respectively before debouching onto the coastal plain behind the Mareth defences. The second stage, codenamed Operation SUPERCHARGE II, began with an attack during the night of 25-26 March to break into the Tebaga Gap and open the way for a late afternoon assault by the British 1st Armoured Division. On 28 March *Generale* Messe was obliged to order a withdrawal from the Mareth Line to new postions to the north, leaving Gabès to be captured by New Zealand troops the following day.

A further 8th Army attack on 6 April codenamed Operation SCIPIO broke through the new Axis position on the Wadi Akarit, running west from the Chott el Djerid salt lake to the coast, prompting a further Axis fighting withdrawal 150 miles through more verdant coastal terrain to Enfidaville, just fifty miles or so from Tunis.[46]

Perhaps fittingly, the main and final blows to *Heeresgruppe Afrika* came from Lieutenant-General Kenneth Anderson's 1st Army, beginning with Operation VULCAN on Thursday 22 April. Orchestrated by General Sir Harold Alexander, VULCAN envisaged a move in the north to take Bizerte by the US II Corps while the British V and IX Corps advanced toward Tunis in conjunction with a renewed attack by the 8th Army from Enfidaville. The terrain and Axis defences north of Enfidaville proved inimical to a rapid 8th Army advance and it took V and IX Corps five days of stiff fighting to finally secure the Djebel el Ahmera or Longstop Hill and clear the way into Tunis. At this point General Alexander allowed the US II Corps to press on against stiff resistance while calling a temporary halt to reorganise the British attack, cancelling further attacks by the 8th Army and transferring the 7th Armoured and 4th Indian Divisions to the 1st Army in order to strengthen the attack along the Medjerda Valley. The attack was resumed as Operation STRIKE on Wednesday 5 May with a preliminary night attack to secure the Djebel Bou Aoukaz that formed the right flank of the attack frontage, with artillery preparation for the main attack commencing at 03:00 on 6 May. Over 600 guns fired 16,632 rounds in the first two hours, with each gun firing an average of 368 rounds over the first twenty-four hours.[47] The artillery was backed with intensive air support which was so effective that armoured patrols from C Squadron 1st Derbyshire Yeomanry and B Squadron 11th Hussars reached the centre of Tunis at 15:40 on Friday 7 May 1943; vehicles from the US 894th Tank Destroyer Battalion spearheaded the US 9th Infantry Division's entry into Bizerte thirty-five minutes later.[48]

The loss of the two ports effectively marked the beginning of the end of Axis resistance in Tunisia. The 8th Army reported taking in excess of 5,000 prisoners, including increasing numbers of German personnel, during the first day of the advance to Enfidaville on 6 April.[49] The cornered Axis forces nonetheless remained a dangerous and potent foe; 167th Infantry Brigade lost sixty-three dead, 221 wounded and 104 missing in an unsuccessful attack on elements of *1ª Armata Italiana* as late as 9 May.[50] Overall however, the effect was a series of surrenders by units, formation HQs and senior commanders beginning in the US II Corps sector in the north. *334 Infanterie Division*, encircled near Tebourba, surrendered on 8 May; *Division von Manteuffel*, *10* and *15 Panzer Divisions* and 40,000 men including *5 Panzerarmee's* final commander *General der Panzertruppe* Gustav von Vaerst surrendered just after midday on 9 May; and *schwere Panzer Abteilung 501*, by this point subsumed into *schwere Panzer Abteilung 504*, surrendered at Cape Bon three days later. *Generaloberst* Hans-Jürgen von Arnim and his *Heeresgruppe Afrika* HQ passed into Allied captivity in the late morning of Thursday 13 May 1943, while a newly promoted *Maresciallo d'Italia* (Marshal of

Italy) Giovanni Messe officially surrendered all the German and Italian troops under his command at 12:20 the same day.[51] Axis casualty figures across the 186 days of the campaign in Algeria and Tunisia are unclear owing to a dearth of accurate Axis records, although one source refers to 8,500 German and 3,700 Italian dead, and a combined total of between 40,000 and 50,000 wounded.[52] With regard to prisoners, the US official history cites an estimated 275,000 Axis personnel passing into Allied captivity while the British counterpart cites 89,442 Italian, 101,784 German and 47,017 'Nationality unspecified', totalling 238,243.[53] On the other side of the ledger, British 1st and 8th Army casualties totalled 6,233 killed, 21,528 wounded and 10,599 missing while the US losses totalled 18,221, breaking down to 2,715 dead, 8,978 wounded and 6,528 missing.[54] The material cost was also high. Between 22 April and 16 May a total of 290 *Regia Aeronautica* and *Luftwaffe* machines were destroyed in action for example, and a further 600 were captured on airfields around Bizerte, Cape Bon and Tunis; across the same period the RAF lost fifty-nine aircraft and the USAAF ninety-five.[55]

The final German radio transmission from Tunisia closing the *Heeresgruppe Afrika* station was received at *OB Süd* in Rome at 13:12 on Thursday 13 May 1943. Four minutes later, at 13:16, General Alexander signalled news of the victory to Churchill in London: 'Sir, it is my duty to report that the Tunisian campaign is over. All enemy resistance has ceased. We are masters of the North African shores'.[56] With that, the stage was set to carry the fight into Axis home territory in mainland Europe, beginning with the island of Sicily.

4

Wrangling and Rancour

The Evolution of the HUSKY Plan from Staff Paper to Fully Fledged Invasion Scheme, June 1942–May 1943

The idea of invading Sicily pre-dated the actual Allied invasion by a year, and it originally arose from British War Cabinet Joint Planning Staff discussions in London in mid-1942. These discussions were intended to identify future strategic objectives in the Mediterranean and pinpointed Sicily and Sardinia, dubbed Operations HUSKY and BRIMSTONE respectively, and Sicily also featured in Mediterranean Command level talks on 8 July 1942 as a possible target for an all-British operation. Developments in North Africa precluded the operation at that point but both islands were the subject of outline planning and feasibility studies across the remainder of the year, and while HUSKY became the preferred British option prior to Casablanca, the Sardinia option remained popular with some in the British senior echelons; British members of the Joint Planning Staff championed the latter as a more easily achievable alternative to HUSKY during the Conference for example, to the chagrin of the Chief of the Imperial General Staff (CIGS), Field Marshal Sir Alan Brooke.[1] The decision to proceed with HUSKY was taken while Operation TORCH was still in full swing, at the Casablanca Conference held just two months after US Major-General Jonathan W. Anderson and Force BRUSHWOOD had secured the city on 11 November 1942.

Codenamed SYMBOL, the Conference was conducted at the Anfa Hotel in central Casablanca across the ten-day period 14-24 January 1943, almost exactly a year after the First Washington or ARCADIA Conference that had agreed to and set TORCH in motion. The Conference was originally planned as a tri-partite affair but Marshal Stalin declined to attend, reportedly because he was preoccupied with the closing stages of the epic battle for Stalingrad. The British delegation was headed by Prime Minister Winston Churchill accompanied by CIGS Field Marshal Sir Alan Brooke, First Sea Lord and Admiral of the Fleet Sir Dudley Pound and the Chief of the Air Staff, Air Chief Marshal Sir Charles Portal; the US delegation was headed by President Franklin Roosevelt accompanied by US Army Chief-of-Staff General George C. Marshall, Commander-in-Chief US Fleet and Chief of

Naval Operations Admiral Ernest J. King and Lieutenant-General Henry H. Arnold, Commanding General of the USAAF and Deputy Chief of Staff for Air.[2] As the Conference agenda included leadership of what were to become the Free French Forces and planning for post-war North Africa, it was also attended by *Général de Corps d'Armée* Henri Giraud and *Général de Brigade* Charles de Gaulle, representing what was to become the *Comité Français de Libération Nationale* from 3 June 1943 before de Gaulle took sole charge four months later.

The French presence at Casablanca was problematic. De Gaulle reportedly had to be forced to attend the Conference and he and Giraud did not get on personally, to the point that the publicity photograph of the French leaders shaking hands was so perfunctory that it had to be staged twice; Roosevelt referred to the entire arrangement as a 'shotgun wedding' and the arrangement was not considered especially satisfactory by the British or US delegations for differing reasons. Although he officially favoured an equal split of responsibility between the French leaders, Roosevelt thought Giraud the better choice for US interests for example, and ironically, given subsequent events, he also viewed de Gaulle as a British puppet and did not formally recognise him as the head of the Free French until the middle of 1944; presumably as a result of all this, neither of the French leaders was permitted to participate in the military planning discussions at the Conference.

The main focus of the Conference was of course on the future prosecution of the war against the Axis Powers however, with topics for discussion including the ongoing U-Boat threat in the Atlantic, maintaining aid to the Soviet Union and the allotment of manpower, ships and aircraft across the various global theatres of war. With regard to strategic bombing policy, discussions by the Combined Chiefs of Staff led to the formulation of the Casablanca Directive on 21 January, which co-ordinated the activities of RAF Bomber Command and the US 8th Air Force operating from bases in the UK. The Directive prioritised German U-Boat construction yards, aircraft factories, transportation links and oil production facilities and specified additional priorities for attention as and when necessary including the U-Boat bases on the French Atlantic coast, targets in northern Italy and France in support of landing operations and Berlin. The Directive was disseminated to the various RAF and USAAF commanders and HQs on 4 February 1943 and formed the template for European strategic bombing operations until the bomber force was redirected to assist in the preparations for the Normandy invasion in June 1944. Toward the end of the Conference Roosevelt also unilaterally announced the more politically oriented Casablanca Declaration, which enshrined the principle of accepting nothing short of unconditional surrender from the Axis Powers as a guiding tenet for future Allied strategy. The term 'unconditional surrender' was reportedly borrowed from General and future US President Ulysses S. Grant who had employed it during the American Civil War and it featured in the final press conference on 24 January. Roosevelt later clarified the term to mean Allied efforts were focussed not upon punishing the Axis civilian population but on destroying their military forces and bringing their political and military leaderships to book in a national radio broadcast on 2 February 1943. Initially intended to apply solely to Germany to reassure Stalin that the Western Allies were not intending to make a separate peace, the Declaration was presumably rooted in the US preference for decisive military victory over political arrangements and more specifically to avoid a repeat of the perceived half-measures at the end of the First World War. However, while the Declaration was presented publicly as a united Allied effort, there was some underlying disagreement.

Although Roosevelt had broached the matter with the US Joint Chiefs of Staff a week before the Conference on 7 January, General Marshall later remarked to Lieutenant-General Eisenhower that 'only time could determine its wisdom' and the latter considered it to be one of the key Allied errors of the entire war.[3] Churchill does not appear to have objected in principle, although discussion of exempting Italy in order to hasten her collapse prompted him to seek counsel from the War Cabinet on 20 January, which recommended Italy be included in the Declaration to avoid damaging relations with Turkey and other Balkan states; he was nonetheless surprised by Roosevelt's unilateral announcement at the final press conference.[4]

While US internal discussions had continued up to December 1942, no unified US position had emerged; according to one source this was directly attributable to President Roosevelt failing to formulate a strategy in favour of waiting to see how matters developed.[5] Admiral King and the US Naval lobby was more concerned with the Pacific Theatre, while President Roosevelt had already agreed to consider British proposals to carry the war into the southern fringes of the European mainland via Sardinia, Sicily, Italy, Greece or the Balkans; the option of seizing Sardinia was also favoured by Eisenhower at Allied Forces HQ (AFHQ). For his part, General Marshall saw the Casablanca Conference as an opportunity to persuade the British to accept a modified Operation ROUNDUP, the scheme for a cross-Channel invasion in 1943, and move the Allies away from what he considered to be a Mediterranean diversion; Marshall was supported in this by Major-General Thomas T. Handy from the US Staff Operations Division (OPD), who considered further Mediterranean operations to be 'logistically unfeasible and strategically unsound' and favoured redeploying all resources from there into ROUNDUP or failing that, the Pacific Theatre.[6] In addition to lacking unity, the US delegation to Casablanca was ill-prepared for serious discussion and debate, not least because the bulk of the US staff officers and specialists that could normally be called upon had been left behind in Washington, obliging a hurried trawl of US units and HQs in North Africa to assemble a provisional staff capability.[7] None of this was the case with their British counterparts who came to Casablanca with a united aim, apart from the last-minute digression by elements of the British Joint Planning Staff led by Admiral Louis Mountbatten arguing for an attack on Sardinia rather than Sicily near the end of the Conference, and after the Sicily invasion had been agreed; as the proposal threatened to undo all his painstaking work at a stroke an angry Field Marshal Brooke successfully argued it down, and the incident also seriously undermined Admiral Mountbatten's stock with the British Chiefs of Staff Committee.[8] The British intention was to exploit the success of Operation TORCH to knock Italy out of the war via an invasion of Sicily, a position reached through exhaustive debate and discussion by the Chiefs of Staff and subordinate Committees, backed by extensive staff work to provide all the necessary facts, figures and lines of argument. British preparations appear to have begun with the venue, the Hotel Anfa, which was selected by Brigadier Ian Jacobs, a Military Assistant Secretary to the War Cabinet despatched to Casablanca by Churchill for that specific purpose. Jacobs later justified selecting a relatively small provincial establishment on the grounds that it was surrounded by nearby villas for accommodation and while the Hotel successfully provided all the necessary hospitality, the relatively restricted nature of the venue also raises the suspicion that it was selected to assist the British in controlling proceedings.[9]

Whatever the rationale for selecting the Hotel Anfa, the British delegation nonetheless proceeded to dominate the proceedings; as one of General Marshall's chief advisors, Brigadier-General Albert C. Wedemeyer put it, the British 'swarmed down upon us like locusts...it was apparent that we were confronted by generations...of experience in committee work, diplomacy, and in rationalizing points of view. They had us on the defensive practically all the time.'[10] Despite this the US delegation fought hard for four days until Monday 18 January before agreeing to an invasion of Sicily as soon as TORCH was concluded in return for British agreement to ROUNDUP, albeit without committing to a firm date for the latter. Although he was wary of being drawn into 'interminable operations in the Mediterranean' General Marshall's agreement stemmed from the realisation that the British were unlikely to agree to anything more concrete connected to ROUNDUP and because he considered Sicily as a better prospect than Sardinia from a strategic perspective; on that basis he therefore regarded HUSKY as a reasonable compromise because it would free up sea lanes across the Mediterranean, could be mounted with troops and assets already in North Africa and seemingly avoided commitment to an invasion of the Italian mainland.

There then remained the matter of command appointments and dates. Lieutenant-General Eisenhower was appointed Allied Commander-in-Chief for HUSKY with General Sir Harold Alexander serving as Deputy Commander-in-Chief and ground force commander, overall command of Allied naval forces was allotted to Admiral of the Fleet Sir Andrew Cunningham while Air Chief Marshal Sir Arthur Tedder became Commander-in-Chief Allied Air Forces. The date for HUSKY was guided by the conflicting needs of the naval and airborne forces, with the former requiring maximum darkness for the final approach on the Sicilian coast while the latter needed a modicum of natural illumination to allow paratroopers and glider pilots a degree of depth perception. The British delegation initially suggested 22 August to take advantage of a last quarter moon, but subsequently agreed to a revised date of 25 July under a waning crescent moon suggested by Admiral King.[11]

The Casablanca Conference was an overwhelming success for Field Marshal Brooke and the British delegation. Commitment to ROUNDUP had been restricted to agreement in principle with no specific date or location, a future invasion of the Italian mainland had not been definitively ruled out, the agreement on the Sicily invasion maintained focus on the Mediterranean Theatre, all the senior appointments for HUSKY bar commander-in-chief were filled by British officers, and the parallel insertion of the British committee command system into the joint command structure provided a means for them to dominate future proceedings. Brigadier Jacobs, who added drafting the final Casablanca agreement document to selecting the venue, later commented that had he noted down his aspirations for the Conference prior to attending he could 'never had written anything so sweeping, so comprehensive, and so favourable to our ideas [which] prevailed throughout'.[12]

Perhaps understandably, the US side were less happy with the outcome. Lieutenant-General Eisenhower was reportedly 'infuriated' by the appointments and was especially exercised by the 'intrusion of the British Committee system' into the running of his AFHQ as it placed him in charge of a group of committee heads rather than directly commanded subordinates and because it undermined the 'centralization of command in his own person' that had worked well in the early part of Operation TORCH. He went as far as drafting a cable for despatch to the Combined Chiefs of Staff but was persuaded to discard it before transmission by his own Chief-of-Staff, Major-General Walter Bedell Smith, who suggested that it was not the best time to be 'creating any fuss'.[13]

In spite of all this, commitment to Operation HUSKY was confirmed and reinforced at the next Allied conference held in Washington between Wednesday 12 and Tuesday 25 May 1943. Codenamed FORCE 545, the conference discussed a number of topics including continuing aid to Nationalist China, the Casablanca Declaration on unconditional surrender and the global allocation of resources. The most contentious element was the argument for a cross-Channel invasion as a prelude to a climactic campaign in North-Western Europe, championed again by General Marshall, versus the long-standing British preference for a peripheral strategy that involved seizing Sicily as a means of knocking Italy out of the war and drawing the Germans into defending southern Europe prior to any cross-Channel invasion, if at all.[14] The outcome, announced on Tuesday 18 May, was again a compromise. Operation HUSKY was confirmed with an open-ended declaration that could be used to justify moves onto the Italian mainland while the cross-Channel attack, codenamed Operation NEPTUNE, was to be launched against the Normandy coast on 1 May 1944. The delay was due primarily to the bulk of the available landing craft being assigned to HUSKY, and seven divisions were also to be withdrawn from the Mediterranean Theatre to participate in NEPTUNE by 11 November 1943.[15] Unsurprisingly, given the depth of feeling in the British and US camps, the high-level discussion and arguments rumbled on, notably at another Anglo-US meeting held in the immediate aftermath of TRIDENT at Algiers from Friday 28 May to Friday 4 June; incidentally General Marshall left Algiers at 17:45 on 4 June and arrived in Washington DC at 18:00 on 7 June travelling via Accra in what is now Ghana, Ascension Island, Recife and Belém in Brazil, Antigua and Bermuda, covering 9,399 miles in three days, a journey that highlights the punishing schedules that attendance at the various high-level Allied conferences involved.[16] Be that as it may, the important point here is that the die was finally cast over the invasion of Sicily, although the detailed planning process for HUSKY was to prove no less acrimonious.

Preliminary outline planning for an invasion of Sicily had begun in London prior to Casablanca, presumably building on the British War Cabinet Joint Planning Staff and Mediterranean Command discussions in mid-1942, and the results were submitted to the Combined Chiefs of Staff at the Conference. An attack upon Messina at the north-eastern tip of the island and just four miles from the Italian mainland would simultaneously isolate Sicily and cut the primary conduit for Axis reinforcement; the planners estimated that the existing ferry service alone could lift up to a division and a half per week. However, this option was ruled out by the lack of sea room for an invasion fleet and the presence of fixed defences along both sides of the Straits of Messina and two simultaneous assaults were suggested instead, one near Catania on the south-eastern coast and the other near Palermo at the western end of the island. Two landings at opposite ends of Sicily would divide the Axis defence and raise the prospect of rapidly nipping off Messina and the north-eastern tip of Sicily from the rest of the island, thereby cutting the Axis conduit for supply and reinforcement and isolating the estimated eight divisions deployed in its defence. It offered rapid access to those major ports and a number of airfields for Allied use. On the down side, launching assaults at opposite ends of the island ruled out Allied mutual support in the initial stages and required sufficient strength to avoid the two invasion forces being defeated in detail, as well as more shipping to deliver them and two powerful naval covering forces to protect them if the *Regia Marina* had not been rendered ineffective by the time of the invasion. In addition, a backstop plan for a single landing near Catania was also created for implementation if Allied bombing and other preparatory measures reduced the Axis force defending Sicily significantly below the expected eight divisions; according to one source there was also a scheme for a single landing at Palermo.[17]

This was not quite all there was to the matter, given that post-Casablanca General Marshall and his War Department planners also pressured Lieutenant-General Eisenhower to launch a surprise ad hoc strike against Sicily to secure the island before the Axis could reinforce and organise a co-ordinated defence; this was based largely on ULTRA and signals intelligence that indicated that the Italian forces were in a 'woeful state' generally and that there were only approximately 5,000 German troops on Sicily, most of whom were not formed into combat units. Eisenhower was not enthusiastic however, which Marshall attributed to his 'conservative nature', lack of adaptability and because the AFHQ commander had permitted boldness to be replaced by orthodoxy. On the other hand, Eisenhower was perhaps equally if not more justified in considering the idea 'too risky and too difficult to carry out at short notice', not least because it would be he who carried the can for failure rather than Marshall and the Washington-based War Department planners although the latter continued to agitate in favour of the idea until mid-May.[18]

Nevertheless, the Combined Chiefs of Staff accepted the outline preliminary planning presented at Casablanca and on 23 January 1943 issued a Directive to guide further developments. The Directive confirmed General Eisenhower's appointment as Commander-in-Chief of Operation HUSKY and that of General Alexander as his Deputy with overall command of the ground element of the invasion. Eisenhower was also tasked to establish the overall chain of command for HUSKY, to nominate commanders for the command slots created and to set up the requisite staff and planning machinery for HUSKY. In line with the way command arrangements had evolved in Tunisia, the Combined Chiefs of Staff also decreed that the ground portion of the HUSKY invasion force would be divided along national lines into separate British and US task forces; the British Eastern Task Force was initially dubbed FORCE 545, later retitled the 8th Army with its HQ in Cairo while the US Western Task Force, dubbed FORCE 343 and subsequently US 7th Army, was initially headquartered in Rabat, Morocco. Eisenhower's nomination for FORCE 545's commanders were the existing commander of the 8th Army, General Sir Bernard Law Montgomery as Ground Force commander, along with Air Vice-Marshal Harry Broadhurst and Vice-Admiral Sir Bertram Ramsay as Air and Naval Force commanders respectively; the former had served as a fighter pilot during the Battle of Britain and commanded the Desert Air Force while the latter had been recalled from retirement in 1939 and as Flag Officer Dover planned and executed Operation DYNAMO, the evacuation of the British Expeditionary Force from Dunkirk. The choice for FORCE 343's US Ground Force commander was a little less straightforward. Eisenhower initially favoured Lieutenant-General Mark W. Clark, commander of the new US 5th Army activated at Oujda on 5 January 1943, but he was ruled out because his formation was already tasked to control French Morocco and guard against possible incursions from adjacent Spanish Morocco. Choice instead settled on then Lieutenant-General George S. Patton, who had commanded the Moroccan side of Operation TORCH and was currently commanding US I Armored Corps from a HQ in Casablanca. The US Air Command was allotted to Colonel Lawrence P. Hickey USAAF who had commanded a number of fighter units and formations from 1939 including US 8th Fighter Command from 1 February 1942, while Vice-Admiral Henry Kent Hewitt USN, who had commanded the US Navy component for TORCH, became FORCE 343's Naval Commander. Eisenhower submitted his nominations to the Combined Chiefs of Staff on 11 February 1943 who granted formal approval two days later, on Saturday 13 February.[19]

In addition to being Deputy Commander-in-Chief and overall Ground Commander, General Alexander was also responsible for 'detailed planning and preparation and with the execution of the actual operation when launched', which required the requisite facilities and staff.[20] As AFHQ in Algiers was still fully occupied with prosecuting the Tunisian campaign, Eisenhower initially established a dedicated planning staff for the Sicilian operation within AFHQ's G3 Operations Section dubbed FORCE 141 after the room number in the St George's Hotel in Algiers where it was first convened, before moving to the *École Normale* at La Bouzaréa, three miles north of the city.[21] On 15 May, two days after the Axis surrender in Tunisia, FORCE 141 was separated out into an independent operational HQ and absorbed General Alexander's 18th Army Group HQ on its disbandment, with additional British staff personnel being posted in from the UK and elsewhere in the Middle East theatre. Their US counterparts were drafted in from US 5th Army and US I Armored Corps HQs at Oujda and Casablanca in Morocco respectively, and as far afield as the Continental United States. Although Alexander was technically in charge of FORCE 141 and its activities, he was preoccupied with the fighting in Tunisia, particularly with keeping Lieutenant-General Kenneth Anderson on 'a tight rein' and monitoring the activities of Major-General Lloyd R. Fredendall and his US II Corps.[22] Command of the planning staff therefore devolved onto the Chief-of-Staff, initially Major-General Charles H. Gairdner who had been brought in from Field Marshal Sir Archibald Wavell's staff in India, although he proved unequal to the task and was eventually reposted as Prime Minister Churchill's Personal Emissary to General Douglas MacArthur's HQ in the Pacific Theatre.

When Gairdner resigned from his post at FORCE 141 in May 1943, due in large part to difficulties working with Montgomery, Eisenhower replaced him with US Major-General Clarence R. Huebner, who then also became the senior US officer at FORCE 141 HQ. Huebner's reign as Deputy Chief-of-Staff was also marred by a difficult working relationship, in this instance with his direct superior General Alexander, due to the latter's reportedly low opinion of the fighting quality of US troops; this remained the case until Huebner was replaced by Brigadier-General Lyman L. Lemnitzer in July 1943. FORCE 141 was renamed 15th Army Group HQ on 10 July 1943, the day the invasion of Sicily commenced.[23]

FORCE 141 commenced detailed planning for Operation HUSKY on Friday 12 February 1943, using the British War Cabinet Joint Planning Staff scheme presented to the Combined Chiefs of Staff at the Casablanca Conference as a template.[24] However, this scheme had originated as a hastily concocted staff study rather than a fully fledged plan, and as a result lacked much of the necessary detail; according to a historian of Combined Operations, much of it was drawn up in haste at Casablanca to provide the 'rough skeleton plan' with a patina of credibility. The FORCE 141 staff thus rapidly identified the flaws and omissions in the scheme, but on raising their concerns with Eisenhower's AFHQ they were overruled by a senior British staff officer who reportedly informed them that the plan had been sanctioned at the highest level and ordered them to 'get on with the job'.[25] This they then did, although their efforts were hamstrung to an extent by a lack of higher-level guidance as Alexander, Montgomery and Patton were fully occupied in the final stage of the fighting in Tunisia, which left the FORCE 141 planners operating in something of a vacuum. They nonetheless began by identifying suitable landing areas, which involved examining over 300 miles of Sicilian coastline; this identified thirty-two suitable beaches, of which twenty-six met the twin criteria of being suitable for landing vehicles and personnel with good exits inland.

The seaborne portion of the landing was carried over virtually unchanged from the Joint Planning Staff scheme and involved the British Eastern Task Force landing four infantry divisions, two infantry brigades, three Commandos, two armoured regiments and a tank battalion onto five separate locations along the hundred-mile stretch of coastline running from Catania on the eastern coast around the south-eastern tip of the island to Gela on the southern coast over a four-day period; the landings varied in size from single brigade to reinforced division. Apart from assigning the landings near Catania to British rather than US units, the major addition to the Joint Planning Staff template was the employment of airborne landings to secure airfields at Comiso, Ponte Olivo and Gerbini on D-Day, D Plus One and D Plus Two respectively. The US Western Task Force employed a slightly smaller force made up of three infantry divisions, two Ranger battalions and two armored combat commands. One division was tasked to land between Marinella and Sciacca on the south-western aspect of the island on D-Day, with the remainder landing at four separate locations along a sixty-mile stretch of coast on the north-western aspect between Castellammare and Cape Zaffarano, ten miles east of Palermo, on D Plus Two. The two westerly landings were divisional affairs while the two easternmost were allotted to detached regimental combat teams from the divisions. A parachute landing was tasked to seize the airfield at Milo near Trapani on the western tip of Sicily on D Plus Two, utilising aircraft employed for the earlier British operations. The chronological and geographical dispersal of the landings was intended to diffuse the Axis response and thereby reduce the possibility of simultaneous counter-attacks across the board, even at the cost of the defenders massing against a single individual landing and defeating it in detail.[26]

The FORCE 141 planners completed their work by 28 February 1943, when Major-General Gairdner travelled the 500 miles from Algiers to see General Alexander at 18th Army Group HQ in Tunisia, who gave his approval to the scheme after suggesting a number of modifications. The most important of these was concentrating both Task Force landings in the south-eastern portion of the island, although this was temporarily withdrawn because the planners considered the ports of Augusta, Catania and Syracuse to be inadequate to support landings on the scale envisaged.[27] Other suggestions included avoiding landings in less than division strength where possible, creating a reserve for unforeseen circumstances and refocusing the airborne portion of the plan from securing airfields to neutralising beach defences to ease the passage of the seaborne landing forces inland; this switch was intended to make up for the inability of naval gunfire support to operate during the hours of darkness when the landings were scheduled to commence. When these revisions had been endorsed by Admiral Cunningham and Air Chief Marshal Tedder, the plan was passed to Lieutenant-General Eisenhower, who in turn approved it in principle at a meeting with the three senior HUSKY commanders on Saturday 13 March; copies were also despatched to FORCE 545 and 343 HQs, although it is unclear whether this was done before or after the latter meeting. Montgomery and Patton were summoned to attend a briefing on Thursday 18 March.[28] Perhaps unsurprisingly given its flawed foundation, the FORCE 141 scheme received a mixed reception. Admiral Cunningham was especially enamoured with the multiple and widely dispersed landings because that diluted the potential Axis air and surface threat to his naval forces, as was Tedder because the scheme accorded with his preference for denying the Axis use of the airfields and securing them as rapidly as possible to facilitate the establishment of Allied air superiority.

This was emphatically not the case with General Montgomery, however. Preoccupied as he was with the ongoing fight in Tunisia, Montgomery does not appear to have paid much attention to his copy of the FORCE 141 plan, but that all changed on the afternoon of 13 March when FORCE 545 Chief-of-Staff Lieutenant-General Miles Dempsey and naval commander Vice-Admiral Sir Bertram Ramsay called in at his field HQ after the conference with Eisenhower and his HUSKY senior commanders. On being briefed on the plan, Montgomery immediately signalled Alexander his misgivings in no uncertain terms: 'In my opinion the operation breaks every commonsense rule of practical battle-fighting and is completely theoretical. It has no hope of success and should be completely recast.'[29] He also relayed his reservations to CIGS Field Marshal Brooke, pointing out that 'the real trouble is that neither Alex [General Alexander] nor myself have time to bother about HUSKY at the moment.'[30]

Montgomery's not unjustified objections began the process of recasting HUSKY, one that was reportedly greeted with enthusiasm by the FORCE 141 planners: 'One of the rare occasions when the planners were overjoyed to see their homework being torn to tatters: they were being delivered from a nightmare.'[31] On the other hand, the process turned into more of a nightmare for FORCE 141's Chief-of-Staff Major-General Gairdner, who found himself increasingly trapped between his direct superior Alexander and an increasingly vociferous Montgomery. Gairdner chaired the 18 March meeting in Eisenhower and Alexander's absence and while Montgomery was also absent co-ordinating Operation PUGILIST against the Mareth Line, he delegated Lieutenant-General Dempsey and Vice-Admiral Ramsay to argue his case. This was that the planned scheme was unsuitable for execution against weak, solely Italian opposition, the proposed landings in the south-east of Sicily would be of insufficient strength and breadth to guarantee sufficient supply for the landing force and that the remedy for this was to scrap the proposed landing to the west at Gela and add the British division slated for it to the south-east landing.

All of this flew directly in the face of Admiral Cunningham and Air Chief Marshal Tedder's insistence that eliminating the airfields around Ponte Olivo inland from Gela was vital to protect the Allied fleet and landing force from Axis air attack, and the meeting descended into an acrimonious deadlock with no progress possible due to Alexander's absence. On being briefed on the meeting the following day, Alexander backed Montgomery's case, but instead of scrapping the Gela landing he sought Eisenhower's permission to replace the British formation with the US 3rd Infantry Division by cancelling the latter's landing to the west at Marinella and Sciacca, and also postponing the Palermo landings until further notice. Eisenhower approved the revised plan on Saturday 20 March.[32]

Eisenhower's approval did nothing to smooth the waters over the HUSKY plan, however. Patton, again not without justification, objected to losing one of his divisions and to the open-ended postponement of the Palermo landing that would have left his formations hanging with no firm timescale, while as early as 23 March Montgomery was lobbying to include more of his veteran formations in the invasion force and to rename the Eastern Task Force the 8th Army. The arguments and disagreements in Algiers rumbled on through April and into May and reached as far as Cairo, from where Commander-in-Chief General Sir Henry Wilson cabled Field Marshal Sir Alan Brooke, although the CIGS chose to remain aloof. Brigadier-General Arthur S. Nevins, the senior US planning officer at FORCE 141 HQ, formally requested Eisenhower to rethink his approval of the revised scheme. A group of British and US staff officers at that HQ unsuccessfully raised their own objections to Major-General Gairdner and on 25 March the British Chiefs of Staff joined Patton in objecting to the possible permanent postponement of the Palermo landing, albeit on the grounds that this would increase the burden on the British contingent and exacerbate the existing shortage of landing craft.

Prompted in part by such uncertainties, Alexander drew up another outline plan with the assistance of Montgomery, which was revealed on 5 April. This again cancelled the Marinella and Sciacca landing, pushed the US landings at Palermo back to D Plus Five due largely to the shortage of landing craft and shipping and envisaged putting a single division ashore at Gela. The main British landing, employing two divisions and a separate brigade, was concentrated on a fifteen-mile stretch of coast running south to the tip of Sicily between Avola and Pachino, with another division going ashore at Pozallo, thirteen miles west of Pachino on the southern coast. Two days later, on 7 April, Eisenhower despatched a pessimistic signal to London and Washington that claimed that the FORCE 141 planners and Alexander, Cunningham and Tedder considered there was little prospect of successfully prosecuting HUSKY '…if the region [Sicily] contained substantial well-armed and fully organized German troops… By the term substantial forces is meant more than two German divisions.'[33]

The signal was presumably intended to garner more resources in order to break the planning impasse, but it drew a blistering response from Churchill directed at his Chiefs of Staff, which one source refers to as 'one of the most sharply worded memos ever written by the Prime Minister'.[34] The memo began by contrasting Eisenhower's timidity with his enthusiasm for a cross-Channel invasion against much higher German odds, criticised the elevation of two German divisions as an operation-abandoning obstacle, and cast doubt on Montgomery and Alexander sharing Eisenhower's pessimistic outlook. He trusted that the Joint Chiefs recipients did 'not accept these pusillanimous and defeatist doctrines', which he considered the result of 'Planning Staffs playing upon each other's fears, each Service presenting its difficulties at the maximum, and Americans and Englishmen vying with each other, in the total absence of one directing mind and commanding willpower'. The memo ended by pointing out that Arctic convoy supplies to the hard-pressed Soviets had been cut because of HUSKY and contrasting Eisenhower's reaction to two German divisions with Stalin facing 185.[35] It is unclear if Eisenhower actually saw Churchill's memo, but he was aware of the reaction to it from the British recipients and the Combined Chiefs of Staff. The former responded by pointing out that the risks of HUSKY were understood, accepted and considered worth running for the likely rewards, and criticised Eisenhower for suggesting that the Allies '*cannot* take on the Germans in combined operations' (original emphasis), while the latter reinforced this by stating bluntly that under no circumstances would they even consider abandoning HUSKY.[36] Presumably prompted by this, Eisenhower approved Alexander's plan on Saturday 10 April 1943, and two days later engaged in some backpedalling in a signal to the Combined Chiefs of Staff, assuring them that the 'HUSKY operation will be prosecuted with all means at our disposal. There is no thought here except to carry out our orders to the ultimate of our ability.'[37]

In the meantime, Montgomery continued to harbour misgivings about the 10 April Plan despite his role in formulating it, which in a matter of days not only resulted in him withdrawing his support for the Plan but actively working against it. To that end he despatched the 8th Army's Chief-of-Staff Francis 'Freddie' de Guingand, promoted to Major-General for the purpose, to become Chief-of Staff at FORCE 545 HQ in Cairo on 17 April. Ostensibly this was to allow the existing incumbent Lieutenant-General Dempsey to return to his existing command of XIII Corps in Tunisia, but de Guingand's real mission was to carry out an in-depth feasibility study of the 10 April Plan. Two days later, Montgomery attended a private meeting with Eisenhower and Alexander in Algiers where he informed them of de Guingand's new role and mission, reiterated his general dissatisfaction with the course of HUSKY planning, again stressing the urgent need for high-level guidance and suggested that a compromise was required, specifically withdrawing his 50th and 51st Divisions and XXX Corps in its entirety from the fighting in Tunisia to begin preparations for HUSKY. According to one source Montgomery came away from the private conference erroneously 'believing he had been given a mandate to take over HUSKY', a view reflected in a despatch he sent to CIGS Brooke the following day, stating that his own 'compromise was the only course of action capable of leading to success' and expressed sympathy for Alexander's inability to concentrate upon the Sicily operation because he was preoccupied with operations in Tunisia and specifically ensuring that the 1st Army 'remained on the rails'. The incompetence of the 1st Army's commander, Lieutenant-General Anderson, was specifically cited as the underlying reason for Alexander's inability to pay more attention to planning for HUSKY.[38]

While all this was going on Major-General de Guingand had been busy analysing the 10 April Plan and after several days concluded that 'a much greater concentration would be required if the Allies were to overcome resistance on a scale similar to that encountered in North Africa'.[39] With his misgivings confirmed, Montgomery therefore travelled covertly to Cairo to be briefed on de Guingand's findings on Friday 23 April and the following day informed Alexander that he was unwilling to prosecute HUSKY in its current form and laid out his specific objections in a detailed, nine-point signal. This acknowledged his own failure to dedicate sufficient time to the Sicily planning, noted that all planning hitherto was based on an assumption of weak Axis opposition and highlighted the grave risk inherent in such assumptions before insisting that the formations and units of his landing force be deployed in sufficiently close proximity to permit mutual support. To that end he again recommended abandoning the Gela and Pozallo landings and informed Alexander that he had already issued orders for the 8th Army to plan for a concentrated landing along the fourteen-mile stretch of coast running south from Avola to the Pachino Peninsula at the very south-eastern tip of the island, with XXX Corps tasked to secure the latter; the signal also stressed the need for haste to offset Axis and particularly German defensive preparations, claimed the unconditional support of Vice-Admiral Ramsay, demanded unlimited access to support from Air Vice-Marshal Broadhurst's Desert Air Force and direct control of the 8th Army in its entirety, with the formations not employed in the initial landing being held in readiness at Algiers for immediate deployment on demand.[40]

Montgomery's summary of the situation to CIGS Field Marshal Brooke at around the same time was more succinct and echoed his sentiments from mid-March, pointing out that the HUSKY planning was a 'dog's breakfast [which] breaks every common-sense rule of practical fighting, and would have no chance of success...unless someone will face up to this problem and give a decision, there will be a first-class disaster.'[41] Montgomery's appreciation was not flawless given that his claim that HUSKY planning was based upon the assumption that Axis opposition would be light contradicted warnings from the Combined Chiefs of Staff that Italian troops on Sicily were likely to fight hard in defence of their home soil and that appreciations from all sources had also repeatedly predicted stiff resistance from German units stationed on the island.[42] On the other hand it should be noted that while Montgomery's action provoked outrage in some quarters, as we have seen the 10 April Plan was essentially a mish-mash of mutually exclusive requirements that pleased no-one – including the planners tasked to draw it up – and on that basis Montgomery was merely acting as a lightning rod for the overarching dissatisfaction of all concerned. The underlying problem was that while Montgomery's misgivings over HUSKY were legitimate, they were mixed with demands that could be construed as self-serving, which undermined their validity, particularly with his US Allies; as the British Official History put it, 'It was one of Montgomery's unfortunate habits often to advocate and secure sound policies and courses of action in a manner that suggested to others that he was blind to every interest except his own.'[43]

Montgomery's withdrawal of support for the 10 April Plan obliged General Alexander to call another conference in Algiers on Tuesday 27 April 1943 to discuss the new proposals although the meeting had to be postponed for forty-eight hours after Major-General de Guingand, who was standing in for Montgomery after the latter reportedly came down with a bout of tonsillitis, was concussed in an aircraft crash en route to the conference; he was replaced as Montgomery's proxy by Lieutenant-General Oliver Leese, commanding British XXX Corps. In addition to Leese, the 29 April conference was attended by Montgomery's US opposite number Lieutenant-General Patton, Vice-Admiral Ramsay, the commander of the Northwest African Tactical Air Force Air Marshal Sir Arthur Coningham and the HUSKY air and naval commanders Admiral Cunningham and Air Chief-Marshal Tedder. The meeting achieved little overall, apart from providing the latter two with the opportunity to ignore Lieutenant-General Leese's presentation on behalf of the absent Montgomery's position and a platform to reprise their insistence that HUSKY was impossible without seizure of the dozen or so airfields around Ponte Olivo inland from Gela; they also emphatically and publicly disagreed with Montgomery's revision when explicitly asked their opinion by Alexander.[44] Perhaps the most unimpressed was Lieutenant-General Patton who was reportedly dismayed by Alexander's lack of control over proceedings and considered the HUSKY Deputy Commander-in-Chief to be a 'sorry figure' and a 'fence walker'.[45] It thus finally fell upon Eisenhower as HUSKY Commander-in-Chief to adjudicate in his capacity as senior Allied commander to break this all-British deadlock, which he did by calling yet another conference in Algiers two days later on Sunday 2 May, at Montgomery's prompting according to one source.

This conference was attended by Eisenhower, Cunningham, Tedder and Montgomery, with Alexander and Coningham initially absent, stuck in Tunisia due to poor flying weather. Montgomery seized the opportunity to present another iteration of his revised scheme that maintained the Eastern Task Force's focus on the Avola-Pachino area while discarding the proposed US landing at Palermo in favour of landing the Western Task Force at Gela and Pozallo.[46] After reading a copy of Montgomery's 24 April signal to Alexander in the run up to the 2 May conference Eisenhower had initially sided with Tedder and Cunningham, but Montgomery's revised scheme prompted a change of stance in favour of the latter. AFHQ Chief-of-Staff Major-General Walter Bedell Smith later claimed this was because Eisenhower was not in favour of the Palermo landing, but he appears to have been swayed by Montgomery elucidating the valid military reasons for his new scheme after cornering Bedell Smith in a toilet at AFHQ. The discussion was rapidly relayed to Eisenhower in Algiers who was also fully aware that compromise was the only way out of the impasse and that Montgomery's latest revised scheme was at least partly acceptable to all parties.[47] Eisenhower therefore instructed FORCE 141's planners to examine the scheme and, after discussing the matter with Alexander after he finally arrived in Algiers from Tunisia, officially approved it the day after the conference, on Monday 3 May. Alexander issued formal orders the same day and Montgomery was informed via signal: 'Your Plan has been approved by the C-in-C.'[48] Acceptance of the compromise was not universally positive. Admiral Cunningham reportedly forbade Montgomery's name to be mentioned in his presence and tried unsuccessfully to gain Patton's support for an attempt to overturn Eisenhower's decision, while Major-General Gairdner resigned as FORCE 141 Chief-of-Staff later in May, citing Montgomery's refusal to accept anything from him that did not accord with the 8th Army commander's preferences.[49] For his part, Patton, while maintaining a 'placid façade' during the various meetings, reserved his ire for Eisenhower in part because he had taken Patton's agreement over the latest HUSKY plan for granted with no consultation, and partly because he considered Eisenhower's actions to be skewed toward British sensibilities and thus 'a betrayal of American forces'; on returning to his FORCE 343/Western Task Force HQ at Mostaganem, 170 miles west of Algiers, he finally publicly vented his spleen by informing his staff that 'This is what you get when your Commander-in-Chief ceases to be an American and becomes an Ally.'[50] Nonetheless, after three months of acrimonious wrangling Operation HUSKY finally had a viable overall plan acceptable to all those tasked to carry it out, at least to some extent.

Eisenhower's decision did not bring an immediate halt to higher level dissent regarding the timing of HUSKY and wider Allied strategy in the Mediterranean. With regard to the latter, the TRIDENT or Third Washington Conference held from 12-25 May 1943 rehashed US objections to Mediterranean operations as a distraction from a cross-Channel invasion for example, although in the event Churchill succeeded in obtaining a firm commitment to HUSKY, a twelve-month postponement of the Normandy invasion and agreement to continue with the strategy of eliminating Italy from the war after Sicily had been secured.[51] With regard to HUSKY specifically, although the Combined Chiefs of Staff had agreed on 13 April to a launch window of 10-14 July to take advantage of a waxing moon, General Marshall continued to push for a hasty ad hoc operation to seize Sicily until Eisenhower finally ruled it out on 10 May 1943, on the grounds that there were insufficient landing ships and assault landing craft to carry a single division and land a single regimental combat team; in Eisenhower's considered and not unjustified opinion, 'An attack with less than two divisions [was] too great a risk.'[52] In the meantime General Alexander and the FORCE 141 planners had been busy drawing up a full operational plan around Montgomery's revised scheme following Eisenhower's decision on 3 May, which was approved by the Combined Chiefs of Staff ten days later on 13 May.[53] With this approval General Alexander issued the plan on Monday 17 May under the heading FORCE 141 Operation Instruction No. 1, with a revised FORCE 141 Operation Instruction No. 2 following four days later on Friday 21 May.[54]

The plan was divided into five separate stages, beginning with a preparatory Phase One during which Allied air and naval forces were to prosecute operations to 'neutralize enemy activities at sea, and...gain air supremacy'. Phase Two involved seaborne landings by the US 7th and British 8th Armies concentrated on the south-eastern coast of Sicily. The 7th was tasked to put the three US Divisions ashore along a shallow forty-mile-wide bay running east from the port of Licata to just east of Scoglitti, while the 8th put two divisions onto the Pachino Peninsula at the south-eastern tip of the island and two more divisions twenty miles to the north between Avola and Cassibile. The seaborne assault was to be preceded by landings by two airborne divisions intended to interfere with Axis movement and communications and secure specific objectives to assist the sea landing including Axis defences, airfields, road junctions and bridges. Phase Three envisaged converting the initial landing lodgement into a firm base for further exploitation and specifically for Phase Four, the seizure of the ports of Augusta and Catania, thirteen and thirty-two miles north of Syracuse respectively. In contrast to this, Phase Five was a vague intention toward the 'reduction of the island', ostensibly due to Alexander's predilection for reacting as required to events as they took their course, rather than trammelling matters with pre-conditions that might be rendered obsolete by events.[55]

According one source both Patton and Montgomery were committed to securing Catania in order to cut the Axis line of supply and reinforcement from the Italian mainland and isolate the remainder of the island and any Axis forces deployed therein, merely differing on the means by which the goal was to be achieved.[56] Montgomery at least had transmitted his intentions in this regard to his Corps commanders from the outset; the commander of XXX Corps, Lieutenant-General Leese, was informed that the object of the invasion was to 'dominate the Messina Straits as soon as possible and to get a footing in...the mainland of Italy' at a meeting at 8th Army HQ on 9 June, and he passed the information on to Major-General Guy Simonds, commanding the 1st Canadian Division, the following day.[57]

The HUSKY landing was preceded by an extensive Allied strategic deception effort with the overall code name Operation BARCLAY. The effort was prompted by ULTRA intelligence gleaned from *Luftwaffe* Enigma signals in March 1943 that revealed the Germans had correctly surmised that the Western Mediterranean would be the focus of future Allied operations, with Sicily as the prime target followed by Crete, Sardinia and Corsica in that order of likelihood; additional ULTRA intelligence the following month showed observation of Allied air, ground and naval concentrations and activity in Gibraltar, Malta and North Africa had confirmed the initial German assessment, with Allied action in the Eastern Mediterranean judged unlikely apart from a possible move to secure Crete.[58] In an effort to distract Axis and particularly German attention away from the Western Mediterranean and mislead them from redeploying their forces there, the Allies therefore decided to launch a more extensive version of Operation CASCADE, a wide-ranging deception operation that grew out of measures to conceal the relative weakness of British forces in the Western Desert in 1941. Carried out by a dedicated undercover unit dubbed 'A Force' commanded by Lieutenant-Colonel Dudley Clarke, who had played a leading role in the raising of Commando raiding units the previous year, CASCADE was launched in 1942 and built upon earlier, small-scale disinformation efforts in order to convince Axis intelligence that British strength in the Western Desert was double the five armoured and ten infantry divisions actually available by creating a wholly fictitious order of battle. This involved A Force fabricating formation and unit insignia, inventing bogus movement records from as far afield as the UK and Australia backed up with manned 'advance parties', spurious radio traffic and information disseminated via a network of double-agents. The effort had the desired effect, given that analysis of German documents captured during and after the Battle of El Alamein by A Force released in November 1942 showed that Axis intelligence had consistently overestimated British armoured and infantry strength by forty and forty-five per cent respectively.[59]

Operation BARCLAY was approved by the Combined Chiefs of Staff in April 1943 with revisions on 20 May, and it provided an umbrella for a wide variety of deception efforts. Arguably the most esoteric was Operation LEYBURN, which purported to show Allied concern for works of art in proposed invasion areas via enquiries in neutral countries, while the most Machiavellian was Operation MINCEMEAT, a scheme conceived to persuade the Germans that HUSKY was actually the codename for an Allied attack on Greece and that plans for an assault of Sicily were merely a cover. The means was a bogus letter penned by Vice-CIGS Lieutenant-General Sir Archibald Nye to General Alexander explaining to the latter why formations promised to him had been diverted to the Greek assault force. The letter was to be delivered into German hands via the body of a deceased Welsh vagrant named Glyndwr Michael dressed in the uniform of a fictitious Royal Marine officer, Acting Major William Martin; the letter and additional genuine documentation for authenticity was contained in a briefcase handcuffed to the corpse's wrist, which was also furnished with an inflatable life vest, a wallet, photograph of a fiancé and other details for realism. (Some today question whether it really was Glyndwr Michael.)

The cadaver was carried from Scotland in a vacuum-sealed container aboard HM Submarine *Seraph* and released into the sea off Huelva on the southern Spanish Atlantic coast in the early hours of Friday 30 April 1943, along with a capsized inflatable aircraft emergency dinghy to support the fiction that 'Major Martin' was the victim of an air crash; Huelva was chosen because the offshore currents were likely to carry the corpse ashore and because an *Abwehr* agent was known to be operating in the vicinity. The body was discovered a few hours later and after an autopsy the following day attended by the local British Vice-Consul Francis Haselden, was buried with full military honours in the local cemetery on Sunday 2 May. As the briefcase was missing at the autopsy the British then initiated a series of pre-prepared signal cables between London and Vice-Consul Haselden stressing the importance of its recovery using a cipher the Germans were known to have broken; as an extra measure *The Times* listed 'Major Martin' among the casualties from a fortuitous air crash in the vicinity on 4 April. The briefcase was returned to Haselden on 11 May and subsequent examination in London showed it had been tampered with. In fact the Germans had fully swallowed the bait, with *Oberkommando der Kriegsmarine* (*OKK*) issuing translated summaries by 7 May which within four days led Hitler to consider a Sicilian invasion less likely and encouraged his long-standing preoccupation with Greece and the Balkans; wider results included fostering disagreement with Mussolini and his *Comando Supremo*, and the redeployment of German armoured formations from France and Russia to Greece, headed briefly by Rommel.[60] Much of this only became apparent through post-war analysis of German records, but the most immediate sign that Hitler and the German High Command had been persuaded by MINCEMEAT came on 14 May via an ULTRA decrypt of a signal from *Oberkommando der Wehrmacht* (*OKW*) to *Generalfeldmarschall* Albert Kesselring at *Oberbefehlshaber* Süd (*OB Süd*) in Rome and other senior German commanders in the Mediterranean, informing them that an Allied operation against Greece was confirmed and that moves on Sicily were a feint.[61] Churchill, who was attending the TRIDENT Conference in Washington, was informed of the success of the operation via a cryptic signal simply stating 'MINCEMEAT SWALLOWED WHOLE'.[62]

In addition to MINCEMEAT, Operation BARCLAY encompassed a number of more conventional deception operations intended to draw Axis attention and forces away from Sicily as the next Allied target in the Mediterranean. BARCLAY itself involved the creation of a fictitious British 12th Army Group with an order of battle that included a dozen armoured, infantry and airborne divisions headquartered in Cairo with the supposed mission of retaking Crete and leading an invasion of the Greek mainland as a prelude to a push north into the Balkans. The threatened Greek invasion was lent physical form by Operation WATERFALL, which maintained deception units in the areas of Egypt within range of Axis reconnaissance aircraft to ensure their activities were monitored by the enemy. These included a bogus 8th Armoured Division complete with fake vehicle parks, camps and training areas, a fleet of dummy and real gliders sufficient to lift an airborne division, up to a hundred replica landing craft moored in a variety of ports all protected by several squadrons of mocked-up fighter aircraft spread across a number of mock airfields protected by real anti-aircraft units. Signals units maintained a net of radio signals commensurate with an Army Group and associated infrastructure, and the deception units also moved physical locations to mimic working up exercises and other preparatory activity in synch with spurious movement orders and bogus launch dates and postponements.

The deception effort in Egypt was complemented by a more kinetic element on the ground in Greece proper. Operation ANIMALS was a co-ordinated sabotage campaign against communications and transport links by the British Special Operations Executive (SOE) and the ELAS Resistance group across Greece. Beginning on 20 June 1943, ANIMALS was intended to replicate preparations for an invasion of Greece, concentrating primarily upon the demolition of railway bridges and ambushing Axis road convoys in the face of the usual German reprisals against the local civilian population. Despite this the operation continued until 11 July, at which point the SOE called a halt as the invasion of Sicily had rendered it superfluous. Overall, the impact of the Allied deception effort varied. *OKW*'s acceptance of the supposed Allied threat to Greece and the Balkans was driven at least in part by Hitler's preoccupation with the region, and it is interesting to speculate how much attention German senior commanders would have paid to it without the *Führer's* involvement, given that ULTRA decrypts showed that German commanders in the Western Mediterranean continued to expect an Allied assault in that region throughout the period of Operation BARCLAY. For their part the Italians had never been convinced of the threat to Greece, likely because Rome was significantly closer to the likely seat of Allied action than Berlin. Both the head of *Comando Supremo*, *Generale d'Armata* Vittorio Ambrosio and *Generale d'Armata* Alfredo Guzzoni commanding the *6ª Armata* on Sicily remained certain that the next Allied blow would be against Italian territory, the only question being whether the blow would fall on Sardinia or Sicily.

Extensive as the Allied deception effort was, it was merely background to the genuine preparations for HUSKY, most of which were carried out from the air. By the time the invasion force arrived on the Sicilian beaches these preparations had involved 3,462 aircraft ranging from single-engine fighters to four-engine heavy bombers and the total included a number of bomber units deployed into the Mediterranean Theatre specifically for that mission.[63] These included sixty Vickers Wellingtons from Nos. 420, 424 and 425 Squadrons RCAF posted in on loan from the UK to RAF No. 205 Group in Tunisia, which deployed them on a new airfield at Zina and an existing base at Kairouan, and approximately 144 B-24s spread across the twelve squadrons of the US 44th, 93rd and 389th Bombardment Groups drafted in from the US 8th Air Force's 2nd Bombardment Division, also located in the UK. These were housed on airfields belonging to the US 9th Bomber Command near Benghazi in Libya; it is unclear if the Command's two organic B-24 units, the 98th and 376th Bombardment Groups, were also in residence there or had moved to Tunisia.[64] Accommodating this host within effective striking distance of Sicily involved some relocation and airfield construction, with Malta being selected as the primary fighter base for the invasion. It was roughly sixty miles from Sicily and a steady programme of construction to permit the housing of up to thirty air squadrons had been ongoing there since January 1943. Relocation of the largely British Desert Air Force's (DAF) ground support echelon to Malta was well underway by

8 June, the first five Spitfire squadrons from RAF No. 244 Wing flew in on 14 and 15 June and by the end of the month had been joined by RAF Nos. 322 and 324 Wings. By the beginning of July 1943, RAF machines had taken up all the thirty-squadron accommodation with Malta providing a home for at least twenty squadrons of Spitfires, five night-fighter squadrons, two Fleet Air Arm torpedo squadrons, two medium bomber squadrons and a photo-reconnaissance wing augmented with at least three P-40 squadrons from the US 57th Fighter Group and the US 47th Bombardment Group's three squadrons of A-20 light bombers, with ground-crews in place preparing for the arrival of three fighter-bomber wings. Malta had thus become 'the equivalent of an unsinkable, giant-sized aircraft-carrier, strategically positioned to provide air support for the Sicily invasion'.[65] Additional fighter capacity was also provided on two other islands. US Army engineers constructed an airfield for the US 31st Fighter Group's three Spitfire-equipped squadrons from scratch on the small adjacent island of Gozo, five miles off Malta, over a period of between seventeen and twenty days in June depending on the account source, and the airfield on Pantelleria, 145 miles north-west of Malta was occupied by the P-40 equipped US 33rd Fighter Group by 26 June, fifteen days after the island had been captured from its Italian garrison. A total of 670 'first-line aircraft' were based across the three islands by the end of June.[66]

The aerial build up was not confined to the islands. The aircraft so located were slated to protect the initial invasion and move onto forward airfields on Sicily as soon as they were secured, and the build-up to provide successive waves and support thus extended to the North African mainland. The DAF's contingent of RAF Hurricane, Kittyhawk and US P-40 fighter-bombers was stationed around Tripoli in readiness to provide air support for the invasion and to move to Malta once space allowed, while three US Fighter-Groups totalling nine squadrons of A-36 and P-40 fighter-bombers were deployed in Tunisia as part of the US 12th Air Support Command, alongside RAF and US bombers assigned to the Northwest African Strategic Air Force (NASAF). The US contingent of the latter included the 5th Bombardment Wing made up of sixteen squadrons of Boeing B-17 heavy bombers and the 47th and 2686th (Provisional) Bombardment Wings, consisting of eight squadrons of B-25 and twelve squadrons of B-26 medium bombers respectively.[67] The RAF provided No. 205 Group which deployed six squadrons of Vickers Wellingtons based at Kairouan and Zina in Tunisia and an RAAF squadron equipped with Handley Page Halifax heavy bombers based in Libya.

In addition, there were numerous other fighter, medium bomber, transport, reconnaissance and maritime strike units belonging to a confusing variety of formations and commands that included the Middle East Air Command (MEAC), the Northwest African Coastal Air Force (NACAF), the Northwest African Tactical Air Force (NATAF), the Mediterranean Allied Photographic Reconnaissance Wing (MAPRW) and Northwest African Troop Carrier Command (NATCC) among others. Northern Tunisia was thus a larger and more geographically dispersed version of Malta with the existing Vichy French air bases employed by the *Luftwaffe* for their Tunisian air bridge being augmented with new scratch-built airfields; the Cap Bon peninsula jutting into the Mediterranean east of Tunis alone housed a total of twelve airfields in a space forty-five miles long and nineteen miles wide, for example.[68]

The employment of this mighty technological host was no less fraught by argument and dispute than the remainder of the HUSKY planning, albeit in this instance with the dispute divided between the largely British advocates of air power and the rest, rather than along national lines. The font of the disagreement was the Commander-in-Chief Allied Air Forces Air Chief Marshal Sir Arthur Tedder. A founder member of the RAF and a bomber squadron commander in 1919, Tedder was something of an independent air power zealot, in common with many of his senior RAF contemporaries, and he was determined to prosecute operations on that basis; as one of his long-standing aides Wing-Commander Leslie Scarman put it long after the war, Tedder was simply unwilling to allow any ground or naval commander to 'dictate to him either the strategy or the deployment of the Air Forces under his command. His attitude was "Tell me what you want done and I will deliver in my own style."'[69] Tedder was enthusiastically supported in this by the commander of the NATAF Air Marshal Sir Arthur Coningham, another fervent believer in independent air power and to a lesser extent by US officers, notably Major-General Carl Spaatz and Major-General James Doolittle, commanders of the Northwest African Air Force (NAAF) and Northwest African Strategic Air Force (NASAF) respectively, as they were trammelled by the USAAF's subordinate status within the US Army, unlike their independent RAF counterparts. Coningham was especially alert for any backsliding from the independent air power ideal by his subordinates and came down hard on the head of the DAF, Air Vice-Marshal Harry Broadhurst, who he considered too wedded to providing direct support for ground forces.[70] His preferences in this regard also crossed national lines with a number of officers being censured for the crime of working too closely with their ground counterparts, most notably USAAF Colonel Lawrence P. Hickey who Coningham had removed from command of the US 12th Air Support Command because of his close interaction with Lieutenant-General Patton and the staff at US 7th Army HQ. Coningham declared the relationship to be a 'weakness', had Hickey declared *persona non grata* at Mediterranean Air HQs and personally prevented him from attaining another command; he was replaced by the presumably more amenable Major-General Edwin House, although Coningham was careful to retain overall operational control to offset further problems.[71]

In line with this fetish for maintaining the spirit of independent air power, Air Chief Marshal Tedder decided that the best contribution air power could make to HUSKY would be to concentrate on dealing with the Axis air forces; as the US Official History put it Tedder's position was that 'air strength should not be parceled [sic] out...but should instead be kept united under a single command to insure the greatest possible flexibility' with the 'enemy air forces...the overriding target'.[72] Given the difficulties the *Luftwaffe* and *Regia Aeronautica* had caused during Operation TORCH and the winter fighting in

Tunisia this was a not unreasonable, if perhaps narrowly focussed, position. The problems arose over the manner in which the decision was implemented, for in contrast to the close liaison between naval and ground planners, Tedder set his staff and subordinates to work drawing up a unilateral Air Plan with absolutely no liaison with or input from the other Service planners, staffs or senior commanders. So the latter were drawing up their own plans without '...concrete information on the amount and type of air support they could expect' and the unveiling of the Air Plan at a joint conference toward the end of June 1943 left them none the wiser; no details of air cover or support were provided and no aerial bombing targets were revealed, apart from the diversionary bombing missions in support of the proposed airborne landings.

Unsurprisingly the ground commanders in particular were less than unimpressed. One of Eisenhower's AFHQ staff officers, US Major-General Harold R. Bull, described Tedder's Air Plan as a 'most masterful piece of uninformed prevarication, totally unrelated to the Naval and Military Joint Plan', and Patton was reportedly especially vexed at Coningham's refusal to provide any assurances as to what support the invasion force could expect from NATAF's 400 aircraft.[73] The assembled land and naval commanders were thus left in the dark and that remained the case up until the HUSKY invasion force went ashore; to quote the US Official History again: 'When the assault troops set sail for Sicily, their commanders had not the faintest idea of when, where, under what circumstances, and in what numbers they would see their own aircraft.'[74] In fact Tedder's Air Plan was a four-phase affair, three phases of which were dedicated to reducing Axis air power while the fourth involved the exponents of independent air power's Holy Grail, the destruction of a ground target primarily by aerial bombing. The first phase commenced on Sunday 16 May 1943 and consisted of geographically widely spread strategic bombing operations involving NASAF's B-17 heavy and B-25 and B-26 medium bomber units by day and Wellingtons from the attached RAF No. 205 Group by night, augmented on occasion by US B-24s from the US 9th Air Force and the Halifaxes from the attached RAF No. 240 Wing under MEAC command. Targets included general Axis shipping, a number of ports and the islands of Lampedusa and Pantelleria midway between Tunisia and Sicily and numerous airfields including those on Sardinia and at Castelvetrano, Sciacca and Trapani in western Sicily and Comiso in the south-east of the island. Airfields on the Italian mainland were also targeted at Naples and Grosseto on the west coast and Foggia and Grottaglie on the southern Adriatic coast with the latter two being hit by MEAC aircraft.[75]

The second phase of the HUSKY Air Plan was the most concentrated and intense episode of the invasion preparations and was targeted largely away from Sicily. The primary focus was codenamed Operation CORKSCREW, a scheme for the seizure of the small Italian island of Pantelleria by a British landing force at the beginning of June 1943. Just over five miles long, three miles wide and located midway between Tunisia and Sicily, Pantelleria had been extensively fortified at Mussolini's personal order from 1938 to act as a counter-balance to the major British base at Malta, 145 miles to the south-east.[76] By 1943 the island hosted a garrison of approximately 12,000 Italian troops from *Generale di Brigata* Achille Maffei's *Brigata Mista Pantelleria* that included twenty-one artillery batteries deploying 109 assorted guns, spread across 112 fortified gun emplacements backed by a reported 600 German troops; the island also contained approximately 10,000 Italian civilians, a modern airfield with underground hangers and radar installations capable of monitoring air and sea movement between Tunisia and Sicily. Given all this, Lieutenant-General Eisenhower unsurprisingly considered Pantelleria an intolerable threat to HUSKY and after consulting with Professor Sir Solomon 'Solly' Zuckerman, a scientist acting as an adviser to British Combined Operations HQ, he authorised the novel solution of eliminating the threat primarily via aerial bombardment.[77]

Eisenhower's motivation from a military perspective was based on the reported impact of constant Japanese artillery fire on the US garrison of the Corregidor fortress in Manila Bay in the Philippines and specifically whether intensive and prolonged aerial bombardment could produce the same effect; on a personal level Eisenhower also appears to have been stung by criticism of his alleged 'lack of adaptability' by General Marshall and selected the novel approach to counter the criticism.[78] Be that as it may, the British had briefly considered seizing Pantelleria in January 1941 but abandoned the idea as impractical at that time. It was heavily bombed over the three days 8-10 May 1943 as part of the operation to hinder the Axis evacuation of Tunisia and Professor Zuckerman was in turn tasked to'reduce the defences of the Island to an extent which would permit the landing of the Ground Forces without undue opposition'.[79] Having clarified that by reducing the defences the military meant degrading the enemy artillery's ability to function, Zuckerman drew up a carefully calculated bombing plan specifically targeting Pantelleria's guns. Using aerial photographs and other intelligence the plan specified the precise tonnage of bombs required to reduce the number of guns in any given battery by thirty per cent, the amount calculated to render it ineffective; overall this involved delivering 1,000 tons of bombs per square mile onto eight square miles of the island.[80] The operation involved almost a thousand RAF and USAAF aircraft including four-engine B-17 bombers, B-26, Baltimore, Boston and Wellington medium bombers and P-38 Lightning and Hurricane fighter-bombers, all of which dropped a total of 6,400 tons of bombs in the course of 5,218 sorties spread over twenty-four days.[81]

The bombardment of Pantelleria was divided into two stages, beginning on Tuesday 18 May 1943 with a preliminary phase spread over the eighteen days to 5 June that systematically struck the island's infrastructure, delivering 1,076 tons of bombs in the course of 1,506 aircraft sorties. By 1 June this had knocked out the island's power station and water supply, destroyed its road network and reduced Pantelleria town and its port facilities to ruins in addition to hitting the nearby airfield and gun positions, with a concomitant impact on military and civilian morale.[82] The bombing was augmented by bombardment from a number of Royal Navy vessels, beginning with the cruiser *Orion* and two escorting destroyers on 31 May. The cruiser *Penelope* and her escorts repeated the shelling the following day, although on that occasion the *Penelope* was hit by counter-fire from Italian coastal defence guns, followed by the destroyers *Ilex* and *Isis* on 3 June and the cruiser *Newfoundland* and escorting destroyers on 5 June. The engagement was not totally one-sided as Italian and German aircraft based in Sicily and the Italian mainland attempted to interfere with the bombing; across the twenty-four days of CORKSCREW fifteen Allied machines were lost in exchange for twenty-three Axis aircraft. The effort had little tangible impact on the ground on Pantelleria, however, and the second stage of the assault saw the bombing increased by an order of magnitude from Sunday 6 June with 3,712 sorties delivering 5,324 tons of bombs over the six-day period to Friday 11 June.[83] It was during this second stage that Professor Zuckerman's bombing experiment was conducted. Sixteen artillery batteries deploying eighty guns were selected for specific attention and deluged with 14,203 assorted bombs totalling 4,119 tons; post-operation analysis showed this smashed ten guns beyond repair, damaged a further thirty-three and destroyed much of the associated fire control and communication equipment, ammunition stores, emplacements, personnel bunkers and reduced the batteries' collective combat effectiveness by fifty-three per cent.[84] This was all paralleled by an increase in the naval bombardment, with the cruisers *Aurora*, *Newfoundland*, *Orion* and *Penelope*, the anti-aircraft cruiser HMS *Euralyus* and eight escorting destroyers adding their weight on 8 June, for example.

On the night of 10-11 June attack convoys from Sfax and Sousse carrying Brigadier John James' 3rd Infantry Brigade and commanded by Rear-Admiral Rhoderick McGrigor closed up to a few miles off the island. Pantelleria's Governor, *Ammiraglio di Squadra* Gino Pavesi, was likely expecting an invasion at some point as Allied aircraft had begun dropping leaflets urging surrender on 8 June; on being informed of this development the *Regia Marina's* general staff, the *Supermarina*, promptly informed *Comando Supremo* that the island would continue to resist 'to the utmost', and Pantelleria's surviving radio transmitter assured *Supermarina* that 'despite everything Pantelleria will continue to resist' on 10 June. Although he had ignored repeated Allied radio requests to surrender, *Ammiraglio* Pavesi was less sanguine, and spent that night despatching a score of telegrams to Rome stressing the island's 'crumbling endurance' before informing *Supermarina* that 'the situation is desperate, [and] all possibilities of effective resistance have been exhausted' in the early hours of Friday 11 June. Pavesi then ordered a large white cross of surrender to be laid out on the airfield at his morning staff conference and all units to cease hostilities with effect from 11:00; the delay was to allow time for the order to reach all the battered unit locations across the island.[85]

In the meantime Rear-Admiral McGrigor's force had closed up to a point eight miles off the ruined harbour at Pantelleria where the assault troops debarked onto their landing craft observed by Lieutenant-General Eisenhower and Admiral Cunningham aboard the cruiser *Aurora*, and *Ammiraglio* Pavesi, who received his first view of the invasion fleet on emerging from his staff conference during a pause in the bombardment. At 11:35 a formation of B-17s pounded the island in 'the most perfect precision bombing of unimaginable intensity' and five minutes later the first wave of landing craft carrying the 3rd Infantry Brigade began its run in to the shore. The landing force included several Ground Controlled Interception (GCI) stations controlling the fighter aircraft tasked to protect the landing, operating from a number of Landing Craft Tank (LCT) vessels; the experiment was deemed so successful that it was subsequently incorporated into the HUSKY landing plan.[86]

Due to a combination of *Ammiraglio* Pavesi's order and the unremitting bombardment Brigadier James' men encountered no resistance when they stormed ashore at around midday on Friday 11 June 1943, with the sole British casualty being bitten and/or trampled by a recalcitrant mule depending on the source; the surrender was made official when *Ammiraglio* Pavesi signed a surrender document at 17:30 in one of the underground hangars at the airfield. Although Professor Zuckerman's experiment had specifically targeted the island's guns and associated infrastructure, it was the human rather than materiel element of Pantelleria's defences that had failed. While the island's garrison only lost between thirty-five and fifty-six dead and 116 wounded, the remainder were 'virtually stupefied' by the sheer weight and longevity of the bombardment, the impact of which was multiplied by the fact that many of the garrison were inexperienced and over-age troops with homes and families on the island.[87] The relative ease with which the island was secured also proved to be a double-edged sword, as it raised unrealistic expectations of the efficacy of aerial bombing among the Allied senior commanders and while this did not prevent the air power lobby from exploiting it for their own purposes, some in their ranks recognised the fact; as Air Chief Marshal Tedder put it in a private communication to Chief of the Air Staff, Air Chief Marshal Sir Charles Portal, 'I can see Pantelleria becoming a perfect curse to us in this manner.'[88]

With Pantelleria secured there remained the task of seizing the three islands of the Pelagie group, located just under a hundred miles south-east of Pantelleria, in an operation codenamed GUITAR. The 4,600-strong garrison of the largest island, Lampedusa, surrendered on 12 June to a ninety-five man party from the 2nd Battalion Coldstream Guards landed by the destroyer HMS *Lookout* after being subjected to aerial bombing and sustained bombardment by the cruisers *Aurora*, *Newfoundland*, *Orion*, *Penelope* and five destroyers; the understandably piqued garrison commander ordered the surrender when Rome responded to requests for air support with a signal reading 'We are convinced that you will inflict the greatest possible damage on the enemy. Long live Italy.'[89] The island of Linosa surrendered to the destroyer *Nubian* the following day and the unoccupied island of Lampione was secured on 14 June. With that, Eisenhower's 'intolerable threat' was lifted, the surface route from Tunisia to Sicily was open and little time was lost in integrating the new acquisitions into the Sicily invasion plan. RAF aircraft were operating from Lampedusa airstrip eight days after its capture, and as we have seen the US 33rd Fighter Group was ensconced on Pantelleria by 26 June, just fifteen days after *Ammiraglio* Pavesi had signed the surrender.[90]

Bombing sorties against targets on Sardinia had been suspended altogether and those against targets primarily in western Sicily scaled back to an eighth of the first phase during Operation CORKSCREW, but with Pantelleria bludgeoned into submission and secured, the HUSKY Air Plan moved into its third phase on Sunday 13 June. This involved a resurgent and tightened focus on Axis airfields primarily in western Sicily but including Catania in the east of the island and raids as far afield as Greece that reinforced the BARCLAY deception plan, although it is unclear if this was the actual intent; on 24 and 27 June US 9th Air Force B-24s under MEAC control bombed airfields at Sedes and Eleusis near Salonika and Athens respectively, destroying a total of twelve *Luftwaffe* machines on the ground and damaging thirteen more.[91] The final phase of the Air Plan ran for the six days up to the invasion from Saturday 3 July to Friday 9 July and saw a limited resumption of attacks against airfields on Sardinia and the airfields around Trapani in Sicily's western extremity but was primarily directed against the Axis air bases closest to the HUSKY landing areas at the eastern end of the island, and with a significant increase in intensity; this phase alone accounted for eighty per cent of the total bombing sorties overall.

Bombers from the NAAF and MEAC flew a thousand sorties against the complex of airfields at Gerbini near Catania over the week up to the invasion with one attack on Monday 5 July involving a hundred B-17s and 136 B-25 and B-26s for example. A total of 624 sorties were flown against airfields at Biscari and Comiso forty miles to the south near Gela and an attack by US 9th Air Force B-24s on 9 July destroyed the central *Luftwaffe* telephone exchange at Taormina, twenty-six miles north of Catania and thus paralysed *Luftwaffe* communications on the very eve of the invasion. By that point all the airfields on Sicily had been rendered unusable as repairs were unable to keep pace with the damage inflicted by the repeated attacks, the exceptions being the bases at Milo and Sciacca near Trapani which remained partially open.[92] Its impact on inter-service relations and support aside, by 10 July Air Chief Marshal Tedder's Air Plan had achieved its aim of reducing the Axis air force's ability to interfere with the HUSKY landings. At the beginning of the final phase Axis air force units deployed around 1,750 combat aircraft excluding transports and maritime machines on bases across Sardinia, Sicily and the Italian mainland. Approximately 960 of these machines belonged to the *Luftwaffe* and were based within striking distance of Sicily while 289 of the latter were actually based on the island along with 145 *Regia Aeronautica* aircraft; fighter and fighter-bomber aircraft made up around seventy-five per cent of the 434 total, the remainder being Junkers 88 twin-engine bombers.[93] The damage inflicted on this force by the Air Plan was considerable. Excluding machines shot down, the bombing of Sardinia and mainland Italy destroyed sixty-two German and fifty Italian aircraft and damaged thirty-five and fifteen respectively. The toll was heavier still on Sicily, where fifty-eight *Luftwaffe* machines were destroyed and a further thirty-one damaged while the *Regia Aeronautica* lost fifty-five destroyed and eighty-five damaged, and by 10 July the bulk of the surviving machines had been withdrawn to bases in mainland Italy.[94] This was particularly serendipitous with regard to the *Luftwaffe's* Focke-Wulf 190 fighter-bombers which were capable of carrying a 500 kilogram bomb at speeds of up to 500 miles per hour in shallow dive-bombing attacks, and thus presented a potent threat to the Allied surface fleet. The Allied bombing obliged their withdrawal to airfields near Naples, around 200 miles from the Allied landing areas on Sicily, which put the machines at the limit of their range for a round trip and thus 'effectively neutralized' the Focke-Wulf threat.[95]

It is unclear to what extent the Germans divined anything of Allied intentions from Tedder's Air Plan, but the fall of Pantelleria appears to have persuaded them that whatever might happen in Greece, the Allies were also set to strike in the Western Mediterranean. On Sunday 27 June 1943 *Generalfeldmarschall* Kesselring issued an Order of the Day to all German forces in the Mediterranean theatre warning that all should stand ready for a fight 'on Italian soil' and in the week running up to the launch of HUSKY signals intelligence showed that while the Germans were unable to definitively rule out Allied landings on Sardinia or the Italian mainland, 'They regarded Sicily as the most probable Allied objective.'[96] While the Germans may have been initially less certain of the Allied destination, over time they came around to considering Sicily to be the most likely target and were aware of the scale and location of Allied preparations. By Monday 5 July, ULTRA decrypts showed *Luftwaffe* reconnaissance had located 120 landing craft, 250,000 tons of shipping and the naval escort force spread across several North African ports and three days later *Supermarina* estimated that the Allies had embarked over a division in the eastern Mediterranean, a division at Malta and seven divisions in North Africa. Based on this, analysis of Allied bombing activity and other intelligence Kesselring decided an Allied invasion was imminent and ordered Axis readiness increased at 16:30 on Thursday 8 July, and the alert status on Sardinia was increased to the highest level on Friday 9 July after sightings of a 200-strong Allied convoy sailing north of Malta.

On Sicily, following *Luftwaffe* reports of several high speed convoys near Pantelleria the same day, *Generale d'Armata* Guzzoni presciently determined that landings were imminent in the vicinity of Catania and Gela and ordered an alert at 19:00.[97] The time for deception was over and Operation HUSKY was inbound, but before moving on to examine how the invasion unfolded it is necessary to examine the attacking and defending forces and their various plans and missions.

5

The Tip of the Spear I

British Airborne Preparations for Operation HUSKY, March 1943 to Friday 9 July

After three months of international, inter and intra-service wrangling the HUSKY plan for the invasion of Sicily had finally been agreed by Lieutenant-General Eisenhower and the other senior Allied commanders on Monday 3 May 1943.[1] This was just under ten weeks short of the launch window of 10-14 July agreed by the Combined Chiefs of Staff on 13 April in order to take advantage of a waxing half-moon for illumination, and due process reduced the lead time yet further.[2] The Combined Chiefs of Staff did not approve the plan until 13 May, the initial FORCE 141 Operation Instruction No. 1 was not issued by General Sir Harold Alexander's planners until four days after that and the final version, entitled FORCE 141 Operation Instruction No. 2, did not appear until Friday 21 May, just seven weeks before the start of the launch window.[3] The final plan envisaged simultaneous landings by the US 7th Army and British 8th Army in two areas in the south-east of the island. The seaborne assault was to be preceded by the British 1st Airborne Division and US 82nd Airborne Division, although the scale of the airborne landings was subsequently reduced to a single brigade/regiment from each formation.[4]

Some of the British Airborne units slated to participate in HUSKY were already present in North Africa. The 1st Parachute Brigade had suffered 1,700 casualties after deploying to North Africa at the beginning of Operation TORCH in a series of ill-thought out and arguably needless parachute operations and employment as conventional infantry, including at least 202 killed in the winter fighting in Tunisia between 12 December 1942 and 18 April 1943. The 2nd Parachute Battalion's experience clearly illustrates the point. On 28 March during the fighting in the Tamera valley the 2nd Parachute Battalion was reduced to just 150 All Ranks and had to be reinforced with a company from the 3rd Parachute Battalion. 16th Parachute Field Ambulance treated 170 casualties in the three-day period 28-30 March.[5] By the time the 2nd Parachute Battalion was withdrawn from the line in mid-April 1943 it numbered 360 All Ranks from an Establishment of 612 All Ranks including a 230-strong reinforcement in January, a casualty rate of eighty per cent.[6] Across the entire six-month deployment in Algeria and Tunisia the 1st Parachute Brigade's Officers amassed eight Distinguished Service Orders and fifteen Military Crosses while the Other Ranks were awarded nine Distinguished Conduct Medals, twenty-two Military Medals along with three *Croix de Guerre* and a *Légion d'honneur*, 'a record never surpassed by any formation of the British Army going…into action for the first time'.[7]

While the 1st Parachute Brigade was being withdrawn from the fighting in Tunisia moves were afoot to move its parent formation to North Africa in readiness for future operations in the Mediterranean. The despatch of the 1st Parachute Brigade to North Africa in October 1942 involved stripping the still-forming 2nd Parachute Brigade and the 1st Airborne Division's other units of parachute-trained personnel and equipment, and the impact was exacerbated by the formation of the 3rd Parachute Brigade on 5 November 1942. All this delayed the 1st Airborne Division's progress toward completing its mobilisation, scheduled for 1 July 1943, to the degree that Major-General Browning submitted a frank report on the matter to GHQ Home Forces and the War Office on 11 January 1943; he followed up with proposals for a reorganisation of the Division and its constituent units and formations on 25 February 1943. The upshot of all this was the transfer of the 3rd Parachute Brigade, two Airlanding infantry battalions and the Airborne Light Tank Squadron to the new 6th Airborne Division. Its creation was the result of a decision on 24 February 1943 by Chief of the Imperial General Staff, Field Marshal Sir Alan Brooke, in the wake of the SYMBOL Conference at Casablanca in mid-January 1943 which determined that the minimum future British Airborne requirement would be two Airborne divisions, one for deployment in the Mediterranean and one to be held in the UK.

Predictably, Brooke's decision prompted opposition from the Chief of the Air Staff, Air Chief Marshal Sir Charles Portal, but after a month-long discussion on organisation and timings Brooke's proposal was finally authorised on 23 April 1943. As the formation selected for Mediterranean service, the 1st Airborne Division's mobilisation deadline was brought forward to 1 May 1943 and the Division travelled to North Africa in two increments, the first of which departed before the Division had technically completed its organisation. The first increment consisted of Brigadier Eric Down's 2nd Parachute Brigade, accompanied by a slice of Divisional units that included the 9th Field Company RE, 261 Field Park Company RE, part of the 1st Airborne Division Provost Company CMP and twenty-six Officers and 254 Other Ranks from the 1st Battalion, Glider Pilot Regiment. The Glider Pilot contingent was included at the insistence of Major-General George Hopkinson, commander of the 1st Airborne Division, despite pleas by Battalion commander Lieutenant-Colonel George Chatterton and the senior RAF representative on the Division staff for the Glider Pilots to be allowed to travel later, to permit them to accrue more much-needed flying hours. The increment sailed from the River Clyde on Friday 16 April aboard a subset of fourteen ships in the twenty-six-vessel strong Convoy WS29.

Dubbed KMF13, the sub-convoy split off from the main convoy for the Mediterranean on 21 April and while the bulk of the vessels docked in Algiers on Friday 23 April, four or five vessels carrying the 1st Airborne Division contingent, including the Dutch MV *Boissevain* and SS *Nieuw Holland*, docked at Oran the previous day. There they spent two days disembarking and unloading equipment, in some instances at the adjacent French naval base at Mers el Kébir.[8]

The new arrivals were greeted in Oran by the 1st Airborne Division's Commander Royal Engineers (CRE), Lieutenant-Colonel Mark Henniker RE, who had been posted to Eisenhower's AFHQ on 12 April 1943 in anticipation of the Division's arrival.[9] As the huge influx of Allied troops into Algeria had put a premium on accommodation, the Airborne units were allotted space at a vast former POW camp administered by the US 5th Army at Tizi, around fifty miles south-east of Oran and seven miles south of Mascara in what was to be the 1st Airborne Division's initial concentration area in North Africa. The transformation of the camp and the reception of the Airborne newcomers was so efficiently managed that it earned the US units involved a 'congratulatory order of the day' from Brigadier Down, although facilities were limited and austere due to the camp's origins; the entire camp was tented and at least some of the newcomers were housed in US Army two-man pup tents.[10] The immediate problem facing the newly disembarked was transportation, as Airborne units were not abundantly equipped with motor transport to begin with and the 2nd Parachute Brigade's vehicles had been left in the UK to travel with the convoy carrying the Division's second increment. Lieutenant-Colonel Henniker and Brigadier Down solved the problem by unofficially prevailing upon a US HQ in Oran who generously provided double their tentative requirement of brand-new trucks, reportedly on the proviso they sourced their own drivers, although some accounts refer to vehicles being driven by African American personnel.[11] The next problem was the discovery that the Tizi camp had been pitched in a dry wadi, which turned into a raging torrent after a night thunderstorm that carried away tents, personal equipment and a quantity of lumber and other materials Lieutenant-Colonel Henniker had appropriated from US Army sources to render the austere POW facilities into something more appropriate for housing operational units.[12] In the event he was able to replace the materials from the same source with some bureaucratic sleight of hand, and the Airborne units provided their own labour, although by 6 May the Provost Company managed to procure more permanent accommodation in a large garage in Mascara. The Redcaps were kept fully occupied with security and patrol duties, including policing paratroopers inebriated on 'cheap and potent' local wine indulging in what Lieutenant-Colonel Henniker euphemistically described as 'rough behaviour'.[13]

The next arrival at the 1st Airborne Division's concentration area south of Mascara was Brigadier Lathbury's 1st Parachute Brigade, which arrived at Tizi from Bou Farik on Monday 10 May 1943.[14] According to Saunders' semi-official history, Lathbury realised 'that his new command were tired after the strenuous North African campaign [and] wisely did not at first demand too much in the way of training'.[15] This was undoubtedly true, but Lathbury's delicate handling may also have been due to his new command, as veterans of operational parachute drops and the harsh Tunisian winter fighting were not enamoured of training methods more suitable for the raising and initial training of parachute units in the UK. This was certainly the attitude displayed by the 1st Parachute Brigade on its return from the Mediterranean in November 1943. Low-level indiscipline was endemic across the Brigade between November 1943 and its departure for Arnhem in September 1944, with the 1st Parachute Battalion apparently the epicentre; the latter's Orderly Room had to be evacuated and the local fire brigade summoned after a smoke marker was ignited outside on 12 February 1944 for example, and on 28 May 1944 the Battalion NAAFI canteen was burgled and the funds therein stolen.[16] The indiscipline extended into the operational sphere with the 3rd Parachute Battalion's commander being replaced on 4 July 1944 ostensibly for health reasons, although Frost's account refers to the replacement as the result of the Battalion being unable to march during a three-day test exercise at the end of June.[17] For its part, the 1st Parachute Battalion had two successive commanders replaced in February and March after attempting to instil discipline with the aid of a new Regimental Sergeant-Major, possibly a Guardsman, which the Battalion rank-and-file considered to be 'treating battle hardened men like children'.[18] Their response was self-termed a 'strike' but was more accurately a mutiny; they refused to draw parachutes for a familiarisation jump from USAAF C-47s on 30 March 1944.[19] Lathbury reacted by hearing the men's grievances and then exchanged the Battalion commander with Lieutenant-Colonel David Dobie who had commanded the Battalion in North Africa.[20] The 1st Parachute Brigade's more than exemplary performance at Arnhem clearly shows all this was largely a matter of good field soldiers making poor garrison soldiers, and Lathbury's careful handling of his new command in the initial stages of taking command in Tunisia was arguably a wise measure before embarking on a period of intensive training intended to integrate untried replacements, with particular emphasis on familiarising All Ranks with handling and firing enemy weapons as a contingency measure.[21]

The 1st Airborne Division's second increment, the 1st Airlanding Brigade accompanied by the 181 Airlanding Field Ambulance RAMC and the remainder of the Divisional units including the 21st Independent Parachute Company and 1st Airborne Division Provost Company CMP rear party sailed from the UK with Convoy WS30, which left the River Clyde on Wednesday 19 May 1943; it is unclear where the Airlanding Brigade and Provost Company boarded its transport but the Field Ambulance and Pathfinders reportedly embarked at Liverpool, the former at least aboard the MV *Stirling Castle*, a Union-Castle Line liner pressed into service as a troopship.[22] The eleven vessels of the convoy earmarked for North Africa, codenamed KMF15, separated from WS 30 in the late morning of Tuesday 25 May and the vessels carrying the 1st Airborne Division contingent docked at Oran two days later while the remainder docked at Algiers on Friday 28 May.[23] With the possible exception of the Provost Company Rear Party, which may have rejoined its parent unit at Mascara, the Airborne contingent moved initially to a tented transit camp near Fleurus, fourteen miles north-east of Oran where training began to assist acclimatisation.[24] Major John Lander ordered the 21st Independent Company on a route-march almost immediately on arrival at Fleurus and within a week units of the Airlanding Brigade were making roundabout-routed marches through the mountains to the seaside town of Kristel, five miles north-west of Fleurus to spend the day swimming on the beach before marching back 'in the cool of the evening'.[25] Facilities at Fleurus were less than ideal, however. In addition to the camp being a 'dustbowl' regularly reaching 110 degrees Fahrenheit, 181 Airlanding Field Ambulance also reported that 'sanitary arrangements were quite inadequate and it was quite impossible to fly-proof the kitchens,' leading to an outbreak of diarrhoea, although the Independent Company's semi-official account suggests that the affliction might also have been due in part to over-imbibing the rough local wine.[26]

On 9 June 1943 the second increment moved fifty miles south-east to a camp in the 1st Airborne Division's concentration area at Froha, six miles south of Mascara, although conditions were not much improved; as the Independent Company's semi-official account put it 'dust, flies, mosquitoes and chlorinated water [were] not the best of companions.'[27] The conditions at Froha were 'rendered even more uncongenial' by the total lack of amenities including the normally ubiquitous NAAFI canteen, which obliged commanders to organise recreational trips to destinations up to fifty miles away including Sidi bel Abbes, the depot of the French *Légion Étrangère*; in addition, the local civilian population rapidly gained a reputation for audacious and unrelenting theft.[28]

The final arrival at the 1st Airborne Division's concentration area was the 4th Parachute Brigade, which began to form at RAF Kibrit alongside the Great Bitter Lake twenty miles north of Suez, from 1 December 1942.[29] The new Brigade was temporarily commanded by Lieutenant-Colonel Kenneth Smyth from 4 December while newly promoted Brigadier John Hackett underwent his parachute qualification course at RAF No. 4 Middle East Training School, also based at Kibrit, before assuming command on 4 January 1943. The first of the Brigade's sub-units was Lieutenant-Colonel H. C. R. Hose and 151st Parachute Battalion, posted to Kibrit from India in October 1942 and renumbered 156th Parachute Battalion reportedly as a disinformation measure, followed in December by the 10th Parachute Battalion commanded by Lieutenant-Colonel Smyth; the latter was built around a hundred volunteers from the 2nd Battalion, The Royal Sussex Regiment, after it was discovered that Regular Army units could not simply be reallocated and incorporated into the Army Air Corps. It took a recruiting campaign across the Middle East to secure sufficient volunteers to bring the 10th Battalion up to strength and to replace a considerable number of pre-war Regulars from 156th Battalion who were eligible for repatriation to the UK. The process was not complete until May 1943.

Meanwhile the Brigade's establishment had been expanded to include the 4th Parachute Squadron RE and 133 Parachute Field Ambulance RAMC, and as the facilities and terrain at Kibrit had proved unsuitable for parachute and tactical training the Brigade and the RAF Training School moved 240 miles to Ramat David in what is now northern Israel at the end of February 1943. The Brigade's third infantry unit, Lieutenant-Colonel R. M. C. Thomas's 11th Parachute Battalion, was not established until March 1943 and remained in the Suez area when the Brigade moved to Ramat David. As the Battalion was still forming it was left behind when the 4th Parachute Brigade moved to join the 1st Airborne Division in Tunisia on 10 June 1943 and did not rejoin its parent formation until December 1943, after leaving the Mediterranean Theatre for the UK. The 11th Battalion conducted a number of small parachute operations in the eastern Mediterranean between August and December, the most notable being a company drop on the Greek island of Kos on Wednesday 15 September 1943; the paratroopers remained on the island for ten days with resupply from the air until being withdrawn by sea on Saturday 25 September.[30]

The 1st Airborne Division's initial concentration area south of Mascara was chosen despite its lack of amenities in part for security and in part as a disinformation measure. Maintaining an Airborne formation in Algeria presented a potential threat to the wider western Mediterranean area, whereas placing it in Tunisia narrowed the possible options to Sicily or the Italian mainland. More importantly from a practical perspective, the entire area inland from the coast between Algiers and Sousse was crammed with Allied troops, along with their support and logistics units and associated dumps, and it therefore made sense to locate the concentration area further west away from the congestion but within easy distance of the docks at Oran. In addition, the Mascara location was not permanent, as it had always been intended to launch the 1st Airborne Division from the area of Sousse in Tunisia, with the move being postponed to as close as possible to the HUSKY launch date. Similarly, the airfields in Tunisia were also crowded with fighter and bomber units tasked to carry out the Allied Air Force HQ's Air Plan in support of HUSKY and in addition to accommodation for the Division, the Mascara area also contained four airfields. Three of these, at Froha, Matemore and Thiersville, were just four and seven miles east, and nine miles south-east, of the 1st Airborne Division's main camp at Tizi respectively.[31] They were built from scratch by US Army engineers, ironically on land hitherto judged unfit for the purpose by the *Armée de l'Air* due to the presence of malarial mosquitoes, although the fine, talcum-like dust that coated the entire region proved to be more of a problem than the local insects. The dust reduced visibility with the slightest disturbance and proved especially detrimental to machinery and particularly aero-engines; counter-measures including pegged metal sheeting and soaking runways and taxiways with waste oil proved only partially effective.[32] The fourth airfield, located at Relizane forty miles north-east of Tizi, was a pre-war *Armée de l'Air* installation that notably boasted permanent buildings rather than the tented accommodation of the other three airfields.[33]

As with accommodation, supplies and ground transport, the 1st Airborne Division were also to be reliant on US largesse for its air transport into battle. At some point on or around 6 May it was decided that the US 51st Troop Carrier Wing would supply the Division's airlift, in part because aircraft from that formation had provided the aircraft for the 1st Parachute Brigade's three drops in November 1942 and were therefore familiar with British procedures.[34] As a result, the four squadrons of Lieutenant-Colonel Aubrey S. Hurren's 62nd Troop Carrier Group, which had delivered the 2nd Parachute Battalion Group to Depienne in November 1942, took up residence at Matemore on 16 May 1943. At around the same time Lieutenant-Colonel Frederick H. Sherwood's four squadrons from the 60th Troop Carrier Group, which had dropped the 509th Parachute Infantry Regiment near Oran at the outset of Operation TORCH and again at Youks les Bains, relocated to Thiersville from the permanent airfield at Relizane; the reaction of the Group's personnel to the primitive accommodation at their new home is unclear. The 51st Wing's third element, Lieutenant-Colonel Claire B. Collier's 64th Troop Carrier Group, remained at Blida.[35] The 60th and 62nd Groups then embarked upon an intensive programme of flight training, parachute dropping and learning the new art of glider towing over the seven weeks or so before HUSKY was launched, although this was hindered by a shortage of time and the condition of the 51st Troop Carrier Wing's C-47s. The latter had seen heavy use throughout the seven months since the beginning of TORCH and were in need of an overhaul which circumstances could not permit, and the local fine dust doubtless exacerbated the wear and tear. The compromise solution was to limit flying hours in an effort to slow engine hours accruing, at the cost of an inevitable impact upon flying and troop training.[36]

The burden on the 51st Troop Carrier Wing was eased to an extent by a contribution from RAF No. 38 Wing, the formation created on 15 January 1942 to support the British Airborne Force. No. 296 Squadron was formed on Saturday 24 January 1942 at RAF Netheravon by the simple expedient of renaming the Glider Exercise Unit at the Airborne Forces Establishment at RAF Ringway and modifying its role to include dropping parachute troops; the parallel Parachute Exercise Unit became No. 295 Squadron via the same process and a reverse re-roling to include glider towing seven months later on Monday 3 August 1942, also at RAF Netheravon.[37] Initially equipped with Hawker Hector and Hawker Hart biplanes, No. 296 Squadron was re-equipped with Armstrong-Whitworth Whitley twin-engine bombers in June and July 1942 and then with Armstrong-Whitworth Albemarles. A modern-looking aircraft with a tricycle undercarriage, the first domestically produced machine of that type in RAF service, the Albemarle had a wingspan of seventy-seven feet, a cruising speed of 170 miles per hour and a ceiling of 18,000 feet. Produced to meet Air Ministry specification B.9/38 for a backstop aircraft for production in case of shortages of strategic materials, the Albemarle featured stressed plywood skin.

When the machine's speed, payload and range fell short of expectations the Air Ministry followed its usual practice with obsolete or unsuitable aircraft and bequeathed the initial batch of around a hundred Albemarles to Airborne Forces.[38] The first machine arrived at Netheravon on 27 January 1943 and while the re-equipment was complete by the end of April 1943, there were sufficient operating alongside the Whitleys by 9 February for Albemarles to partake in the operational side of the Squadron's duties, which at this point involved carrying out night raids over occupied Europe alongside their glider-towing and parachute dropping activities; between 9 and 28 February 1943 the Squadron's aircraft carried out five leaflet drops and one bombing mission on targets including Nantes, Orleans, Paris and Rouen involving single or up to nine machines.[39] Comparative tests between the Albemarle and Whitley towing a Horsa glider on 7 February showed the former to be the superior machine capable of climbing to 2,000 feet in five minutes, less than half the twelve minutes required by the latter.[40] However, although it was officially configured to carry up to ten paratroopers, the Albemarle was poorly configured for parachute dropping. The narrow fuselage was accessed via a small hatch at the rear underside and lacked headroom or seats, and paratroopers were obliged to half-crawl, half-drag themselves and all their kit backwards up the fuselage from the hatch to sit on the floor pressed up against the bulkhead separating the crew compartment. Exiting the aircraft involved moving rapidly in an uncomfortable squatting position carrying loaded kit bags back along the fuselage to the hatch; the process was referred to as 'bunny-hopping' and while considered routine was no mean feat in itself, especially in darkness in a pitching aircraft.[41]

No. 296 Squadron learned it was to move to Algeria via a briefing from the commander of No. 38 Wing, Air-Commodore Sir Nigel Norman, on 17 May 1943.[42] Codenamed Exercise BEGGAR, it involved moving the Squadron's thirty-three Albemarles with all the ground crew, equipment and stores to the airfield at Froha, four miles east of the 1st Airborne Division's main base at Tizi. The first Albemarle departed on Sunday 23 May carrying Group-Captain Thomas Cooper DFC from No. 38 Wing as a passenger, while the Squadron 'advance party' of two aircraft departed from RAF Hurn in Dorset eleven days later, on Thursday 3 June; one machine broke the journey at Gibraltar and arrived at Froha the following day while the other made the ten- to twelve-hour flight straight through to Algeria.[43] The Squadron's remaining aircraft followed spread over ten days, all flying from RAF Hurn, six machines on 5 June, two on 6 June, ten on 7 June, eight on the 10th and single machines on 11, 18, 19 and 21 June.[44] The aircraft were loaded to approximately 36,500 pounds of passengers and freight with most loads including an allocation of 1,186 gallons of fuel. The move was completed without loss, although one Albemarle landed at Gibraltar for repair after its radio set and the propeller constant speed unit failed en route.[45]

The Squadron began familiarising the 1st Airborne Division's personnel with the new Albemarle and providing refresher parachute training before all its aircraft were present at Froha. The 21st Independent Parachute Company had not jumped for the month since leaving the UK on 19 May 1943 and possibly not since Exercise CRAFTY II on 11 February, for example.[46] No. 296 Squadron provided aircraft for the Company to jump from on 17 and 19 June 1943, just fourteen days after the Squadron advance party had left RAF Hurn.[47] Participation in tactical drops and exercises was even swifter. The Squadron provided nine Albemarles for Exercise CACTUS III on 12 June, sixteen for Exercise OYSTER four days later and nineteen machines for Exercise CACTUS IV on 18 June. OYSTER was especially successful, with the first six Albemarles dropping their loads within one minute and all sixteen sticks being delivered onto the Drop Zone (DZ) just after dusk; as a result US 51st Troop Carrier Wing HQ assessed No. 296 Squadron to be 'fit to drop paratroops by night'.[48]

The exercise period was not without risk. On 11 June an Albemarle piloted by Flying-Officer G. L. Wilson had a tyre burst while landing at Froha, but none of the crew were injured. Six days later Flight-Lieutenant Houchin crashed his aircraft while attempting a low-speed landing after suffering brake failure.[49] Nonetheless the Squadron successfully provided individual parachute training and battalion- and brigade-scale exercises for the 1st and 2nd Parachute Brigades. Between 8 May and 30 June 8,913 parachute descents were carried out with a relatively low casualty count of 302, including two deaths, a hundred seriously injured and 200 less severe injuries such as twisted ankles or knees. All this was only possible due to the unsung efforts of RAF No. 1 Mobile Parachute Servicing Unit, which had accompanied the 1st Parachute Brigade to North Africa in November 1942, and No. 2 Mobile Parachute Servicing Unit, which arrived in Algeria at the beginning of May 1943; the Units provided and repacked 12,688 troop and container parachutes between 8 May and 8 June 1943.[50]

The process of providing aerial transport for the 1st Airlanding Brigade proved more fraught, the root of the problem and what followed on Sicily being the 1st Airborne Division's new commander, Major-General George Hopkinson. Hopkinson's selection is curious in itself, given that there were better qualified candidates available such as Brigadier Ernest Down or the battle-tested Brigadier Edwin Flavell; Major-General Richard Gale would perhaps have been an ideal choice, but he was appointed to command the new 6th Airborne Division in May 1943. Given the tight control he exercised over his burgeoning Airborne fiefdom Browning presumably selected Hopkinson as his successor because he thought he would be easy to control, but as we shall see, this turned out to be far from the case. Browning had used his command of the 1st Airborne Division as a springboard for ongoing personal advancement, which was ultimately to lead to the highest Army appointment in the Allied Airborne hierarchy. Hopkinson, a qualified pilot, amateur glider pilot and commander of the 1st Airlanding Brigade from its inception, used his command of the Division as a platform for a personal crusade to raise the profile of glider troops and gliders as the best and most accurate method of inserting troops from the air. Both men possessed a degree of ruthlessness, but while Browning's was harnessed to efficient empire building, Hopkinson's was underlaid by immaturity and petulance, traits that he was soon to clearly demonstrate.

The original FORCE 141 scheme envisaged three brigade-scale parachute operations in the British sector, Operation LADBROKE to seize the Ponte Grande bridge across the River Anapo and adjacent Mammaiabica Canal and capture the port of Syracuse just north of the invasion beaches on the night before the invasion; Operation GLUTTON to secure the bridge over the River Mulinello and the port of Augusta twelve miles to the north, to be carried out on the first night of the invasion; and Operation FUSTIAN to secure the Ponte Primosole bridge across the River Simeto and Gornalunga Canal near Catania, fifteen miles north of Augusta, launch date dependent on the ground advance.[51] This all-parachute scheme did not suit Hopkinson at all and, as an 'ardent exponent' of glider insertion as a superior method to the parachute, he was set upon having the HUSKY plan reconfigured to include an airlanding operation.

The then Brigadier Hopkinson initially travelled to North Africa on Sunday 7 March 1943 accompanied by Wing-Commander Wallace Barton DFC from RAF No. 38 Wing, ostensibly tasked to advise the FORCE 141 planners at Eisenhower's AFHQ on the capabilities and requirements of the 1st Airborne Division; he was also promoted to Major-General and appointed to command of the Division at some point before the end of April, with effect from 6 May.[52] Barton and Hopkinson were joined on Monday 29 March by Major-General Browning, wearing two hats as commander of the 1st Airborne Division and Major-General Airborne Forces with effect from 6 April 1943, and soon to be Airborne Advisor to Allied Forces HQ (AFHQ); Browning was accompanied by the commander of No. 38 Wing, Air-Commodore Sir Nigel Norman and a number of staff officers.[53]

Quite what advice Browning or indeed Hopkinson were able to offer Eisenhower is open to question as Hopkinson's glider force was still in its infancy, US forces were *au fait* with almost all British operational parachute experience as they had provided the airlift for the 1st Parachute Brigade in Algeria and Tunisia, and Browning's role in the expansion of the British Airborne Force had been restricted to the administrative and bureaucratic rather than the practical and operational. This though was incidental, as dispensing Airborne advice and expertise was not Browning's primary intent. Rather, he was using his new status as titular head of the British Airborne Force as a platform for further self-promotion, as he had done as commander of the 1st Airborne Division, and his real purpose in North Africa was therefore to obtain and maintain a place at the top table of Allied decision making.

For his part, Hopkinson used his new rank to plough his own furrow outside Browning's control, specifically to realise his longstanding desire to have an airlanding operation included in Operation HUSKY; this appears to have been the underlying reason for his overruling Lieutenant-Colonel Chatterton's concerns that his 1st Battalion Glider Pilots needed more flying hours before being deployed, and including them in the first increment of the 1st Airborne Division to sail for North Africa on 16 April. According to Chatterton, Hopkinson deliberately avoided Browning, who was looking to discuss arrangements for HUSKY, until the latter was obliged to return to the UK at the beginning of May to take over the newly created HQ Major-General Airborne Forces; neither does he appear to have been available to his subordinates, as Chatterton also noted that Hopkinson had absented himself from 1st Airborne Division HQ 'for weeks'.[54] With Browning out of the picture, Hopkinson circumvented the chain-of-command to engineer a meeting with General Montgomery in Algiers on 7 May. There he portrayed glider troops as the 'wooden Excalibur' necessary for the success of the HUSKY plan that Montgomery had gained approval for, and focussed specifically upon the LADBROKE operation in support of the initial sea landings. To that end he explained the drawbacks of parachute drops for *coup-de-main* operations like the seizure of the Ponte Grande crossings, and advised the 8th Army commander that only glider insertion could provide the pin-point accuracy and concentrated delivery that such missions required.

The pitch worked and Montgomery authorised the amendment of the HUSKY plan to make LADBROKE a glider operation, assigned to Brigadier Philip Hicks' hitherto redundant 1st Airlanding Brigade.[55] Interestingly Montgomery appears to have subsequently raised Hopkinson's parachute objections to the FORCE 141 planning staff, where his conversion to the assault glider cause also created some consternation; Wing-Commander Cooper from No. 38 Wing pointed out that 'night glider assaults were not part of British airborne doctrine', that such complex operations could not be mounted at short notice and that both the glider pilots and airlanding troops lacked the requisite experience. Montgomery refused to reverse his decision however, and LADBROKE remained an airlanding operation.[56]

Lieutenant-Colonel Chatterton learned of the Hopkinson's initiative and Montgomery's acquiescence when he was summoned to the former's HQ in Algiers, possibly on the same day as Hopkinson's audience with Montgomery.[57] According to Chatterton's account Hopkinson began by informing him of the date of the upcoming Sicily invasion, that the 1st Airlanding Brigade was to perform a night landing near Syracuse and invited him to examine aerial photographs of the selected Landing Zone (LZ), which Chatterton was horrified to see was bounded by cliffs, strewn with rocky outcrops and criss-crossed with stone walls. When the Glider Pilot commander tentatively pointed out that his men had not flown for at least three months and had no night flying experience whatever, Hopkinson airily dismissed his concerns and informed him that the USAAF would be providing tugs and gliders for the operation. When Chatterton unwisely queried this on the grounds his men were barely familiar with British machines, Hopkinson responded with a heated 'Well you'll have to put up with it, won't you.' When the Glider Pilot commander compounded his error by pointing out the hazardous nature of the LZ, Hopkinson informed him that he had thirty minutes to examine the LZ photographs and that if he still considered the mission too difficult at the end of that time, he would be relieved of his command. After some soul searching Chatterton felt obliged to accept the mission despite his reservations for the sake of his men, and when Hopkinson returned to the meeting room the discussion continued more amicably as if the earlier disagreement had never happened; Chatterton noted that Hopkinson 'was like a little boy, he was so pleased'.[58] Hopkinson's pettishness was on clear display in this incident, and it is thus difficult to disagree with the verdict of a historian of the Italian campaign who described Hopkinson as an 'overgrown boy scout...a classic example of a commanding officer who posed a greater threat to his men than did the enemy'.[59] The men of the 1st Battalion Glider Pilot Regiment and the 1st Airlanding Brigade were to pay a high price on Sicily for Hopkinson's enthusiasm and impetuosity.

The gliders that Hopkinson had gained access to were WACO CG4A machines, dubbed the Hadrian in British service. Of canvas-covered tubular steel and wooden construction, the CG4A was just under fifty feet long with a wingspan of eighty-four feet, a payload in the region of 4,250 pounds and a towing speed of 125 miles per hour. Named after the initials of the Weaver Aircraft Company from Troy, Ohio, that designed and carried out the initial manufacturing and the official design specification of Cargo Glider 4A, the machine was the fourth most produced US aircraft of the Second World War, with sixteen contractors producing 13,909 machines at a cost of $18,800 each.[60] The CG4A was considerably smaller than the British Airspeed Horsa gliders the Glider Pilot Regiment had trained on in the UK, being capable of carrying fifteen men excluding the crew of two or smaller numbers of passengers alongside a number of cargo combinations. These combinations included a Jeep around which the design was formulated, a loaded Jeep trailer, a 75mm Pack Howitzer and twenty-five rounds of ammunition or a small bulldozer; in a unique touch, the CG4A's largely Plexiglass nose hinged upward to allow the loading and unloading of large items.[61]

An initial batch of crated machines were delivered to Accra in the Gold Coast on 24 March 1943, but when US pilots and groundcrew were despatched from North Africa to assemble and ferry them north it was discovered that a combination of seawater damage, inadequate maintenance and poor storage had rendered most of the machines unserviceable.[62] Four airworthy machines were salvaged and assembled by 23 April and at least one of these, piloted by a USAAF Lieutenant Allen, was successfully towed the 3,600 miles from Accra to the airfield at Thiersville where Lieutenant Allen was subsequently involved in familiarisation flights for members of the 1st Battalion, Glider Pilot Regiment.[63] In the meantime a further 500 crated CG4As were despatched direct to North Africa from the US, according to one source at the request of the FORCE 141 planners in mid-March 1943, for supply-carrying missions after the invasion of Sicily. The machines were preceded by a detachment of 110 USAAF glider pilots despatched from Norfolk, Virginia, on 21 December 1942, who arrived at Port Tewfik in Egypt via the Cape of Good Hope and Suez Canal on 1 February 1943 where they remained until the last week of March, when they moved to Algeria to await the arrival of the gliders.[64]

It is unclear if all the machines were offloaded at Oran or at other ports as well; given that each machine was packed into five separate crates the offloading may have been dispersed to spread the burden. Whichever, by the time Montgomery amended the HUSKY plan at the beginning of May some 240 machines were present in North Africa, thirty of which had been assembled and test-flown, and by 13 June 1943 a total of 346 CG4As had been assembled, flight tested and delivered to airfields in Algeria and Tunisia ready for use.[65]

Lieutenant-Colonel Chatterton did not return to the new camp his Glider Pilots were constructing from scratch adjacent to the airfield at Froha to ease access for flying training, following the fraught meeting with his Division commander. Instead, he travelled to La Sénia airfield just south of Oran, where a USAAF officer had informed him the gliders for British use were cached; on finding crated machines there he despatched a party of his pilots to unpack whatever gliders they could find among the stores dumped at the airfield and assemble them ready for flight.[66] By 8 May 1943 sixty Glider Pilots were so engaged and their task was eased by an unnamed USAAF ground crew Corporal who discovered that the crates contained not only glider components but, with typical American industrial efficiency, an instruction book and full set of construction and maintenance tools for every machine; for their part the Glider Pilots also exercised their Airborne Initiative (ABI) to turn the roomy crates into temporary accommodation as no billets were available at La Sénia.[67] The construction effort was assisted by a number of seconded USAAF ground crew and fatigue parties drawn from the 2nd Battalion, South Staffordshire Regiment and presumably other units from the 1st Airlanding Brigade, and completed machines were being test flown within four days, given that on 12 May 1943 Chatterton became the first British pilot to test fly a CG4A.[68] While noting the different construction method and materials Chatterton reported that the machine was 'a pleasant aircraft to fly and handled very easily', and he went on to make two successful night flights and landings, the first in bright moonlight from a height of 2,000 feet at La Sénia on 14 May while the second, carried out four days later on 18 May, involved a ten-mile free flight after release over Mascara to land at Thiersville.[69]

Positive British opinion on the CG4A was not universal. Squadron-Leader Lawrence Wright from RAF No. 38 Wing agreed the CG4A was easy to fly but found the machine 'a disappointment' for a number of reasons, including its lack of air brakes and consequent long landing runs and lack of blind-flying instruments, as the CG4A's instruments were not luminescent and co-pilots were obliged to provide torchlight during night flights.[70] Wright also objected to the WACO's towing-speed limit of 150 miles per hour, which was dictated by the glider's airframe limitations, because the Albemarle was difficult to fly below its 170 miles per hour cruising speed. At least some of the glider pilots were not enamoured with their new steed either; Staff-Sergeant Michael Hall from the 1st Battalion Glider Pilot Regiment simply considered the machine to be 'vastly inferior' to the Horsa due to its smaller size, payload and construction.[71] Be that as it may, within fifteen days the makeshift production line had assembled fifty-two CG4As that were then towed by USAAF C-47s to the airfields around Mascara with glider pilots at the controls, initially the sixty-six miles to Relizane and subsequently the shorter fifty-mile hop to the airfields at Froha, Matemore and Thiersville.[72]

Chatterton was equally swift in creating and implementing what was dubbed the WACO Conversion Programme to make best possible use of the available gliders, which involved some relocation and allotting specific duties and responsibilities. Major John Place, OC 3 Squadron, was designated Chief Instructor for the initial transition training located at Relizane, tasked to provide day and night flight training for sixty pilots in a three-week period assisted by USAAF Lieutenant Allen, who had piloted the first CG4A from Accra in April. The Squadron move to Relizane began on 19 June 1943, where the Glider Pilots found six newly assembled CG4As awaiting them, and training commenced around 22 June. Both Major Place and Staff-Sergeant Victor Miller commented on the 'luxurious' nature of the permanent accommodation there, the high standard and plentiful nature of the rations provided from US stocks and the proximity to the town in comparison to the dusty wilderness at Tizi and Froha. Interestingly, Lieutenant-Colonel Chatterton's account refers to the food at Relizane being 'limited and almost inedible', to glider pilots being obliged to sleep on bare concrete floors and to the airfield being a 'danger spot' for cholera.[73]

Froha was allotted to 2 Squadron with flight training underway by the end of June and over the same period the assembling and testing regime at La Sénia was wound up, presumably because all the cached machines had been assembled, tested and despatched; between 8 May and 18 May a total of fifty-two CG4As were assembled there.[74] The La Sénia Glider Pilots were relocated to Matemore, although 3 Squadron's assembly teams were reportedly despatched to the coast to continue their work wherever crated machines could be found, while Thiersville became home to the Advanced Phase of the Conversion Programme.[75] Much of the towing was performed by C-47s from the 51st Troop Carrier Wing but No. 296 Squadron became involved immediately on arrival in Algeria. The first test tow of a CG4A by an Albemarle was carried out on 9 June, before the Squadron had fully completed its move to Froha from the UK, and fuel consumption test tows were conducted on 16 June; by 20 June the Squadron was able to contribute twenty-two Albemarles to the lift for airlanding Exercise EVE and tow the gliders back to Froha from Thiersville the following day.[76]

While the CG4A was accepted as a matter of necessity, Hopkinson, Chatterton and presumably Brigadier Hicks and his men from the 1st Airlanding Brigade nonetheless continued to harbour reservations about the US machine's limited payload, particularly with regard to carriage of anti-tank guns and their Jeep prime movers, which were the Airborne troops' only defence against enemy armour. While the Horsa could carry both, the CG4A could only carry one or the other and there were consequently justifiable fears that Jeeps and guns carried in separate machines would be unable to rendezvous during operational landings, and especially night landings as envisaged for Operation LADBROKE. 1st Airborne Division HQ thus made two successive requests for forty Horsa gliders to be provided from the UK to remedy the problem, but these were initially denied by the War Office, on the grounds that no seagoing cargo space was available and that towing gliders to North Africa was impossible because it involved flying well over the 1,000 miles considered to be the upper towing limit; getting the Horsas in place for LADBROKE involved a 1,350-mile flight from the UK to the US airfield at Salé near Rabat in Morocco, followed by 350 miles to Froha and then a final 570-mile leg from Froha to airfields near Sousse in Tunisia, approximately 2,270 miles in total. However, when 1st Airborne Division HQ insisted that LADBROKE could not be carried out without Horsas the problem was passed to No. 38 Wing HQ, which in turn passed it on to No. 295 Squadron, specifically to Squadron-Leader Arthur Wilkinson and the Squadron's A Flight and Major Alastair Cooper's hundred-strong 1 Squadron, 1st Battalion Glider Pilot Regiment.[77] It appears to have been selected because it was newly formed and thus available, A Flight was selected because it had been officially designated the Squadron's Handley Page Halifax sub-unit with effect from 22 April 1943 and was equipped with the four-engine machines rather than the obsolete Armstrong Whitworth Whitleys used by the rest of the Squadron, and Wilkinson because he had survived the experience of towing a Horsa over 700 miles to Rjukan in Norway for Operation FRESHMAN.[78]

Access to the Halifax tugs was complicated by A Flight still carrying out conversion training, but between 15 May and 6 June 1943 Wilkinson was able to employ two or three machines and Horsa gliders to perform five 'consumption tests' involving ten-hour flights to try out the concept of long duration towing, with ten hours being the estimated time for the flight to Morocco. The final test on 6 June involving two combinations was carried out after the first operational flights for North Africa and was presumably abandoned after one glider was cast off near Luton due to tug engine problems and the other over North Wales for reasons that are unclear.[79] The trials identified a number of technical faults not apparent in routine Halifax operations, most seriously a tendency for the oil and coolant connectors to vibrate loose, and modified maintenance schedules were despatched to Algeria with a fifty-strong ground crew advance party tasked to service the tugs before their return flights to the UK. They also led to modifications to both tugs and gliders, notably the fitting of auxiliary fuel tanks in the Halifax bomb-bays to extend range, although this ruled out emergency belly-landings and meant the Halifax could not fly on three engines in the event of combat damage or mechanical failure. The Horsas were modified with the 'Cable Angle Indicator Mk. 1' to permit the glider pilots to monitor the tow-rope angle and thus the relative position of the tug in cloud, fog and darkness, and also carried replacement undercarriages as cargo to permit jettisoning the existing items on take-off as a drag-reducing measure, with interim landings employing the glider's built-in central skid; each machine also carried an additional glider pilot to provide relief from the sheer effort involved in piloting the Horsas for such long periods.[80]

The trials, training and routine shuttle flights were not without risk in themselves. On 16 May a Halifax engaged in the routine transfer of Horsas across the six miles or so between the Squadron's base at RAF Holmsley South and RAF Hurn crashed after losing an engine shortly after take-off, three days later another Halifax engaged in a consumption test crashed at Fordingbridge, ten miles north-west of Holmsley South and on 11 June a third crashed in fog en route to Portreath; everyone aboard the first two machines was killed and all but the pilot and flight engineer aboard the third.[81] Nonetheless, on 21 May a conference at No. 38 Wing HQ was able to confirm that No. 295 Squadron would have a minimum of ten Halifax tugs and twenty-one Horsas in place in North Africa by 21 June 1943, with No. 296 Squadron tasked to provide a further thirty Albemarle tugs by the same date if required.[82]

After an eight-day delay due to bad weather the first flight of four Exercise BEGGAR combinations finally departed from RAF Portreath in Cornwall on Thursday 3 June 1943 at 08:00, 08:10, 08:15 and 08:20. The overall result was less than auspicious. The first combination returned to Portreath after more than seven hours in the air at 15:15, reportedly due to Horsa undercarriage problems, although another source refers to the abort being due to the combination being unable to fly clear of fog extending to 11,000 feet.[83] The second combination with the Horsa piloted by Major Cooper and Sergeants Sotiris Antonopoulos and Dennis Hall covered around 650 miles to a point off Cape Finisterre in Spain where the tug entered cloud, the glider lost station and the overstrained tow-rope parted, obliging the three glider pilots to ditch and take to the machine's dinghy. They were located after a few hours by a Coastal Command Sunderland that could not land due to the sea conditions but vectored the destroyer HMS *Teviot* to pick them up twelve hours after ditching; the destroyer then attempted to sink the still floating Horsa with gunfire, depth-charges and finally ramming all to no avail, and the stricken glider was abandoned to its fate.[84]

The third and fourth combinations made the flight to Salé unscathed, although the last to leave Portreath piloted by Staff-Sergeant Gordon Jenks and Sergeants Percy Attwood and Harry Flynn was damaged during take-off when the prematurely jettisoned undercarriage bounced against the underside of the glider, wedging debris in the starboard wing's control surface linkage and flap itself. The damage made the Horsa very difficult to fly – but Staff-Sergeant Jenks had included a trumpet in his kit and proceeded to entertain his fellow glider pilots and the tug crew with jazz music, relaying the concert via the telephone link woven into the tow-rope. The glider was the first to reach Salé but crash landed when the undercarriage jettison parachute that had remained attached throughout the flight deployed on touchdown and the debris embedded in the wing touched the runway before the landing skid, pivoting the machine through ninety degrees although the crew emerged without injury; the final Horsa piloted by Sergeants Nigel Brown, Dennis Galpin and a Sergeant Granger landed unscathed.[85]

With the validity of the concept proven, the task of ferrying the remaining Horsas to North Africa went ahead under the code-name TURKEY BUZZARD, although No. 295 Squadron Operations Record Book continued to refer to the flights as Exercise BEGGAR. In order to reduce wear and tear on the Halifax tugs the task of ferrying Horsas to RAF Hurn for loading and RAF Portreath for despatch was delegated to No. 295 Squadron's Whitleys, and from Sunday 6 June 1943 a total of thirteen flights were despatched to Salé ranging in size from a single to five combinations, with the final leaving on Wednesday 7 July. Not all the combinations reached Salé. A single-combination flight on 14 June was attacked by two Focke-Wulf 200 maritime patrol aircraft 140 miles off Cape Finisterre and the tug released the Horsa before being shot down. The glider was piloted by Sergeants Antonopoulos and Hall on their second attempt accompanied by Staff-Sergeant Paddy Conway and this time the three glider pilots spent eleven days adrift in their dinghy before being picked up by a Spanish trawler twenty miles off the Portuguese port of Oporto; all three were eventually repatriated to the UK via Gibraltar.[86]

On 26 June, a two-combination flight was aborted after one tug developed engine trouble three hours in and the other released its Horsa shortly after take-off. One combination of three despatched the following day simply disappeared with no radio communication and the final single-combination flight was aborted two hours in due to engine trouble on 6 July, before continuing successfully the following day.[87] The twenty-one Horsas promised by No. 38 Wing HQ were present in North Africa by the due date of 21 June 1943, and by 7 July the number had risen to twenty-seven, with only three being lost during due to accidents or enemy action, although merely getting the Horsas there was not the whole story. A test tow of an unladen Horsa by a No. 296 Squadron Albemarle on 19 June from Rabat to Froha saw the glider being prematurely released when the tug's engine oil temperature rose to excessive levels, for example; the tug reached its destination without further mishap, the Horsa was presumably recovered and on 21 June modifications were carried out on the oil coolers fitted to all the Squadron's Albemarles, which delivered an average temperature reduction of five degrees when glider towing.[88] Exercise BEGGAR was undeniably a 'remarkable feat of airmanship, planning and logistics' and the 1st Airborne Division had the heavy-lift gliders it required for the Sicily invasion.[89]

The 1st Airborne Division was training for its allotted HUSKY missions south of Mascara. The glider pilots and Airlanding Brigade were busy preparing for the upcoming Operation LADBROKE, and between 21 May and 13 July the pilots clocked up 521 hours and 54 minutes flying time, 130 hours at night, spread over 1,873 separate lifts, 510 of them at night. In the process 116 pilots had been trained to fly the CG4A, in the course of which two pilots were killed and four injured in accidents.[90] The fruits of this training were on display on Monday 14 June 1943 when HQ and three Rifle Companies from the 2nd Battalion South Staffordshire Regiment, augmented with elements from Brigade units, were lifted from Matemore and Thiersville in fifty-six CG4As towed by C-47s from the US 60th and 62nd Troop Carrier Groups for Exercise ADAM. Fifty-four gliders put down at Froha over a twenty-eight minute period ending at 19:45, with one casting off during take-off and another en route; the passengers were deployed ready for action in twenty minutes, none were injured during the landing and only five gliders suffered minor damage.[91] The following day the 1st Battalion, The Border Regiment carried out Exercise VIN BLANC, a dry run for an upcoming equivalent to ADAM substituting 3-ton trucks for gliders, each carrying a CG4A load and a pair of glider pilots rehearsing their role. It is unclear if the truck-borne rehearsal was a standard measure or whether it was connected to a six-day suspension of glider training and airlanding exercises ordered by Lieutenant-General Carl Spaatz's Northwest African Air Forces HQ on or around 16 June, to permit additional glider maintenance due to 'a dramatic increase in mechanical failures on the WACO fleet'.[92]

Parachute training continued unabated, however. On 16 June the 2nd Parachute Brigade carried out a mass dusk drop dubbed Exercise OYSTER at Orleansville, ninety miles north-east of Froha in preparation for Operation GLUTTON, involving US C-47s and sixteen Albemarles from No. 296 Squadron, mentioned earlier.[93] Two days later the 1st Parachute Brigade carried out Exercise CACTUS IV in rehearsal for Operation FUSTIAN which involved US C-47s and nineteen Albemarles from No. 296 Squadron delivering the entire Brigade, the 1st Parachute Squadron RE and 16th Parachute Field Ambulance RAMC closer to home near Ain Fekan, nine miles south-west of Froha. The result was less successful than OYSTER. Confusion over ground marking resulted in several sticks being despatched a mile and a half short of the DZ, leading to unfavourable comment by 1st Airborne Division HQ, and two crewmen from an Albemarle bailed out over Froha after the pilot reported a possible undercarriage problem, although the machine subsequently landed safely.[94]

Airlanding exercises resumed on 20 June with Exercise EVE, which involved 632 men from the 1st Battalion The Border Regiment being lifted from Froha to Thiersville aboard seventy-two CG4As, twenty-two of them towed by No. 296 Squadron Albemarles. The EVE landing area was selected for its similarity to the terrain on Sicily where the 1st Airlanding Brigade was to carry out a spearhead landing for Operation HUSKY; the exercise was thus a full dress rehearsal for the 1st Border's participation in Operation LADBROKE, using the same number and types of gliders, tugs and loading.[95] A pointer to events nineteen days hence, Exercise EVE ran less smoothly than its predecessor ADAM, with fourteen CG4As failing to reach the LZ and RAF tug pilots referring to a number of gliders casting off early 'owing to alleged unserviceability'; officer observers from the South Staffords reported a dozen gliders going astray and that the 1st Border's post-landing reorganisation took forty minutes.[96]

The final glider exercise was carried out the following day by the South Staffords. Sometimes referred to as Exercise EVE II, the flight was intended to test the feasibility of 'mass landings' in moonlight and was also the first British night landing by fully laden gliders in North Africa. It involved twelve CG4As towed by US C-47s, carrying sixty-six men from the 2nd South Staffords and personnel from 1st Airlanding Brigade HQ and Major-General Hopkinson, who opted to join the trial personally. It commenced at 01:00 in the morning of Monday 21 June. One combination aborted before take-off due to 'technical problems' and one CG4A went astray, but the remaining ten gliders successfully formed up at 1,700 feet before casting off over a single illuminated marker and setting down on the designated LZ, with three machines being damaged on landing. The trial was judged a success, spectacularly so according to the South Staffords, who also considered it to have saved their participation in the operational landing at Syracuse; interestingly, their War Diary refers to the landing being carried out with 'no moon'.[97] While the trial may have been a success there were still significant gaps in the glider pilot training; none of the 1st Battalion's glider pilots had flown formation at night or over the open sea for example, and none of their flights were close to the duration required to reach Sicily from Tunisia.[98] But time for training had run out, as the latter half of June 1943 was taken up with moving the 1st Airborne Division and its accompanying RAF contingent to the operational concentration area in Tunisia.

The first and most drawn-out move was by No. 296 Squadron, which despatched an advance party by road to an airfield alongside the Kairouan to M'Saken road, codenamed Goubrine II in the Squadron Records, on 15 June. Air movement commenced on Thursday 24 June, with five Albemarles towing CG4As preceded by three loaded with freight tasked to relay weather conditions over the Atlas Mountains. The 530-mile flight was completed in around five hours; no Squadron personnel or equipment were carried in the gliders due to reservations over their reliability following Exercise EVE. The Albemarles returned to Froha immediately on unloading and that night an individual Horsa lift was provided to allow Lieutenant-Colonel Chatterton to perform a moonlight landing without artificial illumination.[99] The airlift continued on a daily basis until the main Squadron road party arrived at Goubrine II on 29 June 1 July, although the final glider lift from Froha occurred on 1 July and three Albemarles were employed moving equipment and personnel for No. 38 Wing the following day.[100] The previously despatched 1st Airborne Division Advanced HQ moved from Cairo to Suez on 26 June and embarked on the troop ship HMS *Dilwara* two days later, while the main Division HQ including Major-General Hopkinson moved from Mascara to the vicinity of Kairouan on 27 June; the 2nd Parachute Brigade completed its concentration in the same area the same day followed by the 1st Parachute Brigade on 30 June.[101]

The largest single move appears to have begun on 27 June with the bulk of the 1st Airlanding Brigade being lifted from Froha using US C-47s and CG4As. The first day's lift included the 2nd Battalion South Staffordshire Regiment in its entirety and although the Battalion's gliders were severely buffeted by turbulence over the Atlas Mountains, all but two reached the Kairouan area. One of these put down safely around half way after a malfunction of some kind but the other crashed when the tail became detached in mid-air, killing all fifteen on board; the dead included Company Sergeant Major Reginald Glynn who had reported in from his sickbed for the flight.[102] In total, the 1st Airlanding Brigade lift carried 1,200 fully-equipped Airlanding soldiers in eighty-four CG4As at a cost of three gliders including the 2nd South Staffords' losses on the first day, with a further five sustaining minor damage, presumably on landing.[103] The last element of the Division to arrive in Tunisia appears to have been its organic artillery component, the 1st Airlanding Light Regiment RA, which left Froha by road on 2 July and was ensconced at a camp near M'Saken, eight miles south-west of Sousse, five days later.[104]

By the beginning of July the 1st Airborne Division was in Tunisia in its entirety, ensconced on or near six airfields codenamed Strip A through Strip F; the newly arrived Horsa contingent and No. 296 Squadron's Albemarles were housed at Strip E near the Sebkra de Hani salt flats and Strip F just to the north on the Kairouan-M'Saken road respectively.[105] There the Division's constituent formations and units embarked on a round of last-minute training, preparation and briefings for their roles in HUSKY, although the intensity of the activity varied. The 2nd South Staffords applied itself to practising disembarkation drills on glider mock ups in the first few days of July for example, while the 1st Border embarked on an enthusiastic live-firing programme employing all Battalion weapons on 1 and 2 July that left five men wounded by PIAT bomb splinters and a prematurely detonated No. 74 grenade; the programme was curtailed after stray rounds hit Sousse lighthouse and wounded an anti-aircraft gunner. Their paratrooper opposite numbers were taking a less energetic approach, given that the 1st and 2nd Parachute Battalions managed to work daily bathing visits to Sousse into their Battalion training programmes.[106] Others were engaged in more routine tasks. The 1st Airlanding Light Aid Detachment REME attached to the 1st Airlanding Brigade spent 1 July collecting a number of Axis light vehicles and motorcycles from a salvage depot and the following day stripping down their engines on discovering sand in the oil as a sabotage measure.[107]

On 3 July a No. 296 Squadron Albemarle conducted a consumption test over the sea with a fully laden Horsa and decided that despite high oil temperatures the machines could be used for Horsa towing in lieu of the Halifax if necessary, and on 4 July embarked on four days of standard forty-flying hour inspections and flight tests as the Squadron's machines had reached their limit during the airlift from Froha. On 8 July an Albemarle crashed during a flight test, killing three of the four crew and writing off another machine parked on the ground.[108] The 1st Airborne Division was in place at its operational concentration area and as ready as time allowed as the clock wound down to HUSKY's launch.

6

The Tip of the Spear II

US Airborne Preparations for Operation HUSKY, March to Friday 9 July

As with the British, elements of the US Airborne force were already present in North Africa before the build-up for Operation HUSKY. After spearheading the TORCH landing at Oran direct from the UK on 8 November 1942 and assisting in the capture of the airfield at Tafaraoui, Lieutenant-Colonel Edson D. Raff's single-battalion 509th Parachute Infantry Regiment carried out a two-company drop to capture the airfield at Youks les Bains on 15 November, which Raff then used as a patrol base to launch a series of unsanctioned forays deep into Axis-held Tunisia, penetrating eighty-five miles south-east to Gafsa on one occasion and ninety miles east to Sidi Bou Zid on another, taking two hundred prisoners in the process. Having received a field promotion to Colonel from Lieutenant-General Eisenhower in person on 27 November, Raff only curtailed his activities following a direct order from Eisenhower's Deputy, Major-General Mark W. Clark, who was concerned that Raff and his men would be cut off and destroyed.[1]

The 509th Regiment's final parachute operation in North Africa continued the raiding theme, albeit with a sabotage mission focussed on a specific target. In December 1942 Allied intelligence identified the railway bridge at El Djem, forty miles north of Sfax, as a chokepoint on the Axis supply line running south from the ports in the north of Tunisia to Rommel's *Deutsch-Italienische Panzerarmee* in Libya.[2] When the bridge proved impervious to Allied bombing including low-level attacks by P-40 fighter-bombers from the USAAF 33rd Fighter Group, AFHQ passed the mission of destroying it to Colonel Raff with a deadline of 26 December, who in turn delegated it to 1st Lieutenant John R. Martin on 20 December.[3] Originally scheduled for 20 December and then Christmas Eve, the mission finally took off from Tébessa at 20:30 on Saturday 26 December in two C-47s carrying thirty-one men including five demolition experts and two Arabic-speaking French paratroopers tasked to lead the party back to friendly lines after the mission, commanded by 2nd Lieutenant Daniel DeLeo in Lieutenant Martin's stead. The lead transport was piloted by Lieutenant-Colonel Philip G. Cochran, the commander of the 58th Fighter Squadron that had attacked the bridge previously; according to one source the formation also included a third C-47 carrying equipment bundles containing between 400 and 500 pounds of TNT explosive, anti-tank mines and a M1903 rifle with grenade launcher and four rounds.[4]

Despite encountering anti-aircraft fire during the 150-mile flight to El Djem and from German road convoys on the final approach to the DZ alongside the railway line, the drop went ahead without incident some time between 22:00 and 23:59, although things then went increasingly awry. One man went missing but reached the rendezvous after thirty minutes, it took until 01:30 to locate one of the explosive containers after it also went astray, a number of Arabs appeared while the raiders were burying their parachutes and after a night of marching, dawn revealed that the C-47s had delivered the party on the opposite side of the bridge as planned and Lieutenant DeLeo had been inadvertently leading his men away from their objective. As they were by now twenty miles or more from their target with no realistic prospect of reaching it without being detected and intercepted, DeLeo therefore elected to expend his explosives on demolishing a 100-yard section of railway track, a hut containing electrical switching equipment, some switchgear and three telegraph poles before splitting his force into smaller groups to exfiltrate back to friendly territory.

Only Lieutenant DeLeo, Sergeant John Betters, Privates Frank Romero and Ronald Rondeau and the two French paratroopers, *Sergent-Chef* Jean Guilhenjoven and *Caporal* Paul Vullierme, reached safety after a four-day odyssey followed by Privates Charles Doyle and Michael P. Underhill who managed to escape shortly after capture. The remainder were hunted down and captured by Axis troops attracted by the demolition. Sixteen either escaped subsequently or were liberated at the end of the Tunisian campaign, one was killed while a Prisoner of War and the remainder were posted missing presumed killed.[5] Lieutenant DeLeo visited the target bridge after the Axis surrender and, given the structure consisted of sixteen forty-foot high stone and concrete pillars carrying a double railway line, concluded that its destruction would have been beyond his means even had his party reached their target; the incident illustrates that despatching highly trained men on speculative missions was not a solely British preserve.

Be that as it may, despite Colonel Raff's vehement objections the 2nd Battalion 509th Parachute Infantry Regiment was split into penny-packets and employed as ground shock troops through the Tunisian winter fighting until the Axis surrender; the Battalion was commanded by former Executive Officer Lieutenant-Colonel Doyle R. Yardley from 1 December 1942 as part of Raff's Tunisian Task Force alongside elements of the 26th Infantry Regiment from the US 1st Infantry Division and the 701st Tank Destroyer Battalion. When the fighting in Tunisia ceased the 2nd Battalion concentrated before moving by rail to Oujda in Morocco, where its accommodation was christened Camp Kunkle in honour of the first member of the Battalion and first US paratrooper killed in action, Lieutenant David Kunkle, who was killed during the operation to secure the airfield at Tafaraoui on 8 November 1942.[6] By this point Colonel Raff appears to have been working for Major-General Browning in his capacity as Airborne Advisor at AFHQ, and Lieutenant-General Eisenhower visited Camp Kunkle to congratulate the paratroopers on their performance.[7]

As with their British counterparts the 1st Parachute Brigade, the 509th Parachute Infantry Regiment was joined by a much larger force direct from their home country. Originally activated on 25 August 1917 and earning its famous AA insignia and the nickname 'All American' due to its ranks including men from every state in the Union, the US 82nd Infantry Division served in the fighting at St. Mihiel and the Meuse-Argonne in France before being inactivated on 27 May 1919. It was reactivated as a motorised formation at Camp Claiborne, Louisiana, on 25 March 1942 from a draft of 2,000 men drawn from the 9th Infantry Division, augmented by 16,000 draftees drawn directly from induction centres in Alabama, Georgia, Mississippi and Tennessee. Initial commander Major-General Omar Bradley was succeeded by his deputy Major-General Matthew B. Ridgway in June 1942, and Ridgway remained in command when the formation was redesignated the 82nd Airborne Division on 15 August 1942, the first such formation in the US Army.

The Division moved to Fort Bragg, North Carolina in mid-September 1942 to be closer to the USAAF's 52nd Troop Carrier Wing based at the adjacent Pope Field and by February 1943 the Division had settled into the two parachute and one glider infantry formations it would take to North Africa and later into Europe; Colonel Reuben H. Tucker's 504th Parachute Infantry Regiment, Colonel James M. Gavin's 505th Parachute Infantry Regiment and Colonel Harry Lewis' 325th Glider Infantry Regiment.[8] The original Washington plan had been for the running mate 101st Airborne Division, activated on 16 August 1942 with a cadre from Ridgway's formation, to be deployed overseas first, but US Army Chief of Staff General George C. Marshall reversed this following the January 1943 SYMBOL Conference at Casablanca for reasons that are unclear, possibly due to Ridgway's close relationship with the Chief of Staff.[9]

Whatever the reason for the policy change, the 82nd Airborne Division was thus slated to participate in Operation HUSKY and Ridgway was despatched to AFHQ in Algiers with a small planning staff, arriving on 8 March 1943 and returning to Fort Bragg on 24 March after spending time with the forward elements of the US 1st and 9th Infantry Divisions, including accompanying front-line patrols.[10] In mid-April, three weeks after Ridgway's return from AFHQ and after seven months of uncertainty, reorganisation and arduous training the 82nd Airborne Division began its move to North Africa.[11] The first stage was a 650-mile railway journey from Fort Bragg to Camp Edwards, Massachusetts, under strict operational security conditions that involved replacing or covering the division patches on uniforms and forbade the display of Airborne insignia, clothing and equipment, parachute qualification badges and wearing the coveted high-leg jump boots; regulation infantry low boots and canvas leggings were issued instead, an imposition the paratroopers considered especially heinous.

Concentrated at Camp Edwards by 23 April, the Division spent four days training before another rail move on 27-28 April for docks at Hoboken, New Jersey and Staten Island, New York where it embarked on the transports *George Washington*, *Monterey* and *Santa Rosa* and sailed on Thursday 29 April as part of a twenty-two transport Convoy UGF.8, along with the Escort Carrier HMS *Tracker* ferrying aircraft and escorted by the battleship USS *Texas* and nine USN destroyers.[12] The convoy divided at 09:05 on Monday 10 May with one section continuing through the Straits of Gibraltar to Oran. The other, including the three transports carrying the Division, headed for Casablanca where it docked at 17:30 the same day.[13] After a two-day stopover Ridgway's Division began the move east to Oujda on 12 May, some men travelling for three dust-filled days by road but most stifled in the standard French *40 hommes ou 8 chevaux* (forty men or eight horses) railway box cars their forebears had likely used in France in 1917-1919.

On arrival the 504th and 505th Parachute Infantry Regiments took up residence in tented accommodation at Oujda near the 509th Parachute Infantry Regiment, while the 325th Glider Infantry Regiment and the Division support units were similarly housed at Marnia, fourteen miles to the north-east and just across the border in Algeria.[14] The troops were preceded by Colonel Harold L. Clark's 52nd Troop Carrier Wing, consisting of the 61st, 313th, 314th and 316th Troop Carrier Groups which had arrived from Pope Field on 8 May, along with a detachment from the 315th Troop Carrier Group based at Aldermaston in England. The 313th and 316th Groups were located at Nouvion airfield seven miles north of Oujda while the 61st and 314th were based at satellite fields at Lourmel and Berguent respectively, although the satellite airfields were reportedly not operational for a further sixteen days; this may also have applied to the presumably expanded facilities at Nouvion.[15]

As with their British counterparts from the 1st Airborne Division a month earlier, the arrivals discovered that their new home, which had been specifically selected by Major-General Ridgway, was a 'potent combination of extreme heat, wind, sand and flies'. The perennially lukewarm water available 'was so heavily chlorinated it burned the trooper's throats'. Private William H. Tucker from one of the Division's replacement units swore he would 'give ten dollars for a glass of cold water, cold beer, or cold anything'.[16] The conditions made eating a particularly fraught chore; according to Private Russell McConnell from the 3rd Battalion, 505th Parachute Infantry Regiment bread or other comestibles were immediately settled on by 'yellow jackets and hornets...almost in your mouth. It was absolute misery'. Private William Blank from the same Battalion recalled that every day 'at mealtime a dust storm would blow right down the mess line and the food would be full of dirt'.[17] Sheep dung in the sand and dust led rapidly to a severe outbreak of dysentery that obliged all ranks to keep their entrenching tools to hand in readiness for the inevitable and frequent toilet emergencies.[18] Despite this, Ridgway instigated an intensive programme of weapons instruction on all US and enemy weapons and unit tactical training using live ammunition, albeit with the concession of allowing the troops to sleep in the intense heat of the day and train in the cool of the night, an improvisation that was to pay dividends in the night landing on Sicily.

Parachute training was constrained by the delay in getting the satellite airfields around Oujda operational, which meant the 52nd Troop Carrier Wing was unable to provide C-47s for jump training until 1 June, and thereafter by the requirement to put on special demonstrations for a string of visiting dignitaries; as Private Allen Langdon from the 505th Parachute Infantry Regiment put it: 'Suddenly it seemed as if every General officer in North Africa wanted to see what this new-fangled outfit was all about.'[19] The process began with a visit by Major-General Mark W. Clark in the Division's first week at Oujda.[20] Clark was followed in quick succession by Lieutenant-General Carl A. Spaatz, commander of the Northwest African Air Forces, Major-General Browning and on 3 June 1943 the Division laid on a review for Lieutenant-General Eisenhower, his deputy Clark, Lieutenant-General George S. Patton, Major-General Omar Bradley and a number of high-ranking French and Spanish officers. The review was intended as a demonstration of Allied capabilities aimed particularly at the Spanish, whose territory in Morocco and pro-Axis sympathies presented a potential threat to Allied lines of communication.[21] The review included a demonstration combat jump by the 1st Battalion, 505th Parachute Infantry Regiment from thirty-six C-47s codenamed EYEWASH, which was the debut of the camouflaged T-10 parachute canopy that became the US Airborne standard. It also introduced the US paratroopers to the perils of parachuting in the thin desert air, especially when burdened with operational loads of weapons, ammunition and equipment; twenty-two of the participants were hospitalised with jump injuries, three of them including a concussion being classified as serious.

Conditions for a practice jump by the 505th Regiment's 3rd Battalion two days later were made more hazardous by thirty mile-per-hour winds across the DZ, resulting in fifty-three hospitalisations and a fatality during a jump by the 505th's HQ Company on 7 June, when Private Gilbert C. Smith's canopy failed to deploy fully, an event referred to as a 'streamer' in US parlance, and the attrition rate prompted Gavin to limit practice jumps to the minimum necessary for his Regiment's upcoming HUSKY mission.[22] The theme was taken up by Ridgway, who forbade 'key leaders' from participating in practice jumps. Gavin prided himself on not expecting his men to do anything he would not do himself. On one occasion Ridgway was obliged to personally order him off a C-47 he had sneaked aboard just before it took off for a practice jump.[23]

The 52nd Troop Carrier Wing arrived in North Africa 'qualified for daylight operations over familiar terrain, but unqualified for night operations'.[24] Colonel Clark rapidly instigated an intensive training programme to rectify this omission beginning with the time-consuming skill of night formation flying, using a combat formation he had developed especially for the purpose. This divided the C-47 squadrons into nine-strong V formations subdivided into vics of three aircraft, with each nine-aircraft formation carrying a company of paratroopers; the V formations flew in convoy at approximately ninety second intervals and four or five such formations made up a serial, flying at ten minute intervals.[25] Time constraints meant there was little opportunity for the C-47 crews to hone the equally vital skills of night navigation including navigating over the open sea and identifying and orienting on DZs, to the extent that Gavin fully expected a proportion of his men to miss their DZs 'by a great deal'.[26]

The primary purpose was to provide practice for pilots and navigators in the C-47s, and drops were thus largely carried out on a reduced scale. Thus on the night of 9 June exercise DODGER saw the 505th Regiment's 1st and 3rd Battalions delivered to the drop area on the ground while Battery A, 456th Parachute Field Artillery Battalion and the 1st Battalion's jumpmasters and equipment bundles were dropped at 22:00 followed ninety minutes later by a second drop by the 3rd Battalion's jumpmasters and equipment bundles and the 456th Parachute Field Artillery Battalion's Battery C. The exercise permitted the C-47 crews to practise night flying, navigation and dropping skills, the artillerymen to practise recovering and assembling their 75mm Pack Howitzers and the infantry to practise their equipment bundle gathering drills and test the efficacy of new luminous markers attached to the bundles. Both Battalions then conducted a two-mile night march to a defensive location followed by a six-mile approach march and attack using live ammunition the following night.[27] A full-scale rehearsal codenamed PIRATE repeated the process with another double night drop on 14 June, the first involving the full battalion staffs, company and platoon commanders from the 505th Regiment's Battalions and the second personnel from the 3rd Battalion, 504th Parachute Infantry Regiment, which was attached to Gavin's Regiment for HUSKY. The participants were issued with maps to plot their landing spots in order to assess the compactness of the drop, and while the first confirmed Gavin's prediction of scattering wide of the DZ, the 504th Battalion's jump 'had somewhat improved results and was deemed a success'.[28] The remainder of the force were again pre-placed and went on to practise 'night organization of a defensive area', followed by a group critique of the exercise at the Paris Theatre in Oujda in the evening of 16 June.[29] The same day two USN Ensigns posted to act as naval gunfire liaison for the 505th Regiment in the invasion reported for parachute training. Gavin held a review of the 505th Regiment on 18 June followed by a Division parade before Lieutenant-General Eisenhower the following day, and with that, training time at Oujda came to a close after six frenetic weeks.[30]

Major-General Ridgway's time at Oujda was not only marked by friction over time, terrain and air transport resources, but also with his British Allies, specifically AFHQ Airborne Advisor Major-General Browning. Ridgway appears to have met Browning during his pre-deployment visit to North

Africa in March 1943 and rightly deduced that the British officer was using his position on Eisenhower's staff to 'exert undue influence' operationally and with regard to accessing USAAF aircraft, while on a personal level finding him 'a bit patronizing...toward those who had considerably less airborne experience than he'.[31] Browning confirmed Ridgway's opinion by turning up unannounced at the latter's HQ at Oujda near the end of May 1943, shortly after the 82nd Airborne had taken up residence there. The visit was ostensibly a courtesy call but was more likely intended to impress upon the US commander where the power resided, given the course and tone of the meeting.

Browning began by laying out his intentions for the British end of the HUSKY airborne landings before demanding to see Ridgway's plans, even though the two men were nominally equal in rank. When Ridgway responded by claiming that he as yet had no plan and pointed out that he took his orders from Lieutenant-General Patton as commander of the US 7th Army, the meeting became heated, with Browning claiming that Eisenhower would likely accept his recommendations without question and that his self-appointed position as Airborne Advisor to AFHQ effectively granted him 'command status' over all airborne operations and the units assigned to them; when Ridgway remained obdurate the meeting ended on a 'testy note'.[32] Browning then compounded matters by contacting Lieutenant-Colonel Yardley directly around 6 June 1943 and informing him that the 509th Parachute Infantry Regiment had been made honorary member of British Airborne Forces, that arrangements were underway to have the Regiment issued with maroon berets to mark the occasion and that he would be 'pleased to inspect the unit'. Such cavalier sidelining of Ridgway and the US chain of command was a blatant breach of military etiquette and – given Browning's reputation as a military diplomat – was likely a deliberate further demonstration of his influence; whether or not, an understandably outraged Ridgway blocked the beret plan and inspection after it was somehow brought to his attention, although for their part the 509th Parachute Infantry Regiment's members were happy to unofficially accept the accolade and continue to celebrate it.[33]

The episode had repercussions. During a subsequent visit to AFHQ Ridgway was 'forcefully reminded' by Eisenhower's Chief-of-Staff, Major-General Walter Bedell Smith, of the need for the utmost co-operation with their British Allies and warned that further transgressions would result in his dismissal; this was presumably the result of Browning bringing the matter to Eisenhower's attention. Ridgway did not take the reprimand well and responded by somewhat histrionically announcing that he was 'fighting for the needs of his command' and refused to permit the lives of his men to be endangered 'for the sake of Allied "harmony"'. The argument grew heated to the point Ridgway called upon Patton for support, who backed Ridgway by reiterating his view that Browning's machinations were aimed at imposing British control over the US Airborne Force in North Africa and likely elsewhere; Ridgway later considered that Patton's rapid and forceful support saved him from an official admonishment at best or being relieved of his command and despatched back to the Continental US at worst.[34] Most of the backwash fell upon the hapless 509th Parachute Infantry Regiment, which had been attached to the 82nd Airborne Division after the latter's arrival at Oujda. Like its counterpart 1st Parachute Brigade, the 509th Regiment had developed a rather superior attitude toward unblooded newcomers, in this instance the remainder of the 82nd Airborne Division, on the back of its eight months combat experience and three combat jumps, with individuals loudly opining that the 82nd Airborne was attached to the 509th rather than vice versa.[35] Ridgway was not enamoured with the unit as a result and retaliated by side-lining the 509th Regiment from involvement in HUSKY despite its combat experience because he believed, possibly not without justification, that Browning was using it as a front to expand his influence over the US Airborne Force.

The backwash applied especially to Colonel Raff, who was doubly tainted by his working for Browning at AFHQ and as Ridgway shared Patton's jaundiced view of US officers who ceased to be American in favour of being Allies, Raff was despatched back to the Continental US to a post at the Airborne Training Centre, ostensibly because Ridgway did not have an opening for a full Colonel.[36] Part of the problem was undoubtedly a personality clash between the senior British and US commanders. Ridgway was a typically entitled West Point graduate of his time, in addition to being a rather pompous individual, convinced, albeit perhaps justifiably with hindsight, that he was destined for greatness. For his part Browning the Grenadier Guards officer was a privileged stereotype virtually guaranteed to upset American egalitarian sensibilities, even without the arrogance and Machiavellian demeanour. Although he later characterised Browning as 'an exceedingly capable officer', at the time Ridgway confided that he could not stand him to Major-General Alexander D. Surles, Director of the US War Department's Bureau of Public Relations. He referred to Browning as 'a dilettante of the first water'.[37] Eisenhower succeeded in keeping the lid on the Anglo-US Airborne animosity, but the friction between the Browning and Ridgway did not end with HUSKY it cropped up again in the run up to the Normandy invasion and before and during the subsequent Operation MARKET GARDEN in Holland.

Despite Ridgway's denial to Browning, the 82nd Airborne Division also worked out its plan for participation in HUSKY while at Oujda, although this, too, was overshadowed by the dispute between the two senior officers. Patton had wanted his 7th Army landings on the southern aspect of Sicily, straddling the ports of Gela, Licata and Scoglitti, to be spearheaded by the 82nd Airborne Division's parachute component, at Ridgway's prompting for a larger role for his Division according to one account.[38] The problem was that although there were sufficient USAAF C-47s in North Africa to deliver the 504th and 505th Parachute Infantry Regiments and the Division parachute support units in a single lift, the USAAF was also committed to providing transport for the British 1st Airborne Division and there were insufficient C-47s available to lift both formations on that scale simultaneously. Like

Patton, Ridgway was of the opinion that US forces should have first call on US resources and assets. This was a reasonable assumption from the US perspective, as the Air Ministry's consistent policy of avoiding providing airlift for more than a fraction of the British Airborne Force was not really a US problem, and a combination of Browning's manipulations at AFHQ and Hopkinson's insistence on mounting an airlanding operation despite a total lack of gliders and then sequestering the bulk of the US-produced CG4As in North Africa to make up the shortfall added insult to injury. CG4As made up 135 of the 144 gliders employed by the 1st Airlanding Brigade for Operation LADBROKE.[39]

On the other hand, British industrial resources and production capacity were finite in comparison with the burgeoning might of US industry, it had already been agreed that the USAAF would provide airlift for the British 1st Airborne Division, and the wrangling directly undermined Eisenhower's efforts to establish and maintain a harmonious Anglo-US working relationship. The upshot was therefore a compromise delivered by Eisenhower in person that allotted around 250 C-47s for the 82nd Airborne's drop and around 110 USAAF machines to the 1st Airborne Division to act as glider tugs for the 1st Airlanding Brigade; a further twenty-eight Albemarles and seven Halifax from Nos. 295 and 296 Squadrons respectively brought the British overall total up to 145 tug aircraft. Even though the compromise gave his Division the lion's share of the airlift, Ridgway still viewed it as taking aircraft from him and gifting them to the British, primarily because 250 C-47s was insufficient to lift both of his Parachute Infantry Regiments and he was thus obliged to deliver them in two separate lifts on successive nights.[40]

This was the beginning of a recurring problem that was to dog large-scale Anglo-US Airborne operations throughout the remainder of the war. While the US airlift capacity especially increased, the size of the Allied Airborne force and scale of the operations it was assigned increased in parallel; the delivery of the three divisions deployed for MARKET GARDEN in Holland in September 1944 in multiple parallel lifts spread across several days provides perhaps the clearest example of the problem and its associated impacts.

That lay in the future however, and at the beginning of June Ridgway selected Colonel James M. Gavin's 505th Parachute Infantry Regiment to carry out the initial night drop into Sicily, and despatched him to the US 7th Army's HQ at Mostaganem, 170 miles west of Algiers to lead the Division's planning effort.[41] A West Point graduate from a Pennsylvania Irish mining background, Gavin had served briefly on the Airborne Command staff, where he wrote the first US manual on 'The Employment of Airborne Forces'. His Regiment was selected for the Sicily mission because Gavin was the senior regimental commander and more importantly, because thanks to his intensive training and exemplary leadership the 505th Parachute Infantry Regiment was widely acknowledged to be among the best units in the US Army, albeit one with a rather high opinion of itself.[42] This and Gavin's leadership style were well illustrated by the 82nd Airborne's senior

Signals Officer, Lieutenant-Colonel Frank W. Moorman, who recalled of the Division's senior commanders: 'Ridgway would cut your throat and then burst into tears. [Maxwell D.] Taylor would cut your throat and think nothing about it. Gavin would cut your throat and then laugh.' Moorman also recalled a Lieutenant from the 505th Regiment reporting to a somewhat taken aback Ridgway while the Division was at Fort Bragg with the words 'Sir, Colonel Gavin sends his regards and told us he wants us to co-operate to the utmost with the 82nd Division.'[43] This was not mere macho posturing; Ridgway's Chief-of- Staff Lieutenant-Colonel Ralph P. Eaton recalled that he had 'never seen such killers' as the 505th Regiment and that they reminded him 'of a pack of jackals'.[44]

As his allotment of 250 C-47s was insufficient to lift both his parachute infantry regiments simultaneously, Ridgway was obliged to make his initial landing in Sicily a two-stage affair, imaginatively codenamed HUSKY ONE and HUSKY TWO, although the latter is sometimes referred to as MACKALL WHITE.[45] D-Day overall for Operation HUSKY was set for Saturday 10 July 1943, with H-Hour at 02:45 to permit the initial waves of landing craft to run into the beaches under cover of darkness. HUSKY ONE was to commence two hours and forty minutes earlier at 00:06 to allow the C-47 pilots and paratroopers to use illumination from the waxing quarter-moon before moonset at 00:31, with the two-fold mission of preventing Axis interference with the US sea landings at Gela and Scoglitti and holding the DZs for HUSKY TWO, a reinforcing drop by the remainder of the Division's parachute infantry component provisionally scheduled for evening of D-Day.[46]

HUSKY ONE was assigned to Gavin's 505th Parachute Infantry Regiment, reinforced with the 3rd Battalion, 504th Parachute Infantry Regiment, the 456th Parachute Artillery Battalion, Company B, 307th Airborne Engineer Battalion, and detachments from the 82nd Airborne Signal Company and 307th Airborne Medical Company.[47] Gavin decided that the best way of protecting the US sea landing was to block access to the sparse road network that ran through the rugged terrain behind the beaches and to that end his reinforced Regiment, now dubbed the 505th Regimental Combat Team (RCT), was to be delivered onto six separate DZs in the area north-east of Gela up to Niscemi, ten miles inland from the coast. The most easterly drop onto DZ X was allotted to a small demolition party tasked to secure the road and rail bridges across the River Acate, ten miles south-east of Gela, with orders to demolish the structures if attacked in strength.[48] The 505th Regiment's Company I was to drop onto another small DZ five miles to the north-west, tasked to secure and hold a junction on the coast road five miles south-east of Gela and to light a bonfire on the adjacent Piano Lupo high ground to guide the US 1st Infantry Division's amphibious landing. The remainder of the 3rd Battalion, 505th Regiment and the 456th Parachute Artillery Battalion's Batteries C & D were to drop on DZ T, three miles north-west of Company I, and secure high ground overlooking one of the RCT's main objectives, Codenamed Objective Y, from the south. The latter was a fortified junction on the *Strada* 115 coast road where the smaller *Strada Provinciale* 11 branched north to Niscemi and was to be secured by the 505th Regiment's 1st and 2nd Battalions dropping onto two adjacent zones collectively dubbed DZ S on the west side of the Niscemi road, along with Batteries A and B, 456th Parachute Artillery Battalion. Finally, the 3rd Battalion, 504th Parachute Infantry Regiment was tasked to secure Objective X, another junction on the *Strada Provinciale* 11 just south of Niscemi after dropping onto the most northerly landing area, codenamed DZ Q.[49]

The 505th RCT was tasked to hold these objectives until relieved by the US amphibious landing force during D-Day, and to protect the DZs for the arrival of HUSKY TWO in the evening; the latter consisted of the 1st and 2nd Battalions of Colonel Tucker's 504th Parachute Infantry Regiment accompanied by the 376th Parachute Field Artillery Battalion and Company C, 307th Airborne Engineer Battalion. Tucker's force was to become the 504th Parachute RCT when reunited with its 3rd Battalion and Gavin's 505th Parachute RCT was then to be temporarily attached to the US 1st Infantry Division on D-Day Plus One, provisionally tasked to assist in securing the airfield at Ponte Olivo, four miles north-west of Objective Y. The remainder of the 82nd Airborne Division was to be brought into Sicily via two glider lifts. The first, scheduled for the evening of D-Day Plus One, was to carry the Division's various HQ staff elements and HQ Company, the Division Artillery HQ and HQ Battery, the 407th Quartermaster Company, the 782nd Ordnance Maintenance Company and the remainder of the 82nd Airborne Signal Company, the 307th Airborne Engineer Battalion and the 307th Airborne Medical Company. The second was scheduled to take place as and when practicable and was to consist of Colonel Harry L. Lewis' 325th Glider RCT and Major Raymond E. Singleton's misleadingly titled 80th Airborne Antiaircraft Battalion.[50] Three of the latter's six Batteries were equipped with Browning .50 calibre machine-guns configured for the anti-aircraft role while the remainder were equipped with M1 57mm anti-tank guns, newly issued to replace the obsolescent M3 37mm guns that had hitherto provided the Division's organic anti-armour protection.[51] The exception to all this was Major-General Ridgway, who elected to travel with a small staff aboard the Western Naval Task Force flagship the USS *Monrovia*, with Lieutenant-General Patton, ostensibly because of the latter's 'excellent communication facilities' and because the flagship was scheduled to anchor at the DIME Landing Area off Gela on D-Day, closest to the 505th Parachute RCT's objectives; as a contingency measure some of Ridgway's staff commanded by Major Emory S. Adams sailed with Major-General Bradley and his US II Corps staff aboard the HQ ship USS *Ancon*, bound for the adjacent CENT Landing Area.[52]

Gavin set his attack force to practising their tasks on full-size lay-outs of his objectives modelled from aerial reconnaissance photographs that included barbed wire entanglements, trenches and bunkers rendered exactly as they were on the ground in Sicily. The men repeatedly attacked their objectives by day and then in darkness after simulating post-drop reorganisation, using live ammunition, Bangalore Torpedoes and satchel charges.[53] While all this was going on Gavin undertook a convoluted journey to Malta on 10 June accompanied by Lieutenant-Colonel Charles W. Kouns and Major Edward Krause commanding the 3rd Battalion 505th and 3rd Battalion 504th Parachute Infantry Regiments respectively, along with at least two and possibly three Group commanders from the 52nd Troop Carrier Wing. On the night of 11-12 June, the party undertook the approximately eighty-five mile flight from Malta to HUSKY ONE's objectives near Gela, with Gavin travelling in the navigator's seat of an RAF de Havilland Mosquito night-fighter, likely from No. 256 Squadron based on Malta; according to one source Lieutenant-Colonel Arthur F. Gorham, commander of the 1st Battalion, 505th Parachute Infantry Regiment left Oujda on 12 June to carry out a similar reconnaissance flight from Malta.[54] The reconnaissance flights permitted the paratroop commanders and USAAF officers to identify all the projected DZs and objectives under similar moonlight conditions forecast for the invasion, and to gauge the Axis defences, which consisted of a handful of searchlights and anti-aircraft guns.[55]

The US Airborne contingent began moving east to its staging area in Tunisia at the same time as its British counterpart, beginning with the 52nd Troop Carrier Wing. It is unclear when the Wing HQ relocated but the 313th Troop Carrier Group departed Oujda for airfields around Kairouan, just over thirty miles west of Sousse, on Wednesday 16 June followed by the 61st and 314th Troop Carrier Groups on 21 and 26 June respectively; the 316th Troop Carrier Group moved to Enfidaville, thirty-five miles north-east of Kairouan, on 21 June.[56] The 82nd Airborne Division began its move east on Major-General Ridgway's order on Thursday 24 June 1943, just six weeks after it had arrived at Oujda, and was fully ensconced at ten separate locations around Kairouan within ten days; it is unclear how close the locations were to the 52nd Troop Carrier Wing's airfields. While some of the Division's personnel and equipment again moved by road or rail, a considerable portion was also moved by the 52nd Wing's C-47s, which provided a running shuttle between the locations that impacted on overall aircraft maintenance and readiness as well as taking up already scarce training time.[57]

While the heat at the Division's new home was potentially as draining as at Oujda, it was offset to an extent by the bivouacs being located in shady almond, olive and pear groves, and Kairouan was sufficiently close to the sea for a relatively cool breeze in the evenings. The troops were able to enjoy a USO show featuring Bob Hope and Frances Langford, units appear to have been shuttled by truck to open air showers and on 6 July the 505th Regiment celebrated its first anniversary with a barbecue featuring steak from three cattle purchased from local Arabs and sufficient beer obtained from unofficial sources to provide every man in the Regiment with at least a canteen cup apiece.[58] There were drawbacks however. One of the bivouac areas was surrounded in part by a large Moslem cemetery and the stench of decomposing bodies from the shallow and specially vented graves permeated the area, and for a while the supply system broke down, obliging some to subsist largely on Spam and marmalade.[59]

For the remainder of the time the paratroopers slated for HUSKY ONE and TWO attended to their weapons and equipment and, from 7 July, received detailed briefings on their unit missions and studied accompanying aerial photographs and sand-table models. Time had run out and like their counterparts in the 1st Airborne Division, the paratroopers of the 82nd Airborne Division were as ready as circumstances allowed. As Major-General Ridgway rather dramatically put it: 'By takeoff time...the men were so lean and tough, so mean and mad, that they would have jumped into the fires of torment just to get out of Africa. Gavin had done a prodigious job... and we were ready, right down to the last round of ammunition.'[60]

7

The Haft of the Spear

The HUSKY Sea Landing Force, March 1943 to Friday 9 July

The final plan for Operation HUSKY, entitled FORCE 141 Operation Instruction No. 2, appeared on Friday 21 May 1943. This was just seven weeks before the start of the launch window agreed by the Combined Chiefs of Staff the previous month, which scheduled the invasion to commence in the four-day period 10-14 July 1943.[1] D-Day was fixed at the beginning of the window for Saturday 10 July 1943, with H-Hour set for 02:45 to permit the initial waves of landing craft to run into the beaches under cover of darkness while allowing the airborne landings illumination from a waxing quarter-moon.[2] Initial planning had envisaged British and US landings at ten separate locations on the north-western, southern and eastern Sicilian coast staggered over several days, but the final plan discarded this in favour of simultaneous landings by the US 7th Army and British 8th Army, initially dubbed the Western and Eastern Task Forces respectively, concentrated in two areas in the south-east of the island. The US landings were to take place at three locations along the shallow, forty-mile-wide Bay of Gela on the eastern end of Sicily's southern aspect including the ports of Licata, Gela and Scoglitti; the British were to go ashore at two points on a thirty-five-mile length of coast extending from the Pachino Peninsula at the south-eastern tip of the island and extending up the Gulf of Noto on the east coast to just short of Syracuse.[3]

The initial wave of General Bernard Montgomery's 8th Army was to be delivered to its landing areas by three Royal Navy formations grouped under the Eastern Naval Task Force commanded by Vice-Admiral Sir Bertram Ramsay, sailing in the Forward Operations ship HMS *Antwerp*. These were FORCE A, commanded by Rear-Admiral Thomas Troubridge from the HQ ship HMS *Bulolo*; FORCE B commanded by Rear-Admiral Rhoderick McGrigor from the HQ ship HMS *Largs*; and FORCE V commanded by Rear-Admiral Sir Philip Vian from the HQ ship HMS *Hilary*.[4] Excluding RN warships, the Eastern Naval Task Force deployed ten assorted Landing Ships, 1,034 assorted landing craft and 171 transports and cargo vessels.[5] Responsibility for delivering the initial wave of Lieutenant-General George

S. Patton Jr.'s US 7th Army to its landing areas in the Bay of Gela lay with the Western Naval Task Force, commanded by Vice-Admiral Henry K. Hewitt from the converted Attack Transport USS *Monrovia*. The US landing force was divided across three sub-formations; Naval Task Force 86, sometimes referred to as JOSS FORCE, commanded by Rear-Admiral Richard L. Connolly from the converted seaplane tender USS *Biscayne*; Naval Task Force 81 commanded by Rear-Admiral John L. Hall, sometimes referred to as DIME FORCE, from the Attack Transport USS *Samuel Chase*; and Naval Task Force 85, sometimes referred to as CENT FORCE, commanded by Rear-Admiral Alan G. Kirk from the HQ ship USS *Ancon*.[6]

General Montgomery's 8th Army landings were grouped into two main areas, each assigned to a separate Corps with Commando and Special Air Service (SAS) troops attached to carry out special missions at the extremities of the thirty-five-mile landing front in the Gulf of Noto. Two of these special missions were to deal with Italian artillery batteries overlooking the beaches at its northern extremity. The 1st SAS Regiment's Special Raiding Squadron (SRS) commanded by Major Robert 'Paddy' Mayne was allotted the mission of landing on the rocky Maddalena Peninsula, seven miles north of the main landing area between it and Syracuse, before the main ACID landings began.[7] Carried aboard the LSI (H) HMS *Ulster Monarch*, the SRS was tasked to eliminate the Lamba Doria Battery, commanded by *Maggiore* Antonino Pandolfo equipped with three 152mm naval guns, and a suspected observation post located in a lighthouse at the tip of the Peninsula at the *Capo Porco di Murro*. The latter mission appears to have been codenamed Operation NARCISSUS but it is unclear if this label also included the attack on the Lamba Doria Battery. As a fail-safe, eliminating the Battery was also included in the 1st Airlanding Brigade's list of objectives, which also included a military radio station; the precise location of the latter is unclear.[8] The second mission was assigned to Lieutenant-Colonel John Durnford-Slater's No. 3 Commando, veterans of the raids on the Lofoten Islands, Vaagsö and Dieppe and now part of the 1st Special Service Brigade. No. 3 Commando was to land from the LSI HMS *Prins Albert* and the Hired Military Transport (HMT) *Dunera* and eliminate another gun battery north-west of Cassibile, three miles inland from the northern end of the British invasion frontage.[9]

The main landing was assigned to Rear-Admiral Troubridge's FORCE A carrying Lieutenant-General Miles Dempsey's XIII Corps, which had participated in the fighting in the Western Desert, Cyrenaica, Libya and Tunisia. Dempsey's primary mission was to secure the port of Syracuse in preparation for a general advance north to take the ports of Augusta and Catania, and XIII Corps was to land on an eight-mile stretch of coast between Avola and Cassibile, approximately ten miles south of Syracuse on the other side of the Maddalena Peninsula. The landing area, codenamed ACID, was divided into two adjoining sections, each of which was subdivided into two Sectors containing one or more Beaches, sometimes divided again into colour-coded sub-sectors. ACID NORTH, oriented on Cassibile, was assigned to Major-General Horatio Berney-Ficklin's 5th Division, a Regular formation that had joined Dempsey's Corps in Egypt in June 1943 after serving in Norway, France, Madagascar, India, Iraq and Syria over the three preceding years, an odyssey that earned the Division the nickname 'The Globetrotters'. All three of the Division's constituent infantry formations were to land on D-Day. 17th Brigade was allotted GEORGE Sector and 15th Brigade HOW Sector, the latter being sub-divided into GREEN, RED and AMBER Beaches while 13th Brigade, the Division reserve, was to land as directed according to the situation on D-Day.

The Division's mission was to establish a firm lodgement, relieve the 1st Airlanding Brigade holding the crossings over the River Anapo and parallel canal on the southern outskirts of Syracuse and secure the port. Major-General Sidney Kirkman's 50th (Northumbrian) Division, a veteran of the fighting across North Africa from November 1941, was to go ashore on the ACID SOUTH Landing Area, oriented on Avola. Only one of the Division's three constituent formations, 151st Brigade, was to land on D-Day, tasked to establish a firm beachhead and cover the left flank of the 5th Division's advance to Syracuse. Landing on JIG Sector, 151 Brigade was to put two battalions onto JIG GREEN Beach and the third onto JIG AMBER Beach; 69th Brigade and 168th Brigade were to land on subsequent days as part of XIII Corps' follow-up force, after which the 50th Division was to participate in the general advance on Augusta and Catania. Both Division's landings were designated ship-to-shore, meaning their troops, vehicles and equipment were carried to the invasion area aboard troop ships to be unloaded onto smaller landing craft just offshore for the final run in to the landing beach.[10]

Rear-Admiral McGrigor's FORCE B was tasked to deliver Lieutenant-General Oliver Leese's XXX Corps onto the rugged Pachino Peninsula at the south-eastern tip of Sicily, sixteen miles south of Avola. Leese was tasked to secure the airfield at Pachino, relieve XIII Corps at the Avola-Cassibile landing area, secure the latter's left flank by establishing a line twenty-five miles inland running west from Syracuse through Palazzolo Acreide to Ragusa and make contact with the US 7th Army landings to the west. The landings were to take place at two main locations on the Pachino Peninsula with a subsidiary flank landing further north. Major-General Douglas Wimberley's veteran 51st Highland Division, which had played a leading role in the fighting in the Western Desert, Libya and Tunisia, was to land at Portopalo Bay on the south-eastern aspect of the Peninsula, codenamed BARK SOUTH. Tasked to establish a secure beachhead, capture the town of Pachino before moving north to relieve XIII Corps and securing Palazzolo Acreide, the Division was to put two of its formations ashore on D-Day. 153rd Brigade was land on QUEEN Sector, RED or GREEN Beach, while 154th Brigade landed on QUEEN Sector, spread over GREEN 2, 3 and 4 Beaches, RED 2 Beach and RED 3 Beach; a small party from the Brigade may also have been detailed to secure Passero Island, a mile or so beyond Portopalo Bay's eastern headland. 152nd Brigade was to come ashore on the same beaches subsequently as part of the follow up force.

The 51st Division's right flank was to be protected by a subsidiary landing by Brigadier Roy Urquhart's 231st Brigade, formerly the 1st (Malta) Brigade, which was attached to the Division for the purpose. All three of 231st Brigade's battalions were to go ashore on NAN Sector of the BARK EAST Landing Area astride the small port of Marzamemi, five miles north of the main Division landings. The 51st Division landing was a shore-to-shore operation, with the bulk of the formation's troops, vehicles and equipment being carried aboard vessels that would deliver them directly onto the beach, including large capacity Landing Craft Infantry (LCI) backed by larger Landing Ships Infantry (LSI).[11] 231st Brigade's landing was a ship-to-shore operation, with the Brigade being shuttled ashore from the LSIs HMS *Keren* and HMS *Otranto* and troopship RMS *Strathnaver*.[12]

The second landing on the Pachino Peninsula involved Major-General Guy Simonds' 1st Canadian Division being delivered by Rear-Admiral Vian's FORCE V onto a landing area codenamed BARK WEST, located in the middle of the four-mile-wide bay between the *Punta Castellazo* (Castle Point) and *Punta delle Formiche* (Point of the Ants) on the western aspect of the Peninsula. Simonds' overall mission was to establish a secure lodgement, capture Pachino airfield west of the town and prepare to advance north-west to secure Ragusa and link up with the US 7th Army landings to the west. He, too, chose to land two-thirds of his force on D-Day, keeping the 3rd Canadian Brigade back aboard its LCIs and LCTs to be landed later when and where convenient as a follow-on force. BARK WEST was divided in two at a rocky central point known as *le Groticelle* (the Caves), into SUGAR Beach on the left and ROGER Beach on the right, the latter being assigned to the 1st Canadian Brigade and the former to the 2nd Canadian Brigade. The approach to the Landing Area was partially blocked by sandbars around eighty yards offshore, more severely off the right-hand ROGER Beach, and as a contingency measure Major-General Simonds ordered that the 1st Canadian Brigade's assault companies should be landed from Landing Craft Tank (LCT) carrying DUKWs in case of grounding; the landing was to be a ship-to-shore operation, with the division being carried ashore from its transport vessels in LCT, LCI and LCAs.

The 1st Canadian Brigade was tasked to eliminate an Italian gun battery around two miles inland from ROGER Beach near Maucini, secure the airfield west of Pachino, link up with the 51st Highland Division there and eliminate a second Italian artillery position a mile or so north-west of the town. The 2nd Canadian Brigade was to clear the enemy defences covering SUGAR Beach, advance inland through an area of marshland behind the beach and establish a line around two miles inland in readiness to advance west.[13] The Brigade was to be assisted in this by Nos. 40 and 41 Royal Marines (RM) Commandos from Brigadier Robert Laycock's 1st Special Service Brigade, which also included No. 3 Commando tasked to assist with the landings at the other end of the 8th Army landing frontage near Syracuse. The two RM Commandos sailed directly from the River Clyde to participate in the HUSKY landings – the former after suffering heavy casualties at Dieppe

– and were slated to land from the LSI HMS *Derbyshire* and transport MV *Durban Castle* onto a stretch of rocky shore just west of *Punta Castellazo*. Their task was to eliminate Italian artillery positions reportedly located just inland, reorganise and dig in on the high ground overlooking the landing place.[14]

Lieutenant-General Patton's US 7th Army landings were spread over three separate landing areas in the Bay of Gela codenamed JOSS, DIME and CENT, centred on the ports of Licata, Gela and Scoglitti respectively. The initial landings allotted a reinforced division to each of the three landing areas, JOSS under Patton's direct control initially from Vice-Admiral Hewitt's Flagship, the converted Attack Transport USS *Monrovia*; DIME and CENT were commanded by Major-General Omar Bradley's US II Corps, travelling aboard Rear-Admiral Kirk's Flagship, the HQ ship USS *Ancon*. The objectives of the initial US landings were relatively limited because 15th Army Group HQ considered the British drive north to the Strait of Messina from their landings on the south-eastern coast to be the primary focus of the invasion, with the US force acting in a subsidiary role as outlined in Alexander's Directive issued on 19 May 1943.

This sidelining generated discontent among some senior US officers, although perhaps surprisingly they did not initially include Patton, who assured General Sir Harold Alexander that he would do his 'goddamndest' to carry out his orders.[15] To this end the US initial objectives were to secure the ports of Gela and Licata for rapid reuse, capture the airfields at Biscari, Comiso, Licata and Ponte Olivo and establish a perimeter roughly twenty miles inland from the beaches. Dubbed the Yellow Line, the western end of this perimeter was anchored on a ridgeline west of Licata near Palma di Montechiaro on the coast and ran around fifty miles east near Campobello, Mazzarino, Caltagirone and Grammichele to the boundary with Montgomery's 8th Army near Vizzini.[16]

The most westerly US landing involved Rear-Admiral Connolly's Naval Task Force 86 delivering Major-General Lucian K. Truscott's US 3rd Infantry Division to the JOSS Landing Area astride Licata, at the western extremity of the Bay of Gela; as we have seen, due to its pivotal role of securing the western flank of the entire invasion frontage the 3rd Division remained under Lieutenant-General Patton's direct control. After landing at Fedala in November 1942 the 3rd Division had remained in French Morocco with its 30th Infantry Regiment providing security for the Casablanca Conference before Major-General Truscott assumed command two months later, on 8 March 1943. For his part, Truscott had headed a US Army Mission to British Combined Operation HQ where he conceiving the idea of forming US Army Ranger units as the equivalent to the British Commandos, worked on planning for Operation TORCH and commanded Task Force GOALPOST during the landing at Port Lyautey. After taking over the 3rd Infantry Division he instituted a rigorous training regime and introduced a requirement for all ranks to be capable of covering five miles in an hour on foot and maintain a rate of four miles an hour thereafter, which became known as the 'Truscott Trot'.

For HUSKY the 3rd Division's three Infantry Regiments were redesignated Regimental Combat Teams (RCTs) and in recognition of the Division's key role in protecting the western end of the landings, JOSS FORCE was reinforced with Major Hermann W. Dammer's 3rd Ranger Battalion and Combat Command A from the 2nd Armored Division. The latter was added on Patton's specific order, while the remainder of the 2nd Armored Division was designated as the US 7th Army's Floating Reserve, along with the 18th RCT from the US 1st Infantry Division. Combat Command A was initially designated as the 3rd Division's floating reserve along with the 900-strong 4e *Tabor de Goums Marocains*, a French-led Berber irregular mountain unit with 117 horses and 126 mules; they were included in the US Order of Battle on Lieutenant-General Eisenhower's orders as a sop to the Free French, scheduled to land on the fifth day of the invasion.[17]

Truscott's immediate mission was to secure the port of Licata with its road and rail crossings over the River Salso and nearby airfield by nightfall on D-Day, before extending his perimeter inland to the Yellow Line to protect the left flank of the US landings and establishing contact with the US II Corps landings to the east. To those ends the Division was to carry out a shore-to-shore landing operation at four separate locations on a ten-mile stretch of coast centred on Licata, two located on either side of the port. The most far flung was codenamed RED Beach, located west of the *Punta San Nicola* five miles west of Licata, which was allocated to the 7th RCT tasked to secure the immediate landing area and establish blocking positions to the west and north. GREEN Beach, straddling the *Rocca Mollarella* headland just over a mile to the east, was assigned to the 3rd Ranger Battalion and the 2nd Battalion, 15th RCT tasked to envelope Licata from the west. The remaining two battalions of the 15th RCT were to complete the envelopment of Licata by moving in from YELLOW Beach three miles east of the port, while the 30th RCT landed on the adjacent BLUE Beach tasked to establish protective positions to the north and east of the JOSS Landing Area and make contact with the adjacent DIME Landing Area at Gela.[18] In addition to the landing force's troops, vehicles and equipment, the assault convoy also carried sufficient food, fuel and other supplies, calculated as 'days of maintenance', to support them for seven days, along with ammunition for one and one-sixth units of fire; the latter was the estimated amount of ammunition a unit or formation was expected to expend from all weapons in a day of heavy fighting. This was to be augmented by a follow-up convoy carrying the same amount of maintenance and units of fire on D-Day Plus Four and another with the same payload on D-Day Plus Eight.[19]

The other two US landings to the east of Licata were under the auspices of Major-General Bradley's US II Corps. On the left, Rear-Admiral Hall's Naval Task Force 81 was to land Major-General Terry Allen's US 1st Infantry Division, a veteran of Operation TORCH and the fighting in Tunisia, on the DIME Landing Area at Gela, eighteen miles east of Licata. The landing was to be a mixture of shore-to-shore and ship-to-shore operations and Major-General Allen's formation was reinforced with FORCE X, made up of the 1st and 4th Ranger Battalions, elements of the 1st Battalion 39th Combat Engineer Regiment, the 1st Battalion 531st Engineer Shore Regiment and three companies from the 4.2-inch mortar equipped 83rd Chemical Battalion, all under the command of Lieutenant-Colonel William O. Darby.[20] Patton considered Gela would be the hardest of the projected landings and he specifically requested Eisenhower to employ Allen's veteran formation in the initial HUSKY landing in place of the originally slated US 36th Infantry Division, an untested Texas National Guard formation; Patton reportedly informed Eisenhower: 'I want those sons of bitches' from the veteran Division, at least in part because the US II Corps' other D-Day assault unit, the US 45th Infantry Division, was also an untested National Guard formation.[21]

Major-General Allen's DIME FORCE was tasked to secure Gela, capture the Gela-Farello airfield two miles inland from the landing area, link up with the 505th Parachute Infantry Regiment on the high ground north of the port toward Niscemi and dominate the airfield at Ponte Olivo seven miles north of Gela. While the 1st Division's 18th RCT was designated US II Corps' floating reserve, the remainder of Major-General Allen's formation was to be delivered onto six beaches along a five-mile stretch of coastline running east from Gela. RED and GREEN Beaches, directly on the port frontage, were allotted to the Rangers of Lieutenant-Colonel Darby's FORCE X, tasked to secure Gela. The remaining four beaches were located east of the port and of the mouth of the River Gela. The 26th RCT was assigned YELLOW and BLUE Beaches on the left with the 1st Battalion tasked to assist FORCE X if required, while the remainder of the RCT secured the beach area, captured the Gela-Farello airfield and pushed north toward the second airfield at Ponte Olivo; the 16th RCT was tasked to advance north-east from RED 2 and GREEN 2 Beaches on the right, toward Priolo and Niscemi to link up with the 505th Parachute Infantry Regiment.[22] With regard to logistics, the US 1st Infantry Division was allotted additional resources to resupply the 505th Parachute Infantry Regiment operating in its area, and the DIME assault convoy therefore carried seven days' maintenance and two and one-third units of fire to cover combined Divisional and Airborne requirements. This was again scheduled for augmentation by a convoy carrying an additional seven days' maintenance and one and one-sixth units of fire on D-Day Plus Four and a further fourteen days' maintenance and two and one-third units of fire on another convoy on D-Day Plus Eight; it is unclear if the latter two convoys also included supplies and ammunition for the Airborne units in the DIME FORCE area or whether they were supplied separately from the 'emergency stockpile' of seven days' maintenance and two and one-third units of fire cached near Kairouan for use by the 82nd Airborne Division.[23]

The most easterly US landing was to be carried out by Major-General Troy C. Middleton's US 45th Infantry Division, an Oklahoma National Guard formation that sailed from Hampton Roads on Tuesday 8 June 1943 aboard between eighteen and twenty-five attack transports as part of Convoy UGF-9, accompanied by the HQ ship USS *Ancon*, three cruisers and nineteen destroyers; the convoy arrived in North Africa without incident on 22 June where Major-General Middleton's formation was assigned to the HUSKY invasion force.[24] The Division's combat-loaded vehicles and equipment were left aboard the transports while the troops trained for the invasion at Arzew in French Morocco, and were integrated directly into the HUSKY landing plan as a complete and ready entity.[25] The 45th Division was thus to be delivered in a ship-to-shore operation by Rear-Admiral Alan G. Kirk's Naval Task Force 85 onto the fifteen-mile long CENT Landing Area running from the mouth of the River Acate, seven miles south-east of Gela, to the *Punta Braccetto*.[26] Kirk's force also carried US II Corps HQ, with Major-General Bradley and a few key staff officers travelling aboard the *Ancon* while the remainder were spread between five LSTs in the main assault convoys. CENT FORCE was tasked to relieve elements of the 505th Parachute Infantry Regiment holding road and rail crossings over the River Acate, capture the port of Scoglitti and town of Vittoria, drive inland to capture the airfields near the towns of Biscari and Comiso and make contact with British XXX Corps on the right of the US landings.

The landings were spread over six beaches grouped into two clusters of three at either end of the CENT Landing Area, one on the east side of the mouth of the River Acate and the other astride the *Punta Braccetto*. At the former, RED Beach was allocated to the 180th RCT, tasked to relieve the paratroopers holding the Acate crossings before driving inland to secure the town of Biscari and the nearby airfield while the 179th RCT was to land on the adjacent GREEN and YELLOW Beaches and despatch a battalion eight miles south-east along the coast to secure Scoglitti, while the remainder of the RCT moved inland to capture Vittoria and assist in capturing Comiso if required. The second cluster of smaller beaches at the *Punta Braccetto*, codenamed GREEN 2, YELLOW 2 and BLUE 2, were allotted to the 157th RCT tasked to push twelve miles inland to capture Comiso town and airfield, protect US II Corps' right flank and establish contact with the 1st Canadian Division at Ragusa, fifteen miles north-east of the beaches on the boundary between the British and US Corps.[27] For reasons that are unclear the CENT assault and D-Day Plus Four follow-up convoys carried a larger logistic load than the other two US Divisions, amounting to twenty-one days' maintenance and ten units of fire, while the D-Day Plus Eight supply convoy scaled this back to seven days' maintenance and one and one-sixth units of fire. In addition, for all three Divisions three floating reserves were set up at Algiers, Bizerte and Oran, each consisting of seven vessels pre-loaded with twenty days' maintenance and four units of fire to be delivered over the beach after D-Day Plus Fourteen as called, and an additional large reserve was established near Bizerte containing fifteen days' maintenance and three and a half units of fire for 140,000 men along with twenty per cent of the combat vehicles, ten per cent of the general purpose vehicles and ten per cent of weapons for the entire US 7th Army contingent.[28]

Assembling the naval force to carry and protect the land invasion force was a prodigious task in itself, involving up to 3,370 assorted vessels ranging from the 37,000-ton battleships HMS *Rodney* to nine-ton Landing Craft Assault.[29] Vice-Admiral Ramsay's Eastern Naval Task Force deployed 320 Royal Navy warships including six battleships, two Fleet carriers, ten cruisers, seventy-one destroyers, 229 assorted escort, minesweeper and coastal craft and twenty-three submarines, seven of the latter being stationed off the Landing Areas as beacon vessels. This armada was spread across the three assault formations, FORCES A, B and V and two covering formations. Vice-Admiral Sir Algernon Willis' FORCE H was a semi-autonomous heavy formation based in the Mediterranean, divided into the 1st, 2nd and 3rd Divisions based at Mers-El-Kébir, Alexandria and Gibraltar respectively. The 3rd Division, temporarily dubbed FORCE Z and including the battleships HMS *Howe* and *King George V*, remained in the Western Mediterranean tasked to escort the HUSKY invasion convoys approaching Sicily from the west and to make a demonstration against the western end of the island as a deception measure. The 1st and 2nd Divisions, including the battleships HMS *Nelson*, *Rodney*, *Valiant* and *Warspite* and the aircraft carriers HMS *Formidable* and *Indomitable*, rendezvoused north of the Gulf of Sirte at 06:00 on 9 July before moving north to take up station in the Ionian Sea between Italy and Greece; this positioning was intended in part to counter any Axis surface moves against the Eastern Naval Task Force's invasion fleet to the west, and in part to support Operation BARCLAY, the ongoing Allied strategic deception effort, by supporting the possibility of Allied landings in Greece.[30] FORCE K, commanded by Rear-Admiral Cecil Harcourt from the cruiser HMS *Cleopatra*, deployed four cruisers including the *Cleopatra*, HMS *Aurora* and HMS *Newfoundland*, and six destroyers to provide close protection to the Eastern Naval Task Force's assault convoys before providing gunfire support for the landings and protecting the northern extremity of the 8th Army Landing area.[31] As it was not involved in providing vessels for the covering Forces, Vice-Admiral Hewitt's Western Naval Task Force deployed fewer vessels, although the US force was still substantial, numbering at least 147 US Navy warships including five cruisers, forty-eight destroyers, eight minesweepers and eighty-three assorted coastal craft.[32]

In addition to the British covering forces all the invasion convoys also contained a good deal of combat power in their own right. On the US side Naval Task Force 81 included two cruisers, thirteen destroyers and the monitor HMS *Abercrombie* for example. Naval Task Force 85 included one cruiser and sixteen destroyers and Naval Task Force 86 two cruisers and eight destroyers. The situation was similar in the British assault convoys where the anti-aircraft cruiser HMS *Carlisle*, cruisers HMS *Mauritius* & *Uganda* and the monitor HMS *Erebus* were seconded to FORCE A, the cruiser HMS *Orion* and anti-aircraft cruiser HMS *Colombo* to FORCE B and the monitor HMS *Roberts* to FORCE V, all supported by a number of destroyers assigned to each FORCE.[33] This firepower was not to be deployed in softening the Axis defences prior to the landings however. In the US case there was some disagreement, with the Army planners feeling such pre-preparation would compromise the element of surprise for the sea assault and more especially the airborne landings behind the landing areas, while the Navy planners felt that a combination of large surface forces approaching the landing areas in moonlight, the ongoing aerial bombing campaign and the airborne landings would negate any surprise in any case. In the event the Army view prevailed and there was to be no sea bombardment until the landing force was going ashore, although a detailed gunnery programme with targets pre-selected by the Army planners was prepared as a contingency against enemy countermeasures, should the landing forces be detected well out to sea.

The Army also intended to make full use of naval gunfire support once the landings were underway and to that end each division HQ staff was allotted a Naval Gunfire Liaison Officer, special fire control and aerial observation arrangements were made and the Army artillery battalions involved formed special fire control parties trained in observing and controlling naval gunfire on ground targets.[34] The embargo on pre-landing sea bombardment also appears to have applied to the British landing beaches and the landing forces there appear to have planned to make less use of naval gunfire support for reasons that are unclear; as the British Official History put it '...the Americans on the whole were prepared to use naval gun-fire more freely than the British in support of troops.'[35] The British preference appears to have been to put artillery units ashore in the forefront of their landings, with guns from the 165th Field Regiment RA, 11th (HAC) Regiment RA and 142nd Field Regiment RA scheduled to be in action at BARK EAST, BARK SOUTH and BARK WEST Landing Areas respectively shortly after the landings commenced, for example.[36]

Unsurprisingly, landing vessels were the most numerous craft in the invasion force, in terms of both numbers and variations. The Eastern Naval Task Force included 1,042 assorted RN-crewed landing vessels, two-thirds of the entire force and the 1,124 US landing vessels included in the Western Naval Task Force made a up a similar proportion of the overall US naval force.[37] Leaving aside the large transport vessels configured as troopships such as the custom-built HMS *Dilwara* or converted liner RMS *Strathnaver*, landing vessels were generally divided into two basic categories; larger ocean-going landing ships capable of moving landing forces directly from friendly ports to landing areas, and smaller landing craft for delivering troops, vehicles and equipment onto the beach from transports moored offshore. At the larger end of the scale for shore-to-shore operations were the various British Landing Ship Infantry (LSI), converted merchant vessels sub-designated Small, Medium and Large, dependent on capacity. The LSI (L) HMS *Glengyle* was a converted 10,000-ton cargo ship, capable of carrying 700 troops and equipped with twenty-four Landing Craft Assault (LCA) and three Landing Craft Mechanized (LCM) for example; the LSI (M) HMS *Princess Beatrix* was a 4,000-ton converted North Sea ferry capable of carrying 370 troops equipped with six LCA and two Landing Craft Mechanised while the LSI (S) HMS *Prins Albert* was a converted 3,000-ton cross-Channel ferry capable of carrying 250 troops equipped with eight LCA.[38]

The other class of large ocean-going landing vessel was configured to carry vehicles, specifically tanks, grouped under the unsurprising heading of Landing Ship Tank (LST); as they were also designed to deliver their loads directly onto the beach they blurred the distinction between landing ships and landing craft. The first such vessels, dubbed LST Mk. 1, were a British initiative that involved modifying the shallow-draught Maracaibo tankers *Bachaquero*, *Misoa* and *Tasajera* by stripping out their oil tanks to create a well deck and modifying their bows with a large door that doubled as a ramp for unloading vehicles directly onto the beach; all three vessels had participated in the TORCH landings at Oran with mixed results. HMS *Misoa* was 380 feet long, displaced just under 4,800 tons fully laden, could accommodate 217 troops along with eighteen thirty-ton tanks or thirty-three heavy trucks, and for HUSKY was slated to deliver elements of British XIII Corps onto the ACID Landing Area on D-Day.

The subsequent LST Mk. 2 was a standardised US-built vessel that came out of discussions between the Admiralty and US Navy's Bureau of Ships in November 1941, with the first batch of completed vessels leaving their construction docks eleven months later in October 1942. Just over a thousand were built in the course of the war, mainly by five concerns with works in Illinois, Indiana and Pennsylvania and were employed by the US Navy and the RN and Royal Canadian Navy (RCN) via the Lend-Lease programme. 328 feet long, displacing 3,880 tons fully loaded and capable of twelve knots, the LST Mk. 2 carried between two and six nine-ton Landing Craft Vehicle Personnel (LCVP), could accommodate approximately 140 troops and carry up to twenty M4 Sherman Medium tanks, thirty-nine M3/M5 Light tanks or twenty-two DUKWs on its internal tank deck; approximately thirty light vehicles could also be stowed on the upper deck for unloading by crane. Many of the Sicilian landing beaches were fronted by substantial sandbars or false beaches, which prevented the standard LSTs from running ashore despite their shallow eight-foot draught, a problem that had also manifested during the landings at Oran. To counter this, some vessels carried pontoon sections to form a bridge across the deep runnels while others were modified with hinged sections at the bow to permit vehicles to be driven directly onto smaller Landing Craft Tank (LCT); it is unclear how many LSTs were so modified.[39]

At the other end of the scale were a confusing plethora of British- and US-designed and produced landing craft which frequently duplicated each other in form and function; all were intended to ground themselves on the shore to permit their loads to be disgorged directly onto the beach before hauling themselves back off using winches and kedge anchors, for example. With regard to tank carriers, the British produced four successive Landing Craft Tank (LCT) versions, the Mk. 3 being the largest with a length of 192 feet, displacement of 640 tons and a draught of just under four feet; the vessel was capable of nine knots while carrying five M4 tanks for unloading via a bow ramp and 235 were built in the course of the war. A notable variant of the British vessel employed in the Sicily landings was the Landing

Craft Rocket (LCR) which featured a welded-up ramp and a modified tank deck filled with launcher racks for over a thousand 5-inch RP-3 rockets, a 60-pound projectile with a five-pound explosive warhead; the rockets were fired in salvoes as the vessel approached the beach, with the vessel carrying sufficient ammunition for twenty-four salvos capable of blanketing an area up to a thousand yards inland. The US equivalent LCT Mk. 5 was also equipped with a bow ramp and was significantly smaller at 117-feet long with a displacement of 286 tons and a draught of just under three feet, but with a tank deck also capable of accommodating five M4 Mediums or nine trucks and a speed of eight knots; in all, 956 Mk. 5s were constructed and the subsequent US LCT Mk. 6 was essentially identical but with the addition of a stern gate that permitted it to be used as an unloading bridge by linking with other craft.

Additional vehicle transport capacity was provided by the smaller Landing Craft Mechanised (LCM). The British LCM 1 was forty-eight feet long, displaced twenty-one tons and could carry vehicles up to sixteen tons or 100 troops at ten knots, while the US LCM 2 was heavier at twenty-nine tons but slightly shorter and slower at forty-five feet long and seven and a half knots top speed, and a slightly smaller payload at thirteen and a half tons. The largest personnel carrying craft was the US-built Landing Craft Infantry (Large) or LCI (L), of which 293 were built in three minor variations at ten US shipyards from early1943 in response to an Admiralty requirement for a craft with a larger capacity than their existing assault craft; 211 of the total were supplied to the RN via Lend-Lease. 158 feet long and with a displacement of 386 tons, the LCI(L) had a draught of just under six feet, a top speed of sixteen knots, a range of 500 nautical miles and a capacity of 180 troops who initially disembarked via gangways on either side of the bow and via a narrow bow ramp in the final variation that also increased the troop capacity to 210; the restricted egress usually led to the LCI(L) being assigned to follow-on waves rather than assault missions.

At the smallest end of the scale were the US Landing Craft Vehicle Personnel (LCVP) and British Landing Craft Assault (LCA). The former are often referred to as Higgins boats after the manufacturer Higgins Industries of New Orleans, which produced or sub-contracted the building of 23,358 examples, while approximately 2,000 of the latter were built or sub-contracted by John I. Thornycroft Co. Ltd. at Woolston near Southampton. With a length and displacement of 36 feet & eight tons and 42 feet & nine tons respectively, a draught of around two feet, egress via a large bow ramp and a troop capacity of thirty-six, the craft were essentially the same, apart from the LCVP being capable of carrying a Jeep and reduced complement of twelve troops and its twelve-knot top speed being two knots or more faster than the British craft. Both were of wooden construction, the latter of mahogany and the US craft of plywood. Finally, the lower-level ship-to-shore movement of supplies was to be augmented with the first large-scale deployment of the new amphibious DUKW, imaginatively nicknamed the 'Duck'; the acronym was derived from the manufacturer's administrative codes, specifically **D**esign (year 1942) **U**tility (amphibious) **K** (all-wheel drive) **W** (dual rear axles). Specifically designed for resupplying units engaged in amphibious operations, the DUKW was a standard US Army 2.5 ton GMC truck factory-modified with a specially manufactured reinforced windscreen atop a boxy watertight hull with a propeller and bilge pump, and was capable of carrying just over two tons of cargo, up to fifty troops or an M2A1 105mm howitzer at a top speed of just over six miles per hour on water and fifty miles per hour on roads. A total of 21,147 examples were built before production ceased in 1945 by General Motors and Chevrolet plants in Michigan and Missouri respectively, 2,000 of which were supplied to Britain under Lend-Lease.[40] Lieutenant-General Eisenhower had requested 400 of the vehicles at the beginning of March 1943 and the first examples so impressed their testers that Lieutenant-General Patton doubled the requirement; by the time HUSKY was launched over a thousand were present in the Mediterranean Theatre.[41]

It is unclear if the latter total included the approximately 350 British DUKWs employed in the HUSKY landings. Of these, XIII Corps deployed 140 vehicles, ninety to the 5th Division and fifty to the 50th Division while XXX Corps allotted nine to 231 Infantry Brigade and 105 to the 51st Highland Division. The 1st Canadian Division employed ninety-six from a batch of 100 delivered to the Division in the UK shortly before deploying to the Mediterranean and the last-minute arrival of these vehicles in the UK in early June caused some concern for the Division's combat loading; the training of driver/mechanics was also affected as although instructors were flown in especially from North Africa, there were only two DUKWs in the UK, based at the No. 1 Combined Training Centre at Inverary, but the batch arrived in time to provide their crews with some basic training.[42]

Impressive as it was from a numerical and technical standpoint, the Allied landing armada was not without problems, largely connected to the untried nature of new equipment and lack of time for familiarisation training and to work out the operational details and procedures. Despite its promise the DUKW had not been intensively tested under operational conditions for example, and one DUKW reportedly sank immediately on launching from an LST off Sicily because it had been overloaded with ten rather than two tons of ammunition.[43] Neither was there data on how many personnel could be safely and comfortably embarked on LSTs or LCTs or for how long, and some naval officers thought the LCI(L) s might be obliged to shuttle their troops ashore in small boats because none of those craft had been beached successfully close enough to shore for their passengers to debark as planned.[44]

The HUSKY plan required the fast assault convoys to be on station off the six landing areas by 00:15 on Saturday 10 July, in order to permit time for loading and launching the initial waves of landing vessels, forming up and running in to hit the landing beaches under cover of darkness at 02:45.[45] Given the sheer number of vessels involved and the fact they were leaving from locations spread over more than 2,500 miles of coastline from Algeria to Egypt and beyond, this was a highly complex and impressive piece of staff work in its own right, that began days before the landings were to commence. On 4 July the US 45th Infantry Division began re-embarking on the thirteen transports docked at Oran in Algeria that had delivered them there from Hampton Roads just thirteen days earlier. Dubbed NCF-1, the convoy sailed from Oran at around 17:40 accompanied by Vice-Admiral Hewitt's flagship the *Monrovia* on Tuesday 6 July, D-Day Minus Four, bound for the Western Naval Task Force rendezvous area west of Malta, a journey of a thousand miles.[46] At least five more transports carrying elements of the US 1st Infantry Division destined for the DIME Landing Area sailed from Algiers on Wednesday 7 July accompanied by the oiler USS *Niobrara* and the LSI's HMS *Prince Charles* and HMS *Prince Leopold*; the grouping joined Convoy NCF-1 north-east of Djidjelli, 150 east of Algiers just after 13:30 the same day.[47] In the east Rear-Admiral Troubridge's FORCE A also sailed on 6 July, carrying XIII Corps' assault elements about 1,300 miles from Port Said in Egypt to the Eastern Naval Task Force rendezvous area fifty miles south of Malta, having previously sailed from the Clyde in March 1943 to Suez via the Cape of Good Hope.[48] FORCE A was accompanied by the LSIs HMS *Keren* and HMS *Otranto* and the troopship HMS *Strathnaver* carrying 231st Infantry Brigade from XXX Corps ultimately bound for the BARK EAST Landing Area.[49]

The remaining assault convoys had shorter journeys and consequently shorter transit times to their rendezvous area. The US 3rd Infantry Division's assault elements bound for the JOSS Landing Area sailed for the western rendezvous area north-west of Malta on 8 and 9 July in three convoys dubbed TJF-1, TJM-1 and TJS-1 sailing from Bizerte, Tunis and Sousse in Tunisia respectively, while FORCE B carried the 51st Highland Division to the eastern rendezvous in two convoys from Sfax codenamed SBF-1 and SBM-1; the former sailed on 8 July, D-Day Minus Two, and included the HQ ship HMS *Largs*, the LSI(L) HMS *Royal Scotsman* and HMS *Royal Ulsterman* and the LSI(S) HMS *Princess Beatrix* and HMS *Queen Emma*.[50] The exception to this was Rear-Admiral Vian's FORCE V carrying the 1st Canadian Division to the BARK WEST Landing Area. The latter had sailed from the Clyde on 18 June 1943 and then to Gibraltar as part of Convoy WS31/KMF-17 before heading directly for Sicily. Renamed Convoy KMF-18, the Sicily-bound force consisted of eight LSI including a HQ variant, three LST(1), five cargo vessels, two troopships and the LSI (Gantry) RFA *Derwentdale* escorted by the anti-aircraft cruiser HMS *Ulster Queen*, twelve destroyers, two frigates, five sloops and a minesweeper.[51] It is unclear precisely when KMF-18 set out from Gibraltar but it overhauled NCF-1 approximately seventy miles east of Djidjelli just after 18:00 on Wednesday 7 July, en route to the Eastern Naval Task Force rendezvous area.[52] On 6 July KMF-18 was followed from Gibraltar by the slower follow-up Convoy KMS-19, which had also sailed earlier from the Clyde. Scheduled to arrive off the ACID Landing Area on 16 July, D-Day Plus Six, KMS-19 was commanded by Rear-Admiral Edward

Cochrane and was made up of thirty-nine cargo vessels, six LST and a tanker escorted by the corvettes HMS *Bluebell* and HMS *Camellia*.[53]

The fast convoys destined for the British and Canadian Landing Areas rendezvoused as arranged at midday on Friday 9 July 1943 and their US counterparts two hours later. Up to this point the entire enterprise had been under the command of Admiral of the Fleet Sir Andrew Cunningham, Naval Commander-in-Chief Mediterranean, but the rendezvous marked the point where control of the assault forces devolved to the individual Task Force commanders. The Eastern Naval Task Force thus came under command of Vice-Admiral Sir Bertram Ramsay in the Forward Operations ship HMS *Antwerp*, who in turn devolved control of the individual landing forces to their commanders. Rear-Admiral Thomas Troubridge thus directed FORCE A forty to fifty miles east of Malta before heading north to the ACID Landing Area in the Gulf of Noto along with Rear-Admiral Rhoderick McGrigor's FORCE B destined for the eastern BARK Landing Area on the Pachino Peninsula, while Rear-Admiral Sir Philip Vian directed FORCE V to the west of the island of Gozo near Malta en route to the western BARK Landing Areas on the other side of the Peninsula.[54]

Shortly thereafter, command of the Western Naval Task Force devolved to Vice-Admiral Henry K. Hewitt aboard the Attack Transport USS *Monrovia*, who also directed JOSS, DIME and CENT FORCES west of Gozo toward their respective landing beaches; the US flagship passed the island at just after 16:30.[55] By this point nature was taking a less than helpful hand in proceedings. The Mediterranean weather had been calm in the three days or so while the invasion fleet had been concentrating, but the wind began to rise in the morning of 9 July and by the time the two Naval Task Forces had rendezvoused and set off for their landing areas it had risen to Force 6, almost forty miles per hour.

The result was 'a short, steep sea' that tossed the heavily laden vessels and grew worse when the invasion force began to move north, as the change of course put the convoys broadside on to the full fury of the wind and waves, which affected the lighter, shallow-draught landing vessels especially badly.[56] The LSIs rolled even more than normal to the discomfort of the hapless troops occupying the cramped on-board accommodation, the vehicles aboard some LSTs began to shift against their chain lashings while some the blunt-nosed LCTs were unable to keep up with their convoys despite operating their engines at full power and began to drop out of formation.[57] This confirmed and heightened Admiral Cunningham's previously expressed concerns that the overall slow speed of the invasion convoys and consequent long transit time would compromise surprise, which were borne out; Axis reconnaissance aircraft spotted five convoys moving north of Malta at around 17:30 on 9 July with two further sightings at 19:10 and 20:30, which prompted a garrison stand-to between 17:40 and 19:30 and again at 22:20.[58]

The straggling by the landing vessels prompted Admiral Troubridge to prepare for the ACID landings to go ahead without the assault force's support weapons to hand, and the ripples caused by the inclement weather reached to the very top of the Allied hierarchy. Admiral Cunningham's HQ was located in tunnels beneath an artillery fort in Valletta Harbour in Malta and he was joined there for the launch of HUSKY by Lieutenant-General Eisenhower, his deputy and commander of the 15th Army Group General Alexander, General Montgomery and Air Chief Marshal Tedder. The foul weather led to discussion on whether the invasion should be postponed for twenty-four hours, rendered the more urgent by the fact it would take an estimated four hours to disseminate the postponement order to all vessels in the invasion convoys; in the event Eisenhower decided against postponement after conferring with Cunningham's meteorological experts and cabled his decision to General Marshall in Washington. The die was cast and the three thousand ships and many more thousands of men of the HUSKY invasion force continued on their now less than serried way toward their target to the north.

8

The Other Side of the Hill

The Axis Defenders of Sicily, March to Friday 9 July

Fewer than a hundred miles north of the rolling and pitching Allied invasion convoys ploughing their way through the heavy seas, the Axis garrison of Sicily were awaiting developments. Responsibility for defending the island lay with the Italian *6ª Armata* based on Sicily with additional responsibility for an area of Calabria on the Italian mainland, but concentration on the island as a distinct defensive entity in its own right began with the appointment of *Generale di Corpo d'Armata* Mario Roatta, a former *Regio Esercito* Chief-of-Staff, to the post of *Comandante Designato d' Armata* to the *6ª Armata* with effect from 5 February 1943. Initially, *6ª Armata* control only extended to the *Regio Esercito* elements on the island, totalling two corps fielding eight assorted divisions, two brigades and over a dozen smaller groupings; the *Regia Aeronautica*, *Regia Marina* and Blackshirt *Milizia Volontaria per la Sicurezza Nazionale* (*MVSN*) personnel on the island continued to operate independently under their own command arrangements. Roatta was initially obliged to liaise with seven military or paramilitary and nine civilian provincial authorities. This changed when the status of *6ª Armata* HQ was upgraded to *Comando delle Forze Armate Sicilia* (Armed Forces Command Sicily) which gave Roatta authority over all Italian military forces on the island as well as the civilian authorities, with the exception of the three *Piazze Militari Marittime* (roughly Naval Fortress Areas) straddling the Straits of Messina, encompassing Augusta and Syracuse, and at Trapani which remained under control of *Comando Militare Marittimo Autonomo della Sicilia*; two similar defended areas at Catania and Palermo did come under *6ª Armata* control.[1]

With the command and control question rectified, *Generale* Roatta set about organising his defence. Every military unit was assigned a designated sector of coastline to defend, military personnel and civilian labour was set to work improving and expanding existing beach defences and constructing a backstop line of fortifications twelve to fifteen miles inland from the beaches, improving communications and building supply stockpiles. Measures for the evacuation of civilians from potential battle areas were also put in place. Progress was hampered by shortages of weapons, materiel and manpower however, and local politics proved to be Roatta's undoing after the Sicilian population took umbrage at a perceived slur to their patriotism in one of his proclamations.

Comando Supremo addressed the resultant furore by replacing *Generale* Roatta as head of *6ª Armata* on 30 May 1943. His replacement was sixty-six-year-old *Generale d'Armata* Alfredo Guzzoni, a former Undersecretary of War and Deputy Chief of *Comando Supremo* who had been recalled from retirement in October 1942; Roatta was elevated to *Superesercito* (Chief of the Army General Staff) in Rome.[2] Guzzoni's report on taking command of the *6ª Armata* highlighted how little his predecessor had been able to achieve during his three months in Sicily. The island was receiving a maximum 2,000 tons of supplies per day to meet a daily minimum requirement for military and civilian purposes of 8,000 tons, which inevitably impacted on morale and prompted widespread black-market activity. There were no continuous lengths of defence works outside the naval fortress areas and the coastal defence units were badly led, poorly equipped and understrength, with battalions being allotted frontages of up to twenty-five miles. The *206ª Divisione Costiera* (coastal division) was responsible for defending an approximately ninety-mile stretch of coast that included the ACID and BARK Landing Areas with just thirty-four mortars and fifty-six field guns.[3] The situation inland was even worse. Only a handful of roadblocks of dubious tactical utility had been completed and few weapons and personnel had been deployed; a twelve-mile stretch of road running inland from Licata to Campobello was defended by a single 47mm anti-tank gun. The inland blocking line consisted of 'a beautiful colored pencil mark on a map.'[4]

By 10 July 1943 *Generale* Guzzoni was commanding approximately 200,000 Italian personnel from his HQ at Enna in the centre of the island divided into two corps, *Generale di Corpo d'Armata* Mario Arisio's *12° Corpo* headquartered at Corleone in the west of the island, and *Generale di Corpo d'Armata* Carlo Rossi's *16° Corpo* with its HQ at Piazza Armerina, twenty miles north of Gela.[5] The former included the *202ª*, *207ª* and *208ª Divisioni Costiere*, deployed respectively along the coast running west from Licata, around the western tip of the island, the Trapani fortress area and along the northern aspect to the boundary with the *Comando Porto* Palermo defensive zone. *Generale* Arisio's main combat power resided in the *26ª Assietta Divisione* and *28ª Aosta Divisione*, deployed to the south-west and north-west of Corleone respectively. The *Assietta Divisione*, commanded by *Generale di Divisione* Francesco Scotti, was recruited largely from the Asti region in the Italian Piedmont and had participated in the invasions of southern France and Yugoslavia before being posted to Sicily in May 1941, while *Generale di Divisione* Giacomo Romano's *Aosta Divisione* had been stationed on the island throughout the war and was made up largely of Sicilians; both formations were understrength, over reliant on horse-drawn transport and lacked modern artillery, artillery ammunition and communications equipment. The *Aosta* was considered especially poorly trained.[6]

The two divisions were augmented with three *Gruppi Mobili* (mobile groups) lettered A through C and four *Gruppi Tattici* (tactical groups). The former were each built around units of light armoured vehicles, generally up to company size, equipped with Italian L3 tankettes, *Semovente* 47mm self-propelled guns or captured French Renault R35 tanks, in some instances augmented with towed anti-tank guns and light artillery while the latter were built around *Bersaglieri* or *MVSN* elements up to battalion size reinforced with machine-gun, light artillery and motorcycle elements.[7] The mobile and tactical groups were stationed around the periphery of the *12° Corpo* area, presumably to act as a tripwire to allow the larger formations time to deploy in the event of an invasion.

The *16° Corpo* was of a similar size and composition but divided into more elements and was responsible for more ground. *Generale di Divisione* Achille d'Havet's *206ª Divisione Costiera* was responsible for the coastline running from the eastern end of the Bay of Gela, around the Pachino Peninsula and north up the Gulf of Noto to the southern boundary of the Augusta-Syracuse *Piazze Militari Marittime*, while *Generale di Divisione* Carlo Gotti's *213ª Divisione Costiera* covered the area north of the fortress area, straddling the *Comando Porto* Catania and running up to the boundary with the Messina *Piazze Militari Marittime*. Two smaller coastal defence units were responsible for areas on the northern and southern aspects of the island. In the south the *18° Brigata Costiera* (coastal brigade) was deployed along the Bay of Gela while the *19ª Brigata Costiera* was responsible for half of the northern coast running east from the Messina fortress area, with the remaining half up to the boundary with the *Comando Porto* Palermo defences being allotted to the *136° Reggimento Costiera* (coastal regiment); the latter may have been an independent unit as it does not appear in the Italian order of battle cited in the British Official History.[8]

Generale Rossi's main combat power was also concentrated in two divisions. *Generale di Divisione* Giulio Gotti-Porcinari's *54ª Napoli Divisione* was roughly equivalent to the *Aosta Divisione*, insofar as it was recruited predominantly from southern Sicily, had been stationed on the island throughout the war and was understrength, poorly trained and lacked weapons, ammunition, transport and other equipment; it was stationed in the south-east of the island with its HQ at Palazzolo Acreide, twenty miles west of Syracuse, backing the *206ª* and *213ª Divisioni Costiere* with elements deployed toward the Pachino Peninsula.

The second formation was the exception to all this. Commanded by *Generale di Divisione* Domenico Chirieleison, the *4ª Livorno Divisione* had participated in the 1940 invasion of France and had been retrained as an assault formation in readiness for the invasion of Malta in mid-1942, codenamed *Operazione C3* by the Italians and *Herkules* by the Germans. When that invasion was cancelled the formation was posted to Sicily en route to North Africa in February 1943 and remained there when the Axis defeat in Tunisia rendered the move superfluous. Although it suffered from the endemic shortages of artillery and ammunition, the *Livorno Divisione* was fully up to strength with well trained, high-quality manpower, possessed sufficient organic transport to be rated a mobile formation and was one of the few Italian formations considered competent by their German allies. On that basis *Generale* Guzzoni designated the *Livorno Divisione* as *6ª Armata* reserve and stationed it in the area of Caltanissetta close to his HQ at Enna. This placed *Generale* Chirieleison's formation close to what Guzzoni considered to be the most likely Allied avenue of attack, twenty-five miles inland from the coast between Gela and Licata, with one regiment deployed forward to the south-east at Mazzarino, sixteen miles north of Gela. Again, the divisions were augmented with five *Gruppi Mobili*, this time lettered D through H and four *Gruppi Tattici*. One of the former was stationed near Catania on the east coast while the remainder were deployed along the south-east coast, two near Niscemi, one near Comiso ten miles inland from Scoglitti and the fifth midway between Ispica and Noto on the neck of the Pachino Peninsula; the latter were again deployed in widely spaced locations on the southern and eastern aspects of the *16° Corpo* area of responsibility.[9]

Generale Guzzoni's *6ª Armata* thus required substantial reinforcement if it were to have any prospect of mounting a realistic defence of Sicily. Circumstances decreed that reinforcement could only come from the Germans, an option that brought a whole raft of complications in its train, not least a particular quandary for the Italians. One faction at the top of the Italian military hierarchy that included the head of *Comando Supremo* from 1 February 1943, *Generale d'Armata* Vittorio Ambrosio, was intent on loosening ties with the Germans; Ambrosio's appointment in itself reportedly prompted a cooling of relations between *Comando Supremo* and the *Oberkommando der Wehrmacht* (*OKW*).[10] Soliciting German reinforcements thus ran counter to this intent, as it would require more political and military interaction with the Germans and more importantly, an increase in the number of German units stationed on Italian soil. On the other hand, a second, more pragmatic faction that included the erstwhile commander of *6ª Armata*, *Generale* Roatta, actively lobbied for an increased German presence on the not unreasonable grounds that an effective defence of Italian territory was simply not feasible without it.[11] For their part the Germans were willing to expand their presence on Italian soil if only because, also not unreasonably, they harboured serious reservations on the competence and reliability of their Axis partner. These reservations dated back to the fighting in North Africa but were exacerbated by the poor Italian performance at Pantellaria and more especially the adjacent islands of Lampedusa, Lampione and Linosa that surrendered without a fight in the first half of June 1943; as the US Official History put it, the Germans 'could not understand why the outlying islands had not been sufficiently stocked for war [and it was] difficult for them to comprehend why the Italians, fighting on their own soil, had offered so little resistance'.[12]

These questions were overridden by pragmatism on both sides. Hitler had already offered Mussolini up to five divisions before Pantelleria fell and *Generalfeldmarschall* Albert Kesselring at *Oberbefehlshaber Süd* (*OB Süd*), the senior German command in the Mediterranean, had obtained Italian agreement on 22 May 1943 for a total of four German divisions to be deployed on the Italian mainland, Sardinia and Sicily.[13] Implementation of the agreement proved to be less straightforward however, as Ambrosio quibbled and stalled during further discussions in Rome in early June, even when Kesselring cited calls for Sicily to be reinforced with German troops from *Generale* Guzzoni and *Generaloberst* Hans-Valentin Hube; the latter had recently arrived in Italy from the Eastern Front to command *14 Panzer Korps*, the operational HQ located in southern Italy tasked to 'administer and supply the German units in Sicily' under direct control from *OB Süd*.[14] The fall of Pantellaria on 11 June prompted a sharp reversal of tack from the head of *Comando Supremo* however, possibly prompted in part by Hitler ordering the reinforcement of Sardinia and Sicily, and things moved rapidly thereafter. Following a pessimistic report from Guzzoni on 14 June, *Comando Supremo* officially asked *OKW* to send two additional armoured or motorised formations to Italy on 17 June, leading to the despatch of *26 Panzer Division* and *29 Panzergrenadier Division*. By the end of the month permission had been sought and granted to establish a further armoured HQ, *76 Panzer Korps*, in Italy, five German divisions were present in whole or part on Italian territory and a further two were en route.[15] Despite the fears of *Generale* Ambrosio and others, events had run ahead and as a result 'Italy was beginning to resemble an occupied territory.'[16]

Be that as it may, the Italian change of tack resulted in substantial reinforcement for *Generale* Guzzoni's *6ª Armata* on Sicily. The first German reinforcement was in place by 14 May 1943 in the shape of *panzergrenadier*, artillery and anti-aircraft elements of *15 Panzer Division* that had escaped from the debacle in Tunisia, initially dubbed the *Division Sizilien* organised and commanded by *Oberst* Ernst-Günther Baade.[17] On 1 July 1943, command devolved to *Generalleutnant* Eberhard Rodt and the formation was expanded and renamed *15 Panzergrenadier Division*, which by 10 July had an atypical and expanded order of battle that included an armoured reconnaissance battalion, an artillery regiment, a mortar regiment equipped with 120mm mortars and thirty-six 150mm *nebelwerfer* rocket launchers, a pioneer battalion, two *panzergrenadier* regiments and a *panzer* regiment equipped with between thirty and sixty *Panzer III* and *Panzer IV* tanks, depending on the source.[18] This was a powerful formation, especially in comparison with the Italian divisions on Sicily but the second German reinforcement was more powerful still. Commanded by *Luftwaffe Generalmajor* Paul Conrath, the *Hermann Göring* (*HG*) *Panzer Division* was reconstituted on 21 May 1943 around elements of the original *Hermann Göring Division* that had not been lost in Tunisia. It included only a single *panzergrenadier* regiment, although this shortfall was addressed by cross-attaching one of *15 Panzergrenadier Division*'s regiments, an armoured reconnaissance *bataillon*, a pioneer *bataillon* and artillery and anti-aircraft regiments, but the formation's most significant combat power lay in in its armoured component. *Panzer Regiment HG* consisted of two *bataillonen* fielding forty-six *Panzer III* and thirty-two *Panzer IV* tanks respectively, latterly alongside a *kompanie* of seventeen Tiger I heavy tanks dubbed *Panzer Abteilung 215*; nine of the latter were an attached *Kompanie* from *schwere Panzer Abteilung 504* that had not been deployed to Tunisia, bolstered with two replacement vehicles from *schwere Panzer Abteilung 501* that had also been left in Sicily and six additional vehicles issued directly to *Panzer Abteilung 215*. A variety of units drawn from *1 Fallschirmjäger Division* and three fortress battalions, one of them possibly Italian, were also attached to the *Division* with elements of *Panzergrenadier Regiment 382*, another unit reformed on Sicily after destruction in Tunisia with reinforcements flown in from Rome.[19]

All this represented an impressive increase in combat power for *6ª Armata*, but there still remained the vexed questions of under whose command the German formations were to operate, and how and where they were to be deployed. Technically, the German formations were under the command of *Generale* Guzzoni's *6ª Armata* and its subordinate *Corpo* HQs, the same arrangement that had existed between the Axis allies in North Africa, although the reality differed somewhat in practice. Rommel had been notorious for simply ignoring his Italian supposed superiors when it suited him for example, and German higher HQs frequently if less blatantly issued orders directly to German commanders, with the pragmatic compliance of their Italian counterparts. In late May, *Generalfeldmarschall* Kesselring ordered German commanders on Sicily to take immediate action against any Allied invasion force as soon as their objectives were clarified, irrespective of any orders or lack thereof emanating from *6ª Armata* HQ at Enna for example, and the impulse appears to have been not unpopular with German senior commanders; on receiving Kesselring's instruction, possibly at the same meeting, *Generalmajor* Conrath responded 'If you mean go for them, Field-Marshal, then I'm your man.'[20]

The fall of Pantelleria appears to have prompted the Germans to expand and formalise this tendency with a parallel chain of command in order to retain fuller operational control over their formations, which resulted in *Generalleutnant* Fridolin von Senger und Etterlin being attached to *6ª Armata* HQ on 26 June 1943, tasked to report directly to Kesselring and to co-ordinate the German formations deployed to Sicily.[21] Senger und Etterlin's first job on arrival in Sicily was to mediate between *Generalfeldmarschall* Kesselring and *Generale* Guzzoni over the deployment of the German formations he was tasked to co-ordinate.

There was a fundamental disagreement on the best way to react to the upcoming Allied landings. The Germans favoured defeating the invaders on the waterline by deploying close to likely landing beaches and launching immediate attacks before the invaders were properly established, while the Italians expected the frontage of the Allied landing to be too broad to immediately divine their intentions, and thus envisaged sacrificing the coastal defence units for time while marshalling their mobile reserves to attack inland when Allied intentions had been clarified. There was a difference of opinion on the deployment of the German reinforcements. Guzzoni favoured deploying the less experienced *Hermann Göring Panzer Division* in the west and the more experienced *15 Panzergrenadier Division* in the east of Sicily, where he expected the main Allied blow to fall, whereas Kesselring, possibly due in part to his *Luftwaffe* background, wanted the opposite because he considered the *Hermann Göring* formation more suitable for the tank-friendly terrain in the east of the island.[22] Interestingly, Guzzoni's deployment plan was preferred by the commander of *15 Panzergrenadier Division*, *Generalleutnant* Rodt and, perhaps surprisingly, by *Generalleutnant* von Senger und Etterlin, but Kesselring's view prevailed and he also succeeded in imposing his view on how to tackle the Allied invasion.

Summarised at the 29 June meeting, the Axis response was fixed to have the battle commence at the waterline with the Italian coastal defence units taking the immediate brunt of the landings, supported by rapid attacks by the Italian mobile divisions backed by the more powerful German formations, which were to complete the job by driving the invaders back into the sea; the policy of swift counter-attack was also intended to prevent the Allies establishing a continuous invasion front by wiping out the individual landings in turn.[23]

By 10 July, Kesselring's edicts had *15 Panzergrenadier Division* divided into three *kampfgruppen* named after their commanders. The groups commanded by *Oberst* Karl Ens and *Oberst* Fritz Fullriede, built around *Panzergrenadier Regiments 104* and *129* respectively were deployed at the western end of Sicily between the *Aosta* and *Assietta Divisioni* with *Generalleutnant* Rodt's Division HQ, although *Kampfgruppe* Fullriede was a recent arrival, having been originally stationed with the *Livorno Divisione* HQ at Caltanissetta, twelve miles south-west of *6ª Armata* HQ at Enna. *Oberst* Theodor Körner's group, built around *Panzergrenadier Regiment 115* was attached to the *Hermann Göring Panzer Division*, as well as the Tiger I-equipped *Panzer Abteilung* 215; a third group dubbed *Kampfgruppe Neapel* (Naples) was also stationed near Caltanissetta and may have been a shorthand term for German units from all sources deployed to *Generale* Guzzoni's *6ª Armata* reserve.[24] Approximately two-thirds of the *Hermann Göring Panzer Division* was stationed in the south-east of the island with its HQ at Caltagirone, eighteen miles northeast of Gela, with the *Livorno Divisione* on its right flank and the *Napoli Divisione* on its left, oriented to cover the Bay of Gela. The remaining third of *Generalmajor* Conrath's formation was stationed between Adrano and Paterno on the lower slopes of Mount Etna, fifteen miles north-west of Catania and oriented to back the *213ª Divisione Costiera* covering the twelve-mile stretch of the Gulf of Noto between the Syracuse-Augusta *Piazze Militari Marittime* and the *Comando Porto* Catania. Dubbed *Kampfgruppe* Schmalz after its commander *Oberst* Wilhelm Schmalz and using the Division's *Panzergrenadierbrigade (z.b.V.)* HQ, it included *Kampfgruppe* Körner from *15 Panzergrenadier Division*, two *bataillonen* from *Panzergrenadier Regiment 382* which were en route from elsewhere in Sicily or the Italian mainland, three fortress units, *Festung Bataillonen 904* and *923* and the *Regio* fortress battalion, which may have been Italian and a number of *Fallschirmjäger* units from *Luftwaffe Generalleutnant* Richard Heidrich's *1 Fallschirmjäger Division* based at Avignon in southern France, which was deployed to Sicily in the immediate aftermath of the Allied landing. These included *Fallschirmjäger Regiments 3* and *4*, *Fallschirmjäger MG Bataillon 1*, *Fallschirmjäger Pionier Bataillon 1*, a *bataillon* from *Fallschirmjäger Artillerie Regiment 1* and a *Kompanie* from *Fallschirm Kommunication Bataillon 1*.[25]

The process of deploying *1 Fallschirmjäger Division* to Sicily began at midnight on 10 July when *Generalleutnant* Heidrich was summoned to *OB Süd* in Rome by *Generalfeldmarschall* Kesselring. The following day Heidrich received orders to move his formation to the island as a rapid reinforcement directly from *Reichsmarschall* Göring in Berlin, with *Oberstleutnant* Ludwig Heilmann's *Fallschirmjäger Regiment 3* spearheading the move. Leaving at 05:00 on 12 July after issuing a Warning Order to his Regiment and *Luftwaffe* transport units across southern France, Heilmann flew the 700 miles from Avignon to Catania accompanied by just two of his Staff Officers, *Hauptmann* Franz Stangenberg and a *Hauptmann* Sprecht. After avoiding being shot down by marauding Allied fighters and being caught in a bombing attack on Catania airfield, Sprecht began scouring the town for motor transport to commandeer while Heilmann and Sprecht set about locating suitable landing zones to the south, quickly settling on an area adjacent to the *Strada* 114 coast road between the River Simeto and Gornalunga Canal, just west of the Ponte Primosole crossing around seven miles south of Catania; ironically the same area had been selected for the British 1st Parachute Brigade's Operation FUSTIAN landing, also originally scheduled for the late evening of 12 July. The intention was for *Fallschirmjäger Regiment 3* to drop at dusk to take advantage of the Allied practice of withdrawing their fighters at that time and Stangenberg's telephone message to the airfields around Avignon arrived within minutes of the take-off deadline. After narrowly avoiding a rerun of the *Palmsonntag Massaker* at the hands of a score of P-38s as the USAAF fighters were low on fuel, the fleet of Heinkel 111 and Junkers 52 transports began running in to the improvised drop zone shortly after 18:00, guided by bonfires lit by *Oberstleutnant* Heilmann and his two companions; 1,400 men were delivered with just a handful of jump injuries and Heilmann's Regiment was moving south-west to confront the British 50th and 51st Highland Divisions at Lentini and Vizzini aboard *Hauptmann* Sprecht's commandeered vehicles within forty-five minutes of the jump.[26]

The much needed German reinforcements were thus in Sicily before or very shortly after HUSKY began and over half the Axis defenders were serendipitously deployed in locations that corresponded to the Allied landing areas; the Axis commanders had also correctly placed the date of the invasion in the middle of July 1943.[27] The prediction was based on a variety of intelligence and reconnaissance reports in the week leading up to the invasion, which indicated that '90 per cent of available Allied troops, 60 per cent of the air forces, and 96 per cent of the landing craft were concentrated in the western-central Mediterranean.'[28] However, *OKW* and *OB Süd* were still labouring under the influence of Operation MINCEMEAT, and therefore interpreted the evidence to support their contention that the Allied blow would fall simultaneously on Sardinia, Sicily and Greece at some point. *Generale* Guzzoni felt that the threat was focussed specifically on Sicily and, in combination with the moon phase, he correctly divined that the invasion of Sicily would commence in the days leading up to 10 July. Events soon confirmed the accuracy of his prediction.

On Sunday 4 July a twenty-five-strong Allied convoy was spotted off North Africa followed by *Regia Aeronautica* reports of another the following day, along with intelligence that the number of Allied hospital ships in the region had increased from two to sixteen. An erroneous *Luftwaffe* reconnaissance report of a large Allied convoy four miles off Licata in the evening of Wednesday 7 July prompted Guzzoni to order his coastal defence formations to man their positions and the following day he ordered the port facilities at Sciacca, Porto Empedocle and Licata on the southern aspect of the island to be prepared for demolition; apparently following the *6ª Armata* lead, *Comando Supremo* ordered the harbours at Marsala and Trapani on the western tip of the island to be filled with earth and rocks to render them unusable on the same day and when this proved impractical, the port facilities were demolished instead. By Friday 9 July it was becoming increasingly clear that the invasion was imminent. In the morning *Luftwaffe* reconnaissance reported up to ninety Allied landing and transport vessels moving at speed near Pantellaria and sightings continued through the day despite the bad weather. At 13:30 a routine *Luftwaffe* patrol reported five convoys, each consisting of up to ninety landing craft, transports and naval escorts, south of Malta, including at least two battleships. The same convoys were spotted again north of Malta and Gozo at around 17:30 and another sighting at 18:10 confirmed the presence of the battleships along with an aircraft carrier and four cruisers, prompting Guzzoni to order a preliminary alert across Sicily at around 19:00. In the evening Allied bombers struck the HQs of the *Livorno and Napoli Divisioni* at Caltanissetta and Palazzolo Acreide respectively, and *Regia Marina* installations at Catania and Syracuse; these two also came under Allied naval gunfire in the early hours of Saturday 10 July along with Augusta, Taormina and Trapani. Further convoy sightings came in at 19:10 and 20:30 followed by reports of two convoys moving east near Bône and Tabarka at 21:00 and of a score of vessels approaching Cape Passero at the south-eastern tip of the island at 23:10. *Generale* Guzzoni had ordered all Axis forces on Sicily to full alert at around 22:00.[29] Time had run out and the German and Italian commanders on Sicily were about to find out how effective their anti-invasion measures were, just fifty-eight days after the Axis surrender in Tunisia.

9

Ill Met by Moonlight at the Ponte Grande

The Operation LADBROKE Glider Landing, Friday 9 July to D-Day, 10 July

Both the Algerian portion of Operation TORCH and the subsequent push east into Tunisia had been preceded by battalion-scale airborne operations, and while the utility and benefit of those operations were arguable the theme was continued for HUSKY by the Allied Forces HQ (AFHQ) planners, albeit on a larger scale. So while the US parts of the Algerian and Tunisian invasions were led by the single-battalion 509th Parachute Infantry Regiment, the US Sicilian invasion force was spearheaded by a reinforced 505th Parachute Infantry Regiment. Similarly, the British push east along the Algerian coast was led by the newly arrived 3rd Parachute Battalion, but while the British portion of the Sicily invasion was also to be preceded by a brigade-level airborne operation, a different means of delivery was selected. The commander of the British 1st Airborne Division from 6 April 1943, Major-General George Hopkinson, was, as previously noted, from a glider rather than parachute background and was also something of a zealot for that method of insertion. Hopkinson therefore personally ensured that the initial British airborne landing in support of HUSKY would be a glider-borne operation, to the extent of giving his glider pilot commander Lieutenant-Colonel George Chatterton the choice of accepting the hazard-strewn landing area he had unilaterally selected or being relieved of his command. Responsibility for carrying out the British Army's first brigade-sized Airborne operation, codenamed Operation LADBROKE, thus devolved onto Chatterton's 1st Battalion The Glider Pilot Regiment and Brigadier Philip Hicks' 1st Airlanding Brigade. By the beginning of July 1943 the latter, No. 296 Squadron and the detached A Flight from RAF No. 295 Squadron were ensconced on or near six airfields inland from Sousse with the CG4A and Horsa gliders that would carry them into battle.[1]

Operation LADBROKE was intended to secure the right/northern flank of British XIII Corps' landings at the ACID NORTH Landing Area and to assist egress from the beaches to the north along the *Strada* 115 coast road and thence onto the Catania Plain north of Syracuse. This was to be achieved by eliminating Italian artillery batteries, possibly including the Lamba Doria Battery on the Maddalena Peninsula and a military radio station in the same area, to prevent them interfering with XIII Corps' sea landing; seizing the double Ponte Grande bridge, codenamed WATERLOO, over the River Anapo and parallel Mammiaibica Canal; seizing the railway bridge over the Mammiaibica Canal just under a mile to the west, codenamed PUTNEY; and securing a number of locations in the southern portion of the port city of Syracuse (codenamed LADBROKE) located on a small peninsula just over a mile north-east of the Ponte Grande including the railway station, codenamed BULFORD, and adjacent sea plane base codenamed CALSHOT.[2]

The mission involved Brigadier Hicks' Brigade HQ and the 1st Airlanding Brigade's entire infantry component, consisting of Lieutenant-Colonel George Britten's 796-strong 1st Battalion The Border Regiment and Lieutenant-Colonel Derek McCardie's 711-strong 2nd Battalion The South Staffordshire Regiment.[3] The infantry component was to be supported by eighty-two men drawn from Major Basil Beazley's 9th Field Company RE, divided into two parties commanded by Captains Duncan Williams and John Holmes, allocated to the 1st Border and 2nd South Staffords respectively.[4]

Medical support was to be provided by the seventy-six men from Lieutenant-Colonel Graeme Warrack's 181 Airlanding Field Ambulance. Two of the Field Ambulance's Sections, commanded by a Captain Greaves and Lieutenant Brian Brownscombe, were attached to each of the infantry battalions as complete units, one Medical Officer and twenty-four men were assigned to augment each battalion's integral RAMC contingent, all accompanied by a surgical team led by Captain Guy Rigby-Jones; Lieutenant-Colonel Warrack and a skeleton Ambulance HQ were to travel with Brigadier Hicks and Brigade HQ.[5] In addition, the operation involved 273 men from the 1st Battalion The Glider Pilot Regiment, two Naval Bombardment Detachments and a detachment from No. 4 Army Film and Photography Section.[6] The Brigade and attachments were to be carried in 135 CG4As and eight Horsa gliders, towed by 109 C-47s from the US 60th and 62nd Troop Carrier Groups and seven Halifax and twenty-eight Albemarles from Nos. 295 and 296 Squadrons respectively; another four CG4As were loaded in readiness in case additional tugs became available by the launch date.[7] As this was insufficient to lift the Brigade in its entirety personnel and equipment were trimmed to suit, with the 9th Field Company leaving behind half a platoon; it is unclear how many if any men were left out of battle by the two infantry battalions. Brigade transport was pared down to seven Jeeps, six of them as prime-movers for six 6-Pounder anti-tank guns, two from the 1st Border and four from the 2nd South Staffords, although 181 Field Ambulance included two more Jeeps and a single stretcher trailer in its lift and 9th Field Company RE another Jeep, nine vehicles in all. Apart from a single motorcycle combination, the remainder of the *coup-de-main* force's transport was muscle-powered, consisting of ninety-nine Airborne bicycles, ten mortar trolleys and 103 Airborne handcarts.[8] In all the LADBROKE force totalled 2,075 officers and men, just over 1,500 of whom were infantrymen.[9]

Brigadier Hicks' plan to achieve his Brigade's mission was a three-stage affair.[10] Phase One was the seizure of the Ponte Grande bridge and adjacent railway bridge by 23:15 on D-Day Minus One, two hours before the arrival of the rest of the 1st Airlanding Brigade and three and a half hours before the sea landings were scheduled to begin. The seizure was tasked to the 2nd South Staffords' A and C Companies and sixteen glider pilots under the overall command of C Company OC Major Edwin Ballinger; as the bridge was known to be rigged for demolition the party also included four Sappers from the 9th Field Company under Lieutenant Eric O'Callaghan spread individually overflown in four separate gliders.[11] The 270-strong *coup-de-main* party was to be carried in eight Horsa gliders towed by seven Halifax from No. 295 Squadron and a single Albemarle from No. 296 Squadron. Given that the 1st Airborne Division's insistence on having Horsas specially flown out from the UK was justified by the need for Six-Pounder anti-tank guns to be delivered with their Jeep prime movers, it is interesting to note that the Horsas were used solely as assault transports and it is also ironic that the six 6-Pounder guns deployed on LADBROKE fell victim to the very problem the Horsas were supposed to prevent; as the British Official Airborne History put it, in the LADBROKE glider landings 'unfortunately, guns and jeeps were separated'.[12]

The eight Horsas were to deliver their passengers onto two Landing Zones (LZs), collectively dubbed LZ 3. Four gliders carrying Major Ballinger's C Company were to land on LZ 3 SOUTH, centred approximately seven hundred yards west of the Ponte Grande crossing on the south bank of the Mammiaibica Canal, tasked to seize that crossing. The remaining four Horsas, carrying Major Thomas Lane's A Company tasked to seize the railway bridge over the Mammiaibica Canal, were to come down on LZ 3 NORTH actually located approximately a mile west-north-west of the Ponte Grande in a loop in the River Anapo between the river and the Mammiaibica Canal and around six hundred yards from the north end of the railway bridge.[13]

Phase Two was the arrival of the 135 Waco CG4A gliders carrying the remainder of the 1st Airlanding Brigade at 01:15, onto a Landing Area located three miles south-east of the Ponte Grande in an area of cultivated land and orchards at the neck of the Maddalena Peninsula.[14] The Landing and Assembly Area, codenamed ANDOVER, was divided into two separate LZs. LZ 1 was the most westerly, in the centre of the one and three-quarter mile neck connecting the Peninsula to the mainland, near the village of Fanusa; LZ 2 was located just over a mile to the south-east on the edge of the Peninsula proper, just two or three hundred yards north of low cliffs marking the coastline and a mile from the seaside hamlet of Punta Milocca. Both LZs were approximately 1,000 yards long and 500 yards wide, irregular in shape and included small extensions located off their south-east corners.[15] Brigadier Hicks' Brigade HQ and Lieutenant-Colonel McCardie's 2nd South Staffords' HQ and support elements, B, D and a composite E Companies were allocated LZ 1 while LZ 2 was allocated to Lieutenant-Colonel Britten and the 1st Border.

There is some confusion over the scheduled landing times; the 1st Border War Diary refers to a twenty-minute window beginning at 22:17, which was the timing for the *coup-de-main* force while the 1st Airborne Division After Action Report refers to the 2nd South Staffords being tasked to reach the Ponte Grande by 01:15, the main force arrival time according to the 1st Airlanding Brigade's Operation Order No. 1.[16] After reorganising, the 2nd South Staffords were tasked to secure the ground around the Landing Area before moving off for the Ponte Grande bridge, completing a number of missions en route; Major Robert Cain's B Company was to eliminate a strongpoint two miles south of the Ponte Grande, likely on the junction of the *Strada* 115 and road running east to the Maddalena Peninsula, Major John Phillp's D Company was tasked to deal with a coastal artillery battery a mile to the south codenamed GNAT and Major James Neilson's E Company, a composite unit formed from elements of H Company and the Battalion Reconnaissance Platoon, was to eliminate another strongpoint on the *Strada* 115 a mile short of the Ponte Grande, codenamed WALSALL.[17]

The 1st Border was to trail the South Staffords from the Landing Area to the Ponte Grande and pass through that location to execute Phase Three of the LADBROKE mission at 01:45. This involved Lieutenant-Colonel Britten's Battalion moving into Syracuse and securing a number of objectives in the city between 02:45 and 03:30 including the railway station, seaplane depot, power station (codenamed BATTERSEA) and the bridge linking the city's two halves (codenamed SOLENT); according to the Battalion War Diary the intention was 'to gain a foothold in SYRACUSE containing the garrison there if possible, until relieved by sea-borne forces'.[18] Wellingtons from RAF No. 205 Group were to carry out diversionary bombing of targets in Syracuse in the thirty-minute period between 02:15 and 02:45 to ease the ground advance into the city, and the 1st Border was to have occupied 'all key buildings and likely enemy approach routes' by 05:30.[19] A further diversionary measure intended to sow confusion on the ground was the dropping of dummy parachutists, following tests at Strip F alongside the M'Saken-Kairouan road on 7 July; the idea was plagiarised from the Germans, who had employed such devices in their airborne operations in Holland in May 1940.[20] The dummies were twenty-inch high hessian outlines with sand-weighted legs attached to small cotton parachutes, some with pyrotechnic gunfire simulators on a ratio of one in three, augmented with small metal bombs containing a Verey pistol flare fused to detonate on impact; both devices were to be despatched from the aircraft's escape hatch by a gunner at a height of 1,000 feet and speed of approximately 180 miles per hour. Three groups of eighty dummies were to be dropped north-west of Catania at 22:00 on D-Day Minus One followed by two further groups of forty dummies west of Augusta by sixteen Douglas Boston twin-engine light bombers, four each drawn from Nos. 18 and 114 Squadrons from RAF No. 326 Wing and Nos. 21 & 24 Squadrons from SAAF No. 3 Wing.[21]

There were two obstacles to overcome before the 1st Airlanding Brigade was ready to set about achieving its objectives on the ground. First was the 290-mile fly-in from Tunisia. After rendezvousing over the Kuriat Islands twenty miles east of Sousse, the glider combinations were to fly east for 200 miles to Malta, overflying the Delimara Peninsula on the south-eastern tip of the island before turning north-north-east for the seventy-one-mile leg to a point off Cape Passero. There the tug pilots were to alter course slightly to almost due north for the final eighteen-mile leg paralleling the Gulf of Noto coast to stay clear of anti-aircraft fire to the release point, two and a half miles short of the *Capo Porco di Murro* at the tip of the Maddalena Peninsula. The release height was determined by the glider's destination with the Horsas carrying the *coup-de-main* force to release at 3,500 feet and the Waco CG4As bound for LZs 1 and 2 at 1,500 and 1,100 feet respectively, dictated by to the distance between the release point and the individual LZs.[22] On release the tugs were to break right, away from the Sicilian coast, to begin their return journey to Tunisia while the gliders continued on to the *Capo Porco di Murro* before turning sharp left, with those allocated to LZs 1 and 2 having just two to three miles flight and a few minutes to identify their LZ in the illumination from a waxing quarter-moon and put down. Leaving aside that the routing carried the combinations directly over the invasion convoys with the consequent risk of fratricidal anti-aircraft fire, the run-in to the release point was problematic for a number of reasons.

The final two legs to the release point had to be made entirely by dead reckoning over the sea with no markers or reference points for guidance, a rather tall order given the relative dearth of night flying experience and training among some of the tug pilots. More importantly, the lack of reference points or other means to identify the correct release point was especially serious because releasing early would result in gliders failing to reach the designated landing area at best, and coming down in the sea or crashing into the sheer cliffs at the *Capo Porco di Murro* at worst; releasing late ran the risk of the gliders overshooting the Peninsula and again ending up in the sea, or travelling too high and fast to make the LZ. These critical points were swiftly noted by the three senior RAF officers despatched to Tunisia by No. 38 Wing to assist with HUSKY, Wing-Commander Wallace Barton, Group-Captain Thomas Cooper and Squadron-Leader Lawrence Wright, all of whom had a good insight into the practicalities and hazards; Group-Captain Cooper had commanded the epic if unsuccessful Operation FRESHMAN in November 1942 and had flown as co-pilot in the surviving Halifax tug for example, while Squadron-Leader Wright had been involved in the British combat glider effort from its inception in 1940.[23] For his part, Cooper was consistently forthright in his criticism of LADBROKE as it was planned and executed from the outset, initially by bluntly pointing out glider night operations were not part of British Airborne doctrine when General Montgomery raised the idea at Hopkinson's prompting in May 1943. Cooper's objections to the LADBROKE fly-in were equally frank: 'The release was over water, and involved judging distances from the shore...

the glider pilots were to make a straight glide in and would have no surplus height...no marks were going to be put on the ground because the Americans said they would cause confusion, and the Army considered they would attract the enemy, and that the release run was made down moon.'[24]

The second challenge was the landing areas, and specifically LZs 1 and 2 on the neck of the Maddalena Peninsula, selected for the bulk of the 1st Airlanding Brigade's landing. As we have seen, Lieutenant-Colonel Chatterton's reaction on being shown aerial photographs of the proposed Landing Area by Major-General Hopkinson resulted in him being given the choice of compliance or being relieved of his command. The area was criss-crossed with stone walls, orchards, lemon groves and tall trees. A sketch map of LZ 2 in the LADBROKE briefing materials shows that the eastern half was bisected by a tree-lined stone wall that enclosed the entire south-eastern quadrant including four stone huts, while the western end included another structure, an area of orchards and a curving line of thirty-foot tall trees; any of these obstacles was sufficient to seriously damage or even destroy the relatively flimsy Waco CG4As machines in a collision at landing speed, with serious and potentially fatal consequences for pilots and passengers alike. Overall, the terrain was so unsuitable that on examining stereoscopic images of the LZs Squadron-Leader Wright initially assumed he had been given the wrong photographs due to a clerical error. Wright was so alarmed he raised the matter with Wing-Commander Barton and Group-Captain Cooper and all three officers brought their misgivings to the attention of their superiors at AFHQ and No. 38 Wing, but to no avail; Wright also took his reservations to a sympathetic Chatterton, who informed him of his own reaction when first confronted with the LADBROKE plan and Hopkinson's response.

There were consequences to this boat rocking and despite the purpose of his presence in Tunisia, Squadron-Leader Wright found himself *persona non grata* at subsequent 1st Airborne Division planning meetings; Wright speculated that this was at Hopkinson's personal intervention, motivated by the Division commander's determination to have LADBROKE go ahead at all costs.[25] If so, the episode was a parallel to events a year later when Browning, by then promoted to Lieutenant-General and commander of the British 1st Airborne Corps and deputy command of the 1st Allied Airborne Army, deliberately suppressed photographic intelligence of German armour in the vicinity of Arnhem. On that occasion the Intelligence Officer who alerted Browning to the evidence was swiftly diagnosed with exhaustion and sent away on enforced sick leave; as with Hopkinson for LADBROKE, the motivation in 1944 was Browning's determination that Operation MARKET should go ahead at all costs, irrespective of the risk to those detailed to carry it out.[26]

The process of briefing the LADBROKE force on its various missions began on Thursday 1 July 1943, with a co-ordinating conference at 1st Airborne Division HQ; 181 Airlanding Field Ambulance held a Regimental Medical Officers conference the following day.[27] On 3 July Lieutenant-Colonels Britten and McCardie briefed the 1st Border and the 2nd South Staffords

Company commanders and Major Beazley briefed all his 9th Field Company Officers, with the rest of the South Staffords' Officers being briefed the following day; it is unclear when the remainder of the 1st Border's Officers were briefed.[28] All Ranks of the 1st Airborne Division were confined to camp on 5 July and the briefing of the Other Ranks involved in LADBROKE was again staggered according to unit.[29] Lieutenant-Colonel Britten addressed all the 1st Border's Officers and NCOs on 6 July and OR briefings took place by Company later, and on the following day of the 2nd South Staffords. The 9th Field Company briefed Captain Holmes 3 Section on 6 July, Captain William's 2 Section on 7 July and held further unspecified briefings the day after that; 181 Field Ambulance briefed All Ranks detailed for LADBROKE on 7 July.[30] According to the 1st Border War Diary 'All ranks [were] very enthusiastic and full of confidence.'[31]

Lieutenant-Colonel Chatterton's glider pilots were also briefed on Tuesday 6 July, beginning at 13:00 with an overview of HUSKY and the 1st Airlanding Brigade's role within it, followed by the Air Plan including routes, timings and loading schedules for Waco CG4As and Horsas; the former were given a maximum payload of 3,700 pounds equating to a maximum of fourteen fully-equipped men and a loaded Airborne handcart and the latter to a payload of 6,900 pounds equivalent to a maximum of thirty-two men. As all the RAF tug crews included a trained navigator the eight Horsa combinations carrying the *coup-de-main* force were to fly independently as a stream; the USAAF tug crews were not so well provisioned and were obliged to fly in formations of four, with one navigator between them. Take-offs were staggered to accommodate the varying distances between start points, calculated to synchronise the arrival of the coup-de-main force at LZ3 in a twenty-minute window between 22:10 and 22:30, and the main force on LZs 1 and 2 two hours later at around 01:15. To assist in the fly-in after release and identifying the unmarked LZs, every glider pilot was issued with a black-and-white 'moonlight map' specially prepared by No. 38 Wing.[32]

The backdrop to the briefings was a mixture of loading, preparation and last-minute planning. The five No. 295 Squadron Halifaxes joined the Horsa contingent at Strip E near the Sebkra de Hani salt flats on Monday 5 July for example, and 181 Airlanding Field Ambulance spent the same day packing medical stores and equipment into their Jeep, trailers and Airborne handcarts.[33] Gliders were accessible for loading on the six airfields on 8 July, under the supervision of glider pilots to ensure loads were correctly distributed for balance. The process was complicated by most Waco CG4As lacking lashing rings and others only being equipped with a floor opening for rope lashing; the problem was circumvented by employing issue lashing sets for heavier elements and rope lashing for lighter items. Preparations were also hindered by high winds, up to thirty miles per hour, that created large clouds of floating dust.[34]

At 14:45 on 6 July the Division reserve ammunition dump located 400 yards from the 1st Airlanding Reconnaissance Squadron lines and three-quarters of a mile from the 1st Battalion Glider Pilot Regiment lines caught fire, with the 1st Border, 2nd South Staffords and other nearby troops being called out as impromptu fire-fighters while 181 Field Ambulance stood to in anticipation of mass casualties. In the event Captain Graham Roberts from the Reconnaissance Squadron suffered a fractured arm from shrapnel and three Glider Pilots suffered minor injuries, but blast from the resultant series of explosions and fire destroyed the glider pilot's tented camp along with personal kit and effects as well as 'showering mortar bombs and phosphorous grenades all over the landscape'; the blaze was not brought under control until 18:00. The fire may have been the reason for 1st Border complaints of being unable to secure sufficient ammunition and particularly No. 36 grenades and Verey light cartridges on Wednesday 7 July; the sting of the situation was presumably soothed by a visit from a mobile cinema unit in the evening of the same day.[35]

Two days later on 8 July an Albemarle from No. 296 Squadron piloted by Flying-Officers Geoffrey Hopkinson and Oscar Coates stalled and crashed after pulling up from a landing approach; according to eyewitness Lieutenant Edward Newport, commanding the 1st Border's 2nd Anti-Tank Platoon, the Albemarle pulled up to avoid a C-47 coming in to land from the opposite direction. Both pilots along with Flight-Sergeant George Hutchins and Sergeant John Charley were killed in the crash and resultant fire, while Sergeant J. R Hayes escaped 'without serious injury'. The fire-fighting effort was hampered by the dust and wind, which by the afternoon of 8 July was gusting up to forty-five miles per hour.[36]

At 10:30 on the day of the Albemarle crash the 1st Airlanding Brigade's constituent units, along with the remainder of the 1st Airborne Division, had paraded for a Jeep-borne visit from General Montgomery accompanied by Major-General Browning, Major-General Hopkinson, Brigadier Hicks and his second-in-command, Colonel Osmond Jones, during which he welcomed the Airlanding Brigade to the 8th Army; the 1st Battalion's glider pilots were visited on the airfields where they were supervising the loading of their machines.[37] The visit was something of a whistle stop given that Montgomery also visited the 1st, 2nd and 3rd Parachute Brigades over the following hour to ninety minutes and is unclear if he made the same address on every occasion, but according to the 1st Parachute Battalion War Diary he asked the troops if they were getting enough beer (to a resounding response of No!) and told the 2nd Parachute Battalion that the Italians were nasty rather than nice people, that the 8th Army had killed quite a lot of them and that they were easy to kill.[38] Whatever its actual content, it is interesting to speculate what the Airlanding soldiers made of Montgomery's pep talk, or indeed being diverted from glider loading and other final preparations just twenty-four hours before leaving for battle.

Possibly due to the destruction of their tented accommodation in the ammunition dump fire, the 286 Glider Pilots slated for LADBROKE spent the night of 8-9 July on the airfields with their part-loaded machines, where they also received their final briefings before the arrival of their chalks of passengers.[39] The gliders were marshalled into their take-off order along their respective runways by 16:00 on 9 July by detachments of twenty-eight men equipped with six Jeeps detailed to each of the six airfields from 1st Airlanding Reconnaissance Squadron; each of the 143 machines was marked with a large chalked number running from 1 to 128 with fifteen extra inserts with an existing number with superscript letter or a letter spread in sequence across all six airfields, and the Reconnaissance Squadron Troopers also assisted in directing chalks to their designated glider. The process of moving the Airlanding Brigade units to the airfields commenced at 15:20, timed to deliver the chalks approximately an hour before take-off; the 2nd South Staffords began embussing at 15:10 after a Church Parade led by the Battalion Padre, Captain Alan Buchan, and an address by Lieutenant-Colonel McCardie, for example; according to Lance-Corporal Reginald Brown from A Company they were fed 'quite a good meal' before embussing and were issued with sandwiches and a rock cake for the journey.[40] The 181 Airlanding Field Ambulance contingent paraded later at 16:15, embussed at 16:30 and moved off for the airfields thirty minutes later.[41] The troops were divided into their glider chalks before moving off, with each chalk being allotted its own 3-ton truck provided by the Division RASC contingent marked with a chalked number corresponding to those on the gliders to ease the process of marrying passengers to machines.[42]

All Ranks paraded in their maroon berets with Airborne helmets, Denison smocks and webbing over their khaki drill hot weather uniforms, later to be topped with a lifebelt in case of ditching. At the Section level each rifleman carried a No. 4 rifle with 120 rounds including a fifty-round cloth bandolier, at least one No. 36 fragmentation grenade and two No. 77 white phosphorous grenades, ostensibly for making smoke; men equipped with Sten Guns carried eight magazines of 9mm ammunition totalling 256 rounds and Section second-in-commands carried six Bren magazines in addition to their own load to augment the ammunition carried by the two-man Gun Group. Each Platoon was equipped with a PIAT anti-tank projector and nine rounds – a considerable burden given that the PIAT weighed thirty-two pounds and the rounds three pounds apiece – a pole-charge for demolishing obstacles and Bangalore Torpedo for breaching barbed-wire entanglements or minefields; it is unclear if the latter were pre-stowed in the gliders or carried from the unit lines. The glider pilots were also equipped to participate in ground combat, as the plan tasked them to rally at the Ponte Grande to become the Brigade reserve under Colonel Jones. Approximately seventy were armed with Sten Guns with six magazines and two No. 36 grenades while the remainder carried No. 4 Rifles with seventy rounds and two grenades. The glider pilot's kit, equipment, weapons and ammunition had been lost in the ammunition dump fire but the losses were made up so far as possible by the 1st Airborne Reconnaissance Squadron's Quartermaster (QM), as for some reason the Glider Pilot Battalion's QM was not present in Tunisia. Even then, the replacement kit, weapons and ammunition did not reach the increasingly nervous glider pilots until 15:00, allowing just enough time to strip the weapons of their packing grease but with insufficient time or ammunition for test firing.[43]

On arrival at their designated airfield the Airlanding chalks were provided with hot tea before being delivered to their designated glider. There they received a final briefing from their glider crew that including being issued with lifebelts and were put through a ditching drill improvised individually by the glider pilots, as there was no standardised version.[44] The drill was reportedly accompanied by a good deal of horseplay and the usual cynical soldierly humour. The immediate pre-take off period also brought the final modification to the LADBROKE Air Plan. At approximately 17:30 reports of high winds of up to thirty-five miles per hour at the release point east of Sicily prompted Brigadier-General George H. Beverley, commander of the US 51st Troop Carrier Wing, to order increases in release height; gliders destined for LZ 1 were now to release at 1,800 feet, LZ 2 at 1,400 and LZ 3 at 4,000 feet. The new heights were passed to Lieutenant-Colonel Chatterton who distributed them to the glider and tug crews on the airfields before take offs commenced on schedule shortly before 19:00.[45] C-47s from the 60th Troop Carrier Group Airstrips towing the 2nd South Staffords were the first away from Strips A and B, beginning at 18:53 and 18:48 respectively. Thirty combinations, one a late addition towed by a No. 296 Squadron Albemarle piloted by a Flight-Lieutenant Jamieson, were airborne from Strip B by 19:15 with two, both carrying Jeeps, suffering problems. Glider No. 41, carrying a Jeep prime mover for a 6-Pounder anti-tank gun, cast off after nine miles, but the tug landed alongside and ferried the passengers back to the airfield where another glider was hurriedly loaded with a replacement Jeep and took off again at 20:59; Glider No. 42, carrying a Jeep and Sappers from the 9th Field Company RE, was obliged to cast off when the Jeep became unshipped after sixty miles and was unable to take off again. At Strip A, twenty-nine combinations were aloft by 19:05 and the Mortar Platoon chalk from Glider No. 27 that cast off on take-off was also lifted in another machine by the same tug at 19:35.

Next was Strip C, where at 19:05 twenty-six C-47s from the 62nd Troop Carrier Group began lifting gliders carrying the 1st Border with Glider No. 69 casting off on take-off; its chalk from A Company were loaded aboard another Waco CG4A and took off with a different tug at 19:38. The lift from Strip C also included Major-General Hopkinson, flying as second pilot in Major John Place's Glider No. 55; Place noted that as LADBROKE was a 'brigade job' his Division commander 'had no business to be there at all... But our "Hoppy" wasn't going to be left out of any fun that was available.'[46] Twenty-five combinations from the same units began lifting off from Strip D at 19:20 and all were airborne by 19:55 apart from Glider No. 90 carrying a chalk from D company, which cast off during take-off due to tail flutter; it was towed aloft successfully by the same tug at 20:08.

The remaining twenty-six 1st Border gliders towed by No. 296 Squadron from Strip F, lifting off between 19:35 and 20:12 included the highest number of failures. Glider No. 127 suffered a collapsed wheel during take-off but with no injury to its Battalion HQ chalk, Glider No. 113 carrying anti-tank elements from Support Company damaged its undercarriage after casting off during take-off, Glider Nos. 121 and 126a carrying elements from the anti-tank and Mortar Platoons respectively cast off due to aileron problems, one shortly after getting airborne and one near M'Saken, Glider No. 120 and its chalk from B Company landed safely after the tow-rope snapped shortly after take-off and Glider No. 125 returned to base with its chalk from the Mortar Platoon after its Albemarle tug developed engine problems approaching the Tunisian coast. For reasons that are unclear, Brigadier-General Beverley personally forbade any of the six machines from attempting to take-off again. In all, seven of the 141 Waco CG4As slated for LADBROKE, the Jeep carrier from Strip B and the six from Strip F, failed to cross the Tunisian coastline.[47]

The first of the eight Horsas carrying the Ponte Grande *coup-de-main* force, Glider No. 128, lifted off from Strip E at 19:25, towed by the sole No. 296 Squadron Albemarle involved piloted by the Squadron commander, Wing-Commander Peter May.[48] The Albemarle was despatched thirty minutes in advance because it was slower than the Halifax tugs; the No. 38 Wing Operation Order specified the Albemarle to fly the outbound leg at 125 miles per hour and the Halifaxes at 145 miles per hour.[49] In addition, as the Albemarle was operating toward the limits of its engine power the Horsa was to jettison its landing gear on take-off to reduce drag and make a skid landing at the LZ. The jettisoning was witnessed by Lance-Corporal Brown from the 2nd South Staffords A Company, who initially thought someone had fallen from the glider.[50] The remaining seven combinations, towed by Halifax tugs from No. 295 Squadron, began taking off at 19:55 and all were airborne without incident by 20:07.[51]

While the glider pilots rated what followed as a good or very good tow, the strong wind compelled some tugs to fly higher than their allotted altitudes and the flight also had its share of incidents. Flight-Lieutenant Thomas Grant's Halifax, towing Lieutenant Lennard Withers and 15 Platoon in Glider No. 133, aborted shortly after take-off due to engine trouble but reversed the decision when the engines began to function properly again on the approach to Strip E, even though the tug's auto-pilot was unserviceable and its compass faulty.[52] More alarmingly, the starboard outer engine of the Halifax towing Glider No. 135 carrying Lieutenant John Badger and 18 Platoon caught fire after turning north over Malta, obliging the pilot to fly on three engines for the remaining forty minutes to the release point and to order the jettisoning of equipment to lighten the load; it is unclear if this related to the tug, the glider, or both. Despite this and the high winds the eight Horsas cast off between 21:55 and 22:20, apart from the Albemarle and Glider No. 128 combination, which suffered a broken tow-rope at 22:16 and thus presumably close to the release point. The tugs then released their tow-ropes, executed a 180-degree turn to the right, climbed to 6,000 feet and began the return journey to Tunisia at a mandated speed of 160 miles per hour.[53] The first tug set down at Strip E at 00:20 on 10 July and the last at 01:25, including the Halifax flying on three engines; Wing-Commander May's Albemarle landed with just fifty gallons of fuel from the 769 gallons with which it had taken off.[54]

The eight Horsas did not fare as well as their tugs. Three of the gliders carrying A Company to LZ 3 NORTH failed to reach the Sicilian coast and came down in the sea. Glider No. 128, carrying Lieutenant Robert Barrett's 7 Platoon, Major Lane and Company Sergeant Major (CSM) Robert Woollhouse came down prematurely due to the broken tow-rope; CSM Woollhouse and Lance-Sergeant James Baird from 9th Field Company RE were drowned, Major Lane and four companions successfully swam to shore and were fortuitously picked up later by a Royal Navy ship along with the rest of the chalk from the still-floating glider. Lieutenant R. G. William's thirty-strong 9 Platoon aboard Glider No. 130 lost fourteen drowned, nine were picked up from the floating wreck and made prisoner by an Italian patrol boat and seven made it to shore under their own steam, while the whole of Lieutenant Alfred Clowes' 10 Platoon were lost with Glider No. 131.[55] Glider No. 129, carrying 8 Platoon commanded by Sergeant Victor Williams accompanied by Company second-in-command Captain John McCooke, was the only A Company machine to make landfall on Sicily and came down safely a thousand yards or more south of LZ 3 NORTH. Captain McCooke and his batman then became separated in a clash with Italian troops while ascertaining their position and were captured, while Sergeant Williams and the 8 Platoon party reached their objective, the railway bridge over the Mammiaibica Canal west of the Ponte Grande, but after an abortive attempt to secure the structure were obliged to surrender at around 15:00 on 10 July.[56]

By contrast, the four Horsas carrying C Company all reached dry land, although two came down a significant distance from LZ 3 SOUTH. Glider No. 135, whose Halifax tug had suffered the engine fire, overshot its destination and delivered 2nd Lieutenant John Badger's 18 Platoon and Company second-in-command Captain Ernest Wyss between two and six miles west of the LZ. The Horsa damaged its undercarriage in the landing before striking a brick wall with one passenger suffering a broken leg; this may have been Captain Wyss who was captured with his batman, while Lieutenant Badger, who had suffered a hand injury, led 18 Platoon east and reached the Ponte Grande in the late afternoon of the following day.[57] Glider No. 134 carrying Lieutenant Ronald Robey and 16 Platoon was hit by automatic fire soon after casting off, tracer rounds from which set fire to the port wing. The Horsa also overshot the LZ and came down further afield, around ten miles to the south-west, striking a six-foot wall in the process. The fire spread to the Horsa's fuselage, igniting stowed ammunition panniers and setting off a No. 77 phosphorous grenade, and the burning machine came under intense machine-gun fire which killed Lieutenant Robey, twelve of his men, both glider pilots and wounded seven more. The intense heat and detonating ammunition made it impossible to recover more casualties from the burning wreck and the survivors withdrew eastward toward the coast, where they linked up with the seaborne advance the following day.[58]

Following the cancelled abort by its Halifax tug, Glider No. 133, carrying Lieutenant Lennard Withers' 15 Platoon, was the only Horsa from the *coup-de-main* force to reach its assigned landing place. Pilots Staff-Sergeant Dennis Galpin and Sergeant Nigel Brown put the Horsa down squarely on LZ 3 SOUTH at 22:45 just south of the Ponte Grande, with its passengers suffering no more than a few cuts and bruises and Lieutenant Withers a sprained ankle; after a covert celebratory nip of whisky the glider pilots assisted 15 Platoon's commander in ascertaining their location.[59] At around this time the final Horsa, Glider No. 132 carrying Lieutenant H. D. Scott's 17 Platoon, a party of Sappers from the 9th Field Company RE and the *coup-de-main* commander Major Ballinger, appeared out of the darkness at low altitude, with flaps extended and slowing to touch down. As the horrified members of 15 Platoon looked on, a stream of machine-gun fire stitched the length of the Horsa's fuselage and detonated something onboard, possibly an RE Bangalore Torpedo; the stricken machine exploded in mid-air and the burning wreckage came to a halt on the edge of the Mammiaibica Canal 400 yards west of the Ponte Grande. All on board were killed apart from Lieutenant Scott and two of his men, all three badly injured; Staff-Sergeant Galpin and Sergeant Brown administered morphine to at least one of the casualties.[60]

Undaunted, Lieutenant Withers led his Platoon north to their objective where he swam the Canal and River Anapo with a five-strong Section and attacked a concrete bunker at the north end of the bridge while the remainder of the Platoon simultaneously attacked the south end. The ferocity of the attack overawed the Italian bridge garrison who promptly surrendered and Lieutenant Withers immediately cut the telephone lines and set his Sappers to severing the wiring and removing the detonators from the demolition charges rigged to the structure, the latter with enthusiastic assistance of a Private Curnock, a nursing orderly and former miner attached from 181 Airlanding Field Ambulance.[61] The precise time Objective WATERLOO was secured is unclear, but it was likely around 23:30, given that the Battalion War Diary refers to an Italian truck loaded with troops driving onto the north end at 23:45, 'fifteen mins after the capture' and while the work of removing the detonators was still underway. The truck was comprehensively shot up by Lance-Corporal George Pratt's Section including Bren Gunner William Charlesworth, who personally despatched five of the passengers before reportedly engaging the survivors using his Bren as a club after the magazine was exhausted.[62] Lieutenant Withers and 15 Platoon then settled down to await further enemy reaction or reinforcement from the rest of the 2nd South Staffords.

In the meantime the rest of the LADBROKE force gliders were undergoing their own trials and tribulations. Of the 131 tugs towing the remainder of the 2nd South Staffords and the 1st Border to LZs 1 and 2, four, two from each cohort, returned their CG4As rather than cast them off. Of two C-47s from the 60th Troop Carrier Group, towing Glider Nos. 41 and 52 carrying chalks from the 2nd South Staffords H and E Companies respectively, the former failed to locate Malta and after a fruitless six hour search returned to North Africa, landing eighty miles south of Sfax, while the latter cast the glider free over Malta after failing to locate the release point off Sicily. The other two C-47 tugs were from the 62nd Troop Carrier Group. One, towing Glider No. 83 and its chalk from the 1st Border's A Company, also delivered its charge to Malta after failing to locate the release point while the other, towing Glider No. 85 carrying men from C Company, insisted on towing the glider back to Tunisia after repeatedly failing to locate the release point; on running short of fuel due to the unforeseen extra consumption the tug pilot released the glider just offshore near Sfax where it landed without mishap.[63] The root problem here was presumably the C-47s becoming separated from their four-aircraft formations and thus losing contact with the aircraft carrying the qualified navigator.

The bulk of the remaining 127 CG4As were not so lucky. Of the fifty-seven gliders carrying the 2nd South Staffords, twenty-eight came down in the sea. The 1st Border fared even worse, with forty-three gliders from a total of seventy-two failing to reach the Sicilian coast and most of seven machines listed as missing, four from the former and three from the latter groupings, likely also came down in the Mediterranean. In some instances, the sea landings were the result of accident or miscalculation and in some the gliders almost made it to dry land. Glider No. 23 carrying a chalk from the 2nd South Staffs Mortar Platoon probably suffered a snapped tow-rope for example, Glider No. 62 carrying men from 181 Airlanding Field Ambulance came down a hundred yards off *Capo Ognina* after the tug pilot mistook that headland for the *Capo Porco di Murro* five miles to the north, and Glider No. 7 with its chalk from the South Staffords Battalion HQ came down 600 yards offshore due to the high wind. Glider No. 2, piloted by Lieutenant-Colonel Chatterton and carrying the 1st Airlanding Brigade's commander Brigadier Hicks, just failed to clear the *Capo Porco di Murro's* sheer 100-foot cliffs and the resultant avoiding action put the glider into the sea; both Senior Officers reaching the shore safely. Glider No. 124 was less fortunate and crashed into the cliffs, injuring two men from the 1st Border's B Company with another nine missing.[64]

In many instances, however, the glider ditchings were directly attributable to tug pilots releasing their charges too far out to sea, again in some instances after becoming separated from their four-strong formations and qualified navigator; a key determinant in whether a glider reached land was release distance, given that sixty-three gliders released beyond the recommended 3,000 yards limit from the coast landed in the sea compared with just four ditchings by gliders released within the limit.[65] Glider No. 54a came down eight miles from land for example, Glider No. 54 was released five miles out and came down around three miles short and Glider No. 111 was released just under three miles out and came down a mile off the Maddalena Peninsula.[66] Glider 112, piloted by Sergeant William Bayley and carrying men from the 1st Border, ditched nearby, whereupon the pilot gathered his passengers on the glider's wing, dived into the submerged fuselage to recover arms and equipment and swam around the wreck encouraging the passengers until they were picked up; Sergeant Bayley was subsequently awarded the Distinguished Flying Medal for his actions.[67]

Some of the tug pilots do not appear to have been keen to venture close to the Sicilian coast or were looking to avoid anti-aircraft fire. The C-47 towing Glider No. 16 ordered the glider pilots to release five miles offshore, and the pilots of Glider No. 119 were obliged to cast off when their Albemarle tug turned eastward while still six miles or more from the coast, resulting in the glider ditching between three and four miles short.[68] In the latter instance the glider pilots were unable to communicate with their tug because the intercom had ceased to function, a problem that may also have contributed to other instances, given that twenty-seven glider crews reported intercom failure or malfunction during the fly in, and the after action report recommended that a more robust and reliable cable be procured.[69]

Major Place and Lieutenant-General Hopkinson piloting Glider No. 55 were also obliged to cast off after distant anti-aircraft fire prompted their tug pilot to reverse course and extinguish the C-47's navigation lights, which made station-keeping impossible. Major Place ditched two miles south-east of Avola, twelve miles from their intended destination on the Maddalena Peninsula and all seventeen occupants spent an uncomfortable night atop the increasingly waterlogged and unstable wreck before being picked up by a passing LCA.[70] In addition, Glider No. 3 carrying Lieutenant-Colonel McCardie, commander of the 2nd South Staffords, came down two miles short of the *Capo Porco di Murro* while Glider No. 57, carrying the 1st Border's commander Lieutenant-Colonel Britten, ditched just 200 yards short of it. Both battalion commanders reached the shore safely, Lieutenant-Colonel McCardie after a two-mile swim. This meant that none of the division, brigade or battalion commanders involved in LADBROKE succeeded in reaching Sicilian soil by glider.[71] The key point here is that while four USAAF tug pilots were unwilling to release their charges without accurately ascertaining their location, many more tug pilots were less diligent and released their gliders in uncertain circumstances with potentially serious and frequently fatal consequences for the pilots and passengers. This was not purely a USAAF failing, given that seven of the twenty-six Waco CG4As towed by Albemarle tugs from No. 296 Squadron came down in the sea, all of them after being released beyond the 3,000 yard limit.[72] For their part, as almost fifty of their number had drowned as a result of being released outwith the 3,000 yard limit, the glider pilots rescued from the sea returned to Tunisia intent on dispensing physical retribution to the tug pilots; feelings were running so high that when the USAAF units involved held an awards parade for their participants, Brigadier John Hackett, tasked to look after the LADBROKE returnees, was obliged to confine them to camp until tempers cooled.[73]

Of the remaining fifty or so Waco CG4s that came down on Sicilian soil, nine were released over the 3,000 yards limit from the coast and others were cast off in random releases that scattered the Waco CG4As far and wide across the Sicilian countryside.[74] The farthest flung was Sergeants James Wallwork and Dick Richards' Glider No. 24 carrying a chalk from D Company 2nd South Staffords, which came down near Portopalo on the very south-eastern tip of the island, twenty-five miles south of its intended destination. Glider No. 108 carrying men from the 1st Border's B Company came down fifty yards inland from the beach twelve miles astray near Avola, with four men suffering broken legs. Glider No. 105 carrying Sappers from the 9th Field Company RE came down safely eight miles south-west of the landing area near Cassibile.[75] The random releases led to some interesting exchanges between the glider and tug pilots over the intercom cables that functioned. When the C-47 towing Glider No. 33 and its chalk from the 2nd South Staffords turned off track for the Maddalena Peninsula on seeing anti-aircraft fire from Syracuse, glider pilots Sergeant Thomas Davidson and Sergeant Victor Langton repeatedly requested that the tug head inland while the tug pilot insisted they cast off as they were at the release point. The glider pilots were shocked by the tug pilot ending the exchange with 'Fuck you! I've got to get this kite back to Africa, you're going!' and even more so when he then released the tow-rope, a dangerous action in itself as the heavy rope and metal end linkage were capable of inflicting serious damage on the glider. In the event, the glider reached land and although unable to identify its landing area made a fast and hard landing two miles south-west of LZ 1, fortuitously without setting off the two Bangalore Torpedoes stowed on the floor of the passenger compartment.[76]

Staff-Sergeant Jack Barnwell and USAAF Flight-Officer Russell Parks elicited a more favourable outcome for Glider No. 52a and its passengers from the 2nd South Staffords E Company when their C-47 pilot repeatedly ordered them to cast off five miles from the coast. Staff-Sergeant Barnwell pointed out the glider could not reach land from that far out and when that failed to make any impression threatened to have the tug pilot 'court martialled for cowardice in the face of the enemy'; this did the trick and Glider 52a came down two and a half miles south-west of LZ 1, although two men were badly injured when the machine struck a wall toward the end of its landing run.[77]

As the latter example shows, merely reaching land was not the end of the matter, as gliders that came in anywhere near their intended destination then had to deal with the obstacle-strewn terrain that Major-General Hopkinson thought constituted a suitable landing area. The pilots of Glider No. 8, Staff-Sergeant Dawkins and Sergeant Kelly, both suffered broken legs after running into a wall at the end of its run, as did Glider No. 35, injuring three men from the 2nd South Staffords' Pioneer Platoon. While Glider No. 106 came in alongside LZ 2 as planned, it scraped under power cables to do so before crashing into a tree; all but two of its chalk from the 1st Border's HQ were injured, although pilots Staff-Sergeant Kay Cawood and Sergeant Bert Holt were unscathed.[78] Lieutenant-Colonel Henniker, the 1st Airborne Division's CRE travelled aboard Glider No. 10 with the 1st Airlanding Brigade's Deputy Commander Colonel Osmond Jones and while all aboard emerged unscathed, gave a graphic description of landing south-west of LZ 1. The glider 'jerked upwards, bounced down again, flashed past a searchlight, hit a tree, smashing the portside wing and spun to a halt almost overhanging the cliffs. The glider...did not burst into flames. It simply crumpled up with a sound of breaking twigs.'[79] In fact, the glider came to rest in a cliff-top vineyard with its starboard wing touching a tree, hard up against a single-strand wire fence atop the fifty-foot cliff and a hundred yards from an Italian searchlight emplacement whose operators promptly opened fire.[80]

Even coming down without striking obstacles was a risky business. Sergeant Victor Miller was flying as second pilot to Lieutenant Arthur Boucher-Giles in Glider No. 110, carrying a 6-Pounder anti-tank gun with Sergeant Hodge and two men from the 1st Border's H Company. Miller was chanting out the diminishing airspeed and height and noted the glide was a little fast at 200 feet when 'there came an exploding crash and a brilliant red flash...A noise like thunder filled my ears and blackness descended.' The 6-Pounder had broken loose from its moorings, seriously injuring Sergeant Hodge and pushing Sergeant Miller's head into the glider's instrument panel. On exiting the stricken machine Sergeant Miller gave a graphic description of its condition: 'It lay like some grotesque prehistoric monster, the nose tilted up in the air. It had almost broken away from the rest of the body, connected only by some twisted tubular steel. The underside of the body had been ripped clean away and...pieces of it scattered along the gouged earth for some fifty yards.' After coming under enemy rifle fire the Glider Pilots left one man to tend Sergeant Hodge and set off for the Ponte Grande, linking up with a party of twenty from the 1st Border en route.[81] Landing injuries equated to almost a fifth of the 1st Border's personnel that came down on dry land; according to their War Diary about thirty-five men, eighteen per cent of the total that came down on land, were injured in landing accidents, many caused by Airborne handcarts becoming unlashed by the impact of landing.[82]

Nonetheless, by the early hours of Saturday 10 July at least fifty chalks of Airlanding soldiers were on the ground in south-eastern Sicily despite the weather, the failings of some tug pilots, the terrain and bad landings.[83] This included approximately 160 men from the 1st Border who emerged from their gliders on land relatively unscathed, subsequently augmented by a further hundred or so who made it ashore from ditched gliders and joined the fight; figures for the 2nd South Staffords are less detailed but were in the region of 290 in all according to the Battalion War Diary.[84] Surprise was compromised by the military radio station on the *Capo Porco di Murro* broadcasting news of the landings to *16° Corpo* HQ before being overrun, although circumstances conspired to nullify any benefit from the timely warning. *Generale* Rossi immediately ordered four of his mobile units to converge on Syracuse and the Ponte Grande, but as transmission of the order was via telephone rather than radio, it was blocked by the 1st Airlanding Brigade's personnel diligently cutting every telephone line they came across.

The impact of this was magnified by the inability of Italian sub-HQs to identify the focus of the glider landings because of their widely scattered nature; according to the British Official Histories only eleven Waco CG4As came down on their allotted LZs and while many came down within five miles of them, landings were scattered across the twenty-five miles between the

Capo Porco di Murro and the Pachino Peninsula at the south-eastern tip of the island.[85] Wherever they came down, the Ponte Grande was the magnet for the Airlanding soldiers and the single-minded diligence with which they went about this and taking the fight to the Axis defenders at every opportunity was a tribute to their training and aggression in itself, irrespective of rank or unit. As the 9th Field Company RE War Diary put it, 'Gliders were very dispersed [and] instead of the ensuing battle being a co-ordinated Brigade effort, it turned into innumerable fights, [with] the Commanders of the Glider Loads attempting to reach their Company objectives.'[86]

The activities of Lieutenant-Colonel Henniker and the officer-heavy chalk from Glider No. 10 provides a clear example of this.[87] Having survived their cliff edge landing and an exchange of fire and hand grenades with the nearby searchlight crew during which Brigade Padre Captain David Hourigan was killed, Brigade deputy commander Colonel Jones ordered their transport set ablaze with a No. 77 grenade and led the party along an east-west track until it bisected the Cassibile-Syracuse railway line. They then followed the tracks northward, at some point looting Glider No. 79, abandoned partly on the line by its chalk from the 1st Border's C Company. The Airlanding Brigade HQ War Diary refers to the loot comprising a pair of wire cutters, a No. 77 grenade, a two-gallon container of tea and a 'much appreciated' melon, whereas Lieutenant-Colonel Henniker's account refers to 'melons, fruit and several bottles of wine'; the precise point when the looting took place also varies between accounts. At 02:30 Colonel Jones' party caught up with Lieutenant William Budgen and No. 2 Section from the 1st Border's Reconnaissance Platoon accompanied by glider pilots Staff-Sergeant Chapman and Sergeant Kelly, who had come in on Glider No. 123 and were also following the tracks north.

A few hundred yards later the group, now numbering over thirty men, came under fire prompting a hasty attack that cleared a group of Italian troops, described as 'miserable "Home Guards"' by Lieutenant Budgen, from a position just short of the Santa Teresa Longarini railway station, killing at least one and capturing several more. Lieutenant-Colonel Henniker had inadvertently charged into a group of four Italians before being rendered unconscious by the blast from a No. 36 grenade thrown by Colonel Jones from the opposite side of the cutting. He regained consciousness next to a dead Italian with three more standing over his inert body with their hands in the air, to find he had suffered seven grenade fragment wounds in the right leg, but he remained ambulatory thanks to the efforts of Medical Orderly Lance-Corporal Hill from Lieutenant Budgen's Section.

When access to the nearby main Cassibile-Syracuse road proved to be blocked by barbed wire entanglements, Colonel Jones led the party to a nearby farm to await full daylight at around 04:00, where they washed, shaved and rested after a meal of freshly gathered fried onions, tomatoes and melon. Their rest was interrupted at around 07:00 by a nearby Italian gun battery opening fire, followed more alarmingly by counter-fire from Allied warships landing within a hundred yards of the farmhouse. This prompted

Colonel Jones to despatch Brigade Signals Officer Captain R. S. Roberson to the main Cassibile-Syracuse road at around 08:00 to make contact with the sea landing force, and then lead Lieutenant Budgen and a Private Cox on a reconnaissance to locate the Italian gun battery. On returning from the reconnaissance Jones organised and briefed a fifteen-strong party for a deliberate attack which went in at *c*.11:15 under smoke and covering fire from two Bren Groups. Despite Allied naval gunfire falling on its location, the attackers penetrated and overran the battery, grenading gun pits, slit trenches and bunkers, killing five or six Italians, wounding six more, taking forty to fifty prisoner and liberated an unnamed glider pilot being held captive in one of the grenaded bunkers; it is unclear if he was wounded or killed in the incident. The attackers then removed the sighting mechanisms from the five guns, burned maps and ranging data and set fire to everything flammable including the ammunition dump, which finally exploded around midday, thirty minutes after the attackers had withdrawn.

While the fight was underway a Company from the 2nd Battalion The Northamptonshire Regiment, which had come ashore at the ACID NORTH Landing Area at *c*.04:00 with 17th Brigade, appeared west of the battery position and engaged the Italian machine-gun posts on that section of the battery perimeter. The Company commander informed Colonel Jones that the battery position was one of his Brigade's objectives and Jones set off to make contact with the commander of 17th Brigade, Brigadier Gerald Tarleton, while the rest of the attacking party withdrew with the wounded and prisoners to their farm start point. There, according to Lieutenant Budgen, they found 'a well earned cup of tea waiting' along with more elements of the 2nd Northamptons. At around 14:00 the party resumed its move northward, linking up with other scattered elements en route and finally reached the Ponte Grande at 22:00, where they were absorbed into the re-established defensive perimeter.[88]

Back at the Ponte Grande itself, Lieutenant Withers and his little band from 15 Platoon spent an anxious five hours after securing the structure at 23:30, seemingly unmolested after shooting up the Italian truck at 23:45; the quiet was presumably at least in part due the continuing inability of *16° Corpo* HQ to transmit its orders to concentrate in the area of Syracuse and the bridge. Their first contact with the remainder of the 1st Airlanding Brigade came at 04:30 with the arrival of Lieutenant Gordon Welch and between seven and fourteen men from the Brigade HQ Defence Platoon, who had come down at *c*.22:15 on the *Capo Porco di Murro* in Glider No. 6, flown by Lieutenant Frank Barclay and Sergeant Ronald Owen. Landing unscathed apart from a collapsed undercarriage that delayed unloading the chalk's Airborne handcart, the party then clashed with an Italian patrol, killing two and taking one prisoner in exchange for one lightly wounded. The prisoner was then persuaded to act as a guide by a Staff-Sergeant Taylor and led the chalk safely around the intervening enemy posts to the Ponte Grande via a pause with a chalk from 181 Airlanding Ambulance and Major Thomas du Boulay from the 1st Border's H Company.[89] Shortly after Lieutenant Welch's arrival, three Italian armoured cars approached the bridge in what was described as a determined attack. This was a serious development given that the Airlanding soldiers lacked any anti-armour weapons, but the blizzard of small-arms fire they brought down on the vehicles reportedly killed the commander of one and all three then withdrew. There then followed a period of small groups of men from the 1st Airlanding Brigade trickling into the Ponte Grande perimeter, some by their own navigational skills, some guided by the bombing of Syracuse by Wellingtons from No. 205 Group and some drawn in by the efforts of the men holding the bridge; Staff Sergeant Cawood recalled hearing a vehicle horn, presumably that on the Italian truck shot up on the bridge, spelling out 'WATERLOO Taken' in Morse code.[90]

At 05:00, possibly while the armoured car attack was underway, Major Beazley and a party of fifteen Sappers from his 9th Field Company RE arrived, having landed in Lieutenant James Dale and Sergeant David Baker's Glider No. 38 just short of LZ 2 in a tomato plantation; the Sappers immediately set about removing the demolition charges still rigged to the bridge.[91] The Sappers were followed ten minutes later by fifteen glider pilots, Borders and South Staffords led by Lieutenant-Colonel Arthur Walch and Lieutenant Boucher-Giles, who had already met Major Beazley's chalk en route; the fifteen included Staff-Sergeant Cawood, his co-pilot Staff-Sergeant Bert Holt and Sergeant Miller, having recovered from his close encounter with Glider No. 110's instrument panel.[92] As Lieutenant-Colonel Walch was a GSO1 on Browning's Major-General Airborne Forces staff he was presumably there in an observer role. Whatever the rationale, as Senior Officer present he assumed command of the bridge defence with Major Beazley as his deputy, likely to the relief of Lieutenants Withers and Welch, and reorganised the defence to cover both ends of the bridge.[93] Small parties and individuals continued to drift into the perimeter including a further substantial reinforcement at 06:30 with the arrival of twenty-three men led by Lieutenants Ernest Deucher and Jack Reynolds from the 2nd South Staffords' 12 Platoon and Reconnaissance Platoon respectively, fresh from eliminating an enemy machine-gun position en route. This brought the strength of the force defending the Ponte Grande up to approximately seven Officers and eighty Other Ranks, equipped in addition to their personal weapons with four Bren Guns, a Two-Inch Mortar with a handful of smoke rounds, a Three-Inch Mortar with a similarly small number of high-explosive rounds earmarked for emergencies, and a solitary No. 74 anti-tank grenade, better known as the Sticky Bomb.[94]

With the sun up, the scales began to tilt slowly and inexorably against the Airlanding soldiers. At 07:00 another truck carrying Italian troops approached from the north along the *Strada* 115 and slowed almost to a stop at the end of the bridge. It was then comprehensively shot up, swerving off the road and stalling on the grass verge.[95] Most on board were killed but some wounded passengers were rescued despite fire by 15 Platoon's Medical Orderly, Private Reginald Tyrer; Tyrer was assisted over the course of the defence by Privates Charles Weate and James Eden, and presumably Private Curnock from 181 Airlanding Field Ambulance who had assisted in removing the demolition charge detonators the previous night.[96] The bridge perimeter then came under heavy and accurate mortar fire and while the defenders' Three-Inch Mortar succeeded in knocking out an Italian mortar dug in by the railway bridge over the Mammiaibica Canal, the duel reduced their stock of ammunition to just three rounds.

The mortar exchange was followed by a ground attack by two companies of *Regia Marina* infantry from the Syracuse garrison and while this was rebuffed, the defenders were obliged to withdraw south at 08:00 to a tighter perimeter on the canal bridge, with Lieutenant Withers and two Sections covering the eastern sector and the remainder covering to the west.[97] Major Beazley was killed by a mortar bomb an hour later and from 10:00 the number of British casualties steadily increased in parallel with the volume of Italian mortar and small-arms fire, augmented until midday by 'very heavy and accurate fire' from a field gun sited on a ridge 300 yards north-west of the bridge; from 11:30 the attackers also received substantial reinforcement from *Generale di Divisione* Giulio Porcinari's *54ª Napoli Divisione*, specifically the *75° Reggimento di Fanteria*.[98]

There was a growing shortage of ammunition. At 12:45 the mounting pressure obliged a further British withdrawal to the east side of the canal bridge, in part to avoid enemy enfilading fire from the loop in the Mammiaibica Canal west of the bridge site, although this was undone at 14:00 by an Italian machine-gun located at the north end of the bridge and over the following half-hour the attackers pressed forward to within 300 yards of the glider soldiers' position. By 15:45 all the defender's outlying positions had been eliminated and systematic mortar fire had driven the fifteen to twenty able-bodied survivors east to an open and thus indefensible area at the confluence of the canal and the sea. There, having exhausted their remaining ammunition, they were overrun and captured around fifteen minutes later by elements of *Colonnello Comandante* Francesco Ronco's *75° Reggimento di Fanteria*, along with a small group of glider pilots commanded by Lieutenant Boucher-Giles holding out on the bank of the River Anapo.[99] The Airlanding Brigade prisoners were marched away by their captors, collecting others during the march until the party numbered eighty-eight including Lieutenant-Colonel Walch and three US Army personnel who had played a full role in the defence of the Ponte Grande.[100] The three were War Correspondent Roderick McDonald and Flight-Officers Sam Fine and Russell Parks, who had co-piloted Glider No. 13 and Glider No. 52a respectively; Flight-Officer Fine had been wounded twice in the right shoulder and once in the neck in the fighting, and was down to the final two rounds in his .45 automatic pistol when captured.[101]

Not all the glider soldiers were rounded up. Despite being wounded in the hip Lieutenant Welch led a party of six or seven men including Private Sam Sidebottom from the 1st Border's Mortar Platoon up a drainage ditch paralleling the canal east of the bridge where they concealed themselves under a small concrete culvert, while Bren Gunner Private Charlesworth also concealed himself despite having been wounded in the stomach. All escaped detection as *Colonnello* Ronco's men failed to carry out a systematic search for fugitives, but they were trapped in situ when the Italians set up a machine-gun post overlooking their hiding places.[102]

Thus at *c*.15:30 on Saturday 10 July 1943 the Ponte Grande passed back into Italian hands, seventeen hours after Staff-Sergeant Galpin and Sergeant Brown brought Horsa Glider No. 133 to a halt on LZ 3 SOUTH and sixteen hours after Lieutenant Withers and 15 Platoon had secured the structure. Across that time frame Operation LADBROKE had incurred a heavy cost. Despite 'less than half' of the formation being involved in the ground fighting, the 1st Airlanding Brigade lost approximately 313 dead, 252 drowned and sixty-one killed in action, 133 wounded and forty-four missing.[103] Within these totals the 2nd South Staffords War Diary reported a loss of 332 men on 20 July, including fifty-four killed, sixty-nine missing, twenty-one missing believed killed and seven missing. The 9th Field Company RE War Diary reported losing four dead and sixteen missing, with Major Beazley being the sole officer casualty.[104] The 1st Battalion The Glider Pilot Regiment lost fourteen dead, twenty-nine wounded and fifty-eight missing, 101 men in all; the number of missing initially included fifteen Officers and fluctuated between ninety and seventy-four NCOs over the period 11-24 July as individuals and reports drifted back to the Battalion lines near Sousse.[105] In return and despite the accumulated confusions, Operation LADBROKE achieved its purpose insofar as the coastal gun batteries were prevented from interfering with the sea-borne landings and the Ponte Grande remained intact to facilitate the British ground advance northward toward Syracuse and Augusta. That, however, was dependent on the success of the British amphibious landings south of the Ponte Grande, and in the wider sense that of the US parachute landings before Gela and the US amphibious landings on Sicily's south-eastern aspect.

10

'A Self Adjusting Foul Up'

The US 505th Regimental Combat Team and the HUSKY ONE Parachute Drop, D-Day Minus One, Friday 9 July to D-Day 10 July

The amphibious landings by the US Western Task Force involved putting three divisions from Lieutenant-General George Patton's US 7th Army ashore at three Landing Areas along the Bay of Gela, on the south-eastern aspect of Sicily. These were Major-General Lucian K. Truscott's US 3rd Infantry Division, assigned to the four Beaches of the JOSS Landing Area astride the port of Licata at the western extremity of the Bay; Major-General Terry Allen's US 1st Infantry Division, assigned to the DIME Landing Area's six Beaches fronting and running east from Gela in the centre; and in the east Major-General Troy C. Middleton's US 45th Infantry Division, assigned to the CENT Landing Area of six Beaches straddling the mouth of the River Acate. The JOSS landings were intended to protect the western flank of the invasion, the CENT landings in the east to link up with the British Eastern Task Force landings on the eastern aspect of the island, while the DIME landings were placed to exploit the limited local road network for an advance inland.

An Airborne landing to shield the amphibious landing from Axis interference was allotted to Major-General Matthew B. Ridgway and the 82nd Airborne Division. As noted earlier, there were insufficient USAAF C-47s available to deliver the Division in its entirety in a single lift due to providing aircraft for the British Operation LADBROKE, so Ridgway was committed to two drops, HUSKY ONE and HUSKY TWO, over two successive days. The former was to take place immediately before the amphibious landings and was to be a night drop, as the amphibious landings were to commence at 02:45 for concealment. The mission was assigned to Colonel James M. Gavin's 505th Parachute Infantry Regiment, upgraded to Regimental Combat Team (RCT) with the attachment of the 456th Parachute Artillery Battalion, a company from the 307th Airborne Engineer Battalion, the 82nd Airborne Signal Company and 307th Airborne Medical Company and reinforced with the 3rd Battalion, 504th Parachute Infantry Regiment. The mission employed six Drop Zones (DZs) north-east of Gela to secure a major road junction and the road and rail bridges across the River Acate five and ten miles south-east of Gela respectively, two junctions on the Gela-Niscemi road north of the DIME Landing Area and an adjacent area of high ground overlooking the coast, which were to be held until relieved by the sea-landing forces. Gavin's force was also tasked to hold the DZ for HUSKY TWO in the evening of D-Day involving the remainder of the Division's parachute elements, followed by the rest of the 82nd Airborne Division in two glider lifts, the first on D-Day Plus One and the second to be carried out as and when practicable.

After two days of intensive briefings, Friday 9 July began with a pre-dawn reveille and breakfast for the paratroopers assigned to carry out HUSKY ONE at the ten satellite camps around Kairouan, after which they were issued their supplies and equipment for the operation.[1] In addition to personal weapon and ammunition, twenty-one en bloc clips totalling 168 rounds for a Garand M1 armed rifleman and with the addition of a .45 Colt automatic pistol for Officers and NCOs, a typical load consisted of a bayonet and/or a trench knife along with a folding-blade M2 jump knife in its special jump jacket pocket, one smoke and four fragmentation grenades, a Hawkins anti-tank mine, a gas mask, two first aid kits, a blanket, a canvas shelter-half, a thirty-foot rope, an entrenching tool, a full canteen with Halazone water purifying tablets, gloves, a wrist watch, a Paratrooper M1C helmet and a M1942 jump suit with a sewn-in compass and silk escape map of Sicily. At the suggestion of Lieutenant-Colonel Arthur F. Gorham, commander of the 505th Regiment's 1st Battalion, every man sewed a strip of luminous tape onto the inside of a cuff on their jump jacket as a recognition measure.[2] Each man carried a small pack called a musette-bag containing spare underwear, two pairs of socks, a mess kit, a K-Ration boxed meal, a D-Ration chocolate bar, toothbrush and toothpowder, soap, razor with spare blades, pencil and paper, ten packs of cigarettes and a Zippo lighter and matches; all were also issued with metal clickers for use as an additional identification measure, one click for challenge, two clicks in response. The individual loads were augmented in many cases with a can of belted .30 machine-gun or other type of ammunition, giving each paratrooper an average burden in the region of ninety pounds including their T5 main and reserve parachutes. Heavier items including .30 machine-guns, M1 Bazookas, 60mm and 81mm mortars, radios, field telephones and wire, demolition materials and equipment, ammunition and medical supplies were packed into equipment bundles carried in drop racks under the C-47's fuselage, which were attached before take-off.[3]

The exception to this may have been the 456th Parachute Field Artillery Battalion, which appears to have despatched a detachment to its carrier unit's airfield to load its twelve M1A1 75mm Pack Howitzers during the day. Each gun weighed 1,440 pounds and could be broken down into nine loads, although according to Private First Class Douglas Bailey from the Battalion's Battery B there were eight; six were carried in bundles attached to the racks under the C-47's fuselage and two more, one consisting of the two pneumatic wheels lashed together and the other containing the breech block and sight in a special padded box, were carried inside the aircraft to be dropped from the door.[4] In the afternoon the paratroopers received a final detailed briefing to ensure every man knew his mission and each was issued an armband bearing the US flag to be worn on the right arm and a strip of white cloth to be worn on the left arm as a night recognition measure. They then donned their jump uniform and equipment and after an evening meal served early at 16:00 were driven out to the airfields in trucks that delivered each stick to its designated C-47. There they drew their parachutes, loaded equipment bundles onto drop racks, were issued the D-Day challenge and password of 'George/Marshall', an inflatable T4 Life Vest to be worn under the parachute harness and a mimeographed sheet bearing a pre-jump message from Colonel Gavin.

Gavin also made a personal address to the 505th Regiment's 2nd Battalion from the bonnet of a Jeep two hours or so before take-off, presumably at the Kairouan satellite airfield used by the 64th Troop Carrier Group; the 64th Group belonged to the 51st Troop Carrier Wing but was temporarily attached to the 52nd Wing for HUSKY ONE.[5] The final task of donning life vests, blacking faces with burnt cork and fitting main and reserve parachutes was done beside the C-47s, with the arrival of the aircrew and their performing final pre-flight checks around thirty minutes before take-off being the signal for the paratroopers to begin the strenuous process of boarding. As many men were still suffering from dysentery each machine had been thoughtfully provided with a 'honey bucket' for use by the afflicted, some of whom left fitting their parachutes until immediately prior to jumping to ease use; some reportedly did not bother and 'jumped into Sicily with more in their pants than they started out with'.[6] Many of the troops were likely too busy for last-minute trepidation, although Private Irvin W. Seelye from the 505th Regiment's 2nd Battalion recalled 'No one knew what to expect or what was about to happen. Each was nervous and frightened.' Some, on the other hand, were positively eager to be away from Kairouan including Private Russell McConnell from the 3rd Battalion whose considered opinion was that 'Africa was a living hell. We knew that Sicily couldn't be any worse… By the time we were ready to go to Sicily, we were more than glad to go.'[7]

The C-47 pilots and paratroop jumpmasters received a final briefing at joint conferences, presumably on a Group or Squadron basis, on 9 July where all were briefed on timings, formations, routing and a myriad of other details for the fly-in. Gavin's 3,405 paratroopers were to be carried in 226 C-47s from Colonel Harold L. Clark's 52nd Troop Carrier Wing in five serials, one from each of the Wing's five constituent Groups, with each serial of around forty-five C-47s divided into five flights of nine aircraft; the multiple vee-formation was presumably in part to offset the same shortage of navigators that had obliged the glider tugs from the 51st Troop Carrier Wing to fly in four-strong formations on the LADBROKE fly-in.[8] In the lead was the 61st Troop Carrier Group carrying Lieutenant-Colonel Charles W. Koun's 3rd Battalion 504th Parachute Infantry Regiment, followed by Major Edward C. Krause and the 3rd Battalion 505th Parachute Infantry Regiment aboard aircraft from the 314th Troop Carrier Group. Next came the 313th Troop Carrier Group carrying Lieutenant-Colonel Gorham and the 505th Regiment's 1st Battalion, then the 316th Troop Carrier Group carrying Gavin's Regimental HQ, part of the 456th Parachute Field Artillery Battalion and other attached elements, and finally the 64th Troop Carrier Group carrying Major Mark J. Alexander and the 2nd Battalion, 505th Parachute Infantry Regiment.[9]

The most problematic element of the fly-in plan was the route. Ridgway had originally envisaged flying the direct 250-mile line from Kairouan to Gela and then ten miles inland to the various DZs and, as this involved flying directly over Vice-Admiral Hewitt's Western Naval Task Force, assumed the US Navy would agree to refrain from firing anti-aircraft guns for the time the C-47s were passing overhead. Vice-Admiral Hewitt and the US Navy representatives at Allied Force HQ (AFHQ) refused however, on the grounds it would leave the invasion fleet defenceless in the face of possible Axis air attack as the troop carriers were passing over, because they could not guarantee sufficiently tight control over the merchant vessels and smaller craft, and insisted that the airlift remain at least five miles from Task Force ships at all times. They then relented and permitted access to a 'certain designated route' that almost tripled the initial fly-in distance but refused to countenance a 'safe corridor' for subsequent supply drops, the D-Day evening reinforcement drop and the planned glider lifts. This sparked an intense bureaucratic battle over the four days up to 6 July that drew in Patton, USAAF Lieutenant-General Spaatz and eventually Eisenhower; the resultant last-minute compromise only appears to have come about because Vice-Admiral Hewitt was en route to the landing area under strict radio silence and thus unable to raise further objections.[10]

As a result of all this the length of the HUSKY ONE fly-in was extended to approximately 640 miles, beginning with a roughly fifty-mile leg from the Kairouan satellite airfields and Enfidaville to the forming up point over Kuriat Island twenty miles off Sousse. The serials were then to fly 200 miles east past Linosa and the eastern tip of Malta before turning north-north-east for sixty miles to a point short of Cape Passero and then turn west-north-west to parallel the Sicilian coast for thirty-six miles to the edge of the Bay of Gela. The formations were then to turn north-west for around sixteen miles to just short of the mouth of the River Acate before turning north for the run-in to the various DZs; after delivering their sticks the C-47s were to perform a wide 180-degree turn, cross the coast west of Gela for a 120-mile run to a point just south of Pantelleria followed by a final 130-mile leg back to Kairouan.[11] Following this convoluted routing would have been a challenge for fully trained aircrew in daylight; doing it at night, at low level in limited illumination over the open sea was a tall order, especially given the shortage of trained navigators and the limited amount of night flying training the C-47 crews had been able to complete before HUSKY was launched. As Ridgway put it in a post-war interview 'At war's end we still could not have executed [the] first SICILY mission, AS LAID ON, at night and under like conditions' [original emphasis].[12]

The five serials were to commence take off at 19:30 in order to be over the DZs in Sicily in the thirty-six minute window beginning at 23:30, and form up into a convoy with a ten-minute gap between each serial stretching back around a hundred miles from the lead C-47 flown by USAAF Colonel Willis W. Mitchell, commander of the 61st Troop Carrier Group. The transports were then to fly in formation at low level to avoid radar detection, before climbing to 600 feet for the final leg and to identify a mile-long body of water near the mouth of the River Acate called the *Biviere di Gela*, the final check point for the run-in to the DZs.[13]

With their pre-flight checks complete and their sticks of paratroopers aboard complete with honey buckets, the C-47s started their engines and began taxiing to their take-off positions, stirring up the omnipresent fine dust into huge clouds visible five miles away, in some instances so thick that pilots were obliged to take-off on instruments. The process of getting the 52nd Troop Carrier Wing into the air began thirty minutes before sunset at 20:15, with the C-47s taking off in increments of three at thirty-second intervals, and was complete by *c*.20:45.[14] Some machines may have taken off earlier. According to Captain Edwin M. Sayre, commander of the 505th Regiment's Company A, the first aircraft from the 313th Troop Carrier Group lifted off at 19:30; the disparity was presumably due to the Kairouan satellite airfields staggering take-offs to assist in forming up.[15] Whatever the precise timings, the overall process went well in spite of the dust; as one Fifth Army observer put it: 'Planning for the final takeoff [sic] had been complete and thorough [and] went off like clockwork.'[16] Thereafter matters ran less smoothly, however. The C-47s were able to maintain station while the light remained but the onset of darkness made it increasingly difficult. Illumination from the quarter moon proved to be less than anticipated, the mandatory low altitude reduced visibility further by coating windscreens with salt thrown up by the wind and propeller-wash, and the C-47s' wingtip navigation lights also proved difficult to see, along with the standard practice of using Aldis lamps in the aircraft's astrodomes as a beacon for stragglers; station keeping was eroded further by winds of up to thirty-five miles per hour, twenty miles per hour above the safe jumping limit, which interfered with dead-reckoning navigation and added airsickness to the woes of the men being carried in the pitching, blacked-out transports.[17] The pilots of the C-47s understandable reaction was to increase distance from nearby aircraft to avoid collisions, but this led to a general loosening of formation that in some instances resulted in individual or small groups of machines losing contact with their serials altogether.

All this impacted on the Group serials but in different ways and with varying degrees of severity. The lead serial from the 61st Troop Carrier Group reached and identified the first way point on Malta twelve minutes ahead of schedule, albeit with several stragglers, two of which became separated and ended up making landfall on the Italian mainland before realising their error and turning west for Sicily. By the final stages of the journey only Colonel Mitchell's flight of nine C-47s remained on course and dropped their sticks from Lieutenant-Colonel Charles W. Koun's 3rd Battalion 504th Parachute

Regiment at 23:32 an estimated mile east of their designated DZ Q, just south of Niscemi.[18] The landing pattern was also somewhat wide, due to a combination of formation separation, high wind and in at least one instance being despatched significantly above the scheduled jump altitude of 500 feet; Lieutenant Roy. M. Hanna from the 3rd Battalion's Machine-Gun Platoon later recalled that it was 'the highest jump I ever made – must have been at least 2,000 feet'.[19] Despite all this and the darkness the paratroopers were generally able to locate their fellows without enemy interference and gravitated toward high ground.

Lieutenant-Colonel Kouns came down close to a road three miles south-east of Niscemi and after gathering in nine of his men set up on a nearby hill where he was joined by another group led by Lieutenant James C. Ott; the latter had landed approximately a mile and a half from the 504th Regiment's target, a road junction just south of Niscemi dubbed Objective X, and after ascertaining his position and leaving four jump casualties in the care of friendly Italian civilians, patrolled eastward from around 02:00 on 10 July before coming upon Lieutenant-Colonel Kouns.

On recovering consciousness after a hard landing Private First Class Shelby R. Hord and his three-man machine-gun squad from Company H set up their weapon on a ruin-topped hill known as the Castello Nocera and gathered in a number of equipment bundles before being relieved by Lieutenant Willis J. Ferrill with a party of seventeen men. By 09:00 the Castello Nocera force had grown to twenty-four and was augmented by a further fifteen men led by Lieutenant George J. Watts from Company G, who had landed a mile and a half from Niscemi. High-flying Lieutenant Hanna spent several fruitless hours searching for the equipment bundles containing his machine-guns before setting in on another hilltop to await daylight with seven men from his Platoon.[20] The remainder of the 3rd Battalion 504th Regiment was scattered across a fifty-mile swathe of south-eastern Sicily, with six sticks remaining unaccounted for a month after the drop.[21] The C-47 carrying Battalion S2 Intelligence Officer, 1st Lieutenant T. Moffatt Burriss and his stick from HQ Company came under anti-aircraft fire as it approached Sicily from the east, prompting the pilot to illuminate the red stand-by light and green jump light in quick succession rather than some minutes apart according to regulations. Burriss's prompt order of 'Go' was consequently met with complaints that some men had not yet hooked up but all made a dispersed exit apart from a Lieutenant Rosenthal and two men who were unable to jump, as the C-47 was back over the sea; Rosenthal prevailed on the pilot to make a second run and the three were despatched some fifteen miles from the rest of the stick. Burriss landed alone in a vineyard and after meeting up with two men from his stick ambushed a party of enemy troops with hand grenades before retiring back through the vineyard.[22]

The second serial, from the 314th Troop Carrier Group carrying Major Edward C. Krause's 3rd Battalion 505th Parachute Infantry Regiment and elements of the 456th Parachute Field Artillery Battalion to DZ T, had the most successful fly-in of the night. The serial maintained cohesion and successfully identified all the navigational way points until the last one for the final run-in to the DZs; unable to identify the mouth of the River Acate or the *Biviere di Gela*, the serial wheeled back out to sea to go around for a second run. The problem was again likely illumination, for while the C-47 pilots had been issued a black and white aerial photograph of the river mouth from Colonel Gavin's personal reconnaissance on the night of 11-12 June, the moonlight was substantially weaker on the night and the target was obscured by dust and smoke from pre-landing bombing and anti-aircraft fire.[23] The serial lost one C-47, carrying elements of Battery C, 456th Parachute Field Artillery Battalion, on its second run in to the coast, presumably to anti-aircraft fire; the machine ditched just offshore and all aboard made it to the beach by rubber dinghy.[24] Again failing to identify the river mouth, the serial became fragmented with some sticks being delivered close to the designated DZ T but most coming down near Vittoria, fourteen miles to the south-east.

The exception to this was the trailing flight of nine C-47s commanded by Captain William R. Bommar, carrying Captain Willard Follmer and the 3rd Battalion's Company I. Tasked to drop into a small DZ to secure a defended crossroad junction five miles south-east of Gela and light a beacon to guide the amphibious landing, Follmer was dissatisfied with the allotted DZ and disobeyed a direct order from Major Krause to approach Bommar in person. The two officers then selected a more accessible and recognisable DZ, and Follmer also prevailed upon the pilot to ensure his flight was assigned the rear location in the Group serial, to drop from smaller, trailing groups of three C-47s rather than one large vee formation, and for Bommar to fly in the co-pilot seat to allow visual confirmation on a white building selected as a final waypoint to the new DZ.[25]

The ad hoc planning worked so well that Company I was the only unit from the 505th Regiment's 3rd Battalion to be delivered accurately onto its assigned DZ that night, at 23:49, with just one C-47 dropping a stick commanded by Lieutenant Walter B. Kroener further inland.[26] However, landing in a narrow valley in high wind led to some men making sudden and hard landings on the slopes; Captain Follmer broke his right leg while Corporal Harry J. Buffone from his stick crashed into a tiled farmhouse roof before being dragged off and dropped to the ground by a gust of wind, fortunately without serious injury.[27] Utilising a mule commandeered by one of his men for transport, Captain Follmer led a group from his HQ group to Company I's road-junction objective where another group led by Lieutenant Joseph W. Vandevegt was clearing an accommodation and ablutions block occupied by the Italian garrison, taking a number of prisoners in the process. Follmer set his group to clearing the two bunkers protecting the road junction, only one of which was occupied and the occupants of which promptly surrendered, before establishing a defensive perimeter around the crossroads.

While this was going on Privates Howard C. Goodson and Joseph Patrick were making their way to the designated high ground overlooking the DIME Landing Area, gathering up another seven or eight paratroopers en route. The group then moved to a farm on the Piano Lupo high ground north of the *Biviere di Gela* and set fire to the barn and a nearby haystack to create a navigation marker for the amphibious landing before presumably moving to the main Company I location. By 02:00 on 10 July Captain Follmer and Company I had thus achieved all their assigned objectives within the scheduled time limit, the only element of the 505th Parachute RCT to do so that night. The paratroopers then settled down in their newly occupied position to await enemy reactions or the arrival of the US 1st Infantry Division.

The third and fourth serials, from the 313th and 316th Troop Carrier Groups respectively, were the most badly affected by the wind and navigational errors to the extent that most aircraft missed Malta, some by a margin of over twenty miles. They ended up flying parallel to Sicily's east coast, with twenty-three C-47s from the 313th Group dropping their sticks near Avola and Noto, just inland from the British ACID SOUTH Landing Area. The exception was a flight of nine machines, in this instance carrying Lieutenant-Colonel Gorham, his HQ group from the 1st Battalion 505th Regiment and Captain Sayre's HQ and two platoons from Company A, that had managed to maintain formation during the fly-in. Alerted to their navigation error by distant anti-aircraft fire to port rather than starboard, the flight turned back out to sea, located the *Biviere di Gela* checkpoint and set course for the final two-minute run-in to DZ S; at that point the formation was disrupted by heavy anti-aircraft fire but nonetheless despatched its sticks of paratroopers within two miles of the DZ at 00:35.[28] Captain Sayre was able to locate his Company assembly point, contact his two platoon leaders by SCR-536 radio, gather them in by using rifle shots as a rallying guide and by 05:00 on 10 July had conducted a probing attack on a nearby strongpoint as well as gathering in forty-five men, three .30 machine-guns with 2,000 rounds apiece and two 60mm mortars with fifty rounds of ammunition.[29] The strongpoint, dubbed Casa del Priolo, was located a mile and a half north of the 1st Battalion's assigned target Objective Y and was initially manned by a small counter-airborne landing unit, the *455a Squadra Anti-Paracadutisti*. Sayre cleared it in a subsequent attack at 06:00, by which time the small garrison had been reinforced by *Capitano* Alfonso Della Minola and two platoons from *4a Compagnia, 429° Battaglione Costiero*; after being driven out of the bunkers the Italians took shelter in a farmhouse at the centre of the strongpoint, where the survivors surrendered to the paratroopers.

The fight cost the Italians fifteen dead including *Capitano* Della Minola and between forty and fifty prisoners including ten Germans, in return for four US wounded and, more importantly for the lightly armed paratroopers, twenty machine-guns and 50,000 rounds of ammunition; a brief interrogation revealed that the German prisoners were a reconnaissance party for the *Hermann Göring Panzer Division* scouting a concentration area for a planned attack toward Gela.

Realising that the Casa del Priolo strongpoint was a key location dominating the road running south from Niscemi to the coast, Sayre decided to remain in place and hold it until relieved rather than move south to his assigned target, the junction of the *Strada Provinciale* 11 and coastal

Strada 115 codenamed Objective Y. His appreciation was confirmed by Lieutenant-Colonel Gorham, who arrived shortly thereafter with a party of thirty men including two Regimental surgeons and a number of wounded paratroopers; Gorham then assumed command of the force.[30]

The serial from the 316th Group, carrying Colonel Gavin in a C-47 piloted by Group commander Lieutenant-Colonel Burton R. Fleet with the 505th Regiment's HQ group, along with part of the 456th Parachute Field Artillery Battalion and the Regiment's engineer, signal and medical attachments, fared the worst of all. Dispersed into ad hoc groupings and individual aircraft by the weather and navigational errors, the serial proceeded north up the Gulf of Noto to make landfall near Syracuse, which three C-47s mistook for Gela and promptly despatched their paratroopers; the rest of the serial spread their passengers across south-east Sicily in groups and individual sticks. Lieutenant-Colonel Harrison B. Harden Jr., commander of the 456th Parachute Field Artillery Battalion, came down near Ragusa, twenty-three miles east of DZ S, accompanied by Lieutenant Richard S. Aiken from Battery D and fifteen men; Lieutenant Aiken was wounded in the head while attacking the station defences that saw him medically evacuated back to Africa after treatment in a Ragusa hospital. Although he was unsure if he was actually on Sicilian soil, Colonel Gavin landed somewhere south of Vittoria around fifteen miles south-east of DZ S and managed to gather up his Personnel and Operations Officers, Lieutenant-Colonel Alfred W. Ireland and Major Benjamin H. Vandervoort respectively, and around twenty men before moving north toward the sound of heavy firing. The fight was 1st Lieutenant Harold H. Swingler, commander of the 505th Regiment's HQ Company, leading a party of forty men in an attack on a fortified road junction south of Vittoria on the road leading to the coast. The fight yielded over a hundred Italian prisoners, many from a nearby field artillery battery who surrendered en masse at the paratroopers' approach, and after clearing the junction Lieutenant Swingler occupied the fortifications and awaited relief from the US 45th Infantry Division advancing inland from the CENT Landing Area.[31]

The final serial, from Colonel John Cerny's 64th Troop Carrier Group carrying Major Mark J. Alexander and the 2nd Battalion, 505th Parachute Infantry Regiment, also missed the Malta checkpoint but maintained cohesion and crossed the Sicilian coast in formation near Marina di Ragusa, twenty miles short of the *Biviere di Gela* checkpoint. Colonel Cerny had promised to put Alexander's Battalion down together and this he did at 00:25, but there were two problems.[32] First, the 2nd Battalion were delivered over an area roughly ten miles long and six miles wide running north-east from Marina di Ragusa, over twenty miles south-east of its allotted DZ S.[33] Second, that area included high ground that led to a number of sudden and hard landings and a defensive strongpoint with trenches, barbed wire and at least five concrete bunkers. Major Alexander and his HQ Company landed directly atop the strongpoint and immediately came under heavy close range machine-gun fire that killed the Assistant Battalion Medical Officer Lieutenant Kurt B. Klee. Corporal Fred Freeland from Company D escaped the same fate by feigning death after becoming hooked up in barbed wire while Battalion Executive Officer Captain John Norton also narrowly escaped with his life on approaching the sound of voices near what he took for a house and issuing the challenge 'George': the house was actually a bunker and the Italian occupants reportedly responded with 'George, hell!' and a barrage of machine-gun fire. After organising men from HQ Company and Company D in the immediate area, including mortars for fire support, Major Alexander set about eliminating the strongpoint starting with a large forty-foot diameter pillbox. The hazardous process continued through the early hours into the morning and involved the paratroopers working through the barbed wire to close in on the bunkers and silence them with grenades through firing ports and entrances, and was the more dangerous because the bunkers were sited to provide mutual support; Lieutenant John D. Sprinkle from Company D was killed with three of his men as they closed in on one bunker by cross-fire from another.[34]

Not all members of the 2nd Battalion serial landed in such close proximity to the enemy, and at least one exited his C-47 in an unconventional manner. Colonel Gavin had given an explicit order that no-one was to return to Tunisia in a C-47 unless wounded or dead and when Staff-Sergeant Reed R. Satterstrom from the 456th Parachute Field Artillery Battalion stood up on the red light he discovered the snap-link on his parachute strop was defective, meaning he was unable to hook up to the static-line cable in the aircraft for opening his parachute. Mindful of Gavin's order he handed his strop to the presumably startled USAAF Crew Chief with instructions to 'hang on to it' before launching himself out of the C-47's door with one hand on his reserve parachute.[35] Lieutenants Waverley W. Wray and James J. Coyle from Company E rounded up their 1st Platoon and equipment bundles without difficulty or injuries despite hard landings due to jumping at an estimated four hundred feet; believing they had come down on DZ S they set out north along a nearby road to carry out their mission of establishing a roadblock on the route to Gela. After the platoon column became temporarily split when some men in the middle fell asleep during a pause in the march, the two Officers located a road junction they assumed to be their objective and settled down to await daylight.

Private First Class Russell W. Brown, a member of a 60mm Mortar Squad from Company F, enjoyed a more bucolic introduction to Sicily. While searching unsuccessfully for the equipment bundles containing their weapons the Squad was waylaid by a civilian in an olive grove, who insisted on them accompanying him to his nearby home where he provided the paratroopers with a hot meal of spaghetti cooked over an open fire. Back at the strongpoint Major Alexander completed the task of clearing the position by mid-morning and by midday had gathered 515 men from his Battalion along with Lieutenant-Colonel Harden and twenty-one men from the 456th Parachute Field Artillery Battalion equipped with a single 75mm Pack Howitzer and thirty rounds of ammunition. He then moved south-west and attacked a fortified Italian coastal artillery position at Marina di Ragusa, which was overrun with fire support from Colonel Harden's Pack Howitzer and after removing and disposing of the breech blocks from the captured Italian guns, began to move north-west in search of his Airborne colleagues.[36]

The first of the returning C-47s touched down at the Kairouan satellite airfields at 01:25 on 10 July and the remainder came in over the following four hours, the last putting down at 06:20; ten machines from the 64th Troop Carrier Group that became separated over Licata while evading searchlights on the return leg of the mission landed at Sfax.[37] They included three machines still carrying their sticks, totalling fifty men, because the pilots had refused to despatch them without a precise locational fix; despite Colonel Gavin's express order that everyone was to jump the paratroopers were not sanctioned and they were slated to jump in with the HUSKY TWO lift later that day. Ten of the returning aircraft were damaged by anti-aircraft fire and eight C-47s were reportedly shot down over Sicily, presumably including the machine from the 314th Group that ditched just offshore on the second run-in to the coast.[38] The bulk of the returning pilots claimed to have successfully located their DZs to the extent that Brigadier-General Paul L. Williams, commander of the Northwest African Troop Carrier Command, reported to Allied Force HQ that eighty per cent of Gavin's men had been delivered accurately. The reality was somewhat different. Of the around 226 C-47s involved in HUSKY ONE, only Captain William R. Bommar's eight machines, from the 314th Group serial carrying Company I from the 3rd Battalion 505th Regiment, delivered their sticks accurately onto the correct DZ and only the 2nd Battalion 505th Regiment was delivered in a reasonably compact group, albeit over twenty miles from its assigned landing area. Of the remainder only fifty-three sticks, approximately 425 men or twelve per cent of the 505th Regiment's 3,405 jump strength, were dropped in the area of Gela. A further 127 sticks were dropped miles to the south-east in the vicinity of Vittoria and thirty-three more were delivered even further afield around Avola in the British zone on the eastern edge of the island.[39] As the US Official History put it, the HUSKY ONE drop was 'dispersed to the four winds'.[40]

However, as with the Ponte Grande glider mission, the scattering of the HUSKY ONE drop proved to be beneficial because the confusion it generated prevented *6a Armata* forming an accurate appreciation of the situation, which in turn obliged *Generale d'Armata* Guzzoni to hold back from initiating counter-moves until matters were clarified. The confusion was exacerbated by the US paratroopers cutting every telephone line and signal cable they came across; *Generalmajor* Paul Conrath, commander of the *Hermann Göring Panzer Division*, was informed of the Allied invasion via a radio signal from *Oberbefehlshaber Süd* (*OB Süd*) in Rome for example, even though his Caltagirone HQ was only twelve and twenty-five miles respectively from *16° Corpo* and *6a Armata* HQs, and just eighteen miles from Gela.[41] Even more important was the determination with which the paratroopers pursued their assigned missions and, when that was not possible, the way they adapted to circumstances and aggressively carried the fight to the enemy, a process Colonel Gavin later referred to as a 'self-adjusting foul up' which played particular havoc with Axis road communications.[42] For example, despite landing ten miles south-east of DZ Q at Biscaris, Lieutenant Peter J. Eaton from the 3rd Battalion 504th Parachute Infantry Regiment gathered up a party of thirty-six men and set out for his unit rendezvous, picking up a further fourteen and capturing two Italian 47mm anti-tank guns en route. Eaton then set up a roadblock using the guns and ambushed an Italian column, inflicting numerous casualties and knocking out an accompanying tank with a Bazooka before withdrawing; Eaton's party later linked up with elements of the 180th Infantry Regiment, US 45th Infantry Division and fought on until 12 July before returning to their own unit. Similarly, Captain James P. McGinity, commander of the 505th Regiment's Company G, came down around four miles short of DZ T in the vicinity of the Ponte Dirillo bridge on the *Strada 115* over the River Acate; along with the railway bridge a mile and a half downriver the bridge should have been secured by a demolition section dropping from three C-47s from the 316th Group onto the nearby DZ X, but navigation errors resulted in the team being dropped by a bridge south of Syracuse, fifty miles away on the east coast.[43] Captain McGinity gathered up eighty men, secured the road bridge and held until relieved by elements of the US 45th Infantry Division.[44]

The impact of these examples and the efforts of other roving bands of Gavin's paratroopers were noted by their opponents both anecdotally and officially. A captured German officer from the *Hermann Göring Panzer Division* told his captors that 'It has been unsafe to use the roads for the past forty-eight hours' while a report issued by *OB Süd* on 20 July noted that 'Paratroops have greatly delayed the advance of our own troops and have inflicted considerable casualties on our troops. Some small groups of parachutists who had jumped into overgrown country made themselves noticed in a particularly unpleasant manner.'[45] For their part, senior German commanders tended to avoid acknowledging the disruption wrought by the US paratroopers in favour of minimising the impact of the parachute operation overall. *Generalmajor* Walter Fries, commander of *29 Panzergrenadier Division*, insisted that there was 'little prospect of their being able to intervene decisively', while *Oberst* Helmutt Bergengruen from the *Hermann Göring Panzer Division* staff claimed that the parachute landings 'might have helped cause panic among some Italian units' but 'did not interfere with the conduct of the battle'. At the very top, *Generalfeldmarschall* Kesselring took a different tack. While acknowledging the losses and delay inflicted by the paratroopers, Kesselring placed the blame squarely upon *Generalmajor* Paul Conrath, commander of the *Hermann Göring Panzer Division* and his senior commanders who employed 'incorrect armour tactics' by failing to properly integrate tanks and *panzergrenadiers* in their 'march groups'.[46]

While the HUSKY ONE drop may have gone disastrously awry, the persistence, initiative and aggression of the men of the 505th Parachute RCT arguably caused as much confusion and disruption to the enemy than if it had proceeded as planned. Moreover, despite the minimising protestations of senior German officers, Gavin's paratroopers were also to impact upon the course of immediate German counter-measures against the subsequent Allied seaborne invasion.

11

Cruisers, Submarines and Landing Vessels

The Initial HUSKY Landings, D-Day Minus One, 11:00 Friday 09 July to D-Day, 08:00 Saturday 10 July

While the paratroopers of the 505th Regimental Combat Team (RCT) were being scattered to roam across south-east Sicily causing mayhem, Vice-Admiral Hewitt's Western Naval Task Force spent D-Day Minus One, Friday 9 July, closing on the US 7th Army's landing areas in the Bay of Gela. The journey was complicated by bad weather, with wind states increasing from Force 3 to Force 6 during the day and increasing to Force 7 fifteen minutes after Admiral Hewitt's Flagship, the converted Attack Transport USS *Monrovia*, reported sighting Gozo at 16:30. The westerly wind impacted especially badly on the shallow draught landing vessels with the LSTs and LCIs being driven out of station to the south and east, and the blunt-bowed LCTs suffering particularly with regard to speed. Naval Task Force 86 heading for the western JOSS Landing Area reported difficulties with LCT stragglers as early as 11:00 on 9 July and the eastern CENT FORCE landings had to be postponed by an hour as the rough sea interfered with launching and loading landing craft there; weather may also have been the reason for the JOSS FORCE minesweepers being ordered to cancel sweeping operations until daylight on 10 July.[1] The weather proved less of an impediment to larger vessels given that the cruisers USS *Birmingham*, USS *Boise*, USS *Brooklyn* and USS *Savannah* joined the Task Force at 11:00, to be assigned later to Naval Task Forces 81 and 86. The wind began to slacken with the onset of darkness, dropping to Force 4 by 22:30 and Force 3 by 01:00 on 10 July.[2] Despite the weather the bulk of the Western Naval Task Force arrived at its various assigned positions at 00:40 on 10 July and ten minutes later the Attack Forces began their final adjustments and preparations prior to launching their assault waves in time to reach the beach on H-Hour, which was set for 02:45. The exception to this was Rear-Admiral Alan G. Kirk's

Naval Task Force 85 carrying CENT FORCE, which delayed its H-Hour to 03:45 on the request of the Force's Commander Transports.[3]

The task of delivering Major-General Lucian K. Truscott's US 3rd Infantry Division onto the western JOSS Landing Area astride the port of Licata was allotted to Naval Task Force 86, commanded by Rear-Admiral Richard L. Connolly from the converted seaplane tender USS *Biscayne*. The Landing Area consisted of four colour-coded beaches, two each side of Licata: RED Beach, five miles west of the port allocated to the 7th RCT; GREEN WEST and GREEN EAST Beaches straddling the *Rocca Mollarella* headland just over a mile to the east, allotted to the 3rd Ranger Battalion and the 2nd Battalion 15th RCT ; and YELLOW Beach three miles east of Licata and BLUE Beach adjacent to the east, allotted to the remainder of the 15th RCT and the 30th RCT respectively.[4] The process of delivering the invasion force to the JOSS Landing Area began at 19:32 on 9 July when Rear-Admiral Connolly authorised his warships to expend eighty per cent of their ammunition on Italian railway artillery batteries sited on the Licata Mole. Eight minutes later Task Force 86 was joined by the cruisers USS *Birmingham* and *Brooklyn* with their escorts, which were ordered to steam ahead of the transports and landing vessels and make contact with the submarine acting as a beacon for the JOSS Landing Area; the destroyer USS *Bristol* established radio communication with HM Submarine *Safari* at 22:30, the marker lights for RED and GREEN Beaches were sighted at 23:25 & 23:37 and those for YELLOW and BLUE Beaches at 00:44 & 00:50 respectively.[5] Admiral Connolly released the two Attack Groups assigned to the RED and GREEN Beaches west of Licata for their transport areas at 23:59, ordering them to make full speed to ensure making the deadline for H-Hour, before moving his Flagship USS *Biscayne* with the remainder of the JOSS invasion force toward the YELLOW and BLUE Beaches east of Licata, dropping anchor two miles offshore at 01:35.[6] The arrival of the *Biscayne* and company did not go unnoticed, with multiple Italian searchlights illuminating the flagship and other vessels at 01:55 and again at 02:50, although no fire was detected.

The LSTs carrying troops for YELLOW and BLUE Beaches began lowering landing craft at 01:15, the first waves moved off from the rendezvous area for BLUE Beach fifty minutes later and made landfall there at 03:15: some LCVPs reportedly landed on schedule at 02:45 in unexpectedly high three-foot surf, presumably on YELLOW Beach. They were covered by salvoes of rockets from LCT(R)s and gunfire from destroyers, the latter specifically targeting Italian searchlights.[7] Matters ran less smoothly at the JOSS RED and GREEN Beaches to the west, where strict radio silence had prevented Admiral Connolly from being informed that the RED and GREEN Attack Groups were behind schedule despite running at full speed. As a result they did not anchor until 02:04, with some LSTs not arriving in their loading areas until 02:15; all the latter anchored further out than planned, some by over two miles, which obliged a longer run-in to the beach for the landing craft.[8] The still-high westerly wind complicated the process of loading and lowering the LCVPs, and nine men were drowned when a davit broke and pitched the passengers of one craft into the sea.[9] Sea conditions also impacted station keeping; the destroyers USS *Roe* and USS *Swanson* collided at 02:55 and were so badly damaged that they requested permission to withdraw to Malta; their duties were taken over by the destroyer USS *Buck* an hour later, although the destroyer did not arrive on station until after 06:00 when the JOSS RED landing was well underway.[10]

The first wave of LCVPs carrying Lieutenant-Colonel Roy E. Moore's 1st Battalion, 7th RCT set off for RED Beach at 03:00, fifteen minutes after they were supposed to have made landfall, and took another ninety minutes to reach the beach due to the extra run-in; there was some concern they might be run down by the larger LCIs that were scheduled to land at 03:30 but this was offset by the LST mother ships anchoring out of position, which inadvertently directed the LCVPs to the right-hand side of the RED Beach frontage. The shallow gradient and soft sand caused additional problems, with many LCTs becoming stuck on unloading, and when sending in LCTs in batches of five failed to alleviate the problem, unloading was switched to YELLOW and BLUE Beaches and Licata harbour once it was secured.[11] The more serious problem was that RED Beach was heavily defended by elements of the *207a Divisioni Costiere* which promptly poured machine-gun and more seriously artillery onto the beach and approaches as the LCVPs came in; the shelling was reported to be 'continuous' at 04:00 and sufficiently heavy for the RED Beachmaster to request a delay in landing LCTs at 05:10, which was ordered twenty-five minutes later.[12] Air attacks began from just after 04:30 with beaches and landing craft being strafed and bombing attacks on larger vessels. The minesweeper USS *Sentinel* was struck by a dive-bomber at 04:50 and suffered several near misses twenty minutes later that overall killed nine, wounded fifty-one and caused her to sink just over five hours later. The aerial traffic was not all one way; the collision-damaged destroyer USS *Swanson* shot down an attacking Messerschmitt 110 just after 05:00 for example. At 06:30 Major-General Truscott was able to report that his 3rd Infantry Division had two battalions from the 7th RCT ashore at RED Beach, that landings were continuing at GREEN Beach despite the narrow and rugged beach frontage, and that progress was satisfactory at BLUE and YELLOW Beaches, all for fewer than a hundred casualties by mid-morning.[13]

Major-General Terry Allen's US 1st Infantry Division and the attached FORCE X, made up of the 1st and 4th Ranger Battalions reinforced with engineer and heavy mortar elements, were delivered to the centre DIME Landing Area by Rear-Admiral John L. Hall's Naval Task Force 81. At the western end of the frontage FORCE X were to land directly in front of Gela on RED and GREEN Beaches, while the bulk of the 1st Division was allotted a stretch of beach to the east of the port on the other side of the River Gela. On the left the 26th RCT was to put a battalion apiece onto YELLOW and BLUE Beaches, while on the right the 16th RCT put a battalion each onto RED 2 and GREEN 2 Beaches.[14] The DIME FORCE LSTs and LCIs were released from their collective convoy with the CENT FORCE vessels off Gozo to make their way north at 16:00, followed by Naval Task Force 81 and the remainder of the DIME FORCE vessels at 18:50. The two elements married up into a central column of transports headed by the cruisers USS *Boise* and USS *Savannah*, with the LCIs and LSTs forming columns on either side, although the flanking columns became badly drawn out due to the weather.[15] Flak and fires from the preparatory bombing of Gela and vicinity provided a useful navigation aid and the destroyer USS *Cole* made contact with HM Submarine *Shakespeare* at 22:15 followed by Hall's flagship the *Samuel Chase* fifty-three minutes later at 23:08. All the DIME FORCE transports were in their areas by moonset at 00:44 where they were joined thirty minutes or so later by eleven of the FORCE's fourteen LSTs and all twenty LCIs; the three errant LSTs turned up in the CENT FORCE area later.[16] The first wave of LVCPs and LCAs carrying the Rangers of FORCE X to RED and GREEN Beaches set off at 02:15.[17] Gela pier was demolished by the Italian garrison as per standing orders from 6ª *Armata* HQ during the run in, and covering fire from the destroyer USS *Shubrick* eliminated two searchlights before switching fire to Italian artillery and mortar positions with the assistance of the cruiser USS *Savannah* before the FORCE X reached shore at 03:35, almost an hour behind schedule presumably due to the sea state; the *Savannah* was joined in turn by the USS *Boise* firing in general support from 03:00 before both cruisers switched to bombarding pre-arranged targets an hour later.[18]

The approach to the four Beaches east of the River Gela was also eased by illumination from the preparatory bombing and the fire ignited at Piano Lupo by Private Goodson and his colleagues from the 505th Parachute Infantry. The first wave of LCAs and LCVPs carrying the 26th and 16th RCTs landed on schedule at 02:45, although the three-foot surf whipped up by the Force 4 wind and a strong current made controlling the craft difficult and resulted in some broaching and becoming stranded. They were followed forty-five minutes later by sixteen larger LCIs, eight of which were able to deliver their loads directly onto the beach and back off without becoming stuck apart from *LCI-220* which lost its stern anchor and also broached sideways on GREEN 2 Beach after artillery fire damaged her port screw; the remaining eight LCIs unloaded their cargo just off the beach via LCVPs and rubber boats. All initial DIME landings were reported complete at 03:35, although this was not the end of the matter.[19] At 04:58 the USS *Maddox* was sunk by a single bomb delivered by a Junkers 88 from *Kampfgeschwader* 54 that detonated the destroyer's aft magazine and sent her down in under two minutes; 211 of her crew went down with the ship, 209 of which were officially posted as Missing, with just seventy-four survivors being picked up by the tug USS *Intent*.[20] Allied fighters were scheduled to be on station over the invasion fleet by 04:20, twenty minutes after first light, but the USAAF Spitfires from the Gozo-based 31st Fighter Group tasked to cover the DIME Landing Area became entangled with Axis aircraft en route over the CENT Landing Area and as a result did not arrive until 05:15, fifteen minutes after the sinking of the *Maddox* and almost an hour behind schedule.[21] Nonetheless, by 05:10 DIME FORCE was able to report that all initial landings had been successful apart from YELLOW Beach, the latter likely due to the presence of mines, and a Situation Report issued just under two hours later confirmed Major-General Allen's 1st Division Command Post was established ashore and that while there was no contact with the Rangers in Gela, the Division's phase lines had been achieved and no opposition had been encountered since 04:00.

The situation was not as secure as all this suggested, given that at 07:10 another report warned of accurate Axis artillery fire on the beaches close to Gela and that BLUE Beach was also heavily mined, with personnel casualties and the loss of bulldozers, DUKWs and other vehicles, but within five hours of the first wave landing the US 1st Infantry Division was firmly ashore with little opposition, the DIME FORCE transports were moving inshore for unloading and landing craft and DUKWs were lifting men and equipment onto RED 2 and GREEN 2 Beaches.[22]

Major-General Troy C. Middleton's US 45th Infantry Division was assigned to land on the third and most easterly CENT Landing Area, spread across five beaches grouped into two clusters at either end of the landing frontage framing the small fishing port of Scoglitti, which was located slightly off the centre of the frontage. The three larger beaches were located side-by-side at the leftward extremity, running east from the mouth of the River Acate. RED Beach, adjacent to the river mouth, was allocated to two battalions from the 180th RCT while the 179th RCT was to put a battalion apiece onto the adjacent GREEN Beach and neighbouring YELLOW Beach. The second cluster of two smaller beaches, allotted to the 157th RCT, was located fifteen miles to the south-east at the other extremity of the landing frontage, running north-west from the sandy *Punta Braccetto* promontory; a battalion each was to be put ashore on GREEN 2 and YELLOW 2 Beaches, a stretch of sandy shore just over a mile long to the left of the headland.[23] Getting Major-General Middleton's CENT FORCE to its designated Landing Area was the responsibility of Rear-Admiral Alan G. Kirk's Naval Task Force 85, which shepherded the main transport convoy past Gozo nine minutes behind schedule at 19:20 in the wake of the FORCE's LSTs and LCIs, which had been released at the same point just over three hours earlier. The heavy seas caused some LST cargoes to shift, there was some confusion and manoeuvring during the mating of the assault convoy's two sections and further delay was incurred when the Attack Transport USS *Thomas Jefferson* stopped for twelve minutes to offload a support boat, holding up the four transports steaming astern.[24] Nonetheless the convoy, headed by the cruiser USS *Philadelphia* and the minesweepers USS *Sustain* and USS *Steady*, turned onto the approach to the CENT transport area at 22:57, Admiral Kirk's Flagship the USS *Ancon* spotted the homing beacon from HM Submarine *Seraph* at 23:16 and the convoy reached its assigned location on schedule at 00:40, where the *Ancon* dropped anchor.[25]

Naval Task Force 85 had succeeded in making up the lost time and delivered the CENT assault convoy to its loading area on schedule but matters then went awry, initially as the exposed nature of the loading area led to the weather interfering with the hoisting out and launching of the landing craft with a number of vessels being damaged in the process, and clearing the initial assault wave took well in excess of the thirty to forty-five minutes required at the adjacent DIME Landing Area. Admiral Kirk was thus obliged to request an hour postponement of H-Hour for the CENT landing at 02:39 which was granted by Admiral Hewitt from the *Monrovia* four minutes later, with the proviso that the landing should commence as soon as possible.[26] The 180th RCT's 1st Battalion was embarked in time to depart at 03:00 in line with the revised schedule but the 2nd Battalion had much more difficulty and its landing craft were not loaded and ready to depart for RED Beach until 03:37; the remainder of the CENT landing force, the 179th and 157th RCTs, allotted to GREEN & YELLOW Beaches and GREEN 2 and YELLOW 2 Beaches respectively, were also ready to proceed on time.[27] In contrast to the JOSS and DIME landings which were carried out with no preparatory bombardment, the CENT landings were preceded by fifteen minutes of pre-targeted fire from the 5-inch guns of Naval Task Force 85's destroyer contingent, nine vessels from DesRon 15 and seven from DesRon 16, and by fire from a number of Landing Craft Rocket (LCR).[28] The destroyers opened fire at 03:30, H-Hour Minus Fifteen, and continued through the final run in, lifting just as the assault wave made landfall.[29] The landing on one of the CENT Beaches, it is unclear which, was also screened by smoke from Landing Craft Support (Smoke) (LCS(S)) using rockets and smoke pots; this method does not appear to have been employed elsewhere, although destroyers used white phosphorous shells to create a smokescreen screen twice at the JOSS Landing Area.[30]

In the event, the CENT Landing Force's passage ashore did not proceed altogether smoothly for all the units involved. The landing craft carrying the 1st Battalion 180th RCT had already crossed the line of departure for RED Beach when the hour postponement order was received and the recall, poor visibility and rough seas scattered the four assault waves so badly that the depleted first wave did not make landfall until 04:45, while just six craft from the 2nd Battalion's first wave reached RED Beach six minutes earlier thanks to a combination of loading difficulties and scattering due to the sea state; the remainder ended up scattered along the twelve-mile stretch of coast running north-west from Scoglitti to the DIME Landing Area. In contrast, the 179th RCT was delivered accurately onto GREEN and YELLOW Beaches on time, and the 157th RCT with mixed results due to being carried east of its intended destination. After setting off for GREEN 2 Beach at 03:03 the 2nd Battalion 157th RCT was carried east by the wind and current and the first wave touched down at 03:55 on the far end of the adjacent YELLOW 2 Beach, next to the *Punta Braccetto*. The second wave was carried even further awry onto the rocky headland with its ten- to twelve foot-high surf which tossed the two leading landing craft sideways onto the rocks; both craft capsized, drowning twenty-seven men.

The rest of the second wave managed to unload onto the headland followed by four of the seven landing craft in the third wave, which unloaded safely but remained stuck. Of the remaining craft, two beached on sand close by and the seventh went wildly astray and delivered its load in the 179th RCT's

Landing Area west of Scoglitti. While the 157th RCT's 1st Battalion was delayed by difficulties loading and launching its landing craft, it reached YELLOW 2 Beach as assigned at around 04:55 without incident, suggesting that the preceding 2nd Battalion's difficulties may have been due to navigation errors as well as the sea conditions.[31] The CENT initial landings were reported complete at 04:55 without encountering enemy resistance, a circumstance credited to the pre-landing bombardment by DesRon 15 and 16.[32] Enemy resistance was not totally absent. Attacks on the CENT Force vessels and beaches by *Luftwaffe* and *Regia Aeronautica* aircraft began at 04:24, with the cruiser USS *Philadelphia* and Attack Transport USS *Thomas Jefferson* coming under attack from eleven Junkers 88 dive-bombers, but the threat was countered by the arrival of Allied fighters from just after 05:00 and the routine shuttling of men and materiel onto the CENT beaches was able to commence at 06:00.[33] Within seven hours of the Western Naval Task Force arriving on station off the southern coast of Sicily the assault wave of the US 7th Army's three-division landing force was successfully ashore on all planned locations and reorganising in readiness to begin the advance inland.

On the British side of the operation the approximately 1,530 assorted vessels of the Eastern Naval Task Force, commanded by Vice-Admiral Sir Bertram Ramsay from the Forward Operations Ship HMS *Antwerp*, rendezvoused at Midday on Friday 9 July fifty to seventy miles south of Malta after travelling from Egypt, various points on the Tunisian coast and in the case of FORCE V's ten vessel Fast Assault Convoy, after a nine-day voyage direct from the UK. At that point Vice-Admiral Ramsay devolved control of the fast assault convoys carrying the landing force to make their way independently, all scheduled to be in place at the designated Release Positions off their respective Landing Areas by 00:15 on Saturday 10 July. The assault convoys were divided into two overall groupings. FORCE A, commanded by Rear-Admiral Thomas Troubridge from the HQ Ship HMS *Bulolo*, was heading for the ACID Landing Area between Cassibile and Avola at the northern end of the twenty-mile wide Gulf of Noto, carrying Lieutenant-General Miles Dempsey's XIII Corps; Rear-Admiral Troubridge's Force was also accompanied by two LSIs and a troopship from FORCE B, detailed to peel off and deliver 231st Brigade to the BARK EAST Landing Area at Marzamemi at the southern end of the Gulf.

Rear-Admiral Rhoderick McGrigor aboard the HQ Ship HMS *Largs* commanded FORCE B, tasked to deliver the 51st Highland Division from Lieutenant-General Oliver Leese's XXX Corps to the BARK SOUTH Landing Area on the south-eastern aspect of the rugged Pachino Peninsula, at the southern extremity of the Gulf of Noto and the very tip of the island. Finally, FORCE V, commanded by Rear-Admiral Sir Philip Vian from the HQ Ship HMS *Hilary* was tasked to deliver the 1st Canadian Division to the BARK WEST Landing Area, a four-mile wide bay between the *Punta Castellazo* (Castle Point) and *Punta delle Formiche* (Point of the Ants) on the western aspect of the Peninsula; FORCE V and eighteen-vessel Fast Assault Convoy carrying the Canadian division had sailed from the Firth of Clyde on 1 July, passed Gibraltar on 5 July, steamed on along the North African coast to make the Midday rendezvous on D Minus One, and thence the final leg of the journey to Sicily in company with the rest of the Eastern Naval Task Force.[34]

The first troops ashore on the 8th Army landing frontage on Sicily's eastern coast were those detailed to carry out preparatory missions in support of the main landings, two of which were located at the northern extremity of the landing frontage; both involved eliminating Italian artillery batteries that presented a threat to the ACID Landing Area. LCAs from the LSI HMS *Ulster Monarch* landed approximately 220 men from the 1st SAS Regiment's Special Raiding Squadron (SRS), commanded by Major Robert 'Paddy' Mayne, onto the southern aspect of the rugged Maddalena Peninsula, seven miles north of the ACID Landing Area. Their task was to eliminate the three 152mm naval guns of the Lamba Doria Battery and a suspected observation post in a lighthouse at the tip of the Peninsula at the *Capo Porco di Murro*; the latter mission appears to have been codenamed Operation NARCISSUS, but it is unclear if the codename also included the attack on the Battery. The SRS landed safely but twenty minutes behind schedule and at separate locations; No. 3 Troop and the Mortar Troop landed accurately at the western end of the designated landing beach while the assault element, consisting of Nos. 1 and 2 Troops, came ashore a half a mile or more to the east and significantly closer to the Battery than planned. Despite this, the SAS troops stealthily surmounted the rocky face backing the beach, which involved either climbing sheer cliffs or scaling broken rocky terrain, and deployed around the Battery. The move to the assault positions was masked by the noise generated by Allied preparatory bombing; the Battery was stood-to by an air raid warning at 21:30 and began to engage Allied aircraft with its organic 20mm guns thirty minutes later, along with other anti-aircraft positions in the vicinity.

Once deployed Major Mayne's men silently eliminated the Italian sentries and launched their assault at 02:15 under a covering barrage from the Mortar Troop's 3-inch mortars, sparking a two-hour fight that ended at approximately 04:00 with the Battery in British hands. SAS Sappers then destroyed the Battery's three 152mm guns before the SRS withdrew toward Cassibile to link up with the main ACID landing, accompanied by approximately sixty Italian prisoners; the SRS came out of the fight without suffering any casualties, but the Lamba Doria Battery's garrison reportedly lost seven dead and twelve wounded. At least one of the Italian wounded was shot by his own side; range-finder operator *Caporale* Paolino Carmelo was hit by three rounds from a burst fired accidentally by Battery commander *Maggiore* Antonino Pandolfo as he loaded his weapon in the Battery Fire Direction Centre.[35]

The second northerly landing was carried out by Lieutenant-Colonel John Durnford-Slater's No. 3 Commando, which was tasked with a dual mission. Half the Commando, dubbed No. 1 Group commanded by Colonel Durnford-Slater, was tasked to eliminate an Italian artillery battery located in the almond and olive groves north-west of the town of Cassibile, three miles from the sea while Major Peter Young's No. 2 Group was tasked to secure the nearby beach defences and exits at Scoglio Imbiancato. Colonel Durnford-Slater and Nos. 4, 5 & 6 Troops set off from the LSI HMS *Prins Albert* at 01:15 aboard assault craft from the 503rd LCA Flotilla commanded by Lieutenant George Holt RNVR, with Durnford-Slater travelling aboard the naval commander's LCA. By mutual agreement the two officers ignored a misplaced red marker light from a submarine-launched Folbot canoe, likely HM Submarine *Unruffled* which was acting as beacon vessel for the ACID landing force, and Lieutenant Holt brought No. 1 Group ashore exactly where envisaged without incident apart from some machine-gun fire during the last three-hundred yards of the run in to the beach, which was swiftly suppressed by the LCAs' own weapons.[36] Colonel Durnford-Slater was one of the first ashore, moving so smartly that he was almost run down by Holt's LCA, and discovered that the lack of application by the immediate defenders was fortunate given that the beach was covered by 'masses of barbed wire and many pill-boxes'.[37] After a rapid reorganisation on the beach Captain Anthony Ruxton and No. 6 Troop cut a path through the wire and moved off for the target battery trailed by Nos. 4 and 5 Troops through orange and lemon groves divided by thick, five-foot high banks and over stone terraces and walls. The terrain turned the move into 'a severe test of endurance' as the Commandos were weighed down with a number of 2-inch and broken-down 3-inch mortars, hundreds of assorted mortar bombs and 'several thousand' rounds of .303 ammunition; the only incident appears to have involved an unfortunate Sicilian farmer who was despatched with a Thompson gun after rashly firing on the heavily armed interlopers with a shotgun as they passed through his farmyard.[38]

The final stage of the advance was masked by the noise of the guns firing, and the Commando's Mortar Section set up 400 yards short of the battery, where the remainder of the Group dropped off their mortar ammunition in passing. At 04:10 the battery was inundated with mortar bombs and small arms fire to cover Captain John Pooley's No. 5 Troop moving into position for the assault, which was launched by a bugle call at 05:00 covered by another deluge of mortar and small arms fire. Defending fire dropped away rapidly as the fight moved to close-quarters and the battery was rapidly overrun with the gun crews, some in their underwear, eagerly surrendering to the Commandos, apart from the occupants of a building to the rear of the battery attacked by Lieutenant Brian Butler and a party from No. 4 Troop; they also surrendered when Butler's men set the roof alight with an improvised incendiary device known as a Flower-pot Bomb.[39] The Commandos then disabled the guns with explosives and set charges to detonate the battery ammunition dump containing a thousand shells, supervised by Lieutenant-Colonel Durnford-Slater; on returning to the main Group location the Commando commander was gratified to discover that his batman had prepared him 'a very good breakfast'.[40] Major Young and No. 2 Group, carried in six LCAs from HMT *Dunera* and an additional craft from the *Ulster Monarch*, did not fare so well. The little flotilla set off south-west of its intended course and became hopelessly lost in the darkness after failing to detect signals from a designated sonic buoy; Major Young's chagrin was doubtless increased by the RN flotilla commander '...repeating at intervals that he did not know where he was'.[41] In the end the LCAs located the correct beach and landed safely but again after coming under machine-gun fire and after daylight, making contact with a fighting patrol from No. 1 Group shortly thereafter.[42]

The third preliminary operation took place at the southern extremity of the 8th Army landing frontage, west of the Pachino Peninsula. Lieutenant-Colonel James Manners' No. 40 RM Commando and Lieutenant-Colonel Bruce Lumsden's No. 41 RM Commando were to go ashore just west of the *Punta Castellazo*, which demarcated the left-hand edge of BARK WEST Landing Area, from the LSI HMS *Derbyshire* and transport MV *Durban Castle* respectively, accompanied by Brigadier Robert Laycock and his 1st Special Service Brigade HQ. Their mission was to protect the western flank of the 1st Canadian Division's landing and to eliminate a number of Italian artillery emplacements overlooking the BARK WEST landing beaches, which had been identified from aerial reconnaissance photographs although not everyone was convinced; Brigadier Laycock's GSO 1, Colonel Thomas Churchill, was convinced that the artillery positions were machine-gun emplacements at best. Be that as it may, the Commandos offloaded onto twenty-two LCAs in a heavy swell that slowed and complicated the transfer, before setting off for the beach at 01:10.[43] The swell also caused some dispersal among the assault craft during the run-in to the beach, soaked the heavily-laden Commandos and caused numerous cases of sea-sickness that exacerbated the already miserable conditions.

The craft carrying No. 40 RM Commando initially proceeded too far east, and regaining the proper heading was complicated by becoming intermingled with waves of craft carrying elements of the 1st Canadian Division onto BARK WEST proper. As a result, No. 41 RM Commando was first ashore, albeit thirty minutes behind schedule at 03:00 and east of their intended landing beach, on that allocated to No. 40 Commando; the shallow gradient of the landing beach also obliged the Commandos to wade a significant distance through the swell to reach dry land, and several radio sets and a quantity of mortar bombs were rendered unserviceable by water ingress in the process. Nonetheless, after organising impromptu forming up areas in the dunes Lieutenant-Colonel Lumsden's men cut their way through the barbed wire entanglements bordering the beach and moved off for their objectives, leaving Brigadier Laycock to establish his Brigade HQ in a house just inland from the beach. By 05:00 No. 41 Commando had secured all its own objectives and those of its running mate unit as well, which turned out to be either machine-gun posts or empty artillery emplacements, as predicted by Colonel Churchill; four hours later both No. 40 and 41 RM Commandos were in their designated positions, the latter in contact with elements of the Seaforth Highlanders of Canada on its right flank, and Brigadier Laycock was shaving while his batman prepared a can of self-heating soup for breakfast.[44] The operation cost the two RM Commandos a combined total of between six and nine dead and between nineteen and thirty-seven wounded in return for approximately fifty Italians killed and around a hundred taken prisoner; many of the former were despatched as a result of continuing to fire on the Commandos until the last minute before trying to surrender.[45]

Besides the three preliminary support missions, the 8th Army landings involved putting four divisions and a separate brigade onto two separate Landing Areas with multiple beaches at each end of the Gulf of Noto. At the southern end guided by lights deployed by HM Submarine *Unrivalled*, Rear-Admiral Sir Philip Vian's HQ Ship HMS *Hilary* dropped anchor west of the Pachino Peninsula at 00:48 on 10 July, seven miles off the BARK WEST Landing Area. The eighteen transports from FORCE V's Fast Assault Convoy, carrying Major-General Guy Simonds' 1st Canadian Division, dropped anchor nearby in its assigned Release Position. The Landing Area was divided into two sections located either side of a central rocky feature known as *le Groticelle* (the Caves). The left-hand westerly section, dubbed SUGAR Beach, was allotted to Brigadier Christopher Vokes' 2nd Canadian Brigade and the LCAs carrying the two assault battalions, the Seaforth Highlanders of Canada and Princess Patricia's Canadian Light Infantry (PPCLI), set off from the LSIs HMS *Circassia*, HMS *Durban Castle* and the transport MV *Llangibby Castle* at 01:34, covered by salvos of 15-inch shells from the Monitor HMS *Roberts*; the Brigade's third battalion, The Edmonton Regiment, remained in reserve aboard ship. In this instance the heavy swell was beneficial as it carried the assault Battalion's LCAs over the offshore sandbars that had caused the planners concern, although this was offset to an extent by navigation errors that put the Seaforth Highlanders on SUGAR Beach but to the right of the PPCLI rather than to the left. Despite this mix-up the landing was uneventful apart from some scattered machine-gun fire in the final yards of the run-in that ceased as the LCAs ran up onto the beach; the attackers then quickly disembarked, breached the barbed wire obstacles blocking egress from the beach and pushed inland, overrunning a number of less than zealously manned machine-gun emplacements in the process. By 03:00 the initial wave was completed by the arrival of the outstanding HQ and remaining company elements and an hour later Brigadier Vokes was informed that both his assault battalions were successfully ashore, the PPCLI were moving inland while the Seaforth Highlanders moved west to rectify their crossed-over landing before also pushing inland toward their first phase objectives.[46]

The landings on the adjacent ROGER Beach by Brigadier Howard Graham's 1st Canadian Brigade did not run so smoothly. ROGER Beach was fronted by a 600-yard long sandbar eighty yards offshore covered by just eighteen inches of water, which prompted Major-General Simonds to order that the 1st Canadian Brigade's assault companies should be carried in three LCTs carrying a total of twenty-one DUKWs so that if the larger vessels become grounded the latter could ferry the infantry over the final stage of the journey; as an additional contingency measure Brigadier Graham was ordered to land his assault force via LCA if the three LCTs were not in place at the Release Position by 00:15. As predicted by the Senior RN officer aboard LSI HMS *Glengyle*, from where Brigadier Graham was commanding the landing, the LCTs did not appear as scheduled due to the weather and Graham was obliged to order his assault wave to proceed aboard LCAs. This switch involved reorganisation and consequent delay and the LCAs carrying the assault wave from the Hastings and Prince Edward Regiment were not ready for lowering from the *Glengyle* until 02: 26, nineteen minutes before they were scheduled to reach the more distant beach. In the meantime two of the LCTs arrived at 01:40 and came alongside the troopship MS *Marnix van Sint Aldegonde* to allow elements of the Royal Canadian Regiment to embark. The late arrival was compounded by the heavy swell which delayed the operation to the extent that Rear-Admiral Vian signalled the *Glengyle* 'Will your assault ever start?' at 03:15. Twenty minutes later Major-General Simonds despatched a messenger from the *Hilary* in Admiral Vian's personal barge, ordering Brigadier Graham to get his assault waves away immediately by whatever vessels were available.

The LCAs moved off from the *Glengyle* between 03:15 and 03:35 and the LCTs finally cast off from the *Marnix van Sint Aldegonde* at *c*.04:00, approximately an hour and ninety minutes late respectively. By this time it was full daylight and both elements of the assault wave were shelled by an Italian battery at Maucini, a mile or so inland from ROGER Beach, but the guns were swiftly suppressed by return fire from FORCE V's escort vessels. The Hastings and Prince Edward Regiment's LCAs do not appear to have encountered difficulty with the sandbar, and the LCTs carrying the Royal Canadian Regiment confirmed the wisdom of equipping the vessels with DUKWs as a contingency measure; both LCTs became grounded and immediately launched their fourteen DUKWs pre-loaded with infantrymen. The LCAs touched down on the Beach in the correct location at 04:45 followed by the first DUKWs forty-five minutes later, with no resistance encountered and at 06:45 Major-General Simonds was able to inform Lieutenant-General Leese's XXX Corps HQ aboard HMS *Largs* that his Division had secured all its initial objectives.[47]

Five miles away Rear-Admiral Rhoderick McGrigor's FORCE B was delivering XXX Corps' second divisional landing by Major-General Douglas Wimberley's 51st Highland Division onto the BARK SOUTH Landing Area astride Portopalo Bay, on the south-eastern aspect of the Pachino Peninsula. HM Submarine *Unison*, the beacon vessel for the Portopalo landing, made visual contact with the four assorted LSIs from the FORCE B Fast Assault Convoy at 00:11 and were in their designated Release Position a mile offshore by 00:30, fifteen minutes behind schedule due to the bad weather; it is unclear if this also applied to Admiral McGrigor's command ship, HMS *Largs*. Whether or not, the LSIs compensated for their late arrival by having the first wave of LCAs, carrying men from 154th Brigade, fully loaded and lowered in just six minutes. Suspecting that the wide and sandy Portopalo Bay would be extensively sown with mines and submerged barbed-wire obstacles, Major-General Wimberley had opted to land on either side of the

Bay. Two of 154th Brigade's constituent battalions, the 7th Battalion Argyll & Sutherland Highlanders and the 7th Battalion The Black Watch, were to land on three RED Beaches spread along the one and a quarter mile stretch of narrow beach and rocky outcrops stretching to *Capo Passero* on the left, while the 1st Battalion Gordon Highlanders attached from 153 Brigade landed on two GREEN Beaches on the right; a further GREEN Beach was located on the adjacent Passero Island, but it is unclear if this was also used by 154th Brigade. The Brigade's third constituent battalion, the 1st Battalion The Black Watch, was to initially remain afloat as the Brigade floating reserve along with tanks from the 50th Royal Tank Regiment (RTR) and 11th (HAC) Regiment, Royal Horse Artillery (RHA). The LCAs proceeded in to the beach under cover of salvoes from LCT(R)s with the 7th Argyll & Sutherlands coming ashore on the correct beach exactly on schedule at 02:45; the adjacent 7th Black Watch landed late due to difficulties locating the correct Beach and on the other flank the 1st Gordons landed a whole hour behind schedule, presumably due to the same problem.

In the event the assault wave was unopposed; General Wimberley later commented that 'no real attacking was necessary, and opposition was either very slight or negligible.'[48] This was perhaps fortunate given that there was some confusion with the follow-up waves that led to some congestion just off the beach but despite this and arriving two hours behind schedule due to the heavy seas, the LCTs carrying the Brigade's attached armoured vehicles began to beach at 04:00. Within two hours Honey Stuart tanks from the 50th RTR and self-propelled Priest 105mm guns from B Battery, 11th Regiment RHA, were ashore and in action, and by 07:00 154th Brigade had secured its initial objective, a ridge a mile inland from the beach, and the 7th Argyll & Sutherlands had established contact with elements of the 1st Canadian Division on the left flank.[49]

The third XXX Corps landing was a flank protection mission that involved delivering Brigadier Roy Urquhart's 231st Brigade onto the BARK EAST Landing Area astride the small port of Marzamemi, five miles north of Portopalo Bay. 231st Brigade's constituent units included the 1st Battalion Hampshire Regiment, the 1st Battalion Dorsetshire Regiment and the 2nd Battalion Devonshire Regiment which were carried aboard the LSIs HMS *Keren*, HMS *Otranto* and the troopship RMS *Strathnaver*, which sailed for Sicily in company with FORCE A. At 23:35 on 9 July they split off with their escort vessels toward Marzamemi and were guided into their Release Position on schedule just after Midnight by lights and sonic buoys deployed by HM Submarine *Unseen*.[50] The sea state again complicated matters but did not delay the loading and launching of LCAs and the bulk of the assault waves arrived accurately, on schedule at 02:45 and achieved complete surprise, although there was some scattered resistance; Captain A. P. Boyd and a Corporal Higgins from the 1st Hampshires reportedly stormed a barbed-wire protected bunker firing on the beach.[51] Other scattered resistance was suppressed by escorting vessels, with the Dutch gunboats HNLMS *Flores* and *Soemba* working together to silence an Italian gun battery, and the Brigade's infantry units were then able to push inland toward the road running north from Pachino to Noto, covered by the 165th Field Regiment RA's 3.5-inch howitzers from 07:30.[52]

The furthest travelled component of the Eastern Naval Task Force from the rendezvous south of Malta was Rear-Admiral Thomas Troubridge's FORCE A, which included the Fast Assault Convoys carrying Major-General Horatio Berney-Ficklin's 5th Division and Major-General Sidney Kirkman's 50th (Northumbrian) Division from Lieutenant-General Miles Dempsey's XIII Corps. After sailing north almost the length of the Gulf of Noto Admiral Troubridge's FORCE A made visual contact at one minute after midnight with the beacon vessel HM Submarine *Unruffled*, which had been on station six nautical miles from the *Capo Porco di Murro* lighthouse since 23:05 on 9 July.[53] The transport vessels carrying the assault Divisions then made for their respective Release Positions for the two ACID Landing Sectors, guided by navigation-light equipped Folbot canoes launched by the *Unruffled* at 21:45 and 22:20. The 5th Division's landing, oriented on Cassibile, was to take place on the ACID NORTH Landing Area with two brigades and their support elements landing on adjacent Beaches while the Division's third constituent formation, Brigadier Lorne Campbell's 13th Brigade, was held back aboard ship in reserve to land as directed according to the situation. Brigadier Gerald Tarleton's 17th Brigade was allotted the right-hand GEORGE Sector, but while the first wave hit the beach just after the 02:45 deadline it came ashore well to the south of its target beach and while the succeeding waves were delivered accurately they were up to an hour behind schedule for reasons that are unclear; despite this, GEORGE Sector was secured by 05:00 and the bulk of the Brigade was then able to advance on Cassibile as envisaged. Matters went even more awry for Brigadier George Rawstorne's 15th Brigade on the left-hand HOW Sector. The Brigade's initial wave was unable to locate its assigned landing point and consequently came ashore in the wrong place and almost an hour behind schedule, with a similar knock-on effect for the succeeding waves. The 15th Brigade landing also came under fire from Italian shore batteries until they were successfully suppressed by gunfire from the destroyer HMS *Eskimo*, and Brigadier Rawstorne's formation was established in the vicinity of Cassibile alongside 17th Brigade by 10:00.

The final Eastern Naval Task Force landing, by the 50th Division onto the ACID SOUTH Landing Area oriented upon Avola twenty miles to the south, was intended as a flank protection measure for the 5th Division landings to the north. It was consequently a smaller scale affair, involving only Brigadier Ronald Senior's 151st Brigade; the 50th Division's other constituent formations, 69th and 168th Brigades, were to land later as part of XIII Corps' follow-up force. 151st Brigade was tasked to put two battalions onto JIG GREEN Beach and the third onto JIG AMBER Beach, but matters went seriously awry from the outset. The RN guides were obliged to commandeer other craft when their specially fitted-out motor-launches failed to appear on time and the strong wind and resultant rough sea complicated and slowed the process of launching and marshalling the LCAs. The sea state continued to be problematic during the run in from the Release Position. Troops aboard the LCAs were obliged to bale continuously, water ingress rendered numerous pairs of binoculars, radio sets and electrically illuminated compasses unserviceable and interfered with navigation to the extent that the first wave missed the landing deadline of 02:45 by more than an hour and were scattered and intermixed along the landing frontage.

The Brigade was ashore by just after 06:00 with naval gunfire from the escorts suppressing fire from Italian coastal batteries and the advance inland went ahead in the face of scattered and irresolute opposition from Italian troops, who tended to melt away after the first exchange of fire. Neither Brigadier Senior travelling in a landing craft nor Major-General Kirkman aboard the landing ship HMS *Winchester Castle* were initially aware of the landing's success due to patchy radio communication until they went ashore, the former shortly before 06:00 and the latter at 08:20. Even then the 'build-up from the sea was unpunctual and confused' with stores and equipment arriving in the wrong order at best and going completely astray at worst, to the extent that by the end of D-Day only nine field guns from the Division's three RA Field Regiments were ashore and in action.[54]

Thus by around 08:00 on Saturday 10 July 1943 a British Airlanding Brigade, a reinforced US Parachute Infantry Regiment and elements of three British, one Canadian and three US Divisions were on Sicilian soil. The question now was how the Italian and German commanders on Sicily would react, and how this would impact on the Allied interlopers transforming their beach front footholds into larger defensible lodgements to support extending the advance inland.

12

The Sword in Alexander's Right Hand

The Supporting Air Effort and the British 8th Army Landing Area, D-Day, 08:00 Saturday 10 July to D-Day Plus Five, 23:59 Thursday 15 July

Operation HUSKY had commenced during the night of 9-10 July 1943 with the insertion of a British Airlanding Brigade and a reinforced US Parachute Infantry Regiment into south-eastern Sicily. By the early morning of 10 July the Airborne trail blazers had been joined by the lead elements of three US, three British and a Canadian Division distributed across five separate landing areas; these were spread over a hundred miles of the island's south-eastern and eastern coast, running from Licata at the western extremity of the Bay of Gela to the edge of the Pachino Peninsula near Syracuse in the east. The US Official History recorded: 'By 09:00, 10 July, infantry battalions were pushing inland. The assault had been accomplished with a minimum of casualties against only minor enemy resistance.'[1] With the initial landing waves ashore in the face of generally minimal resistance the immediate task for the HUSKY landing force was to link up with the Airborne elements and fully secure and enlarge their beach front footholds into properly defensible lodgements; these could then be expanded laterally in turn to create a base area from which to break out and overwhelm the remainder of the island.

The initial HUSKY landings were supported by a huge Allied air effort employing aircraft operating from bases in Malta, Pantelleria and North Africa, totalling 2,543 sorties across the twenty-four hours from dusk 9 July to dusk 10 July.[2] During the hours of darkness these included nine intruder sorties over Axis airfields on Sicily and southern Italy by Mosquito night-fighters likely from RAF No. 256 Squadron attached to Malta Air Command, while other Mosquitos and Bristol Beaufighter night-fighters, likely from the Malta based RAF No. 108 Squadron and RAF Nos. 219 and 255 Squadrons flying from North Africa, flew eighteen patrol and six ground-attack sorties over the invasion beaches.[3] The Malta based machines were controlled by Ground Controlled Interception (GCI) stations carried aboard modified

Landing Craft Tank (LCT) vessels travelling with the invasion fleet, a technique successfully trialled during the invasion of Pantelleria a month earlier on 11 June 1943.[4] The night activities also included 203 sorties by heavy, medium and light bombers that delivered 259 tons of bombs onto a variety of targets.[5] On the British 8th Army landing frontage Vickers Wellingtons from the Tunisia-based RAF No. 205 Group carrying out missions in direct support of the 1st Airlanding Brigade's Operation LADBROKE. A third of the Group's strength was tasked to bomb Augusta and the airfield and communication links at Catania to the north between 22:00 and 23:30 on 9 July as a diversion from the glider *coup-de-main* against the Ponte Grande, the remainder were to bomb targets in Syracuse between 02:15 and 02:45 on 10 July to assist the Airlanding Brigade in securing the city while to the south of Syracuse twelve Liberator heavy bombers from RAF No. 178 Squadron hit a number of targets around Avola and Noto. To the west behind the US 7th Army landing frontage North African-based US B-25 medium bombers from North African Strategic Air Force (NASAF) and North African Tactical Bombing Force (NATBF) units hit the airfield at Biscari and communication targets in the surrounding area while RAF Martin Baltimore and Douglas Boston light bombers also from the NATBF bombed targets around Niscemi, ten miles inland from Gela; the latter units also attacked airfields at Sciacca and Milo, fifty-five miles west of the US landing area and at the western extremity of Sicily respectively.[6]

The bombing effort intensified with the onset of daylight, with a total of 367 sorties across the day delivering 415 tons of bombs onto roads, railways and airfields with the latter absorbing two-thirds of the total.[7] The sorties included at least one supporting attack on the south-western tip of the Italian mainland, where twenty-one B-24 heavy bombers from the US 9th Air Force's two Heavy Bombardment Groups carried out a supporting raid on an airfield network at Vibo Valentia. On Sicily a force of fifty-one B-17 heavy bombers from the US 5th Heavy Bombardment Wing struck the network of airfields and landing grounds around Gerbini, sixteen miles west of Catania, sixty B-25s divided their attention between the rail marshalling yards in Catania and communication targets around Palazzolo, ten miles to the west and a further seventy-one B-25s struck the airfields at Sciacca and Milo again; it is unclear if the B-25s were from the US 47th Medium Bombardment Wing, the NATBF's US 12th and 340th Medium Bombardment Groups, or both. In addition, fighter-bomber aircraft were tasked to 'interfere with enemy movements toward the areas of landing'. Over the course of D-Day A36 fighter-bombers from the US 27th and 86th Fighter Groups flew 111 sorties against communication targets and defensive positions around Barrafranca, twenty miles north of Gela and a further forty-one sorties against similar targets over a wider area that included Vallelunga thirty miles to the north and Agrigento on the coast thirty-five miles to the west.[8] A detachment of twelve P-38 fighter-bombers on loan from NASAF performed the same mission in the area around Grammichele, twenty-five miles to the east; it is unclear if the loaned machines belonged to the US 1st, 14th or 82nd Fighter Groups.[9]

The daylight bombing was paralleled by an extensive Allied fighter cover and escort effort that totalled 1,891 sorties over the course of 10 July, with fighters units being given responsibility for protecting specific Landing Areas.[10] On the US side, defence of the JOSS Landing Area astride Licata was allotted to the four P-40-equipped Wings from the 33rd Fighter Wing flying from recently captured Pantelleria, while the Spitfire-equipped three Wing-strong 31st Fighter Group based on Gozo was responsible for the DIME Landing Area around Gela.[11] The most easterly US CENT Landing Area centred on Scoglitti and the Anglo-Canadian ACID and BARK Landing Areas were protected by RAF fighters, with five Squadrons of Spitfires flying from Malta being allotted to each Landing Area with a further five Squadrons held initially in reserve before being released to escort bomber sorties. The identity of these Spitfire units is unclear, but as Malta Air Command had only a single Spitfire Wing of five Squadrons the remainder were presumably drawn from other formations and based temporarily on the island for the beginning of HUSKY. The fighter cover was initially controlled by the various FORCE HQ ships and Ground Controlled Interception (GCI) stations carried in modified LCTs and then specially configured RAF Forward Fighter Control (FFC) units made up of a GCI station, two Light Warning Sets radars (LWS) and a Wireless Unit (WU) made up of five individual posts each equipped with a Jeep which could also act as a forward early-warning screen. One FFC was allotted to each of the three Landing Areas covered by the RAF and went ashore during D-Day, while a similar USAAF forward control unit was deployed in the 7th Army landing sector; it is unclear if this unit went ashore on the JOSS or DIME Landing Area.[12]

Allied fighters were scheduled to be on station over the invasion fleet and Landing Areas by 04:20, twenty minutes after first light, but Axis aircraft were faster off the mark, attacking the ships off the CENT Landing Area at 04:24 using parachute flares for illumination and at least one fighter element was late on station; the USAAF Spitfires from the Gozo-based 31st Fighter Group did not arrive over the DIME Landing Area as assigned until 05:15, after becoming involved in the fighting over CENT.[13] The rapid Axis reaction might have been countered by expanding the night-fighter intruder missions over Axis airfields and standing patrols over the invasion fleet and Landing Areas from the twenty-seven night-fighter sorties flown on the night of 9-10 July, but there was a relative dearth of night-fighters. Mediterranean Air Command included only six RAF night-fighter Squadrons equipped with ninety-six Beaufighters and six Mosquito night-fighters detached to Malta from the UK-based RAF No. 256 Squadron from 4 July 1943.[14] This was a relatively small force with which to carry out intruder missions, cover the invasion fleet and sea lanes and carry out defensive patrols over ports and other installations on the North African mainland; while the US 350th Fighter Group deployed four squadrons equipped with a further forty-eight inherited Beaufighters, these were equipped with older and less efficient radar sets and were tasked to defend ports in North-West Africa.[15] The US 7th Army landings, and especially the DIME and JOSS Landing Areas, attracted the most attention from the Axis air arms, due to the geographical spread and number of ships deployed there. The cruiser USS *Philadelphia* and the Attack Transport USS *Thomas Jefferson* emerged unscathed from the initial attacks by eleven dive bombers, including Junkers 88s likely from *Kampfgeschwader* 54, but at 04:50 the minesweeper USS *Sentinel* was severely damaged and sank later at 10:50, and at 04:58 the destroyer USS *Maddox* was hit by a single bomb that detonated her aft magazine, sending her down in two minutes and killing 211 of her crew.[16]

Other air attacks were reported on the JOSS anchorage at 05:12 and 05:20 after which things appear to have tapered off until the early afternoon, when the JOSS Landing Area again came under strafing and bombing attack. *Luftwaffe* Messerschmitt 109 and Focke-Wulf 190 fighter-bombers conducted intermittent tip-and-run attacks against all three US Landing Areas over the course of the afternoon, followed by high level bombing of the anchorages off the CENT and DIME Landing Areas at 15:47.[17] The air attacks on both shipping and beaches continued until dusk. At 18:35 a bombing attack damaged LST 312 and LST 313, setting the former on fire in return for a bomber shot down by the destroyer USS *McLanahan*, and at 19:30 a tip-and-run attacker scored a direct hit on another unidentified LST also setting it ablaze.[18] The Allied anti-aircraft fire proved to be something of a two-edged sword; as the British Official History put it, 'In general, the anti-aircraft artillery was too excitable [and] persistently engaged Allied fighters, thus distracting them from their protective duties.'[19] In some instances the distraction could be fatal; at 14:15 off the CENT Landing Area a Spitfire, presumably from the US 31st Fighter Group, '…was accidentally shot down in flames by [an] LST' while attempting a forced landing.[20]

In addition to Axis aircraft and 'friendly' anti-aircraft fire the covering fighters also had to contend with attempts to expand their defensive mission while it was underway. At 09:45 Vice-Admiral Hewitt, commanding the Western Naval Task Force from the converted Attack Transport USS *Monrovia*, ordered his cruiser commanders to report the 'disposition of cruiser spotting planes…in advance so that our fighters can give them protection against anticipated enemy air attacks'. The order appears to have prompted some dissent, given that five hours later Hewitt was obliged to reacquaint his cruisers and Task Force Flagships with the fact that the primary mission of the covering fighter force was the protection of the landing beaches and invasion shipping, with the rider that spotter aircraft needed to align their flights and dispositions with the fighter schedules and remain within five miles of the anchorages if they wished to be protected. The dissent was likely caused by the loss of catapult-launched Vought OS2U observation floatplanes engaged in gunfire spotting for their cruisers; two were shot down at around 08:30, three more reported at 13:35 and a further two at 15:35.[21]

Aerial events developed in a less frenetic manner at the British 8th Army landing area in the Gulf of Noto, which according to the British Official History suffered 'one [air] attack in the morning and a few more during the rest of the day'; the disparity was presumably due to the much larger assemblage of shipping off the adjacent US landing areas being a more attractive target.[22] In fact Axis air attacks on the 8th Army landing areas reportedly totalled twenty-three spread over the first forty-eight hours of Operation HUSKY, with the first occurring at 09:00 on 10 July followed by a number of heavier attacks starting at 11:00; on the Canadian BARK WEST Landing Area the 09:00 attack destroyed one beached LCT and badly damaged another.[23] The most damaging attack occurred after dark on D-Day when the hospital ship HMHS *Talamba* was bombed at anchor five miles off Avola, despite being fully floodlit and marked as a Red Cross vessel. The vessel sank approximately twenty minutes after being hit at *c*.22:00, possibly by a single bomb, although the 400 casualties aboard were successfully rescued along with all but five of the *Talamba's* 168-strong crew.[24] A combination of the larger and more target-rich environment off the US landing beaches and less extensive nature of the 8th Army landing area appears to have made the latter easier to defend, reinforced by the efficiency of the Malta-based Spitfire Squadrons which flew a total of 1,346 sorties on 10 July.

The final interception of the day, by machines from No. 229 Squadron, rebuffed a formation of eight Italian Macchi C200 *Saetta* fighters, shooting down three. In all the Malta-based Spitfire Squadrons reported encountering just fifty-seven Axis fighters in the course of the day from an estimated hundred deployed. According to *Comando Supremo*, 141 *Regia Aeronautica* machines of all types were deployed against the landings on 10 July along with 370 *Luftwaffe* machines spread over *c*.300 sorties. Sixteen *Luftwaffe* and eleven *Regia Aeronautica* machines of all types were destroyed, with all the Italian aircraft reportedly shot down, in return for a total of twenty-five Allied aircraft lost.[25] The low Axis sortie rate was a testament to the effectiveness of the HUSKY Air Plan and D-Day bombing effort. The *Luftwaffe* response on 10 July was hamstrung by the destruction of the central *Luftwaffe* telephone exchange at Taormina near Catania by USAAF B-24s on 9 July for example, which paralysed *Luftwaffe* communications on the very eve of the invasion.[26] The limited damage the Axis air sorties managed to inflict was in turn a testament to the efficiency of the Allied covering fighter effort; while pre-invasion estimates placed likely Allied shipping losses in the region of 300 vessels to Axis air attack, only six were lost on D-Day Minus One/D-Day, rising to just twelve over the three day period 10-12 July.[27] Naval Commander-in-Chief Mediterranean, Admiral of the Fleet Sir Andrew Cunningham wrote in his post-HUSKY report: 'To one who had fought through the Mediterranean campaign from the beginning it appeared almost magical that great fleets could remain anchored on the enemy's coast, within forty miles of his main aerodromes... The navies (and consequently the armies) owed a great debt to the air for the effectiveness of the protection offered them throughout the operation.'[28]

The effectiveness of this protective Allied air umbrella not only permitted the initial amphibious landings to proceed with minimal interference but also allowed the immediate post-landing consolidation and movements inland to proceed largely unhindered as well. This was particularly the case with the British 8th Army advance inland from the initial beach lodgements. At the 5th Division's ACID NORTH Landing Area the bulk of Brigadier Gerald Tarleton's 17th Brigade moved on its primary objective, the town of Cassibile just over a mile inland from the beach, after reorganising, and simultaneously despatched the 2nd Battalion Royal Scots Fusiliers (RSF) north toward Syracuse to relieve the 1st Airlanding Brigade at the Ponte Grande. With Cassibile secured, Brigadier Tarleton handed over to Brigadier George Rawstorne's 15th Brigade, which was tasked to hold the beachhead, and directed the 2nd Battalion The Northamptonshire Regiment and 6th Battalion Seaforth Highlanders northward in the wake of the 2nd RSF; they were subsequently followed north by the 5th Division's floating reserve, Brigadier Lorne Campbell's 13th Brigade, in the afternoon of D-Day.[29]

The bulk of 17th Brigade made good time covering the four miles or so to the Santa Teresa Longarini railway station, roughly midway to the Ponte Grande by late morning, apparently dealing with subsidiary objectives en route; a Company from the 2nd Northamptons linked up with a party from the 1st Airlanding Brigade led by the Brigade Deputy Commander, Colonel Osmond Jones, in attacking an Italian gun battery in the vicinity of the railway station at some point before Midday, for example.[30] For their part the 2nd RSF reached the Ponte Grande at c.16:15, just an hour or so after the 75° *Reggimento di Fanteria* had finally overcome the elements of the 1st Airlanding Brigade that had seized the crossing, codenamed WATERLOO, shortly before Midnight on 9 July. The approach of 17th Brigade's lead elements was heralded by Italian troops withdrawing northward in 'complete disorder' including a party of approximately twenty that retired up the beach before attempting to swim across the mouths of the River Anapo and parallel Mammiaibica Canal. Their passing alerted Lieutenant Gordon Welch, sheltering in a nearby concrete drainage culvert with half a dozen 1st Airlanding Brigade evaders, of the 2nd RSF's imminent arrival at the Ponte Grande. Despite being mortared as they debussed from their transport just short of the bridge, the Fusiliers secured the structure in around thirty minutes before establishing a defensive perimeter. According to one source this was done with the assistance of Lieutenant Welch, who made himself known to the RSF lead elements and guided them through the attack to clear the area and secure the bridges. Thereafter Lieutenant Withers, who was also presumably an evader, supervised the gathering in of all the wounded in the vicinity with the assistance of a RSF Corporal and their evacuation south for treatment using a captured Italian ambulance, while Lieutenant Welch reported to the 1st Airlanding Brigade HQ at 18:00. The precise location of the HQ at this point is unclear.[31]

At *c.*17:00 17th Brigade's lead elements overtook and released the party of approximately eighty-eight 1st Airlanding prisoners who been marched away when the bridge was overrun. The party's senior officer, Lieutenant-Colonel Arthur Walch, immediately sought and was granted permission from Brigadier Tarleton to move the party back to the Ponte Grande and resume a role in its defence, which was done using recycled enemy weapons.

At 21:00, 17th Brigade resumed the advance north to secure Syracuse and Brigadier Tarleton formally handed responsibility for the bridges to Colonel Walch and his party and Walch in turn handed over command of the bridge defence and the liberated POWs to Brigadier Philip Hicks and 1st Airlanding Brigade HQ at 08:00 on Sunday 11 July; the Brigade HQ had moved up to just south of the Ponte Grande at *c*.21:00 the previous night, where Brigadier Hicks finally joined it at 22:00 after regaining dry land from his ditched glider, accompanied by Brigade second-in-command Colonel Osmond Jones fresh from eliminating the Italian gun battery near the Santa Teresa Longarini railway station.[32] In the meantime the British advance up the Sicilian coast from the ACID NORTH Landing Area continued to gather pace. 17th Brigade secured Syracuse after an hour-long fight and continued to press north toward Augusta, leaving the 1st Airlanding Brigade to move up and garrison the port at 09:00 on 11 July, while Brigadier Lorne Campbell's 13 Brigade moved rapidly up on the left flank and secured Floridia, eight miles west of Syracuse, also during the night of 10-11 July. The ease of the British advance was due in part to the continuing inability of *16° Corpo* HQ at Piazza Armerina, over fifty miles from the scene of the action in central Sicily, to concentrate Italian reinforcements in the east of the island; this in turn induced a rolling collapse of the defence of the Augusta-Syracuse *Piazze Militari Marittime* (roughly Naval Fortress Areas), although some reinforcements did arrive in the area. At 20:00 on 10 July the lead elements of *Kampfgruppe* Schmalz, made up of *Fallschirmjäger* and *Panzergrenadier* units arrived in Melilli, twelve miles north of Syracuse after travelling forty miles from its concentration area west of Caltagirone. The *Kampfgruppe* fought a successful day-long delaying action against 17th Brigade the following day at Priolo Gargallo, seven miles north of Syracuse; two *battaglioni* from the *75° Reggimento di Fanteria*, the erstwhile conquerors of the Ponte Grande, fought another delaying action the same day against 13th Brigade at Solarino, three miles north of Floridia, inflicting casualties on the 2nd Battalion Inniskilling Fusiliers and 2nd Battalion The Wiltshire Regiment.

The delay proved negligible as 17th Brigade pushed on to enter Augusta in the early hours of Monday 13 July, supported by a landing by the SAS Special Raiding Squadron from the LSI *Ulster Monarch* covered by the RN destroyers *Nubian*, *Tetcott* and the Greek *Kanaris*. The advance also reacquainted the 5th Division's infantry elements with a staple of their trade that had been minimised in the Desert campaigns by distance and motor transport; the British Official History recorded that by 13 July 17th Brigade's constituent battalions had marched over a hundred miles in 'boots which had been sodden in sea water'.[33]

Twenty miles to the south the 50th Division landing at the ACID SOUTH Landing Area was a smaller scale affair intended to protect the left flank of the larger landing at ACID NORTH, involving Brigadier Ronald Senior's 151 Brigade; the remainder of the Division was to land later as part of the follow-up force for Lieutenant-General Miles Dempsey's XIII Corps. Despite the bad weather scattering the landing, to the extent that one battalion was delivered among the 5th Division landing on ACID NORTH, 151st Brigade was ashore in its entirety by 06:00 and after mopping up Italian troops at the landing area set off to achieve its initial objective of securing Avola, a mile or so inland from the beach, and establishing a blocking position west of the town.[34] In the event the Brigade's passage inland was eased by assistance from an unexpected source. Due to a navigational error twenty-three C-47s from the USAAF 313th Troop Carrier Group scattered their sticks from the 1st Battalion 505th Parachute Infantry Regiment in the vicinity of Avola. After rallying, a party of paratroopers between sixty-five and seventy-five strong commanded by a group of junior officers decided to secure the town on their own initiative, a decision that sparked a fierce street-by-street fight with the well emplaced Italian garrison, likely from the *206a Divisione Costiera*, that went on through the morning and beyond. Handicapped by a lack of support weapons, the paratroopers became pinned down in an open square but the situation was saved by the arrival of a Bren Carrier and men from 151 Brigade's lead elements in mid-afternoon, although that was not quite the end of the matter. As the British troops were unfamiliar with US Airborne uniforms and accoutrements and were not expecting to encounter US troops in their area, they made the not unreasonable assumption that the paratroopers were in fact Axis troops and opened fire on them; fratricide was only averted by the paratroopers loudly and fervently shouting their nationality while waving their helmets on weapon muzzles. The identification problem arose frequently due to the scattering of the US paratroopers across the British zone, and it was exacerbated by the British and US forces employing different passwords; this was addressed subsequently by issuing a common challenge and response for use British and US troops alike, which became a feature of all future joint operations.[35]

The 50th Division joined the advance north, still acting as left flank-guard, once all its constituent formations came ashore with the follow-up force landings, with Brigadier Edward Cooke-Collis' 69 Brigade in the lead. By 13 July the latter had covered the twenty miles from Avola to Sortino, fourteen miles west of Augusta and after clearing the town continued to push north toward Lentini, while 151st Brigade followed up by clearing Axis elements in the area of Solarino and Sortino bypassed in the 5th Division's push to Augusta. After repelling an attack by elements of the *54a Napoli Divisione* on 12 July 151st Brigade's 6th Battalion Durham Light Infantry (DLI) attacked high ground held by the Italian formation at 04:45 the following day. The high ground was secured by 07:30 on 13 July and thirty minutes a column of Carriers from the 6th DLI and a Troop of Sherman tanks likely from the 44th RTR moved off to rendezvous with elements of the 51st Highland Division at Palazzolo to secure XIII Corps' left flank. The column knocked out two Italian R35 tanks and three anti-tank guns and captured staff cars carrying the commander of the *54a Napoli Divisione*, *Generale di Divisione* Giulio Gotti-Porcinari and his staff before making contact with the 51st Highland Division at 12:30.[36]

The most northerly of the BARK landings, by Brigadier Roy Urquhart's 231st Brigade at the BARK EAST Landing Area centred on Marzamemi, approximately twelve miles south of Avola, was also a peripheral supporting affair intended to protect the 51st Highland Division's right flank. Despite loading problems 231st Brigade landed on time and in the right place apart from the LCT-borne armoured element, which was running six hours behind schedule due to bad weather, and by midday the Brigade had secured its final initial objective by reaching the coast road running north from Pachino. Urquhart's Brigade came under the operational control of 51st Highland Division and participated in the general division advance north and north-west from the landing area in the wake of the British 5th and 50th Divisions. The first stage to Noto, twelve miles north of Marzamemi, was led by the 2nd Battalion Devonshire Regiment which reached the town at dawn on 11 July, while the 1st Battalion Dorsetshire Regiment accompanied an armoured column advance on Palazzolo, sixteen miles to the northwest. After regrouping, 231st Brigade passed through Palazzolo on 12 July and moved a further thirty miles north-west over twisting mountain roads, reaching a point three miles short of Vizzini at 10:00 on 13 July. It was at that point, after a sixty-mile advance and with resupply becoming increasingly difficult in the rugged terrain, that the Brigade ran into its first serious opposition, as Vizzini's defenders included elements of the *54a Napoli Divisione* and also the first German troops encountered, elements of the very recently arrived 1 *Fallschirmjäger Division* seconded to *Kampfgruppe* Schmalz. Brigadier Urquhart said later: 'After the comparative ease with which we overcame the opposition on the first three days – mostly Italian – it was a shock to the system to be rebuffed at Vizzini, and here we met the Germans.'[37] The attack was resumed by 153rd Brigade with support from 154th Brigade and artillery belonging to the 1st Canadian Division and Vizzini was finally secured in the early hours of 15 July, after which 231st Brigade was granted a day to rest and recuperate.[38]

The larger scale landing by Major-General Douglas Wimberley's 51st Highland Division at the adjacent BARK SOUTH Landing Area astride Portopalo Bay, on the south-eastern aspect of the Pachino Peninsula, also proceeded relatively smoothly. While the 7th Argyll & Sutherland Highlanders came ashore right on schedule at 02:45, the 7th Black Watch and 1st Gordon Highlanders were delayed by difficulties locating the correct beach, the latter by an hour, but resistance proved to be negligible. The assault waves suffered just a handful of casualties from mines and a single hand-grenade attack on an LCA, in exchange for 'two or three hundred rather antiquated Italian prisoners' and 154th Brigade was in place on its initial objective, a ridge a mile inland from the beach, by 07:00.[39]

In the meantime the LCTs carrying the Division's armoured component, again two hours behind schedule due to bad weather, began landing the 50th Royal Tank Regiment (RTR) at 04:00 followed two hours later by the first of 11th Regiment RHA's self-propelled guns and, according to the Division history, 153 Brigade at 06:30. Major-General Wimberley's

Tactical HQ and 152nd Brigade, appear to have come ashore directly from LSIs in the early afternoon, with around 4,000 men being landed 'almost simultaneously', by which time 154th Brigade had pressed four miles inland to Pachino.[40] The Division then spearheaded XXX Corps' advance north out of the Pachino Peninsula on 11 July on an eight-mile front to the towns of Rosolini and Noto, the latter being secured by the temporarily co-opted 231st Brigade, and the Division continued to lead the way thereafter, moving north-west on an eight- to ten-mile front to broaden the coastal advance by XIII Corps. By Tuesday 13 July the advance had covered around sixty miles and reached the towns of Vizzini and Francofonte on the left and right respectively. On the left adjacent to the US 45th Infantry Division boundary, Vizzini sat atop a 2,000-foot height surrounded by terraced orange groves, orchards and vineyards, many of them on steep, razor-back ridges. When 231st Brigade's initial attempt to secure the town off the march on 13 July was rebuffed, 153rd Brigade launched a deliberate two-battalion attack with artillery support from the 1st Canadian Division the following day. Despite the difficult terrain and lack of water on the hottest day the invaders had experienced since landing, the 5th Black Watch secured the western half of the town while the 1st Gordon Highlanders succeeded in securing Vizzini's cathedral tower and cemetery on the eastern side by 21:00; when the attack was renewed in the early morning of 15 July after a preparatory artillery barrage it was discovered the German defenders had withdrawn during the night, leaving a quantity of stores and a number of prisoners. The cost of the hard-fought action was increased by the 1st Black Watch from 154th Brigade suffering thirty casualties to friendly artillery while moving up to support the attack.[41]

On the right, Francofonte proved to be an even harder nut to crack. Defended by elements of *Oberstleutnant* Ludwig Heilmann's *Fallschirmjäger Regiment 3*, which had parachuted onto a drop zone just west of the Ponte Primosole near Catania as a rapid reinforcement in the evening of Monday 12 July, the town was also located on a steep hilltop surrounded by terraced olive groves, with access via a single road with a tight hairpin bend overlooked by a cemetery.[42] In the morning of Tuesday 13 July 152nd Brigade, accompanied by Sherman tanks likely from C Squadron, 50th RTR approached Francofonte from the south with the 5th Seaforth Highlanders in the lead. An anti-tank gun deployed in the cemetery knocked out the first Bren Carrier in the column before withdrawing and as the 5th Seaforth Highlanders attempted to move up the steep slope toward the cemetery they came under withering flanking fire from *Fallschirmjäger* located in the town; when the German defence then rebuffed their attempts to enter the town, the 5th Seaforths withdrew to the road below Francofonte for the night. Following a heavy artillery bombardment in the morning of Wednesday 14 July the attack was taken over by the 2nd Seaforth Highlanders who fought their way into Francofonte, sparking a close-quarter, house-to-house battle that continued through the day, with a building dubbed the 'Red House' putting up particularly stubborn resistance; by nightfall the *Fallschirmjäger* were still holding a portion of the town including the Red House and the fierce fighting had reduced the 50th RTR Squadron supporting the attack to a single serviceable Sherman tank. A night attack, likely by the 5th Cameron Highlanders, was planned to maintain the pressure but proved superfluous as the surviving elements of *Fallschirmjäger Regiment 3* quietly broke contact and withdrew under cover of darkness, and the 5th Camerons instead resumed the advance on 15 July towards Scordia, five miles to the north.[43]

On the western aspect of the Pachino Peninsula Major-General Guy Simonds' 1st Canadian Division landing at the BARK WEST Landing Area also proceeded generally as planned. BARK WEST was located in a shallow, four-mile-wide bay bounded by the *Punta Castellazo* (Castle Point) on the left and the *Punta delle Formiche* (Point of the Ants) on the right, divided in two by a rocky central point known as *le Groticelle* (the Caves). The assault wave from Brigadier Christopher Vokes' 2nd Canadian Brigade reached the left-hand SUGAR Beach on time and in good order after the heavy swell carried the assault craft over an offshore sandbar, apart from some units being put ashore in the wrong sectors and the Brigade was moving on its initial objectives in the face of minimal Italian resistance by 04:00. However, events on the adjacent ROGER Beach on the right proved more problematic. The loading and consequent departure of Brigadier Howard Graham's 1st Canadian Brigade was delayed for almost two hours by a last-minute switch to LCAs, due to the non-appearance of some of the slated DUKW-carrying LCTs, which prompted some tetchy signals and courier-carried messages from FORCE V's commander, Rear-Admiral Sir Philip Vian aboard the HQ Ship HMS *Hilary*, demanding to know if the assault would ever start. Despite shelling by an Italian battery at Maucini, a mile or so inland from ROGER Beach, the assault wave touched down on ROGER Beach between at 04:45 and 05:30 with no resistance, allowing Major-General Simonds to report that his Division had secured all its initial objectives at 06:45. The assault waves were trailed by the 1st and 2nd Brigades' reserve battalions followed by support units; by 10:15 a complete Squadron of Sherman tanks from the Three Rivers Regiment was ashore and ready for action on ROGER, and self-propelled guns from the attached 142nd Field Regiment RA were driving ashore forty-five minutes later.[44] The Division's third formation, Brigadier Howard Penhale's 3rd Canadian Brigade, also began to disembark at *c.*11:00 and moved to a holding position at Burgio, three miles west of Pachino

The 1st Canadian Brigade began to push inland from ROGER Beach as soon as post-landing reorganisation was complete, with the Royal Canadian Regiment (RCR) in the lead shadowed by the Hastings and Prince Edward Regiment. The former swiftly cleared Maucini and overran the nearby Italian gun battery, capturing the entire thirty-eight-strong garrison in the process and by 09:00 had covered the three miles to Pachino airfield, which proved to be ploughed over and deserted; it was handed over to the 15th Airfield Construction Group RE attached to the Canadian Division shortly thereafter, which had an emergency landing strip functioning on the site by the early afternoon. In the meantime the RCR's A Company cleared some barrack buildings north of the airfield with the assistance of the Hastings before moving on to secure an Italian artillery battery position north of the town while C Company made contact with elements of the 51st Highland Division's 154th Brigade in Pachino proper. The four 150mm guns at A Company's objective had been silenced by naval gunfire after ineffectually shelling the RCR at the airfield, but the advancing Canadians came under 'considerable' machine-gun fire on approaching the position and were obliged to mount a deliberate attack. The resulting fight cost the RCR two dead and two wounded in exchange for 130 prisoners and saw the first Canadian gallantry awards of the Sicily campaign; Privates Joseph Grigas and Jack Gardner were awarded the Distinguished Conduct Medal and the Military Medal respectively for their actions during the battle. While this was going on C Company had taken a further hundred prisoners while securing high ground north-east of the airfield and by 18:00 the 1st Canadian Brigade had established a defensive perimeter in the grape vines north of Pachino town and airfield, which allowed the troops to enjoy their first meal since leaving their landing ships in the early hours.[45]

The 2nd Canadian Brigade's move inland from the left-hand SUGAR Beach was less eventful. After sorting out their mixed up delivery the Seaforth Highlanders of Canada and Princess Patricia's Canadian Light Infantry (PPCLI) set out for their initial objective, high ground north and west of Pantano Longarini, five miles north-west of the Beach, followed by The Loyal Edmonton Regiment after it came ashore with the reserve elements: the 48th Highlanders of Canada, who came ashore with Regimental pipers in the lead, moved north toward Pachino to rejoin the 1st Canadian Brigade. The 2nd Brigade's advance was unopposed, with the only contact with Axis troops being frequent surrenders to the advancing patrols. The exception to this were No. 40 & 41 RM Commandos from the 1st Special Service Brigade moving along the coast on the left of the 2nd Brigade's advance, which ran into determined resistance from a Blackshirt *Milizia Volontaria per la Sicurezza Nazionale* (*MVSN*) unit which not only pinned the lightly-armed RM Commandos down with heavy and effective fire from mortars and anti-tank guns, but also began to push into the space between them and the Seaforth Highlanders of Canada. The situation was saved by the passing presence of a Canadian Heavy Mortar Detachment, reportedly from the Division Support Battalion, The Saskatoon Light Infantry, which quickly deployed its weapons following a request from the Commandos and delivered 160 rounds onto the advancing Italians in short order; an RM Commando counter-attack then sparked a precipitate withdrawal by the *MVSN* unit, which abandoned its horse-drawn guns and a large quantity of ammunition. The second phase of the initial landing operation commenced after dark on D-Day. While the 1st Canadian Brigade appears to have remained in place around Pachino, the 2nd Canadian Brigade advanced a further three to four miles north-west to Pantano Longarini, again without encountering resistance and scooping up a number of Italian prisoners in the process. The advance was paralleled on the right by the 3rd Canadian Brigade moving up from Burgio, which resulted in a fight between a force of Italians and the West Nova Scotia Regiment; the latter suffered no casualties and took twenty-five prisoners. The total number of Italian personnel captured by the 1st Canadian Division on 10 July is unclear, but Division HQ reported holding a total of 650 prisoners including twenty *Luftwaffe* aircrew by 06:45; a further hundred were estimated killed. Canadian casualties for the day totalled seven killed and twenty-five wounded, while the 1st Special Service Brigade lost a further six dead and nineteen wounded.[46]

The 2nd and 3rd Canadian Brigades night move was in preparation for the 1st Canadian Division's advance out of the immediate landing area. As we have seen, one of Lieutenant-General Oliver Leese's XXX Corps' immediate post-landing missions was to despatch the 51st Highland Division northward to widen XIII Corps' advance up the eastern Sicilian coast and act as a flank guard, the other mission being to expand the BARK WEST Landing Area westward to make contact with US forces advancing inland from the CENT Landing Area. The 1st Canadian Division was tasked to address the second mission by advancing on Ragusa, a mountain town 1,680 feet above sea level with a 48,000 population around twenty miles north-west of Pantano Longarini, with the 1st Canadian Brigade on the right initially moving in the wake of the 51st Highland Division before striking west, the 2nd Canadian Brigade on the left still pressing west and the 3rd Canadian Brigade in reserve.[47] As it paralleled the Sicilian coast the Canadian advance was to be covered by naval gunfire from the cruisers HMS *Delhi* and *Orion*, the monitor HMS *Roberts* and the destroyers HMS *Brecon*, *Brissenden* and *Blankney*, controlled by RN forward observers moving with the lead elements at the forefront of the advance. Brigadier Graham's 1st Canadian Brigade moved off from its positions near Pachino in the afternoon of Sunday 11 July with the 48th Highlanders of Canada in the lead for the first nine-mile bound to Rosolini, which was already held by a detachment of Sherman tanks from the Three Rivers Regiment. The Royal Canadian Regiment (RCR) then took the lead using the Three River's Shermans, motor transport drawn from across the Brigade, captured Italian vehicles and requisitioned mules and carts to offset a general transport shortage in the Division.[48] The shortage was the result of the loss of three transports from the KMS-18B convoy carrying Canadian MT elements to U-Boat attacks on 4 and 5 July 1943.[49] Despite this the Royal Canadian Regiment was just four miles east of Ragusa by the early morning of Monday 12 July and after calling down a few artillery rounds from the 142nd Field Regiment RA as a demonstration, despatched a Carrier-mounted reconnaissance patrol into the town to clarify the situation.

The patrol found Ragusa and its population of 48,000 occupied by troops from the US 45th Infantry Division, specifically a company from the 1st Battalion, 157th Infantry Regiment despatched by Battalion commander Lieutenant-Colonel Preston Murphy in the afternoon of 10 July as per his pre-landing orders. The US vanguard of two motorised platoons reached the town at 18:00 that day where they were joined by the remainder of the company shortly before midnight; after arresting the mayor and chief of police and seizing the local telephone exchange the company spent Sunday

11 July replying to anxious telephone enquiries about events closer to the coast from surrounding Italian garrisons.[50] With the link up with US Forces complete the 1st Canadian Brigade paused at Ragusa for the 48th Highlanders and Hastings and Prince Edward Regiment to catch up before pushing north in the evening of 12 July with the Hastings in the lead, and by daylight on Tuesday 13 July the Brigade were set in around the hill village of Giarratana, ten miles north of Ragusa and thirty miles north-west of ROGER Beach.[51]

On the left-wing of the Canadian advance Brigadier Vokes and the 2nd Canadian Brigade's move on Ragusa proved to be less straightforward. The Brigade advance began with an eight-mile move on Ispica just after Midday on 11 July, led by The Loyal Edmonton Regiment which entered the town without a fight in the mid-afternoon following an ultimatum from the Edmonton's commander, Lieutenant-Colonel James Jefferson, backed by a warning salvo from the cruiser HMS *Delhi*; the naval gunfire was called down by Captain G. D. Mitchell's Forward Observer Team from No.1 Naval Bombardment Unit which was accompanying the Canadian advance. On entering the town Colonel Jefferson's men were met with the 'enthusiastic greetings of the civil population and the frantic endeavours of the military population to surrender'; the Italian eagerness was due in part to extensive aerial bombing and naval bombardment along the Brigade's planned line of advance the previous night and earlier in the day.[52]

A company from the Seaforth Highlanders of Canada was detached to assist in securing the coastal town of Pozzallo, five miles or so south-west of the Brigade's line of march; the town had surrendered to landing parties from the destroyers HMS *Blankney* and *Brissenden* after being bracketed by a 160-round demonstration bombardment from the destroyers. On arrival in the afternoon of 11 July the Seaforths not only captured 260 prisoners and a quantity of military equipment, but also found the civilian population suffering from a severe food shortage as the local government had broken down after the mayor and town council fled their posts. Enlisting the assistance of the local Catholic priest and the town postmaster, the Canadians located and broke open a granary before overseeing the distribution of supplies of bread, grain and pasta to the locals. To maintain momentum the PPCLI resumed the main advance from Ispica at 17:15, marching west through the night along *Strada* 115 and by the early morning of 12 July had covered approximately ten miles as the crow flies to occupy high ground overlooking the town of Modica. They were preceded by Captain Mitchell's intrepid Forward Observer Team which, after reaching the outskirts of Modica shortly before midnight, informed Major-General Simonds' Division HQ that there were no German troops in the town and later that it was seeking to surrender; the information was relayed to 2nd Canadian Brigade HQ shortly after midnight and at 01:25 on Monday 12 July Brigadier Vokes ordered the PPCLI to accept the surrender.

The PPCLI thus despatched a fighting patrol into Modica in the morning of 12 July after a fifteen-minute bombardment from 142nd Field Regiment RA, which quickly secured a 'considerable number' of Italian prisoners.

Thereafter, however, matters went awry. It is unclear if the culprits were Italian troops resurfacing after taking shelter from the bombardment or elements re-entering the town after withdrawing, but the result was an upsurge of fighting driven in part by the fact that Modica housed *Generale di Divisione* Achille d'Havet's *206^a^ Divisione Costiera* HQ, the formation tasked with defending the ninety or so miles of the Sicilian coast from the Bay of Gela to Syracuse. Small motorised elements from the Seaforth Highlanders of Canada and the RCR entered the town in the mid-morning in search of their parent units and under the mistaken assumption that it had been secured. After being ambushed the elements joined forces and fought back using a mortar and fire support from142nd Field Regiment RA to gain the town's central square. This sparked a mass Italian surrender, and the combined band of fifteen Canadians also captured thirteen assorted artillery pieces sited to cover roads running into the square; all were handed over to relieving elements from the Loyal Edmonton Regiment. Obtaining an overall Italian surrender then descended into something of a comic opera, with *Generale di Divisione* d'Havet insisting that he would only formally surrender to an officer of 'appropriate rank', despite being initially captured by the PPCLI Sergeant commanding the first fighting patrol; the impasse was overcome by the 2nd Canadian Brigade's Brigade Major, Major Richard Malone, personally escorting *Generale* d'Havet to General Simonds' HQ where he became 'the first general officer to be captured by Canadian troops in the Second World War'.

The presence of US troops in Ragusa rendered further advance westward redundant so the 2nd Canadian Brigade reoriented its line of advance northward, apart from mopping up known pockets of Italian troops. A platoon from The Loyal Edmonton Regiment supported by a Troop of Sherman tanks was despatched to the small town of Scicli, six miles south-west of Modica, for example; after the tanks fired three rounds over the town around 1,100 Italian troops emerged from positions in the surrounding hills to surrender. By nightfall on 12 July the 2nd Brigade had covered the five miles to Ragusa where it spent the night before pushing on the further ten miles to join the 1st Canadian Brigade at Giarratana on 13 July, trailed by the 3rd Canadian Brigade. By this point the 1st Canadian Division had collectively travelled approximately forty miles from the BARK WEST beaches as the crow flies and many more in reality due to the broken terrain, and after four days of continuous movement the troops were badly in need of rest; the PPCLI reported its men falling asleep at every stop during the night march to Modica for example, and on 13 July the Royal Regiment of Canada calculated its men had slept for an average total of eight hours since coming ashore four days earlier. The impact of this, the near constant movement and the rugged terrain was multiplied by the heat and dust of the Sicilian summer, and the fact that the 1st Canadian Division had not only launched into the invasion after ten days in cramped conditions aboard attack transports, but it was also the sole 8th Army formation not acclimatised to tropical weather. The troops had nonetheless 'marched well' as the British

Official History put it, but cognisant of the above, General Montgomery ordered left flank operations to hold in place at Giarratana on 13 July and granted the Division a thirty-six hour rest period, during which he visited the formation in person.[53] The halt not only permitted the troops to rest but also allowed the Royal Canadian Army Service Corps (RCASC) to bring up ammunition, rations, supplies and replacement vehicles from the follow-up convoys; in the twelve days or so after 10 July 3,700 assorted vehicles and 23,400 tons of stores for the 1st Canadian Division were unloaded across the BARK WEST beaches.[54]

Within five days of landings the British 8th Army had thus expanded its lodgement twenty miles north along the Sicilian coast, thirty miles into the mountains to the north-west and around twenty-five miles west to establish contact with the US 7th Army landings. It is now necessary to investigate the progress of the US landings at the JOSS, DIME and CENT Landing Areas to complete the picture of the HUSKY landings overall.

13

The Eastern Flanking Shield in Alexander's Left Hand

The CENT Landing Area, D-Day, 08:00 Saturday 10 July to D-Day Plus Five, 23:59 Thursday 15 July

While General Bernard Montgomery's British 8th Army was landing and pushing inland from its ACID and BARK Landing Areas along the Gulf of Noto on the eastern aspect of Sicily, Lieutenant-General George S. Patton's US 7th Army was doing the same along the shallow, forty-mile-wide Bay of Gela at the eastern end of the island's southern aspect. The US landings were spread over three separate locations in the Bay running west to east centred on the ports of Licata, Gela and Scoglitti, with each landing area being assigned to a reinforced division. The western JOSS Landing Area was allotted to Major-General Lucian K. Truscott's US 3rd Infantry Division, which remained under Lieutenant-General Patton's direct control due to its pivotal role of securing the western flank of the entire HUSKY invasion frontage. The centre DIME Landing Area at Gela was assigned to Major-General Terry Allen's US 1st Infantry Division while Major-General Troy C. Middleton's US 45th Infantry Division was tasked to land at the eastern CENT Landing Area straddling the small port of Scoglitti; the two divisions were under the auspices of Major-General Omar Bradley's US II Corps. The US initial objectives were to secure the ports of Gela and Licata for rapid reuse, capture the airfields at Biscari, Comiso, Licata and Ponte Olivo and establish a perimeter roughly twenty miles inland from the beaches dubbed the Yellow Line, the western end of which was anchored on a ridgeline west of Licata on the coast and ran around fifty miles east to the boundary with the British 8th Army near Ragusa.[1] These were relatively limited objectives because the British drive to the Strait of Messina was considered the primary focus of the invasion with the US acting in a subsidiary role; as the US Official History put it: 'Patton's army would be the shield in [General Sir Harold] Alexander's left hand; Montgomery's army the sword in his right.'[2] Perhaps ironically given this characterisation, the US 7th Army shield and particularly the central sector before Gela was to see the bulk of the fighting in the initial phase of the invasion, some of it the heaviest in the entire campaign.

The US 45th Infantry Division's CENT Landing Area was a fifteen mile stretch of coast roughly centred on the small fishing port of Scoglitti, running east from the mouth of the River Acate to a promontory known as the *Punta Braccetto*. The most easterly of the landings was that by Colonel Charles M. Ankcorn's 157th Regimental Combat Team (RCT), which was to put Lieutenant-Colonel Preston J. C. Murphy's 1st Battalion and Lieutenant-Colonel Irving O. Schaefer's 2nd Battalion onto the adjacent YELLOW 2 and GREEN 2 Beaches respectively. Collectively nicknamed 'Bailey's Beach' the landing area stretched for just over a mile to the left of the *Punta Braccetto*, was only ten to twenty yards deep backed with sand dunes and rocky outcrops that extended down to the waterline in some instances; neither beach was suitable for landing vehicles and later a third, codenamed BLUE 2, was opened on the east side of the *Punta Braccetto* while the original two beaches were closed. The initial landings by the 2nd Battalion from the Attack Transport USS *Thomas Jefferson*, which were supposed to come ashore on the left-hand GREEN 2 Beach, went awry. Lieutenant-Colonel Schaefer's first wave actually made landfall far to the right of its intended location at the eastern end of YELLOW 2 Beach at 03:55, the second wave was carried onto the rocky *Punta Braccetto* causing two craft to capsize and drowning twenty-seven men, although the remaining landing craft were able to unload directly onto the promontory along with four craft from the third wave; two of the remaining three from the third wave beached nearby while the third eventually came ashore in a different Regiment's landing area twelve miles or more up the coast past Scoglitti.

The confused, scattered and misplaced landing was unopposed apart from a few scattered rifle shots and an Italian machine-gun team that surrendered without firing a shot, although it still took the 2nd Battalion several hours to complete its mission of clearing Italian positions along the shore line and reorganise its scattered elements. In contrast, although delayed by difficulties loading and launching its landing craft from the Attack Transport USS *Charles Carroll*, the 1st Battalion's first wave landed safely on YELLOW 2 Beach as tasked at around 04:55 and all six succeeding waves including Colonel Ankcorn's Regimental staff followed over the next hour. Lieutenant-Colonel Murphy's unit was ready to move first thanks to its less fraught landing, but both battalions were on the move toward their initial objectives by 09:00.[3]

The 157th RCT's far-flung landing location, ten miles from the next nearest US beach, was not only the most easterly of the 45th Infantry Division's landings but also of the US 7th Army overall, and marked the boundary with the British 8th Army's area of responsibility. Colonel Ankcorn's RCT thus 'constituted an almost independent task force', the more so as it was also assigned the 45th Division's attached 753rd Tank Battalion; Ankcorn was tasked to protect the US II Corps' right flank, establish contact with British XXX Corps advancing inland from the BARK Landing Area fifteen miles further east and to assist in securing wider Divisional objectives. To that end the 157th RCT was to make a two-pronged advance inland with Lieutenant-Colonel Murphy's 1st Battalion on the right tasked to secure the town of Santa Croce Camerina, just under four miles inland from the landing beach, while on the left Lieutenant-Colonel Schaefer's 2nd Battalion was to by-pass Santa Croce Camerina to the left and press north to assist in securing the town and airfield at Comiso, twelve miles to the north-west of the landing area.

The 1st Battalion secured Santa Croce Camerina in the early afternoon of D-Day with the serendipitous assistance of Major Mark J. Alexander and his 2nd Battalion 505th Parachute Infantry Regiment who had been misdropped twenty miles from their intended DZ atop a strongly fortified Italian strongpoint north-east of Marina di Ragusa. After reducing the strongpoint Major Alexander moved south-west and overran an Italian artillery battery at Marina di Ragusa before moving north-west in search of the remainder of his Regiment, carrying sufficient weapons and ammunition liberated from the battery to equip perhaps an additional battalion in 'a heavily armed gypsy caravan' made up of wheelbarrows, donkey carts and animals.[4] On approaching Santa Croce Camerina Alexander immediately set about organising an attack from the east, unaware that Lieutenant-Colonel Murphy's 1st Battalion was closing in from the west; the Italian town garrison were also fixated on the seaborne invaders and the resultant accidental pincer movement prompted an immediate surrender. With the town secured Major Alexander continued his journey north-west while Lieutenant-Colonel Murphy despatched a rifle company to Ragusa, technically on the British side of the XXX Corps boundary, spearheaded by two motorised platoons that reached the town outskirts at 18:00. On being joined by the remainder of the company shortly before midnight the Americans occupied the town, arrested the mayor and chief of police, seized the telephone exchange and spent Sunday 11 July replying to anxious telephone enquiries about events closer to the coast from surrounding Italian garrisons; they were relieved by the Royal Canadian Regiment early the following day. In the meantime Lieutenant-Colonel Schaefer's 2nd Battalion, trailed by the RCT's newly landed 3rd Battalion, had pressed on to overrun an Italian strongpoint at Donnafugata five miles north-east of Santa Croce Camerina and by nightfall had pushed a large motorised patrol on a further four miles to Hill 643 overlooking Comiso, where it prepared a battalion assembly area in readiness for the move on the town and nearby airfield the following day.[5]

The US 45th Infantry Division's remaining two RCTs, each with an initial wave of two battalions, came ashore at the other end of the CENT Landing Area fourteen miles up the coast from the *Punta Braccetto*, on three adjacent beaches running south-east from the mouth of the River Acate collectively nicknamed 'Woods Hole' by the US Navy planners. The left-hand RED Beach was assigned to Colonel Forrest E. Cookson's 180th RCT, while the remaining centre and right-hand beaches were allotted to a battalion apiece from Colonel Robert B. Hutchins' 179th RCT. Lieutenant-Colonel Earl A. Taylor's 3rd Battalion was tasked to land on the central GREEN Beach from the

Attack Transport USS *Florence Nightingale*, move ten miles inland and secure Vittoria and then press on a further four miles and assist the 157th RCT in securing the town and airfield at Comiso; the right-hand YELLOW Beach was allotted to Lieutenant-Colonel Edward F. Stephenson's 1st Battalion landing from the Attack Transport USS *Leonard Wood*, tasked to move eight miles down the coast and seize the small fishing port at Scoglitti.

Both Battalion landings were accurate and on the revised H-Hour with the first wave going ashore at 04:03, the three succeeding assault waves were ashore within an hour, follow-up landings commenced at 06:00 and Colonel Hutchins was ashore and had set up a Regimental Command Post a mile inland from the beach by 09:30. Due at least in part to the fifteen-minute pre-landing bombardment from Naval Task Force 85's sixteen destroyers and a number of Landing Craft Rocket (LCR) Italian resistance was largely restricted to a few scattered shots before surrendering or making off, although on YELLOW Beach one such shot wounded Captain Gavrice L. Robison, commander of the 1st Battalion's Company C, in the stomach. Captain Robison thus earned the dubious honour of becoming the 179th RCT's first combat casualty of the Second World War.[6]

After reorganising, Lieutenant-Colonel Stephenson detailed a company to remain at YELLOW Beach to finish clearing enemy positions and led the rest of his 1st Battalion south-east along the dune line eliminating Italians positions on the way including a fortified artillery position at the *Punta Zafaglione*, an area of high ground two miles short of Scoglitti. The port was secured by 14:00 by which time Lieutenant-Colonel Stephenson's men had inflicted 187 Italian casualties and taken 800 prisoners in exchange for fifteen US casualties.[7] Lieutenant-Colonel Taylor's 3rd Battalion were equally swift off the mark, securing the dune line behind GREEN Beach with no resistance apart from a brief fight when a by-passed machine-gun position briefly opened fire on the fifth wave of landing craft. After a hasty reorganisation the 3rd Battalion moved inland for around four miles to the *Strada* 115 coastal highway and then angled along it toward Vittoria, seven miles or so to the south-east, picking up sixty men from Company G, 3rd Battalion 505th Parachute Infantry Regiment and three 75mm Pack Howitzers from Battery C, 456th Parachute Field Artillery Battalion en route, and arrived at the town in the late afternoon; according to one source Major Alexander's 'heavily armed gypsy caravan' from the 2nd Battalion, 505th Parachute Infantry Regiment was also involved.[8] The initial attempt to enter Vittoria was rebuffed by small arms fire and being reluctant to subject the 36,000 civilians in the town to artillery bombardment unless forced, Lieutenant-Colonel Taylor initially intended to persuade the garrison to surrender; unfortunately he was unable to convince any locals to enter the town to contact the mayor or other authorities.

The town surrendered at 16:40 just as Lieutenant-Colonel Taylor was about to begin shelling thanks to the efforts of 1st Lieutenant William J. Harris from the 2nd Battalion 505th Regiment's HQ Company. Captured after being misdropped the previous night, Harris had been held in Vittoria with two companions who proceeded to get 'roaring drunk' while he persuaded the Italian commander to surrender, unknowingly in the nick of time.[9] Vittoria was the first sizeable Sicilian town to fall to the invaders, although the formal surrender was not quite the end of the matter. Sniper fire continued through the night and some opposition to the US invaders was more substantial. Lieutenant James H. Cruickshank's platoon from the 3rd Battalion's HQ Company came under fire from enemy troops manning two light anti-aircraft guns while moving through the town; unable to approach at ground level, Lieutenant Cruickshank moved single-handed across the rooftops to where he could fire down on the enemy gun position, killing three and prompting the remainder to abandon their gun positions.[10] The 179th RCT resumed the advance in the morning of 11 July, with the 1st Battalion moving north from Scoglitti and taking up positions to protect the left flank by occupying high ground overlooking Biscari to the north.

The 3rd Battalion, now accompanied by Lieutenant-Colonel Charles D. Wiegand's 2nd Battalion, moved north-east toward Comiso airfield in two battalion columns and despite stops and delays due to enemy artillery and long-range machine-gun fire, were in position to the south and west of the airfield. The other pincer in the move on the airfield was provided by the 157th RCT, which occupied Comiso town without a fight in the early morning before approaching the airfield from the south-east. The airfield was subjected to a co-ordinated bombardment from the 158th and 160th Field Artillery Battalions which also used their radio net to co-ordinate moves by the two RCTs, thickened with naval gunfire support controlled by forward observers. At around 16:00 the bombardment lifted and the 179th RCT's 2nd and 3rd Battalions attacked acting as the hammer against the 157th RCT's anvil and the airfield was overrun in just twenty minutes, yielding between 120 and 125 assorted Axis aircraft, twenty of them in working order, 200,000 gallons of aviation fuel and a substantial amount of bombs and other ammunition.[11]

With their initial post-landing objectives achieved, both RCTs appear to have paused for the night at Comiso before resuming the advance in the morning of Monday 12 July to establish the initial post-landing perimeter; the 'Yellow Line' was roughly twenty miles inland from the US 7th Army Landing Areas, running from a ridgeline on the coast near Licata in the west to the boundary with Montgomery's 8th Army near Vizzini in the east.[12] 157th RCT reached Chiaramonte Gulfi, around fourteen miles north-east of Comiso and ten miles or so short of the Yellow Line without incident; Colonel Ankcorn then paused to draw in the scattered elements of his formation, but events developed less favourably for the 179th RCT which made its first major contact with German rather than Italian troops. Lieutenant-Colonel Taylor's 3rd Battalion was attacked by armoured vehicles likely from the *Hermann Göring (HG) Panzer Division's Panzer Aufklärungs Abteilung* (armoured reconnaissance battalion) while moving northward; the attack was fought off with fire from anti-tank guns and Bazookas which destroyed a tank and another unidentified vehicle. Back at Comiso Colonel

Hutchins had ordered Lieutenant-Colonel Wiegand's 2nd Battalion to relocate just over a mile to the north of the airfield to protect USAAF elements working to make it operational where it was attacked at around midday, likely by elements of *15 Panzergrenadier Division*. The fight was so fierce that Colonel Hutchins had to reinforce the 2nd Battalion with Lieutenant-Colonel Stephenson's 1st Battalion and even then the situation was not stabilised until the late afternoon. The 179th RCT assumed the fighting was an Axis counter-attack aimed at recapturing the airfield, but in fact the German units were looking to keep open escape routes to the north to avoid being cut off by the US 1st Infantry Division's advance inland from Gela and the DIME Landing Area on the US 45th Infantry Division's left flank.[13]

The third, left-hand prong of the US 45th Infantry Division's advance should have involved Colonel Forrest E. Cookson's 180th RCT putting its 1st and 2nd Battalions, commanded by Lieutenant-Colonels William H. Schaefer and Clarence B. Cochran respectively, onto RED Beach immediately adjacent to the mouth of the River Acate; Colonel Cookson's formation was tasked to relieve elements of the 505th Parachute RCT holding road and rail crossings over the River Acate and secure Biscari, just over eight miles inland and the airfield five miles north of the town. The 180th RCT's 1st Battalion aboard the Attack Transport USS *Calvert* had its first four assault waves loaded aboard their landing craft, launched and on the way to the beach shortly after 02:00, but then paid an unfair price for the efficiency of the *Calvert's* crew. The commander of Naval Task Force 85 carrying CENT FORCE, Rear-Admiral Alan G. Kirk, put H-Hour back an hour to 03:45 at the request of the Force's Commander Transports, just as the 1st Battalion was approaching RED Beach.[14] The resultant recall order, combined with poor visibility, rough seas and a dearth of experienced coxswains badly scattered the four assault waves to the point the depleted first wave did not make landfall until 04:45, three storm-wracked hours after launching, with the other three waves trickling in piecemeal thereafter.[15]

Loading difficulties delayed the 2nd Battalion's departure from the Attack Transport USS *Neville* until 03:37 and the sea state scattered them badly; just five craft from the first wave reached RED Beach at 04:34 followed by three, seven and eight from the second, third and fourth waves. The remainder were scattered along the twelve-mile stretch of coast straddling the mouth of the River Acate and included Colonel Cookson and part of his RCT staff, which came ashore in the DIME Landing Area near Gela. They were joined by 300 men from the first, second and fourth follow-up waves from Lieutenant-Colonel Bryan W. Nolan's 3rd Battalion which had launched from the Attack Transport USS *Frederick Funston* at 07:00; on sighting landing craft moving on a north-westerly heading the first wave commander assumed that RED Beach had been closed and followed the craft to the DIME Landing area trailed by the second and fourth waves, while the third wave continued to make landfall on RED Beach.[16] The chaos extended onto land as the shore parties tasked to control the flow of men, vehicles and materiel onto and over the beach were not in place until *c*.08:00 and as a result RED Beach became 'a mass of stranded boats and...milling...men and vehicles'.[17] As one US historian observed, the '180th [RCT] was the only combat team in the entire American assault-force which had been completely disorganized by faulty landings.'[18]

Despite this unpromising start and the absence of their Regimental commander the elements of the 180th RCT rapidly set about making the best of the bad situation. Lieutenant-Colonel Cochran gathered up the 'relatively intact' Company F and part of Company E from his 2nd Battalion and, after clearing some bunkers overlooking the beach, set off up the River Acate to relieve the demolition party from the 505th Parachute RCT holding the rail and road and crossings three and five miles inland respectively. As the demolition party had been misdropped fifty miles away near Syracuse the 2nd Battalion men found the rail crossing unguarded, but the concrete slab Ponte Dirillo carrying the *Strada* 115 across the steeply banked river was held by a similarly misdropped party of between sixty and eighty-five paratroopers from the 505th Regiment's Company G, led by Company commander Captain James P. McGinity. Lieutenant-Colonel Cochran assumed command of the combined groups, detailed Company F to hold the bridge and moved the remainder of his Battalion to a blocking position on high ground to the north of the crossing overlooking the *Strada* 115 while Captain McGinity and his paratroopers occupied another piece of high ground south of the bridge near the seaward end of the Biazzo Ridge.[19] Lieutenant-Colonel Schaefer was equally swift in getting his 1st Battalion on the move. After a lone reconnaissance by landing craft crewman Seaman 1st Class Francis Carpenter, who had visited the landing area before the war, Lieutenant-Colonel Schaefer moved the men he had gathered through the dune line to a minor road identified by Seaman Carpenter to reorganise; by 06:00 he had gathered in his entire Battalion bar a platoon mislanded near Gela and moved off for Biscari, ten miles inland and the airfield five miles north of the town.[20]

Unfortunately, this line of advance carried the 1st Battalion directly into the path of a counter-attack by an infantry-heavy *kampfgruppe* from *Generalmajor* Paul Conrath's *HG Panzer Division* made up of two *bataillonen* likely from *HG Panzergrenadier Regiment 1*, supported by the *HG Panzer Artillerie Regiment* and seventeen Tiger I tanks from the *kompanie*-sized *Panzer Abteilung 215*. Launched late at 14:00, the initial attack was brought to a standstill at 15:30 by dogged US resistance, fire from the 180th RCT's 171st Field Artillery Battalion, poor German armour-infantry co-operation and difficulty manoeuvring the sixty-ton Tiger tanks in the terraced terrain and dense olive groves. *Generalmajor* Conrath responded by replacing the *kampfgruppe* commander and a renewed, better co-ordinated attack later in the afternoon met with more success, overrunning the 1st Battalion and capturing Lieutenant-Colonel Schaefer and a number of his men in the process, before pushing on toward the 45th Infantry Division's landing beaches. The situation was saved by the arrival of Lieutenant-Colonel Nolan and his mislanded 3rd Battalion after its forced march from the DIME Landing Area, which formed a hasty defensive line along the south side of the *Strada* 115 that held until the momentum of the German attack ebbed with the onset of darkness; the attackers then appear to have panicked and withdrew in some confusion to Biscari to regroup.[21]

The night of 10 July nonetheless found the 180th RCT in a precarious position, pressed back to within four miles of its landing beach with no reserves to hand, no contact with the US 1st Infantry Division on the left or the 179th RCT on the right and its 1st Battalion largely captured or put to flight; it is unclear if Colonel Cookson was aware that Lieutenant-Colonel Schaefer had been captured and his battalion overrun, and communications with Lieutenant-Colonel Cochran's understrength 2nd Battalion holding the Ponte Dirillo were 'tenuous at best'. On the other side of the hill *Generalmajor* Conrath was being ordered to launch a concentrated attack on Gela by *Generalfeldmarschall* Kesselring at *Oberbefehlshaber Süd* (*OB Süd*) in Rome and nearer to home by the senior Axis commander on Sicily *Generale d'Armata* Guzzoni, who also attached the *HG Panzer Division* to the Italian *16° Corpo* for the purpose; Guzzoni's original plan involved wiping out the Gela landings before wheeling right to do the same to the Licata landing but subsequently amended this to a left wheel to deal with the Scoglitti landing. Conrath's reorganisation to meet the new order impacted on the 180th RCT by restating his order for the *HG kampfgruppe* east of the River Acate to cross the river at the Ponte Dirillo in order to join the attack on Gela.[22]

Advancing from Biscari at 06:15 on 11 July the *HG kampfgruppe* secured the road junction with the *Strada* 115 near Biscari Railway Station and an adjacent section of the Biazzo Ridge as a flank guard. The attackers then turned north up the highway, drove back the 2nd Battalion's Company F, unknowingly opening an avenue directly to RED Beach in the process, recaptured the Ponte Dirillo and were only prevented from overrunning Lieutenant-Colonel Cochran and the less than 200-strong remainder of the 2nd Battalion on the high ground north of the crossing by artillery fire from the 171st Field Artillery Battalion and gunfire support from the destroyer USS *Beatty*. The destroyer put down an intense barrage on the advancing German column in the vicinity of the Ponte Dirillo with its four 5-inch guns from 07:38 to 08:11; when relieved at 11:00 by the destroyer USS *Laub* the *Beatty* had expended 799 rounds of 5-inch ammunition and had only 192 rounds left in her magazine.[23] The situation was saved by the appearance of Colonel James Gavin and a large group of his paratroopers from 505th Parachute RCT from the east at *c*.09:00. Dropped fifteen miles or more south-east of his designated DZ S with Lieutenant-Colonel Alfred W. Ireland, Major Benjamin H. Vandervoort and six men from his Regimental staff, Gavin had no idea of his location and spent 10 July and much of the following night searching for friendly forces before happening on elements of the 179th RCT five miles south-west of Vittoria at 02:30 in the morning of 11 July.

With his location finally clarified, Colonel Gavin rapidly set about getting himself and his scattered paratroopers to DZ S near Niscemi. After gathering in the paratroopers at Vittoria, which included sixty men from his 3rd Battalion's Company G, the three 75mm Pack Howitzers from the 456th Parachute Field Artillery Battalion and possibly Major Alexander's gypsy caravan from the 2nd Battalion, Gavin despatched them in the direction of Gela and set off westward along the *Strada* 115 in a commandeered Jeep accompanied by Ireland and Vandervoort. Happening across 250 men from the 505th Regiment's 3rd Battalion bivouacked at the roadside under an unexpectedly passive and unresponsive Battalion commander Major Edward C. Krause, Gavin ordered them to move in his wake immediately before moving on.[24] He then ran into Lieutenant Benjamin L. Wechsler and twenty men from the 307th Airborne Engineer Battalion with a larger group from the 180th RCT, who informed Gavin that German troops were on the high ground to their front. Immediately sensing the tactical importance of the high ground Gavin led Lieutenant Wechsler's paratroopers forward on a personal reconnaissance and captured two German officers on a motorcycle combination near Biscari Station, which confirmed the rumour of German troops in the vicinity. Gavin despatched Major Vandervoort on the double mission of hurrying Major Krause's party forward and finding the 45th Division's command post to request reinforcements before leading the Airborne engineers and the sixty newly arrived men from Company G in a hasty attack that drove the German detachment off the crest at the cost of several US casualties including Lieutenant Wechsler.[25]

The stage was set for what became known as the Battle of Biazzo Ridge.[26] The contingent from the 505th Regiment's 3rd Battalion reached the Ridge around twenty minutes after it had been secured, now led by Battalion Executive Officer Captain William H. Hagan as Major Krause had gone to seek out the 45th Division's HQ and inform them of developments.[27] Over the same space of time the commander of the *HG kampfgruppe* decided that leaving the Ridge in US hands presented an intolerable threat to his left flank and rear as the *kampfgruppe* moved north-west over the Ponte Dirillo, and set about regaining it, while Gavin, correctly surmising that a German counter-attack would be swiftly forthcoming, chose to forestall it with a spoiling advance. Meeting Captain Hagan at Biscari Station, Gavin ordered him to cross the ridge and advance toward the river at some point between 10:30 and 11:00, but after moving around a mile beyond the ridge the 3rd Battalion paratroopers ran into a large force of *panzergrenadiers* moving in the opposite direction supported by between four and six Tiger I tanks according to the source.[28] The counter-attack appears to have been covered by artillery shelling and smoke, given that Lieutenant Robert A. Fielder from the 3rd Battalion referred to 'ineffectual' white phosphorous rounds that 'started to burn the foliage and grass'.[29] Lacking anti-tank weapons apart from M1 Bazookas firing 2.36-inch rockets that proved ineffective against the Tigers' thick armour, the 3rd Battalion contingent was driven back to the ridge. A flow of ambulatory casualties included Captain Hagan.

Gavin personally prepared the relative handful of troops occupying the ridge to withstand the oncoming German attack, with some equally ad hoc assistance. On arrival at the Ridge Lieutenant Raymond A. Grossman from the 456th Parachute Field Artillery Battalion assisted the crew of a 75mm Pack Howitzer in manhandling their gun to the crest of the ridge on hearing that 'the Germans had a Tiger tank ...kicking the hell out of our boys' and engaged a Tiger among buildings down the slope. The first howitzer round fell short, as did the tank's response that temporarily drove the crew from their gun before returning for a second shot that struck the tank or the building it was sheltering behind and prompted it to reverse out of sight; Lieutenant Grossman and the gun crew cheered as if they 'had just scored a touchdown'.[30] Two paratroopers who attempted to distract the Tigers by driving a captured Italian personnel carrier over the ridge line were not so lucky as an 88mm shell demolished the vehicle killing both men; the driver, Corporal Lewis W. Baldwin from Battery C, 456th Parachute Field Artillery Battalion was posthumously awarded the Distinguished Service Cross.[31] Another captured Italian truck commandeered for use as an ambulance by the 505th Regiment's surgeon Captain Daniel P. McIlvoy, assisted by Privates First Class Murray Goldman and Marvin L. Crosley, was machine-gunned by a Tiger firing down the *Strada* 115 despite the truck being clearly marked with a Red Cross; all three men escaped from the vehicle unscathed although Goldman was subsequently wounded in the back by mortar fragments.[32]

With the intense German machine-gun and mortar fire and Tiger tanks picking off individual paratroopers with their 88mm guns, maintaining a presence on the forward slope and crest of the Biazzo Ridge was tantamount to suicidal; the intensity of the German fire was illustrated by US observers seeing individual tanks withdrawing from the firing line to re-supply with ammunition from support vehicles.[33] Gavin therefore ordered a withdrawal to a new line just back from the crest on the ridge's reverse slope from where the paratroopers would be able to engage the *panzergrenadiers* and tanks as they came over the crest at close-quarters, thereby nullifying the German advantage in firepower. The tactic worked and the US line held in place against three separate attacks spread over a two- to three-hour period with Gavin moving constantly back and forth along the line encouraging, cajoling and personally deploying piecemeal reinforcements as they became available, despite pleas from a newly arrived Major Vandervoort to move his command post back slightly to a more protected location.[34] Although Gavin was unaware of it, his right flank was protected by Captain McGinity's party from Company G atop the hill between the ridge and the River Dirillo, and the left flank was secured by a party from Company H led by Lieutenant Arthur T. Laird who had been drawn from the east by the noise of the battle. On reporting to a reappearing Major Krause at the 3rd Battalion Command Post on the reverse slope Lieutenant Laird was directed to deploy among olive trees on a hill on the left of the ridge and the men were digging in when approached by a ten-strong German machine-gun group; reacting first, Laird's party killed three of the interlopers, wounded several and took the rest prisoner.[35]

Needing more substantial reinforcement than co-opted 'clerks, cooks, truck drivers' and paratroopers drawn in by the sound of the battle, Gavin despatched Lieutenant-Colonel Ireland on a commandeered civilian bicycle to find and obtain assistance from 45th Division HQ, where he found not only Division commander Major-General Middleton but also visiting US II Corps commander Major-General Bradley. On hearing Ireland's report the latter instructed Middleton to give the paratrooper officer 'whatever he wanted'.[36]

Shortly thereafter Lieutenant-Colonel Ireland was on his way back to the Biazzo Ridge in a Jeep accompanied by artillery observation teams, arriving at *c.*15:00 to find a heavy German attack in full swing; at around the same time the first increment of reinforcements from the 45th Division arrived, two half-tracks towing 57mm anti-tank guns from the 179th RCT. The observer teams rapidly brought down fire from destroyers augmented by 155mm fire from the 189th Field Artillery Battalion that stopped the assault and drove the attackers back part way down the ridge's forward slope.[37] On learning at 18:00 that 45th Division trucks were ferrying 1st Lieutenant Harold H. Swingler and a hundred men from his HQ Company from the fortified road junction south of Vittoria and that between six and eleven M4 Medium tanks from the 753rd Tank Battalion were also en route, Gavin set about organising a counter-attack to drive the *HG kampfgruppe* off the ridge altogether. Lieutenant Swingler's party were immediately rushed up to the start line on arrival at some point between 19:00 and 20:00, paratroopers and M4s advanced over the crest at 20:45 preceded by a concentrated artillery barrage and overran the German machine-gun and mortar positions in a series of close-quarter encounters. The *HG* survivors retreated into the growing darkness, some back toward Biscari and others across the Ponte Dirillo, where some paused to set up blocking positions.

With that the epic ten-hour battle for the Biazzo Ridge was over.[38] The German attackers left behind two half-tracks, a dozen 120mm mortars and an intact Tiger tank captured by Lieutenant Swingler, who came upon its crew having a discussion outside the vehicle and despatched them with a well-placed hand grenade before taking possession of the 82nd Airborne Division's first captured enemy tank.[39] Another Tiger was disabled by radio operators Technician Fifth Grade George Banta and Private First Class Dick Symonds from HQ Company who crept to within twenty yards of the armoured behemoth and broke its right track with a well-placed Bazooka rocket; the Germans recovered the disabled Tiger during the night, but Banta and Symonds were both subsequently awarded the Bronze Star for their actions.[40] Their feat was the more noteworthy as the M1 Bazooka's 2.36-inch rockets were incapable of penetrating the Tiger's thick frontal armour, obliging gunners to engage from close quarters in the hope of scoring a flank or rear hit; a number of crushed US dead were reportedly found with the broken remains of Bazookas to hand.[41] In total the battle cost the *HG kampfgruppe* fifty dead and another fifty taken prisoner; Gavin's scratch force lost forty-three dead and a hundred wounded, a number of whom had remained in the fighting line despite their injuries.[42]

The retreat from the Biazzo Ridge was part of a wider withdrawal northward by the entire *HG Panzer Division* prompted at the top by a series of vacillations by *Generale d'Armata* Guzzoni on 11 July. Initially elated by erroneous reports that the US landing force at Gela had been forced to temporarily re-embark and following discussion with *Generalleutnant* von Senger und Etterlin, the *OB Süd* representative at *6ª Armata* HQ, Guzzoni had instructed *16° Corpo* HQ to direct the Division east to the Syracuse sector via Vittoria during the morning, but this was undermined by reports of US reinforcement landings, the failure of the *HG* and the *4ª Livorno* divisions to retake Gela and concern that US 45th Infantry Division's advance to Comiso not only blocked the planned move east but raised the prospect of the *Luftwaffe* formation being cut off. In the afternoon Guzzoni therefore ordered *16° Corpo* to cease offensive operations before Gela, pull the *Livorno Divisione* back to a covering line running east from Mazzarino and withdraw the *HG Division* to Caltagirone, sixteen miles to the north, in readiness to move against the British 8th Army advance toward Vizzini on 12 July.

For his part *Generalmajor* Conrath had been informed of the move east by von Senger und Etterlin in person, but his initial agreement with the plan was nullified by the losses suffered in the Gela fighting, which reportedly included over a third of his Division's tanks and the mauling of his eastern *kampfgruppe* on the Biazzo Ridge; he therefore appears to have decided to comply with Guzzoni's order but via a deliberate, staged withdrawal, despite Guzzoni's requirement for urgency.[43] The latter attempted to hasten Conrath with another order in the morning of 12 July instructing him to hurry to the line of the *Strada* 124 in the area of Caltagirone-Vizzini-Palazzolo Acreide, which was repeated later in the day and reinforced with three radio instructions from von Senger und Etterlin, the last at 21:40. The chivvying was driven by growing concern at *6ª Armata* HQ over the ramifications of the British and US advances from Ragusa and Comiso, which just before midnight on 12 July prompted Guzzoni to order Conrath to attack south-east toward Palazzolo Acreide the following day. By the morning of 13 July however, only the lead elements of Conrath's formation were in the vicinity of the Vizzini jump-off point, with the remainder stretched out over twenty miles west to the *Strada* 117 west of Caltagirone and it took until well into the night for it to close up, with some units still deployed to counter the US advances from Niscemi, Biscari and Comiso. In the short term, *Generale* Guzzoni also had to cope with the result of Allied bombing of *6ª Armata* HQ at Enna in the late evening of 12 July, which obliged a fifty-five-mile relocation to Passo Pisciaro, twenty-five miles north of Catania on the east coast that was not complete until late the following day.[44]

With the exception of 2nd Battalion at the Ponte Dirillo, the Biazzo Ridge battle gave the 180th RCT a twenty-four-hour respite to regroup and reorganise before resuming the advance inland on Monday 12 July. The area of the 1st Battalion's debacle at Biscari was retaken by 20:00 and in the late evening Major-General Middleton tied the RCT's further advance into the 45th Infantry Division's overall scheme by ordering Colonel Cookson to cross the River Acate, secure Biscari airfield five miles north of Biscari proper and push on a further ten miles north to Caltagirone; the 180th RCT was thus to form the left wing of the 45th Division's advance to the Yellow Line, the US 7th Army's initial objective around twenty miles inland from the US landing beaches. However progress north from Biscari was slowed by a combination of rugged terrain, a single narrow road and *HG Division* rearguard units which prevented Colonel Cookson from crossing the River Acate until the late afternoon of 13 July. Progress was slowed again the following day as the German rearguard had demolished the bridge over the River Ficuzza and the road leading down to the crossing, but the 2nd and 3rd Battalions began an all-night march at 23:00 that got them to Biscari airfield by late morning the following day. This caught the *HG* rearguard and Italian garrison by surprise and allowed the US units to seize the airfield and hold it in the face of a series of counter-attacks.

When the German rearguard finally withdrew in the evening of 14 July Colonel Cookson launched a swift pursuit that caught up with it at Caltagirone in the early morning of 15 July, resulting in the 2nd Battalion engaging in 'quite a tussle' in the outskirts of the town; they were prevented from securing it altogether by an order from Major-General Bradley at US II Corps HQ instructing the 45th Division to hold two miles short of the *Strada* 124 as the road now marked the boundary between the US 7th Army and the British 8th Army advancing north-west from Vizzini.[45] Nonetheless, by the morning of Thursday 15 July the US 1st and 45th Infantry Divisions were 'stood at or near the Seventh Amy's Yellow Line across the entire II Corps front'.[46]

Major-General Middleton had been so dissatisfied with the 180th RCT's initial performance that he tried to have Colonel Cookson replaced but was prevented by US II Corps HQ being unable to provide a suitable candidate, prompting Middleton to despatch his deputy division commander to monitor Cookson.[47] Given that the 180th RCT's badly scattered landing was the root of the problem and that lay outside Colonel Cookson's control this seems unfair, but the dissatisfaction was presumably reinforced by the RCT's relatively slow progress between 12 and 15 July and possibly two separate instances of killing Axis prisoners by members of the depleted 1st Battalion during the drawn-out fight at Biscari airfield on 14 July. Captain John T. Compton, commanding Company C, organised a firing squad for thirty-six Italian prisoners on the assumption that they were the snipers who had killed or wounded twelve members of Company C including wounded and medics, while Sergeant Horace T. West from Company A executed a party of thirty-five Italian and two German prisoners he had escorted to the rear, using a Thompson gun borrowed from the Company First Sergeant Haskell Y. Brown.

On learning of the incidents, a reportedly 'horrified' Major-General Bradley reported them to US 7th Army HQ, refused Lieutenant-General Patton's suggestion that it would be best to claim the dead had tried to escape on the grounds that the incident 'would make a stink in the press and...would make the [US] civilians mad' and had both men brought before a court-martial charged with multiple counts of murder.[48] Both men pleaded not guilty and claimed to have been obeying indirect orders from Patton, based on a 'dynamic pep talk' the 7th Army commander gave to the entire 45th Division in two increments on 27 June 1943; the speech warned the inexperienced GIs about Axis troops using feigned surrender to gain advantage and specifically referred to unsuspecting Allied troops being killed by such ruses.[49] Captain Compton was acquitted of the charges and transferred to the 179th Infantry Regiment; he was killed in action in Italy on 8 November 1943. Sergeant West was found guilty and sentenced to life imprisonment, although the sentence was remitted on 24 November 1944 and West returned to service before obtaining an honourable discharge at the end of the war; he died in Oklahoma in January 1974. The friction generated by the incident at the top of the US chain of command was not restricted to Bradley and Patton; Allied Commander-in-Chief Lieutenant-General Dwight D. Eisenhower later admonishing Patton for 'talking too much' in reference to the pre-invasion speech to the 45th Division.[50]

14

The Western Flanking Shield in Alexander's Left Hand

The JOSS Landing Area, D-Day, 08:00 Saturday 10 July to D-Day Plus Five, 23:59 Thursday 15 July

Thirty miles up the coast north-west of the Scoglitti landings, at the opposite extremity of the US 7th Army landing area, the US 3rd Infantry Division came ashore across the roughly twelve-mile-wide JOSS Landing Area straddling the port of Licata. The JOSS landing also employed four separate landing beaches but while those in the CENT Landing Area were separated by fifteen miles, the JOSS beaches were in much closer proximity with two landing beaches located either side of and within five miles of Licata; they were paired either side of the port to meet specific missions. The forces landed on the two outer beaches, codenamed RED and BLUE to the west and east of Licata, were tasked to secure the flanks of the landing and the latter were to make contact with friendly forces to the east. The extreme left of the Landing Area five miles west of Licata RED Beach, bounded by the cliff top *Torre di Gaffe* tower to the west and the *Punta San Nicola* headland to the east, was assigned to Colonel Henry B. Sherman's 7th RCT. Referred to by the US Navy planners as the Gaffi Assault Group after the *Torre di Gaffe*, the 7th RCT was reinforced with elements of the 1st Battalion 36th Combat Engineer Regiment and M4 tanks from Company G, 66th Armored Regiment, all tasked to secure the immediate landing area, establish blocking positions to its west and north to protect the left flank of the JOSS Landing Area and the US 7th Army landings overall, and ultimately provide a secure anchor for the western end of initial invasion phase, the Yellow Line.

At the other end of the JOSS Landing Area BLUE Beach was assigned to the three battalions of Colonel Arthur R. Rogers' 30th RCT reinforced with elements from the 1st Battalion 36th Combat Engineer Battalion, tanks from Company I, 66th Armored Regiment, Company C 3rd Chemical Battalion and the 41st Field Artillery Battalion; the US Navy planners dubbed this the Falconara Assault Group after the highly visible *Punta Falconara* promontory to the east of BLUE Beach, with the rocky *Punta della due Rocchi* marking the actual eastern extremity.[1] Colonel Rogers' formation was tasked to eliminate Italian strongpoints east of Licata, secure the Monte Desusino heights around five miles north-east of the landing beach and then establish contact with the US 1st Infantry Division at the DIME Landing Area to the east.[2]

Responsibility for delivering the 7th RCT onto RED Beach was allotted to Captain Lorenzo S. Sabin USN, employing seven LSTs, seventeen LCIs and twenty-one LCTs. The JOSS RED vessels were delayed by bad weather and as a result the lead element, seven LSTs commanded by Lieutenant-Commander Samuel H. Pittie carrying the assault battalion, did not reach the loading area until between 02:00 and 02:15 and on arrival anchored between two and a half and six miles from shore; the more distant than planned anchorages may have been made necessary by a group of LCIs led by the minesweeper USS *Seer* anchoring in the loading area first.[3] Whatever the reason, the additional distance lengthened the time required for the run-in to the beach and the delay was compounded by the anchorage being open to the heavy westerly surf which complicated loading and launching the LCVPs carrying the 7th RCT's assault element. Nine men were drowned when a davit failed and pitched men from an LCVP into the sea.[4] Lieutenant-Colonel Roy E. Moore's 1st Battalion set off at 03:00, fifteen minutes after they were supposed to have made landfall and was ashore on RED Beach by 04:35, clustering toward the right side of the 2,800-yard beach frontage rather than the centre due to the non-appearance of a US Navy guide party equipped with homing lamps. The final forty minutes of the run-in was under fire from the Italian beach defences manned by elements of the *207a Divisione Costiere*; RED Beach was 'probably the most heavily fortified and defended of the JOSS beaches' with concrete bunkers set in the high cliffs overlooking the beach from the flanks, more bunkers and machine-gun positions along the beach frontage, a mobile artillery battery a mile or so from the beach and four more gun batteries located on the lower slopes of the high ground ringing Licata just over three miles inland. Fortunately for the assault wave, the pre-dawn darkness rendered the fire largely ineffective.[5] Carrying only weapons, ammunition, two canteens of water and K-Rations to enhance mobility the 1st Battalion immediately set about opening the beach exits and eliminating or keeping the immediate beach defences occupied to allow the 7th RCT's other two battalions to pass through for their own objectives. One of Lieutenant-Colonel Moore's companies turned left and began clearing the defences covering the beach exits, one moved right and set about clearing and securing the *Punta San Nicola* while the third swept the centre sector to occupy three low hills overlooking the beach; all three tasks were completed by *c.*06:00, within ninety minutes of touching down.[6]

The 7th RCT's second wave, Major Everett W. Duvall's 2nd Battalion travelling in six LCIs commanded by Lieutenant-Commander Edward W. Wilson, set off for the beach on schedule at 02:40, but seeing no sign of the assault wave's delayed LCVPs Lieutenant-Commander Wilson led his charges back round to the loading point to check if H-Hour had been postponed and, realising that the assault wave had been delayed, paused for twenty-five minutes before setting off again at 04:15.[7] By that point visibility had improved and as the LCIs began to form an extended line around 450 yards out for the final run-in onto the centre of the beach they came under intense machine-gun and artillery fire concentrated on the left of the line. *LCI-218* ran aground on a sandbank and after three unsuccessful attempts to break free began transferring its passengers ashore via rubber dinghies, although the bulk were taken off and landed by an LCI from the third wave. The remaining five craft all reached the beach, albeit not all in the manner intended. Lieutenant Carl F. Robison's *LCI-1* on the left end of the line received a direct hit that killed the helmsman and engine room telegraph operator and destroyed her controls, resulting in a full speed run up onto the beach. There her bow ramps were cut away in an unsuccessful effort to prevent the vessel broaching sideways that left her angled stern first in the surf; Lieutenant Robison then directed his Oerlikon gunners in a duel with the Italian positions on the *Punta San Nicola* until they exhausted their ammunition while the infantry disembarked over the stern. Another vessel, possibly Lieutenant John T. Ogilby's *LCI-2*, also became beached losing both bow ramps in the process and was only able to disembark her passengers after salvaging and remounting one of the ramps. The bulk of the 2nd Battalion was on the beach by 05:00.[8]

While the intact second wave craft were leaving the beach Commander Robert G. Newbigin's third wave of nine LCIs, six carrying Lieutenant-Colonel John A. Heintges' 3rd Battalion and three carrying elements of the 36th Combat Engineer Battalion, came ashore at *c.*05:15 on the left side of the beach under similarly heavy fire from emplacements near the *Torre di Gaffe*, which had remained unmolested by the first wave. Lieutenant Richard W. Caldwell's *LCI-5* carrying Colonel Sherman and his HQ group was hit by a 90mm shell that killed several men in a troop compartment and more were drowned trying to disembark after one bow ramp was carried away by the surf and the other became entangled with another LCI; Caldwell rectified the problem by deliberately broaching his vessel so the infantry could disembark over her port side. The disembarkation was only possible due to covering fire from the Oerlikon 20mm guns mounted on the LCIs, which reportedly killed an Italian lobbing grenades from the cliff top and netted the presumably surprised crew of one vessel five prisoners when the occupants of a bunker they had engaged came forward across the fire-swept beach to surrender.

At 05:10 the RED Beach Beachmaster judged the enemy fire too heavy for further landing in view of the lack of gunfire support from the destroyers USS *Roe* and USS *Swanson* which had been withdrawn after a collision at 02:55; he therefore requested the fourth wave carrying the 7th RCT's vehicles, the 10th Field Artillery Battalion's self-propelled 105mm guns and the tanks of the 66th Armored Regiment be held back and that naval gunfire support be provided to suppress the Italian artillery, repeating the request at 06:45. Serendipitously, Commander E. R. Durgin's twenty-one LCTs carrying the fourth wave had been delayed by the rough seas, although the three or four lead vessels carrying the 10th Field Artillery Battalion either did not receive the pause order or simply ignored it and carried on to beach at 06:30. At around 06:45 the destroyer USS *Buck* and cruiser USS *Brooklyn* began firing on the gun positions, the destroyer's high-speed passes so close to shore that her backwash refloated the stranded *LCI-128* from the second wave.[9] Within thirty minutes the volume of Italian fire had slackened to the extent that at 07:22 the commander of Naval Task Force 86, Rear-Admiral Connolly, ordered all the remaining LCTs 'to "charge the beach" and land whatever the cost'.[10] Covered by a smokescreen laid by the *Buck* and the destroyers USS *Bristol* and USS *Edison* the LCTs beached as ordered by 08:00 and by 09:00 the tanks from the 66th Armored Regiment's Company G were ashore and the 7th RCT's vehicles and support units were unloading.[11]

Once ashore the 7th RCT's battalions set about moving out to reach their various objectives. With its initial objectives secured by 06:00, Lieutenant-Colonel Moore's 1st Battalion moved on to establish positions to safeguard RED Beach for the follow-up waves and logistical effort, one inland just short of the *Strada* 115 almost a mile from the beach and the other on the right to the east of the *Punta San Nicola*, just short of GREEN Beach. Major Duvall's 2nd Battalion moved north across the *Strada* 115 before dividing in two, with one company moving north-east to set up a blocking position at Stazione Sant'Oliva five miles north of Licata, astride the railway line and *Strada* 123 running through the mountains to Campobello di Licata, eight miles to the north. The remaining two companies secured the summit of the Monte Morotta, on the west side of the *Strada* 123; both blocking positions were in place by 10:00 and the force at Stazione Sant'Oliva rebuffed a half-hearted attack by elements of the *207a Divisione Costiere* later in the day. Lieutenant-Colonel Heintges' 3rd Battalion also moved out to the *Strada* 115 before heading west toward Palma di Montechiaro and by 11:00 was set in a mile short of the crossing over the River Palma where the coast railway crossed the road, with one company deployed south of the *Strada* 115, two to the north oriented north-west and an anti-tank block on the road itself. So by the late morning of D-Day and within just a few hours of landing the 7th RCT had pushed its 2nd and 3rd Battalions out to the Initial Beachhead Line and Colonel Sherman had achieved his mission of shielding the left half of the JOSS Landing Area and had laid the foundations for a firm western anchor for the US 7th Army landing overall.[12]

Events unfolded in a less fraught manner at JOSS BLUE Beach east of Licata, in part because the Italian gun batteries overlooking the beach from the area of Monte Desusino five miles to the north-east were silenced at the outset; the cruiser USS *Brooklyn* expended 713 rounds of 6-inch ammunition on the positions as soon as it was light enough for effective aerial spotting at 04:45.[13] The LSTs from Commander Roger E. Nelson's Falconara Assault Group carrying Colonel Rogers and the 30th RCT were the first JOSS LSTs to arrive, anchoring in their loading area on schedule at 01:15, albeit further south than planned. Although the US Navy guide party again arrived too late for marking, BLUE Beach was clearly identifiable thanks to the

Punta Falconara and Monte Desusino and the LCVPs carrying the assault wave, Lieutenant-Colonel Lyle A. Bernard's 2nd Battalion, beached at 03:15, thirty minutes behind schedule; all the LCVPs were able to retract apart from four that became beached on rocks at the *Punta della due Rocchi.* Despite scattered small-arms and machine-gun fire and shelling from guns on the Poggio Lungo high ground three miles to the east, Colonel Barnard's unit immediately set about destroying the Italian beach defences, most notably a strongpoint and separate bunker on the landward side of the intertwined *Strada* 115 and railway line that paralleled the coast just a few hundred yards from the waterline.

The LCIs carrying the second wave, Lieutenant-Colonel Fred W. Sladen's 1st Battalion, landed at 04:22 followed shortly thereafter by Lieutenant-Colonel Edgar C. Doleman's 3rd Battalion as the third wave; all but one of the LCIs were able to back off the beach. DUKWs from LST-318 began coming ashore from 05:30 and the LCTs carrying the tanks of 66th Armored Regiment's Company I and the 41st Field Artillery Battalion, again delayed by the weather, began offloading vehicles at 06:27. With the elimination of a final Italian battery on Monte Desusino by the *Brooklyn* at 09:18 the way was clear for Colonel Rogers' formation to secure all its initial objectives, which was done by 09:30. By 11:00 the 30th RCT was ensconced on high ground overlooking Licata from the north and east with the 3rd Battalion spread over three separate locations to the north-west and north of BLUE Beach, the 1st Battalion in a perimeter around a plateau four miles to the north-east and the 2nd Battalion occupying a blocking line straddling the *Strada* 115 and the Poggio Lungo five miles to the east.[14] The eastern flank of the JOSS Landing Area was thus secure and on or near the Initial Beachhead Line by midday on D-Day.

The two inner beaches bracketing Licata, codenamed GREEN and YELLOW to the west and east respectively, were selected to facilitate a rapid envelopment and seizure of the town and its harbour. On the right YELLOW Beach was a mile-long stretch of sandy shore running from a point two miles east of the mouth of the River Salso to the *Punta della due Rocchi* that divided it from the adjacent BLUE Beach. Narrowing from sixty yards to fifteen yards deep west to east, the beach gave way to a 200- to 300-yards-wide strip of harvested wheat fields and tomato plantations running up to the *Strada* 115, backed by several bunkers and machine-gun posts on the landward side of the road; an Italian railway battery mounting four 76mm guns located on the Licata harbour mole with a direct line of sight over YELLOW Beach was obliterated in place by the destroyer USS *Bristol* shortly after daybreak. Commanded by Commander William O. Floyd, the Salso Attack Group was a smaller affair than the neighbouring BLUE Beach landing with just three waves made up of two battalions from Colonel Charles E. Johnson's 15th RCT travelling in LSTs and the tanks of Company H, 66th Armored Regiment and elements of the 39th Field Artillery Battalion carried aboard nine LCTs. Despite one of the marker vessels being off station Commander Floyd had his LSTs anchored and ready to load and launch their LCVPs by

01:41. In this instance the beach was clearly marked by a party of US Navy Scouts and Raiders led by Ensign Phil H. Bucklew and the assault wave, Lieutenant-Colonel Ashton Manhart's 3rd Battalion, touched down accurately on YELLOW Beach at 03:40; all but one of the LCVPs involved reversed off the beach safely.[15]

Opposed only by some scattered machine-gun fire the 3rd Battalion rapidly crossed the *Strada* 115, overran the beach defences and established a covering position to the north; an Italian-speaking reporter attached to the 3rd Battalion answered a ringing telephone in an abandoned command post and assured a grouchy Italian senior officer that there was no truth in reports of US landings near Licata. The second wave, Lieutenant-Colonel Leslie A. Pritchard's 1st Battalion, came ashore at 04:45 and immediately moved off through the 3rd Battalion for its primary objective, an Italian gun battery a mile and a half north-west of the beach, which was secured by 08:00; ninety minutes later Lieutenant-Colonel Pritchard was ordered to cross the River Salso, detach a platoon to guard the bridge and prepare to move on Licata from the north while the 3rd Battalion moved in from the east. The only confusion involved nine of the LCTs from the third wave which were mistakenly led to the DIME Landing Area at Gela by a guide vessel; the error was realised in time for them to reach YELLOW Beach at 08:00 and by 09:14 all the Salso Attack Group LSTs were putting vehicles ashore.[16]

Located three miles west of Licata at the western end of the Monte Sole heights overlooking the port, GREEN Beach was not only the smallest but also the most difficult to access of all the JOSS beaches, consisting of two separate beaches codenamed GREEN EAST and GREEN WEST on the flanks of a sandy 300-yard isthmus tipped by the rocky, eighty-foot high outcrop of the *Rocca Mollarella*. The eastern beach was 400 yards wide and forty yards deep, accessed by a cove mouth around half that width, but with good vehicle exits giving access to the *Strada* 115 just over a mile inland; the western beach, 350 yards wide, was narrower at twenty yards deep and was also largely rocky apart from a 150-yard stretch of sand. Both beaches were at least partially blocked with barbed-wire entanglements. Machine-gun positions on the *Rocca Mollarella* dominated the western beach and a network of trenches and machine-gun positions protected with more barbed wire had been constructed in the body of the isthmus.[17] Further north, a chain of three bunkers were located roughly midway to the *Strada* 115 backed by a large strongpoint straddling the road, another smaller strongpoint straddled it closer to Licata and an artillery battery and several bunkers were located in the lee of the Monte Sole north-east of the landing beach.[18]

Commander Robert M. Morris' Molla Attack Group was the smallest of the JOSS landing forces, consisting of eleven vessels: six LSTs, three LCTs and the British LCIs HMS *Prinses* (then *Princess*) *Astrid* and HMS *Princess Josephine Charlotte*, Belgian civilian craft requisitioned by the Royal Navy in 1940 and converted into landing ships. The landing component, under the overall command of the 15th RCT's Executive Officer Lieutenant-Colonel Brookner

W. Brady, was made up of Major Herman W. Dammer's six-Company 3rd Ranger Battalion carried in the British LSIs and Lieutenant-Colonel William H. Billings' 2nd Battalion, 15th RCT travelling in the six LSTs, all tasked to move on Licata from the west. Colonel Brady's force also included a platoon of 75mm Pack Howitzers from the 15th RCT's Cannon Company, Company B 3rd Chemical Battalion equipped with 4.2-inch mortars and 105mm guns from Battery B, 39th Field Artillery Battalion, but they were not scheduled to begin landing from the three LCTs along with the infantry force's vehicles until 06:05, four hours after the assault.[19]

Led by the destroyer USS *Edison* and minesweeper USS *Sentinel*, Commander Morris's little fleet reached the loading area without incident despite the weather and was anchored ready to load and launch landing craft by 01:20, with Major Dammer's Rangers making up the assault wave in sixteen British LCAs. Guided by marker lights set up by a group of Scouts and Raiders on the *Rocca Mollarella*, the sixteen LCAs deftly steered their way into the restricted beaches despite the violent surf and delivered all six Ranger Companies simultaneously onto both beaches at 02:57, just twelve minutes behind schedule. Three Companies immediately set about clearing the defences in the immediate area of the beaches while the remaining three pushed north out of the isthmus to the western end of the Monte Sole where they set up a jumping-off point for an advance onto the heights. LCVPs from the LSTs delivered Lieutenant-Colonel Billings' 2nd Battalion onto GREEN WEST at 03:42 and after reorganising moved through the Rangers to begin clearing the Monte Sole ridge while Major Dammer's Rangers moved along the northern edge, eliminating the smaller strongpoint straddling the *Strada* 115 in the process.

By 07:35 the Rangers had covered the three miles or so to the outskirts of Licata and secured the Castel Sant'Angelo and, unable to proceed further due to naval gunfire falling on the port, took down the Italian flag flying over the Castel and replaced it with a Stars and Stripes in full view of the landing fleet. In the event the final concentric advance into Licata from the west, north and east met little resistance as the overawed Italian garrison largely chose to surrender rather than fight; in all the JOSS landing netted some 3,000 Italian prisoners whom a US officer involved in shuttling them out to ships for transport to North Africa described as 'the happiest crowd you ever saw'.[20] Licata was firmly in US hands by 11:30 and by midday Major-General Truscott and his staff had come ashore from the Naval Task Force 86 flagship USS *Biscayne* and set up a HQ in the Palazzo La Lumia in the town centre while the 15th RCT reorganised and moved rapidly north, through the 7th RCT blocking position at Stazione Sant'Oliva and up the *Strada* 123 before being blocked later in the day by a scratch force of motorcyclists and artillerymen short of Favarotta, roughly halfway between Stazione Sant'Oliva and Campobello di Licata.[21]

Licata harbour proved too small to accommodate large vessels but was open for LSTs and smaller craft to unload by late afternoon/early evening on 10 July; transport vessels were unloaded over YELLOW and BLUE Beaches using LCTs and over pontoon causeways that permitted vehicles to drive straight off their landing vessels onto dry land; RED and GREEN Beaches were closed on D-Day, the former presumably due to enemy fire and the latter because of the difficult access and relatively limited egress.[22] Securing Licata port and adjacent landing area achieved one of the US 3rd Infantry Division's primary initial objective within eight hours of the start of the JOSS landings and events over the first three days of the invasion underlined the necessity and wisdom of this; by 12 July 20,470 troops had passed through Licata harbour or over the adjacent YELLOW and BLUE Beaches along with 3,752 assorted vehicles and 6,614 tons of supplies.[23] In addition to securing the harbour and beaches, by the end of D-Day the 3rd Infantry Division had also reached its Initial Beachhead Line, all for a cost of fewer than a hundred casualties.[24] As one of the US Official Histories put it: 'Thus, the left flank of the entire Allied assault was secured by a bold offensive, and an ample beachhead with a feeder port was obtained for the conquest of western Sicily; and all this with minimum air support'.[25]

The seizure of Licata and the threat posed by the US 3rd Infantry Division's progress north and west from the JOSS landing beaches was quickly noted by the Axis commanders. *Generale d'Armata* Guzzoni was especially concerned that the 15th RCT's advance north toward Campobello di Licata not only threatened the *Hermann Göring Panzer* Division's right flank but also had the potential to cut off the Axis forces in the west of Sicily. Guzzoni therefore despatched First World War veteran *Colonnello* Alessandro Venturi and a *battaglione* from his *177° Reggimento Bersaglieri* to Favarotta on the *Strada* 123 south of Campobello di Licata in the evening of 10 July; on arrival the *Bersaglieri* commander integrated the elements holding the town into *Gruppo Tattici* (tactical group) Venturi and began organising a counter-attack toward Licata for the following morning. To counter the threat posed by the 7th RCT's move west the *207ª Divisione Costiere* was ordered to establish another *Gruppo Tattici* near the River Naro crossing on the *Strada* 115, also tasked to counter-attack east toward Licata; other Italian units moving in behind the forming line at nearby Agrigento and Canicatti, fifteen miles further inland, were warned to stand-by to move south through Naro to Palma di Montechiaro on the coast to reinforce the attack.[26]

The German reaction was more potent. Alerted by retreating Italian units and reports that the counter-attack toward Gela was not proceeding according to plan, *Generalleutnant* Eberhard Rodt ordered the bulk of his *15 Panzergrenadier Division* to move toward the US landings from its concentration area around Salemi in the western tip of Sicily on his own initiative and relocated his HQ seventy miles east to Pietraperzia, twenty miles north of Licata, arriving there at 04:00 on Sunday 11 July. As he, too, was concerned with the implications of the Licata landings and especially the advance north toward Campobello di Licata, Rodt divided his force in three groups to counter it. The primary block was to be executed by *Kampfgruppe* Fullriede, built around *Oberst* Fritz Fullriede's *Panzergrenadier Regiment*

129, which was ordered to deploy along an eight-mile line running east from Canicatti through Delia to Sommatino in order to block the main routes running north through the mountains from Campobello di Licata six miles to the south, and thus the US 3rd Infantry Division's northern line of advance. Behind and to the west of this line *Kampfgruppe* Neapel was ordered to deploy as a backstop covering the roads running east and north from Canicatti; the composition and commander of *Kampfgruppe* Neapel are unclear but it may have been built around the *Aufklärungs Abteilung* belonging to *15 Panzergrenadier Division*. Finally, *Kampfgruppe* Ens, built around *Oberst* Karl Ens' *Panzergrenadier Regiment 104*, was tasked to cover the east flank against interference from the US advance from Gela, and to detach a *bataillon* to move south-east and secure Riesi before doubling back west to attack the flank of the US advance on Campobello di Licata.

On the US side, with the JOSS Initial Beachhead Line achieved by midnight on 10 July attention turned to expanding the lodgement for additional security and to reaching Patton's Yellow Line. Major-General Truscott therefore summoned his senior commanders to his HQ in Licata in the evening of 10 July to issue his orders for the following day's operations, which were intended to carry his formation forward to the Yellow Line. On the 3rd Infantry Division's right flank Colonel Rogers' 30th RCT was to maintain its role of protecting the Division's exposed eastern flank by despatching a battalion fifteen miles north to secure the hilltop town of Riesi and thereby block access through the rugged terrain on its front. The Division's other two RCTs were also to continue their existing activities. Colonel Johnson's 15th RCT was to continue to advance north up the *Strada* 123 and secure Campobello di Licata while Colonel Sherman's 7th RCT, regrouped to the west after its initial blocking mission, was to move along the coastal *Strada* 115, over the River Palma and secure Palma di Montechiaro and the high ground just beyond the town to the west; both towns lay on the Yellow Line. However, this left a considerable gap between the northern and western lines of advance that was vulnerable to exploitation by Axis units that aerial reconnaissance reported moving in from the west of the island.

General Truscott therefore decided to plug the gap with his floating reserve, Brigadier-General Maurice Rose's Combat Command A from the 2nd Armored Division, which came ashore through Licata port and the adjacent YELLOW and BLUE Beaches in the late afternoon or evening of 10 July.[27] Combat Command A had been attached to Truscott's formation for HUSKY at 7th Army commander Patton's specific order and consisted of the 1st and 2nd Battalions 66th Armored Regiment, the 2nd and 3rd Battalions from Colonel Sidney R. Hinds' 41st Armored Infantry Regiment, Company B 82nd Armored Reconnaissance Battalion and the 14th Armored Field Artillery Battalion.[28] Having been previously briefed to be ready to advance on Agrigento, Campobello di Licata or Gela to the west, north and east respectively, perhaps typically Brigadier-General Rose was directed to seize the town of Naro, approximately seventeen miles north-west of Licata, and occupy the high ground to the north and east; Naro was also located on the Yellow Line.[29]

All elements of Major-General Truscott's formation attained the Yellow Line by nightfall on 11 July, twenty-four hours ahead of schedule, although some units encountered more difficulty than others. The least opposed move was on the 3rd Infantry Division's right flank where Lieutenant-Colonel Edgar C. Doleman's 3rd Battalion, 30th RCT advanced north fourteen miles in the face of 'scattered resistance' and secured Riesi by the end of the day, unwittingly pre-empting *Kampfgruppe* Ens' projected flanking attack in the process. In the centre the 15th RCT's attack toward Campobello di Licata began at 04:45 on 11 July with the 3rd Battalion moving on the town up the meandering *Strada* 123 tasked to secure the high ground overlooking Campobello from the west, while the 1st Battalion hooked to the right over a concealed route via a series of rugged draws on the right intended to envelop the town from the east; the 2nd Battalion followed in reserve, with support provided by the 39th Field Artillery Battalion and an attached battery from the 9th Field Artillery Battalion.

The 3rd Battalion's advance up the *Strada* 123 ran headlong into *Gruppo Tattici* Venturi's counter-attack at Favarotta, sparking a four-hour battle for the town during which US artillery fire pounded the Italian guns and vehicles in the surrounding area. A move to outflank the town from the west was stymied when several Italian machine-guns emplaced in dead ground and thus impervious to artillery fire pinned down the company involved; Colonel Johnson responded by calling up a platoon from the RCT's Cannon Company to provide direct fire support, which involved the three T30 HMC half-tracks racing forward at full speed through several hair-pin bends and pre-registered Italian artillery fire.[30] With the impasse broken the 3rd Battalion swiftly overran Favarotta and *Gruppo Tattici* Venturi withdrew to Campobello di Licata leaving three artillery pieces and numerous machine-guns behind; the *Bersaglieri battaglione* in particular had suffered heavy casualties in the fighting, possibly including a wounded *Colonnello* Venturi.[31]

While all this was going on and despite starting an hour late the 1st Battalion had advanced unopposed and unseen through the rugged terrain alongside the *Strada* 123 to arrive east of Campobello di Licata at 13:00, joined around the same time by the 3rd Battalion moving onto the high ground to the west of the town. Both Battalions launched a simultaneous advance on Campobello at 15:00 after an intensive artillery bombardment by the 39th Field Artillery Battalion; between this and the earlier fighting at Favarotta the 39th and the 9th Field Artillery Battalion fired a total of 1,570 rounds on 11 July, the vast majority by the former unit.[32] Securing the town proved problematic as the advance was halted on the outskirts by concentrated automatic fire from the defenders, elements of *Kampfgruppe* Neapel whose presence was due to a change in the local Axis overall command structure. During the morning of 11 July *12° Corpo* HQ at Corleone ordered the commander of the

207ª Divisione Costiere, *Generale di Brigata* Ottorino Schreiber, to hand over his formation to *Colonnello* Augusto de Laurentiis and assume command of the effort to block the US advance from Licata, and thus all the Axis units at and en route to the vicinity of Canicatti. Arriving at the latter at 11:30 *Generale* Schreiber immediately despatched *Kampfgruppe* Neapel to Campobello di Licata in the wake of the already engaged *Gruppo Tattici* Venturi with orders to launch a joint attack down the *Strada* 123 at 13:30 but he was subsequently obliged to abandon the attack, in part due to *Gruppo Tattici* Venturi's rough handling at Favarotta and in part because a developing US advance on Naro, five miles south-west of Canicatti, threatened the right flank of any move down the *Strada* 123. Schreiber therefore initiated a withdrawal back toward Canicatti covered by *Kampfgruppe* Neapel at Campobello, which thus became embroiled in defending the town from the 15th RCT. The attack was renewed after a further round of artillery preparation, although the German defence remained tenacious. The 3rd Battalion's Company L was held up by a concealed machine-gun that wounded three officers and 2nd Lieutenant Robert Craig single-handedly located and charged the position, killing the three-man crew with his M1 carbine. When his platoon was subsequently pinned down on a forward slope by another gun, Lieutenant Craig repeated his feat to cover his men's withdrawal to cover, killing eight of the enemy and wounding three more before being killed himself; he was posthumously awarded the Medal of Honor for his gallantry.[33] After an hour-long fight the 3rd Battalion was able to enter Campobello at 16:00, while *Kampfgruppe* Neapel withdrew to the north.[34]

On the 15th RCT's left Brigadier-General Rose's Combat Command A moved on Naro with a screen from the 82nd Armored Reconnaissance Battalion covering Lieutenant-Colonel Marshall L. Crawley's 3rd Battalion, 41st Armored Infantry Regiment reinforced with a company of M4 Medium tanks from the 66th Armored Regiment. Due to the poor state of the secondary roads and trails running the sixteen or so miles north-west from Licata progress was relatively slow with a brief strafing attack by two German aircraft being the primary opposition encountered, and presumably in an effort aid mobility the 'Armored Doughs' from the 3rd Battalion travelled for the last leg of the journey on the decks of the M4 tanks. The US column was greeted just short of Naro by a Sicilian civilian accompanied by his small son, who informed Colonel Hinds that the town was undefended; a perhaps understandably sceptical Hinds promptly placed the pair on the bonnet of his command half-track and after despatching teams to secure the flanks and exit routes led the way into the streets. The Sicilian's claim proved to be accurate and Naro was in US hands by mid-morning, although a subsequent attempted move on to Canicatti proved less successful. A unit of M4 tanks was strafed by P-38 fighter-bombers that mistook them for elements of *15 Panzergrenadier Division* despite the tanks deploying yellow smoke as mandated to identify friendly vehicles; the misidentification was the first of a series of such incidents that cost Combat Command A seventy-five casualties and fourteen vehicles in the week beginning 11 July, and was only mitigated by 15th Army Group HQ replacing yellow smoke with day-glo panels as a recognition measure. More importantly, the lead elements of the column ran into resistance two miles north of Naro from a *battaglione* of Italian infantry holding a narrow defile; the Italians had arrived from Agrigento just minutes before the US unit arrived. Lieutenant-Colonel Crawley's 3rd Battalion deployed to clear the roadblock but the Italians held them back until the onset of darkness before withdrawing. Nightfall on 11 July thus found Combat Command A just north of the Yellow Line, four miles short of Canicatti.[35]

The 7th RCT's move along the *Strada* 115 coast road to Palma di Montechiaro was spearheaded by Lieutenant-Colonel Heintges' 3rd Battalion advancing west from its D-Day position just short of the River Palma. After crossing the river without incident, the Battalion ran into Italian positions along a line of low hills just short of Palma di Montechiaro, which by 11:00 had been cleared by a combination of individual attacks, the survivors withdrawing to the outskirts of the town. A number of white flags were then seen on the outlying buildings, but a patrol despatched by Lieutenant-Colonel Heintges to clarify the situation was fired on, losing two dead and two wounded; the flags were reportedly the work of local civilians rather than the Italian garrison. An 'enraged' Colonel Heintges responded by personally leading a team forward through heavy fire to a large building housing Italian troops, which was collapsed by a demolition charge. The detonation of the charge signalled the 3rd Battalion's attack into the town, although clearing it proved more complicated as the defence had been bolstered by the arrival of the *Gruppo Tattici* from the River Naro. A ferocious two-hour fight then ensued, focused along Palma's main street, that continued until 13:00 when the Italians began to withdraw west along the *Strada* 115. After a hasty reorganisation the 3rd Battalion went in pursuit before digging in on high ground south of the road to await reinforcements; by the late afternoon of 11 July the 7th RCT was also firmly ensconced on the Yellow Line.

As a result of all this the night of 11-12 July was another period of shifting priorities on both the Axis and US sides. *Generale* Schreiber found his efforts to erect a coherent defence after the reverses at Favarotta and Campobello di Licata obstructed, initially by an Allied bombing raid on Canicatti at 18:00 that damaged the railway station and inflicted heavy casualties upon *Gruppo Tattici* Venturi located in the town. Shortly afterward, *12° Corpo* HQ instructed him to resume the attack in the morning of 12 July using reinforcements provided for the purpose, including an infantry *battaglione* from the *26ª Assietta Divisione*, another *battaglione* and anti-tank company drawn from the *28ª Aosta Divisione* backed by two *battaglioni* of artillery. The attack instruction originated with *Generale* Guzzoni at *6ª Armata* HQ, who was still seeking to block the US advance into central Sicily to prevent the island being cut in two. However, the arrival of *Oberst* Fullriede at Schreiber's HQ at 20:00 caused some confusion; along with reporting that his *Kampfgruppe* was concentrated north of Canicatti as ordered with flank guards deployed at Delia and Sommatino to the east and warning of the US armoured advance from Naro, Fullriede also referred to instructions from *6ª Armata* HQ to adopt a defensive role in the Canicatti area and await the arrival of further German reinforcements. Understandably puzzled, Schreiber sought clarification and discovered that the *volte face* also originated with Guzzoni, who had simply changed his mind; the following day's attack was thus to be abandoned and activities were to be restricted to 'local thrusts...that would not seriously deplete his [Schreiber's] manpower and material'.[36]

On that basis Schreiber went a step further and set about withdrawing all his units south of Canicatti behind *Kampfgruppe* Fullriede's line, although the process was complicated by aggressive US patrolling; one Italian 105mm gun battery, unable to break contact, opted to destroy its guns and surrender. The additional German reinforcements, in the shape of *Kampfgruppe* Ens, arrived in the course of the night. *Oberst* Ens was slightly wounded in an Allied bombing raid on *15 Panzergrenadier Division* HQ at Pietraperzia while reporting to *Generalleutnant* Rodt but continued in command and deployed his formation north and east of *Kampfgruppe* Fullriede's line, in a fourteen-mile arc blocking the main roads running north from the Licata and Gela landing areas; one *bataillon* was posted south of Pietraperzia astride the *Strada Provinciale* 10, one seven miles to the south-west astride the *Strada* 191 at Barrafranca and the third ten miles east at Piazza Armerina beside the *Strada* 117 tasked to make contact with the *Hermann Göring Panzer* Division's right flank. It is unclear if the reinforcements from the *Aosta* and *Assietta Divisioni* also arrived or were directed elsewhere.

On the other side of the hill, achieving the Yellow Line effectively left the US 3rd Infantry Division without a mission. In the absence of additional orders and in an effort to avoid losing the initiative, Major-General Truscott instructed Combat Command A to carry out reconnaissance toward Canicatti in readiness for a continued advance on the town the following day; this may have been part of the patrol activity that interfered with the Italian withdrawal behind *Kampfgruppe* Fullriede. Official permission to seize Canicatti was obtained from the US 7th Army's Deputy Commander, Major-General Geoffrey Keyes, who arrived at 3rd Infantry Division HQ in the morning of Monday 12 July; Truscott appears to have sold the concept by pointing out that Canicatti marked the junction of the *Strada* 123 and *Strada* 122 running north from Agrigento to Caltanissetta which, in conjunction with the minor roads linking Licata and Naro, provided perfect routes for a mechanised advance into the heart of the island. Losing no time, Truscott set his Division in motion.

The 7th RCT was to remain in place as a left flank guard while patrolling forward to the west, Combat Command A was to move directly on Canicatti, the 15th RCT was to move up on the right and secure Delia and Sommatino while the 30th RCT, minus the 3rd Battalion holding Riesi, moved across to Naro. Combat Command A moved off through the defile that had prompted the previous evening's fight at 13:30, after a five-minute preparatory artillery bombardment from the 14th and 62nd Armored Field Artillery Battalions and again with infantry riding the decks of the lead M4 tanks; the 15th RCT presumably moved off at around the same time. While some distance short of Canicatti Colonel Hinds came under shell fire while personally investigating reports of a white flag flying from what turned out to be a hospital, prompting him to order a thirty-minute systematic bombardment of the rest of the town and German positions identified on the high ground to the north. The bombardment did the trick and a company of M4s from the 66th Armored Regiment secured Canicatti without a fight at 15:00, but an attempt to push further ran into *Kampfgruppe* Fullriede's main blocking line on the ridge a mile or so north of the town, sparking a fight that cost one M4 knocked out and obliged the US tank company to withdraw after expending all its ammunition. A subsequent right-flanking attack pushed the German defenders off the ridge by 20:00 despite stubborn resistance, while to the east the 15th RCT had overrun and secured Delia and cleared much of Sommatino by nightfall, inflicting heavy losses on the elements of *Kampfgruppe* Fullriede deployed there. Lacking the strength to continue in place – the *bataillon* at Canicatti had reportedly been particularly badly mauled – *Oberst* Fullriede sought and was granted permission to withdraw seven miles to a new blocking line along the railway linking Serradifalco with San Cataldo six miles to the east.[37]

The US 3rd Infantry Division's repeated success on 12 July achieved all the formation's objectives in short order, but also again left Major-General Truscott in a quandary. The 7th RCT's location maintained the option of moving west along the coast to Agrigento, and the seizure of the Canicatti-Delia-Sommatino line allowed the additional option of further advance northward to take Caltanissetta and Enna to dominate the heart of the island, and potentially cut it in two. However, at this point the 3rd Division was also holding a fifty-mile front with open flanks, the right flank being of particular concern due to the unsecured area around Riesi, with Axis units known to be east of the town and *Kampfgruppe* Ens to the north. Addressing the situation required the US advance from the DIME Landing Area to close up to the Yellow Line. Simply holding in place was therefore not an option, but further movement required at least an RCT in reinforcement, as Truscott's Division was not only geographically stretched but was also fully committed, with the 3rd Ranger Battalion being its only uncommitted reserve. The problem was that authorisation and reinforcement had to be sought from 7th Army HQ, and Lieutenant-General Patton was in turn awaiting instructions from 15th Army Group HQ, where General Alexander was still concentrating on the British 8th Army advance in the east and particularly the prospect of a 'massive' Axis counter-attack; he was therefore content for the US 3rd Division to remain in place to provide 'a solid block on the army group left'.[38]

The situation was again saved by Major-General Keyes, who had remained at Truscott's HQ on 12 July to witness the capture of Canicatti and briefed Patton on the developing situation by radio that evening. Keen to avoid increasing the 3rd Division's vulnerability and relinquishing the initiative, Keyes authorised Truscott to clear the reported enemy roadblock east of Riesi, the high ground north of Canicatti and, most significantly with hindsight, to prosecute a battalion-strength reconnaissance in force west toward Agrigento on his own authority. He then departed for 7th Army HQ, which was now operating from a mansion on the outskirts of Gela after Patton moved ashore from the Western Naval Task Force flagship USS *Monrovia* in the afternoon of 12 July. Patton approved Keyes' provisional instructions and requested permission to seize Agrigento and nearby Porto Empedocle from Alexander in person during a meeting the following morning; Alexander acquiesced but with the strict proviso that the seizure was achieved using only reconnaissance assets and provided it 'did not cost too much in manpower or material'.[39] Keyes therefore confirmed his provisional authorisation to Truscott for the advance west in writing in the afternoon of 13 July.

Back to the west of Licata Major-General Truscott had ordered Lieutenant-Colonel Moore's 1st Battalion, 7th RCT to conduct a reconnaissance-in-force toward Agrigento on 13 July on receiving Keyes' provisional authorisation, which revealed that the eastern outskirts of the town were defended by around a regiment of Italian infantry and a dozen or so high-velocity guns, with more infantry dug in along the River Naro to the east, all supported by an estimated *battaglione* of field artillery. Despite this relatively formidable defence, the reconnaissance persuaded Truscott that an operation to take Agrigento and Porto Empedocle was feasible and the opportunity to sell the idea occurred the following day. Patton made his first visit to Truscott's HQ shortly after midday on 14 July and while briefing Truscott on General Alexander's justification and restrictions for keeping the 7th Army in place on the British 8th Army's left flank, he also mentioned needing Porto Empedocle to support a future advance on Palermo to the north-west; Patton had been increasingly fixated on securing the Sicilian capital since its designation as an objective in the early iterations of the HUSKY plan, and the more so as his US 7th Army was repeatedly side-lined while Montgomery's rival British formation maintained the operational lead. Truscott responded by seeking Patton's approval for a larger reconnaissance-in-force to seize the port and Agrigento, which was granted on the proviso that the operation would be on Truscott's responsibility and the 3rd Infantry Division commander immediately swung into what was by now customary rapid action.

As the strength of the Italian defences at Agrigento precluded a frontal approach along the *Strada* 115, Truscott chose to outflank them by moving Colonel Sherman's reinforced 7th RCT through Favara, five miles to the east of Agrigento on the *Strada* 122 running north to Caltanissetta, to attack Agrigento from the north-east; Favara had been occupied by a company from the 1st Battalion during the night of 13 July. Colonel Sherman's Regimental HQ and Lieutenant-Colonel Heintges' 3rd Battalion were ordered to move up the east side of the *Strada* 115 to high ground overlooking the River Naro while to the right Lieutenant-Colonel Duvall's 2nd Battalion marched to Favara directly from Palma di Montechiaro; Truscott also despatched his Division reserve, Major Dammer's 3rd Ranger Battalion, to Favara via Naro, seven miles to the east. Support was to be provided by the 10th Field Artillery Battalion reinforced with a battalion from the 77th Field Artillery Regiment, backed by naval gunfire support from the US cruisers *Birmingham*, *Brooklyn* and *Philadelphia* and the monitor HMS *Abercrombie*; the *Birmingham* and *Brooklyn* had been firing against targets in Agrigento and Porto Empedocle since 12 July. The night march proceeded without incident and before dawn on Thursday 15 July the 7th RCT was in position to begin the assault on Agrigento.[40]

The attack began with Major Dammer's 3rd Ranger Battalion departing Favara at dusk on 15 July to perform a right flanking move around Agrigento to Montaperto, six miles to the west, which would allow the Rangers to approach Porto Empedocle from the north. At 00:30 on 16 July the Rangers ran into an Italian roadblock position just east of the *Strada* 118 and *Strada* 122, which was taken in under an hour with 165 prisoners. They ambushed an Italian column of two trucks and ten motorcycles moving down the *Strada* 118 toward Agrigento just after dawn, killing a number and taking another forty prisoner and then engaged four Italian artillery batteries in the valley below after moving into Montaperto; most of the gunners opted to trek up the slope to surrender while some fled to the south. The 7th RCT's main attack on Agrigento was initially less successful, for while Lieutenant-Colonel Duvall's 2nd Battalion secured high ground overlooking the town from the east at 09:00 despite communication difficulties, a night move on Agrigento by Lieutenant-Colonel Moore's 1st Battalion was blocked by elements of two Italian infantry battalions withdrawing into the town, with the resultant fighting continuing into the afternoon of 16 July.

The impasse prompted Major-General Truscott to deploy Lieutenant-Colonel Heintges' 3rd Battalion in support of the stalled 1st Battalion at 14:00, which tipped the balance against the defenders in conjunction with US land and naval bombardment that had silenced the Italian artillery by the time the 3rd Battalion became involved, and had also damaged Italian commander *Colonnello* Augusto de Laurentiis' command post and set parts of the town on fire. Surrounded and with the 1st Battalion pushing into the town, *Colonnello* de Laurentiis surrendered to Lieutenant-Colonel Moore with the remainder of his men, while to the west Major Dammer and the 3rd Ranger Battalion pushed south from Montaperto and secured Porto Empedocle. By nightfall on Friday 16 July Major-General Truscott's reconnaissance-in-force had achieved its objectives.

The JOSS landing force was arguably the most successful of the three US 7th Army landings. The flanking pincer movement secured Licata within eight hours of the first landing craft coming ashore, the protective blocking position to the west that was to provide a foundation for the entire 7th Army left flank was in place within nine hours and the port and eastern beaches were open to traffic within approximately fourteen hours. The Initial Beachhead Line was achieved by midnight on D-Day and the Yellow Line by nightfall on D-Day Plus One, twenty-four hours ahead of schedule. The subsequent aggressive twenty-mile advance north from

Licata stymied the planned Italian counter-attack at Favarotta, secured Campo di Licata and fought back the German blocking line at Canicatti to secure the town in just forty-eight hours. To the west the blocking line on the *Strada* 115 was pushed forward via Major-General Truscott's imaginative interpretation of the reconnaissance-in-force concept to secure Agrigento and Porto Empedocle, despite 15th Army Group's intention for the US 7th Army to remain passive as a secure anchor and western flank guard for the British 8th Army's advance up Sicily's east coast. Within 120 hours of HUSKY commencing, Major-General Truscott and his 3rd Infantry Division had achieved all of their pre-invasion missions on or before time, pushed aggressively against Italian and German forces to the north of the JOSS Landing Area, disrupting their counter-measures in the process, and had laid the groundwork for a break out of the initial invasion area into the west of Sicily in the event of a change of US focus.

The underground Lascaris War Rooms complex, Valetta, Malta. Lascaris was the advance Allied HQ from where Eisenhower, Cunningham, and Montgomery directed Operation HUSKY. Tedder remained at Marsa: see page 411. (Courtesy Frank Vincentz under Creative Commons 3.0)

Above left: General Harold Alexander. (Courtesy National Archives)

Above right: War Office official photograph of General Sir Bernard Montgomery in 1943.

Above: Patton strikes a pose on Sicily, 11 July. 'We will not be stopped.' (Courtesy LOC)

Below left: Omar Bradley portrait by Clarence Lamont MacNelly (1920-1986).

Below right: George C. Marshall. (Courtesy Marshall Foundation Archives)

Above left: Lieutenant-Colonel John Frost, 2nd Parachute Battalion, later to be captured at Arnhem. (Public domain)

Above right: General Carlo Rossi, commander of the XVI Army Corps. (Public domain)

1938 image of *Generaloberst* Hans-Valentin Hube as Kommandeur *Infanterie-Ausbildungsstabes* Döberitz, Infantry Training School staff, third from left. Hube commanded the XIV Corps during the Soviet counter-offensive, Operation URANUS, November 1942, before creating Gruppe Hube in Sicily. (Public domain)

Far left: Mugshot of *Generaloberst* Hans-Jürgen von Arnim, image taken by the US Signal Corps. He replaced Rommel as commander of Army Group Africa on 10 March 1943. He surrendered to British forces on 12 May. (Public domain).

Left: Generalleutnant Fridolin von Senger und Etterlin. (Public domain)

Kesselring (left) and Hube in southern Italy. After setting up the Gustav Line, Hube would be reassigned to the Eastern Front in command of *1 Panzerarmee*. (Public domain).

Above: General Matthew Bunker Ridgway, CG of the 82nd Airborne in Sicily and later commander of the XVIII Airborne Corps. He would eventually take over as Supreme Allied Commander Europe (SACEUR) from General Eisenhower. (Public domain)

Below: Monty as he would like to be remembered; 1st Viscount Montgomery of Alamein, with black beret and badge of the Royal Tank Regiment. (Public domain)

Rear Admiral Alan G. Kirk with Alexander, General Middleton and Patton aboard a landing craft in Mers el Kabir Harbour in Algeria watching preparations for HUSKY. (Public domain)

LSTs waiting to load tanks two days before the invasion of Sicily at the French Naval Base La Pecherie, Tunisia. (Public domain)

Troop carrier pilots' briefing immediately before the invasion. (Courtesy LOC)

Liberty ship *Robert Rowan* (K-40) explodes after being hit by a German Ju 88 bomber off Gela, Sicily, on 11 July. All 421 men on board were safely evacuated by PT boats and transferred to nearby destroyers before her cargo of ammunition blew up. (Public domain)

A US Combat Camera team took this shot of the nose section of the wrecked glider on 3 August, recording: 'Note tree knocked down by impact with wing'. (Courtesy LOC)

Taken from the deck of a Coast Guard-manned transport that has just unloaded, a picture of the bomb-pocked waters off Sicily. (Public domain)

Above: Driving onto the beach in safety. (Courtesy LOC)

Below: An American ship exploding after being hit by dive bombers. Is this also the *Robert Rowan*? (Courtesy LOC)

51st Highland Division disembark, 10 July. (Courtesy LOC)

Bird's-eye view of the invasion seen from almost directly overhead, Allied landing boats on the shores of Sicily during the early days of the invasion. It would be fascinating to know who took the picture. (Courtesy LOC)

Not long after the opening of the Sicilian invasion, the beach near Scoglitti presented this peaceful appearance as an LCI and DUKW drew up to deliver and take on loads. (Courtesy LOC)

Above: Moving inland, here through Scoglitti. In part, simply a lack of Jeeps forced Anderson to temporarily halt the US advance at some point in the late afternoon or early evening, allowing transport and heavy weapons to catch up. (Courtesy LOC)

Left: Tired from his march to Brolo, Sgt. Norwood Dorman from Benson, North Carolina, falls into the pose of the memorial to the Italian soldier of the First World War. (Courtesy LOC)

Above: The island of Pantellaria is totally obscured during the bombing that led to its swift surrender in Operation CORKSCREW. The adjacent islands of Lampedusa, Lampione and Linosa also surrendered without a fight in the first half of June. (Courtesy LOC)

The operation involved almost a thousand RAF and USAAF aircraft including four-engine B-17 bombers, B-26, Baltimore, Boston and Wellington medium bombers, plus Hurricane and the unmistakable P-38 Lightning fighter-bombers. (Courtesy CindyN under Creative Commons 4.0)

Private Roy Humphrey of Toledo, Ohio, treated for wounds in Sicily. (Courtesy LOC)

Evac. (Courtesy LOC)

French-Canadian troops in Sicily, with French-speaking Italians. The Italian soldier in the centre was a veteran of many Italian engagements. Following the signing of the Armistice of Cassibile on 3 September, he became a firefighter in his local village. (Courtesy LOC)

Captured Italian soldiers. Something like 117,000 Italian combatants were listed as captured or missing after HUSKY. (Courtesy LOC)

Map courtesy Paul Hewitt, @www.battlefield-design.co.uk, and Dudley Giles.

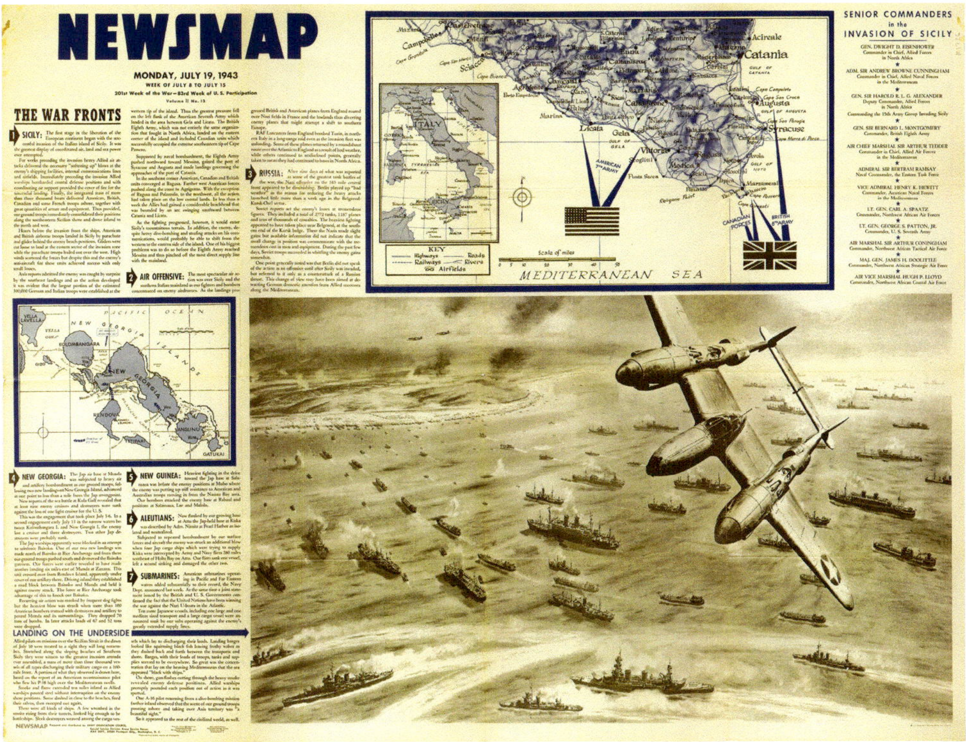

NEWSMAP

MONDAY, JULY 19, 1943

WEEK OF JULY 8 TO JULY 15

201st Week of the War—83rd Week of U.S. Participation

THE WAR FRONTS

1 SICILY:

2 AIR OFFENSIVE:

3 RUSSIA:

4 NEW GEORGIA:

5 NEW GUINEA:

6 ALEUTIANS:

7 SUBMARINES:

LANDING ON THE UNDERSIDE

SENIOR COMMANDERS in the INVASION OF SICILY

GEN. DWIGHT D. EISENHOWER
Commander in Chief, Allied Forces in North Africa

ADM. SIR ANDREW BROWNE CUNNINGHAM
Commander in Chief, Allied Naval Forces in the Mediterranean

GEN. SIR HAROLD R. L. G. ALEXANDER
Deputy Commander, Allied Forces in North Africa
Commanding the 15th Army Group Invading Sicily

GEN. SIR BERNARD L. MONTGOMERY
Commander, British Eighth Army

AIR CHIEF MARSHAL SIR ARTHUR TEDDER
Commander in Chief, Allied Air Forces in the Mediterranean

ADMIRAL SIR BERTRAM RAMSAY
Naval Commander, the Eastern Task Force

VICE ADMIRAL HENRY K. HEWITT
Commander, American Naval Forces in the Mediterranean

LT. GEN. CARL A. SPAATZ
Commander, Northwest African Air Forces

LT. GEN. GEORGE S. PATTON, JR.
Commander, U. S. Seventh Army

AIR MARSHAL SIR ARTHUR CONINGHAM
Commander, Northwest African Tactical Air Force

MAJ. GEN. JAMES H. DOOLITTLE
Commander, Northwest African Strategic Air Force

AIR VICE MARSHAL HUGH P. LLOYD
Commander, Northwest African Coastal Air Force

MEDITERRANEAN SEA

Above: Ten days in and (some of) the details are made public. (Courtesy LOC)

Right: Somewhere on the way to Catania, a General Sherman tank and a German 88 mm gun. (Courtesy LOC)

Below right: An American soldier who found his relatives in Palermo: Vincent J. Orivello of Milwaukee, Wisconsin, eating ice-cream with three of his cousins. (Courtesy Nick Parrino, LOC)

The Axis evacuation. The Germans and Italians operated separate evacuation routes. The Italians utilised the existing civilian ferry routes (including the rail ferry) whilst the Germans created entirely new routes. Map courtesy Paul Hewitt and Dudley Giles.

A temporary US cemetery on Sicily's north coast. (Courtesy LOC)

15

Epicentre of the HUSKY D-Day Fighting

The DIME Landing Area at Gela, D-Day, 08:00 Saturday 10 July to D-Day Plus Five, 23:59 Thursday 15 July

The US 7th Army's third Landing Area, codenamed DIME, was allotted to Major-General Terry Allen's reinforced US 1st Infantry Division with the landings focussed on the fishing port of Gela in the centre of the US invasion frontage, around sixteen miles from Licata and Scoglitti to the west and east respectively. With a population of about 32,000, Gela was located just west of the mouth of the River Gela atop a 150-foot high plateau overlooking a 300-yard-long steel pier projecting from middle of the port frontage; as the port lacked a harbour the pier served as a mooring point for fishing vessels and was linked to the town by a winding road up the steep bluff. The coast line running west from Gela was predominantly made up of narrow beaches backed by rugged and steep slopes or cliffs unsuitable for landing large numbers of personnel and vehicles, but a mile or so east of the mouth of River Gela lay a three-mile stretch of wider, sandy beach backed by dunes and scrub, although fronted by numerous sandbars; the locals used the dunes to grow melons and the fruit was to provide some GIs with a welcome respite from the Halazone-disinfected African water that came up the US supply chain.

Inland from Gela a treeless plain used for growing wheat stretched north for four miles or so to the foothills of the island's mountainous interior, flanked by olive groves and vineyards. The coastal railway and *Strada* 115 ran through the centre of the town and across the River Gela to the east where the road veered inland. The *Strada Provinciale* 81 and *Strada* 117 also ran north from Gela, the former to Mazzarino and the latter paralleling the west bank of the River Gela via Piazze Armerina toward Enna at the centre of the island, where *Generale d'Armata* Alfredo Guzzoni had established his *6ª Armata* HQ.[1]

Although it utilised six separate beaches, the DIME landings were the most compact of the US HUSKY landings, as all the beaches were contained within five miles of coast. As the coastline running west from Gela was unsuitable for large-scale personnel and vehicle landing, the left-hand boundary of the DIME Landing Area was the port frontage itself, divided into RED and GREEN Beaches to the left and right of the pier respectively. These were allotted to the composite FORCE X attached to the 1st Infantry Division for the assault, commanded by Colonel William. O. Darby who also retained command of the 1st Ranger Battalion; the remainder of FORCE X consisted of Major Roy Murray's 4th Ranger Battalion, the 1st Battalion 39th Combat Engineer Regiment, a battalion from the 531st Engineer Shore Regiment and three companies from the 83rd Chemical Battalion equipped with 4.2-inch mortars, all tasked to secure Gela. The remaining four beaches were located immediately adjacent to one another on the stretch of sandy beach a mile or so east of the mouth of the River Gela. Two were assigned to Colonel George A. Taylor's 16th RCT and two to Colonel John W. Bowen's 26th RCT; as the 1st Infantry Division assault plan involved employing an initial wave of two battalions from the two assaulting RCTs, each beach was assigned to a single battalion.

On the left, Major Walter H. Grant's 1st Battalion, 26th RCT was assigned YELLOW Beach, tasked to assist FORCE X in securing Gela if required, while Lieutenant-Colonel Darrell M. Daniel's 2nd Battalion 26th RCT, next in line on BLUE Beach, was to secure the beach area, capture the Gela-Farello airfield just north of the *Strada* 115 coastal highway and push toward a second airfield at Ponte Olivo, six miles to the north. The next beach in line, codenamed RED 2, was allotted to Lieutenant-Colonel Joseph Crawford's 2nd Battalion 16th RCT while the final right-hand GREEN 2 Beach was assigned to Lieutenant-Colonel Charles L. Denholm and the 1st Battalion, 16th RCT. The 16th RCT was tasked to advance north-east onto the Piano Lupo high ground held by elements of the 505th Parachute RCT, before moving through Priolo and on to Niscemi, ten miles inland, to link up with other elements of the 505th Parachute RCT holding high ground and road junctions in the vicinity of the town. The 16th and 26th RCTs' 3rd Battalions were to come ashore in the second wave while the US 1st Division's third constituent formation, Colonel George A. Smith's 18th RCT, remained aboard the transport USS *Chateau Thierry* as US II Corps' floating reserve, along with the US 2nd Armored Division's Combat Command B aboard the transport USS *Orizaba*.[2]

The task of delivering the reinforced US 1st Infantry Division onto the DIME beaches in a mixed shore-to-shore and ship-to-shore landing was the responsibility of Naval Task Force 81, sometimes referred to as DIME FORCE, commended by Rear-Admiral John L. Hall from the converted Attack Transport USS *Samuel Chase*. Naval Task Force 81 carried the invasion force aboard five Troop Transports, two Attack Cargo ships, an Attack Transport, two British LSIs, HMS *Prince Charles* and HMS *Prince Leopold*, fourteen LSTs and twenty LCIs; the transport echelon was escorted by the cruisers USS *Boise* and USS *Savannah*, destroyers including the USS *Jeffers*, *McLanahan* and *Shubrick*. Admiral Hall's force was also accompanied by the commander of the Western Naval Task Force, Vice-Admiral Henry K. Hewitt aboard his flagship, the converted Attack Transport USS *Monrovia*. Travelling in three columns with the transports in the centre and separate LST and LCI columns on the flanks, DIME FORCE moved in to its loading area using the fires from the preparatory bombing and the bonfires lit on the Piano Lupo heights above Gela by Privates Goodson and Patrick from the 3rd Battalion 505th Parachute RCT as navigation aids, until the destroyer USS *Cole* and Admiral Hall's flagship the *Samuel Chase* made contact with marker vessel HM Submarine *Shakespeare* at 22:15 and 23:08 respectively.[3]

The transports were anchored in the DIME loading area by 00:44, followed by the LCIs and all but three of the LSTs by 01:15 due to the rough seas, with the three missing vessels turning up at the CENT Landing Area later.[4] Despatched as the transports were anchoring, the US Navy Scouts and Raiders party tasked to mark RED and GREEN Beaches before Gela reached their objective ahead of schedule, while FORCE X was unloading the 1st Ranger Battalion aboard thirty LCVPs from the Attack Transport USS *Joseph T. Dickman* and the 4th Ranger Battalion aboard fourteen LCAs from the LSIs *Prince Charles* and *Prince Leopold*; the reserve for the Gela landing, the 1st Battalion 39th Combat Engineer Regiment, was carried in three LCIs along with the carts containing the 83rd Chemical Battalion's 4.2-inch mortars and ammunition and Colonel Darby's HQ element.[5]

While all forty-four assault craft were in the water by 01:25 in spite of the rough seas, the control craft to lead them in were delayed and the Ranger's assault wave did not reach the Line of Departure for the final run in to the Beaches until 02:45. Despite the supporting warships holding their fire at Major-General Allen's request in an effort to maintain the element of surprise, the units from the *18a Brigata Costiera* defending Gela appear to have become aware of the approaching assault craft, given that they demolished the pier in line with standing orders from *6a Armata* HQ during the Rangers' run in. Searchlights had repeatedly skimmed the larger vessels out to sea but when one locked on the assault craft at 03:10 the destroyer *Shubrick* eliminated it with five salvoes of 5-inch gunfire and knocked out a second light a few minutes later with a further three salvoes. Accurate Italian artillery and mortar fire then began to fall among the assault craft despite the *Shubrick* and cruiser *Savannah's* efforts to suppress it, augmented with machine-gun fire when the range closed to around five hundred yards; as the rough seas had calmed somewhat during the run in some Rangers reportedly responded by firing their M1 Bazookas.

The 4th Ranger Battalion's LCAs touched down first on the right-hand GREEN Beach at some point between 03:15 and 03:35, around an hour behind schedule, in the face of a fully alerted and functioning defence; most if not all the LCAs appear to have managed to winch themselves back off the beach, although some may have been broached by the three-foot surf.[6] Company F were immediately pinned down by withering cross-fire that killed and wounded the equivalent of a platoon and while the adjacent Company D was spared the gunfire an attempted rush revealed the beach was also sown with mines that killed the lead platoon commander Lieutenant Walter Wojak and four of his men and wounded several more; fortunately for the attackers, the Gela beaches were only thinly sown with mines because the civilian labour recruited to lay them refused to complete the task after two of their number were killed during the work.

Despite being wounded, Sergeant Randall Harris, accompanied by Corporal Howard Andre, made his way forward to a dyke housing the machine-gun bunkers and knocked out two with hand-grenades, opening the way for the rest of Company D, which then temporarily abandoned its mission of pushing into Gela in favour of dealing with the remaining beach defences firing on the hapless Company F, possibly assisted by men from the 39th Combat Engineer Regiment; the defences were manned by *Capitano* Domenico Mascherpa's *112° Battaglione di Mitragliatrici* (Machine-gun Battalion). With the beach defences cleared, both Ranger Companies then pressed on for their objectives in Gela, with Company F heading for the town's main square.[7]

On the adjacent RED Beach, two LCVPs carrying the 1st Ranger Battalion were hit by mortar fire on the run in that caused heavy casualties, and again some of the LCVPs may have been broached by the surf. Events on landing followed a similar pattern as the Rangers negotiated the mines and barbed wire and penetrated the beachfront defences before taking the fight to the elements of *Maggiore* Arnaldo Rabellino's *429° Battaglione Costiero* deployed in Gela itself. The fighting was house-to-house with that around the main church square, where the local *Carabinieri* had occupied the Hotel Trinacria and were dug into the nearby public gardens, being especially intense, but the defenders were overcome by around 06:00 and within two hours all remaining resistance had been eliminated leaving Gela in US hands. The four-hour battle for the town cost the *429° Battaglione Costiero* 197 dead and wounded, almost half of its strength, with another 200 taken prisoner, including *Maggiore* Rabellino, who surrendered at around 09:00. The 4th Ranger Battalion immediately moved on to establish a defensive perimeter around the north and east of the town while to the west the 1st Ranger Battalion's Companies A and B under Captain James B. Lyle organised a position blocking the *Strada* 115. Three 77mm field guns were overrun with a large stock of ammunition at the Capo Soprano on the western edge of the town plateau. The Italian gunners had removed the sights and elevation mechanisms before abandoning the pieces, but after ascertaining they could be fired Captain Lyle had them moved out to his position and manned by scratch crews of Rangers; the Rangers also took over a nearby two-storey building for use as an artillery observation post.[8]

Back at the waterline *LCI-188*, one of the three landing craft carrying the follow-up wave, grounded on a sandbar off GREEN Beach but later floated free. One of the other LCIs had great difficulty in offloading two dozen carts loaded with 4.2-inch mortars; the process took nearly four hours under machine-gun and artillery fire that killed and wounded a number of the vessel's crew. Nonetheless, by 08:00 mortars had been landed and set up ready to fire in support of the Ranger perimeter around Gela.[9]

The main US 1st Infantry Division was landing on the beaches a mile or so to the east on the other side of the River Gela. The initial assault wave from the 1st and 2nd Battalions, 26th Infantry Regiment, travelling aboard LCVPs from the Attack Transport *Barnett* and Transport *Lyon* respectively, left the loading area at 02:15 and landed accurately on YELLOW and BLUE Beaches on time thirty minutes later, in spite of the rough seas and again aided by the illumination from the preparatory bombing and the 505th Parachute RCT's two bonfires.[10] There was no opposition until the invaders began to receive scattered small-arms and machine-gun fire twenty minutes after landing, while the remaining three LCVP assault waves were still coming in; all were ashore by 03:30.[11] The fire did cause some problems. The thirty-six men from the 1st Battalion aboard Seaman 2nd Class Thomas B. McMonagle's LCVP refused to debark onto YELLOW Beach into enemy machine-gun fire, obliging him to winch his craft back off the beach and silence the Italian gun with the craft's .30 guns before landing again, at which the passengers disembarked; Seaman McMonagle was seriously wounded in the process and passed out from blood loss en route back to the USS *Barnett*. He was subsequently awarded the Silver Star for his actions.[12]

Italian fire, and particularly mortar and artillery fire, increased on YELLOW and BLUE Beaches as visibility improved from around 04:00, and matters were further complicated by the sea and the terrain. The three-foot surf again broached some LCVPs and while some of the LCIs delivering the 3rd Battalion as the follow-up wave from 03:30 beached and retracted successfully, some became grounded on sand bars and had to offload their passengers via LCVPs and rubber boats. When DUKWs from a battalion launched from LSTs offshore reached the beach it was discovered that it was heavily sown with anti-vehicle mines that destroyed or disabled a number of the amphibious vehicles, along with bulldozers and trucks offloaded from other LSTs directly onto the beach; the disruption was so serious that at 09:19 it was decided to divert traffic from YELLOW and BLUE Beaches onto RED 2 Beach until the mines were cleared; both beaches were declared clear and open to vehicles three hours later at 12:12.[13] Nonetheless, by 09:00 Major Grant's 1st Battalion was on the move toward Gela and the 2nd and 3rd Battalions were across the *Strada* 115 and moving north to secure the Gela-Farello airfield and link up with the elements of the 505th Parachute RCT expected to be blocking access to Gela from the north along the *Strada* 117.[14]

Events at the adjacent RED 2 and GREEN 2 Beaches were more frantic. The assault waves carrying the 2nd Battalion 16th RCT to RED 2 from the Troop Transport USS *Thurston* and the 1st Battalion 16th RCT to GREEN 2 from the Transport USS *Elizabeth C. Stanton* made landfall at 02:47, just two minutes behind schedule. While the LCVPs had been illuminated during the run in by Italian searchlights, the defences held back until the craft hit the beach before opening fire briefly with machine-guns and small arms on the first assault wave; the positions then fell silent to be bypassed before opening more effective fire against the second assault wave, and repeated the tactic against the third and fourth assault waves as they came ashore after 03:00.

The Italian fire was augmented with mortar and artillery fire as visibility improved at around 04:00, at which point Admiral Hall ordered Naval Task Force 81's support vessels to commence their pre-planned fire support programmes; the destroyer *Jeffers* and cruiser *Boise* also bombarded targets of opportunity at RED 2 and GREEN 2 Beaches, destroying a beachfront bunker firing on the invaders and targeting Italian artillery positions on the high ground inland from the coastline.

While the naval gunfire diminished the incoming fire, it did not silence it altogether and on occasion the Italian fire was sufficiently heavy to again interfere with offloading over RED 2 Beach; at 09:40 Admiral Hall ordered the *Boise* and *Savannah* to move in to 3,000 yards from the beach to silence a particularly troublesome enemy battery, fire from which obliged the closing of RED 2 to incoming traffic for twenty minutes at 10:10, for example.[15] In addition to enemy action, the 16th RCT landing suffered the same tidal challenges, with some LCVPs becoming broached in the surf and some LCIs also grounding on sandbars and unloading via LCVPs and rubber boats. The initial phase of the DIME landing was complete with the arrival of the final six LCIs at GREEN 2 at 04:30 just as it began to grow light. Five unloaded and retracted successfully but *LCI-220* grounded briefly on a sandbar and did not reach the beach until 05:00, where a near miss from an Italian artillery round sprang a hull plate, damaged the port propeller and cut away the craft's kedge anchor, its loss preventing the LCI retraction and she ended up stranded sideways on the beach. Mindful of orders from DIME FORCE LCI flotilla commander Captain John H. Leppert that any beached vessel was '...still a fighting unit as long as it has guns and is above the surface of the water', the crew remained aboard employing the vessel's four Oerlikon 20mm guns until *LCI-220* was refloated in the afternoon of D-Day Plus One with the help of bulldozers and tugs. The minesweepers attached to DIME FORCE began clearing the closer approaches to the beaches beginning at 06:00, which permitted the LSTs to access to the beach and the larger transports and cargo vessels to anchor closer inshore for unloading between 08:30 and 10:00.[16]

In the meantime the 16th RCT was ashore in its entirety and Colonel Taylor elected to keep one battalion in reserve at the beachhead while despatching the other two battalions north onto the Piano Lupo high ground to link up with the 505th Parachute RCT. En route they found Captain Willard Follmer and Company I dug in holding their road junction objective at around 08:45; Company I was the only one of the 3rd Battalion's units delivered onto its designated DZ in a compact group apart from a single misdropped stick, although Captain Follmer had broken his right leg in a hard landing. There was no larger Airborne force on the Piano Lupo high ground where the 16th RCT expected to find them because the paratroopers were scattered far and wide across south-east Sicily, with just two coherent exceptions on the 16th RCT front. These were a party of around twenty-four men from the 3rd Battalion 504th Parachute Infantry Regiment near the Objective X junction on the *Strada Provinciale* 11 just south of Niscemi, led by

Battalion commander Lieutenant-Colonel Charles W. Kouns, and a party of around seventy-five from the 1st Battalion 505th Parachute RCT commanded by Lieutenant-Colonel Arthur F. Gorham and Captain Edwin M. Sayre occupying the Casa del Priolo strongpoint just over a mile north of Objective Y, the junction of the *Strada Provinciale* 11 and coastal *Strada* 115. Although Major-General Allen had no way of knowing at this point that the high ground overlooking the DIME Landing Area and – more importantly, the most direct route to Gela and the DIME Beaches from the Sicilian interior – had not been secured as the HUSKY plan had envisaged. The consequences of that omission were about to become starkly apparent.[17]

At *6ª Armata* HQ at Enna *Generale* Guzzoni, already convinced that Sicily was the Allies' target, had received a steady stream of reports of the armada closing on the island through Friday 9 July, his belief backed up by widespread Allied preparatory bombing. As a result, he ordered a preliminary alert at 19:00, put all Axis forces on Sicily onto full alert at around 22:00 and finally declared a State of Emergency at 01:00 on Saturday 10 July, triggering the firing of demolition charges to create harbour obstacles at Licata and Porto Empedocle.[18] As reports clarified that the Allies had landed in the Bay of Gela as he had predicted, Guzzoni quickly moved to assist *Generale Di Brigata* Orazio Mariscalco's *18ª Brigata Costiera* in weathering the Allied assault, by reinforcing *Generale di Corpo d'Armata* Carlo Rossi's *16° Corpo* to permit a rapid counter-strike. The reinforcement included two *Gruppi Mobili* earmarked for the defence of the airfields at Biscari and Ponte Olivo, the most significant of which was *Gruppo Mobili E* located near Niscemi, which included approximately thirty-two ex-French Renault R35 tanks, a motorised infantry *compagnia*, a motorised anti-tank *compagnia* armed with 47mm guns, a motorcycle *compagnia*, a battery of 75mm howitzers and a section of 20mm anti-aircraft guns attached from the *26ª Assietta Divisione*; this force may have been augmented with between nine and sixteen Fiat 3000 light tanks, a licence-built copy of the two-man Renault FT, from *Gruppo Mobili H*.[19]

The other two formations assigned to *16° Corpo* were of a larger scale. *Generale di Divisione* Domenico Chirieleison's *4ª Livorno Divisione*, serving as *6ª Armata* reserve at Caltanissetta, was widely acknowledged as the best and most powerful Italian formation in Sicily. The *Livorno Divisione* included two motorised infantry regiments, the *33°* and *34° Reggimento di Fanteria*, the twelve-battery strong *28° Reggimento di Artiglieria*, an anti-tank *battaglioni* equipped with 47mm guns, an 81mm mortar *battaglioni*, an engineer *battaglioni* and three 20mm light anti-aircraft batteries.[20] The other formation was *Luftwaffe Generalmajor* Paul Conrath's *Hermann Göring (HG) Panzer Division*, apart from *Kampfgruppe* Schmalz, which was detached to face the British landings near Syracuse. Concentrated in the area of Caltagirone, the *HG Panzer Division* was the most powerful Axis formation on Sicily and included a two-*bataillon Panzer Regiment* equipped with forty-six *Panzer III* and thirty-two *Panzer IV* tanks, *Panzer Abteilung 215* equipped with seventeen Tiger I heavy tanks, a *panzergrenadier* regiment on attachment from *15 Panzergrenadier Division*, artillery and anti-aircraft regiments, an armoured reconnaissance *bataillon* and a pioneer *bataillon*.[21] Finally, Guzzoni overcame his concern at a possible Allied landing in the west of Sicily and ordered *Generalleutnant* Eberhard Rodt's *15 Panzergrenadier Division* to reverse its recent move to the western end of the island and concentrate in the area of Canicatti-Caltanissetta-San Cataldo in the middle of the island, for deployment as and where required.[22]

Generale Guzzoni's plan was for *16° Corpo* to launch a co-ordinated, concentric assault on Gela with the *Livorno Divisione* moving in from the north-west while *Gruppo Mobili E* and the *HG Panzer Division* moved in from the north and north-east. However, while *Gruppo Mobili E* at Niscemi was well placed to carry out Guzzoni's plan, this was not the case with the other two formations; the *HG Panzer Division* was concentrated around Caltagirone, twenty road miles or more from its attack concentration area at Niscemi, and the *Livorno Divisione* at Caltanissetta was around thirty miles from its concentration area near Butera. More importantly co-ordination was hamstrung, notably by communication problems as the already unreliable telephone system virtually collapsed under the impact of targeted Allied bombing and the wire-cutting and other activities of the scattered US paratroopers roaming the Axis rear areas. Reconnaissance parties scouting the *HG Panzer Division* assembly area near Niscemi reported clashes with paratroopers for example, while *Generalmajor* Conrath actually learned of the Allied invasion via radio from *Oberbefehlshaber Süd* (*OB Süd*) in Rome, being unable to contact *16° Corpo* and *6ª Armata* HQs even though they were only twelve and twenty-five miles respectively from his Caltagirone HQ; he was also initially unaware of Guzzoni's plan for a co-ordinated attack, or that his formation had been placed under the operational control of *16° Corpo*.[23]

The overall result was that the 'broad fronted, massive, co-ordinated push visualized against the Gela beaches [by *Generale* Guzzoni] would turn out to be a series of un-co-ordinated independent thrusts by Axis units at varying times and various places along the center of the American front'.[24] In the immediate term, despite Conrath putting his units on alert at 22:00 on 9 July and unilaterally ordering the move to the Niscemi assembly area in readiness to attack toward Gela six hours later, the German counter-attack did not go in until the afternoon of 10 July; the initial piecemeal Axis counter-attacks were carried out by *Gruppo Mobili E* and a *battaglione* from the *33° Reggimento di Fanteria* from the *Livorno Divisione*.

At Niscemi, communication problems also left *Gruppo Mobili E* in the dark regarding *Generale* Guzzoni and *16° Corpo* intentions, but the commander appears to have unilaterally decided to implement pre-existing anti-invasion measures. The *Gruppo* was thus divided into two columns before moving from Niscemi, with one then moving west for the *Strada* 117 to approach Gela from the north while the other, made up of approximately twenty R35 tanks and a number of other vehicles, headed southward down the *Strada Provinciale* 11. This brought the column into contact with Lieutenant-Colonel

Gorham's seventy-five-strong party from the 1st Battalion, 505th Parachute Infantry Regiment occupying the Casa del Priolo strongpoint at around 07:00. With admirable discipline the paratroopers waited until a small Italian scouting party mounted on motorcycles and one or more Fiat 508 field cars were within the strongpoint perimeter before opening fire, killing several men and taking the rest prisoner. When the Italian column despatched a reported two companies on foot to investigate thirty minutes later the paratroopers again held their fire until the Italians were within two hundred yards before unleashing a withering fire, making good use of the twenty machine-guns captured at the strongpoint; the Italians then deployed a self-propelled gun that systematically pounded the strongpoint from outside the range of the paratrooper's weapons. At this point a patrol despatched earlier by Captain Sayre returned to report that Objective Y, the 1st Battalion's designated target, was located a mile and a half to the south defended by around twenty Italian troops manning three defensive bunkers. As the Italian shellfire was rendering the Casa del Priolo strongpoint untenable, Colonel Gorham decided to withdraw to Objective Y, taking advantage of naval gunfire that had fortuitously begun to fall on the stalled Italian column.[25]

The naval gunfire was directed by Lieutenant Cyril G. Lewis USNR flying a Vought OS2U observation floatplane from the cruiser USS *Boise*, who spotted the column moving at 08:26 while dodging enemy fighters that had shot down two spotter aircraft from the USS *Savannah*. He passed the co-ordinates back to the *Boise* at 09:00 with a request for one-turret salvoes, with the first salvo of 6-inch shells landing ten minutes later and continuing for two-minute's rapid fire; the cruiser's commander, Captain Leo H. Thébaud, later commented that had he realised the nature of the target he would have ordered fire from all fifteen main guns rather than three.[26] Lieutenant Lewis, who had served aboard the *Boise* at the Battle of Cape Esperance off Guadalcanal in October 1942, was later awarded the Distinguished Flying Cross for his actions on 10 July 1943.

Lieutenant-Colonel Gorham and his men successfully broke contact to move down the east side of the *Strada Provinciale* 11 apparently moving in two groups with one under Captain Sayre, taking their prisoners and wounded paratroopers with the former carrying the latter; an initial refusal to co-operate by the German prisoners was resolved by a German NCO jabbing one of his recalcitrant colleagues in the buttocks with a bayonet.[27] Six R35 tanks appeared on the paratroopers' left flank moving down a minor road, but before they could close, the tanks themselves came under fire from a small misdropped group from the 1st Battalion 505th Regiment led by Sergeants Timothy Dyas and John Dixon; moving toward the sound of the fight at Casa del Priolo, the group simply stumbled upon the tanks upon cresting a hilltop. Luckily the group included a Bazooka team, which promptly knocked out two R35s and distracted the rest from pursuing the Casa del Priolo party, sparking a two- to three-hour stand-off that ended when another R35 succeeded in moving past its burning colleagues to outflank Sergeant Dyass' group, who were then obliged to surrender.[28]

In the meantime the erstwhile defenders of Casa del Priolo appear to have reached high ground overlooking the Objective Y strongpoint shortly after the main *Gruppo Mobili E* column had passed through the junction, which was under fire from the USS *Jeffers*' 5-inch guns; the destroyer fired nineteen salvoes at the strongpoint directed by Naval forward observers moving with the 16th RCT's lead elements.[29] The column's infantry reportedly sought shelter from the gunfire in the strongpoint while the tanks continued through and turned right onto the *Strada* 115 toward Gela, which brought them into head-on contact with the 16th RCT advancing from the DIME beaches. This stalled the column and after the lead two tanks were knocked out the remainder withdrew north.[30] Back at Junction Y, Captain Sayre, who appears to have been operating independently with his contingent from the 1st Battalion's Company A, noted that the naval gunfire was landing two hundred yards north of the strongpoint as the *Jeffers*' guns lacked sufficiently high trajectory to clear high ground to the south. Although lacking contact with the destroyer, Sayre despatched an Italian prisoner with an ultimatum demanding immediate surrender, or the bombardment would be directed onto the strongpoint.

The bluff worked and at 10:45 on 10 July Objective Y was finally in the hands of the 1st Battalion 505th Regiment as tasked, just in time for Captain Sayre's party to rebuff four enemy tanks that approached from the north, possibly the survivors of the fight with Sergeant Dyas' group.[31] Contact was established with scouts from Lieutenant-Colonel Denholm's 1st Battalion 16th RCT at 11:30, which cleared some outlying Italian positions before digging in around the road junction; Sayre then used the US 1st Infantry Division's communication network to inform Major-General Ridgway aboard the US flagship *Monrovia* of his unit location before rejoining Gorham's group, which had attached itself to Lieutenant-Colonel Crawford's 2nd Battalion, 16th RCT on the high ground just north-west of Objective Y. Captain Edwin M. Sayre was subsequently awarded the Distinguished Service Cross for his actions on 10 July.[32]

At Gela, Colonel Darby's FORCE X found itself assailed by two separate Italian attacks, firstly by the second column from *Gruppo Mobili E.* Also consisting of approximately thirteen R35 tanks and ten other vehicles, the column made it onto the *Strada* 117 before being spotted by a Naval forward observer party at 08:30 as it traversed the open wheat fields north of Gela. The observers called down fire from the destroyer USS *Shubrick*, which hit and set ablaze perhaps three R35s, temporarily stalled the column and drove the accompanying infantry to seek cover. This left the tanks bereft of infantry support when they resumed the advance, with four being observed pausing in a roadside olive grove just under three miles short of Gela by the 1st Ranger Battalion artillery observation post, which called in fire from the 83rd Chemical Battalion's 4.2-inch mortars. After some discussion and improvisation of augmentation charges, one tank was hit and began to burn, prompting the remainder to withdraw deeper into the grove; when they reappeared a few minutes later Captain Lyle engaged them with the three captured Italian 77mm field guns as the mortars were running short of ammunition using improvised ranging. The resultant near misses persuaded the tanks to withdraw altogether.[33]

The other seven R35s had pushed on to enter the northern outskirts of Gela at around 10:30, where they were confronted by the extremely aggressive 4th Ranger Battalion assisted by members of the 39th Combat Engineer Regiment's Company B. Lacking anti-tank guns the Rangers nevertheless immediately embarked on a deadly game of hide-and-seek as the R35s pushed in toward Gela's central piazza, firing small-arms and Bazookas from alleyways and dropping hand-grenades from the flat rooftops; Colonel Darby contributed by firing on the tanks with the .30 machine-gun mounted on his personal Jeep while his driver Sergeant Carlo Contrera skidded and dodged through the narrow streets.

Realising heavier weapons were required, Darby directed Contrera to Gela harbour where they commandeered a recently landed M3 37mm anti-tank gun and a box of armour-piercing ammunition before racing back to the action. There they were assisted in unlimbering the gun by Captain Charles Shunstrom, commander of the 1st Ranger Battalion's Company C, just as an R35 nosed around a nearby corner. The tank fired first but both rounds missed while Captain Shunstrom put a round into the vehicle's turret and another into the hull in quick succession, knocking the tank back bodily several feet; abandoning his loader duties Colonel Darby finished the encounter by igniting an M14 thermite grenade on a hatch, the heat of which swiftly induced the crew to abandon the vehicle and surrender. Another R35 was stalked by a group from the 39th Combat Engineers led by Lieutenant Dee Baker which used a combination of rifle grenades and Bazooka rockets to blow off a track and/or running gear before continuing until the immobilised vehicle was destroyed, and a third tank was knocked out by the same method or possibly utilising a pole charge designed for wall breaching.[34] The battle lasted for around twenty minutes, after which the surviving tanks withdrew from Gela back up the *Strada* 117. The third Italian piecemeal attack against Gela came from the north-west and involved elements of the *Livorno Divisione*. Although *Generale* Guzzoni had intended the bulk of *Generale* Chirieleison's formation to be involved in the attack to retake the port on 10 July, for reasons that are unclear the twenty-three mile move south from Caltanissetta to the attack concentration area near Butera was somewhat tardy; *Tenente Colonnello* Dante Leonardi's *3° Battaglione* from the *34° Reggimento di Fanteria* did not receive the two-hour warning order to move until 17:00, for example.[35] As a result only the *3° Battaglione* from *Colonnello* Mario Mona's *33° Reggimento di Fanteria* appears to have reached the attack concentration area near Butera Station in the morning of 10 July, and attacked down the line of the *Strada Provinciale* 8 directly toward the blocking position held by Captain Lyle and the 1st Ranger Battalion's Companies A and B.

The *Livorno Divisione* may have been the best Italian formation on Sicily but it lacked combat experience and the attack was carried out in 'formal, parade ground formation' against which the two Ranger Companies wrought havoc, first with the provisional Ranger Artillery Battery's three captured 77mm pieces and then with 60mm mortars, machine-guns and small-arms as the range closed; a party of around 200 Italians who sought shelter in a farmhouse north of the blocking position were shelled into a disorderly retreat and the misguidedly courageous attack faded away in the face of the Rangers' concentrated fire without coming close to the US positions.[36]

Generalmajor Conrath was struggling to launch the *HG Panzer Division* counter-attack, which he initially intended to commence at 09:00. Conrath envisaged a pincer movement against Gela with the right pincer moving down the *Strada Provinciale* 11 from Niscemi and the left along the east bank of the River Acate from Biscari to the *Strada* 115 before crossing the Ponte Dirillo to move on the Objective Y junction and thence Gela. The Biscari attack was assigned to an infantry-heavy *kampfgruppe* made up of two infantry *bataillonen* likely from *HG Panzergrenadier Regiment 1*, elements of the *HG Panzer Artillerie Regiment* and seventeen Tiger I tanks from *Panzer Abteilung 215*, while the Niscemi attack was assigned to a tank-heavy *kampfgruppe* made up of *Panzer Regiment HG* with forty-six *Panzer III* and thirty-two *Panzer IV* tanks, most of the Division's engineer and reconnaissance *bataillonen* acting in the infantry role, supported by elements of the *HG Panzer Artillerie Regiment*. Both *kampfgruppen* were on the move from Caltagirone along three secondary roads toward their assembly areas near Biscari and Niscemi by 04:00, but the twenty-mile journey took much longer than anticipated due to the poor roads, persistent Allied air attacks, inadequate junior leadership, general troop inexperience and interference from random groups of US paratroopers.[37] As we have seen, one *HG* scouting party was captured by Lieutenant-Colonel Gorham's party at the Casa del Priolo strongpoint for example, while Lieutenant-Colonel Kouns' group from the 504th Regiment ambushed a convoy of trucks carrying *HG* troops near Objective X south of Niscemi, destroying a field car and its occupants with a Bazooka and halting the convoy before withdrawing.[38] Allied naval gunfire as far north as Niscemi also became a factor as the German columns came closer to the battle area. The monitor HMS *Abercrombie* was transferred to the DIME Landing Area at 11:40 tasked to bombard Niscemi; her commander, Captain George Faulkner, induced a list by adjusting his vessel's ballast to gain more elevation so the monitor's 15-inch guns could hit the eight-mile distant town.[39]

The *HG Panzer Division* attack finally went in at 14:00 with the Biscari *kampfgruppe* being fought to a standstill not far from its start line within ninety minutes; a resumed effort under a replacement *kampfgruppe* commander enjoyed more success, overrunning a battalion from the US 180th RCT and pushing to within four miles of the CENT Beaches before being turned back by a hastily formed emergency defence line along the *Strada* 115. The Niscemi *HG kampfgruppe* fared equally badly. Patrols from Colonel Crawford's 2nd Battalion 16th RCT and Lieutenant-Colonel Gorham's attached contingent from the 505th Parachute RCT spotted the German advance moving down the *Strada Provinciale* 11 near the Casa del

Priolo strongpoint and called down naval gunfire along the road, but the *kampfgruppe* continued to just short of the Objective Y junction, where it deployed scouts and the engineers acting in the infantry role to secure the high ground to the right overlooking the junction. This was occupied by Crawford and Gorham's men, who responded by inflicting heavy casualties on them; the fight also drew in Lieutenant-Colonel Denholm's 1st Battalion dug in around the Objective Y junction. The situation was saved by a deluge of naval gunfire that erected a barrier across the highway north of the US positions through which the German tanks were unwilling to pass, even though they were largely immune to anything less than a direct hit; their hesitance was fortuitous as the 16th RCT lacked anti-tank weapons, with the 2nd Battalion reportedly possessing only a single anti-tank gun, a 57mm M1 according to one source.[40]

The attack stalled and an attempt to restart it by Conrath in person at 15:00 failed to have the desired effect. Unable to make progress against the US infantry and in the face of the naval gunfire and concerned about the non-appearance of the Biscari attackers on the left flank, the attack stalled again at 17:00 and Conrath ordered a dusk withdrawal back toward Niscemi at around 18:45.[41] The withdrawal may have been covered by Axis air attacks, given that US 1st Infantry Division HQ reported being subjected to two hours of continuous dive bombing at 19:30.[42]

Bombing or not, the US DIME front moved rapidly to take advantage of the Axis withdrawals. As soon as it was fully dark Captain Sayre led an eight-strong patrol of paratroopers back to Casa del Priolo in search of a 2nd Lieutenant who had gone missing in the earlier fight and withdrawal from the strongpoint. After finding the officer's body the patrol was literally fallen upon by a ten-man German patrol while resting in a sunken stream bed; in the resultant hand-to-hand struggle the paratroopers killed one, captured three and drove the remainder off before returning unharmed with their prisoners.[43] At midnight, the US 1st Infantry Division's two RCTs began a deliberate two-pronged advance northward; presumably worried by how close the Axis counter-attacks had penetrated, Major-General Allen was seeking to establish a buffer zone to protect the increasingly congested DIME beaches, although it is unclear if the idea originated with Allen or at US II Corps or 7th Army level. On the right the 16th RCT was to secure the Casa del Priolo strongpoint as a preliminary for seizing Niscemi, with Lieutenant-Colonel Denholm's 1st Battalion moving up the *Strada Provinciale* 11 while the 2nd Battalion took over the junction apart from Company G, which was despatched to cover the left flank of the advance. However, while the 1st Battalion reached the junction without incident, Company G unilaterally withdrew back to the main 2nd Battalion position after spotting six German tanks to their north-west; concerned at leaving Denholm with an open flank, Lieutenant-Colonel Crawford ordered his Companies E and F and the 505th Regiment contingent forward to occupy an orchard ridge at Abbio Priolo, a thousand yards north-west of the Casa del Priolo strongpoint, which was reached by 05:30.

On the left, Colonel Bowen's 26th RCT, which had moved across to Gela during the day and early evening, was tasked to move on the Ponte Olivo airfield located just over five miles north-east of Gela. The initial phase involved Lieutenant-Colonel John T. Corley's 3rd Battalion advancing up the *Strada 117* to secure the Monte della Guardia, also known as Hill 300, as a covering position but the advance stalled after thirty minutes when the advance came under heavy enemy fire from the front and flanks; the 3rd Battalion dug in on high ground straddling the road and Lieutenant-Colonel Daniel's 2nd Battalion did the same a mile or so to the south between the highway and the River Gela. Both locations were to play a key role in events in the morning of 11 July.[44]

A pre-emptive advance to create a buffer zone was surely a wise move, given that the absence of the 505th Parachute RCT on the Piano Lupo high ground left the US 1st Infantry Division without an immediate reserve, and that a combination of Axis artillery fire, bombing, lack of manpower, beach access and mine clearing problems had seriously delayed landing the remainder of the 1st Division and reinforcement units; YELLOW and BLUE Beaches were closed to traffic due to mines at 09:19, reopened three hours later only to be closed again at 18:15, for example.[45] As RED 2 and GREEN 2 Beaches were generally unsuitable for LSTs to unload directly owing to offshore sandbars and beach sand too soft for vehicles to traverse unaided, the vessels had to unload vehicles via pontoon causeways. As it had been planned to utilise the demolished Gela pier, only two causeways were provided. One went astray to Scoglitti aboard *LST-337,* but *LST-338* began erecting her causeway onto RED 2 Beach at 08:03 and within ninety minutes had offloaded her 300 troops and sixty three vehicles despite skip-bombing attacks by three Messerschmitt fighter-bombers, giving way to *LST-344* at 10:30. Attempts to erect a second causeway at GREEN 2 Beach in the late afternoon were thwarted at 18:35 when another fighter-bomber scored a direct hit on *LST-313*, which was fully-loaded with the 26th RCT's entire complement of anti-tank guns, fully fuelled and combat loaded Jeeps, trucks, half-tracks and a large stock of 37mm ammunition and land mines. The resultant explosion turned the vessel into a blazing hulk, demolished the partially completed causeway under construction by the adjacent *LST-311* and the fire and secondary explosions rendered much of the beach and cached causeway sections unapproachable. Around twenty troops and one member of the crew died in the explosion. The death toll would have been higher without the actions of *LST-311's* commander, Lieutenant Robert L. Coleman, who swung his bow ramp round into contact with the stricken vessel's stern, allowing eighty men trapped on the fantail to escape. By nightfall on 10 July, only three LSTs had been fully unloaded at the eastern pair of DIME beaches and another, the fully loaded *LST-312*, was broached sideways on the beach, possibly as a result of the explosion that gutted *LST-313*; she was refloated by tugs around midnight.[46]

Aboard the USS *Monrovia* the morning's armoured counter-attacks by *Gruppo Mobili E* were of particular concern to Lieutenant-General Patton.

By midday most of the 1st Infantry Division's anti-tank guns were still aboard ship and none of the M4 Medium tanks from the attached elements of the 67th Armored Regiment had been unloaded at all.[47] At 14:00 he therefore ordered Major-General Hugh J. Gaffey, commander of his Floating Reserve the 2nd Armored Division, to land his formation on YELLOW and BLUE Beaches forthwith.[48] Sometimes referred to as KOOL FORCE, the 2nd Armored Division consisted of two sub-formations: Colonel Isaac D. White's Combat Command B made up of the 3rd Battalion 67th Armored Regiment, 1st Battalion 41st Armored Infantry Regiment, elements of the 82nd Armoured Reconnaissance Battalion, an engineer battalion and two field artillery battalions, and Colonel George A. Smith's 18th RCT attached from the US 1st Infantry Division in lieu of Combat Command A, which had been detached to the US 3rd Infantry Division at the JOSS Landing Area. Most of Combat Command B was aboard the transport USS *Orizaba* and most of the 18th RCT was aboard the transport USS *Chateau Thierry*, the remainder spread across eleven assorted landing vessels. Gaffey immediately despatched his chief-of-staff Colonel Redding L. Perry from the *Orizaba* to assess the situation ashore and on discussing matters with Major-General Allen and Assistant Division Commander Brigadier-General Theodore Roosevelt, he returned to advise switching the landing to RED 2 Beach owing to the original choices being mined.[49]

Major-General Gaffey approved the switch to RED 2 Beach but amending already issued orders generated delay and Combat Command B's command element did not land until 17:00, moving to an assembly area near the Gela-Farello airfield recently vacated by the 26th RCT. An hour later the first wave of the 18th RCT began landing, wading ashore from their LCIs because no LCVPs for ferrying had been made available, despite the Beachmaster's expectations based on the beach's unsuitability for direct unloading; according to the US Navy Official account the oversight was due to 'the sending of the [landing] order by roundabout Army channels rather than from ship to ship', while the Army account refers to delays due to the LCIs remaining in sailing rather than landing formation.[50]

Whatever the reason, three men were drowned and a quantity of equipment lost in the high surf, but the first wave was ashore by 21:30 and by around midnight the entire RCT was in an orchard assembly area at the Gela-Farello airfield site. They were joined there by the dismounted 1st Battalion 41st Armored Infantry Regiment, but landing two platoons of M4 tanks from the 67th Armored Regiment at 02:00 on Sunday 11 July ended with all ten vehicles bogged down in soft sand and then immobilised when attempts to move them using pierced steel matting ended up with the metal entangled in their tracks and running gear; further attempts to land tanks during the early hours were frustrated by a combination of the high surf and congestion on the beach. Landing the US 7th Army Floating Reserve thus did nothing in the immediate to short term to allay Generals Patton and Allen's concern about the lack of armour in the DIME Landing Area; in practical terms, it merely added four infantry battalions without heavy weapons or transport to the 1st Infantry Division and in the process increased the congestion on RED 2 Beach.[51]

On withdrawing to Niscemi, *Generalleutnant* Conrath was summoned sixteen miles north to *16° Corpo* HQ at Piazza Armerina, where he learned his formation had been subordinate to *16° Corpo* for twenty-four hours. He was also informed that *6ª Armata* HQ had again ordered the *HG Panzer Division* and the *Livorno Divisione* to launch a co-ordinated attack on Gela, to commence at 06:00 on 11 July using *Strada* 117 as a boundary, with each formation despatching columns along three separate lines of attack. *Generale* Guzzoni's initial attack order, issued at 20:00 on 10 July and confirmed in the early hours of the following morning, instructed the *HG Panzer Division* to wipe out the landing at Gela before wheeling west to assist the *207ª Divisioni Costiere* in eliminating the landing at Licata. On being informed at 03:00 on 11 July of the British capture of Syracuse, Guzzoni decided to shift focus and issued *16° Corpo* with amended orders that tasked the *HG Panzer Division* to break into the US perimeter at Gela before wheeling east and leaving the *Livorno Divisione* to complete the job; the German formation was then to advance on the British 8th Army landing along the line of Vittoria-Comiso-Palazzolo Acreide, eliminating the Scoglitti landing in the process.

On arriving back at his command post at Niscemi to make his preparations Conrath found an additional attack order, transmitted via the *Luftwaffe* communication network, awaiting him. Having decided, perhaps not unreasonably, that only German units were capable of stemming the Allied invasion *Generalfeldmarschall* Kesselring at *OB Süd* had also ordered the *HG Panzer Division* to attack Gela in the morning of 11 July; in the event the instruction did not interfere with Conrath's preparations to carry out his existing orders from *6ª Armata*.

The *Livorno Divisione* attack west of *Strada 117* was an enlarged repeat of the previous day's effort with the *3° Battaglione, 34° Reggimento di Fanteria* moving down the *Strada 117* on the left flank and the *2° Battaglione, 33° Reggimento di Fanteria* on the right moving down the railway line from Butera Station; the expansion was a third thrust down the *Strada Provinciale 8* from Butera by the *1° Battaglioni* from the *33°* and *34° Reggimenti di Fanteria*. Once again, communications problems, aggravated by a lack of radio equipment and the terrain, undermined attempts at synchronisation; as a result, what was supposed to be a single, concentrated strike was again reduced to a series of unco-ordinated piecemeal attacks. The first to jump-off was the renewed advance down the *Strada* 117, which encountered problems from the outset. *Tenente-Colonnello* Leonardi's *3° Battaglione, 34° Reggimento di Fanteria* was strafed by Allied aircraft at the start of the thirty-mile journey from Caltanissetta to the attack assembly area at Ponte Olivo airfield, which killed two, wounded twenty and damaged five vehicles, and they received only the sketchiest of written orders from *Reggimento* commander *Colonnello* Carlo Martini en route; a slightly more detailed explanation of the overall *16° Corpo* plan was delivered by a junior officer from *Livorno Divisione* HQ on the start line.

The 06:00 start time was delayed for thirty minutes as the artillery unit in support was late arriving, which obliged the attack to begin without artillery preparation; according to one source the *3° Battaglione* started on its own initiative after seeing a *kampfgruppe* from the *HG Panzer Division* advance south from Ponte Olivo at 06:15.[52] The Italians immediately came under intense machine-gun and mortar fire from the 3rd Battalion, 26th RCT position straddling the *Strada* 117 and US artillery fire but pushed on and partly overran the 3rd Battalion's Company K at around 08:00 as the US unit was withdrawing from contact with the *HG kampfgruppe*, capturing equipment and a number of US prisoners. The attack then ran into the 4th Ranger Battalion's outpost line and fire from the 26th RCT's Cannon Company, the 4.2-inch mortars in Gela and the US 5th and 33rd Field Artillery Battalions which had been ferried ashore via DUKW, thus largely avoiding the congestion on and offshore at the eastern DIME beaches. The Italian advance took three hours to cover 500 yards, one company losing all its officers killed or wounded and reduced to just thirty men, another lost two of three platoon commanders killed and the company commander badly wounded, while the third company was similarly badly hit while attempting to dig in. The attack therefore stalled a few hundred yards north of Gela and with no substantial reinforcements forthcoming or indeed available, *Tenente-Colonnello* Leonardi's men withdrew at midnight to their start line. The *3° Battaglione, 34° Reggimento di Fanteria* began the attack with 1,134 men; by the time of the withdrawal, it had been reduced to approximately 400, a loss of almost seventy per cent.[53]

The other two *Livorno Divisione* attacks were similarly handled. In the centre *Generale* Chirieleison delayed for an hour while fruitlessly seeking confirmation that the *HG Panzer Division* had launched its attacks east of the *Strada* 117 boundary line before launching the two *Battaglioni* from Butera toward the 1st Ranger Battalion blocking position north-west of Gela. The result was a bloodier rerun of the previous day's rebuff. The Rangers spotted the advance down the line *Strada Provinciale* 8 at around 09:00 and on reporting it to Colonel Darby at FORCE X HQ, Captain Lyle was informed that his 120-strong party would have to '…fight with the troops and supporting weapons you have at this time' as everything else was involved fighting off an armoured attack in the east; Darby nonetheless took the precaution of forming an inner perimeter with the 39th Combat Engineer Regiment contingent and logistic units in Gela.

As soon as the Italian skirmish line moved into range the provisional Ranger Artillery Battery opened fire with its captured 77mm pieces and Captain Lyle called down fire from the 4.2-inch mortars in Gela, which slowed the enemy advance. At that point Patton, who was en route from the *Monrovia* to the US 1st Infantry Division command post via Gela, appeared in the Ranger observation post. After ordering Captain Lyle to buckle his helmet chinstrap, the US 7th Army commander listened to a situation report before departing with the instruction that Lyle should 'kill every one of the Goddamn bastards'. The 4.2-inch mortar ammunition again began to run low but the situation was saved by the arrival of a US Navy forward observer from the USS *Savannah*, who called down fire on the skirmish line and then the main Italian column moving down the road; the cruiser delivered 474 rounds of 6-inch ammunition onto the hapless Italians between 09:17 and 12:31.[54] The effect was devastating and Captain Lyle immediately ordered a counter-attack to take advantage of the confusion created by the bombardment; the Rangers reported that the bombardment had killed or wounded around half the attackers including a large proportion of the officers, and took 400 prisoners.[55] A subsequent reconnaissance patrol by vehicles from the 1st Battalion, 41st Armored Infantry Battalion that reinforced Lyle's little band in the afternoon of 11 July on Patton's specific orders, came upon a packed Italian field hospital and returned with another 450 prisoners in tow.[56]

The third Italian attack by the *2° Battaglione, 33° Reggimento* down the railway line from Butera Station progressed only a short distance before running into a company-strength patrol from the 30th RCT, likely from Lieutenant-Colonel Lyle A. Bernard's 2nd Battalion, which was moving east along the *Strada* 115 to link up with the DIME Landing Area. The US patrol promptly attacked and inflicted heavy casualties on the Italians, who withdrew to their start line; they may have been hurried on by naval gunfire from the cruiser *Savannah*, which reportedly fired 393 rounds at an Italian attack in the vicinity of Butera between 16:21 and 19:28.[57] Whether or not this was the case, by nightfall on 11 July the *Livorno Divisione* had effectively ceased to be a combat-worthy entity.

Events east of the *Strada 117* boundary proceeded in a different manner and the *16° Corpo* requirement for a three-pronged attack obliged *Generalmajor* Conrath to reorganise his force. To the east of the River Acate, the infantry-heavy *kampfgruppe* at Biscari was left intact and with the same orders to cross the river at Ponte Dirillo but then to move to the area of the *Biviere di Gela* lake six miles east of Gela; attempts to secure the left flank of the move over the bridge resulted in the epic, day-long battle at the Biazzo Ridge with Colonel James M. Gavin's 505th Parachute RCT, which enervated the *kampfgruppe* and prevented it from participating in events west of the river. Instead, Conrath opted to divide the force that had attempted to push south from Niscemi into two *kampfgruppen*, each assembled around a *bataillon* from the *Panzer Regiment HG* and with a different overall mission in line with his orders from *16° Corpo/6ª Armata* and *OB Süd*. The *HG Panzer Bataillon 2 kampfgruppe* was tasked to advance down the east side of *Strada* 117 from Ponte Olivo with a group of tanks carrying on along that line toward Gela as a feint, while the remainder of the force angled across the Gela plain to the Objective Y junction with the *Strada* 115. The *HG Panzer Bataillon 1 kampfgruppe* was allotted the *HG Panzer Division* main effort, which involved renewing the assault down the *Strada Provinciale* 11 from Niscemi to capture the Objective Y junction and two hills on the southern edge of the Piano Lupo high ground overlooking the *Strada* 115 as a rendezvous for the western *kampfgruppe*, before moving south to meet up with the Biscari *kampfgruppe* near the *Biviere di Gela* lake; the entire

HG force was then to roll up the Dime Landing Beaches from east to west all the way to the mouth of the River Gela.[58]

The *Bataillon 2 kampfgruppe* moved off from the Ponte Olivo assembly area toward Gela at 06:15 and twenty-five to forty-five minutes later hit Company K holding the eastern end of the 3rd Battalion, 26th RCT's overnight position straddling the *Strada* 117. The remainder of the 3rd Battalion held its position but Company K was driven back south-west across the highway into the path of the *3° Battaglione, 34° Reggimento* and withdrew in some disorder toward Gela.[59] The *kampfgruppe* then angled south-east across the Gela plain unmolested, until naval gunfire began to fall from the USS *Savannah* at 08:29 and again at 09:02, followed by rounds from the cruiser *Boise* beginning at 10:40. The reason for the delay is unclear but may have been due to a combination of the cruisers lacking spotter aircraft – the *Savannah* reported losing its aircraft at 08:20 for example – and dust and smoke obscuring events from US Navy forward observer teams.[60]

To the east, the *Bataillon 2 kampfgruppe* accompanied by *Generalmajor* Conrath resumed the advance down *Strada Provinciale* 11 from Niscemi at 06:15 and ran directly into the 2nd Battalion 16th RCT and Lieutenant-Colonel Gorham's paratroopers; the latter had resumed the advance north from the Abbio Priolo ridge and were reorganising atop a small rise dubbed Hill 41, half a mile from the Casa del Priolo strongpoint, captured from a German patrol an hour or so earlier. A vanguard of six tanks assaulted the hill directly, prompting a number of the 2nd Battalion's inexperienced replacements to break and run according to Captain Sayre, but the remainder and the paratroopers held and engaged the vehicles knocking out two, one by Colonel Gorham with a Bazooka and the other by two 2nd Battalion officers who manned the unit's sole 57mm anti-tank gun after it was abandoned by its crew. The US force lacked the strength to hold up the entire *kampfgruppe* but the delay they caused allowed warning to be passed to US 1st Infantry Division HQ as the German advance bypassed Hill 41 and did the same to the 1st Battalion at the Casa del Priolo strongpoint; this bought a breathing space for Lieutenant-Colonel Crawford to withdraw five hundred yards and reorganise on a less tank-accessible hill, and both Battalions and Lieutenant-Colonel Gorham's paratroopers withdrew to the Objective Y junction, now held by the 16th RCT's 3rd Battalion, under covering fire from US field artillery and naval gunfire, arriving at around 11:00.[61] In bypassing the 16th RCT the *Bataillon 2 kampfgruppe* moved around twenty tanks onto the high ground to the west of the *Strada Provinciale* 11, which brought them into sight of the naval gunfire observers. The destroyer USS *Glennon*, which had been drafted in with the USS *Butler* at 05:30 to replace the *Jeffers* and *Shubrick* as they were almost out of 5-inch ammunition, began firing on the German vehicles at 08:47, followed by the cruiser *Boise* switching fire to hit another group of vehicles spotted moving south from Niscemi at 11:19.[62]

Despite the naval gunfire which knocked out a number of tanks, the *kampfgruppen* converged at around 10:10 in the vicinity of Santa Spina on the high ground overlooking *Strada* 115, only around 2,000 yards from the waterline, although the dunes obscured the beaches and the unloading activity thereon from direct fire; the elated *HG Panzer Division* HQ nonetheless erroneously informed *16° Corpo*, *6ª Armata* and *OB Süd* that its objective had been achieved and that the Allied landing force was re-embarking.[63] However, by this point General Allen had been able to muster a last-ditch defence fronting the beaches, drafting in elements of the 18th RCT and the 41st Armored Infantry Regiment along with every man on the beaches, including personnel from the Army engineer beach parties and the US Navy Advanced Base Group. In addition, the 155mm guns of the 5th Field Artillery Battalion were emplaced just west of the *Biviere di Gela* and 33rd Field Artillery Battalion's 105mm pieces had been offloaded from DUKWs directly into firing positions in the dunes directly behind the beaches, where they were joined by the half-track mounted pieces from the 16th RCT's Cannon Company; all the guns were able to fire on the perimeter over open sights as an emergency anti-tank defence. The defence also included the first five M4 tanks to reach the DIME frontage in a combat-worthy state, which had been cross-loaded from their LST onto *LCT-197* at around 08:45 and then delivered onto BLUE Beach to avoid the congestion on RED 2 and GREEN 2 at around 10:25; the tanks drove straight into battle without pausing to strip off their waterproofing.[64]

The proximity of the belligerents at the dune line meant that naval gunfire support had to be temporarily suspended, although clearer targets were still hit; the destroyer USS *Butler* fired a concentration of almost fifty rounds on a group of *panzers* spotted reorganising on the Gela plain at 13:16 for example.[65] At the dune line, although the *HG Panzers* succeeded in driving the 18th RCT across the *Strada* 115 to the railway line, they were unable to cross themselves to push into the dunes and beach area. After losing fourteen to sixteen *panzers* to fire from the US field guns and M4 tanks in repeated attempts to pierce the US defence over four hours, *Generalmajor* Conrath called off the attack at around 14:00 and ordered both *kampfgruppen* to withdraw to Niscemi. Four more tanks appear to have been knocked out in the final stages of the attack or during the withdrawal by the 16th RCT's 1st and 2nd Battalions and Lieutenant-Colonel Gorham's paratroopers from their hasty perimeter at the Objective Y junction, and the German withdrawal was harassed by naval gunfire as the distance from friendly forces opened and rendered them viable targets again.

The *Boise* continued to fire through the afternoon until 16:11, the destroyer USS *Laub* fired 343 rounds between 15:47 and 17:11 followed by the destroyer USS *Tillman* for an hour after 18:00 and the *Glennon* delivered another 165 rounds in support of the 16th RCT between 20:25 and 20:57. The fire followed Conrath's *panzers* as far north as Ponte Olivo and Niscemi; the *Boise* moved as close inshore as possible to make the range for the latter, with crewmen taking constant depth soundings with chains as the cruiser manoeuvred.[66] *Generalmajor* Conrath's decision to withdraw was independently seconded during the afternoon by *Generale* Guzzoni, who, fearing the US advance from the CENT Landing Area would cut off the *HG Panzer Division*, cancelled the projected wheel to the east and ordered *16° Corpo* to cease offensive operations; Conrath's formation was to withdraw to Caltagirone for redeployment against the British 8th Army advance near Vizzini while the remnants of *Generale* Chirieleison's *Livorno Divisione* was to reorganise along a line from Mazzarino to Caltagirone to cover the *HG* withdrawal. Conrath initially considered continuing with the advance eastward after discussion with the *OB Süd* liaison officer at *6ª Armata* HQ, *Generalleutnant* von Senger und Etterlin but abandoned the idea on learning of the drubbing his eastern *kampfgruppe* had received from Colonel Gavin's 505th Parachute RCT at Biazzo Ridge and ordered the withdrawal to Caltagirone as per Guzzoni's orders.[67]

The *HG Panzer Division's* performance in the effort to retake Gela and drive the DIME landing force into the sea on 10 and 11 July was variable, due largely to the formation's dearth of combat experience; the approach march from Caltagirone was reportedly delayed by poor junior leadership, Conrath replaced the commander of the eastern *kampfgruppe* for lack of application and he issued an order castigating his men for succumbing to '*panzerangst*' (tank fear), abandoning equipment and supplies, spreading alarm via rumours and retreating to the rear at the sound of isolated shots, in some instances crying hysterically.[68] Nonetheless, the *Luftwaffe* formation still displayed considerable application and courage in its first full-scale action as the loss figures show; the battle for Gela cost the *HG Panzer Division* about 630 men killed, wounded and missing along with approximately half the formation's tank strength of around ninety vehicles.[69]

Sunday 11 July tailed off into patrol actions in the vacuum created by the *HG Panzer Division's* retreat, and the night also brought another fiasco for the remainder of Major-General Ridgway's 82nd Airborne Division. As noted earlier, the original HUSKY plan had envisaged delivering the 82nd Airborne Division into Sicily in two increments, HUSKY ONE and HUSKY TWO. HUSKY TWO was a reinforcing landing onto DZs secured by the first drop scheduled for late on D-Day, made up of the 1st and 2nd Battalions of Colonel Reuben H. Tucker's 504th Parachute Infantry Regiment accompanied by the 376th Parachute Field Artillery Battalion and Company C, 307th Airborne Engineer Battalion; Tucker was to take back control of his 3rd Battalion and operate as an independent formation on arrival. In the event the HUSKY TWO force was stood to for the operation at 18:00 on 10 July as scheduled, but it was postponed around thirty minutes later as 'the situation was not deemed favorable'.[70] The postponement was due to Major-General Ridgway who went ashore from the *Monrovia* in search of Colonel Gavin and his men early on 10 July, accompanied by his ADC Captain Don C. Faith Jr. He found no word of the paratroopers at US 1st Infantry Division HQ and on venturing inland found only Captain Willard R. Follmer from the 3rd Battalion 505th Parachute RCT nursing his broken leg at his road junction objective and a few other groups of two or three, none of whom had any information on Gavin or the bigger picture. After fruitlessly attempting to contact Gavin by radio from 1st Division HQ, Ridgway returned to the

Monrovia and persuaded Patton to postpone HUSKY TWO, which the 7th Army commander had intended to have delivered onto the Gela-Farello airfield just north of the *Strada* 115 three miles east of Gela.[71]

The following morning Patton changed his mind, seeing the 504th Parachute RCT as a useful reinforcement and its parachute delivery as a means of circumventing the congestion plaguing the DIME beaches. Despite his continuing misgivings over the lack of contact with Gavin and concern over the possibility of the naval task force firing upon the second lift, at 08:39 on Sunday 11 July Ridgway therefore signalled the 82nd Airborne Division's HQ in Tunisia to proceed with the MACKALL WHITE variant of HUSKY TWO; Ridgway had set up an elaborate code system to cover the various permutations for the operation, under which MACKALL referred to dropping onto the Gela-Farello airfield and WHITE signifying that Colonel Tucker was to 'be prepared for ground action as ordered'. Due to some unexplained delay the signal did not reach Kairouan until 11:00, although it was acknowledged fifteen minutes later, and there was also a delay in the order being transmitted down to the USAAF troop-carrier units, with one squadron not being informed of the operation until 16:00 and briefing at 17:00, just two hours before take offs were due to begin.[72]

Warning the invasion fleet of the upcoming airborne lift appears to have been similarly tardy. Naval Commander-in-Chief Mediterranean HQ had issued a warning of the original cancelled HUSKY TWO drop at 10:50 on D-Day, but the signal from 52nd Troop Carrier Wing HQ in Tunisia warning of the rescheduled drop did not reach Western Naval Task Force commander Vice-Admiral Hewitt until 17:47 on 11 July; the US Navy Official History noted that this prompted a '...mad scramble to alert all ships and antiaircraft batteries ashore but it was too late to pass the word to everyone'.[73] The possible ramifications of all this were not lost on Ridgway who, having obeyed Patton's orders, returned ashore and visited several anti-aircraft units around 1st Infantry Division HQ and in the vicinity of the Gela-Farello airfield to inform them of the incoming lift; this showed that some units had not received word of the impending airlift, and wider dissemination may have become lost in a conference of anti-aircraft unit officers later in the afternoon.[74] For his part, Patton reportedly came around to Ridgway's misgivings over HUSKY TWO after being caught in an air attack while ashore on 11 July and attempted to cancel the drop, but was unable to establish radio contact with Tunisia on returning to the *Monrovia* at around 20:00. His change of heart came too late: the HUSKY TWO force was in the air and heading east across the Mediterranean toward Malta.[75]

Colonel Tucker's 2,304-strong force was to be carried to Sicily aboard 144 C-47s from Colonel Harold L. Clark's 52nd Troop Carrier Wing, with three machines carrying sticks from HUSKY ONE that had been returned to Tunisia by pilots unwilling to despatch them without a firm locational fix. Take-off time was an hour earlier at 19:00 to make best use of daylight and the fly-in route largely replicated that of HUSKY ONE, with Kuriat Island again serving as the forming-up point for the flight east past Linosa to Malta and then north toward Sicily, but instead of heading for the *Biviere di Gela* lake the C-47s were to make landfall at Sampieri, almost forty miles east of Gela. The serials were then to continue a mile or so inland before turning left and flying along a two-mile wide safe corridor over US-held territory paralleling the coast, which would take them over the *Biviere di Gela* and the Gela-Farello airfield, after which they were to continue paralleling the coast past Licata before angling west out to sea and then south-west past Pantellaria and on to Tunisia.[76]

Take-offs began at thirty-second intervals from 19:00 with the 313th Troop Carrier Group in the lead followed by the 61st, 314th and 316th Troop Carrier Groups at ten-minute intervals, the last beginning at 19:45. Once airborne the C-47s shook out into their customary nine-machine vee formations stepped down to allow those following to silhouette the lead machine against the quarter-moonlit sky, flying at between 700 and 1,000 feet. The formations began passing Kuriat Island twenty miles off Sousse at 20:16 and enjoyed an uneventful flight in clear weather past Linosa, before pivoting around the eastern tip of Malta in formation and on time for the run almost due north for Sampieri, although the formations came under ineffective anti-aircraft fire from Allied convoys during this leg in an ominous portent of what was to come. On reaching Sicily, the C-47s ran into scattered cumulus cloud at around a thousand feet, which obliged some formations to climb above it and a light ground haze complicated waypoint identification; but the lead elements from the 313th Group made landfall in place and on time and successfully navigated their way up the designated corridor without incident.[77]

Passing troop-carrier aircraft over or in the vicinity of the invasion fleet had been a fiercely argued bone of contention before HUSKY commenced, to the extent that Vice-Admiral Hewitt and the US Navy representatives at Allied Force HQ (AFHQ) refused to countenance any mandatory silencing of ship-borne anti-aircraft guns and insisted that any troop-carriers had to remain a minimum of five miles from the surface fleet. This was eventually relaxed to permit a specific one-off route for HUSKY ONE that almost tripled the fly-in distance, which was in turn arguably responsible at least in part for the scattered delivery of HUSKY ONE and Operation LADBROKE. In addition, the concession appears to have been pushed through by Eisenhower after Hewitt had sailed for Sicily under radio silence, and no such arrangement was offered for HUSKY TWO or the two projected glider lifts for the remainder of the 82nd Airborne Division.[78] The arrangement had worked tolerably well on 9-10 July because of the rough weather, because the invasion fleet was still moving or manoeuvring when the airlift went in and because of the widespread scattering of the C-47s. By contrast, in the evening of 11 June the invasion fleet had not only been on station off the landing areas for thirty-six hours or more, but it had also been under near-constant and increasingly heavy air attack during that time.

Axis aircraft were active over the invasion fleet from 05:06. At 06:35 twelve Italian SM79 bombers attacked the shipping off Gela, scoring hits on the transports *Barnett* and *Orizaba*, holing and setting the former on fire and damaging the latter; near misses left the flagship *Monrovia* unscathed but damaged the transport *Joseph T. Dickman*. At 08:10 *LST-158* was hit and left burning off the JOSS beaches, which were bombed and strafed just under an hour later and again at 12:04 and 12:25. The CENT transport area was attacked at 14:22 and the shipping off Gela was attacked by two separate formations of bombers at 14:35 and 14:46 while fighters strafed the beaches. The DIME 14:46 attack hit and set fire to the fully loaded ammunition ship *SS Robert Rowan*, which was abandoned just over an hour later with a warning for nearby vessels to stand clear; the vessel exploded dramatically at 17:00 and the wreck settled in shallow water and continued to burn despite attempts by the destroyer *McLanahan* to douse the fires with gunfire at 17:21.

Axis air attacks continued through dusk and into the night, with the *Robert Rowan's* burning wreck providing a useful navigational marker; German fighter-bombers attacked the CENT shipping at 20:00, fifteen aircraft attacked the shipping off Gela fifty-five minutes later using parachute flares for illumination and again at 22:16, with additional attacks by torpedo-bombers on the destroyers *McLanahan* and *Murphy* on the fringes of the fleet.[79] In all there were twenty-three or twenty-four separate air attacks on the HUSKY beaches on 11 July, the bulk of them against the US landing areas and shipping, employing 198 *Regia Aeronautica* and 283 *Luftwaffe* aircraft.[80] The key point was that by the late evening of 11 July the anti-aircraft gunners aboard ships and in the US 7th Army landing areas were 'operating with frayed nerves and hair triggers', a state of mind that was to have appalling consequences for the troop carrier formations.[81]

Among the heaviest Axis air attack of the day on the US landing area came in two or three waves beginning at 22:16 and was thus underway when the head of the HUSKY TWO lift made landfall. The 313th Troop Carrier Group's lead element dropped their sticks accurately at the Gela-Farello DZ five minutes ahead of schedule at 22:40, but things went increasingly awry thereafter.[82] As the 313th Group's second flight was approaching the final way-point at the *Biviere di Gela*, Jumpmaster Captain Willard E. Harrison from the 504th Regiment's Company A saw a single .50-calibre machine-gun open fire from the dunes.[83] The gunner may have been initially misled by two *Luftwaffe* bombers attacking shipping from the same heading and altitude just two minutes before the C-47s appeared, according to Major Mark J. Alexander, whose 2nd Battalion 505th Parachute RCT was spread along the *Strada* 115 near the Biazzo Ridge; Alexander also reported naval gunners simply switching fire from the enemy targets to the incoming transports.[84]

Whatever the catalyst, every anti-aircraft gunner in sight and beyond commenced firing indiscriminately into the night sky; one Officer from the 504th RCT likened it to 'a mammoth Fourth of July celebration'.[85] The firing spread for miles across the invasion fleet and shore lodgement like wildfire; the rearmost formations of the second in line 61st Troop Carrier Group were up to ten miles offshore in an area that was supposed to be clear of Allied shipping at this point for example, and were hit by heavy fire that ignored the C-47s' recognition signals of red flares and flashing amber belly lights. As it was over or rapidly approaching the release point when the indiscriminate firing began, the 313th Group serial put most of its paratroopers down on or near the DZ and escaped the worst effects, but was still obliged to break for the open sea over Licata and continued to receive fire from the JOSS invasion fleet; some machines reported being fired on for up to thirty miles after leaving the Sicilian coast.[86] The following serials fared much worse, as the amount and adverse impact of the fire increased the further back in the transport stream, with the trailing 316th Troop Carrier Group suffering the worst of all. Eight C-47s, six of them from the trailing 316th Group, turned away in the face of the flak storm and returned to Tunisia with their 104 passengers from the 504th RCT's HQ Company and 2nd Battalion, Division Artillery HQ and the 376th Parachute Field Artillery Battalion still aboard; four dead and six wounded paratroopers were removed from the aircraft after landing.[87]

A further six C-47s carrying seventy-one men were shot down before their sticks had a chance to jump. A complete stick from the 376th Parachute Field Artillery Battalion was lost when their C-47 crashed into the sea but a total of twenty-one men from the other five aircraft survived. Two bailed out using their reserve parachutes when their C-47 was engulfed in flames, three were blown clear when their machines were destroyed in the air, Jumpmaster 1st Lieutenant M. C. Shelly from the 2nd Battalion's HQ Company was thrown clear of the door on impact as the sole survivor from his machine and the 504th RCT's Executive Officer Lieutenant-Colonel Leslie G. Freeman and fourteen paratroopers emerged alive from the wreckage of their C-47, although eleven of the party were wounded. The remaining 130 C-47s took evasive action as best they could, breaking up the carefully maintained vee-formations in the process, dropping their sticks wherever possible before descending to low level and heading back out to sea, although the tactic brought mixed results. Flight Officer J. G. Paccassi's machine from the 61st Group was hit as his stick exited near the DZ, lost its rudder to more hits at low level after crossing the coast and ditched after losing both engines; the wreck was then briefly fired on by the destroyer *Beatty*, which despatched a rescue boat on realising the aircraft was a USAAF machine. The destroyer *Jeffers* picked up the five–man crew of a C-47 from the 316th Troop Carrier Group along with two paratroopers and the destroyer *Cowie* rescued two crewmen from the 314th Group after their C-47 ditched in flames. Not all the low-flying transports were so fortunate. Off Scoglitti a C-47 that flew low over the bow of the transport USS *Susan B. Anthony* was promptly shot down in flames in mistake for an Axis bomber with the aid of the adjacent Attack Transport USS *Procyon*, and another C-47 was brought down in similar circumstances nearby a few minutes later; there do not appear to have been survivors from either machine.[88]

While most of the damage appears to have been wrought by the naval anti-aircraft guns, some was down to fire from Army units and personnel, not all of which was directed at the transport aircraft. Several C-47s turned east on making landfall to avoid the flak and scattered their sticks across the island as far as Vittoria, twenty miles from the Gela-Farello DZ. Many were despatched over US 45th Infantry Division's area where the men on the ground assumed the paratroopers were part of a German airborne attack on the landing area and proceeded to fire on aircraft and descending parachutists alike; matters were compounded further by the infantrymen being unfamiliar with the paratrooper's distinctive uniforms and the 82nd Airborne personnel having different challenges and countersigns to the troops on the ground.[89] The pilot of the C-47 carrying Lieutenant Charles A. Drew from the 2nd Battalion 504th RCT's hurriedly despatched his stick over the 180th RCT just east of the River Acate as the C-47 began to burn; Drew landed within sight of three blazing transport wrecks and reported that three of his men were killed while descending and a fourth was shot dead on the ground after tendering the wrong reply to a challenge.[90]

The 504th RCT's Chaplain, Captain Delbert A. Kuehl and his stick were pinned down by heavy US fire despite repeatedly shouting their password; the firing continued until Chaplain Kuehl worked his way into the GI's position and gently enquired who they were firing at. Neither did the problem lie solely with the inexperienced 45th Division. Colonel Tucker's C-47 from the 314th Troop Carrier Group passed directly over the still burning *Robert Rowan* and continued west as far as Licata before the pilot got his bearings and turned about to deliver the stick onto the Gela-Farello DZ. Immediately on landing, Tucker intervened to stop five M4 tanks near the DZ firing on the passing C-47s with their .50 calibre machine-guns; his own C-47 made it safely back to Tunisia but the crew later counted over a thousand holes in their machine.[91]

The magnitude of what happened over the invasion fleet and landing areas did not become apparent until the C-47s began to arrive back at the Kairouan satellite airfields from 00:41 on Monday 12 July. Twenty-three of the 144 C-47s employed on HUSKY TWO failed to return, twelve of them from the trailing 316th Troop Carrier Group, only one of which is believed to have been due to enemy fire after straying too close to German positions near Comiso.[92] This was a loss rate of sixteen per cent and a further thirty-seven aircraft were badly damaged; in human terms the 52nd Troop Carrier Wing lost seven dead, thirty wounded and fifty-three missing, with thirty-seven of the casualties again coming from the 316th Group.[93] While the haste with which HUSKY TWO was mounted, problems with the Identification Friend or Foe (IFF) systems fitted to the C-47s and poor US Army procedures and fire discipline all undoubtedly played a part, the bulk of the blame lay with a combination of tired and stressed anti-aircraft gunners and poor naval fire control, US Navy claims of short notice notwithstanding.[94] Perhaps unsurprisingly, the US Navy perspective was also supported by Naval Commander-in-Chief Mediterranean, Admiral of the Fleet Sir Andrew Cunningham, who opined that any aircraft approaching ships at night was fair game and that the cause of events on 11 July was 'either bad routing or bad navigation on the part of the aircraft crews'.[95] Cunningham carefully avoided addressing the legitimate issues of why the naval gunners consistently ignored the red flare and amber flashing light recognition signals, why the firing was permitted to continue over an extended period and after the shot-down targets were identified as USAAF machines. It is difficult to disagree with an unidentified and understandably bitter surviving C-47 passenger who opined that 'Evidently the safest place for us tonight while over Sicily would have been over enemy territory.'[96]

The impact on the paratroopers was at least as serious. The 504th Parachute RCT lost eighty-one dead, 132 wounded and sixteen missing, equivalent to ten per cent of Colonel Tucker's force and the scattering was equally as bad as HUSKY ONE; by 07:15 on 12 July Tucker had rallied just the equivalent of a rifle company and a battery of 75mm Pack Howitzers from the 2,304-strong force that had lifted off from Tunisia the previous evening, rising to just 555 by the late afternoon.[97] Lieutenant-General Patton's intent to employ the 504th RCT immediately as effective reinforcement was thus hamstrung, and the situation mirrored Major-General Ridgway's overall plight; by midnight on Tuesday 13 July, four days and forty-eight hours after HUSKY ONE and HUSKY TWO respectively, the portion of the 82nd Airborne Division deployed to Sicily could only muster 3,024 of the 5,307 men delivered to the island across both lifts.[98] Perhaps unsurprisingly given the partisan defensive attitudes on display, the board of officers tasked by Allied Forces HQ to investigate the debacle failed to identify a definable cause, 'uttered only generalities' in its findings and the matter was carefully and deliberately side-lined; as General Ridgway subsequently declared, 'The responsibility for loss of life and materiel…is so divided, so difficult to fix with impartial justice, and so questionable of ultimate value to the service because of the acrimonious debates which would follow efforts to hold responsible persons or services to account, that disciplinary action is of doubtful wisdom.'[99]

Be that as it may, with the exception of the costly fiasco of the HUSKY TWO drop, the events of 11 July generally left the DIME landing force in a better position than hitherto. Consequently, in the afternoon of that day Major-General Allen ordered a resumption of the advance northward and in the early hours of Monday 12 July the three-pronged advance out of the Gela perimeter was resumed with the Rangers of Colonel Darby's FORCE X pushing up the *Strada Provinciale* 8 toward Butera to secure high ground as a flank guard for the 26th RCT resuming the advance up the *Strada* 117, reinforced with the 2nd Battalion, 18th RCT. The latter secured the Ponte Olivo airfield at 08:45, so suddenly that freshly opened wine was reportedly captured in the officers' mess, and by 10:00 the 26th had taken the nearby Hill 300/Monte della Guardia.[100] The hardest fighting of the day again occurred on the right where the 16th RCT's advance from the Piano Lupo heights to Niscemi up the *Strada Provinciale* 11 brought it into contact with the eastern *HG kampfgruppe* attempting to join the general withdrawal northward after crossing the River Acate at the Ponte Dirillo, following its drubbing on the Biazzo Ridge.

A *HG* covering attack petered out by midday in the face of stubborn resistance from the 16th RCT; the 1st Battalion's commander Lieutenant-Colonel Denholm was badly wounded and the 2nd Battalion was reduced to around 200 men including the remainder of Lieutenant-Colonel Gorham's paratroopers from the 1st Battalion 505th Regiment. The fight also cost the US force four M4 tanks lost in exchange for three Tigers from *Panzer Abteilung 215* and the Niscemi road finally claimed Lieutenant-Colonel Gorham's life; he was killed while stalking a Tiger with a Bazooka. Niscemi was taken without a fight at 10:00 on 13 July. This was the culmination of the hardest fighting of the DIME landings, as illustrated by the 16th RCT's losses over the two days 11-12 July, during which the 1st Battalion lost thirty-six dead, seventy-three wounded and nine missing. The 2nd Battalion lost fifty-six dead, 133 wounded and fifty-seven missing.[101] The 16th RCT nonetheless pursued the *HG Panzer Division* as it withdrew to avoid being cut off by the US advances from the JOSS and CENT Landing Areas, and by the early afternoon were nearing Caltagirone almost on the initial invasion phase Yellow Line. On the left, Colonel Darby's Rangers secured Butera early on 14 July while the 26th RCT pushed on to reach its Yellow Line objective at Mazzarino in the afternoon. In the centre the 18th RCT advanced north up the *Strada* 117 to occupy high ground overlooking the junction with the *Strada* 124 by the late afternoon. By the morning of Thursday 15 July, Major-General Allen's US 1st Infantry Division had closed to the Yellow Line and linked up with the US 45th Infantry Division to the east; the stage was set to shift from the HUSKY initial invasion phase to operations aimed at exploiting the gains and overrunning the remainder of the island.[102]

16

The Run-Up to MARSTON TONIGHT

Preparations for the 1st Parachute Brigade's Landing at the Ponte Primosole, D-Day Minus Eight, Friday 2 July to D-Day Plus Three, 19:01 Tuesday 13 July

It took just under a week from the initial HUSKY landings to establish a lodgement of sufficient depth and strength for subsequent exploitation across the entire 15th Army Group frontage. In the west the US 7th Army spent five days pushing out from the JOSS, DIME and CENT Landing Areas toward the initial invasion phase Yellow Line, which was reached by 15 July 1943; the Line was approximately twenty-five miles inland from the invasion beaches, running from Palma di Montechiaro on the coast in the west to Vizzini on the boundary with the British 8th Army in the east. The latter made similar progress over the same period, with the 1st Canadian Division linking up with the US 45th Infantry Division near Ragusa on 12 July before turning north in the wake of the 51st Highland Division and attached 231st Brigade's advance on the left and centre of the British frontage. Francofonte in the centre was secured after two days of hard fighting on Wednesday 14 July and Vizzini on the left in the early hours of the following day.

The advance on the right up the eastern Sicilian coast was spearheaded by the 5th Division with the 50th Division acting as a left-flank guard; the latter secured Avola inland from its landing beaches before advancing twenty miles north to take Sortino and Lentini on 13 July. The main advance by the 5th Division retook the recently lost Ponte Grande in the late afternoon of D-Day, liberating the captured men from the 1st Airlanding Brigade in the process and secured the port of Syracuse during the night of 10-11 July. After successfully pushing back German and Italian delaying actions at Priolo Gargallo and Solarino on 12 July the 5th Division entered the port of Augusta in the early hours of Tuesday 13 July in conjunction with a sea landing by elements of the SAS Special Raiding Squadron.

The original HUSKY plan had envisaged three British airborne operations in support of ground troops. The first was Operation LADBROKE, the ill-starred glider operation by the 1st Airlanding Brigade to secure the right flank of the ACID NORTH Landing Area, assist egress from the beaches north along the *Strada* 115 coast road and access to the port of Syracuse via the Ponte Grande crossings over the River Anapo and parallel Mammiaibica Canal. The second was Operation GLUTTON, which tasked the 2nd Parachute Brigade to seize the road bridge across the River Mulinello west of the port of Augusta along with the town and harbour. Originally scheduled for the night of 10-11 July, GLUTTON was to be launched at 18:45 on 10 July but was put back an hour and then postponed for twenty-four hours. During the stand-down Private Charles Duncan from the 4th Parachute Battalion covered the detonation of an accidentally armed No. 36 grenade with his own body to save his surrounding comrades and died; he was subsequently awarded the George Cross for his selfless action.[1] The Brigade returned to the airfields in the afternoon of 11 July but GLUTTON was cancelled altogether at 17:07, as the 5th Division's ground advance had rendered the operation superfluous.[2]

However, the speed and relative ease of the British ground advance to Augusta also prompted the launch of the third planned operation, the precise date and time of launch of which was to be dictated by the progress of the ground advance from the outset. Codenamed FUSTIAN, the Operation was allotted to Brigadier Gerald Lathbury's recently rebuilt 1st Parachute Brigade and involved seizing the Ponte Primosole, codenamed MARSTON, carrying the *Strada* 114 coast road over the River Simeto sixteen miles north of Augusta and seven miles south of the 8th Army's next major coastal objective, the port of Catania; the bridge was the only intact crossing over that watercourse on British XIII Corps' proposed line of advance. The ground advance to the River Simeto was to be eased by a further *coup-de-main* operation, intended to secure the *Strada* 114 crossing over the River Leonardo at the Ponte Malati, just over six miles south-west of the Ponte Primosole and approximately ten miles north of the British front line. The mission was allotted to Lieutenant-Colonel John Durnford-Slater's No. 3 Commando, which was to go ashore from the LSI (S) HMS *Prins Albert* at Agnone, around five miles east of the bridge, in the late evening at the same time as the FUSTIAN landing to the north. The seaborne operation does not appear to have had a codename, presumably due to the haste with which it was mounted.

No. 3 Commando had just re-embarked on the *Prins Albert* on 12 July after covering the beachhead flank and the next day Lieutenant-Colonel Durnford-Slater was summoned to Syracuse Naval HQ for a briefing with Montgomery and the XIII Corps' commander, Lieutenant-General Miles Dempsey. With barely enough time to issue his men with a warning order, Durnford-Slater was now whisked away in a fast motor launch to the quayside in Syracuse.

According to Durnford-Slater, Dempsey did most of the talking and began the briefing with a tantalising opening: 'We've got a new operation for you tonight. It's an ambitious one, but I think you'll like it.' He then went on to explain that there was only one road which ran directly from Syracuse to Catania and that it was now destined to be the Corps' main axis of advance. However, there were two potential problems. This road crossed two rivers and if the bridges over them were blown or held by the enemy in strength it would impose a serious delay on 8th Army's progress to Catania and Messina. There was to be an airborne drop that night on the Primosole Bridge by the 1st Airborne Division and Durnford-Slater's mission was to seize and hold the Punta dei Melati, a bridge over the Leonardo River which lay two miles north of Lentini. Durnford-Slater now knew the importance of his mission and the fact that his men would be on their own ten miles beyond the forward line of Dempsey's troops without any support to call on. Just before leaving to return the *Prins Albert* Dempsy took him aside and said, 'If, by any chance, 50th Division, who will be our leading troops, don't get through to you by first light tomorrow morning, clear off and hide up for the day.'[3]

The ground relief for the *coup-de-main* missions was tasked to Major-General Sidney Kirkham's 50th Division, specifically Brigadier Ronald Senior's 151st Brigade supported by Sherman tanks of the 44th RTR from Brigadier John Currie's 4th Armoured Brigade; the operation envisaged an advance of thirty miles over a twenty-four hour period and General Montgomery reportedly stressed that Kirkham was to move with 'all possible speed' at the final Orders Group held on 13 July.[4]

The 130-yard-long Ponte Primosole was of steel box-girder construction set on two stone supporting pillars, located approximately five hundred yards downstream from the junction of the River Simeto and the Gornalunga Canal. The bridge defences were garrisoned by elements of *Generale di Divisione* Carlo Gotti's *213a Divisione Costiera*. At the north end the defences consisted of a barbed-wire perimeter roughly 300 by 350 yards set in an area of vines and poplar trees interspersed with farm buildings that stretched along the north bank of the river and canal. The perimeter enclosed a road block consisting of a chicane of concrete blocks with a movable barrier and guard house, covered by a concrete bunker containing an anti-tank gun on the west side of the road; two more hexagonal concrete pillboxes mounting Breda machine-guns, one immediately behind the anti-tank bunker close to the bridge entrance covering the eastern flank and the other on the opposite side of the perimeter, covered the western flank.

The terrain at the south end of the bridge was more open, consisting of a low-lying flood plain interspersed with drainage channels and embanked roads with a smaller defensive perimeter stretching 200 yards along the bank either side of the bridge and extending 150 yards inland to enclose an embanked S-bend in the *Strada* 114 leading onto the bridge itself; it, too, boasted a concrete roadblock and guardhouse, an anti-tank bunker close to the roadblock and two machine-gun pillboxes set either side of the roadway adjacent to the bridge entrance. Another pillbox was located at a Y-junction on the *Strada* 114 750 yards south of the bridge, opposite an Italian flak battery with tented accommodation for the gunners. Italian troops were dug in atop hills straddling the *Strada* 114 a mile or so south of the crossing and others occupied coastal defensive positions just over a mile east of the bridge and a strongpoint alongside the *Strada* 114 roughly the same distance to the north.[5]

The Italian units in the vicinity of the Ponte Primosole also received a substantial and serendipitous reinforcement on the very eve of FUSTIAN. As we have seen, *Oberstleutnant* Ludwig Heilmann's *Fallschirmjäger Regiment 3* had jumped onto a drop zone just west of the Ponte Primosole at 18:00 on 12 July 1943, spearheading the transfer of *1 Fallschirmjäger Division* to Sicily as a rapid reinforcement. The airlift carrying the second increment set off from southern France the following day and included *Major* Werner Schmidt's *Fallschirmjäger MG Bataillon 1*, a *kompanie* from *Fallschirm Kommunication Bataillon 1* and the *Division's* anti-tank guns and crews carried in a number of Messerschmitt 323 transports. The latter were dogged by misfortune as a number of the giant machines crashed on take-off, killing all on board, several more were lost during the long flight over the Mediterranean and two were destroyed by Allied bombing after landing at Catania. *Fallschirmjäger MG Bataillon 1* made Catania airfield unscathed, however, and moved off for a holding position just over a mile south of the Ponte Primosole under second-in-command *Hauptmann* Otto Laun, while *Major* Schmidt obtained orders from *Oberstleutnant* Heilmann's HQ at Carlentini, seventeen miles south of Catania.

Given that by then the 1st Parachute Brigade was at the satellite airfields around Kairouan awaiting take-off for Operation FUSTIAN, Heilmann's orders were prescient if not claivoyant; he warned Schmidt that 'something is bound to happen tonight' and instructed him to remain south of Catania, to hold the Ponte Primosole and to deploy a *kompanie* between the bridge and the coast to prevent any Allied thrust north into the Catania Plain from cutting off German and Italian units south of the River Simeto. The Axis force south of Catania thus received a substantial boost just hours before the 1st Parachute Brigade was due to arrive at the Ponte Primosole, and the initiative and aggression of the newly arrived *Luftwaffe* paratroopers was to play a pivotal role in the subsequent fight for the bridge and the British ground advance to relieve the FUSTIAN force.[6]

The 1st Parachute Brigade included the original British parachute volunteer cadre formed in response to Churchill's order in late June 1940, initially dubbed No. 2 Commando, then 11 Special Air Service Battalion before becoming the 1st Parachute Battalion and being subsumed into then Brigadier Richard Gale's 1st Parachute Brigade at the end of September 1941. Despatched to North Africa to participate in Operation TORCH at the end of October the following year under the command of Gale's successor Brigadier Edwin Flavell, the 1st Parachute Brigade carried out three ill-thought out and arguably needless battalion-scale parachute operations on 12, 16 and 29 November 1942 before being deployed as conventional infantry for the five months from December 1942. Brigadier Flavell was posted back to an Airborne staff appointment on 27 April 1943 and command of the Brigade passed to Brigadier Gerald Lathbury, fresh from a number of staff and training appointments in the UK.

Brigadier Lathbury's appointment to command the 1st Parachute Brigade was not without its ostensible advantages despite his lack of operational experience. While his wartime career prior to joining Airborne Forces in September 1941 had been spent in a series of Staff appointments, he then spent eight months raising and training the 3rd Parachute Battalion from scratch and after serving an eight-month stint at the Air Directorate at the War Office, five months raising and training the 3rd Parachute Brigade, also from scratch. Lathbury was therefore well qualified for the not inconsiderable task of rebuilding the 1st Parachute Brigade, as this involved assimilating large numbers of replacements and bringing them up to the required standard of fitness and tactical expertise, the Brigade having been largely starved of replacement personnel throughout its time in Algeria and Tunisia. The average strength of the Brigade's constituent battalions had only been around 300 men across the North African deployment, around half their official War Establishment, and on occasion their strength was significantly lower. The 2nd Parachute Battalion was reduced to just 120 men and had to be reinforced with a company from the 3rd Parachute Battalion at the end of March 1943 for example, and when it was finally withdrawn from the line in mid-April 1943 with the rest of the Brigade it numbered 360 All Ranks after suffering an overall casualty rate of eighty per cent.[7] Part of the problem was the expansion of the British Airborne Force to Division strength, which had effectively blocked obtaining parachute-trained personnel from the UK, and no volunteers could be sought locally as the British 1st Army was experiencing manpower problems of its own.[8]

In addition to the basics, Lathbury was able to provide refresher parachute training and an introduction to the new Armstrong-Whitworth Albemarle when the Brigade moved with the rest of the 1st Airborne Division to Tizi near Mascara on 10 May, courtesy of the US 51st Troop Carrier Wing, RAF No. 296 Squadron and RAF Nos. 1 and 2 Mobile Parachute Servicing Units. The final move, in readiness for Operation HUSKY, came on 30 June, when the 1st Parachute Brigade again accompanied the rest of its parent Division to the area around Kairouan near Sousse in Tunisia.[9]

Specific preparations for Operation FUSTIAN went back at least as far as 18 June 1943 with Exercise CACTUS IV, a parachute drop involving the 1st Parachute Brigade and attachments allotted to the Primosole Bridge operation and nineteen Albemarles from RAF No. 296 Squadron; it is unclear if the exercise also involved the approximately five CG4A and five Horsa gliders initially slated for FUSTIAN, or if the participants were aware of the underlying purpose of the exercise.[10] At the 1st Airborne Division level a co-ordinating conference was held at Division HQ on 5 July, with another overall conference involving all the Division's Brigadiers and their subordinate Commanding Officers tasked for involvement in HUSKY the following day, though by that point the briefing process for FUSTIAN was well underway.[11]

1st Parachute Brigade HQ issued Operation Order No. 14 containing detailed instructions for FUSTIAN to its subordinate and attached units on 2 July with the 1st and 3rd Parachute Battalion's noting receipt the same day and the commander of the former, Lieutenant-Colonel Alastair Pearson, briefed his Company Commanders on the content at 20:00; 16 Parachute Field Ambulance did not acknowledge receipt until the following day, 3 July, however.[12] Thereafter the briefings were grouped together over several days from 7 July. The 1st Parachute Battalion Officers were briefed at 19:00 on 7 July and the Other Ranks from the evening of 9 July for example, while the 2nd Parachute Battalion stretched the process over five days; Company Commanders were briefed in two stages at 10:00 and 09:00 on 7 and 10 July respectively, Platoon Commanders at 16:00 on 10 July with Other Ranks briefings beginning an hour later and continuing at 11:00 the following day with a final session at 08:30 on 12 July, the originally scheduled day of departure.[13] For its part the 3rd Parachute Battalion's Company Commanders were briefed on 9 July followed by Platoon and Section Commanders twenty-four hours later.[14]

The Operation FUSTIAN force was made up of 109 men from 1st Parachute Brigade HQ and Defence Platoon, 600, 501 and 541 men respectively from the 1st, 2nd and 3rd Parachute Battalions, two Troops from the 1st Parachute Squadron RE numbering around fifty, A and B Troops from the 1st Airlanding Anti-Tank Battery RA numbering seventy-seven men with twelve 6-Pounder guns, fifty-one men from the 16th Parachute Field Ambulance RAMC, three two-man Pathfinder teams from the 21st Independent Parachute Company, the 4th Army Film and Photographic Section, two parachute-trained Naval Forward Observer Teams to control naval gunfire support, a Forward Observer party from the 1st Airlanding Light Regiment RA to liaise with XIII Corps artillery and thirty-eight members of the 1st Battalion, The Glider Pilot Regiment, 1,971 men in all.[15] This force was to be carried to the Ponte Primosole in 116 parachute aircraft, eight CG4A gliders and eleven Horsa gliders; the glider allotment was twice that originally scaled as FUSTIAN inherited the unused machines from Operation GLUTTON.[16] Of the parachute transports, 105 were US C-47s drawn from the 51st Troop Carrier Wing, fifty-one from the 60th Troop Carrier Group, fifty from the 62nd Troop Carrier Group and four from the 64th Troop Carrier Group along with eleven Albemarles from RAF No. 296 Squadron; at least three spare aircraft were also stationed at the airfields as emergency substitutes. The C-47s carried sticks of between fourteen and eighteen men and all but one of the Albemarles sticks of ten, the exception being a single nine-man stick.[17] Interestingly, according to a US official account the optimum load for a C-47 was sixteen paratroopers; as thirty-five of the 1st Parachute Brigade's machines were carrying sticks of seventeen men and a further twenty-eight carried sticks of eighteen, sixty-three or just over half of the British formation's C-47s were technically overloaded.[18]

Eight of the nineteen gliders assigned to FUSTIAN were CG4As, two carrying a 6-Pounder anti-tank gun, two men and eight rounds of ammunition apiece with the remainder each carrying a Jeep and a total of eighteen men, two No. 18 Radio Sets and eighty-four rounds of 6-Pounder ammunition distributed across the six machines. All eleven Horsas slated for FUSTIAN carried five passengers in addition to the two pilots; seven carried a Jeep and 6-Pounder gun with twenty-four rounds, three carried the same load with a stretcher, a No. 18 Radio Set and a No. 22 Radio Set respectively, and one carried two Jeeps, a light motorcycle, two No. 18 Radio Sets and a No. 22 Radio Set. Four of the Horsas were to be towed by Albemarles and the remaining seven by Halifax bombers from RAF No. 295 Squadron.[19] The aerial armada was to again use Kuriat Island as a forming-up point before following the well-worn route east past Linosa to the Delimara Peninsula on the south-eastern tip of Malta and then turn north-east and north for four legs totalling 130 miles past Cape Passero and up the Gulf of Noto and Gulf of Catania.

The course was intended to keep the fly-in ten miles from the Sicilian coast, double the five-mile danger margin requested by the Allied naval commands, and a US official account refers to the pilots being briefed to stay at least six miles from the coast.[20] The fifth and final leg of the approach involved a ninety-degree turn to port and a thirteen-mile run almost due west, making landfall at the mouth of the River Simeto and delivering paratroopers and gliders onto six landing zones, three north of the River Simeto and three to the south of the parallel Gornalunga Canal; none of the landing zones were located between the two watercourses, presumably because the terrain was considered unsuitable, although *Fallschirmjäger Regiment 3* had carried out a 1,400-strong reinforcing jump onto that area without problems on 12 July 1943. After delivering their charges the Allied aircraft were to perform a 180-degree turn to port and fly back out to sea before following the same route back to Tunisia, staggered slightly to the east and south; the outbound flight was to maintain an altitude of 500 feet and the return between 1,000 and 3,000.[21]

Apart from seizing the Ponte Primosole the 1st Parachute Brigade was to secure a number of other objectives, utilising four parachute Drop Zones (DZs) and two glider Landing Zones (LZs). DZ 1 and DZ 2 were located a mile north-west and a mile and a half south-west of the bridge respectively, DZ 3 a mile or so further along the Gornalunga Canal from DZ 2 and DZ 4 almost three miles north-west of the bridge. The perhaps confusingly numbered LZ 7 sat in a loop in the River Simeto a mile or so upstream from the Ponte Primosole. LZ 8 was located at the south-west end of the bridge alongside the junction of the River Simeto and Gornalunga Canal.[22] The operation had three phases. Phase One tasked two Platoons from Lieutenant-Colonel Pearson's 1st Parachute Battalion, augmented with Sappers from the 1st Parachute Squadron RE, to drop onto DZ 1 and DZ 2 at 22:20, seven sticks on the former and two on the latter, to secure the structure by 23:20.[23] Five minutes later at 22:25 two Platoons from Lieutenant-Colonel Eric Yeldham's 3rd Parachute Battalion were to drop onto DZ 4, just over two miles north-west of the bridge and eliminate a nearby battery of four anti-aircraft guns.

Phase Two, the main parachute landing, was in four stages. Colonel Pearson and the remainder of the 1st Parachute Battalion were to drop onto DZs 1 and 2, tasked to complete the seizure of the Ponte Primosole if required by 00:40 and then hold the structure until the Brigade perimeter to the north and south of the bridge was fully established; Pearson and his men were then to become Brigade reserve. Lieutenant-Colonel John Frost and the 2nd Parachute Battalion, accompanied by one of the Naval Forward Observer Teams, were to drop onto DZ 3 to clear and secure the high ground straddling the *Strada* 114 south of the Ponte Primosole, specifically a series of hilltops collectively codenamed JOHNNY. JOHNNY I was located immediately east of and overlooking the *Strada* 114, JOHNNY II to the east of that while the smaller JOHNNY III lay just west of the highway; a fourth peak dubbed JOHNNY IV lay further west, but it is unclear if this was included in the 2nd Battalion's list of objectives. The southern blocking perimeter this would create was to be in place by 04:00 and Frost was also tasked to 'act vigorously southward' from the perimeter to assist the relieving force from British 50th Division if required.

Lieutenant-Colonel Yeldham and the remainder of the 3rd Parachute Battalion were tasked to drop onto DZ 4 and establish a protective perimeter north of the Ponte Primosole anchored on a loop in the River Simeto by 01:35, and to patrol outward toward Catania airfield to the north. Finally, Brigade HQ, accompanied by the Forward Observer party from the 1st Airlanding Light Regiment RA and the other Naval Forward Observer Team, were to drop onto DZ 2 and regroup before moving to the vicinity of the bridge. Phase Three was the arrival of the gliders carrying A, B and D Troops from the 1st Airlanding Anti-Tank Battery RA and their twelve 6-Pounder guns, in two increments. One was to land on LZ 7 in the loop of the Simeto north-west of the bridge at 01:00, with all six guns coming under command of the 3rd Parachute Battalion. The second increment was to land on LZ 8 at the south-west end of the Ponte Primosole at 01:10, from where four 6-Pounders were to move south and come under command of the 2nd Parachute Battalion; the remaining two guns and Battery HQ were to join Brigade HQ in the area of the bridge.[24]

Both the FUSTIAN Air and Ground Plans were problematic as envisaged for a number of reasons. For the transport and tug aircraft to make accurate landfall at the mouth of the River Simeto as proposed in the Air Plan required dead-reckoning navigation at an unrealistic level of accuracy, given that virtually the entire fly-in was over water and the dearth of USAAF night navigation training. According to one account the 1st Airborne Division's RAF adviser suggested that the 51st Troop Carrier Wing abandon flying in formation for FUSTIAN in favour of the RAF night-flying practice of despatching pairs of aircraft in a stream at two-minute intervals.[25] This might have been an option for the thirty RAF machines as their crews were trained in night-flying and included a navigator, but the suggestion was unsurprisingly rejected by their US counterparts due again to the dearth of USAAF night-flying training and because only one in four of the US C-47 crews included a navigator.

Even assuming the parachute transports and glider tugs made landfall at the correct spot, it is difficult to see how the landing force could have been delivered as envisioned due to the short distance between the mouth of the River Simeto and the landing zones. With the nearest, LZ 8, under two miles from the coast and DZ 3 the furthest at under four miles, the pilots had around a minute to get their bearings, identify their zone and orient their aircraft, assuming the C-47s were already throttled back to the optimum dropping speed of between 120 and 135 miles per hour, just above the machine's stalling speed, before crossing the coast; the pilots also had to adjust trim to a tail-high attitude while maintaining the agreed jump height of 500 feet.[26] All this was no easy feat in ideal conditions, but this was a busy and confusing landing area, with separate DZs and LZs in an area two and three quarter miles east to west by three and a half miles north to south bisected by a river and a canal, which were probably too close together for swift differentiation from the air.

Furthermore, for at least the initial flights, the drop and landing zones were to be unmarked. The three two-man Pathfinder teams from the 21st Independent Parachute Company were tasked to lay out marker lights and a EUREKA radar homing beacon on LZ 7 but flew in aircraft in the main body of the transport stream rather than flying ahead; Sergeant Joe Smith, tasked to mark zones south of the Gornalunga Canal, was No. 6 or 8 in Lieutenant-Colonel Pearson's stick while Pathfinder team mate Corporal Stanley Brown was stick No. 1 in another C-47, for example.[27] The need for the landing zones to be marked in advance of the main landings was recognised for subsequent operations, with Pathfinders in dedicated aircraft taking off up to an hour before the main bodies for the landings the following year in Normandy and near Arnhem.

The FUSTIAN ground plan was overly complicated for the task, likely due to a combination of the dearth of British operational airborne experience which, excluding the 1st Airlanding Brigade landing near Syracuse, amounted to two parachute sabotage raids and three independent battalion drops, and the British Airborne Force's roots in small-scale raiding. The various landing zones placed the 1st Parachute Brigade's constituent units unnecessarily far from their specified objectives in some instances and it is difficult to see why two combined DZ/LZs closer to each end of the Ponte Primosole could not have been used instead, with a smaller dedicated DZ for the assault on the anti-aircraft position, although responsibility for this likely lay with the RAF planners. The post-landing plan immediately directed a large proportion of the Brigade's strength to subsidiary tasks rather than concentrating on the key factor of securing the Ponte Primosole, in clear breach of the military maxim about identifying and maintaining focus on the primary aim; having the 3rd Parachute Battalion patrol toward Catania airfield and despatching the 2nd Parachute Battalion to secure high ground a mile and more south of the primary objective immediately on landing were arguably legitimate sub-missions, but only after the primary objective had been secured and not as separate objectives in their own right, as envisaged in the plan.

In a similar vein the plan was criticised for assuming the *coup-de-main* force would automatically succeed in securing the Ponte Primosole within an hour of jumping, with no back-up contingency as the 2nd and 3rd Parachute Battalions were busy with their own parallel missions.[28] The defensive phase of the plan dispersed the Brigade's constituent units in three separate locations spread across more than five square miles placing them too far apart to permit mutual support or reinforcement, and thus risked them being isolated, overwhelmed and defeated in detail if the Allied ground relief did not appear as scheduled. With regard to the source of the plan, it is unclear to what extent if any Major-General Hopkinson was involved given his malign role in the plan for Operation LADBROKE or if it was the work of Brigadier Lathbury alone, although the fact that Lathbury's Brigade plan at Arnhem just over a year later replicated many of the same errors strongly suggests that the Ponte Primosole plan was his, too. In the event the matter is moot, for circumstances were to render the FUSTIAN air and ground plans superfluous.

Operation FUSTIAN was originally scheduled for launch in the evening of Monday 12 July and the participants spent Sunday 11 July making last-minute preparations including practice firing, personnel inspections, loading containers, issuing and fitting parachutes and life jackets before compulsory rest with lights out at 20:00; the 2nd Parachute Battalion held a Catholic Mass at 10:00 with a separate Church of England Service in B Company lines before resuming final briefings at 11:00.[29] The parachute transports and gliders were to launch from the six satellite airfields around Kairouan where they were based, the 60th Troop Carrier Group from Airfields A and B with the borrowed machines from the 64th Troop Carrier Wing flying from the former, the 62nd Troop Carrier Group from Airfields C and D, the seven RAF No. 295 Squadron Halifax and four Albemarles from No. 296 Squadron towing Horsas from Airfield E and the eleven No. 296 Squadron Albemarle parachute transports and eight Albemarles towing CG4A gliders from Airfield F.[30]

Smaller units were lifted from the same airfields in their entirety. The 1st Parachute Brigade HQ element flew in the eleven parachute Albemarles from Airfield F for example, while the 1st Parachute Squadron RE and the 16th Parachute Field Ambulance contingents flew in six C-47s, three for each unit, from Airfield B. However, the Parachute Battalions were distributed across air transport units and/or airfields, presumably to minimise the possible impact of fly-in losses or non-arrivals; for example, half of 2nd Parachute Battalion HQ, A Company and a third of S Company flew in eleven 62nd Troop Carrier Group C-47s from Airfield C, the rest of Battalion HQ, B Company and another third of S Company flew in ten 62nd Troop Carrier Group C-47s from Airfield D while C Company and the remainder of S Company flew from Airfield A in ten C-47s from the 60th Troop Carrier Group. The 1st Parachute Battalion was spread across Airfields A, C and D and the 3rd Parachute Battalion across Airfields A, B and C.[31]

The move to the airfields was made in 120 three-ton trucks provided by the 1st Airborne Division's Royal Army Service Corps (RASC) element, with each vehicle being matched to a specific aircraft serial number and first despatched to the various unit lines. There they were loaded with containers and parachutes by the stick assigned to that aircraft, which then travelled aboard the truck to their designated airfield and out to their assigned aircraft. There the containers were loaded aboard the machines while awaiting the code-phrase MARSTON TONIGHT, indicating that Operation FUSTIAN was to proceed. Movement timing was according to a March Table beginning at 13:45, although the 1st Parachute Battalion reportedly moved off at 13:30, the 2nd Battalion Parachute Battalion at 14:45 and the Brigade HQ element an hour later at 15:45.[32]

The various units arrived at their airfields to be informed that the operation had been postponed for twenty-four hours, although the delay may not have come as a total surprise given that the 1st Parachute Battalion at least had made specific arrangements for that contingency.[33] The process of moving the 1st Parachute Brigade and attachments to the airfields was repeated on 13 July using the same RASC March Table and timings; the 2nd Parachute Battalion reported that the additional briefing time the postponement afforded 'was of considerable advantage'.[34] The process was eased at 1st Parachute Brigade HQ because containers and parachutes were left aboard the motor transport overnight. The 1st Parachute Battalion left its containers mounted on its C-47s and its 'statichutes' aboard the aircraft on Airfields A, C and D, along with one man per two aircraft to ensure unit equipment 'was not tampered with'. Perhaps others did the same.[35]

This time the MARSTON TONIGHT code was issued, apparently at some point in the late afternoon, prompting Brigadier Lathbury to despatch his Brigade Intelligence Officer to 51st Troop Carrier Wing HQ for the latest Situation Report. Lathbury and Brigade Major David Hunter moved to Airfield F independently at 18:30 on his Intelligence Officer's return, while word that FUSTIAN was on filtered down to the Battalion commanders at their respective Airfields at around the same time.[36] After arrival at its Airfields the 2nd Parachute Battalion's stick commanders took over their C-47s from 17:30 and were provided with a hot meal forty-five minutes prior to emplaning from 19:10, a process presumably followed by the other FUSTIAN units.[37] The worn condition of C-47 No. 88, dubbed 'Miss Carriage' belonging to the 60th Troop Carrier Group was noted by Lieutenant Peter Stainforth from the 1st Parachute Squadron RE: 'The fuselage had been peppered with flak and the holes had only recently been hastily patched. Black marks smeared the undersides of the wing behind the exhaust manifold. Her paint was chipped and dingy from long service in the African theatre.' The Crew Chief sought to reassure a mildly unimpressed Stainforth by telling him the 'crate' had seen plenty of service and could probably fly to Sicily and back on its own accord.[38]

The parachute aircraft take-offs were spread over the two-hour period between 19:00 and 21:00, with the 62nd Troop Carrier Group leading the way from Airfields C and D. The Group's first C-47 lifted off from the former at 19:01, ten minutes ahead of schedule, and all twenty-four transports were aloft within twenty-two minutes without incident, apart from one stick being transferred to a spare machine after their original became unserviceable.[39]

Take-offs from Airfield D commenced at 19:25 with all twenty-seven machines airborne by 19:48, two of which aborted. One C-47 returned immediately after take-off with engine trouble, its stick and containers were immediately transferred to a spare machine that took off two hours late; the second C-47 returned at *c*.23:30 also with engine trouble, which could not be resolved.

The first of the 60th Troop Carrier Group's C-47s took off from Airfield A at 19:53 with all twenty-nine machines aloft by 20:05 without incident. The twenty-five C-47s at Airfield B began taking off at 19:55 and all were aloft by 20:22. One machine suffered a burst tyre on take-off, landed immediately and took off again after the ground crew had fitted a replacement in just eight minutes; another returned at 22:25 with engine trouble which again could not be resolved. At Airfield F the eleven parachute Albemarles from RAF No. 296 Squadron were all in the air in just eight minutes beginning at 20:45, although one returned with engine problems at 23:10 and was unable to take off again. Of the glider lift, the eight Albemarles towing CG4A gliders began taking off from Airfield F at 21:43 and seven were airborne by 22:15. The eighth Albemarle crashed and burned at the end of the runway during take-off and while the glider cast off and landed safely, there was no spare tug available; one of the preceding CG4As was also obliged to cast off near M'Saken due to trim problems. At Airfield E the Horsa combinations began taking off at 21:45 and ten were aloft and en route by 22:39. All four of the Albemarle combinations got away without problems but one Halifax combination suffered a broken tow-rope during take-off which was replaced, allowing the combination to carry on late. Another Halifax that took off with a disconnected tow-rope went round again while its Horsa was swapped over to another tug that lifted off without problems, before landing to be connected to another Horsa. The machine appears to have been ill-starred given that the second tow-rope also snapped during take-off, damaging the Horsa's nose and rendering it unserviceable. In all a total of 113 assorted parachute transports, six CG4A and ten Horsa combinations were airborne by 22:39 on 13 July, carrying about 1,865 men.[40] The Operation FUSTIAN force was on its way to Sicily and the Ponte Primosole.

17

Ill Met by Moonlight at the Ponte Primosole

The FUSTIAN Landing and the Fight for the Simeto Crossing, D-Day Plus Three, 22:39 Tuesday 13 July to D-Day Plus Four, 20:00 Wednesday 14 July

After again forming up over Kuriat Island just off the Tunisian coast the Operation FUSTIAN fly-in proceeded east, passing south of the island of Linosa and a sea convoy 'bristling with barrage balloons' without incident to the way point off Malta's Delimara Peninsula, where the route wheeled north into the Ionian Sea for Sicily. Thereafter, matters began to go increasingly awry beginning with an Allied sea convoy firing on the rear of the formation of Albemarles carrying the 1st Parachute Brigade HQ at 21:40, fortunately without scoring any hits.[1] This was a portent of what was to come, although the flight remained benign until the transport stream approached Cape Passero, from where it was to fly for forty miles over the Eastern Naval Task Force stationed in the Gulfs of Noto and Catania. There was fault on both sides for what came next.

At least thirty-three aircraft reportedly strayed close to or within the five-mile exclusion zone, while on the naval side the destroyers and presumably other naval ships had been briefed on the FUSTIAN fly-in but the transports and cargo vessels had not – and an alert for an Axis torpedo-bomber attack was put out just before the transport aircraft began to arrive on the scene. The result replicated the HUSKY TWO fly-in near Gela two days earlier as some vessels, possibly mistaking the containers slung beneath the C-47s for torpedoes, disregarded instructions and opened fire on the slow-moving transport aircraft on their own initiative; as one account put it what began initially 'as a flurry of isolated fire spread rapidly and developed into another ferocious and seemingly uncontrollable fleet-wide barrage of flak'.[2] Fifty-six aircraft reported being fired on by 'friendly' ships, fourteen of them reportedly between five and eight miles from the coast and at least thirty of the remainder between eight and twenty-three miles out to sea.[3] Fortunately and perhaps surprisingly given the volume of fire, only two C-47s were shot down, one carrying a stick from the 3rd Parachute Battalion from which all were saved albeit with six men injured. The other was carrying Captain Arthur Percival's stick from No. 4 Section, 16 Parachute Field Ambulance; Corporal William Amos and Private Arthur White were unable to exit the C-47 despite the best efforts of Captain Percival and a Staff-Sergeant Anderson who were last out after the aircraft had sunk thirty feet beneath the surface. Two more men, Private John Wheeler and Driver Anthony Went, were missing by the time the stick was picked up by a Greek escort vessel, likely the destroyer *Vasilissa Olga*.[4]

The naval anti-aircraft fire prompted around a dozen C-47s to abandon their mission and return to Tunisia, or in one case Malta, with their sticks of paratroopers still on board; the pilot of the C-47 that landed at Malta was wounded by anti-aircraft fire from four or five vessels near Cape Passero that killed his co-pilot and damaged the aircraft's instruments. One C-47 carrying a stick from the 1st Parachute Battalion aborted due to an engine fire that may not have been connected to the friendly flak and two machines carrying sticks from the 1st Parachute Squadron RE also turned away, one after suffering damage to the tail and losing formation and the other because the pilot was wounded and the co-pilot had reportedly never despatched paratroops before. Two C-47s carrying sticks from the 3rd Parachute Battalion turned away after colliding during evasive manoeuvres and damaging a wing and tail respectively and three more carrying sticks from the 1st Parachute Battalion also aborted, one after being hit in the wing, one due to damage to a wing and fuel tank and the third after sustaining hits that wounded the Crew Chief, damaged the tail and blew a three-foot hole in one wing.[5] Four or five C-47 pilots, all from the 62nd Troop Carrier Group carrying sticks from the 1st Parachute Battalion, claimed to have been ordered to abandon their mission by their Squadron commander; it is unclear if this was actually the case and if so, the justification for the order.[6]

Approximately eleven more transports including a No. 296 Squadron Albemarle also ended up returning to Tunisia with their sticks aboard due to a combination of enemy flak, becoming lost and/or being unable to locate the DZ or run-in point at the mouth of the River Simeto; a number of pilots reported it obscured by haze and smoke, perhaps due to incendiary ammunition igniting dry stubble or the enemy deliberately setting fire to haystacks. Six C-47s abandoned their mission after failing to locate the run-in point or DZ but several only after multiple attempts to establish their bearings. Three C-47s carrying sticks from the 1st Parachute Battalion made multiple unsuccessful run ins, up to eight times in one instance, under enemy anti-aircraft fire and one after suffering wing damage from Allied naval flak; another machine carrying men from the 2nd Parachute Battalion made two attempts before flak chopped six feet from a wing while the single Albemarle turned away after four attempts due to lack of fuel. Including the two C-47s shot down into the sea, around twenty-five sticks were removed from the FUSTIAN order of battle by machines aborting for whatever reason after passing Malta, one from 1st Parachute Brigade HQ, eleven from the

1st Parachute Battalion, three from the 2nd Parachute Battalion, seven from the 3rd Parachute Battalion and one out of three from 16 Parachute Field Ambulance.[7] At least one stick and possibly two or a part stick also returned from the 1st Parachute Squadron RE.[8]

Just under ninety aircraft pressed on despite the Axis anti-aircraft fire and navigation difficulties to deliver their sticks of paratroopers.[9] Many pilots displayed great determination by making multiple attempts to break through the Axis anti-aircraft fire or locate their designated DZs; one C-47 from the 62nd Troop Carrier Group carrying a stick from the 1st Parachute Battalion finally succeeded on its fifth run over the DZ for example, and another carrying men from the 2nd Parachute Battalion pressed on to drop close to DZ 3 despite problems with both engines, one of which failed completely on the return flight.[10] A number of machines were travelling so fast and low that they clipped haystacks and trees and a British paratrooper Sergeant acting as Jumpmaster in one C-47 recounted how his machine made two unsuccessful attempts to penetrate the flak barrage and was hit in the process, before breaking through in a steep dive; the machine crossed the coast at just a hundred feet travelling faster than its passengers realised possible in an effort to shake two searchlights before the pilot, a Major Curtis, pulled up to between 400 and 500 feet and despatched his stick in what the Sergeant described as 'a nice jump'.[11]

At the other end of the scale Lieutenant-Colonel Pearson's C-47 appears to have made it to Sicily untroubled by friendly anti-aircraft fire but Pearson awoke from a doze to discover the machine was flying parallel to the coast well north of the landing area and heading in the wrong direction, despite being one of the relatively few with a qualified navigator on board; on accessing the cockpit he discovered that the pilots were deliberately avoiding approaching the DZ due to the flak. Having ascertained that a former RAF pilot in his stick was capable of flying the C-47, Pearson brought the resulting heated argument to a close by drawing his pistol and threatening to shoot the pilots if they did not do their job; this unorthodox approach worked and Pearson and his stick were duly dropped near their objective.[12]

Despite the pilots' best efforts, Axis flak and searchlights shot down nine transports, eight C-47s and an Albemarle, all but one after dropping their sticks.[13] The exception appears to have been a C-47 from the 60th Troop Carrier Group carrying a stick from the 3rd Parachute Battalion, which burst into flames over the DZ when an under-slung container was hit by flak and exploded; after ordering the machine abandoned the pilot discovered several injured men still aboard and threw them out of the door before exiting himself. Another machine carrying a stick from the 2nd Parachute Battalion also reportedly crashed in flames near DZ 3 after ten of its sixteen-strong stick had jumped.[14] In all, five aircraft appear to have been shot down over Sicily and between four and six including the Albemarle ditched out to sea after dropping their sticks.[15] Unsurprisingly, all this seriously affected the accuracy of the drop overall, and not just in the geographical sense. A number of aircraft despatched their sticks above the maximum drop speed of 135 miles per hour and below the agreed jump height of 500 feet; at least five of the latter despatched their sticks at less than half that height resulting in two landing fatalities and thirty-five landing injuries, thirteen of them serious.[16]

The low despatches included Lieutenant-Colonel Pearson's stick from the 1st Parachute Battalion. Pearson jumped in the middle of the stick and his canopy had barely deployed when he hit the ground; all ten men behind him were winded and bruised at best, several were badly injured and the last man was killed by an undeveloped canopy.[17] Of the nearly ninety aircraft that pressed through the anti-aircraft fire, sixty-six were certain that they had despatched their sticks on or close to the correct DZs, but the reality was different. Only thirty sticks were actually dropped on a designated DZ, nine landed within half a mile and forty-eight further out; twenty-two sticks came down within five miles of their assigned DZ and nineteen aircraft dropped their passengers ten miles or more astray.[18] Four sticks, likely one from the 1st Parachute Battalion and three from the 3rd Parachute Battalion, were dropped on the slopes of Mount Etna over twenty miles from the Ponte Primosole, with some unfortunates possibly falling into the volcano's active crater.[19]

The bulk of the parachute drops were carried out in a window of just under two hours, the first reportedly a stick from the 2nd Parachute Battalion despatched at 22:05 and the last a stick from the 3rd Parachute Battalion despatched at 23:55, although at least four individual sticks were delivered later. The latest of all was a C-47 from the 62nd Troop Carrier Group that delivered a stick from the 1st Parachute Battalion almost seven miles south of DZ 2 at 01:50; the delay may have been due to the pilot becoming lost or possibly due to engine trouble, given that the machine put down on Malta.[20] The first returning aircraft touched down in Tunisia at Airfield C at 23:40 with most of the rest landing by 00:45. By 10:00 on 14 July 101 parachute transports had returned to their home bases, ninety-one C-47s and ten Albemarles; another three machines returned later having landed elsewhere and six more were reported missing.[21] A total of fifteen aircraft returned carrying full sticks and individual aircraft entries suggest as many as twenty-three C-47s returned with partial sticks still aboard, six each from the 1st and 2nd Parachute Battalions, nine from the 3rd Parachute Battalion and two from 16th Parachute Field Ambulance.[22]

The cause was usually men being thrown off their feet or becoming entangled in parachute strops and kitbags, although a dozen men were wounded by anti-aircraft fire before they could jump, three of them seriously, and in three instances refusals blocked the door to men behind them in the stick until the machine was past the DZ.[23] Most returns involved one or two men, but several aircraft despatched half or less of their sticks, sometimes because pilots halted the jump for safety reasons; two C-47s carrying men from the 3rd Parachute Battalion managed to despatch just four men from sticks of fourteen, for example.[24] Thirty-five aircraft were damaged, one after colliding with a presumably ship-mounted barrage balloon and the rest by anti-aircraft fire, three so seriously they had to be written off, although the remainder were returned to service within forty-eight hours. The US 60th Troop Carrier Group was reportedly worst hit, losing nine C-47s and another twenty-three damaged. The combined RAF and USAAF aircrew casualty figures for FUSTIAN, compiled around two weeks after the event, listed one known dead, fourteen wounded and thirty-five missing.[25]

In all 1,278 of the 1,856 paratroopers from the 1st Parachute Brigade who left Tunisia jumped over Sicily, of whom 295 men, around twenty per cent of the force, landed close enough to take part in the subsequent battle for the Ponte Primosole.[26] They descended upon a fully alerted enemy, as noted by an unnamed participant from the 3rd Parachute Battalion: 'Red Light – Green Light – we float down into a world of searchlights, tracer bullets and burning corn stacks.'[27] A Lance-Corporal Coster from the 1st Parachute Battalion landed squarely atop a happily unlit corn stack and his abrupt arrival flushed out six hapless Italian troops sheltering beneath it who reportedly 'ran like hares'.[28] The full impact of the scattering on unit cohesion swiftly became apparent on the ground, and mirrored that of the US 82nd Airborne Division's HUSKY ONE and TWO parachute drops. Just 124 men from the 1st Parachute Battalion had rallied by 09:00, while the 2nd Parachute Battalion had gathered in 112 at the unit rendezvous by 01:00 before moving off for the high ground to the south.[29]

The 3rd Parachute Battalion fared worse of all. At 23:20, fifteen minutes after jumping, the 3rd Battalion War Diary noted: '3rd Bn. Para. Regt. Consists of CO and batman, RSM and batman, Int. Sjt. and one Int. Pte.' Realising they had been dropped on the wrong DZ, Lieutenant-Colonel Yeldham led his little band to the Battalion RV location, but on arriving at midnight found it deserted apart from a single member of the 21st Independent Parachute Company waiting to guide in the glider lift.[30] At 01:00 they were joined by six men who had been travelling with a party from the 1st Parachute Battalion and four hours later by Major Mervyn Dennison with a platoon from his A Company and a party of fifteen led by at Lieutenant Peter Waddy, bringing the 3rd Battalion strength up to around forty.[31]

Brigadier Lathbury's Brigade HQ suffered similarly. While nine of its eleven Albemarles reached the landing area and two reported fast exits, one stick clearing the aircraft in just ten seconds, only four reported delivering their sticks accurately onto DZ 2 with the remainder being dropped well over a mile to four miles away.[32] The scattered included Brigadier Lathbury and his batman, a Private Lake, who dropped at 23:32 over high ground as their Albemarle turned abruptly to avoid flak in mid-jump, which put them down around three miles from the DZ and reduced the jump height by half; both men were fortunate to avoid injury. Lathbury found a few men from HQ staff including Brigade Major David Hunter at the open and flame-illuminated DZ before establishing a Command Post in a nearby dry watercourse, from where he tried to clarify the situation while waiting for more men to rally.[33] At 02:15 Lieutenant-Colonel Frost and his 112 men passed Lathbury's location on the way to secure the high ground to the south, after being directed by two men from the Brigade HQ Defence Platoon moving back to DZ 2 in search of a No. 18 Wireless Set; after a brief discussion, Frost wished his commander Many Happy Returns as 14 July was Lathbury's forty-seventh birthday, before pushing on for the JOHNNY I hilltop, passing Major Dennison and a party from the 3rd Parachute Battalion busy cutting signals cables close to the *Strada* 114.[34]

Frost's passing and departure clearly highlights one of the key flaws in the FUSTIAN Ground Plan, and one to which Lathbury was seemingly oblivious. At this point Lathbury was 'a brigadier without a brigade' and was totally out of contact with his subordinate units, not least because all the radio containers were unaccounted for apart from one, which landed in the nearby Gornalunga Canal; the Brigade Signals Section recovered a No. 22 Set from it but the Set was water damaged and unserviceable.[35] Lathbury had no idea whether the 1st Parachute Battalion's *coup-de-main* attack had succeeded in securing the Ponte Primosole, but he appears to have been quite content to allow Frost to go about his business and take over a hundred men in the opposite direction to FUSTIAN's primary objective.

Around fifty men eventually gathered at the Brigade Command Post including Captain Richard Gammon and Lieutenant John Helingoe from the 1st Parachute Battalion and a stick of fifteen from the 1st Parachute Squadron RE commanded by Lieutenant Peter Stainforth. Lathbury and Major Hunter divided them into three assault groups and a fire-support section, each led by an officer, and at some point between Frost's departure and 03:15 moved off to secure the Ponte Primosole via a pre-arranged RV at a road drainage culvert half a mile west of the bridge.[36]

Although Lathbury had no way of knowing it, the bridge had already been taken by his men, beginning an hour before he reached the structure himself. The 1st Parachute Battalion's *coup-de-main* attack did not go ahead, as the two assault platoons failed to arrive but at DZ 1 Captain J. Rann gathered a party of around fifty men from the 1st Battalion and moved off for the bridge at 01:00 on his own initiative, apparently linking up with the small 3rd Parachute Battalion party en route. Arriving at the bridge at 02:00, Captain Rann despatched 1st Battalion Signals Officer Lieutenant James Lasenby and six men to scout the approaches and on learning the bridge appeared to be undefended Rann mounted a hasty assault that swiftly secured the north end; the Italian troops manning the northern defences surrendered, fled or went into hiding and MARSTON was effectively if not completely in British hands from *c.*02:15 on Wednesday 14 July.[37]

Over the next hour or so the north end defences were fully cleared, the roadblock re-established, a 1st Battalion Command Post was set up presumably by Captain Rann, and Lieutenant Lasenby and his party were despatched across the bridge to check the south end, accompanied by a Sergeant from the 3rd Battalion's Intelligence Section tasked to locate Brigade HQ and report developments. Around the same time the bridge was approached by vehicles, a three-truck convoy from the north and a vehicle towing an artillery piece of some kind from the south. The convoy vehicles were attacked and set ablaze with Gammon bombs either before reaching the bridge or after moving onto it, depending on the source; the gun prime mover was machine-gunned to a halt either just short of the south end of the bridge or after moving onto the structure.[38]

The Brigade HQ party approached the bridge at 03:15 fully prepared to attack and secure the structure until Brigadier Lathbury went forward to clarify the situation and discovered men from the 1st and 3rd Parachute Battalions at the south end. The area had not been fully cleared, however, and as Lathbury and Brigade Major Hunter were moving to cross the bridge they were attacked by a 'a stray Italian' with a grenade variously reported as emerging from a pillbox, sheltering near the shot-up prime mover, or by a German escaping from the northern convoy. Whoever was responsible for the deed, the explosion cost Major Hunter's batman three of his toes and peppered Lathbury's legs and back with fragments that left him 'in a good deal of pain' but still mobile, if slow.[39] Lieutenant Stainforth saw his Brigade commander standing 'with his trousers fallen round his ankles' while his batman applied field-dressings to his wounds.

The Sapper officer and his stick were busy removing the bridge demolition charges starting at both ends using 'borrowed pliers, wire-cutters and machetes from the infantry and gunners'. The demolition preparations consisted of charges in metal boxes attached to the girders, fortunately without detonators or connected wiring, and 120 pounds of granular explosive spread equally across six chambers in the two stone supporting pillars, sufficient 'to blow the stone to powder'; all the explosive and associated wiring was unceremoniously dumped in the river.[40] The grenade incident also appears to have prompted a thorough clearing of the defences at the south end and fifty Italian prisoners were then moved across the bridge and incarcerated in a building at the north end; thirty of the prisoners were reportedly Italian engineers rounded up by a small patrol led by Lieutenant John MacFadden, the 1st Parachute Battalion's Intelligence Officer.[41]

The FUSTIAN glider lift was coming in by now. Of the original nineteen gliders slated for FUSTIAN, three dropped out at take-off or shortly thereafter; one CG4A was scratched when its tug became unserviceable with no replacement aircraft available, another cast off over Tunisia with trim problems and a Horsa was damaged beyond use when its tow-rope failed on take-off. A further three machines, a CG4A and two Horsas, appear to have gone missing over the sea with one of the Horsas being cast off without warning two miles off the coast of Sicily, and two more gliders went missing after being successfully released over dry land, a CG4A over LZ 7 and a Horsa over LZ 8. Of the remaining eleven gliders that made landfall on the island six, three of each type, came down wide of the Ponte Primosole, several miles distant in most cases. A CG4A carrying a 6-Pounder gun landed inside the defences of Catania airfield five miles north of the bridge after being hit in the starboard wing by flak on release, and another carrying a Jeep put down north of Lentini, seven miles to the south-west but was unable to extract the vehicle due to landing damage and the proximity of enemy troops. The third CG4A, also carrying a Jeep, made a heavy landing on the beach east of the landing area that left the crew unable to lift the machine's nose for unloading; again, the proximity of Italian defences precluded cutting the vehicle free. Of the three Horsas, one carrying a 6-Pounder gun and Jeep landed seven miles south-west of LZ 7 and unloaded its cargo within thirty minutes. The other two fared less well. One landed safely north-east of Lentini despite being 'riddled' by enemy small-arms and 20mm fire but came to rest at an angle that prevented unloading via the side door; when the crew attempted to cut off the glider's tail using a length of explosive detonator cord, the plywood machine caught fire and was destroyed along with its cargo.[42] The third Horsa crashed north-east of Lentini, reportedly after its Halifax tug was shot down while going around again for another run on the LZ. Four of those aboard the glider including both pilots were killed and the remaining three passengers were badly injured.[43]

According to one source guns from *Major* Schmidt's *Fallschirmjäger MG Bataillon 1* accounted for three tugs, two gliders and captured eighty-two men from the 1st Parachute Brigade in the course of the night.[44] The result of the German automatic fire was graphically described by Brigadier Lathbury: 'One Horsa glider came over our heads at about one-hundred feet; it was clearly visible in the light of the fires and every German machine-gun and light flak gun turned onto it. We could see about five streams of tracer going through the fuselage, then it disappeared into the darkness and a moment later we heard it hit the ground with a crash.'[45]

Of the seventeen gliders that had lifted off from Airfields E and F in Tunisia around four hours earlier, only four Horsas and a single CG4A came down on or close to their assigned LZs. CG4A No. 118C, piloted by Lieutenant Norman Adams and Sergeant Frederick Street, came to rest to the south-west of LZ 7 with a jammed nose that prevented the crew unloading the Jeep it was carrying and all aboard were injured to some degree; Sergeant Street was killed either during the landing or later on during 14 July.[46] Lieutenant William Barrie's Horsa No. 120, co-piloted by Sergeant I. N. Williams, suffered a snapped tow-rope while its Albemarle tug circled looking for LZ 7 but made a safe skid landing 2,000 yards west of LZ 8, where its Jeep and 6-Pounder were unloaded over a three-hour period; the prolonged unloading time was likely due to the glider's rear fuselage having to be cut away with hand tools.[47] Horsa No. 128, crewed by Lieutenant Robin Walchli and Sergeant Wallace Mackenzie, was even less fortunate. Lieutenant Walchli successfully avoided a set of high-tension cables and the edge of the bridge superstructure but clipped the raised bank of the Gornalunga Canal with the Horsa's undercarriage while making his final turn for LZ 7. The glider slammed abruptly into the embankment, catapulting both pilots through its plexiglass nose and into the canal; both survived the unplanned ejection but four of their passengers were killed, two more were injured and just one man emerged unharmed. The glider was too badly smashed for its Jeep and 6-Pounder, both also likely severely damaged, to be unloaded.[48]

The remaining two Horsas landed closest of all to their objective. The Halifax towing Staff-Sergeant David White and Sergeant Henry Webb's

Horsa No. 129 released its charge high over LZ 8 due to anti-aircraft fire, but despite the glider being hit repeatedly by flak Staff-Sergeant White brought it down safely on the *Strada* 114 carriageway around a hundred yards from the south end of the Ponte Primosole. No-one aboard was injured but the machine's shackled cargo shifted severely under the impact of the hard surface landing and it took four hours to extract the 6-Pounder after removing the rear fuselage and a further five hours to remove the Jeep; the machine may have been that observed by Brigadier Lathbury. The pilots and passengers were assisted in their efforts by Lieutenant Lasenby's patrol, which came upon the wrecked Horsa after crossing the bridge.[49] Horsa No. 126, piloted by Staff-Sergeant Harold Protheroe and Sergeant David Kerr, was the only FUSTIAN glider to put down on its assigned LZ. The Horsa made a 'perfect release' from its Halifax tug at 00:45 at an altitude of 500 feet, successfully avoided the electricity pylons and high-tension cables and made a 'heavy landing' on LZ 8, coming to halt just short of a copse that bounded the western end of the zone. Daylight investigation showed that the heavy landing was actually a collision with a telegraph pole that again catapulted both pilots through the windscreen, injuring Sergeant Kerr in the leg and wrecking the glider. The passengers emerged unscathed and immediately set about extracting the cargo, as described by Lieutenant Stainforth who passed by en route to the bridge: 'A Horsa glider was lying on its side…one wing was crumpled into matchwood, while the other pointed at the sky; the nose was crushed…a swarm of men were cutting and wrenching at the tail unit to get their gun and jeep out.' The load was extracted in functioning order by *c*.01:45.[50]

The 2nd Parachute Battalion was now beginning what developed into its own isolated battle on the high ground south of the River Simeto. The action began when Lieutenant Tony Frank from A Company gathered a party of two officers and around forty men from A and B Companies in the vicinity of DZ 3; Lieutenant Frank and half his stick were involved in several clashes with the enemy and one of the gathered-in sticks had been 'very actively engaged' clearing enemy positions along the southern edge of the DZ.[51] At *c*.02:30, after failing to locate any more men or his company or battalion command elements at the DZ or the designated Battalion rendezvous, Lieutenant Frank decided to lead his party in an independent attack on JOHNNY I, the 2nd Battalion's centre objective just east of the *Strada* 114.

After interrogating a captured enemy despatch rider, Frank launched a three-pronged assault on the hill from the north-east at *c*.03:15 that secured the summit against light opposition by 04:00 along with 130 Italian prisoners, forty of whom emerged from caves on the northern slope. Also at 04:00, Lieutenant-Colonel Frost and the main 2nd Battalion party reached their designated Forming Up Point (FUP) for the assault on JOHNNY I, an abandoned pillbox at the base of the hill, where Frost set up a Command Post before despatching Major Richard Lonsdale and his fifty men from A Company to secure the objective. On reaching the summit at 04:30 Lonsdale discovered Lieutenant Frank already in possession. After absorbing

Frank's party, Lonsdale took command of the location as ordered; within half an hour the JOHNNY I position had been consolidated and 2nd Parachute Battalion HQ had been established at the abandoned pillbox occupied by a now immobilised Lieutenant-Colonel Frost. By 05:30 the 2nd Battalion force had grown to around 140 men from A, B and Support Companies along with twenty signallers deployed in a perimeter defence using Italian trenches and wire where possible, albeit bereft of radios or support weapons.[52] A Prisoner of War cage had also been established in a walled farmyard on the north summit; surrendering Italian troops including *Regia Aeronautica* and *Regia Marina* personnel were 'appearing from all directions [and] soon became and remained a nuisance'.[53] The British presence on JOHNNY I did not go unnoticed. At 05:30 a *Luftwaffe* spotter plane flew low over the hill and thirty minutes later the 2nd Battalion positions came under heavy and sustained machine-gun fire from elements of *Fallschirmjäger MG Bataillon 1* ensconced on the JOHNNY II feature 600 yards or so to the east, and from the vicinity of a farmhouse 200 yards to the south-east.[54]

Back at the Ponte Primosole the new tenants were also busy consolidating their defence. By *c.*05:00 approximately 200 men from the 1st Parachute Brigade were present at the bridge including Lieutenant-Colonel Pearson and around 120 men from the 1st Parachute Battalion equipped with a Vickers MMG, two 3-inch mortars, three PIATS and a functioning No. 22 Wireless Set; together with Major Dennison and a platoon from the 3rd Parachute Battalion; Captain Waddy and fifteen men also from the 3rd Battalion; Lieutenant Stainforth's stick of fifteen Sappers from the 1st Parachute Squadron RE; and three 6-Pounder guns and crews from the 1st Airlanding Anti-Tank Battery RA.[55] At 05:30 Lieutenant-Colonel Pearson was placed in charge of the bridge defences and over the next hour the 3rd Battalion HQ was established on the north bank and the 1st Battalion and Brigade HQ Command Posts were established at the south end of the bridge.[56]

Pearson's HQ established radio contact with its S and T Companies and the 3rd Battalion HQ on the north bank, although attempts to contact No. 3 Commando, which was supposed to be en route from the Ponte Malati by this time, or the 4th Armoured Brigade, were unsuccessful; the No. 22 Set was subsequently appropriated by Captain George Rowland, commander of the Brigade HQ Signals Section, along with a No. 68 Set.[57] By *c.*06:30 a coherent defence had been erected on both banks of the River Simeto incorporating the existing Italian pillboxes, trenches and barbed wire, drainage ditches and slit trenches. A Bren gun was stationed covering the *Strada* 114 to the north and two Breda machine-guns which had been captured with 44,000 rounds of ammunition at the south end appropriated by Lieutenant Joseph Gardiner from the 1st Parachute Battalion MMG Platoon were also integrated into the defence.[58]

Heavier support was provided by the three 6-Pounder anti-tank guns from Horsa Nos. 120, 126 and 129; the two guns commanded by Sergeant Harold Doig and a Lance-Sergeant Atkinson were deployed on the north bank while Sergeant John Anderson's gun was deployed at the south end of the bridge. Two bunker-mounted Italian anti-tank guns captured in working order were also pressed into service, manned by scratch crews of glider pilots and paratroopers who were given a crash course in anti-tank gunnery by Lieutenant Eric Clapham from the 1st Airlanding Anti-Tank Battery.[59] The Airborne troops put a large stock of German Teller anti-tank mines discovered in a bunker to good use; after removing the demolition charges from the bridge structure, Lieutenant Stainforth's Sappers spent the remaining hours of darkness inserting fuses into the mines and carrying them out for use on the perimeter.[60]

A Main Dressing Station (MDS) complete with a surgical team was established as planned in a farm near the south end of the bridge, along with a smaller Advanced Dressing Station (ADS) on the north bank to feed casualties back from the individual Battalion Regimental Aid Posts (RAPs). The MDS buildings were initially cleared and secured by Captain Derek Ridler and his stick from 16th Parachute Field Ambulance at *c*.04:45, who were joined shortly after by Major Cedric Longland and his surgical team. The commander of 16th Parachute Field Ambulance, Lieutenant-Colonel Ross Wheatley, landed five miles south of the Ponte Primosole and arrived there at 05:45; he then used a commandeered bicycle to reach the MDS, assumed command at 06:40 and informed Brigade HQ that the Station was open for casualties twenty minutes later.[61] While there was still no sign of patrols from No. 3 Commando advancing north from the Ponte Malati or the 50th Division, after twenty minutes trying as callsign 'Pronto' via the No. 22 Set, Captain Rowland drew a response from the 4th Armoured Brigade Command Net at 09:30 with the immortal words 'Oh, Hullo Pronto, Sorry to keep you waiting.' Rowland immediately passed the handset to Brigade Major Hunter who identified himself: 'Seagull SHO speaking – we cannot tell you who we are but does "Marston One" mean anything to you?' The unknown Armoured Brigade officer responded 'Yes, my God it does, good show, I wish I could get to you now.' Captain Rowland maintained contact with the Armoured Brigade Command Net until the No. 22 Set's batteries gave out, but he was unable to make any contact with the shorter-ranged No. 68 Set.[62]

Through the morning of Wednesday 14 July 1943 there were just three Axis reactions to the presence of the 1st Parachute Brigade at the Ponte Primosole. At 03:45 an Italian armoured car approached the bridge from the north and was promptly knocked out with a Gammon bomb.[63] Five hours later two trucks, again approaching from the direction of Catania, were observed offloading infantry around a mile and a half from the bridge. The paratroopers allowed the infantry to close to within a mile or so before dropping half a dozen 3-inch mortar bombs close enough to inflict a number of casualties; 'the remainder withdrew at speed' at *c*.09:15.[64] The third contact came from the air. At 10:00 the area of the bridge was strafed by two German aircraft, variously reported as Messerschmitt 109 or Focke-Wulf 190 fighters, the first of an ongoing relay that continued for the rest of the day; on expending their ammunition the fighters returned to the nearby

Catania airfield where the paratroopers could see them being rearmed for their next sortie.[65] The strafing attacks were sufficiently troublesome to prompt Lathbury's Brigade HQ to move 200 yards to a culvert under the *Strada* 114 for shelter.[66]

The reason for this relatively quiet morning was that the Axis side, and specifically *Hauptmann* Franz Stangenberg from *Fallschirmjäger Regiment 3* Staff, was busy arranging a counter-attack from scratch. On learning of the British presence at the Ponte Primosole from a despatch rider, *Hauptmann* Stangenberg travelled to the crossing to investigate and after coming under fire from the new tenants immediately set about organising a response. He began by requesting and receiving permission from *Generalleutnant* Heidrich at *OB Süd* in Rome to co-opt the only uncommitted *1 Fallschirmjäger Division* unit in Sicily, *Hauptmann* Erich Fassl's *1 Kompanie* from *Fallschirm Kommunication Bataillon 1*. Stangenberg then began building an ad hoc counter-attack force using the signal unit as a core, not least by despatching a party of *Hauptmann* Fassl's senior NCOs to round up every German serviceman they could lay hands on; there does not appear to have been any effort to co-opt Italian troops into the force at this stage, perhaps understandably given the poor performance of the bridge garrison. By midday *Hauptmann* Stangenberg had gathered around 200 men including administrative personnel from *1 Fallschirmjäger Division* and the *Hermann Göring Panzer Division* and *Luftwaffe* ground crew from Catania airfield. He had Fassl's signallers lay a telephone line to the *Luftwaffe* 88mm anti-aircraft guns deployed at the airfield so they could provide directed fire support for the attack, and he may also have been responsible for the relay of fighters strafing the bridge perimeter.[67]

The Wednesday morning lull did not extend to the 2nd Parachute Battalion at the JOHNNY I feature south of the Ponte Primosole. At 06:30 the heavy machine-gun fire from the adjacent JOHNNY II feature and farm buildings to the east was augmented by increasingly accurate mortar fire that the Battalion was unable to counter due to its lack of support weapons, and a fighting patrol from C Company despatched at 07:30 to deal with the enemy positions to the south-east ran into heavy German fire shortly after leaving the perimeter and was then comprehensively shot up by three enemy armoured cars that inflicted a number of casualties. The German mortar fire fell accurately on a forward outpost manned by a party from A Company located in an olive grove to the south of the main hilltop position overlooking the *Strada* 114, intended to remedy a weak spot in the main perimeter; the party had only just begun digging in when the mortar fire commenced and was so seriously hit that it had to be withdrawn back into the main perimeter at 08:00. By this point the hilltop perimeter was under machine-gun fire from three sides and the enemy were closing in on the British positions using a combination of 'heavy fire power and considerable skill', although the traffic was not all one way.

A party of paratroopers, possibly led by Support Company commander Captain Stanley Panter, attacked an unwary MG34 team, capturing the gun and two members of the team, one of them badly wounded; the capture revealed that the 2nd Battalion's opponents were in fact their *Fallschirmjäger* opposite numbers. At 08:30 the British situation was reportedly 'becoming rather serious' as the approximately 140-strong force were being whittled down by the unrelenting German fire and running short of ammunition, and by 09:00 small groups of *Fallschirmjäger* were engaging the 2nd Battalion positions with automatic fire from within 400 yards.[68] The tide turned at *c*.09:00 when an Observer Team from No. 1 Combined Operations Bombardment Unit headed by Captain Francis Hodge made contact with the cruiser HMS *Newfoundland* from Rear-Admiral Cecil Harcourt's FORCE K; Captain Hodge and his Observer Team had linked up with the 2nd Parachute Battalion's HQ element after parachuting in and had been trying to make contact with the cruiser for at least two hours.[69]

After bringing down a ranging salvo that gave a 'tremendous' boost to British morale, Captain Hodge systematically walked the salvoes from the *Newfoundland's* 6-inch guns back toward the British perimeter, dealing with the German pockets individually until the shells were falling within just 150 yards of the perimeter; two shells hit thirty yards from the improvised Prisoner of War cage, reportedly wounding two or three prisoners and sending the rest into 'a state of hysteria for about five minutes'. The shelling resulted in a marked reduction in the volume of automatic fire directed at the 2nd Battalion perimeter as the closest German elements sought cover or withdrew; as Lieutenant-Colonel Frost later noted, Hodge's actions represented a complete turning of the scales by 'one young officer, a signaller and a wireless set'.[70] An upsurge in German sniping followed with one individual especially 'firing accurately and with considerable zest', but at 10:30 Hodge was able to switch to German machine-guns on the adjacent high ground and enemy-occupied buildings to the south-east; the results of the former were unclear as the targets were difficult to identify and shifted location, but enemy troops were seen evacuating the buildings.[71] Captain Hodge relocated his team several times in order to obtain clearer observation despite the heavy German fire and was subsequently awarded the Military Cross for his actions on JOHNNY I.[72]

The 2nd Battalion's lack of support weapons was partially addressed at 11:00 with the discovery of an abandoned Italian howitzer and a quantity of ammunition in a valley east of the British perimeter. Captain Panter organised a scratch crew from his weaponless 3-inch mortar crewmen and had the gun moved to where it could fire on the encroaching Germans; enemy fire prevented the piece being placed within voice range of Captain Hodge's Observer Team, although how useful this would have been is open to question given that the howitzer's sights were missing. The gun was laid by eye and fired fifteen rounds at German troops spotted on the Johnny II and adjacent features before Frost ordered Panter to cease his activities as they were 'more likely to bring unwelcome retribution than any harm to the enemy'.[73] Captain Panter was nonetheless also awarded the Military Cross for his actions on 14 July.[74] The combination of the *Newfoundland's* gunfire and the efforts of Captain Panter's scratch howitzer crew had the desired effect. By midday the German sniping and machine-gun fire had slackened noticeably and continued to do so over the next hour, when German artillery began shelling the JOHNNY II feature in the belief that it was occupied by Frost's men.[75]

As the action on JOHNNY I died down, the attack on the Ponte Primosole was getting underway. Having gathered his ad hoc counter-attack force, which now included a self-propelled gun of some description and several anti-tank guns, *Hauptmann* Stangenberg divided it in two. The main body, commanded by Stangenberg in person, was to advance down the line of the *Strada* 114 while *Hauptmann* Fassl and his signallers moved on a parallel line east of the road; the concentration on the north end of the bridge was presumably due to the vines and poplar trees that offered cover for infiltration.[76] Preparation for the attack commenced just after noon in the wake of a *Luftwaffe* strafing attack with shelling at both ends of the bridge that went on for almost an hour; the 3rd Parachute Battalion noted that the artillery fire was accurate and consisted largely of air bursts set to detonate at a height of twenty to thirty feet.[77]

The forty-strong 3rd Battalion contingent appears to have borne the brunt of the first German attack shortly after the bombardment lifted at 13:00, possibly by *Hauptmann* Fassl's contingent on the flank of the main German line of advance; Lieutenant-Colonel Yeldham reported the situation was under control at 13:20 and the attack was rebuffed by 14:30, but in the meantime the 1st Parachute Battalion's S Company observed more German troops moving down both sides of the *Strada* 114 under cover of smoke at 13:50 before launching an attack twenty minutes later, beginning on the left flank of the 1st Battalion's frontage and spreading around to the right flank; the attack was again held but at cost of a number of wounded and the perimeter had to be tightened closer to the bridge to maximise the available manpower.[78]

The British Semi-Official History and a more recent account refers to German attacks on the south end of the bridge around this time that continued through the day, but while this may have been the case, the unit War Diaries only refer to enemy infantry attacks against the northern perimeter and to shelling and strafing attacks against the southern.[79] Be that as it may, *Hauptmann* Stangenberg resumed the bombardment of the north bank from 15:00 to cover regrouping in preparation for a renewed attack, which the 3rd Parachute Battalion described as 'intense and accurate'.[80] At this point Captain Hodge and his Observer Team intervened in the fight for the Ponte Primosole from atop JOHNNY I by directing fire from HMS *Newfoundland* or possibly her running mate HMS *Mauritius* onto an Italian coastal battery spotted shelling the bridge perimeter from west of Catania. The 6-inch shells reportedly knocked out two of the enemy guns and set fire to the battery observation post and ammunition magazine, which exploded a few minutes later, putting the remaining guns out of action. Captain Hodge then switched fire to a field artillery battery with less certain or spectacular results due to restricted visibility, and then back to enemy troops and transport spotted near a group of buildings closer to the 2nd Parachute Battalion's hilltop perimeter at 16:00.[81]

In addition to regrouping under cover of the renewed shelling, *Hauptmann* Stangenberg's force received several truckloads of German and Italian reinforcements, which may have included elements of *Major* Ernst Liebach's *Fallschirmjäger Pionier Bataillon 1*.[82] The attackers began infiltrating through the vine groves and trees up to the tightened British northern perimeter from *c*.15:30 and at 16:00 lifted the bombardment onto the south side of the bridge for a sustained and determined attack. The renewed assault was 'held but only just', according to the 3rd Parachute Battalion account, and the volume of defensive fire inevitably slackened as British casualties mounted and the remaining defenders began to run short of ammunition.[83] Lieutenant Gardiner's captured Breda machine-guns and ammunition were an important component of the defence. A Driver D. Reed was instrumental in distributing reserve ammunition to the units on the perimeter under fire using a 1st Airlanding Anti-Tank Battery Jeep. Driver Reed also made at least two trips across the fire-swept bridge from the northern perimeter carrying stretcher cases to the MDS accompanied by Lieutenant Clapham, the erstwhile anti-tank gunnery instructor; he was subsequently awarded the Military Cross for his actions, but Driver Reed does not appear to have been similarly honoured.[84]

Driver Reed's activities were replicated in slower motion by a Corporal F. J. Scott from the Army Dental Corps, who made six trips under fire ferrying wounded and injured from crashed gliders and the Battalion RAPs to the ADS on the north bank, using a commandeered horse and cart.[85] For its part the MDS operated with the assistance of a volunteer Italian Medical Officer from 10:00 and by 22:00 was treating sixty-two British and twenty-nine enemy casualties; Major Longland's surgical team carried out twenty-one operations across the thirteen hours the MDS was at work.[86] Despite all this, within an hour the situation at the north end of the bridge was becoming untenable as the British positions continued to be squeezed by enemy infantry and were under continuous direct fire from numerous anti-aircraft, infantry and self-propelled guns, augmented by heavy automatic fire from an armoured car on the *Strada* 114.[87] In order to prevent them being overwhelmed and destroyed in place, Brigadier Lathbury therefore ordered the men holding the northern perimeter to withdraw across the bridge to the south bank at 17:05, reportedly in an effort to consolidate his force and maintain a partial hold on the objective.

Lieutenant-Colonel Yeldham's contingent from the 3rd Parachute Battalion withdrew first followed at *c*.17:30 by Lieutenant-Colonel Pearson and his larger party from the 1st Parachute Battalion, which had reportedly grown to 160 men by this point, stragglers reaching the bridge perimeter across the day. Both parties reportedly completed the crossing without sustaining casualties, with at least one party wading through the shallow water and mud beneath the bridge rather than using the roadway according to Lieutenant Stainforth; the two 6-Pounder guns from the 1st Airlanding Anti-Tank Battery may have been withdrawn across the bridge as well.[88]

The withdrawal was covered by Sergeant Anderson's 6-Pounder, which appears to have dissuaded the enemy armoured car from pushing across the bridge and knocked out one of the recently vacated pillboxes at the north end when its new occupants proved especially troublesome. The unrelenting Axis artillery fire continued to fall on the southern perimeter, now augmented with machine-gun and small arms fire from the north bank, which proved more effective as the area south of the bridge was largely devoid of cover apart from the road embankments and extensive reed beds along the water's edge, these only providing cover from view rather than fire. The only substantial cover was provided by the concrete roadside pillboxes, although the few paratroopers who gained shelter within them soon discovered they were far from impervious to fire from an enemy anti-tank gun brought up for the purpose. Captain Gammon from the 1st Parachute Battalion noted that the north-facing entrance of his pillbox was only protected by a bead curtain and watched in helpless fascination as enemy solid shot systematically demolished the pillbox on the opposite side of the road, possibly containing one of Lieutenant Gardiner's captured Breda guns. The anti-tank gun then turned its attention to his shelter: 'Suddenly there was a crash, fumes, dust, and something hit me in the chest. I could hardly see... Where's the door? Had it collapsed? A shaft of light and I groped my way out into the blinding sunshine.'[89] The destruction of the pillboxes was witnessed by Lieutenant Stainforth who was stationed between the structures and the riverbank with a 1st Parachute Squadron Bren team and the redeployed Vickers MMG from the 1st Parachute Battalion, tasked to protect them and block any attempt to cross under the bridge; he too noted the repeated armour-piercing hits until the loophole '...crumbled into dust, leaving a gaping socket in place of the oblong slit [and the] Breda spoke no more'.[90] In addition to destroying the pillboxes the attackers also managed to set fire to the reed beds and adjacent cornfields and, more importantly, forded the River Simeto around 400 yards east of the crossing at 18:30.

Within thirty minutes of the crossing the British perimeter was thus being increasingly infiltrated from the east, blocked in part by Lieutenant Stainforth's small riverside group, as well as under constant small-arms and machine-gun fire from the north bank and the JOHNNY IV feature to the south, the latter presumably from elements of *Fallschirmjäger MG Bataillon 1*.[91]

The writing was on the wall and at dusk Brigadier Lathbury ordered the occupants of the bridge perimeter to withdraw to the high ground to the south in small groups and make contact with the 2nd Parachute Battalion. The precise timing of the order is unclear, for while the Brigade HQ War Diary refers to it being issued at 19:15, the Division After Action Report gives a later time of 19:35 and the 1st and 3rd Parachute Battalions refer to the earlier times of 18:30 and 19:00 respectively. The differing timings may have been due to the withdrawal order being formulated earlier and distributed in readiness for a dusk or dark break away, as padre Captain Talbot Watkins from 16th Parachute Field Ambulance reported that 'the situation was very grave, and that the Bde intended to withdrew from the bridge at dusk' on returning to the MDS from Brigade HQ at 16:15; the MDS was officially informed of the withdrawal at 20:00 by the 1st Parachute Battalion's Medical Officer Captain M. H. K. Haggie, who dropped off members of the RAMC who wished to remain at the MDS as his Battalion passed the location.[92] Whenever it was formulated, Lathbury's order also assumed that the 2nd Parachute Battalion was still maintaining a presence to the south, as there had been no contact with Lieutenant-Colonel Frost's HQ since a visit by Brigade Major Hunter to the JOHNNY I position at 09:20 that morning.[93] In the event the 2nd Battalion was still firmly ensconced in its hilltop perimeter, with Lieutenant-Colonel Frost moving his Command Post into the main Battalion perimeter at 18:00 and the arrival of a party of fifteen men from the 3rd Parachute Battalion being the only noteworthy events between Captain Hodge calling down naval gunfire to assist the bridge perimeter and the withdrawal from the latter.[94] In the circumstances, a withdrawal to the south was the only viable option and whenever it was formulated and distributed, the withdrawal order marked the end of the 1st Parachute Brigade's attempt to hold the Ponte Primosole, approximately seventeen hours after Captain Rann's party had secured the north end at 02:15.

The withdrawal period varied between units due to the continuing enemy fire, the time required to organise the small parties, and avoiding enemy patrols. The 1st Parachute Battalion appears to have taken two and a half hours to reach the JOHNNY I location due to taking a circuitous route to the east and lost six men en route, Captain Rowland reported the 1st Parachute Brigade Signal Section was also at Frost's location by 21:00 and Brigadier Lathbury does not appear to have arrived until 06:00 on 15 July; on the other hand the 3rd Parachute Battalion was in place within fifty minutes and by 20:00 was assisting Frost's men on the perimeter.[95] The redoubtable Sergeant Anderson also successfully extracted his 6-Pounder gun, towing it south along the 'bare, fire-swept road' with his fortunately undamaged Jeep. According to glider pilot Staff-Sergeant Protheroe, who had attached himself to Anderson's gun crew after landing on LZ 8, the gun was then abandoned at the edge of the high ground after being rendered unserviceable by removing the striking pin and the party moved south on foot, reaching British lines at some point on 15 July; Protheroe particularly recalled the joy of being provided with drinking water by the friendly troops: 'It tasted like champagne, as our supply had run out the previous day.'[96]

Some did not reach the high ground at all. Captain Gammon, still groggy from his pillbox experience, passed the MDS '...where some orderlies, like vultures, swooped upon me and whipped me inside'. There he remained despite his protestations while the Station was captured by an Italian Medical Officer, liberated by a patrol from the 2nd Parachute Battalion and then closed in the early evening of 15 July with seventy-one British and thirty-eight enemy casualties, presumably including Captain Gammon, being passed over to the 186th Field Ambulance MDS from the 50th Division.[97] A party of twelve surplus personnel including five RASC soldiers that left the MDS at 21:00 led by Padre Captain Watkins and RSM E. W. Brock reached 8th Army lines, as did a party led by Lieutenant Stainforth.[98]

Informed of the withdrawal by Brigade Major Hunter in person at 20:00, Lieutenant Stainforth gathered up all the RE personnel in the vicinity of the bridge and a number of stragglers from the Parachute Battalions totalling approximately twenty men and set off for Lentini at 22:00, moving west across the British and German drop zones where he examined the abandoned enemy parachutes and equipment containers before turning south. After lying up in thick vegetation near a convenient spring through the daylight hours of 15 July, the party set out again at 21:30 and made contact with elements of the British 50th Division north of Lentini in the early hours of Friday 16 July.[99]

Of the approximately 295 men from the 1st Parachute Brigade that fought the seventeen-hour battle to hold the Ponte Primosole, twenty-seven were killed and seventy-five wounded; of this the 2nd Parachute Battalion alone lost sixteen dead, thirty-three wounded and 138 missing, although a number of the latter including four officers turned up later. Overall, 313 men from the Brigade were still missing by 28 July, along with the bulk of the Brigade's heavy equipment including twelve Jeeps, ten 3-inch mortars, nine Vickers MMGs and six 6-Pounder anti-tank guns.[100] The highest ranking casualty appears to have been Lieutenant-Colonel Charles Crawfurd, the 1st Airborne Division's Commander Royal Artillery (CRA), who attached himself to the 1st Airlanding Anti-Tank Battery with the intention of acting as a supernumerary Artillery Forward Observer; he was killed when the glider in which he was travelling crashed in Sicily.[101] The bulk of the survivors of the battle successfully rallied at the 2nd Parachute Battalion's JOHNNY I hilltop perimeter where they remained relatively unmolested until formally relieved by 151st Brigade at midnight on 15 July; during this period Major John Fitch, commander of the 2nd Battalion's B Company, reached the Brigade location with eight men after a twenty- mile journey from their landing spot on the slopes of Mount Etna, Captain Panter was able to fire off the remaining stock of ammunition from his captured Italian howitzer and Lieutenant-Colonel Pearson and an unnamed officer and Sergeant from the 1st Battalion participated in a second, successful British attack to recapture the Ponte Primosole by a Battalion from the Durham Light Infantry.[102]

From 07:00 on 16 July the Brigade was moved to the port of Syracuse by road via a concentration area at Lentini and Augusta, with two truckloads of the Airborne soldiers being treated to one of General Montgomery's morale-boosting speeches and subsequent cigarette distribution en route to embarking on LST 424 from 15:00; at this point the 1st Parachute Battalion contingent took the opportunity for a 'refreshing swim in the harbour'.[103] After a night of bombing during which several bombs landed close to the vessel without causing casualties or damage, the LST sailed for Sousse on 17 July via another overnight stop off at Malta, arriving at the Tunisian port early on Monday 19 July 1943. By mid-morning the survivors of the 1st Parachute Brigade were back in the dusty camps they had left for the satellite airfields around Kairouan in the afternoon of 13 July.[104]

18

Hauptkampflinie, Discord at the Top and the Push to Palermo

The Second Stage of Operation HUSKY, D-Day Plus 3, Tuesday 13 July to D-Day Plus 14, Saturday 24 July

The 1st Parachute Brigade's withdrawal from the Ponte Primosole in the evening of Wednesday 14 July left Major-General Sidney Kirkham's British 50th Division without a passage across the River Simeto to reach the port of Catania, the 8th Army's next major objective. The episode was close-run however, for as the withdrawal from the bridge was getting underway a local farmer informed Lieutenant-Colonel John Frost's 2nd Parachute Battalion holding the JOHNNY I hilltop a mile or so south of the bridge that a German armoured car was approaching their location from the south. Shortly thereafter at 19:30 several armoured vehicles appeared in the olive grove on the southern edge of the 2nd Battalion perimeter, which proved to be Sherman tanks belonging to a Squadron from the 44th RTR attached to Brigadier Ronald Senior's 151st Brigade, the formation tasked by 50th Division to lead the advance from Lentini and relieve the 1st Parachute Brigade at the Ponte Primosole. On learning that the 9th Battalion Durham Light Infantry (DLI) had stopped two miles to the south in readiness to attack the bridge the following morning, Lieutenant-Colonel Frost despatched his Intelligence Officer, Lieutenant Francis Hoyer-Millar at 19:45 to explain the situation and seek reinforcement; as a result a Troop of Shermans were detailed to remain at JOHNNY I as support, joined by a Company from the 9th DLI at 23:40.[1]

The reason for 151st Brigade's late arrival in the vicinity of the Ponte Primosole stemmed from the 50th Division's post-landing move northward past Syracuse as the spearhead of Lieutenant-General Miles Dempsey's XIII Corps. Brigadier Edward Cooke-Collis's 69th Brigade covered the twenty miles from its landing beaches near Avola to Sortino by 13 July and the relative ease of the advance triggered the launch of Operation FUSTIAN, but perhaps predictably, this rapidly ceased to be the case. 69th Brigade's nine-mile road march from Sortino to Lentini, the next hilltop town on the

50th Division line of advance, began at 13:30 on 13 July but ran into two successive blocking positions occupied by elements of *Kampfgruppe* Schmalz on the approach to Monte Pancali at around 16:30. The first position was cleared in a dusk attack by the 6th Green Howards but it took until 04:30 on 14 July to bring up the 7th Green Howards to take over the advance due to the difficult and congested road network; as a result the second blocking position was not cleared until 10:00 and 69th Brigade did not reach Lentini until the afternoon. This in turn delayed 151st Brigade's planned pre-dawn move on the Ponte Primosole, which was supposed to have started from Lentini in the early hours of 14 July.[2]

The delay also impacted adversely on the operation to secure the Ponte Malati crossing over the River Leonardo, three miles north of Lentini and seven miles south of the Ponte Primosole, by Lieutenant-Colonel John Durnford-Slater's No. 3 Commando. After avoiding a torpedo attack by a German E-Boat en route, the LSI(S) HMS *Prins Albert* anchored five miles north-west of Agnone and began landing the 350-strong Commando at *c*.21:30 in two waves, as the *Prins Albert* only carried eight Landing Craft Assault (LCA). The first wave of 200 men, made up of the Commando HQ and Nos. 1, 2, 3 and 4 Troops, landed at *c*.22:30 in the face of intense but largely inaccurate Italian machine-gun fire from four pillboxes, under covering fire from the LCAs Lewis Guns and the destroyer *HMS Tetcott*. The Italian defenders proved more resilient than the Commandos had been briefed to expect, reportedly because elements of *Oberst* Erich Walther's *Fallschirmjäger Regiment 4* were stationed in the vicinity. The landing's second wave, consisting of Nos. 5 and 6 Troops under the overall command of Captain John Pooley, reached the beach at some point after 01:00, again assisted by the *Tetcott* using smoke to blind a particularly troublesome machine-gun on the cliff overlooking the beach. Despite this the entire second wave of LCAs landed safely apart from one vessel that ran aground on rocks at the foot of the cliff, obliging the occupants to swim for shore in twenty feet of water.

The first wave of Commandos exited the beach using Bangalore Torpedoes to blow gaps in the barbed wire and worked their way through the defences, which appear to have been partly manned by *Fallschirmjäger Regiment 4*; Major Ronald Skrine, attached from Combined Operations HQ, was badly wounded knocking out a machine-gun-equipped German motorcycle and sidecar. No. 3 Troop took the direct route to capture Agnone railway station along with a number of Italian prisoners, in exchange for several British casualties including Troop Sergeant-Major Nicholas Wareing killed and Captain Lincoln Leese blinded in one eye by grenade fragments.[3] The remainder of the first wave arrived at the railway station via more circuitous routes, with No. 4 Troop encountering a misdropped stick from of 1st Parachute Brigade making their way north to the Ponte Primosole. The commander of No. 4 Troop's lead element, Lieutenant John Erskine, also reported a party of *Fallschirmjäger* moving on a parallel course on the left flank, complete with hand-cart-mounted supply containers; the enemy were monitored rather than attacked to avoid delay in reaching the Ponte Malati, the Commando's primary mission.[4]

After regrouping at the station the attackers pressed on along the railway line and then cross-country when the line entered a tunnel, before fording the River Leonardo to approach the bridge from the northern end at *c*.03:00. The northern defences were overrun in fifteen minutes, with one pillbox being knocked out by Lieutenant Brian Butler posting a hand grenade through the slit after problems removing the pin, while the other was eliminated by Captain Peter Young repeatedly firing his rifle into a vision slit after running out of grenades.

With the north end of the bridge secured, Lieutenant-Colonel Durnford-Slater ordered Captain Young to establish a defensive perimeter and remove the bridge demolition charges. The problems began when Lieutenant Erskine and a dozen men from No. 4 Troop were despatched over the carriageway, and Captain John Lash and No. 3 Troop went under the structure across the partially dry River Leonardo, in an effort to extend the perimeter to the southern end of the bridge. On occupying a vacant pillbox Lieutenant Erskine observed a large number of *Fallschirmjäger* entrenched along the embanked road within five yards of his location, positioned to cover the southern approach to the bridge, with more deployed in a nearby citrus orchard lined with cypress trees. Lieutenant Roy Herbert and the No. 3 Troop contingent were pinned down by German fire as they emerged from dead ground under the bridge, which inflicted a large number of casualties. Despite this the Germans do not appear to have been initially aware of developments on the north bank, as they permitted a truck and trailer loaded with ammunition to move onto the bridge from the south; it was promptly knocked out part way across by a PIAT and continued to burn and detonate for some time. At this point, around 05:20, Captain John Pooley arrived with Nos. 4 and 5 Troops from the beach and Colonel Durnford-Slater directed them to secure and hold a small house a hundred yards east of the bridge to block a German flanking movement and protect the line of withdrawal back to the beach.

Daylight revealed the exposed nature of the Commando's position, which was underlined by accurate fire from three recently arrived tanks, identified as Tigers, located in the citrus grove. With no sign of 151st Brigade, no effective answer to the German tank fire and casualties mounting, Colonel Durnford ordered a withdrawal to a defensive position organised by RSM William Lowe on high ground eight hundred yards south-east of the bridge, where Medical Officer Captain Edward Moore had established a Dressing Station. The location proved too exposed to be tenable however, and Colonel Durnford-Slater ordered his men to break into small groups and make their way independently to link up with friendly troops. Most appear to have headed south to meet the 50th Division advance, some fighting sharp actions against German and Italian troops on the way.[5] One group of around eight led by Troop Sergeant-Major Angus Stenhouse made their way back to the landing beach to discover there were no LCAs because *Prins Albert* had withdrawn; after a 'brisk battle' with the still-occupied beach defences the

Commandos dug in until relieved by a patrol from the York & Lancaster Regiment from the 5th Division advancing up the coast.[6]

The Ponte Malati operation cost No. 3 Commando almost half its 350 men. Twenty-eight Commandos were dead including seasoned veterans Captain Anthony Ruxton MC and Captain William Lloyd, sixty-six were wounded and fifty-nine were missing or taken prisoner.[7] The latter included Lieutenant Erskine and his party from No. 4 Troop who were ambushed after successfully withdrawing from the bridge, reportedly by the same *Fallschirmjäger* they had observed during the move inland; one Sergeant was killed in the ambush and the Section runner badly wounded in the leg.[8]

69th Brigade reaching Lentini in the afternoon of Wednesday 14 July did not herald a rapid resumption of the 50th Division's advance up the *Strada* 114, and not just due to German delaying parties and Axis strafing attacks. 'Lentini taken was not Lentini cleared' as the British Official History put it. The streets were clogged with rubble, possibly from premeditated demolition, the surrounding roads were deliberately cratered and a demolished bridge to the south near Carlentini hampered the passage of the 4th Armoured Brigade's Sherman tanks. As a result the 9th DLI and supporting tanks from the 44th RTR making up the lead element of 151st Brigade did not move off from Lentini until 18:45, by which time No. 3 Commando had withdrawn from the Ponte Malati and the 1st Parachute Brigade were starting to do the same from the Ponte Primosole.[9] The eight miles or so to the vicinity of the latter were covered in around an hour before a halt short of the high ground south of the bridge held by the 2nd Parachute Battalion. The decision to stop short is excused on the grounds that it was too late to attack the bridge 'with much hope of success' and that the 9th DLI was 'very tired', having been short of sleep over the preceding six days, but was nonetheless curious given the supposed importance of the mission and, more importantly, as the 1st Parachute Brigade was supposedly holding the bridge and urgently awaiting relief.[10] On that basis the stop short looks suspiciously like another example of ground commanders taking a somewhat relaxed and cavalier attitude toward Airborne units and operations, as experienced by the 1st and 2nd Parachute Battalions at Souk-el Arba and Depienne in November 1942, and which was to manifest itself again on a division and corps scale in Holland just over a year in the future.

Be that as it may, the 9th DLI did launch an attack on the Ponte Primosole at 07:30 on 15 July, supported by the 44th RTR tanks and fire from two Royal Artillery Field Regiments that briefly put a single platoon across the bridge but *Hauptmann* Stangenberg's scratch force from *1 Fallschirmjäger Division* rebuffed the penetration and held the attackers on the south bank of the River Simeto through the day while the two sides' artilleries engaged in a protracted duel from Midday. The abortive attack cost the 9th DLI thirty-four dead and sixty-six wounded and missing, and the mauled Battalion was withdrawn from the area of the bridge to relieve the 2nd Parachute Battalion on the JOHNNY I high ground at midnight on 15 July.[11]

The abortive 9th DLI attack was the first in a series of attacks that marked the second phase of the fight for the Simeto crossing by British XIII Corps, the right-hand prong of the British 8th Army's advance up the Sicilian east coast. Brigadier Senior immediately set about organising a second assault on the Ponte Primosole on 15 July, in line with orders from Major-General Kirkham to secure the crossing in readiness for a concerted move on Catania. The 151st Brigade Orders Group was attended by Brigadier Gerald Lathbury and Lieutenant-Colonel Alastair Pearson, commanders of the 1st Parachute Brigade and 1st Parachute Battalion, who were still in area; Brigadier Lathbury had travelled to 151st Brigade HQ after reaching JOHNNY I at 06:00 and learning of its presence from Lieutenant-Colonel Frost. The Orders Group appears to have been at some point before 09:15 on 15 July, given that Lathbury departed to have his back and leg wounds treated at the still functioning 1st Parachute Brigade MDS at that time. Brigadier Senior's initial plan was a repeat of the 07:30 frontal attack employing just the 8th DLI as the Brigade's third unit, the 6th DLI, was two miles to the south guarding the 50th Division's west flank toward Scordia. The plan prompted a testy exchange with Lieutenant-Colonel Pearson, who suggested the plan was a good way to 'see another battalion written off', before offering to guide the DLI over a ford west of the bridge to outflank the German defences; another source refers to Lathbury reining in his subordinate before suggesting the indirect approach. Whoever was responsible, Lieutenant-Colonel Pearson, with the assistance of his Batman, an unnamed Officer and Sergeant from the 2nd Parachute Battalion and 2,000 yards of white marker tape guided the 8th DLI's A and D Companies over the ford at *c*.01:30 on Friday 16 July and secured the north end of the bridge shortly afterward.[12]

Everything then went haywire. According to the British Official History a combination of thick fog, misdirected reports and water-damaged radio sets meant the remainder of the 8th DLI and tanks from the 44th RTR were not be pushed across the bridge until after first light, by which time it was too late and the advantage was lost; Lieutenant-Colonel Pearson referred to the 8th DLI's commander, Major Robert Lidwill, failing to act upon advice to move up to the edge of the cultivated area north of the bridge and to bring up his reserve Company under cover of darkness, for which 'they were hammered the next morning'. Interestingly, the Official History makes no mention whatever of Pearson's involvement, although it is clearly stated in the 1st Airborne Division After Action Report.[13] Unable to make headway in the face of fierce resistance and counter-attacks from *Hauptmann* Stangenberg's *Fallschirmjäger* the 16 July attack ground to a halt. A further attack launched at 01:00 on 17 July by the 6th and 9th DLI supported by tanks from the 3rd County of London Yeomanry cleared a thousand-yard-deep area north of the River Simeto after a day of intense and confused fighting that cost the DLI Battalions 220 casualties and pushed the *Fallschirmjäger* back to a large earthwork ditch just over two miles north of the Ponte Primosole dubbed the *Fosso Bottaceto*.

As his 50th Division was by this point available in its entirety, Major-General Kirkham organised a larger scale assault for the early hours of 18 July intended to open the way to Catania, spearheaded by Brigadier Kenneth

Davidson's 168th Brigade tasked to break through the *Fosso Bottaceto*, supported by eight Royal Artillery Field Regiments and two Medium Batteries. The latter's fire plan was drastically rearranged at the last moment when reconnaissance reports indicated that forward German positions had been withdrawn and that the earthwork was only held by 'weak detachments'. This was not the case and the unmolested *Fallschirmjäger* forward elements fought 168th Brigade to a standstill two hundred yards short of the *Fosso Bottaceto*, obliging the Brigade's lead elements to withdraw half a mile to shelter behind another earthwork and an adjacent orchard area east of the *Strada* 114. It was decided that further movement north along the *Strada* 114 was impossible and the 50th Division dug in to protect its gains.[14] Thus the 50th Division's advance from Sortino to Catania via the *Strada* 114 that triggered Operation FUSTIAN came to an end, just over a mile north of the Ponte Primosole and seven miles short of the port, after five days of fierce fighting that cost in excess of 422 British casualties.

On 18 July General Montgomery endorsed the decision to halt the 50th Division, but in an effort to maintain the momentum toward Catania ordered Lieutenant-General Dempsey to open another northward line of advance oriented on Misterbianco, five miles or so west of Catania, using XIII Corps' other formation, Major-General Horatio Berney-Ficklin's 5th Division; the attack was scheduled to reach Misterbianco by nightfall on 20 July. Sidestepping west from its role covering XIII Corps' right flank, the 5th Division thus carried out a two-stage attack beginning with an assault crossing of the River Simeto and Gornalunga Canal by Brigadier Lorne Campbell's 15th Brigade three and a half miles upstream from the Ponte Primosole during the night of 18-19 July, in the face of fierce resistance from elements of the *Hermann Göring (HG) Panzer Division*.

The second stage, which tasked Brigadier George Rawstorne's 15 Brigade to expand the bridgehead, began at 01:30 on 20 July again supported by eight Royal Artillery Field Regiments but was fought to a standstill by German machine-guns and mortars after covering a mile and half in the course of a confused five-hour battle. An attempt to renew the attack by Brigadier Gerald Tarleton's 17th Brigade was postponed and then abandoned after the preparations were badly shelled by German artillery on 21 July, with Lieutenant-General Dempsey authorising 5th Division to consolidate in place.[15] While all this was going on Lieutenant-General Oliver Leese's XXX Corps, the western half of the 8th Army's northward advance, was also pushing ahead. After securing Vizzini and Francofonte on 15 July, Major-General Douglas Wimberley's 51st Highland Division moved ten miles or so to the area of Scordia and Palagonia and on 17 July launched a twin-track advance on Paterno, twenty miles to the north and eleven miles west of Catania, intended to secure Paterno by 20 July.

A composite mobile column dubbed ARROW FORCE pushed across the River Dittaino while 154th Brigade cleared enemy rearguards from Ramacca to the west but stiffening Axis resistance blocked further advance, despite additional crossings of the Dittaino upstream at Sferro and Catenanuova.[16]

Divining that the town of Gerbini was the key to the enemy defence, and particularly the cluster of five well-defended airfields around it, Major-General Wimberley tasked Brigadier Thomas Rennie's 154th Brigade to attack at 22:00 on 20 July and capture the town, spearheaded by Lieutenant-Colonel Robert Mathieson's 7th Battalion Argyll & Sutherland Highlanders (A&SH) supported by a Squadron of Sherman tanks from the 46th RTR, two Royal Artillery Field Regiments and elements of two Medium Regiments following an extensive Fire Plan. The 7th A&SH secured their objective after three hours of fierce and continuous fighting by 01:00 on 21 July, but the Germans maintained heavy fire to cover repeated infiltration attacks on the British gains. The attackers were reinforced by the 1st Black Watch and the 46th RTR tanks at 04:50, although the RTR Squadron commander, Major John Routledge and Lieutenant-Colonel Mathieson were killed when the Major's Sherman was knocked out.

Brigadier Rennie's appreciation of Gerbini as a key component of the German defence proved to be correct, as a large proportion of the *HG Panzer Division* was in the immediate vicinity after withdrawing from the US II Corps landings at Gela and Scoglitti, including much of *HG Panzer Bataillon 2*, two *bataillonen* from *HG Panzergrenadier Regiment* 2 and elements of the *HG Panzer Aufklärungs Abteilung*; a determined counter-attack by these units at around 10:00 obliged the 154th Brigade units to withdraw to their start line under covering fire from the RA guns.[17] The fight at Gerbini cost the 7th A&SH 178 casualties including eighteen of its twenty-six Officers and the 46th RTR its commander and eight tanks; as with the XIII Corps Divisions to the east, the 51st Highland Division was also placed on the defensive with effect from 21 July.[18]

Matters unfolded in a similar manner for the 8th Army's left flank formation, Major-General Guy Simonds' 1st Canadian Division, albeit over a longer period of fighting and in more mountainous terrain. After thirty-six hours of rest at Giarratana, the Division was ordered to advance toward Enna, forty-five miles to the north-west. The advance was led initially by Brigadier Howard Graham's 1st Canadian Brigade, which moved off at midnight on 14 July for the recently captured Vizzini. There it paused until 06:00 before angling west along the *Strada* 124 to arrive at Grammichele at 09:00 where it encountered a rearguard detachment of tanks and anti-tank guns from the *HG Panzer Division*. The initial ambush destroyed a Sherman from Three Rivers Regiment, three Universal Carriers and several soft-skin vehicles likely from the Hastings and Prince Edward Regiment (Hasty Ps) and held up the Canadian advance for three hours before the rearguard broke contact and withdrew north, leaving behind three knocked-out tanks, several *flak* guns and 'a quantity of equipment and stores' in exchange for twenty-five Canadian casualties.

The advance was resumed in the early afternoon with the Three Rivers Regiment and the 48th Highlanders of Canada in the van and reached the badly bombed town of Caltagirone at Midnight on 15 July from where Brigadier Christopher Vokes' 2nd Canadian Brigade took the lead in the early morning of 16 July, pushing west along the *Strada* 124 through San Michele di Ganzeria before turning north onto the *Strada* 117 toward Piazza Armerina. At midday, after a twenty-mile advance, the Canadians ran into another blocking position on a difficult section of road three miles short of the Piazza Armerina, this time manned by *Bataillon 2, Panzergrenadier Regiment 104* from *15 Panzergrenadier Division*. The block consisted of interlocking machine-gun and mortar positions on high ground overlooking the road which the Three Rivers' Shermans could not engage as their 75mm guns were unable to elevate sufficiently, and Lieutenant-Colonel James Jefferson's Loyal Edmonton Regiment were initially obliged to rely on their 3-inch mortars until fire support from the Royal Devon Yeomanry and 7th Medium Regiment RA came on stream later in the day. The *Panzergrenadiers* broke contact during the night and the 2nd Brigade were in control of Piazza Armerina by 06:00 on 17 July; the fight netted the Canadians a large stock of petrol and signals equipment abandoned by *Generale di Corpo d'Armata* Carlo Rossi's *16° Corpo* HQ, but at a cost of twenty-seven Loyal Edmonton Regiment casualties and a twenty-four-hour delay as Brigadier Matthew Penhale's 3rd Canadian Brigade was not able to resume the advance until noon on 17 July.[19]

The resumption was short lived as the Germans had blown a bridge four miles north of Piazza Armerina that took until 16:30 to bypass, and the advance then ran into a third blocking position, manned by *Panzergrenadier Regiment 104* in its entirety, across a mountain pass called the *Portello Grottacalda*. At this point Major-General Simonds changed tack and expanded the width of his Division's advance, ordering the 3rd Canadian Brigade to continue north-west toward Enna and the 1st Canadian Brigade north to Valguarnera, eight miles from Piazza Armerina.[20] The 3rd Brigade opened the road to Enna at 17:00 on 18 July after a fourteen-hour battle that involved a frontal attack by the Royal 22e Régiment while the Carleton & York and West Nova Scotia Regiments outflanked the German position from east and west, prompting a further withdrawal by the *Panzergrenadiers*. A shift in Allied priorities by General Alexander actually led to Enna becoming part of the US 7th Army sector, although the British 8th Army retained control of the major roads to the east of the town.

The 1st Brigade advance also involved the formation's entire infantry component, beginning with a night cross-country move from the *Strada* 117 by the Hastings and Prince Edward Regiment which put half the unit on high ground less than a mile south of Valguarnera, where they erected a roadblock and ambushed several German vehicles withdrawing from the *Portello Grottacalda*, notably destroying an ammunition truck with a PIAT, possibly the first Canadian success with the new weapon. The other half fought a sharp action on a knoll dominating the immediate approach to the town, again ambushing a number of enemy vehicles before a strong German counter-attack obliged a rapid withdrawal. Starting later at 05:30 on 18 July the Royal Canadian Regiment (RCR) recaptured the knoll before being engaged by three German tanks, which withdrew into Valguarnera after being unsuccessfully stalked by a party armed with a PIAT, while the RCR dug in on the knoll in expectation of a counter-attack. It failed to materialise as the Germans again withdrew northward, leaving Valguarnera to be taken without a fight by the 48th Highlanders. The fighting on 18 July cost the 1st Canadian Division 145 casualties, forty of them dead, the Hastings and Prince Edward Regiment losing twenty killed and wounded with eight taken prisoner; estimates of German losses ranged between 180 and 240 killed with a further 250 taken prisoner plus thirty Italians.[21]

With Valguarnera secured Major-General Simonds continued his twin-pronged northward advance on 20 July, directing the 1st Canadian Brigade to secure the mountain village of Assoro, ten miles from Valguarnera and the 2nd Canadian Brigade to take Leonforte, two miles to the west on a separate area of high ground. Assoro was secured by the Hastings and Prince Edward Regiment during the night of 20-21 July via an imaginative climb up the steeply terraced and consequently unguarded eastern face of the mountain, which placed the Canadians above the village and its unsuspecting garrison. There they repulsed two counter-attacks before being relieved at midday on 22 July by the 48th Highlanders attacking from the south-west and clearing the village; the action cost approximately 114 Canadian casualties.

Leonforte was attacked by the Loyal Edmonton Regiment in the evening of 21 July without tank support as the bridge over the ravine fronting the town had been demolished, blocking access to the Three Rivers Regiment's vehicles. The Loyal Edmonton Regiment crossed the ravine covered by artillery and fire from the Seaforth Highlanders of Canada, whose initial advance on the town had been slowed by a combination of German machine-guns and misplaced friendly artillery fire that cost the Battalion thirty men. They entered the town at 21:00; the interlopers then expanded their lodgement via a night of confused and intense house-to-house fighting that ended with a large party cut off in the town centre.

A Platoon from the 3rd Field Company RCE succeeded in repairing the fifty-foot gap in the bridge and a Troop of four Shermans, C Company Princess Patricia's Canadian Light Infantry (PPCLI) and a Troop of guns from the 90th Canadian Anti-Tank Battery boldly raced across the bridge at 09:00. The force fought through to relieve the isolated party from the Edmonton Regiment at 10:00, reportedly knocking out three German tanks in exchange for a Three Rivers' Sherman and, with the assistance of the remainder of the PPCLI, the town was cleared by the afternoon; the German defenders fell back to two overlooking hills which the PPCLI cleared by *c.*17:30.[22] The fight for Leonforte cost 161 casualties. The rigours of house-to-house fighting saw the Loyal Edmonton Regiment lose seven dead, seventeen wounded and one prisoner; the PPCLI lost twenty-one dead and forty wounded while the Seaforth Highlanders suffered most of all, losing twenty-eight dead and forty-eight wounded.[23]

Twelve days from the initial HUSKY landing the 8th Army advance on the eastern sector of the Allied front thus ran out of momentum, the result of difficult terrain and stiffening resistance. That stronger resistance was not merely the result of the Axis and more especially German forces recovering and regrouping from their rough handling at the CENT and DIME Landing Areas, as the impetus came from the very top. On 12 July, *Generalfeldmarschall* Kesselring travelled from *OB Süd* to see the situation in Sicily for himself, expecting the Allied landings to be equivalent to the Dieppe raid in August 1942; finding the reality somewhat different he reported by telephone to *General der Artillerie* Alfred Jodl at *OKW* the following day that a further concerted attack on the Allied landing sites was impossible, that buying time primarily to keep Italy in the war was the only realistic prospect and recommended that *Luftwaffe* reinforcements including *1 Fallschirmjäger Division* and *29 Panzergrenadier Division* should be despatched to Sicily forthwith. Based on this and after discussion with Jodl, Hitler backed Kesselring by personally redefining the German mission in Sicily to delaying the Allied advance and retaining the eastern portion of the island behind a line running south-east from Santo Stefano di Camastra on the north coast, through Adrano to Catania on the east coast. The *Fuhrer* also ordered the despatch of further elements of *1 Fallschirmjäger Division* to the island, bomber reinforcements to the Italy-based *Luftflotte 2*, *29 Panzergrenadier Division* to redeploy to Reggio Calabria in readiness to move across the Strait of Messina and *Generaloberst* Hans-Valentin Hube to move his *14 Panzer Korps* HQ to Sicily and assume overall command there with effect from 15 July.

Hitler also issued *Generaloberst* Hube with secret instructions, shared with *Generalleutnant* Fridolin von Senger und Etterlin and his liaison staff at *6ª Armata* HQ, to take complete control of operations in Sicily, to 'quietly' exclude the Italians from future German planning and take control of the remaining Italian units on the island.[24] The groundwork was laid in a further meeting between Kesselring, *6ª Armata* commander *Generale d'Armata* Alfredo Guzzoni and *Generaloberst* Hube on 15 July, with the latter assuming command of all German formations in Sicily and *de facto* control of Italian units operating in the same sectors during the night of 16-17 July, with Guzzoni's written agreement issued the following day, 18 July. Overtly, all parties continued the fictional nicety that *6ª Armata* HQ was in overall command of all Axis ground forces in Sicily including tactical control over *Generaloberst* Hube's German formations; on that basis Guzzoni ordered the withdrawal of *Kampfgruppe* Fullriede and *15 Panzergrenadier Division* to the north-east on 16 July and assigned *14 Panzer Korps* responsibility for the north-eastern sector of the island two days later.[25]

At the Axis formation and unit command levels the initiative and tactical acumen of the commanders won through, despite Kesselring and Guzzoni inserting themselves into the orders cycle on occasion, and the upshot on the ground in the north-east of Sicily was the establishment of a *Hauptkampflinie* (Main Battle Line) by *14 Panzer Korps*. Starting on the east coast just below Catania, the *Hauptkampflinie* ran roughly west along the River Simeto and River Dittaino past Gerbini and Sferro to Catenanuova, before angling north-west past Regalbuto and Agira and then north through Nicosia to Santo Stefano di Camastra on the coast. The Line made use of existing terrain features rather than prepared defences, with the eastern thirty miles or so to

Dittaino held by *Generalmajor* Conrath's *HG Panzer Division* (including *Kampfgruppe* Schmalz and elements of *1 Fallschirmjäger Division*), while *Generalleutnant* Rodt's *15 Panzergrenadier Division* occupied the sector to the west centred on Nicosia, with the gap between the two German sectors being held for a time by the remnants of *Generale di Divisione* Chirieleison's *4ª Livorno Divisione* in the vicinity of Agira.

It was the delaying element of the criss-crossed German withdrawal to the projected *Hauptkampflinie* that generated the 8th Army delays at Lentini, Grammichele, Piazza Armerina and the *Portello Grottacalda*, and the establishment of the line for the rebuffs at the *Fosso Bottaceto* and Gerbini. To the west *Generale* Guzzoni assigned the Italian *12° Corpo* responsibility for the western sector with *16° Corpo* in reserve, which resulted in the US 7th Army being faced by *Generale di Divisione* Scotti's *26ª Assietta Divisione* deployed on a line running north-east from Menfi on the south coast through Prizzi and Lercara Friddi to Cerda on the north coast, screened by *Gruppi Mobili* A, B and C deployed forward to block the two major roads and railway running toward Palermo to the north-west. The gap between the northern tip of the *Assietta Divisione* line was occupied by elements of *Generale di Divisione* Romano's *28ª Aosta Divisione* reinforced by *Oberst* Karl Ens' *kampfgruppe* from *Panzergrenadier Regiment 104*, deployed along a line running west from Petralia across a south-projecting loop of the *Strada* 120 and screened by *Generale di Brigata* Schreiber's composite *Raggruppamento*.[26]

The British and Canadian advances that necessitated the creation of the German *Hauptkampflinie* were framed by a Directive issued by HUSKY ground commander General Sir Harold Alexander on Tuesday 13 July. Issued at 20:00 on 13 July, the Directive reiterated the existing stance of employing the US 7th Army as a flank guard to cover the advance of General Montgomery's 8th Army up the Sicilian east coast toward Messina. The US formation was thus tasked to form a protective line running north from Palma di Montechiaro through Canicatti and Caltanissetta to the Army boundary, while the British formation was to establish a line running west from Syracuse to Palazzolo Acreide and then south-west to Ragusa before moving north to capture the ports of Augusta and Catania and secure Gerbini and the cluster of five airfields around it. Given subsequent events, the 13 July Directive was thus somewhat hopeful, being based on optimistic situation appreciations by Montgomery issued in the evenings of 11 and 12 July, but the key point was that it gave Montgomery's formation the primary role in expanding the Allied foothold on Sicily while allotting Patton's formation a subsidiary and supporting role.[27]

Despite his personal reservations Lieutenant-General Patton had acquiesced to the principle of his US 7th Army acting as the flank guard for the British 8th Army while the latter made the initial strategic running, as outlined in General Alexander's Directive of 19 May 1943.[28] Patton had responded to the latter by pledging to do his 'goddamndest' to carry out 15th Army Group HQ's orders and ensured his subordinates toed the same line, even when it complicated matters from the US perspective; Patton complied with General

Montgomery unilaterally appropriating the *Strada* 124 running east from Vizzini to Caltagirone on 12 July for example, even though that section of the road, which marked the eastern section of the US Yellow Line, had been allotted to Major-General Bradley's US II Corps and its appropriation impacted on Bradley's ability to maintain his advance out of the immediate beach head area.[29] Patton also accepted the reiteration of the US 7th Army's subsidiary role in the 15th Army Group scheme as outlined in Alexander's Directive of 13 July 1943 although as his subsequent actions showed, Patton, not unreasonably, considered the arrangement to be a temporary and soon to be jettisoned expedient. This underlay Patton's permitting Major-General Truscott to secure Agrigento and Porto Empedocle on 16 July as an imaginative interpretation of the principle of reconnaissance-in-force as a foundation for a wider US effort to clear western Sicily and secure the island capital Palermo, the seizure of which 'amounted to an obsession' for the US commander.[30] This was to be achieved via a reorganisation and reorientation of the US 7th Army in an equally imaginative interpretation of Alexander's future intentions, which Patton revealed to his subordinates on 15 July while the operation to secure Agrigento and Porto Empedocle was still underway.

At the top, the US command structure was modified to create a US Provisional Corps, headed by the 7th Army's Deputy Commander Major-General Geoffrey Keyes, to stand alongside Bradley's US II Corps. The new formation consisted of the US 3rd Infantry Division, the 82nd Airborne Division and elements of the US 9th Infantry Division; Major-General Hugh J. Gaffey's US 2nd Armored Division became the 7th Army reserve after reintegrating its detached Combat Commands, but was also attached to the Provisional Corps. Patton divided the 7th Army front into two roughly equal parts divided along a line running approximately fifty-five miles north-west from a point near Serradifalco through Mussomeli, Lercara Friddi and Marineo to Palermo on the north coast. The new US Provisional Corps was allotted the left-hand sector running from Porto Empedocle and Agrigento through Favara and Canicatti to Serradifalco, with Major-General Truscott's 3rd Infantry Division tasked to secure the line of the *Strada* 115 by nightfall on 19 July and hand over to the 82nd Airborne Division in readiness for further offensive action; the US 2nd Armored Division was also tasked to stand-by to exploit any opportunities, with particular reference to the US Provisional Corps' frontage.

The right-hand sector, bounded to the east along a thirty-mile line running north from Enna to a point on the coast just west of Santo Stefano di Camastra, was allotted to Major-General Bradley's US II Corps. The reorganisation also involved switching the orientation of the Corps' two constituent divisions, with the US 45th Infantry Division moving to the west of the sector while the US 1st Infantry Division moved to the east along the US 7th and British 8th Army boundary, tasked to make contact with the 1st Canadian Division; once reoriented Bradley's formations were to push forward to the north-west to secure Caltanissetta and a stretch of the *Strada* 122 running east from the town, again by nightfall on Monday 19 July. The switch was achieved by moving the US 45th Division to a concentration area near Riesi, fifteen miles south of Caltanissetta, on 16 July, while the US 1st Infantry Division moved north via Mazzarino and Barrafranca the same day, aided by a fortuitously intact bridge over the River Salso on the *Strada* 191 just north of Mazzarino.[31] The advance sparked a brief fight with a withdrawing *Kampfgruppe* Ens before an abandoned Barrafranca was secured, and the 16th RCT reached the *Strada* 122 east of Caltanissetta in the late evening of 17 July. Caltanissetta was secured by the 157th RCT in the late afternoon of the following day after a two-day advance that began with a ninety-mile road march via Gela trailed by the US 753rd Medium Tank Battalion and two battalions of Divisional artillery; the remainder of the US 45th Infantry Division also closed up to Caltanissetta on 18 July.

Patton's intent had been to maintain his posture as a flank guard as instructed in Alexander's 13 July Directive, while preparing to take advantage of an expected shift in the overall situation to launch thrusts to the west and north; he '…fully intended to be ready to go as soon as General Montgomery had firmly established the 8th Army on a line from Catania to Enna' and had achieved his intention within four days of issuing his own US 7th Army Directive on 15 July.[32]

However, Patton's hopes and assumptions were thwarted within twenty-four hours of outlining them to his senior subordinates. Following another optimistic report from Montgomery on 14 July and a visit to the latter's HQ the following day, Alexander issued a further 15th Army Group Directive on Friday 16 July 1943 that perpetuated the British 8th Army's primary operational role by proposing a three-pronged advance intended to bottle up the bulk of the Axis forces in Sicily into the Messina peninsula. On the right, the advance north up the *Strada* 114 and the strip of land between Mount Etna and the coast was to continue, the centre thrust was to advance just over thirty miles from Leonforte through Regalbuto to Adrano in order to cut the *Strada* 121 running west from Catania, while the left prong was to advance roughly east-north-east along the thirty-two miles or so from Nicosia through Troina to Randazzo, angled to sweep round the western face of Mount Etna and dominate the strip of land between the Mount and the north coast.[33]

The US 7th Army's role in all this was again merely to act as a flank guard for the British advance, tasked in the short term to secure Enna in order to cut the Axis access to the island's central road network and in the longer term to press on to the Sicilian north coast to secure the rear of the British advance to Messina at the north-eastern tip of the island; presumably as a sop to US sensibilities, Alexander also authorised the seizure of Agrigento and Porto Empedocle, seemingly unaware that Patton and Truscott's imaginative reconnaissance-in-force had secured those objectives that same afternoon.[34] Alexander's 16 July Directive thus revealed that the US 7th Army's subordination was to be a permanent rather than temporary arrangement and, while its intentions were stymied in the immediate term by the failure to secure Catania and the rebuffs along the *Hauptkampflinie*, the Directive also appears to have been intended to give the remainder of the campaign in Sicily 'a virtually unalterable shape'.[35]

The problem was that the US party did not consider that shape to be cast in stone. Alexander's 16 July Directive also marked the end of the US 7th Army's acquiescence to being second fiddle while the British 8th Army made all the operational and strategic running and garnered the resultant kudos. The arrival of the 15th Army Group Directive at US 7th Army HQ at midnight on Friday 16 July reportedly left Patton 'mad as a wet hen', not so much because it gave the major prize of Messina to the rival 8th Army, but more because the continuing employment of the US 7th Army as a flank guard precluded it from going after the only remaining significant objective on the island, the Sicilian capital with which Patton was increasingly fixated; as Major-General Truscott put it 'Palermo drew Patton like a lode star'.[36] Patton began by holding immediate early hours discussions with his 7th Army Chief-of-Staff Brigadier-General Hobart R. Gay, the newly promoted US Provisional Corps Commander Major-General Keyes and two observers attached to 7th Army HQ, Brigadier-General Albert C. Wedemeyer and Major-General John P. Lucas, during which he announced his intention to protest to Alexander over what he viewed as the continuing misuse of his formation, and revealed that he also intended to present Alexander with a scheme for the US 7th Army to clear western Sicily and seize Palermo; carefully arranged to avoid interfering with the projected 8th Army attacks focussed on Messina or compromising their security, the scheme envisaged an enveloping attack on the Sicilian capital, with one wing sweeping to the west via Castelvetrano and Corleone while the other took a more direct route north-west toward Palermo via Villafrati and along the *Strada* 113 north coast road.[37]

Patton then flew to Tunis later on 17 July and argued his case in person in an unscheduled meeting sprung on Alexander at La Marsa on the coastal outskirts of Tunis, stressing that continued aggressive action was the surest way to provide security for the British 8th Army's drive on Messina and that a simultaneous drive on Palermo by his 7th Army would 'split the enemy forces irreparably'.[38] Alexander appears to have been genuinely unaware of the depth of US bitterness generated by the perception of being repeatedly side-lined from the action, but he also appreciated the need for inter-Allied harmony and, perhaps more importantly, that the volatile Patton might be provoked into taking matters into his own hands. Consequently – and to Patton's surprise – Alexander therefore approved the Palermo proposal with the proviso that the tasks in the 16 July Directive were also carried out.[39] In Patton's view his projected advance on Palermo obviated the need to secure the road net in the vicinity of Caltanissetta and Enna or cut the island in two, but he agreed on the grounds that 'it's a mean man who won't promise' before returning to Sicily the same evening.[40]

It is interesting to speculate to what degree the US resentment and desire to assuage it by moving on Palermo was attributable to Patton's personal ambition and to what extent it was the case across the wider 7th Army. US II Corps commander Major-General Omar Bradley shared Patton's discontent over playing second fiddle to the British for example, but while he later acknowledged securing Palermo was useful from a logistics perspective and a morale-booster for the troops and wider US public, he nonetheless considered operations in the west of Sicily to be a distraction from the decisive fight in the east and a 'grandstanding' vehicle for Patton.[41] Similarly, the commander of the US 3rd Infantry Division, Major-General Lucian Truscott, considered operations in western Sicily to be strategically irrelevant to the extent of suggesting his Division be employed capturing the central road hub at Caltanissetta before Keyes and Patton authorised the reconnaissance-in-force west toward Agrigento on 13 July; although Palermo was to become the US 7th Army's logistical hub, he also rejected the need for the city's port facilities, on the grounds that the already captured ports along the Sicilian south coast were adequate to support operations and considered that Patton was primarily drawn to the 'glamour' of the Sicilian capital.[42]

That the move on Palermo was driven primarily by Patton's ego and thirst for publicity is a common theme in the historiography. One British historian observed that 'Patton not only had to *be* a good general but *seen* to be a good general through his deeds [original emphasis]. Newspaper headlines were one way to achieve this end. Patton instinctively knew what to do.'[43] One US account took things further by suggesting that Patton deliberately manipulated Alexander into kneejerk compliance with his Palermo scheme solely to 'regain control of his [Patton's] destiny', and reinforces Bradley and Truscott's view that the operation to secure Palermo and western Sicily was a needless distraction and detrimental to the prosecution of the Sicilian campaign overall. While arguably valid, this view is perhaps coloured by hindsight given that there were approximately 60,000 assorted Italian troops in the west of Sicily when the drive on Palermo commenced on 19 July, a potential threat that could not be simply ignored; it also begs the question of how the bulk of the US 7th Army's combat power could have been brought fully to bear against the German force in the rugged and restricted geographical space at the neck of the Messina peninsula, which was at that point already extensively populated by the British 8th Army.[44]

True or not, Alexander's prompt acceptance of the Palermo scheme also possibly averted another bout of inter-Allied wrangling like that which had marked the SYMBOL Conference in Casablanca in January 1943, and more acutely the planning for HUSKY in the first half of the year. A concerned but supportive Major-General Lucas flew to Allied Forces HQ (AFHQ) in Algiers on 17 July to report the matter to Eisenhower, but the latter was absent, ironically in Tunis, and it was 20 July before Lucas was able to deliver his report. By then events had moved on, although Lucas was hardly reassured when Eisenhower responded with a detailed defence of Alexander's past record and caution, before ordering Lucas to ensure that Patton stood up to Alexander in the future on pain of being relieved of command of the 7th Army; the inherent contradiction reportedly left Lucas 'incredulous'.[45]

Having obtained Alexander's sanction for his scheme, Patton wasted no time setting it in motion with an Order issued on Sunday 18 July that formally decreed Palermo to be the US 7th Army's new primary focus. The task of meeting the 16 July Directive missions of securing the western section of the Enna road net and splitting the Axis-held portion of the island was allotted to the US 1st Infantry Division, which was to advance north from the line of the *Strada* 122 on a forty-mile axis running through Alimena and Petralia to Cefalú on the Sicilian north coast, which also marked the US II Corps' eastern boundary; this paralleled the projected axis of British XXX Corps' advance east of the 7th-8th Army boundary along the *Strada* 117 from Enna through Nicosia to Santo Stefano di Camastra, thirty miles east of Cefalú. The US II Corps second formation, the US 45th Infantry Division, was to provide the right wing of the advance on Palermo, tasked to advance the fifty miles or so north-west up the line of the *Strada* 121 to the junction with the coastal *Strada* 113 east of Palermo. The US Provisional Corps was to provide the left wing of the overall advance, with the US 3rd Infantry Division moving north-west up the railway line parallel to *Strada* 118 toward Corleone, before looping north toward Palermo while the 82nd Airborne Division followed a parallel track along the *Strada* 115 coast road toward Castelvetrano in a supporting role; the final assault to secure Palermo was to be commanded by Patton in person, employing the US 2nd Armored Division.

Patton also designated three Phase Lines for the advance overall, but stressed that these were for control purposes only and explicitly forbade his commanders from stopping without specific orders before reaching the third Phase Line, code-named BLUE, overlooking Palermo.[46] Four hours after Patton had issued his Order setting things in motion, a further Directive arrived from 15th Army Group HQ formalising the previous day's meeting in Tunis that included conditions that had not been raised or discussed the previous day. These included specifying that Patton was to secure Petralia before despatching units north through Santa Caterina Villarmosa to Campofelice di Roccella on the coast, and that he establish a firm line extending from the north coast through Caltanissetta to Agrigento on the south coast before launching any move on Palermo.[47] Patton's reaction to this can be well imagined, but in the event he never saw Alexander's Directive as he was absent from 7th Army HQ when it arrived and his Chief-of-Staff appears to have taken an executive decision to keep it that way. Brigadier-General Gay simply issued US II Corps with modified instructions designating Campofelice di Roccella the north coast objective in place of Cefalú and ignored the rest, apparently by drawing out the decoding, claiming the Directive had become garbled during the process and then requesting a resend; by the time this arrived, US troops had reached Palermo.[48]

Although it began well, US II Corps' initial task of securing the western end of the roads running east from Caltanissetta to Enna proved to be problematic, not least because Enna lay within the British 8th Army boundary. In line with existing instructions from US II Corps, the US 1st Infantry Division's 18th RCT moved off from the line of the *Strada* 122 east of Caltanissetta in the evening of 18 July, initially moving eight miles north-west to Santa Caterina Villarmosa and then east along the objective *Strada* 121 the following morning toward Villarosa, six miles from Enna on the US side of the Army boundary. After being held back briefly by German troops at a water course three miles west of Villarosa, the 18th RCT forced a crossing and by midday had reached high ground overlooking the town. It was at this point that Major-General Bradley received Patton's Order refocusing the 7th Army on Palermo and extending II Corps' mission to include an advance to the north coast. This was not welcomed by Bradley who, although he shared Patton's dissatisfaction with the US side-lining, considered operations in the west of Sicily to be condemning the 7th Army to an arena 'where there was no glory in the capture of hills, docile peasants and spiritless soldiers'; his view of his new mission to the Sicilian north coast was equally jaundiced, which he characterised as placing his II Corps where 'we can sit comfortably on our prats while Monty finishes the goddam war'.[49]

Bradley's chagrin was increased by news that British XXX Corps had bypassed rather than secured Enna, as part of the 8th Army reorientation ordered by Alexander in his 16 July Directive; as Bradley's Corps had been closely paralleling the British formation, the deviation to the north-east left the US 1st Infantry Division with an open flank. Bradley decided that securing Enna was the only way to resolve the problem and having informed XXX Corps' commander, Lieutenant-General Leese, of his intention and obtained permission to access British-controlled roads east of the Army boundary for the purpose, Bradley ordered the US 1st Infantry Division to have the 18th RCT secure Villarosa and then push east to Enna, while the 16th RCT moved up to approach Enna from the south. In so doing Bradley deliberately side-lined the mission of advancing north to Petralia and on to the north coast until the situation at Enna was resolved; in the event Petralia was secured by the 18th RCT on 22 July, after which the II Corps reoriented east to participate in the push on Messina and the by then arguably irrelevant act of dividing the island defaulted to the II Corps' other formation, the US 45th Infantry Division, elements of which reached the north coast between Campofelice di Roccella and Termini Imerese, twenty-five miles east of Palermo, on 23 July.[50]

The US units tasked for the advance on Palermo were ready to move by the afternoon of Sunday 18 July. In an early evening meeting at US Provisional Corps HQ Major-General Keyes announced that the attack would begin at 05:00 the following morning, while at the US 3rd Infantry Division HQ Major-General Truscott informed his staff of his intention of being in Palermo within five days before drinking a rare toast in Scotch whisky to 'the American Doughboy'.[51] On the other side of the hill *Generale* Guzzoni, realising that the loss of Agrigento on 16 July raised the prospect of the Italian forces in western Sicily being cut off and overrun, had already initiated steps intended to avoid that eventuality. On 17 July, he ordered *Generale* Arisio's *12° Corpo* to have the *26ª Assietta* and *28ª Aosta Divisioni* and the *Corpo* artillery perform a withdrawal north-east pivoting on Cerda, east of Palermo, and establish a covering line along the *Strada* 120 running eastward to Nicosia; the withdrawal would create a thirty-mile coastal safe corridor ranging between five and twenty miles wide west to east for Italian units to withdraw eastward to the relative safety of the German *Hauptkampflinie* across the base of the Messina peninsula.[52] The order appears to have been implemented the following day with the *28ª Aosta Divisione* moving first by rail and road followed by the *28ª Aosta Divisione*, screened by *Gruppi Mobili* A, B and C and a number of *Bersaglieri*, artillery and coastal defence elements were also swept up in the withdrawal; some of the retiring columns sustained losses or were wiped out in clashes with US units or by Allied air attacks.[53]

At the same time the *202ª* and *208ª Divisioni Costiere* were tasked to remain in place around the western end of the island to counter any additional Allied amphibious landings, although the commander of the latter formation, *Generale di Divisione* Giovanni Marciani, was elevated to command of the *Comando Porto* Palermo defensive zone along with all coastal units in the surrounding area. *Generale* Marciani was specifically tasked to keep the twenty-five mile stretch of the coastal *Strada* 113 running from Palermo to Cerda open; it is unclear if his authority also extended over the *Piazze Militari Marittime* naval fortress area at Trapani. As noted earlier, overall Italian personnel in western Sicily totalled approximately 60,000 men including the *Regia Marina* base personnel at Palermo, Trapani and Marsala.[54] *Generale* Guzzoni's men were to be at the mercy of the Allied air forces. The Axis air effort had waned considerably by 13-14 July, with the daily total of aircraft committed to operations over Sicily dropping from 500 to 170 across the week from 10 July, and the air situation in Sicily itself had become unsustainable by the 15th; on that date *Generalfeldmarschall* Kesselring informed *Generaloberst* Hube that *14 Panzer Korps* could no longer expect daylight air support and the *Luftwaffe* and *Regia Aeronautica* units on the island began moving their aircraft and ground staff to the Italian mainland the same day.[55]

On the right of the US advance on Palermo Major-General Middleton's US 45th Infantry Division was spearheaded by the 180th RCT, which spent 19 July clearing an Italian blocking position at Portella di Recavitto, ten miles north of Caltanissetta, before pressing north-west up the *Strada* 121 the following day; by the morning of 22 July Colonel Cookson's men had covered around thirty-five miles to reach Villafrati and had reconnaissance patrols probing the outskirts of Palermo, just twenty miles distant. At that point the 45th Division's boundary with the US Provisional Corps was altered to give Major-General Keyes' Provisional Corps access to the *Strada* 121 for the final assault on Palermo, and Major-General Middleton was assigned the new mission of reaching the north coast, which was achieved by sidestepping the 157th and 179th RCTs to the right and pushing up the line of the *Strada* 120.

Colonel Ankcorn's 157th RCT reached the junction with the coastal *Strada* 113 near Stazione di Cerda at 09:00 on 23 July and despatched elements to Termini Imerese five miles to the west and Campofelice di Roccella, six miles to the east. Termini Imerese was secured without a fight but the Battalion moving east ran into a *kampfgruppe* from *29 Panzergrenadier Division* commanded by *Oberst* Max Ulich just short of Campofelice di Roccella; elements of the German formation had only just arrived in Sicily after being released for deployment there by *OKW* the previous day. Colonel Ankcorn's men cleared Campofelice di Roccella with the assistance of a Company of M4 Medium Tanks probably from the 753rd Tank Battalion but were then brought to a halt by heavy artillery and small-arms fire from German positions on a ridge just east of the town, on the opposite bank of the River Roccella.[56]

On the US Provisional Corps' frontage Major-General Truscott's 3rd Infantry Division advanced on two general axes with Colonel Rogers' 30th RCT moving up the *Strada* 118 on the left while Colonel Johnson's 15th RCT moved up on the right just inside the boundary with the US II Corps, trailed by Colonel Sherman's 7th RCT. The 15th RCT's initial objective was the junction of the *Strada* 118 and the *Strada Provinciale* 19 at Santo Stefano Quisquina, around twenty miles from the start line and while Colonel Johnson's men secured Santo Stefano on 20 July, the 7th RCT looped to the right and pushed on for Prizzi, ten miles further up the *Strada* 118, after which the Division pushed on another ten miles to Corleone. By midday on 22 July, almost two days ahead of Truscott's provisional schedule, the 3rd Infantry Division had reached Phase Line Blue near the upper reaches of the River Belice around twelve miles from Palermo and was poised to move on the city. Italian resistance was described as 'spotty', but covering around a hundred miles largely on foot over some of Sicily's most rugged terrain at altitudes of up to 4,000 feet in the dust and heat of the Sicilian summer in a little over seventy-two hours was a feat in itself. The 15th RCT's 3rd Battalion covered the initial twenty miles or more to Santo Stefano Quisquina on foot over mountain trails in just thirty-three hours, for example; after Palermo had been secured Patton complimented Truscott by commenting 'Well, the Truscott Trot sure got us here in a damn hurry.'[57]

The 3rd Infantry Division's performance was impressive, but on the US Provisional Corps' left the 82nd Airborne Division's push west along the line of the coastal *Strada* 115 made even more spectacular progress, to the extent Major-General Ridgway later labelled the advance 'a pleasure march'.[58] Colonel Tucker's 504th Parachute RCT jumped off at 03:00 on 19 July, two hours ahead of schedule, trailed by Colonel Gavin and the 505th Parachute RCT. Within six hours Tucker's paratroopers had covered seventeen miles to cross the River Platani near the ancient Greek city of Heraclea Minoa, despite a demolished bridge, and by early afternoon had pressed on a further seven to the River Verdera. There the advance was held up by an exchange with a pillbox-mounted Italian anti-tank gun on the far bank, which was knocked out by a half-track M3 Gun Motor Carriage despite the US vehicle sliding off the road while taking evasive action. US counter-fire from mortars and machine-guns prompted seventy Italians to abandon their positions and surrender before Major-General Keyes ordered a halt for the night at dusk, by which point the paratroopers had covered twenty-five miles from the start line and captured 500 Italian prisoners. Tucker moved off again at 06:00 the following day, moving eight miles to take the port of Sciacca and nearby abandoned airfield by 09:25. By nightfall the 504th RCT had secured Menfi and extended the day's advance to twenty miles, taking a further 745 prisoners in exchange for one paratrooper killed and another wounded.

At this point the 82nd Airborne Division had advanced almost fifty miles in under forty-eight hours and after conferring with Patton, Major-General Keyes decided to deploy the 2nd Armored Division for the final run to Palermo. He therefore ordered Major-General Gaffey to draw together his two Combat Commands, which were spread over the road network along the twenty-five miles from Agrigento to Ribera, and the 82nd Airborne Division to turn north from the *Strada* 115 up the line of the River Belice and secure a concentration area for the 2nd Armored Division between the river and Santa Ninfa on the *Strada* 119 to the west. To facilitate the northward pivot, Major-General Ridgway ordered the 504th Parachute RCT to secure San Margherita di Belice, seven miles north of Menfi and Tucker in turn assigned the task to his most intact unit, Lieutenant-Colonel William P. Yarborough's 2nd Battalion, which moved off just after dawn on 21 July. At the entrance to the Tuminello Pass, three miles or so south of San Margherita di Belice, the 2nd Battalion came under accurate and sustained shell and machine-gun fire from a well-sited and camouflaged Italian artillery battery, likely from the *202a Divisione Costiere*, overlooking the entrance to the Pass.

The Italian fire pinned the paratroopers down for the thirty minutes it took to organise counter-fire before a bayonet charge by Lieutenant Charles Drew's Company F prompted a mass surrender that brought the 'most spirited fight of the westward march' to a close. Six men from the 2nd Battalion were killed and eight wounded while the defenders lost over a hundred dead, thirty-five wounded and over 1,500 prisoners, including fourteen officers. San Margherita di Belice was then occupied and Colonel Gavin's 505th Parachute RCT moved through Tucker's force to complete the eastern flank guard for the 2nd Armored Division's assembly area.[59]

The mission of securing the *Strada* 115 crossing over the River Belice just west of Menfi and establishing a western flank guard for the 2nd Armored Division at Castelvetrano eleven miles further up the highway was devolved to Colonel William O. Darby's reconstituted FORCE X, consisting of the 1st and 4th Ranger Battalions reinforced with artillery elements and Lieutenant-Colonel John J. Toffey Jr.'s recently landed US 39th RCT, attached from the US 9th Infantry Division. Moving off from Menfi in the morning of 21 July, FORCE X discovered that while the road and rail bridges over the hundred-foot-wide River Belice had been demolished, a network of pillboxes and field fortifications covering the crossing had been abandoned. Colonel Darby swiftly pushed elements of one of his Ranger Battalions across the river to establish a presence on the west bank but lacked bridge-building equipment; the problem was solved by the arrival of Brigadier-General Maurice Rose and his Combat Command A en route to the 2nd Armored Division's assembly area, who immediately set his engineer elements to constructing a crossing.

In the meantime, Darby managed to work a reconnaissance element mounted on Jeeps and M3 Light Tanks over the river which, after clearing a minefield, pushed ten miles up the *Strada* 115 to Castelvetrano where the Italian garrison of 400 surrendered without a fight. Once the Combat Command A bridge was in place, Darby despatched the 39th RCT in the wake of the reconnaissance element, which by this time was closing on Alcamo, over twenty miles to the north of Castelvetrano and around the same distance from Palermo to the north-east. Alcamo also appears to have surrendered without a fight, presenting the reconnaissance element with a further 800 prisoners and a large stock of fuel; FORCE X covered approximately thirty-five miles on 21 July, taking almost 4,000 prisoners on the way. The 2nd Armored Division reached the assembly area east of Santa Ninfa and Major-General Gaffey launched his advance on Palermo, with Brigadier-General Rose's Combat Command A advancing directly north-east toward the city; by midday on Thursday 22 July, Combat Command A was on the high ground overlooking Palermo, alongside Truscott's 3rd Infantry Division on Phase Line Blue.

Precisely which formation entered the Sicilian capital first is still debated, with the 3rd Infantry Division claiming that patrols from Colonel Henry B. Sherman's 7th RCT were in Palermo by 14:00 on 22 July.[60] Though a patrol from the 2nd Armored Division's 82nd Armored Reconnaissance Battalion captured *Generale di Divisione* Giovanni Marciani, the commander of the *Comando Porto* Palermo defensive zone, in the city at some point in the afternoon. His successor, port defences commander *Generale di Brigata* Giuseppe Molinero, was also captured in the city shortly thereafter by a patrol from the 41st Armored Infantry Regiment tasked to capture a *Regia Marina* battleship reportedly anchored in Palermo harbour; Regimental commander Colonel Sidney R. Hinds was relieved to find the vessel had departed the previous day, not least because capturing large warships was not a task he or his men had trained for.

Given that Palermo was the largest city on Sicily with a population of almost half a million, it is perfectly possible that elements of both Divisions were in the city at the same time and oblivious of the other's presence.[61] For their part the Italian military and civilian populace were more than willing to surrender, but found the process less than straightforward. A civilian delegation that approached 3rd Infantry Division HQ in the early afternoon tried to surrender to the Deputy Divisional Commander, Brigadier-General William W. Eagles, who declined their offer due to instructions from Major-General Truscott that the honour had been reserved for US Provisional Corps commander Major-General Keyes.

Keyes appears to have been at Combat Command A HQ with Major-General Gaffey when the 41st Armored Infantry patrol delivered *Generale* Molinero, who promptly offered to surrender the city. He then accompanied Keyes and Gaffey by car to the Royal Palace in Palermo where Keyes formally accepted the Italian surrender at 19:00; after obtaining permission from Patton, who was en route, Keyes ordered the 2nd Armored and 3rd Infantry Divisions to occupy the city at 20:00; Patton himself arrived an hour later guided by the 2nd Armored Division's Chief of Staff, Colonel Redding L. Perry.[62] Patton held his own triumphal tour of Palermo in his personal Dodge WC-57 Command Car the following day to much adulation from the locals decrying Mussolini and praising America and, having set up his HQ in the city's Royal Palace, received a series of visitors including a representative of the Cardinal of Palermo in the style of 'a king in times gone by'. One of Patton's aides, Captain Alexander C. Stiller, tried to persuade the 7th Army commander to take over a more modern abode, but Patton preferred the grander residence in part due to his sense of history; his sense of egalitarianism also led him to relish the idea of eating 'K-Rations on china marked with the cross of Saxony' and using toilet facilities previously 'made malodorous by constipated royalty'. With that, Patton's long-standing fixation with Palermo was finally sated and he moved back to Agrigento the following day, 24 July.[63]

With Palermo firmly in US hands and Patton ensconced in the city's Royal Palace, there remained the matter of securing the rest of western Sicily, which Major-General Keyes addressed in a set of orders on Friday 23 July while Patton was making his triumphal motor tour of the Sicilian capital. Colonel Isaac D. White's Combat Command B from the 2nd Armored Division was tasked to secure the ports along the thirty miles or so of north Sicilian coast between Castellammare del Golfo and Palermo, which was accomplished the same day. Mopping up the remainder of the western tip of Sicily was delegated to Major-General Ridgway and the 82nd Airborne Division, reinforced with FORCE X, who in turn tasked Colonel Tucker's 504th Parachute RCT to take Castellammare del Golfo via Alcamo to the north, Colonel Gavin's 505th Parachute RCT to take the *Regia Marina* base at Trapani in the centre and Colonel Darby's FORCE X to take Marsala to the south. The latter despatched Lieutenant-Colonel Toffey's 39th RCT west along the *Strada* 115 from Castelvetrano to Marsala at Midday on 23 July which by the late afternoon had covered around twenty miles to the River Sossio, five miles short of the city, where the advance was halted by demolished road and rail bridges.[64] When Italian artillery began shelling the engineers brought up to build a crossing, Colonel Toffey decided to remain in place overnight before resuming the advance in the early morning of 24 July, pushing two battalions across the River Sossio under covering fire from the 26th Field Artillery Battalion. Marsala was secured shortly thereafter.

In the centre the 505th Parachute RCT moved off for Trapani aboard a convoy of borrowed 2 ½-ton trucks in the morning of 23 July, accompanied by Major-General Ridgway, the 376th Parachute Field Artillery and 34th Field Artillery Battalions and the 4.2-inch mortar-equipped 83rd Chemical Battalion. The column travelled north-east through Santa Ninfa and Salemi on the *Strada 188* before turning north to access the *Strada 113* that ran directly into Trapani; the forty-mile route was lined by locals cheering their 'liberators' and throwing bread, home-grown fruit and chocolate pilfered from Italian military stores to the presumably grateful paratroopers. The dusty road march was otherwise uneventful until it approached the vicinity of Trapani, where Italian troops began to appear. A group of over a hundred promptly surrendered to the 505th Regiment's lead element when the paratroopers assaulted their position and another group of fifty hiding in a tunnel on the adjacent railway line also surrendered when approached by a squad of Colonel Gavin's men.

At 16:00, as the column approached the outskirts of the city, it ran into a defended roadblock covered by minefields and as the paratroopers deployed from their vehicles they came under additional fire from Italian artillery emplaced on high ground overlooking the road. Gavin responded by deploying his attached guns and mortars and during the two- to three-hour artillery duel that ensued set his men to eliminating the Italian positions. Once this had been achieved, Ridgway despatched Lieutenant-Colonel Alfred W. Ireland, now the 1st Battalion 505th Regiment's Executive Officer, into Trapani with his surrender terms, which included ceasing all resistance, placing guards on all military and naval equipment and securing all supply dumps and other stores. The commander of the Trapani naval base area, *Contrammiraglio* Giuseppe Manfredi, promptly agreed to the terms and surrendered the city, the naval base and its contents – and his sword and binoculars – to the US commander, along with 2,639 men.

The column of 2 ½-ton trucks was retracing its route to lift Colonel Tucker and the 504th Parachute RCT to their objective to the north; the paratroopers were in Alcamo by midday on 24 July and had secured their objective, Castellammare del Golfo, by 17:00.[65] The final task of neutralising about 1000 Italian troops stationed on the islands of the Agadi Archipelago off the western tip of Sicily was carried out five days later. On 29 July, two of Ridgway's staff officers sailed to the largest island, Favignana, where they secured the surrender of the senior Italian commander and his force.[66]

The 82nd Airborne's performance at least equalled that of the US 3rd Infantry Division; in the ten days to 24 July the Airborne formation had advanced 158 miles, securing *c.*1,550 square miles and taking 18,836 prisoners.[67] Major-General Keyes' US Provisional Corps in the first ten days of its existence inflicted 2,900 casualties on its Italian opponents, took a further 53,000 prisoner and captured forty-one tanks, 189 guns of 75mm calibre or above, and 359 assorted vehicles. With that, the Provisional Corps HQ took over administration and garrison duties in western Sicily, employing the US 2nd Armored Division and 82nd Airborne Division on occupation duties until the end of the Sicily campaign.[68]

In just fifteen days from setting foot on Sicily, the Allied landing force had fought off a major armoured counter-attack, captured several defended naval base areas, performed numerous river crossings, secured much of the eastern coast of the island, pushed through the rugged central section of the island from south to north, cleared the entire western half including seizing the island capital Palermo and destroyed the bulk of *Generale d'Armata* Alfredo Guzzoni's 200,000 strong *6ª Armata* in the process. The focus of Operation HUSKY now shifted to the more vexed and demanding task of eliminating *Generaloberst* Hans-Valentin Hube's *14 Panzer Korps* corralled in the Messina Peninsula at the north-eastern corner of the island.

19

The Final Push to Messina

The Third Stage of Operation HUSKY – Part One: D-Day Plus 13, Friday 23 July to D-Day Plus 18, Wednesday 28 July

While the British 8th Army's advance was running out of steam on the Catania Plain and the south-western approaches to Mount Etna and the US Provisional Corps was pushing north-west for Palermo, Major-General Bradley's US II Corps was engaged in harassing the Axis withdrawal east to *14 Panzer Korps' Hauptkampflinie* on the British left flank. Originally tasked to secure the road network running east from Caltanissetta to Enna on the boundary with the British 8th Army, Bradley's mission had been expanded to include pushing to Cefalú on the north Sicilian coast via Alimena and Petralia by Patton's Order of 18 July, although he temporarily side-lined that mission in favour of securing Enna in order to close an open flank created by the 1st Canadian Division veering north-east from the Army boundary toward Leonforte. Enna was actually taken without a fight on 19 July by the 16th and 18th RCTs from Major-General Terry Allen's US 1st Infantry Division as *Kampfgruppe* Fullriede had withdrawn from its positions south-west of the city the same day, moving back through *Raggruppamento* Schreiber's position at Alimena and then north-east to a new line along the *Strada* 120 running east from Gangi to Sperlinga; in so doing *Kampfgruppe* Fullriede tied in with *Kampfgruppe* Ens on the left to close the outstanding opening in the middle of the *Hauptkampflinie*. With Enna securely in US hands, Bradley authorised Allen to begin the advance north in the partial wake of *Kampfgruppe* Fullriede and Colonel John W. Bowen's 26th RCT, accompanied by M3 Light Tanks likely from the 70th Tank Battalion, moved off shortly before Midnight on 20 July.

By this time the preparation of the *Hauptkampflinie* (also known as the San Stafano Line) was approaching completion. As previously mentioned, the *Hauptkampflinie* would make use of existing terrain features rather than prepared defences, with the eastern thirty miles or so to the Dittaino being held by *Generalmajor* Conrath's *HG Panzer Division* while *Generalleutnant* Rodt's *15 Panzergrenadier Division* occupied the sector to the west centred on Nicosia. The gap between the two German sectors was, for the time being, held by the remnants of Generale di Divisione Chirieleison's *4ª Livorno Divisione* stationed in the vicinity of Agira.

Events in Rome and the anticipation – if not the expectation – in Berlin that the Italians might suddenly attempt to quit the Axis and seek a separate peace with the Allies now dominated German views on how to proceed in Italy and, in particular, Sicily. For the moment, Hube had a continued need for the Italian formations still engaged in the battle (however unreliable they had been in the past and might prove to be in the future). So, in addition to Chirieleison's *4ª Livorno Divisione* around Agira, Italian troops would continue to retain the sector between Santo Stefano on the northern coastline and Nicosia. This was in order to allow time for the *29 Panzergrenadier Division*, commanded by Major General Walter Fries, to be brought onto the island – the last of the German reinforcements.[1]

Fries was an interesting character. He had joined the Prussian Army in 1912 and was commissioned three years later. During the Great War he had served with distinction on the Western Front but had failed to secure a place in the much-reduced post-war Reichsheer. Instead, he became a policeman in Prussia and in 1934 a police adjutant to General Goering, a man for whom he soon developed a healthy distaste. In 1936 he finally secured a place in the Wehrmacht where his police experience of motor vehicles gained him an entrée into the new panzer arm. As a battalion commander, he had served in the invasions of Poland, Belgium, and France where he once again added to the Iron Crosses he had gained in the First World War. By November 1940 he had achieved regimental command and promotion to full colonel four months later. During Operation Barbarossa, his regiment took part in the assault on the Baltic States and in the defensive fighting south of Leningrad in early 1942; actions for which he was awarded the Knight's Cross.

It was while fighting in the Rzhev salient in late 1942 that Fries was critically injured when his command post received a direct hit from a Soviet artillery barrage. Fries was rushed back to Germany where his left leg and left arm were amputated. His military career was apparently over. However, Fries was not finished yet. He learnt to walk with a prosthetic leg and was soon back in harness, albeit as an instructor at the Doberitz Infantry School. By this time the war was going badly for the Germans on the Eastern Front and Germany needed all its experienced panzer officers. On 1 March 1943, Fries was sent to France to command and train the *29ᵗʰ Panzer Grenadier Division*, the reincarnation of his old 29ᵗʰ Motorised Division which had been destroyed at Stalingrad and in which he had received his first troop command. When the Allies invaded Sicily on 10 July 1943, Fries's Division was sent to Calabria in southern Italy awaiting the call.

Fries's Division was to take up positions on a secondary defensive line – the Etna Line. This line, which began at San Fratello on Sicily's northern coast, was to be the first of a series of fall-back positions through which Hube planned to withdraw his forces to Messina and, in many cases, it would prove to be stronger than the *Hauptkampflinie* itself. The Division was to hold the northern sector of the Etna Line between San Fratello and Troina; thereafter the line would continue on to the Simeto valley below Adrano before ending on the east coast at Catania.

With these interim deployments in place, the Germans now began to execute a plan to gradually eliminate all of the Italian command posts on the Island. Hube's *14 Panzer Korps*, now situated on the northern slopes of Mount Etna east of Randazzo, had already been receiving its orders directly from Kesselring, which meant that Guzzoni, while nominally still in command of all Axis forces on the island, was increasingly being side-lined. Although the 6th Army continued to issue orders and receive reports – indeed, Guzzoni still harboured thoughts of a major counterattack and was pressing the *Comando Supremo* for major reinforcements to be sent to the island – in reality the Italians could do nothing to influence the future direction of the battle.[2]

Eventually, Guzzoni had to be content with concentrating his efforts on ensuring that when the time came, he could extract his troops and equipment across the Messina Strait in good order. Matters would come to a head on 31 July when the *Comando Supremo* ordered Guzzoni to comply in future with German wishes and to hand over to Hube the command of all German and Italian troops in the fighting zone. These arrangements came into effect on 1 August.[3]

Although Italian morale was deteriorating rapidly, German morale remained strong, even though fears that they might be made subject to one of Hitler's infamous 'hold at all costs' orders – as had happened to Paulus's Sixth Army at Stalingrad and von Arnim's forces in Tunis – was clearly preying on some minds. These fears would be assuaged on 2 August when, in direct contravention of an order from Hitler forbidding it, Hube made it generally known to his troops that preparations were already in hand to evacuate them to the safety of the mainland when the time was ripe. We will discuss these events in more detail in a later chapter, but the effect of this announcement on German morale was galvanising. Whereas the coming fighting, with one notable exception, would be categorised by wholesale surrenders by Italian troops, this would not be the case when the Allies faced German opposition. Their defence would be deadly and tenacious.[4]

On the morning of the 25th, Patton, fresh from his victory celebrations in Palermo, boarded a C-47 and flew to Syracuse for a meeting with Montgomery, Alexander and Eisenhower's chief of staff, Walter Bedell Smith. It appears that Montgomery had initiated the meeting; even going as far as cabling Patton, saying, 'We would be very honoured if you will come over and stay with me for a night and bring your Chief of Staff. We can then discuss the capture of Messina.'[5] From this reading of events, it would seem that Alexander's presence at the meeting would simply be to endorse the strategy put to him by his subordinates.

That Monty thought that he could manipulate his superior with impunity reflects the Army Group commander's continuing lack of grip. From the outset, Alexander had resolved not to create a master plan for the campaign but instead to await the outcome of the landings and his subsequent reading of Axis intentions. As Carlo D'Este observed, 'What passed for strategy can be summed up in Alexander's *idée fixe* that Patton would be the shield in his left hand while Eighth Army served as the sword in his right.' As one of Montgomery's principal operational staff officers later wrote, 'The two armies were left largely to develop their operations in the manner which seemed most propitious in the prevailing circumstances. When there is a master plan, the subordinates exercise their initiatives within its framework, and there is thus greater cohesion in seeking to achieve the superior commander's object'[6]

Events earlier in the campaign had already highlighted the weakness of Alexander's approach when on 13 July Montgomery imperiously 'appropriated' *Strada* 124 for the advance of the 1st Canadian Division; even though the route lay within Seventh Army's area of operations and Patton was already intending to use it for the movement of his 45th Infantry Division inland from the beaches. Moreover, Montgomery had tasked Simond's Division with the capture of Vizzini, the self-same objective that Patton had allocated to Middleton's 45th Division! D'Este argues that Alexander had already resolved to order 8th Army to capture Vizzini and implement the requisite boundary changes before Montgomery's actions, but the incident serves to show that Alexander was not the master of events in Sicily. His somewhat patrician attitude simply reinforced Patton's mounting paranoia regarding a British cabal intent on maintaining the demotion of his Army to a supporting role.[7]

Patton, of course, had already shown that he, too, could set his own agenda by inveigling Alexander's support for his march on Palermo, but he was suspicious of Montgomery's intentions. Having claimed one prize already, Patton was eager to add Messina to his list of triumphs and knew that exclusive access to some of the key routes in Sicily's sparse road network would be key to this endeavour; in particular *Strada* 113, the coast road from Palermo to Messina, and *Strada* 120, the interior road which ran from Nicosia and around the western flank of Mount Etna. He was not going to stand for a repeat of the Vizzini experience.

To Patton's surprise, Montgomery was not only happy to make these concessions but also threw in the use of *Strada* 117 north and south of Enna.[8] By the time Alexander and his new American chief of staff, Brigadier-General Lyman L. Lemnitzer, arrived at the meeting, Montgomery and Patton had already struck a deal. That the plan now being proposed was already one that Alexander had formulated independently back in North Africa seems moot. It looked like the tail was wagging the dog. This impression that it was Montgomery and not Alexander who was in the driving seat would be reinforced three days later when Monty flew to Palermo to see Patton to continue their joint planning. It was a journey that nearly cost Monty his life.

Prior to the flight Montgomery had cabled ahead: 'Would arrive airfield 1200 hours in my FORTRESS. Query, is this convenient to you?' Montgomery was ludicrously proud of the fact that he had his own private plane which he had won during the North Africa campaign in a private bet with Walter Bedell Smith, Eisenhower's chief of staff.[9] Monty had part of the plane fitted up with a table as a desk and two armchairs and boasted that 'It is a great thing to have your own aeroplane, to start *when* you like and go *where* you like.' As his ADC, John Henderson, was later to remark, Montgomery's cable to Patton was like saying 'Can I come to lunch in my Rolls-Royce?'[10] Not unsurprisingly, Patton ignored the cable; as he did the follow-up message which queried whether the Palermo airfield could accommodate a B-17. The short answer was – it couldn't. As Henderson recalls: 'We went down the runway and it absolutely ate it up. The hangers were at the end and it wasn't long enough. I remember sitting in the glass dome in which I always sat, and I saw the hangar coming up – the pilot did the most amazing job. He swung the whole thing round and we landed on our side. I mean he put all the brakes on one side and revved one engine and swung the whole thing round – which wrote it off. That was the end of it. It collapsed on one side. We got out pretty shaken.'[11]

Monty appeared unphased by the whole experience. As Broadhurst later observed: 'Monty was sitting there reading, quite unafraid of anything. We should never have gone there in that aeroplane... He should never have had it but he adored it.'[12] Patton deliberately snubbed Montgomery by failing to greet him personally at the airfield, but then went out of his way to impress the British general by laying on a cavalcade of scout cars and motorcycles to take him to his headquarters in the Royal Palace. There he was greeted by a military band, invited to inspect a Guard of Honour and hosted to a sumptuous lunch before the two men got down to brass tacks.[13]

Once again, Montgomery went out of his way to stress the importance of the American thrust on Messina. As Patton later wrote in his Diary: 'Monty kept repeating that the move of the 45th Division along the coast was a most significant operation. I can't decide whether he is honest or wants me to lay off [Route] 120. On the other hand, he said that if we got to Taormina first, we were to turn south. Previously he had insisted that we not come as far as the [eastern] coast.'[14] Patton would remain sceptical of Monty's *bona fides* and that evening penned a memo to Middleton: 'This is a horse race in which the prestige of the US Army is at stake. We must take Messina before the British. Please use your best efforts to facilitate the success of our race.'[15]

What was the plan for what was later to be referred to as Operation HARDGATE?[16] In the east, Dempsey's XIII Corps was ordered to continue to hold firm on the Catania Plain in order to allow simultaneous Allied attacks to develop in the west. Here the US II Corps, led by Bradley, and the British XXX Corps, led by Leese, were to execute the main assaults on the *Hauptkampflinie*. In total, the equivalent of three and a half British divisions, including the newly arrived 78th Infantry Division (the 'Battleaxe' Division) would converge on Adrano, a key town guarding the slopes of Mount Etna, while four US Divisions operating in depth on a two-division frontage would attack the northern sector of the enemy's defence line. To support these operations Coningham, commander of the Northwest African Tactical Air Force, had directed that his forces should concentrate their efforts on three main tasks: disruption of the enemy's supplies (by sea, road, and rail); direct support to the land forces (what today is referred to as CAS or close air support); and fighter protection by day and night for the forward troops and Allied shipping off the east coast of Sicily. These tasks would be performed by AVM Harry Broadhurst's Desert Air Force (DAF) and the US XII Air Support Command, led by Major General Edwin House. Meanwhile, because of the predicted unfavourable night conditions, the Tactical Bomber Force would concentrate its efforts on daytime raids only.

General Middleton's 45th Division had initially been part of the forces assigned to capture Palermo and was to advance to the northwest using *Strada* 121 as its main axis of advance. Once it had reached the north coast road it was to wheel to the west and begin its drive on Palermo. However, as events unfolded the 45th was not needed; Palermo fell more quickly than expected to troops from Truscott's 3rd Infantry Division and Gaffey's 2nd Armored Division, leaving Middleton's troops 30 miles short of the Sicilian capital at Termini Imerese. With Ridgeway's 82nd Airborne assigned to mopping up the few remaining pockets of resistance, the Provisional Corps' short period of combat operations was coming to an end. From 24 July onwards it would spend the rest of the campaign on garrisoning and administering western Sicily. Henceforth, the burden of future US combat operations and the advance on Messina would fall to Bradley's II Corps. And for this task Patton sent him reinforcements in the form of the French 4th Tabor of Guoms (which hitherto had formed part of Truscott's 3rd Division), and the 39th Infantry Regiment together with assorted artillery assets from Major General Eddy's 9th Infantry Division. (At the same time Patton called for the balance of Eddy's Division to be sent over from North Africa.)[17]

On reaching Termini Imerese on 23 July Middleton had ordered his leading troops, the 157th RCT, to turn both left and right along the *Strada* 113 coast road. However, the battalion advancing to the east came across fierce German resistance just west of Campofelice. And although it was subsequently able to clear Campofelice itself, it was then brought to a sudden halt along the line of the Roccella River. The troops the 45th Division found themselves facing were the advance elements of Fries's 29th Panzer Grenadier Division, which Hube had recently deployed to bolster Rodt's already stretched 15th Panzer Grenadiers.

Middleton's axis of advance – *Strada* 113 – lay between the sea and the Caronie Mountain chain. The official US History described it as skirting 'the rim of what resembled a washboard, created by numerous short streams flowing down from the mountain crests at frequent intervals to empty into the sea'.[18] Where it hugged the coastline the road itself would often be built into the cliff face perilously hanging above the sea, crossing the rivers on iron bridges and burrowing through the intervening ridge lines in a series of dark, unlit tunnels. For most of its length, the railway from Palermo to Messina also hugged this coastline route. This terrain would prove to be a dream playground for German engineers who were rapidly building an ominous reputation for sowing their demolitions with inventive improvised booby traps.

The US troops referred to two of these booby traps as the Castrator and the Bouncing Betty. The castrator was a metal tube, about six inches in length, stuck into the ground inside of which was a .45 calibre bullet initiated by a firing pin with a spring. Any soldier unfortunate enough to step on one could expect the bullet to travel through his foot and leg and into his groin area (hence the sobriquet). The Germans placed these booby traps everywhere they expected Allied troops to pass and especially around their machine-gun nests. The Bouncing Betty was 'as wide as a grapefruit and eight inches long'. Packed with black powder, blades, nails, and any other scrap metal the Germans could find, they were attached to a trigger on the ground and then buried. Initiation was by trip wires, some as long as twenty or thirty yards. The black powder charge in the bottom of each mine would send the top part into the air which, when it exploded could kill within a radius of thirty yards.[19]

As previously described, Fries's Division had temporarily halted the advance of Middleton's 157th RCT along the northern coast road and, by blowing the bridge over the Malpertugio River five miles east of Cefalu and planting mines in the riverbed, his engineers had imposed further delays. However, the 179th RCT, moving eastwards six miles south of the coast road on a secondary route, was able to make progress and quickly reached Castelbuono. With Allen's 1st Division already occupying Petralia, eight miles to the south, this now brought Bradley's two divisions into line.

Middleton was ordered to keep up the pressure on the north coast road (*Strada* 113) and on the evening of 24 July he conducted a passage of lines. The 180th RCT crossed the Malpertugio River in the face of fierce resistance, only to come up against a similar problem on the Pollina River where the Germans had established a defensive position based on the 3000-foot-high Pizzo Spina, its vertical cliffs dominating the crossing point. This was a bridge which the Germans had decided not to demolish but instead had surrounded it with infantry and support weapons.

Scaling the heights of Pizzo Spina was slow and dangerous work. Two companies of Colonel Cochrane's 2nd Battalion climbed to almost 3000ft in less than a thousand yards, all the while under artillery, mortar and machine-gun fire and with German defenders rolling hand grenades down the slopes. The attack, which almost petered out in the face of such resistance, was ultimately successful, but although the Americans now held the heights the Germans were reluctant to give up and launched three, ultimately unsuccessful, counter-attacks. The battle raged for most of the day but eventually, just before nightfall, the Germans pulled out. Their attempts to finally blow the bridge were defeated by heavy and accurate American artillery fire.

American efforts to pursue the retiring Germans were thwarted by fears of an Axis amphibious landing. Fourteen unidentified naval vessels had been detected off the coast and fearing that they may enemy vessels, Bradley ordered Middleton to halt and deploy his forces facing the sea. It would not be until the afternoon of the next day, 26 July, that the vessels were identified as American destroyers and minesweepers.[20]

After Patton had managed to change the original concept of operations by swanning off to Palermo and taking 45th Infantry Division with him, it fell to Terry Allen's 1st Division to complete the original mission of driving north towards the coast, thereby protecting Montgomery's western flank and effectively cutting the Island in two. But first, Leese having altered the axis of advance of Simonds' 1st Canadian Division away from Enna and towards Leonforte and Assoro, it was left to Allen to capture the town, which hitherto had been the location of Guzzoni's 6th Army. Enna fell without a struggle; the Germans having abandoned it realising that with the Canadians on their left and Middleton's 45th Division on their right, it no longer held any strategic importance and would only leave their forces vulnerable to encirclement.

The defenders of Enna, *Kampfgruppe* Fullriede, part of Rodt's 15th Panzer Grenadier Division, withdrew north through Alimena to take up new defensive positions along *Strada* 120 between Gangi and Sperlinga. They were closely pursued by Allen's Division. Fullriede's new mission was now to prevent the Americans from sweeping around Rodt's right flank. Alimena itself was defended by an assortment of Italian forces known as Group Screiber. They were all that remained of the Italian 207th Division and despite fighting bravely and with a degree of reckless bravado, they were easily swept aside. However, German demolitions, particularly a blown bridge just south of Bompietro, and fierce resistance by Fullreide's soldiers, continued to slow Allen's progress towards Cefalu and the coast. Petralia, a key town on *Strada* 120, was captured on the morning of 23 July, by which time Bradley had issued fresh orders. With Seventh Army now tasked with operating on 8th Army's left flank, Middleton and Allen were to drive eastwards in tandem; Middleton via the coast road and Allen along *Strada* 120 through Sperlinga to Nicosia on the *Hauptkampflinie* and then on to Troina.[21] The official British History described the *Hauptkampflinie* (and the defensive lines behind it) thus:

> Following roughly the road-line from just west of S. Stefano south to Nicosia -Agira, east to Regalbuto then southerly to Catenanuova – eastwards along the Dittaino River – across the northern edge of the Catanian plain to the coast six miles south of Catania. This unavoidable string of names indicates a useful, coast-to-coast defensive line, taking advantage of mountainous country, a river bank, and the broken Catanian plain. Behind the line [lay] the Etna Line or 'Old Hube Line'. From S. Fratello, a few miles inland from the northern coast – south to Troina, south-east to Aderno [Adrano], and east along the roads girdling Etna to the sea at Acireale. [And behind that the] 'New Hube Line'. Mt. Pelato – Cesaro – Bronte – eastward to the sea near Riposto. This 'line' in fact was the outermost delaying position for the north-eastern evacuation bridgehead. These 'lines' should not be pictured as belts of field-works. They were, rather, excellent natural positions for defence and delay, formidable in themselves, which could readily be made more formidable by demolitions, mines, blasting, pick and shovel – any of the improvements that troops who mean business can make.[22]

As the official history emphasises, the reader should not imagine this line as being a continuous stretch of trenches a la the Western Front in the Great War; instead, they were an inter-connected series of strongpoints based on natural features such as rivers and mountain tops. And, in front of them, the

Germans had created additional defences overlooking obvious avenues of approach. Three examples of these 'outposts' have already been cited earlier (Leonforte/Assoro, Gangi/Sperlinga, and Pizzo Spina) and there would be more to come as the Allies closed in.

In the north, the 45th Division, having paused to counter the fictitious Axis amphibious landings, advanced to yet another of these outposts. Group Ulich, the defenders of the Pollina River, had withdrawn to yet another river line, the Tusa. Their new defences ran from where the river entered the sea at Castel di Tusa, south through Pettineo, and on to Castel di Lucio. The 180th RCT reached this line late in the afternoon of 26 July. Hube had insisted that Fries held the Americans at bay for as long as possible - and at least until the night of 30 July – and Fries in turn was determined to make Middleton's men fight for every yard of territory.

Once again, the Germans had left a bridge intact and while one of his battalions (the 2nd) operated a feint near the bridge the 180th RCT commander sent another battalion (the 3rd) to attempt a crossing two miles further inland. The point chosen for the crossing was dominated by two separate ridgelines which faced each other on either side of the River Tusa. Each ridgeline bore the name of its principal village: Tusa in the west and Pettinco in the east. Tusa fell without much difficulty at 06:00 on 27 July, but the Germans still clung on to much of the ridgeline and nine hours later a reinforced battalion from *Kampfgruppe* Ulich sitting on the Pettinco ridgeline continued to resist all attempts by the Americans to get across the river.

Blocked in the south, the 180th RCT was forced to turn the initial feint on the coast road into a full-blown attack. By now the bridge itself had been destroyed by German artillery fire, although not before the 1st Battalion had successfully managed to get one company across to the eastern side. Despite their best efforts, the Americans could not capitalise on this bridgehead and just before dark on the 27th the company was withdrawn to the western side of the river. Rodt had successfully kept the Americans at bay in the north – at least for the moment.

Bradley, recognising that his divisions had now almost fought themselves to a standstill, decided to relieve them both. In the north, Middleton's 45th Division would soon be replaced by Truscott's 3rd Division whose task it would now be to close up onto the *Hauptkampflinie*. In the south, he planned to relieve Terry Allen's 'Big Red One' with Eddy's 9th Division; but this change would take longer to effect as the 9th had still not completed the process of bringing its remaining units across from North Africa. Allen was therefore told to continue advancing east towards the *Hauptkampflinie* at Nicosia and then onto Cerami and Troina.[23]

On the evening of 28 July, while Truscott's 3rd Division was preparing to move forward and conduct a passage of lines, Middleton continued his attempts to break the German defence on the River Tusa. At 17:45, two battalions of the 157th Infantry, having struggled for much of the day to get its troops forward over a blown section of the coast road west of the Pollina River, finally relieved the 180th Infantry on the Tusa. While the 1st Battalion set about clearing the remaining Germans from the Tusa ridgeline, the 2nd Battalion passed through Tusa itself and began the descent to the river.

In contrast to the opposition faced by its sister Regiment the previous day, the 157th managed to get into Pettineo without much difficulty, the only resistance coming in the form of a small counterattack from elements of the 2nd Battalion 15th Panzer Grenadier Regiment. The reason for this was because Rodt had now pulled back his troops to yet another piece of high ground behind the Pettineo ridge, on which was the Motta d'Affermo-Mistretta road. The attack on the Motta ridgeline began on the morning of 29 July and would take the best part of two days. It was a battle that the 45th Division would later remember as 'Bloody Ridge'. Colonel Ankcorn, the commander of the 157th RCT, was forced to commit all of his resources against an enemy which still had hopes of regaining its lost ground and retaking the Pettineo and Tusa ridgelines. Rodt, convinced that he could easily hold off any American advances along the coast road, knew that the most serious threat to his forces holding the *Hauptkampflinie* at Santo Stefano would come here in the south. And Hube could not have been clearer; Rodt was to keep the Americans at bay until at least 31 July.

Kampfgruppe Ulrich's counterattack began without any preparatory artillery fire at 04:30, 30 July and caught the Americans completely off-guard. However, success was short-lived and very quickly Ankcorn's men regained their composure. By 13:00, supported by the full weight of 45th Division's artillery, they managed to blunt the German offensive. Motta fell without a fight that evening and the next morning troops from the 45th Division entered San Stefano. Rodt had fulfilled his mandate. And so too, one could say, had Middleton's troops. In the words of the US Official History: 'For the 45th Division, Santo [San] Stefano marked the end of active combat operations in Sicily. For a short time, at least, the division could enjoy a respite from the bloody business of war. In its first twenty-one days of combat in World War II, the 45th Division had earned an enviable reputation. It had marched and fought from Scoglitti to the north coast, suffered 1,156 casualties, and taken 10,977 prisoners.'[24]

Middleton's progress towards the *Hauptkampflinie* had been hard-fought and bloody, and Allen's 1st Division now faced a similar prospect. Having chased *Kampfgruppe* Fullriede, part of Rodt's 15th Panzer Grenadier Division, north out of Enna to Petralia, the eastward axis of advance for the 1st Division now lay along *Strada* 120, a road which bordered the southern slopes of the Caronie Mountains. With the exception of Mount Etna itself, this mountain range is the highest in Sicily and its rugged terrain and the paucity of north-south communications would effectively prevent Bradley's forces from providing mutual support. So, until they reached Messina, II Corps' leading divisions would find themselves operating in isolation.

Allen's men had captured Petralia, a key town on *Strada* 120, on the morning of 23 July. The route which faced them as they moved eastwards to Nicosia was narrow and crooked, with steep gradients and turns that were so sharp that vehicles frequently had to three-point turn in order to negotiate the corners. Moreover, the road was dominated on both sides by high mountains. Like *Strada* 113 in the north, this road therefore offered the German defenders endless possibilities for imposing delay and damage on the advancing Americans.

On the morning of 24 July, Allen conducted a passage of lines. Colonel Bowen's 26th RCT took up the vanguard and were charged with capturing Gangi and Sperlinga. Fully expecting to have to fight for every inch of ground, the regiment was pleasantly surprised to find that the Germans had abandoned Gangi. This state of affairs would not last for long. Advancing now on a two-battalion front, one either side of the road, Bowen found his entry into Sperlinga barred by a triangle of hills: Hill 825 (Monte Cannella) to the north; Hill 937 (Monte Caolina) to the south; and, in depth behind them, Hill 962 (Monte Barnagiano). Defending these hills was a recently reinforced *Kampfgruppe* Fullriede.

Major Grant, commanding the 1st Battalion, soon reported that Hill 825 was 'nothing more than a barren slab of rock, impracticable to occupy'. Commenting that 'there is no place to put anyone if we did have it,' Grant suggested that, if necessary, it would be simpler to dominate the feature by fire from already held higher ground to the west. Bowen concurred. But when Colonel Daniel, commanding the 2nd Battalion, made a similar observation and recommendation regarding Hill 937, Bowen demurred and ordered him to secure it. His reason for doing so was that he intended to push his 3rd Battalion further to the south so that they could advance cross-country for eight miles and take Nicosia from an unexpected direction. For this he needed to have a secure flank. No sooner had a company of Daniel's battalion taken Hill 937 than they found themselves being thrown off it again by a counter-attack. It was the start of a fierce battle which would rage for over three days. It also came at a time when the Italian and German strategy for defending the island became irrevocably broken.

As dawn broke on 25 July, heavy German artillery fire began to descend across the whole 26th RCT front. It was the signal for an entire German battalion to advance on Hill 937 and throw the defenders off. With Allen and his deputy divisional commander, Teddy Roosevelt Jr, putting pressure on him from above, Colonel Bowen pressed his men to retake the feature. To this end the 1st Battalion were now told to occupy Hill 825 and the orders for 3rd Battalion to move on Nicosia were cancelled. Instead, this battalion was to swing around the right of Hill 937, thereby squeezing the German defenders in a two-battalion pincer movement.

By mid-afternoon the Germans had been expelled from their positions on the top of Hill 937 but still clung on tenaciously to the eastern slopes. What had previously been an infantry slugfest now turned into an artillery one as both sides tried to use artillery to break the deadlock. As German and Italian artillery fire raked the men of the 2nd Battalion holding the hilltop, Allen's artillery commander, Brigadier-General Clift Andrus, was able to concentrate the fire of six artillery battalions and two 155-mm gun batteries onto the German defenders. It is estimated that over 2,000 rounds of artillery ammunition were fired by the Americans on 25 July. It was to prove too much for Colonel Fullreide's men. In the nick of time, they managed to pull back before becoming enveloped and cut off by Bowen's 3rd Battalion.

Thwarted, Bowen now ordered the 3rd Battalion to capture the German depth positions centred on Hill 962. This move began shortly before midnight and was supported by the 1st Battalion who were told to advance from Hill 825 north of the road and occupy Hills 921 and 825, 800 yards further east. Although initially successful, the Americans did not hold Hill 962 for long. Fullreide's men fought ferociously to recapture it and the battle for Hill 962 would ultimately see-saw for most of 26 July.

As a result, the hilltop itself became a no-man's land swept by opposing artillery fire with the Americans occupying the western slopes and the Germans the eastern ones. Compared to the lightning speed of the Provisional Corps' drive on Palermo, after three days of fighting on two fronts II Corps' advance on Messina had barely got out of first gear. Intent on breaking the stalemate, on the morning of 26 July Bradley returned the two battalions of the 16th RCT from Allen's division which until now he had been holding as his corps reserve. This would allow Allen to fulfil his original intention of bypassing the Germans at Sperlinga and attacking Nicosia overland from the west.

By 16:00 on 26 July all of the 1st Division's three regiments were either engaged or on the move. Bowen's 26th RCT was fighting off yet another German counter-attack on *Strada* 120 as German resistance in front of Sperlinga showed no signs of diminishing; the 18th RCT, reinforced by French troops of the 4th Tabor of Goums, was ordered to move across the mountain slopes to the north of the road and head towards *Strada* 117 which connected Nicosia with San Stefano on the northern coast; and the recently released battalions of the 16th RCT were moving south to outflank Hill 962. But, as darkness fell that night, little progress had been made.

The next day, 16th RCT's drive south was stopped in its tracks. To the north the 18th RCT made better progress. Hills 921 and 825, which had given the 26th RCT so much trouble the day before, were captured, and one battalion supported by the Goumiers was approaching Monte Sambughetti, a towering hill mass 4,500 feet high which hugged the western side of *Strada* 117 and looked down on both Sperlinga and Nicosia. Here they took 300 Italian prisoners and were able to continue down onto *Strada* 117 and the *Hauptkampflinie* and, in the process cut the main line of communication between the Axis defenders on the coast road and those in Nicosia. Allen, judging that the time had finally come to push the Germans once and for all from their positions covering the road west of Sperlinga, now ordered thirty-two light tanks from the 70th Tank Battalion and a platoon of tanks from the 753rd Medium Tank Battalion to sweep the road in front of Hills 825 and 962. The attack itself was a non-event and achieved very little in practical terms, but it bolstered the morale of the American infantryman on the surrounding hills and probably reinforced the German decision to finally pull back from Sperlinga and Nicosia.

On 25 July, punctually at 17:00, Mussolini's car passed through the gates of the Villa Savoia, the King's private home in Rome. It was, the Duce thought, a routine visit. Had the two men not met like this twice a week for the past two decades? But this was to be far from an ordinary meeting; as Mussolini would quickly discover. The King, dressed formally in the uniform of the First Marshal of the Empire, was highly nervous. 'My dear Duce, it can't go on any longer. Italy is in pieces. Army morale has reached rock-bottom and the soldiers don't want to fight any longer... The result of the votes cast by the Grand Council is devastating. Surely you have no illusion as to how Italians feel about you at the moment? You are the most hated man in Italy; you have not a single friend left, except me.'[25]

That wasn't quite true. The King had already decided to remove him. In the past month Generale Ambrosio, head of the *Comando Supremo*, had twice requested the King's permission to arrest Mussolini and replace him with Marshal Badoglio, the erstwhile chief of staff the Duce had forced to retire in disgrace two years previously after the debacle of the Greek campaign. The day before, on 24 July, at the meeting of the Grand Council to which the King had just referred, the Duce had been urged to share power and hand authority over the armed forces to the King. Finally, the King had decided to act. The reins of power, Mussolini was told, would be handed over to Badoglio. He would form a cabinet of career officials 'in order to rule the country and go on with the war'.[26]

Just twenty minutes after arriving at the Villa Savoia, Mussolini was bundled into the back of an ambulance and driven away to a barracks in the city. Here, he was later informed in a letter from Badoglio, he was to be held in protective custody 'since we have information from several sources of a plot against your life'.[27] News of Mussolini's fall spread like wildfire. While many Italians must have thought that the war was surely coming to an end, Badaglio, in bringing the news to the nation by radio, stressed that in fact Italy would continue to fight. Of course, no-one seriously believed him; least of all the Germans. Hitler's first reaction was to pull troops out of Sicily and send a panzer division into Rome to arrest the King, Badoglio, and the whole nest of 'traitors'. Later, after he had calmed down, wiser counsels prevailed. The *OKW* had already anticipated Italy's collapse and had made contingency plans accordingly. All that was needed was time to refine them and bring them into action. In the meantime, German troops on Sicily would continue to fight.[28]

On 26 July, the day after Mussolini had been removed from office, Hube's chief of staff was in Rome receiving instructions from Kesselring for the final stages of the Sicilian campaign. Guzzoni still intended to hold Nicosia as one of the key positions on his main line of resistance and believed that Hube had the same opinion. But already the first indications were emerging that the Germans were adopting an independent strategy. Hube's strings were being pulled by *OKW* and C-in-C South and, as such, he had already instructed Rodt to recce suitable defensive positions in front of the planned Etna Line with the intention of pulling back his forces from Nicosia on the night of the 27th. When Guzzoni got wind of these intentions he immediately asked Hube to amend his orders to *Kampfgruppe* Fullreide. Hube promised to stop the withdrawal and establish a new line between Nicosia and Agira in accordance with Guzzoni's design. This would see the *Aosta Divisione* holding a 3,000-foot-high mountain pass on *Strada* 117 between Nicosia and Mistretta called the Colle del Contrasto, which would continue to prevent Bradley's divisions from supporting each other. There is nothing to suggest that Hube was not completely sincere in giving these assurances to Guzzoni, but in reality, the amended orders were not received by his subordinates and as a result, on the night of the 27th and in accordance with his existing orders, Rodt duly withdrew his troops from Nicosia and established a fresh line of defence six miles east of Nicosia running from Capizzi in the north through Cerami and Serradifalco (both on *Strada* 120) to Gagliano in the south.

Caught off guard, some units of the *Aosta Divisione* failed to withdraw at all and became isolated when American forces entered Nicosia on the morning of the 28th. Although the Americans encountered small pockets of resistance, by the end of the day Allen's troops had taken the town and with it over 700 Italian prisoners, as well as a few German soldiers who had also failed to extricate themselves. Moreover, the Italian division which had been assigned to hold the Colle del Contrasto had also pulled back to the east, giving Bradley free access to the important lateral, which was *Strada* 117.

Leaving the American sector for the moment, we can now turn our attention to Montgomery's 8th Army. By the third week of July, Dempsey's XIII Corps had been fought to a standstill. The 50th Division had failed to make further progress after being held at the Fosso Bottaceto on 18 July and an attempt to use 5th Division on a left flanking attack aimed at Misterbianco had stalled after three days of fierce German defence which had thwarted all efforts to get across the twin obstacles of the River Simeto and Gornalungo Canal. This led to the Division being ordered to consolidate its positions just north of Primosole Bridge. It was now that Montgomery turned to XXX Corps for salvation.

The 51st Highland Division, emerging from the hills which overlooked the western edge of the Catania Plain and tasked with reaching Paterno on the southwestern slopes of Mount Etna, after two bitterly contested engagements had briefly taken the twin villages of Sferro and Gerbini. But these villages could not be held in the face of intense counter-attacks by elements of the Herman Goering Division who were determined at all costs to deny the Allies the use of the Gerbini airfields. Leese had therefore been forced to withdraw the Division behind the line of the Dittaino River and switch the point of his corps' attack further west, where he hoped to capitalise on the Canadian successes at Assoro and Leonforte. These attacks would be led by Maj-Gen Guy Simonds' 1st Canadian Infantry Division. With the exception of Matthew Ridgway, the American commander of the 82nd AA Division, the Canadian Guy Simonds was arguably the most inexperienced divisional commander fighting in the Sicily Campaign. Not that he lacked ambition or ability. But inexperience combined with ambition can be a dangerous combination. Two weeks into the fighting Simonds had yet to find his feet and had already made several errors of judgement.

A pre-war regular Permanent Force artillery officer, Simonds had at a very early stage in his career been earmarked as a rising star. Nevertheless, by 1943 he had yet to gain any valuable combat experience; being too young to have served in the First World War and without yet being blooded in the Second. Still only in his mid-thirties, Simonds was highly regarded for his quick brain, incisive intellect, and incredible application. However, his peers and students found him remote and standoffish. As one of his cadets remarked years later, 'No student would ever have thought of going to Major Simonds with a personal problem.'[29] Major-General Bert Hoffmeister, who served as the commanding officer of the Seaforth Highlanders of Canada under Simonds in Sicily, did not like him and called him 'cold blooded...a bastard... The kind of man who liked to kick people when they were down.'[30]

Deployed to the UK as the GSO2 of the 1st Canadian Infantry Division on the cusp of 1940, by July of that year Simonds had been promoted and given command of the 1st Field Regiment RCA. The regiment had only just returned from the fall of France and although it had managed to save its guns, much of its remaining equipment had been left behind during the evacuation. Morale was subterranean. Simonds made an immediate impact. According to his adjutant, Simonds related well to his gunners who responded positively to a training regime which took them back to the basics of their trade; but, in the process, he terrified his young officers.

With the Canadian Army in UK growing at a prodigious rate in 1940, Simonds' time in command was all too brief. After only four months he was pulled out to fill a series of short-term staff appointments all designed to enhance the capability of what was eventually to become 1st Canadian Army. In August 1941, after only three months as the GSO1 of the 2nd Canadian Infantry Division, he received another promotion and became the Brigadier General Staff (BGS) at Canadian Corps HQ. Thus, from arriving in England at the beginning of 1940 Simonds had, in the space of just nineteen months, risen rapidly from major to brigadier., Simonds soon came into contact with an even greater ego – General Bernard Law Montgomery – as the Canadian Corps was under the command of Monty's South Eastern Command. Montgomery was quickly impressed by the staff work of this young Canadian who, in July and August 1942, had been set the task of planning Churchill's latest 'wizard wheeze' – Operation JUPITER, an attack on Norway. Of course, like many of Churchill's schemes, it came to nothing but it absolved Simonds of any potential contamination as the recriminations flowed from the disastrous Dieppe raid.

A year after becoming BGS, Simonds was given command of the 1st Canadian Infantry Brigade in September 1942 and, seven months later in April 1943, another promotion followed; major general and command of the 2nd Canadian Infantry Division. And that is probably where he would have remained had it not been for the untimely death of Major-General Harry Salmon, the 1st Canadian Infantry Division's GOC, who died in a plane crash en route to the Middle East while preparing for his Division's employment in HUSKY. Salmon needed to be replaced quickly and on 29 April 1943 Simonds returned to a division in which he had been both GSO2 and GSO1 and where he had also served as a regimental and brigade commander. To the 1st Division Simonds was a known quantity, and he had the comfort of knowing all of its key officers. His GSO1, Lt Col George Kitching, had served under him in the Canadian Corps HQ, and Simonds had personally chosen Lt Col Pres Gilbride to come onboard as his chief administrative officer. Of his three brigade commanders, one was an old classmate from RMC (Brigadier Chris Vokes commanding 2nd Brigade) and another was a fellow gunner (Brigadier Howard 'Pen' Penhale commanding 3rd Brigade). Brigadier Howard Graham was now commanding Simonds' erstwhile brigade, the 1st Brigade, and their relationship was to prove stormy, at least initially.

Howard Graham was a peacetime lawyer and a highly experienced militia officer. He had enlisted in the infantry for the Great War and arrived in France in 1917 aged 19, where he was later wounded. In 1923 he took a commission in his local regiment, the Hastings and Prince Edward Regiment (the Hasty Ps), and rose steadily through its ranks, later becoming one of a very few militia officers to attend the Advanced Staff Course at RMC Kingston. In 1939 he once again volunteered for overseas service and in September 1940 he was appointed to command his battalion. It was a popular selection and coincidentally one which brought him into contact with Monty who gained a favourable impression of him. Two years later, Graham took command of the Canadian 7th Infantry Brigade. However, within only a few months he was cross posted to take command of the 1st Brigade. The reason for this was never explained to him, but reading between the lines, it would appear that the GOC, Major General Harry Salmon, who had previously been his CO, had personally asked for him. He was to replace Guy Simonds. Graham duly handed over his brigade to the incoming brigadier and set off to his new command. He had never met Simonds before but had heard that he was 'cool, reserved (perhaps shy), abrupt, didactic, a serious and dedicated student of military science and unquestionably an able staff officer'.[31] At this stage he was unable to form his own opinion as Simonds had shot off the day before to take up his new appointment. There was to be no handover; in fact, it would be several months before the two officers would have any direct communication.

Graham was on duty in Norfolk House putting the final touches to the Sicily planning when news of Harry Salmon's death was received. When Simonds arrived as the new GOC he naturally wanted to be briefed on the divisional 'plan' for Sicily. Graham was the first to brief him. Simonds clearly didn't like what he heard and gave Graham a dressing down in front of the assembled officers. The other two brigade commanders quickly adapted their briefings. Furthermore, Simonds would always refer to his fellow brigade commanders, both regular officers, as 'Chris' or 'Pen' whereas the militia officer, Howard Graham, was always 'Graham'. It irked. And it was noticed. This was not the last occasion that Simonds chose to criticise Graham in front of colleagues and juniors. He did it again during the HUSKY rehearsals in Scotland, much to the annoyance of the Senior Naval Officer Landing (SNOL) assigned to the 1st Brigade. He took umbrage at Simonds' attitude and had no difficulty in calling it out. Graham was thankful for the support, but the writing was on the wall; Simonds clearly had no confidence in him.[32]

Matters came to a head on 15 July. It was the first time that Simonds had visited 1st Brigade since the landings. Once again Simonds harangued Graham, but this time in front of their respective drivers and signallers. Graham was furious and that night, after the daily 'O' Group, he tackled Simonds. The 'conversation' ended with Graham resigning his command. Simonds was taken aback but accepted the situation. And that might have been the end of it had not wiser heads intervened. The next day Graham was summoned to Corps headquarters, he assumed to be told his future. In reality he was met by the Corps Commander, Oliver Leese, who ushered him in to see Monty who wanted to know the full story. Graham proceeded to tell him the whole sorry tale. According to Graham Monty listened in silence and then said: 'Have you ever refused to obey an order?'

'Never, sir.'

'Well, Graham, you will go back with the Corps Commander this morning and resume command of your brigade.'

'But this will be very difficult, sir. I spoke very frankly to the GOC, and although I was respectful, I was quite critical.'

'Don't worry about that. There will be no problem. Both of you are to blame. Just get on with the battle.'[33]

This background is useful because it partly explains what happened next. By 21 July the Allies had achieved air superiority over Sicily and were close to achieving air supremacy. There were no longer any enemy aircraft operating from airfields on the island and very few German aircraft were getting through from either Sardinia or the Italian mainland. Nevertheless, German ground forces continued to stymie Montgomery's efforts to break through their defences on the Catania Plain and so on this day Montgomery issued instructions that all formations of the 8th Army save the 1st Canadian Division were to assume a defensive posture along the line of the Dittaino River. The Canadians, however, were directed to 'continue without restraint directed on Adrano'.[34] The spotlight was now firmly on Simonds who, given his recent experience over the Graham affair, must surely have felt that he was on probation.

On 20 July Simonds had been given an additional brigade to support his efforts, 231st (Malta) Brigade. Commanded by Brigadier-General Roy Urquhart (later of Arnhem fame) the brigade had since the landings on 10 July been operating as an independent formation within XXX Corps advancing northwards between the Canadians and 51st Highland Division. It was currently located on the Dittaino River south of the hilltop town of Agira. Simonds' route to Adrano would require the capture of Agira, yet another of the Sicilian hilltop towns. The vista from the top of Mount Assoro looking east towards Mount Etna is one of confusing ridgelines and hilltops, many of which are indistinguishable from one another, except Agira. Contemporary accounts describe Agira as resembling a multi-tiered, conical 'wedding cake'. Simonds set out his plans on 22 July. The attack on Agira was to be made the next day by a battalion of Graham's 1st Canadian Infantry Brigade (1st CIB) approaching eastwards by night along the winding *Strada* 121 and supported by the full weight of the division's artillery. 2nd CIB would secure the start line and provide a firm base from the newly captured towns of Leonforte/ Assoro while another battalion of 1st CIB would provide flank protection to the attack by sealing off *Strada* 117, which ran north from Leonforte towards Nicosia. The newly attached 231st Bde was well placed to threaten the town from the south and act as a possible distraction to the defenders by advancing to a line about half a mile south-east of Agira, which marked the furthest range of the available artillery. 3rd CIB was to be kept in reserve.

Strada 121 followed a ridgeline separating two river valleys: the Salso to the north and the Dittaino to the south. One of the very few paved roads in the Sicilian interior, it was generally free from the extreme gradients that the Canadians had experienced in their march northwards from the Pachino peninsula, but at least four times in the eight miles of its length between Leonforte and Agira it would curve over the low hills which ran north-south across its path. And it was behind these hills that the Germans lay in wait.

Problems emerged almost immediately for the Canadians when the 48th Highlanders of Canada, advancing out of Assoro, were delayed in getting to their flank protection task on the junction of *Strada* 117 and 121 by heavy enemy artillery, mortars and machine-gun fire. 2nd CIB was also delayed in establishing the firm base that the divisional plan required and by midday on the 23rd Simonds was forced to concede a 24-hour delay in the operation. Meanwhile reconnaissance troops from the 4th Princess Louise Dragoon Guards reported the presence of German troops defending both *Strada* 117 (the road to Nicosia) and *Strada* 121 at the village of Nissoria, a small community of less than a thousand inhabitants midway between Assoro and Agira.

These reports concerned Brigadier Graham who by now was well versed in the German tactics of stationing a minimum force of mobile troops and guns on half-tracked vehicles at strategic points along the axis of advance, thus forcing their opponents to pause and deploy superior forces to combat them. Graham had 'grave doubts' about the feasibility of a plan that assumed he 'could advance ten or twelve miles without serious opposition'. Simonds, however, remained confident.

Part of Simonds' confidence stemmed from a meticulous timed programme of artillery concentrations and smoke screens which would be laid down ahead of the advancing infantry coupled with pre-arranged bombing and strafing attacks on predicted targets along the road by Kittyhawk fighter-bombers of the Desert Air Force. This was textbook stuff, indicative perhaps of the mind of a staff college-trained artillery officer. But Graham operated in the real world: 'In all my military teaching, limited as it was perhaps, this sort of wishful thinking seemed to me not only ridiculous but almost certain to be perilous and wasteful in men and material.'[35]

At 15:00 on 24 July, the artillery barrage from five field and two medium regiments began to fall as the leading companies of the Royal Canadian Regiment (RCR), supported by the tanks of A Squadron of the Three Rivers Regiment set off towards Nissoria, watched by Simonds and his key staff from the vantage point of the Norman castle atop Mount Assoro. The high HE shells were clearly having an effect, but the planned smoke screen dissipated in the strong breeze which blew across the plain below them and despite instructions from Simonds to his Commander Royal Artillery to increase the density of smoke shells from one to three rounds per gun, it was impossible to sustain the masking effect. Simonds was later to criticise his infantry for failing to keep up with the barrage and cited it as the primary reason why his plan immediately fell apart. This was another slight on Graham. And it still rankled over forty years later when Graham came to write his memoirs: 'I still resent the effort to justify a bad plan by putting the blame for its failure on the backs of troops.'[36]

Whether he liked the plan or not, Graham still had to do his best to execute it. By 16:00 his leading troops were in Nissoria and had met practically no resistance. But as soon as they emerged on the far side of the village 'all hell broke loose'. The RCR came under sustained artillery, mortar, and machine-gun fire and the supporting tanks were engaged by well concealed anti-tank guns which had not been previously identified. The RCR adapted quickly and using the ground to great effect managed to outflank the German defences. But when radio communications failed, CO Lt Col Crowe went forward on foot to make contact with his forward companies and was mortally wounded by machine-gun fire. By this time it was dark. The RCR had gone to ground, and Graham returned to his headquarters to prepare a plan of attack for the next day. When he attempted to clear this with Simonds on the radio he was told by the GSO1, Lt Col George Kitching, that the GOC was asleep and not to be disturbed. He was advised to stick with the original plan and press on.

The Hastings and Prince Edward Regiment made an unsuccessful night attack across unreconnoitred ground and lost their CO (Lord Tweedsmuir) in the process. Tweedsmuir had been injured by a mortar bomb and, not for the first time in the Italian campaign, was forced to hand over command to his 2IC, Maj. 'Bert' Kennedy. Once again, Graham asked for time to plan a deliberate and closely coordinated attack by artillery, tanks and infantry and once again this was denied; this time by Simonds himself. Graham was forced to commit his third battalion, the 48th Highlanders, who also failed to dislodge the German defenders. Graham had now committed each of his three battalions, with not inconsiderable losses (including two commanding officers), and although the enemy had clearly suffered severe casualties themselves, they still barred the way out of Nissoria. Finally, on the evening of the 26th, Graham was permitted to execute the deliberate attack he had wanted to plan as soon as the RCR had identified the German positions two days previously. The Germans prudently withdrew, but only to secondary positions. It now fell to 2nd CIB to pick up the baton.

Meanwhile, 231st (Malta) Brigade was approaching Agira from the south. They had had better luck than 1st CIB. On the night of 24-25 July, when the RCR was unsuccessfully trying to exit Nissoria, two companies of the Hampshires had already infiltrated and occupied two key mountain top locations to the south (Mount Gianguzzo) and east (Mount Campanelli) of the town. Here they were able to observe German movements along both *Strada* 121 and the secondary road which led north from Agira to Troina (the latter being in the 7th Army sector). However, their positions on these two hills were too exposed and vulnerable to be held for long and by mid-afternoon they had been forced to withdraw in the face of German counter-attacks. They returned the next night and the night afterwards, each time with orders to retire before daybreak should the expected attack by the Canadians from the west fail to materialise, which it did.[37]

Simonds' new plan required 2nd CIB to advance on Agira in two stages: an advance by a single battalion to seize and consolidate a firm base beyond Nissoria, followed by an exploitation by a second battalion to the high ground which overlooked the western entry to Agira. The leading battalion would advance behind what would be the heaviest barrage yet fired by the division and eventually captured two features of equal height which dominated *Strada* 121 east of Nissoria, codenames 'Lion' and 'Tiger'.[38]

It was now 27 July. Agira, which Montgomery and Leese had been told would be captured on 23 July, was still held by the enemy. 2nd CIB had pressed on down *Strada* 121 and, after heavy fighting during the day which carried on overnight, had successfully captured two hill features (Mount Crapuzza and Mount Fronte) on the western approaches to Agira. On 28 July Agira finally fell. This time 231st (Malta) Brigade did not withdraw their night-time presence from Mounts Gianguzzo and Campanelli. Instead, spirited attacks during the day by both the Dorsets and the Devons allowed it to consolidate its hold on the eastern approaches to the town. By mid-afternoon Commander 2nd CIB was poised to pulverise the town with artillery and mortar fire prior to sending in the infantry to clear the streets. Fortunately, a forward observation officer, having infiltrated the town, found it packed with civilians. The Germans appeared to have fled and the bombardment was called off. In reality, German rearguards still remained in the upper portion of the town and it took more than two hours of stiff street fighting to remove them.

When 231 (Malta) Brigade moved north from the Dittaino River to support the attack on Agira it was relieved in place at Radduasa-Agira station by 3rd CIB. Although the ground to their left had been cleared of enemy troops during the attacks on Leonforte and Assoro by 1st and 2nd CIBs, the terrain on the brigade's right still contained outposts of enemy troops defending the foothills below the hilltop towns of Regalbuto and Centuripe. These two towns lay on the ridgeline which extended from Agira towards Adrano and were to become the next objectives for XXX Corps. However, before they could be assaulted, it would be necessary to clear out all the remaining enemy troops still in the Dittaino River valley. To this end 3rd CIB, moving east, headed towards the village of Catenanuova, while 51st Highland Division prepared once again to attack north to capture the village of Sferro and the hills beyond it.

In this area the Dittaino River meandered along a valley floor which sometimes stretched up to a mile wide. It was occupied by a road and railway line which connected the cities of Enna and Catania. Two hills guarded the entrance to Catenanuova from the west; to the north a bald, rounded hill rising to 800ft (Mount Santa Maria) and to the south a more imposing feature, Mount Scalpello, whose rocky ridge towered nearly 3000ft above the valley floor. Both were captured on the night of 26 July by troops of the French-Canadian Royal 22nd Regiment (Royal 22e) although a successful counter-attack by the Germans managed to recapture Mount Santa Maria, albeit at great cost to themselves. For the moment, further operations to seize Catenanuova were temporarily postponed as these would become part of a much larger operation (Operation HARDGATE).[39]

On 28 July Alexander relocated his headquarters to the island from North Africa occupying 'a dusty but well-concealed site in an almond grove near Cassibile'.[40] By this time British signals intelligence had revealed that with the exception of reinforcements for *1 Fallschirmjäger Division* the Germans had ceased bringing motor vehicles and personnel onto the island; indeed, there were clear indications from signals intelligence that the Axis forces were drawing up plans for an evacuation. However, while the men and women at Bletchley Park were now routinely reading German high level cypher traffic, improved security of field communications by German and Italian tactical formations in the field meant that these Sigint successes were not being replicated on the ground. At the tactical level, the Allies were unable to gain similar actionable intelligence.[41]

After six days of hard fighting the Allies had still not managed to break the enemy's main defensive line. However, in his memoirs Kesselring claimed that he had now taken the decision to evacuate Axis forces from Sicily on his own initiative; a decision which had made him *persona non grata* with his superiors in Berlin.[42] How accurate that statement was is questionable. *OKW* was perfectly able to assess the situation and had already realised that, although Sicily itself could not be saved, a spirited defence designed to inflict maximum casualties on the Allied forces might still deter the Allies from a full-scale invasion of mainland Italy itself. As a contemporary German article written in August 1943 explained:

> The German-Italian command drew the correct conclusions at the correct time from the situation that had arisen. There was no sense in entering into a decisive battle for possession of the island. The factors of power, time, and space were no longer at their disposal to a sufficient extent. They chose, therefore, to employ delaying action, and this was pursued by stages to the northeastern tip of the island. As with every bridgehead, this one had the disadvantage of having but a few routes of retreat, and finally only one: and even this route, on account of the rapid narrowing of the area to the

> rear, was increasingly jeopardized and at last ended at the coast in a narrow pass. This natural route of retreat was the highway through Nicosia and Randazzo.[43]

Although Guzzoni was still nominally in command, Hube had made his own independent appreciation. Mount Etna, which still remained in his hands, would eventually force his enemy to split his forces. While he continued to hold Catania Hube assessed that an approach by Montgomery's 8th Army up the eastern coastline was unlikely; although the threat of an amphibious operation behind his lines there continued to be a worrying prospect, even though the Allies had yet to demonstrate any interest in such an operation. But as soon as Adrano and its southern neighbour Paterno fell, Catania would eventually have to be given up. And then the advantages which Etna had hitherto provided to the defender would start to turn against him, at least in the east.

If the threat of an amphibious operation along the eastern coastline north of Catania worried Hube, he was no less concerned by the possibility of a similar operation somewhere on the northern coastline. Given their maritime and air superiority, and the evidence of the sheer number of maritime forces committed to the invasion itself, the absence of follow-up amphibious operations by the Allies had mystified the Germans. Kesselring himself had anticipated a large-scale encirclement of his forces on the island or, worse, additional landings in Calabria. When these did not come, he found himself with an unexpected opportunity to organise his defences with the very limited resources he had to hand.[44]

The Germans, of course, were not to know just how limited the Allies were when it came to amphibious resources in 1943 or the tensions which existed over the deployment of these scarce assets among the various theatres. Things had become more complicated in the Mediterranean on 16 July when the Combined Chiefs ordered Eisenhower to begin preparing two new operations: the first for an amphibious operation to capture Naples (Operation AVALANCHE) and the second for a similar landing in Calabria to facilitate the exploitation of the expected capture of Sicily. Both would require significant amphibious resources. By 27 July Eisenhower had set this planning in hand.

Only Patton seemed to have given any consideration to an amphibious 'hook'. At his meeting with Alexander and Montgomery on 25 July Patton had specifically asked for some landing craft and warships to facilitate outflanking operations on the north coast. Alexander agreed to the landing craft and said that he would ask for the warships. There is no record of Montgomery making any similar request.[45] For the moment, the Allies continued to put their main effort in the centre. Using *Strada* 120 as its main axis of advance, Patton's Seventh Army was tasked to take Troina, the highest town in Sicily (an intermediate point on the way to Randazzo) while Montgomery's 8th Army continued to follow *Strada* 121 en route to Adrano. Both roads led to the western slopes of Mount Etna.

20

The Final Push to Messina

The Third Stage of Operation HUSKY – Part Two: D-Day Plus 19, Thursday 29 July to D-Day Plus 29, Sunday 8 August

During the first two weeks of the invasion both Hitler and Kesselring had been reluctant to reinforce the garrison on Sicily, at least until Allied intentions had become clearer. But when it became obvious that the Allies had no immediate intention of threatening the Italian mainland – thereby threatening his rear – Hube was to be given sufficient resources to fight a prolonged rearguard action and instructed to inflict as many casualties on the Allies as possible prior to the execution of a controlled, phased evacuation. Now, with Walter Fries's 29th Panzer Grenadier Division complete on the Island, Hube could complete his dispositions and execute the first part of his mission.[1]

The right (northern flank), and what remained of the Assietta Division, was assigned to Fries. He was to hold a sector which stretched from the coast east of San Stefano to a point south of Mistretta. Eberhard Rodt's 15th Panzer Grenadier Division, with the remains of the Aosta and Livorno Divisions and two battalions of the German 382nd Panzer Grenadier Regiment, held the centre, leaving Paul Conrath's *Hermann Göring (HG) Panzer Division*, with elements of the 1st Parachute Division (most notably *Kampfguppe* Schmalz), to defend the southern sector from positions on the ridgeline overlooking the Salso and Dittaino rivers to the coastline south of Catania.[2]

With the Allies now set to advance eastwards towards Mount Etna and thence to Messina Patton's 7th Army would advance along two axes: the northern coastal road *Strada* 113 and the parallel inland route, 120. Separating these two roads were the Caronie Mountains. As previously mentioned, the rugged terrain of these mountains, which contained the highest peaks in Sicily other than Mount Etna itself, meant that once the road between San Stefano and Nicosia had been captured there would be no other roads capable of sustaining meaningful north-south logistic traffic. Bradley's two divisions would be advancing in splendid isolation with no opportunity for mutual support.

Strada 113, the north coast road, had already proved to be a nightmare for the Americans and matters would not improve for Truscott's 3rd Division who had relieved Middleton's 45th Division on 31 July.[3] Although the road itself was paved and capable of taking two-way traffic, the Germans had already demonstrated that they could dominate it at will. As soon as they withdrew from a blocking position their engineers would blow up every bridge and liberally sow every potential crossing point with mines and booby-traps. In places where the road hugged the mountainside, they created landslides to further impede progress. Now, having been pushed out of San Stefano by Middleton's troops, Hube decided to pull back his right flank onto a secondary defensive position, the Etna Line. The Etna Line was anchored on the San Fratello ridge, which overlooked the estuary of the Furiano River, five miles west of the town of Sant Agata. Moving south it followed a secondary road to Cesaro and then via Troina to Adrano and on to Acireale, which lay on the eastern coast north of Catania. With more time to prepare, it was in many places stronger than the *Hauptkampflinie* and, on the northern coast especially, the Furiano River would act like a medieval moat.

Having conducted his appreciation of the situation, Truscott recognised that continuing with the direct approach along the road simply played to his enemy's strengths. He therefore looked at finding ways to outflank Fries's men whilst still maintaining pressure on the enemy forces defending the road and river line. One possibility which presented itself, thanks to Patton's foresight in requesting naval support, was to try to execute an amphibious 'hook' and insert forces behind the German defenders, possibly at Sant Agata. The other was to move the bulk of his forces further inland and to seek a way overland through the mountains. Preparations for these manoeuvres would take time. Meanwhile, Bradley was counting on Terry Allen's 1st Division to complete the break in of the *Hauptkampflinie* and push on to Troina.

As previously described, the 1st Division's approach to the *Hauptkampflinie* had been hard fought, but the fall of Nicosia itself had come surprisingly quickly. However, Rodt's 15th Panzer Grenadier Division continued to fall back in good order, if not considerably weakened. Allen's attempts at pursuit were hampered by further stubborn rearguard resistance and, bizarrely, bad weather. For weeks soldiers of both forces had been fighting under the unrelenting heat and dust of a Sicilian summer. But now, on the night of 28-29 July, the heavens opened for the first time since the invasion, and rain of biblical proportions fell. Allen's forward troops, the 16th RCT, were brought to a standstill. They occupied three hills west of Cerami and awaited further orders.

For Hube, the defences against potential Allied penetrations along *Strada* 120 (by 7th Army) and *Strada* 121 (by 8th Army) were necessarily interlinked. This is explained by the terrain. The ground between the two highways is almost unique in Sicily, a remote high plain with its own rolling countryside of valleys, ridges and gullies. *Strada* 120 follows the northern edge of this plain and, after leaving Nicosia, climbs ever higher as it winds its way up towards Troina. In the distance to the south, and on the other side of the plain, stands the ridgeline which demarcates the watershed between the Salso and Dittaino rivers and on which stand the towns of Agira and Regalbuto.

The Germans had used the time wisely during the clashes with Allen's forces on the approach to Nicosia to prepare their fallback positions on the Etna Line. Under the direction of Colonel Albrecht Grell, Rodt's divisional engineers together with representatives of the panzer grenadier and artillery units had been sent to Troina and its surrounding hills well in advance. Using whatever troops they could lay their hands on, and with men from the *Aosta Divisione* operating as a labour corps, Grell fashioned a web of interlocking defensive posts. Stone sangers were built, trenches dug, mines laid, fields of fire cleared, and artillery, mortar and machine gun positions created; all carefully planned to be mutually supporting.

The keystone of these defences was Troina itself. The highest town in Sicily, it stood on a dominating bluff that gave the defenders excellent fields of observation in all directions. It was surrounded by a series of parallel north-south ridges and dozens of hills, which could all be used to protect Rodt's flanks – most notably to the north Monte Acuto and Monte Basilio, and to the south Monte Pellegrino and Monte Salici. From these hills forward observers would be able to call on artillery and mortar fire to attack the American assembly areas. The intervening valleys were almost completely barren, offering the attackers no cover or concealment from the defenders on the high ground.

Omar Bradley described the battle for Troina as 'the most bitterly fought battle of the campaign'.[4] Part of the reason for this was a misappreciation of German intentions. For the past week American intelligence officers had convinced themselves that Troina would be just another blocking position, like so many that they had already faced on the way to the *Hauptkampflinie*, a position that the Germans would give up in time before falling back to a 'final' defensive zone, perhaps centred on the town of Cesaro. All their intelligence gathering efforts had thus been directed on identifying this mythical zone whereas, in fact, Hube's whole strategy was based on avoiding such a final stand. Hube saw the north-east sector of the island in the round. It was to be ground on which he could establish a succession of strongpoints each populated by small garrisons which would stay in place for as long they were not endangered by the enemy's outflanking manoeuvres. And by outflanking manoeuvres he envisaged not just local manoeuvres to unhinge a particular trouble spot but wider ones, which might in themselves threaten the viability of other garrisons. It was in this respect that he gauged the overall importance of Troina.

The Americans miscalculated. From a defender's point of view Cesaro – which was where the Americans expected the Germans to make a stand – and Troina had similar characteristics. Both offered a series of hill 'clusters' behind which artillery could be positioned in reverse slope positions and from which artillery observers were presented with wide vistas covering almost every possible avenue of approach with observed fire. These surrounding hills also offered fields of fire for well sited machine guns shooting from concealed defilade positions. But the key difference was this. For Hube's plan to succeed, the troops defending against Monty's 8th Army further south must be allowed the opportunity to escape to Messina along two routes, north-west via Randazzo and north-east via Misterbianco. Cesaro was too close to Mount Etna and the road network which skirts its western flanks through Randazzo. Cesaro could only be given up after and not before Adrano. And the best way of achieving this was to defend forward at Troina.

Troops exiting Cerami on *Strada* 120 would be immediately exposed to artillery fire from Troina and the surrounding hills, but after a mile or so the road makes a reverse loop. Here it enters a pocket of ground which is screened from Troina and its surrounding hills and could give Terry's men temporary protection from all but the highest angle howitzers. But whilst they might be safe from fire, they were not safe from observation. For as long as Hube's forces held the small town of Gagliano and beyond it, further south, the larger town of Agira, all of 1st Division's movements could be seen and reported on by Hube's forces guarding *Strada* 121.

However, when Agira fell to the Canadians Rodt's task on *Strada* 120 became more difficult. And should Troina fall prematurely, life would become even more difficult for Conrath's *Hermann Göring Panzer Division* who, defending on *Strada* 121, were now engaged in a struggle to keep the Canadians out of Regalbuto. Equally, should both Troina and Regabulto fall, then Adrano, which was the objective of the newly arrived British 78th Infantry Division, would surely follow in quick succession. And then Hube's whole defensive plan would swiftly unravel.

Rodt's defensive plan for Troina was based on the forward deployment of two of his regiments. The 129th Panzer Grenadier Regiment, *Kampfgruppe* Fullriede, on hills to the north-east of the town, and the 104th Panzer Grenadier Regiment (*Kampfgruppe* Ens) occupying the hills to the southeast. However, *Kampfgruppe* Ens had previously been the main defensive force in Agira and the downside of its successful delaying action there against the Canadians meant that its withdrawal north to rejoin its parent division would be slower than had been anticipated. And this would have consequences; at least in the early stages of the Troina battle.

As well as misreading German intentions, three other factors also came into play which undoubtedly influenced the way in which the American approached the coming battle. All involved the human dimension. The first was Bradley's insistence that, in advance of handing over to Eddy's 9th Infantry Division, Allen should not take a sledgehammer to crack a nut.[5] The next was Terry Allen himself, the legendary commander of 'The Big Red One'; a man who was fully aware that the Sword of Damocles was dangling by a thread above his head. And finally, there was Colonel 'Paddy' Flint, one of Patton's oldest and dearest friends, who had only just taken command of the 39th Infantry Regiment, a 9th Division formation which, after the fall of Palermo, had been attached to the 1st Division.

As early as May 1943 Eisenhower had been considering sending Terry Allen back to the USA, albeit on promotion as a corps commander. He had formed the opinion that, although an excellent combat officer, Allen was now tired and needed a rest. This view was strengthened in his mind when reports of ill-discipline within the division began to surface later that same month; ill-discipline that Allen had failed to grip and seemed almost to excuse. When Allen realised what was being planned, he wrote directly to Eisenhower asking to retain command of his beloved 'Big Red One', at least for the duration of the Sicily campaign. Patton strongly supported this request, and it appeared that, for the moment at least, Allen had gained a stay of execution. But he was clearly on borrowed time. Moreover, his immediate superior, Omar Bradley, had also formed an unfavourable opinion of this hard-drinking and, at times, temperamental officer. Bradley later claimed that, for "'the long-term welfare of the division', he had determined that Allen would need to go as soon as the campaign in Sicily was over.

Bradley could not have relieved Allen without Patton's agreement, but as he and Allen had already clashed in Sicily, this developing fracture with his corps commander may well have been playing on Allen's mind; especially as he knew that his Division would shortly be taken out of the line and replaced by Major-General Eddy's 9th Division. From a military standpoint this made eminent sense. 'The Big Red One', just like Middleton's 45th Division, had been in action continuously since D-Day and it was time for fresh troops to take on the spearhead duties. Initially, the handover to Eddy had been scheduled for 4 August, but Allen and Bradley were now in agreement that this should not take place in the middle of the coming battle.[6] So, for Allen, the campaign in Sicily was drawing to an end. His letter to Eisenhower had merely gained him a stay of execution. Surely it was only natural to believe that a good showing in the coming battle might ensure that Troina would not mark the end of his campaigning days.[7]

Another reason for Bradley delaying the handover to Eddy's 9th Division was the fact that this division had not yet completed its transit from North Africa and the last of its troops were still coming through the port of Palermo. However, the 39th Infantry Regiment had been brought over early in order to bolster the drive on Palermo and then, after its fall, had been assigned to II Corps. It quickly proved to be a 'skittish' formation with a reputation for poor discipline and so when Eddy wanted to replace its commander Bradley appointed Colonel 'Paddy' Flint. And, for the attack on Troina, Bradley assigned Flint's regiment to Allen's 1st Division.

Flint was a veteran of the First World War. At 56 he was older than his peers and had previously been on the staff of II Corps where he had been constantly badgering Bradley for a combat command. His first act as commander was to instruct his Quartermaster to ensure that every soldier in the regiment had his helmet emblazoned with a new regimental motto, AAA-0. When asked what it stood for, he replied: 'It means anything, anytime, anywhere, bar nothing.' Flint was intent on making his mark. And quickly. It was to lead him to over-estimate both his own abilities and that of his men.[8]

Hitherto, the nature of the terrain in Sicily had limited 7th Army's opportunities to deploy its full combat strength. Commanders had become accustomed to attacking in echelon with regiments and battalions on a succession of narrow fronts. Now, perhaps for the first time, the terrain which faced the 1st Infantry Division would offer the scope for attacking on a much larger scale. But – perhaps because he expected minimal resistance until he reached Cesaro – Terry declined the opportunity to do this. Instead, relying on his own divisional intelligence assessments which noted, 'Germans very tired, little ammo, many casualties, morale low', he continued the now established practice of advancing on a narrow front.[9]

Despite his careful preparations, Rodt's position in Troina was vulnerable to attack from the south via a feature known as the Gagliano salient. This stretched northwards from Agira and carried a secondary road towards Troina along which *Kampfgruppe* Ens had made its escape from the Canadians. In the centre of the ridge was the small town of Gagliano itself. Unfortunately for Rodt, it offered few natural defences against a determined attacker and anyway was too far from Troina to be held successfully, even if additional troops had been available. Rodt feared that a powerful strike along this feature might not only pose a serious threat to the left flank of his positions at Troina but, if the Americans could use it as an avenue of approach to capture Monte Pellegrino and Monte Salici, it could also seriously the threaten the highway east of Troina on which Rodt would eventually have to withdraw his division.

Allen began his preparations for the advance on Troina on 30 July by probing the approaches to Cerami and the much smaller village of Capizzi which lay to its north. Patrols from both the 16th and 18th Regiments had noted some artillery and a lot of activity in Cerami and a battalion of French Goums, which Bradley had previously attached to the division, had been prevented from entering Capizzi by small arms and mortar fire. At the start of operations in Sicily, Bradley had detached two troops of his corps recce squadron to Allen's division who now used them to protect his right flank and maintain liaison with the Canadians. B Troop 91 Recce Sqn entered Agira on 30 July and then moved north on the road to Gagliano where, just south of the town, it encountered a large crater in the road. Whilst efforts were being made to repair the crater this troop then came under fire from elements of *Kampfgruppe* Ens. In the action that followed, Sgt Kisters was awarded the Congressional Medal of Honor to accompany the Distinguished Service Cross he had earlier gained in North Africa. In doing so Kisters became the first American soldier to be awarded both of America's highest awards for valor in the Second World War.

Concentrations of mortar and artillery fire brought down on the positions during the night of 31 July/1 August and an attack by the cavalry soldiers later that day forced the Germans to withdraw by late afternoon to new positions five miles further north where the troopers, now acting as dismounted infantry, were again held up by extensive minefields and machine gun fire.[10] Also on 1 August, when Flint's troops entered Cerami unopposed, the French Goums were being held by Italian troops on Monte Scimone, a mile and a half north-east of Capizzi. Allen, emboldened by the ease with which Cerami fell, and encouraged by Flint, now abandoned the plan to pass Bowen's 26th Infantry through for the final attack on Troina and ordered the 39th to continue pressing forward, in the expectation that Troina would fall just as easily. Still convinced that Cesaro would be where that Germans would make their final stand, reports which now began to come into the intelligence cells from civilians and captured POWs that Troina was lightly held by only a few troops, some antitank guns, an antiaircraft battery, and only one heavy gun simply added to their existing confirmation bias. [11]

Whilst *Strada* 120 continued to be the axis of advance, it was clear to Flint that it could not be used by his troops going forward. Instead, his advance on Troina would have to be across the open ground of the surrounding hills. With the French Goums now attached to him, his scheme of manoeuvre was to use them to cover his left flank by advancing on Monte Acuto, then south-east to Monte Basilio, and eventually emerging on *Strada* 120 behind Troina, thereby cutting off the German's avenue of escape. His main attack, however, paralleling the highway to the north, would be spearheaded by a single battalion, Colonel Bond's 3rd Battalion, with the 1st and 2nd Battalions simply following in echelon behind on both flanks of the road. To support the attack, General Andrus, Allen's artillery commander, had planned an impressive array of supporting fire. With the ability to call on not just his own four artillery battalions but also the fire of four artillery battalions of the 9th Division and eight artillery battalions from II Corps, Andrus had 165 artillery pieces at his disposal. But it was not to be. Terrain and the unexpected – and by this time rare – interdiction of the *Luftwaffe* played havoc with the deployment of Allen's artillery support. Nevertheless, in the absence of what was considered adequate artillery support, Flint and Allen decided to press on. After all, everyone still expected Troina to fall quickly.

The battle for Troina was essentially an infantry battle. The rocky terrain intersected with steep gullies did not favour the deployment of American tanks and Rodt decided to group what was left of his tanks east of the town in positions from which they could be deployed as counter-attacking forces should the Americans break through.[12] Bond's 3rd Battalion jumped off at 05:00 on 1 August from start lines which were four miles east of Cerami; they were already halfway towards their destination with Troina just four miles further to go. From the very beginning Bond's men came under effective mortar and small arms fire from *Kampfgruppe* Fullriede, which, with the few artillery assets now available to him, Flint could do nothing to help suppress. By mid-morning he was forced to call off the attack and Bond's battalion returned to their original positions.

There was brighter news elsewhere, however. Flint's 1st Battalion, led by Major Philip Tinley, following up Bond's advance to the south of the road, had met very little resistance from *Kampfgruppe* Ens and Tinley had managed to place two of his companies on Hill 1034, a key feature to the west of Troina less than a mile from the town, and from which they had a clear view not only into Troina but also of the German artillery positions behind the town. The contrasting fortunes of Flint's units north and south of

Strada 120 posed Allen with a dilemma. Should he continue on the northern approach, his preferred route, and implement an earlier plan to exercise a passage of lines using Bowen's 26th Infantry, or should he reinforce the unexpected success in the south? And, if so, how?

Allen spent the rest of the morning perfecting plans to bring both the 26th Infantry and the 16th Infantry into the fight. In effect he would be attempting to use the tactics of a double envelopment which had proved so successful a week earlier at Sperlinga and Nicosia. The northern arm of this manoeuvre would see the 26th Infantry passing around Flint's forces to the north via Monte Basilio to a hill mass commanding the road exiting Troina to the east. In this respect they would be replacing the Goums who, having previously been tasked with cutting off the German's escape route to Cesaro, had been blocked by Axis troops holding Monte Acuto. The southern arm would see Colonel Taylor's 16th Regiment crossing Monte Femmina Morta, an east-west ridgeline running south of *Strada* 120 and, by passing Troina to the south, seek to occupy Hill 1056 about a mile east of the town. This would then cut the other route out of Troina, a road leading southeast towards Adrano.

These plans eventually came to nought, at least initially, because Flint insisted that his regiment could still capture Troina by itself. In this he was clearly emboldened by Tinley's earlier success in capturing Hill 1034. Allen wavered. In the end, he decided to allow Flint's regiment to continue to make the main attack on Troina and also secure Hill 1056. For the moment he would keep the 16th Regiment in reserve. Allen left Bowen to decide how best to proceed. Initially, Bowen proposed advancing with two battalions up, but he was persuaded by Allen's staff that with the Goums operating on his left flank, this would be overkill. In the end, he elected to echelon his battalions.

Although Allen had promised him all possible artillery support (which included four batteries of II Corps' 155mm 'Long Toms', four battalions of the Division's own light artillery, and one battalion of medium artillery) Bowen was still wary. He did not share Allen and Flint's seemingly unbridled optimism and began to think that, rather than bypassing the enemy's strength, he was sending his troops right into their 'teeth': an assessment the Goums had already reached having experienced the ferocity of *Kampfgruppe* Fullriede's efforts to stop them crossing the Troina River, which lay at the base of Monte Acuto.[13] Despite this, Bowen prepared to launch his attack on 2 August.

Flint pressed on. By the afternoon of 1 August the attempts of his 2nd and 3rd Battalions to take the high ground north of Troina were getting nowhere. The enemy's defensive artillery fire was proving too difficult to overcome. Worse was to follow. That night *Kampfgruppe* Ens launched a ferocious counter-attack against Tinley's men on Hill 1034. So effective was it that Tinley sought permission to withdraw his men to safety, a request to which Flint grudgingly felt he had to accede. By midnight, Ens was in possession of this important ridgeline and Tinley's battalion had been reduced to just 300 men. Only 2,000 yards separated the two forces, but Ens, content with his success, chose not to push home his advantage. Instead, he ordered his men to consolidate their newly won positions and, by digging in, strived to block any further attempts by the Americans to approach Troina from either the west or the south.

Having rolled into Cerami on the morning of 1 August, the Americans had expected Troina to fall later that same day. Yet the next day the Goumiers operating on the northern flank had not yet crossed the Troina River, Flint's southern battalion had been thrown off Hill 1034, and there had been no progress in the centre. Only Bowen's 26th Infantry would see any success on this day, and that only minor. To the north, the French continued to be stymied, but jumping off at 05:00, at least Bowen's lead battalion managed to push forward half a mile to occupy the hill feature known as Rocca di Mania. It was a paltry gain, accomplished in the face of heavy enemy artillery, and did nothing to reassure an increasingly frustrated Bradley.

At last Allen realised that he would have to plan a large-scale, coordinated effort if he was to break the Troina defences. Until now he had been content to enable Flint's 39th Infantry to secure the main prize – Troina – with his own headquarters and other elements of the Division merely playing a supporting role. Now, for the first time, he set about constructing a proper divisional plan. The frontage of the attack would now be significantly increased by bringing the 16th and 18th Infantry Regiments out of the reserve and into the fight to the south of the highway. The task of taking Troina itself and then cutting the south-eastern exit road to Adrano would pass to the 16th Infantry with its core three battalions. A fourth battalion, attached to it from the 18th Infantry and advancing from Gagliano, would attack a key German strongpoint on Monte Bianco, about two miles south of the town. Bowen's 26th Infantry was to continue its encircling movement, taking Monte Basolio and then moving south-east to cut the highway behind Troina. In doing so it was to swing past Flint's men, still operating from just north of *Strada* 120, but whose task was now limited to capturing Monte San Silvestro, two miles north-west of Troina; after which they would move into divisional reserve.

H-Hour was scheduled for 03:00 on 3 August. Shortly after midnight, 2nd Battalion 16th Infantry set out for the forming up point situated below the southern corner of the German ridge positions. The 3rd Battalion followed and by dawn leading elements of both battalions were making their way up the slopes, only to be met with a wall of machine-gun and small arms fire which forced the men to take cover. By midday it became evident to Allen that these two battalions could not move and that he would have to adapt his plan. Since the battalion of the 18th Infantry heading for Monte Bianco, though hindered by the terrain, was making steady progress he ordered it to push on beyond its assigned objective and take the high ground half a mile south of Troina. To assist it in this expanded mission, he augmented it with the 1st Battalion 16th Infantry. By instigating this manoeuvre, Allen hoped to divert the German's attention away from the main body of the regiment and thus relieve the pressure on the two battalions which had become bogged down.

Before the hook from the south could gather any momentum, Ens launched a combined infantry and tank attack against Colonel Taylor's two stuck battalions. Only the fire of six battalions of American artillery directed onto the high ground of the ridge saved these battalions from being completely overrun. Although thwarted, at least initially, Ens would not give up. The fighting went on all afternoon, often at very close quarters. Meanwhile, the two battalions coming up from Gagliano were making little progress, due mainly to German raids on both flanks combined with effective artillery, mortar and machine-gun fire. In an effort to maintain the momentum, Allen issued orders for one of these two battalions to make a wider sweep to the east, thereby outflanking Troina completely. However, these orders were quickly withdrawn on the advice of his assistant divisional commander, Brigadier-General Roosevelt, who, having arrived on the ground, took one look at the terrain and the state of the men, assessed that further progress was unlikely.

Progress in the centre looked more promising; at least initially. Bowen's men reached the first objective, Monte Basilio, with surprising ease, as did a battalion of Flint's 39th Infantry who seized Monte San Silvestro. But that was as good as it got. German artillery firing from reverse slope positions outside the range of American counter-battery fire began to take its toll on the attackers. Bowen was able to call down an air strike by half a dozen Spitfires of the Desert Air Force who struck the northern slopes of Monte Castagna and Monte Acuto. Their bombs and strafing had a noticeable effect on the enemy's shelling. But they also managed to engage the Goumiers who were still trying to cross the Troina River and seize Monte Acuto. This was to be the first of a number of blue-on-blue incidents during the battle which, once again, only underlined the nascent and fragile nature of effective allied air-ground liaison in the War.

Although equipped by the Americans, communications between the French troops and their Allies were proving difficult. This was less to do with language and more to do with unfamiliarity. This was demonstrated most noticeably when the commander of the Moroccans personally came back to Capizzi to plead for artillery support to break the deadlock on the Troina River. His request was refused because the artillery staff deemed it unsafe; the exact locations of the French forces could not be determined and the distance separating the French and the Germans was reported as being only 200 yards. The inability of American and French troops to accurately report their locations was symptomatic of the terrain. The hills and gulleys all looked the same to the average GI and a distinguishing feature noted from one angle would tend to disappear when viewed from a different angle. Nor could the maps be relied on.[14] At the same time that the air strike to support Bowen's attack was going in, Flint called for another. He had just been made aware of a road which was not marked on his map and which ran eastwards from Capizzi for some fifteen miles linking Monte Acuto, Monte Pelato, and Monte Camolato. As it was obvious to him that this road would have been used by the German artillery who were making life so difficult for his troops,

Flint wanted air support to deal with them. But as Allen's headquarters could not accurately identify the location of friendly troops, this request was denied.[15] A contributing factor to denying this request may well have been the fact that one of Bowen's battalions from the 26th Infantry had become lost on its way to Monte Basilio and after wandering the hills for some time finally recognised that they had ended up on Monte Stagliata, some two miles west of the rest of the regiment. Despite 'losing' one of his battalions, Bowen managed to capture and then hold on to Monte Basilio in the face of determined German counter-attacks. But he could get no further, and his positions were now vulnerable to enfilade fire both from Troina and Monte Acuto.

After four days of intense fighting, 'The Big Red One' had still failed to capture Troina. Some gains had been made and from its positions on Monte Basilio Bowen's 26th Infantry in particular was now able to call down interdictory fire onto *Strada* 120 beyond the town itself, thereby disrupting Rodt's ability to move and resupply his troops safely. For the fifth day of the battle (4 August) Allen would yet again seek to widen his frontage by instructing the commander of the 18th Infantry Regiment, Colonel Smith, to take responsibility for the extreme right flank of the attack. With one of his three battalions having previously been detached to the 16th Infantry for the attack on Monte Bianco Smith was now given the 1st Battalion 16th Infantry, which was already in the area of the Gagliano salient, in exchange. The plan, however, remained the same; a double envelopment of the town by the 18th Infantry in the south and the 26th Infantry in the north, whilst the 16th and 39th Infantry Regiments continued to exert pressure on Troina in the centre.

Although Allen had not yet managed to complete his mission, his attacks were nonetheless taking their toll on Rodt's 15th Panzer Grenadier Division who had already lost approaching 1,600 men. But, as long as their escape routes behind Troina remained open, the defenders remained determined to resist. By noon it seemed that the Germans had managed to stifle Allen's plan. *Kampfgruppe* Fullriede was particularly effective in taking the battle to Bowen's men in the north, infiltrating American positions and generally knocking the GIs off their stride. And, although less aggressive in its approach, Group Ens continued to rebuff Smith's attempts to breach their defences in the south. Attempting to redress the balance, Bradley and Allen called for support from the skies. Three air strikes by P-51s and A-36s carrying 500lb bombs followed, plastering Troina and the surrounding hills. German morale declined, and yet it was not enough to shift the dial. Although all four regiments managed to take advantage of the temporary dislocation of Rodt's men and make some advances, the Germans continued to hold out.

By this time the 9th Division was forming up in Nicosia and Eddy had begun planning the next stage of the advance along *Strada* 120 to Messina. Bradley's orders to his Division were to attack what was still thought to be the German's next defensive line centred on the town of Cesaro. On the assumption that Allen would finally take Troina by the evening of the 6th, which by then would have been the sixth day of the battle, Eddy planned to avoid the inevitable congestion on *Strada* 120 by executing a wide overland hook to the north. His 60th Infantry Regiment, commanded by Colonel Frederick DeRohan, would advance out of Capizzi, pick up the Goums (who had still not captured Monte Acuto) en route, bypass Monte Acuto to the north, cross over Monte Pelato and Monte Camolato, and then cut the secondary road which came south from Sant Agata to Cesaro. All of this was to be achieved in a single day, 5 August.

As DeRohan's regiment set out on this manoeuvre Allen continued his efforts to capture Troina. Fullriede's troops defending Monte Acuto were still making a nuisance of themselves and Bowen's attempts to neutralise them with air support were frustrated by ground fog on the airfields. Meanwhile, the Germans were attempting to remove his two battalions from their positions on Monte Basilio with a fresh wave of counter-attacks. Although the Americans held on, by late afternoon they were in bad shape. Effectively cut off for the past three days, Bowen's men were running low on food and ammunition. Although they had been partially resupplied by air, their situation was becoming desperate.[16] In the centre, the attacks by Flint's 39th Infantry and Taylor's 16th Infantry Regiments were also proving to be unsuccessful as were Smith's 18th Infantry in the south.

Despite his apparent successes, Rodt knew that his position was ultimately untenable. Now aware of DeRohan's wide flanking manoeuvre to the north and frustrated by his failure to recapture Monte Basilio, it was surely only a matter of time before his badly depleted and exhausted troops would be overwhelmed. Especially as the British were making inroads into the *Hermann Göring (HG) Panzer Division*'s positions further to his south and threatening one of his avenues of escape (via Adrano). A previous plea to Hube for permission to fall back to a new defensive line had been denied, but now even Hube could not put off the inevitable. Although, technically, this was not Hube's decision to make.

When the opening stages of the battle for Troina began, command of all Axis forces on the Island still resided with Guzzoni's Sixth Army HQ. However, on 31 July Guzzoni received a directive from *Comando Supremo* ordering him to hand over the command of all Axis troops in Sicily to Hube. In future he was to comply with German wishes. When this order was confirmed by Kesselring via his liaison officer von Senger, Guzzoni issued an order on 1 August confirming the new command arrangements. With effect from noon on 2 August all Italian fighting troops still at the front were to take their orders from HQ *14 Panzer Corps*, although the Italian XVI Corps was to retain command of what remained of the coastal defences and the Italian XII Corps was to remain at the disposal of his Sixth Army Headquarters. These last two caveats were a fig leaf. The Germans were never going to allow their lifeline across the Messina Strait to the mainland to remain in the hands of what was now demonstrably an unreliable coalition partner. The days of Headquarters 6th Army were clearly numbered and Hube was now calling the shots. On 5 August, Hube suggested to Guzzoni that he should move his headquarters to Calabria in order to make room for his own headquarters; a slight that, even at this stage of the campaign, Guzzoni was not prepared to accept.[17]

Exercising his de facto authority, and despite Guzzoni's protests, Hube now decided to begin withdrawing from the Etna Line, at least in the eastern and central sectors of the front.[18] The troops would begin to pull out during the night of 5 August (although, in fact, Conrath's *Hermann Göring* (*HG*) *Panzer Division* began pulling out of Catania during the evening of 4 August leaving only a small rearguard behind). By nightfall of 6 August the vast majority of Rodt's troops were occupying new defensive positions just west of Cesaro with only a handful of troops left behind around Troina acting as rearguards. Most of the Division's heavy equipment was now en route to Messina bound for the ferries.

Despite signs of German withdrawal – American patrols reported that Monte Acuto had been abandoned on 5 August – Allen was wary. He had been caught out too many times and so he and his staff had spent most of the evening of 5 August making elaborate plans for the renewal of the attack on Troina the next day. All of this proved unnecessary. By dawn on 6 August, the seventh day of the battle, patrols from his 16th Infantry Regiment were in the town and meeting only sporadic small arms fire. Troina had finally fallen.[19] That afternoon General Eddy took over command of the sector, passing his 47th Infantry Regiment through Troina and along *Strada* 120 towards Cesaro. The Big Red One went into reserve. Its days of fighting in Sicily were over.

Returning to the fighting in the north, on 31 July Middleton's 45th Division was in possession of San Stefano and handing over to General Truscott's 3rd Division. A passage of lines takes some time to accomplish, and General Fries took the opportunity presented by this slight pause in the battle to break contact and withdraw his 29th Panzer Grenadier Regiment to its new defensive positions on the Etna Line. Fries's withdrawal was not without incident, however, because the open maritime flank and local air supremacy allowed Allied naval and air assets to continue to engage and harass his troops as they pulled back along *Strada* 113. Nevertheless, at this stage in the battle Fries could still rely on the support of the Italian Assietta Division and so his new defensive line continued to be a mixture of German and Italian troops.

By the morning of 3 August, the 15th Infantry Regiment advancing down *Strada* 113 had driven in Fries's outposts and pushed up to the Etna Line. But now they could proceed no further. Crossing the estuary of the Furiano River would present a completely different challenge to the steep, narrow gulleys which the Americans had previously had to face. The openness of the terrain and the dominating feature of the San Fratello ridgeline which sat behind the river gave the Germans a tremendous advantage. There was nowhere that the Americans could cross unobserved, and every potential crossing point had been liberally sown with minefields, all covered with direct and indirect fire. Behind the river the entire face of the San Fratello ridge was dotted with pillboxes, trenches and gun emplacements giving the defender wide fields of fire onto the plain below. The Germans had an uninterrupted view of *Strada* 113 stretching as far west as Caronia ten miles away. All attempts by two battalions of the 15th Infantry Regiment to get across the river on 4 August failed. The cost had been heavy, 103 casualties and no ground taken. It was enough to convince Truscott that he would have to shift his point of attack further inland. This would mean further delay.

His plan of attack on 6 August involved both the 15th and 30th Infantry Regiments. Whilst the 15th Infantry was ordered to renew its efforts to cross the Furiano River near its estuary, Colonel Rogers' 30th Infantry Regiment was tasked with crossing the river further upstream, capturing the town of San Fratello and thereby cutting the important lateral route of the road to Cesaro. However, the points where Rogers' battalions were to cross the Furiano were close to where the Nicoletta River – a tributary of the Furiano – joined the main course and it was soon apparent that Truscott had severely underestimated the complexity of the terrain into which he had committed Rogers' men. This complex manoeuvre, conducted at night, would involve crossing an intermediate ridge line that separated the two rivers near their confluence: it was ground that would prove to be particularly challenging. It took Rogers' men the best part of 5 August to get to their forward assembly areas. Moving forward in darkness towards the river, crossing the intermediate ridge line in the early hours of 6 August and eventually making their way up the mountainside to San Fratello itself was a nightmare. Troops everywhere quickly became lost. Some never actually crossed the rivers; and those who finally managed to start making the climbs were often stopped in their tracks by heavy enemy fire. What had been planned as a coordinated attack by five battalions across a wide frontage quickly degenerated into a series of 'uncoordinated battalion-size thrusts'.[20] Truscott, having gone forward himself to see what was facing the 30th Infantry, realised that he would need a new plan. And that plan would involve the use of an amphibious hook, an operation which the Germans had long anticipated and feared.

As noted earlier, at his meeting with his Army commanders on 25 July, Alexander had specifically promised Patton that he would try his best to secure him some landing craft and warships in order that the American could facilitate outflanking operations on the north coast should the opportunity arise. Despite Patton's scepticism,[21] Alexander had been as good as his word. The result was Naval Task Force 88 (NTF 88) which was created two days later, on the very day that Palermo opened to Allied shipping. Commanded by Rear Admiral Lyal A. Davidson, NTF 88 consisted of two cruisers, 14 destroyers, 14 MTBs, a number of small escort craft and, crucially, 19 assorted landing craft (two LSTs, ten LCI(L)s and seven LCTs). It would soon become known as 'General Patton's Navy'.[22]

Bradley, perhaps fearful of Patton's well-known impatience, had quickly secured an assurance from his superior that the responsibility for planning any amphibious operations within the II Corps area of operations would rest with his planning staff and not 7th Army HQ. In this way, Bradley wanted to ensure that the distance between the landing force and the main body of the attacking formation would be small enough to guarantee an early link-up, ideally, within the range of supporting artillery fires. An earlier amphibious operation, designed to help Middleton break the deadlock at San Stefano, had previously been cancelled at the last moment after Fries unexpectedly withdrew his forces to the Etna Line, but already Bradley and Truscott had planned – at least in outline – four other potential missions, each designed to place a small force behind a predicted enemy defensive line.[23] And 'small' was the right word. Nineteen landing craft would only be enough to move a battalion-sized force. The force nominated was Lt Col Lyle Bernard's 2nd Battalion, 30th Infantry Regiment, reinforced by two field artillery batteries, a platoon of medium tanks, and a platoon of combat engineers.

Just after noon on 6 August Truscott ordered Bernard to move his men to an embarkation point a mile west of San Stefano. His aim was to launch the force early the next morning and land it on a beach just east of Sant Agata. At the same time Truscott intended that Colonel Sherman's 7th Infantry Regiment, pushing down *Strada* 113, would finally make the expected crossing of the Furiano River, break through Fries's defensive line and effect the link-up. Just as Bernard was marching his men towards the RV, the *Luftwaffe* made one of its increasingly rare forays over the island. Four German aircraft bombed and strafed the loading area. Although two aircraft were subsequently shot down by anti-aircraft fire, enough damage was done during this raid to one of the key LSTs that Truscott was forced to delay the end run for twenty-four hours whilst Davidson called for a replacement craft to be sent forward from Palermo.

Truscott could not afford to allow the enemy any further respite, so, perhaps reluctantly, he set about repeating the aborted attacks of 6 August, this time sending his assistant divisional commander, General Eagles, forward to supervise the operations of the 30th Infantry. Colonel Sherman's 7th Infantry Regiment would still be brought forward to the Furiano river line, but this time it would be poised to strike across the river near the coast to exploit any successes the 30th Infantry might gain on the San Fratello ridgeline. The attacks on 7 August proved to be no more successful than the previous day. Therefore, that afternoon, Colonel Bernard's men once again moved from their bivouac areas and headed to the beaches west of Santo Stefano. Overnight another LST had sailed from Palermo to make up the shortfall created by the previous day's air raid, and the *Luftwaffe* once again attempted to intervene. This second air raid was less successful than the first. Although an LST and one of the escort vessels suffered some damage, it was not enough to derail the operation. At 19:40 ten landing craft, escorted by two cruisers and six destroyers, pulled away from the embarkation beach heading for Sant Agata.

Whilst Bernard's augmented battalion was edging its way down the coast, things were not going well inland. Two battalions, the 3rd Battalion, 15th Infantry and the 3rd Battalion 30th Infantry, had spent the entire morning trying to capture Hill 673 without success. This feature was seen to be the key to the enemy's southern ridge positions; the same objective had eluded both of them the previous day. Then it had been Manhart's 3rd Battalion, 15th Infantry that had spearheaded the attack, supported by Doleman's battalion. Now, on the 7th, the roles had been reversed; but the result was the same. Late in the afternoon, General Eagles worked with both battalion commanders to come up with a new plan which, as the day progressed, finally began to deliver results. Just before midnight on 7 August the Americans were finally able to gain the crest of the hill. They immediately set about digging in knowing full well that the Germans would inevitably counter-attack. But this time, the counter-attacks had a different purpose. Now aware of the amphibious force at sea and cognizant of the situation further south where Troina had fallen, Fries had finally been given authority to withdraw. But to do this successfully he would need to protect his flanks. Ten miles east of Sant Agata, another Sicilian river, the Rosmarino, enters the sea. Convinced that this would provide yet another intermediate defensive position for the Germans, Bradley planned to land Bernard's amphibious force on the eastern side of that river, near the town of Torrenova. By doing so he hoped to deny the enemy a line of retreat.

Although Fries had instructed his service units and other troops operating on his line of communication back to Messina to guard against a surprise Allied landing, it was a forlorn hope to expect them to be anything other than a security watch. Of more importance to him for the moment was maintaining his access to the Cesaro-San Fratello Road, which followed the San Fratello ridge line and was the only route he could use to get his vehicles and equipment off the hill tops, onto the coastal highway and away to safety. He had therefore retained a reinforced battalion of his 29th Panzer Grenadier Division in the Monte San Fratello positions and a regiment of Italian troops from the Assietta Division on the ridge south of the town as rearguards when the remainder of these two divisions began the withdrawal that night. It was these troops that had been resisting all attempts by the Americans to seize the ridge.

In anticipation of their withdrawal the Germans had rigged the bridge over the Rosmarino river for demolition and mined the riverbed. This was to work against them later when one of Davidson's warships attacked the bridge on the evening of the 7th and set off the demolitions. It would take Fries's engineers over six hours to create a bypass across the river; work which was completed by 03:00, 8 August. The exact time that Bernard's force landed ashore. Not for the first time, and certainly not for the last in the Italian campaign, the disembarking troops quickly discovered that they had been delivered to the wrong spot. Instead of being on the east side of the Rosmarino River Bernard's men landed to the west on a beach which was midway between Sant Agata and the river line, in the midst of the now retreating Axis forces. When Barnard discovered the truth, he rapidly adapted the plan. Quickly securing his beachhead he determined to move east and occupy the high ground on both sides of the river, reasoning that this would give him good defensive terrain from which to dominate the road whilst he awaited the advance of the 7th Infantry Regiment.

Fortunately for Fries, most of his division had extracted themselves before the bridge was blown but his rearguards now found themselves isolated and fighting in two directions; west against the advancing 7th Infantry and east against Barnard's men, who were trying to prevent their withdrawal down *Strada* 113. Despite deploying a small infantry detachment supported by four tanks – two Italian Renault and two German Mark IV Panzers – against the Americans defending the Rosmarino crossing, these rearguards could not break the stranglehold from the west and were forced to retreat into Sant Agata, where Bernard now deployed his own artillery and tanks to support the infantry he had tasked with keeping them bottled up. And Fries's men in Torrenova, who were trying to open up the escape route from the east, were equally unsuccessful in breaking the stranglehold.

At San Fratello the remaining Axis forces were completing their withdrawal. This made the task of clearing the ridge easier for the advancing 7th Infantry who by 11:30 were in Sant Agata where they were able to quickly overcome the small force of Germans caught in Barnard's trap. High up on the San Fratello ridge, the soldiers of the Assietta Division were now surrendering in droves, almost a thousand men being captured by Doleman's battalion alone. Although *Strada* 113 west of the Rosmarino crossing was now denied to them, Bernard's forces defending the river line were too stretched to cover every avenue of approach. Concentrating their efforts on the hill mass in and around the inland village of San Marco, the majority of the remaining German rearguard, usually approaching in small parties, managed to infiltrate the American positions and get away. They were aided by determined efforts by relieving troops attacking from the east who successfully engaged and distracted the American defenders. Eventually, except for about one company and a few vehicles from the rearguard, most of Fries's division got away.

By late in the afternoon of 8 August Truscott's 3rd Division had closed up on the Rosmarino river. Bradley's first amphibious end run, whilst achieving surprise, had failed to capture Fries's 29th Panzer Grenadier Division. The best that can be said of it was that it deprived the Germans of an opportunity to impose further delays by holding out on that river, which, considering previous performances, might have delayed the American's advance by an additional day.[24]

Returning now to Montgomery's 8th Army and the operations of Leese's XXX Corps. On 21 July, after being rebuffed at Gerbini, the 51st Highland Division operating on the Corps' extreme right flank had been withdrawn behind the Dittaino River whilst Leese concentrated his attention on the Canadians and their advance towards Agira. Having captured Agira, Leese now had the task of capturing Adrano, a key town on the Etna Line and which lay on the southwestern flank of Mount Etna. The approaches to Adrano were protected by two defensive outposts centred on the towns of Regalbuto and Centuripe. Regalbuto marked the western extremity of Conrath's *Hermann Göring (HG) Panzer Division* defensive line, which stretched from there all the way to the eastern seaboard at Acireale. Conrath had assigned the defence of Centuripe to Colonel Heilmann's 3rd Parachute

Regiment, but with insufficient infantry assets to man the whole of his line in strength and in depth he was forced to assign the defence of Regalbuto to his Armoured Engineer Battalion. Nonetheless, the Engineers, commanded by Lt-Col von Carnap, were capable soldiers and had already fought as a battle group earlier in the campaign.

Leese planned to overwhelm the Germans by launching a two-pronged attack on Adrano, with the Canadians continuing their eastward advance along *Strada* 121 from Agira via Regalbuto supported by a simultaneous attack on Centuripe launched from the valley of the Dittaino. This latter task would be given to the 78th Division, Monty's Army Reserve, only recently brought over from North Africa. Before this division could be launched, however, it would require the 3rd Canadian Infantry Brigade (3rd CIB) to secure its start line at Catenanuova and the 51st Highland Division to clear the Germans off the Sferro Hills, a small but not insignificant feature that dominated the road and railway line running along the floor of the Dittaino River from Catania through Catenanuova and on to Enna.

Earlier we described how, on 26 July and at great cost to themselves, the Royal 22e, part of 3rd CIB, had initially captured both hill features which guarded the western approach to Catenanuova. Whilst the Canadians had managed to consolidate their positions on the 3000ft rocky ridge known as Mount Scalpello that lay to the south of the road and railway line, they had not been able to hold on to Mount Santa Maria on the northern side which, at 800ft, was significantly lower but just as important. This feature would now need to be recaptured before the attack on Catenanuova, which lay a mile to the east, could be instigated. 3rd CIB, now temporarily under the command of 78th Infantry Division, launched its attack shortly before midnight on 29 July. It met relatively little resistance. This was because the defenders, men of the 923rd Fortress Battalion, had uncharacteristically bolted. Despite the best efforts of German paratroopers who were also in the area and on their own initiative launched a series of uncoordinated counter-attacks, the damage had been done. Having successfully captured Catenanuova, 3rd CIB spent the next few days clearing the surrounding hills of the enemy before moving north to rejoin the rest of the Canadians in the fight for Regalbuto.[25]

The 51st Highland Division launched its attack on the Sferro Hills at 02:00 on 31 July. It was to be a full divisional attack and carried out in darkness with 154 Bde on the left, 152 Bde on the right and 153 Bde in reserve. Additional support would be provided by tanks of 50th RTR who were to move forward at first light to provide close support to repel the anticipated German counter-attacks. To achieve their objectives the infantrymen would first have to descend to and cross the wide, but largely dry, riverbed of the Dittaino River and capture the village of Sferro before moving up on to the low hills above the village which represented the main German defensive positions. The area was characterised by terracing and olive groves. The attack was preceded by an intense artillery barrage. This was the 8th Army way, but its predictability was leading to diminishing returns: 'The Germans were by now used to it and their reaction was to get as many men as possible under cover, leaving just a few sentries and look-outs. As the shelling ended, or went over, they reoccupied their defensive positions and came up fighting.'[26] Colonel Schmalz, who was in overall charge of the defence of this sector, estimated that the British fired approximately 30,000 shells on a one-kilometre frontage over a period of 90 minutes – killing only two of his men and wounding eight others.[27]

However predictable the pre-planned artillery barrages may have been, the true value of Monty's artillery could be found in its ability to harass and ultimately thwart the enemy's counter-attacks. The Highlanders' attack was 'stubbornly opposed' by Conrath's *Hermann Göring (HG) Panzer Division* troops who also used tanks to support their counter-attacks. But 'on call' fire from the Scottish Horse Artillery and six other field regiments dealt with these in a deadly and efficient manner leaving twelve panzers destroyed on the battlefield and the Scotsmen as victors. This was to be the last major battle fought by the 51st Highland Division during the Sicily campaign. For the next few days, the Division would take on a flank protection role, supporting the 78th Division in its attack on Centuripe and Adrano. Two of its battalions would be tasked with securing a crossing over the Simento River on 5 August and 152 Bde would capture Biancavilla on the 6th, but essentially its work had been done. Its commander, General Wimberley, known by everyone as 'Tartan Tam', had led them throughout the North African and Sicily campaigns and, in no small measure, ensured that its near mythical reputation had been burnished and sustained. But Monty, having judged him unsuitable for command of a corps, believed that after two years hard fighting, this competent soldier, whom he greatly admired, was displaying tiredness and deserved a rest. He therefore recommended him to Alanbrooke as a strong contender for the prestigious appointment of Commandant at the Staff College; a recommendation that the CIGS accepted.[28]

Many, including Wimberley himself, thought this a poor return for his experience, leadership and endeavour over two trying years but, true to his character, 'Tartan Tam' was more concerned about the effect that this might have on the morale of his men. Ten days earlier, after his division had failed to take Gerbini, Monty had come to see him to tell him that operations were now being switched to the Canadians on the left flank. 'I knew full well that my "Jocks" were more temperamental soldiers than the phlegmatic "Tommies", and it would never do, if they thought we had been brought to a full stop by enemy action, especially after the grand fight the Argylls had just put up.' Wimberley asked Monty to confirm this decision, and the reasons for making it, in writing. Monty duly obliged and, grabbing a pencil, immediately wrote a note of praise for the Scots. After explaining his reasoning for the switch of emphasis he concluded by saying, 'Please tell all your soldiers that I think they have done magnificently. They have marched and fought over a very long distance in great heat, and up to the best standards of the Highland Division. I am sending you 50,000 cigarettes as a present to the Division.'[29] And Monty meant it. He later wrote: 'Of the many fine divisions that served under me in the Second World War, none were finer than the Highland

Division.'[30] It is typical of this division and its commander that as soon as the Sicily campaign was over it immediately began retraining itself. And this included revisiting the ground of Gerbini and Sferro on a battlefield tour to learn its lessons.[31]

The advance parties of the 78th Division, also known as the Battleaxe Division (a reference to its divisional sign), arrived in Sicily on 25 July, the day that Mussolini had been dismissed, and were joined over the next few days by the rest of the division. The first battalion to see action were the 5th Northamptons who reinforced 3rd CIB during the attack on Catenanuova. They were quickly joined by the other two battalions of 11th Bde, 2nd Lancashire Fusiliers and 1st East Surreys, who participated in the expansion of the Catenanuova lodgement. The Division's next objective would be the hill town of Centuripe which was clearly visible on the skyline above and looked to one officer 'like something out of Grimm's Fairy Tales'.[32] Centuripe was on a prominent, but separate, ridge feature which ran nine miles eastwards to Regalbuto and guarded the south-western approaches to Adrano. Seen from the air, the town looks like a prostrate man; his body lying on a narrow ledge and his arms and legs dangling on either side of it, the arms and legs being ridge lines emanating from a central spine. This is how many of the first-hand accounts of the time refer to the routes that were taken during the ascent, with troops frequently mentioning the 'left arm' or the 'left leg'.

The Battleaxe Division had been formed in June 1942 in preparation for Operation TORCH and was commanded by General Vivian Evelegh, 'a tall, bluff man with a commanding presence and a loud laugh'.[33] It had fought in North Africa as part of Anderson's First Army, and this was to be its first action with Monty's 8th Army. Everyone, from the GOC to the OR, was keen to make a good impression and taking Centuripe could not have been a more difficult challenge. It was to prove a real baptism of fire but one, given their previous experiences in Algeria and Tunisia, they felt prepared for. They considered themselves to be the best 'mountain' division in the British Army and now was the time to prove it. The Division would be up against Conrath's *Hermann Göring* (*HG*) *Panzer Division*.

Too many of the secondary sources written after the campaign continue to refer to this as a 'crack' or 'elite' division; most probably based on its reputation when serving under Rommel in North Africa. But this was not the same division, a fact which had been recognised by von Senger and Guzzoni when considering their initial deployments. It was a reconstituted division, and the vast majority of its troops were inexperienced and untested. More worryingly, its leadership was suspect. But their opinions had been overridden by Kesselring. At least initially, their concerns had been justified. The division had performed badly in the early days of the campaign, particularly in the way in which Conrath had handled his armoured units, and had failed to take advantage of the, albeit limited, opportunities which had been presented. But it was learning quickly and had already begun to prove its worth when fighting from prepared defensive positions.

An exception to this overall assessment of the division was *Kampfgruppe* Schmalz which, for the first two weeks of the campaign, had been operating as a semi-independent formation detached from the main body and when reinforced by elements of the *1 Fallschirmjäger Division* had effectively fought Dempsey's XIII Corps to a standstill. And it was primarily the men of 'King Ludwig' Heilmann's 3rd Parachute Regiment, part of *Kampfgruppe* Schmalz, who were now responsible for the defence of Centuripe. Heilmann had led the advance guard of the German paratroopers onto the island and had personally reconnoitred the landing and drop zones. Having joined *Kampfgruppe* Schmalz, he had been given responsibility for the defensive positions between Carlentini and the sea, which, of course, included the Malati and Primosole bridges.

From the south there are only two roads which lead up to Centuripe from the Dittaino valley. In a few places, both followed exposed ridgelines. But in the main, they tracked the contours of the terrain, clinging tightly to the sides of the mountains, climbing to the top via a succession of blind hairpin bends. Both roads had been heavily mined and cratered, and every bend concealed a potential ambush. The left-hand road begins in Catenanuova and eventually reaches the town via the prostrate man's left arm; the second, five miles to the south, begins half-way between Catenanuova and Sferro and enters the town via his outstretched right leg. Neither approach was an enticing prospect. A *Fallschirmjäger* unit had double the number of machine-guns possessed by a normal German infantry unit – one for every five men rather than one for every ten[34] – and Heilmann's men had placed them judiciously. Every fold in the ground had been utilised to maximise the defender's advantage and every avenue of approach covered, not only by interlocking machine-gun posts but also predicted mortar and artillery fire.

Initially, Evelegh had planned his attack as a single brigade operation using Brigadier Howlett's 36th Brigade. It would move at night from the secure lodgement that had been gained in Catenanuova now being held by his 11th Brigade, with the intention of attacking at first light from a secure position south-west of the town's cemetery, a prominent feature which lay on the prostrate man's left wrist. The attack was due to take place on 2 August. However, the unexpected capitulation of the German troops holding Catenanuova presented Evelegh with an opportunity he intended to seize. Knowing that every hour he gave his enemy would be used to reinforce an already formidable position, he decided to advance his plans by twenty-four hours. This was not only a reflection of his own natural self-confidence but also the confidence he had in his division. It was a risky decision. As one artillery officer recalled afterwards, 'It was all rather a rush… We protested vigorously about this lack of time, but were told that it was most vital that the attack should start earlier than was planned as a very great deal depended on it… In the event the guns were ready at about 0030hrs, half an hour before they had been ordered to be.'[35]

Howlett advanced with two battalions, 5th Buffs and 6th Royal West Kents, and one in reserve. Their axis of advance was across the open mountainside to the west of the road. But after a mile or so of steady progress both battalions began to meet fierce resistance. Further progress was slow, made more difficult by the German rearguard who, utilising the many small caves in the area, had lain undetected and would suddenly appear to snipe and harass the leading platoons from behind. By dawn on 1 August neither battalion had reached their jumping-off points and Howlett was forced to commit his reserve battalion, the 8th Argylls. Meanwhile, Evelegh reinforced him by sending forward the 5th Northamptons. What had started out as a two-battalion attack had now become a four-battalion attack.

It was now that the Allied artillery began to deliver. The Argylls having been held up by two determined heavy machine-guns, the CO turned to his FOO for support. Yet, before the FOO could even get to his wireless set, the ground shook with the sound of twenty-four rounds of 25-pdr shells landing on the target, followed almost immediately by a further 240 rounds. Lt Col Usher, the CO of 138 Fd Regt, having already moved forward with Howlett's advance HQ, had spotted the danger. 'First class map reading had done the rest, aided by good survey and intelligent allowance for atmospheric conditions at the guns.' Usher had called a Mike target and with astonishing first round success with his ranging fire (one round per gun) had quickly increased the rate of fire of his 24-gun regiment to 'Ten rounds gun fire'. In a few minutes, the immediate impediment to the Argylls' advance had been eliminated. Artillery support was needed as all four battalions tried to advance over boulder-strewn ground covered in prickly bushes and cactus plants which offered little meaningful cover. The terracing provided another unwelcome obstacle. Moving forward in extended line one infantry officer reported: 'Our position is miserable...every movement we make is spotted and our only hope is artillery. We therefore go to ground and wait for the 25-pounders.'[36]

By mid-afternoon Evelegh had come forward to assess the situation for himself. Aware that his attack was losing momentum, he called forward the 1st East Surreys. What had begun as a two-battalion attack had now become a five-battalion one. The East Surreys were deployed to the left flank and told to take the high ground above the cemetery in order to bring fire down on the Germans who were impeding the progress of the West Kents. The route taken by the East Surreys followed a mule track which the Germans had covered with machine-guns firing on fixed lines. The only way to make any progress at all was to move onto the steep hillside to their right as the ground to the left dropped away sharply. Nevertheless, by nightfall they had achieved their objective and opened a second front against the Germans defending the cemetery. Fighting continued throughout the night under a sky lit up by German flares, but still Evelegh's men were denied access to the town. The battle for Centuripe was now entering its second day and the men were getting very tired; the Argylls and Royal West Kents had been engaged in continuous action for over forty-eight hours. It was worse, of course, for the German defenders, who had been engaged in these fresh assaults for over four days.

For the British an increasing concern was the question of how to get supplies forward to the fighting troops. Until the single road could be repaired and brought into use, the only way to bring forward much needed food and ammunition was by means of carrying parties or mules, the latter always in short supply. It fell to the sappers to get the road open so that it could be used by the division's wheeled and tracked vehicles. Their vanguard was the trusty D7 bulldozer which, later in the Italian campaign, would prove to be as important a piece of battle-winning equipment as the tank. Even as the fighting was taking place on the hills around them, 256th Field Company's D7, affectionately known as 'Tiger Lil', was making its way slowly up the road like a mechanical phalanx, whilst behind it teams of sappers were risking their lives clearing mines, repairing culverts and filling in craters.

By mid-afternoon Evelegh sensed that the Germans had reached breaking point. One last hammer blow should do it. He was right. As a result of the combined pressure being exerted here by the Battleaxe Division, by the Canadians to the west at Regalbuto, and by the Americans further north at Gagliano and Cerami, Hube was becoming increasingly concerned that if the Americans broke through Rodt's defences at Troina it would imperil the *Hermann Göring Division*'s escape routes. He therefore ordered Conrath to begin thinning out his troops beginning at 21:00 on 2 August. This order, however, was a precautionary one. Conrath was to thin out, not withdraw. Centuripe was still to be held for as long as possible.

The task of entering Centuripe now passed to Brigadier Nelson Russell. Russell had taken command of 38th (Irish) Brigade shortly before Operation TORCH and had commanded it with distinction throughout the North African campaign. He knew full well that any frontal attack would be 'a hazardous operation in daylight', especially on a battlefield which was becoming increasingly congested (as a two-battalion attack had now become eight, with only the 2nd Lancashire Fusiliers remaining uncommitted). Once again, artillery supporting determined infantry would prove to be the key to success. Russell's plan was to attack in two phases and on two axes. In phase one the 2nd London Irish Rifles, advancing from the south-west, would pass through the Royal West Kents and secure a start line from which the 1st Royal Irish Fusiliers could attack the cemetery and gain access to the western half of the town. This was phase two. And, as part of this phase, the 6th Inniskilling Fusiliers would cross to the far side of the central valley in front of Centuripe and make a frontal assault onto the spur where the other road into the town entered Centuripe from the east via the 'right leg'.

H-Hour was set for 18:00 and, in addition to his own three regiments of artillery, Evelegh had ensured that Russell's brigade could call on the support of two field regiments and one medium regiment of the Corps' artillery. Russell was keen to get his men into the town before darkness fell as he wanted them to have at least some daylight in which to carry out the inevitable street fighting that would ensue. 2nd Irish London Rifles made steady progress and by 19:00 had captured two of its three objectives, which were all small peaks to the west of the town. However, the third peak was proving to be elusive as the attacking troops were coming under sustained machine-gun fire from above and from the flanks. Rather than accept any further delay, Russell now ordered phase two to begin. At 20:00 the Royal Irish Fusiliers entered the cemetery just as darkness was falling and after an hour of heavy fighting managed to secure a lodgement in the town. While their attack was in progress, the Inniskillings took the last height in front of the town, scaling a 100-foot-high cliff, and entered Centuripe from the east. A third entry into the town was made by a company of the 'Skins' who had made their way onto the road which led into the town from Adrano.

Surrounded on three sides, the Germans nevertheless continued the fight. Two tanks in the town square soon beat a hasty retreat, but the paratroopers were made of sterner stuff and the street fighting that followed was a new experience for troops that had hitherto only experienced 'open' warfare. Fighting went from house to house and street to street. At times it was brutal hand-to-hand, close-quarter fighting with the Irish using bayonet and grenade against paratroopers, many of whom carried submachine guns. As the night progressed, and as more and more of Russell's men entered the town, the outcome was inevitable. Heilmann's men melted away and by first light on 3 August Centuripe had been taken.

It should be noted that at this stage in the campaign the Italian troops fighting on Sicily still did not know their ultimate fate. But high-level German planning for the evacuation had begun as early as 25 July, when Mussolini was removed from office, with secret meetings taking place in Rome two days later. Hube himself did not receive any specific evacuation instructions until 1 August; even then, he had not been authorised to communicate that information to his troops.[37] Nevertheless, on 2 August and in order to maintain the fighting spirit of his troops, he decided to make it 'unofficially' known that an evacuation was planned.[38] In the meantime he required Conrath's division to continue to hold Dempsey's XIII Corps at bay on the Catanian Plain whilst at the same time protecting the withdrawal routes east and west of Mount Etna. Conrath, as well as fighting Leese's XXX Corps, was now anxiously looking over his right shoulder wondering whether Rodt would be able hold the Americans at Troina. If he couldn't, he himself would have to yield and face the prospect of being channelled onto the very narrow roads east of Mount Etna.

It had taken the Canadians four days to cover the eight or so miles which separated Leonforte and Agira. It was another nine miles along *Strada* 121 to Regalbuto, which Simonds intended to capture in much less time. Regalbuto was built around a central crossroads where a secondary road from Troina to Catenanuova, running roughly north-west to south-east, crosses *Strada* 121, running east to west from Agira to Adrano. This crossroads sits in a small saddle at the convergence of three prominent hill features, all of which would play an important in the coming battle. From the south-west, and starting about a mile outside the town, was the Regalbuto Ridge. This ran parallel to *Strada* 121 on its southern side and came to an end just south of the crossroads on a summit called Mount Santa Lucia. To the north-west was a slightly lower spur. This carried the road to Troina, which, after a mile or so, dropped down towards the Salso valley. The end of this spur was known as Mount Serione. And finally, to the east of the crossroads, and once again paralleling *Strada* 121, was the beginning of a nine-mile-long ridge feature leading to Centuripe which, at Regalbuto, ended in a feature known as Tower Hill, so named because of a prominent stone lookout perched on its summit. One other key feature which would play a part in the coming battle – and which significantly did not appear on any of the Canadian maps – was a deep ravine which ran southwards from the outskirts of the town and effectively separated Mount Santa Lucia from the road to Catenanuova and, on the other side of that road, Tower Hill.

In his original orders for the capture of Agira Simonds had given Brigadier Urquhart's 231 (Malta) Brigade the task of leading the advance on Regalbuto and seizing a bridge beyond it which carried *Strada* 121 over the River Salso west of Adrano. Urquhart chose the Dorsets and the Hampshires to lead the advance, which would be across countryside eerily similar to that which had faced 1st CIB as they exited Nissoria; a succession of rocky ridges crossing the road at right angles and offering a multitude of ambush opportunities. The surrounding countryside was a thick covering of olive and almond groves and, starting out in daylight on 29 July, both battalions progressed cautiously. As night approached, they had barely covered six miles but could now see the looming Regalbuto Ridge. Urquhart ordered the Hampshires to make an immediate night attack against the ridge but, approaching in darkness, their presence was soon discovered and they were met with withering fire from machine-guns, mortars, and the deadly *nebelwerfer*, one salvo of which practically wiped out a platoon as they formed up on their start line. In the face of mounting casualties, the Hampshires were forced to call off their attack.

The next day, Friday 30 July, the task of taking the Regalbuto Ridge passed to the 2nd Devons. They at least had the luxury of time to prepare for the attack which again would take place at night; but this time with the support of 144 guns from four field and three medium artillery regiments. Simonds, the gunner, was leaving nothing to chance. Lt-Col Valentine, commanding the Devons, chose an indirect approach. Rather than attacking directly down the road, the most likely axis of advance, he led his men into a valley to the north where they emerged not at the point of the ridge but some way down, before then crossing the road and climbing the ridge. The attack was a complete success, but the Devons would spend most of the following day in a bitter fight to hold onto their gains as the Germans, now using elements of Heilmann's 3rd Parachute Regiment, mounted a succession of counter-attacks in an ultimately unsuccessful bid to retake the ridge.

Whilst this fighting was taking place, Urquhart sent the Dorsets in to capture Mount Serione, the end of the spur on which lay the road to Troina. Their route also utilised the same valley employed by the Devons, albeit slightly further down, and took them past the town's uncompleted railway station, work on which had ceased in 1940, then uphill, via the town cemetery, onto the spur. This movement, carried out in daylight, necessitated two company-sized attacks, one to capture the railway station and another to subdue strong German resistance in the cemetery. The objective was taken by mid-afternoon and soon afterwards the Dorsets were relieved by the 48th Highlanders of Canada, who had been temporarily attached to the Malta Brigade. Urquhart's brigade now occupied two of the three hill features commanding Regalbuto, but it was clear that the Germans were still not prepared to surrender the town. They had issued instructions for the removal of transport to the rear areas, but von Carnap's orders to his troops were very clear: 'The present position must be held at all costs... There must be no doubt about this point. The abandonment of the present position and a fighting withdrawal to the bridgehead position will only be carried out on express orders from division.'[39]

Regalbuto itself was a shambles. Prior to the invasion, Alexander and Montgomery had sought advice from Allied air commanders on the most efficient means of hindering Axis movements by creating traffic blocks on key roads. Three options were offered, one of which was to use bombers to attack houses on either side of narrow streets in small towns with no bypass routes and few through routes. This option was accepted but, as the Allies were soon to learn to their cost, would prove to be a double-edged sword as it offered defensive opportunities for troops holding these towns and would ultimately impede the forward movement of Allied troops. On 26 and 28 July the Tactical Bomber Force launched 211 and 82 sorties respectively against Regalbuto and achieved the aim of blocking routes in the town. More strikes went in to support the attacks on Regalbuto Ridge on 30 and 31 July and continued on subsequent days.[40] Fighter bombers were now circling overhead in readiness to attack German transport, tanks, and other vehicles expected to flee the town in the direction of Adrano.[41]

German tanks, carefully sited and concealed amongst the town's rubble, were now making life extremely difficult for the Allied infantry operating to the south of the town. They were covering the ravine which separated Mount Santa Lucia from the Catenanuova road and so far had frustrated all attempts by the Devon's to capture Tower Hill. So, whilst anti-tank guns were being manhandled forward to deal with this threat, Simonds and Urquhart agreed to launch a reconnaissance in force that night with the aim of drawing fire and thereby identifying enemy positions prior to a subsequent attack on Tower Hill by the Royal Canadian Regiment (RCR). This battalion, having lost their previous CO during the advance to Agira, was now under the command of Lt-Col Powers. Called forward from Agira, the battalion undertook a 'hellish' seven-mile cross-county march arriving in Regalbuto on the evening of the 31st.

The reconnaissance in force, carried out by a company of the Dorsets, failed to make contact with the enemy, but Urquhart, not wishing to delay matters any further, decided to send in the RCR regardless. The Canadians, anticipating a descent into a ravine of no more than ten feet or less, began their attack at 02:00, 1 August. The leading company soon got into difficulties. The ravine turned out to be about one hundred feet deep and terraced, each terrace separated by sheer sides four foot high. The noise of their descent quickly drew enemy fire, which forced the men to take cover. The remaining companies, unsure of the situation because of a breakdown in radio communications, pressed on and hoped for the best. The next company to enter the ravine took thirty minutes to reach the bottom and the same amount of time to climb up the other side. Instead of scrambling out into open countryside, they found themselves in a cluster of houses at the southern edge of the town where they were immediately engaged at close quarters by a tank. Whilst most of the company was now pinned down by this tank, one platoon, led by Lt Bowman, managed to evade its fire and carried on to the top of Tower Hill. However, realising that the rest of his company would not be able to join him unless something was done about the tank, Bowman immediately turned around, and leaving a section behind under the command of his sergeant, set off to deal with it.

A third RCR company had by now entered the ravine, and the plan was completely unravelling. When daybreak approached, three of Powers' companies were dug in on the eastern side of the ravine and unable to move, Bowman's platoon was isolated, unable to get either up or down Tower Hill, and the section on top of Tower Hill, having held out for a few hours, was finally forced to surrender.[42] The RCR attack had ended in complete failure and the battalion would spend the rest of the day sheltering either side the ravine with battalion HQ and one company on the western edge and the three remaining companies on the eastern side. The battalion finally managed to extract itself that night, the withdrawal being completed by 22:30.[43]

The Germans had turned Regalbuto into a fortress and it was believed that there were at least eight tanks in the town. Having failed to take Tower Hill by direct assault, Simonds now needed to come up with a new plan. It was abundantly clear to him that the enemy would not surrender the town unless ordered to do so by higher authority or until he, Simonds, had forced their hand by taking Tower Hill, thereby threatening their only line of retreat. The 48th Highlanders on Mount Serione were without their supporting arms and running low on food and ammunition, so, until his sappers could construct a makeshift track from *Strada* 121 in order for supplies to reach them, an attack from the north, at least initially, was impractical. But what if this could be combined with a wider, flanking manoeuvre to the south? One which was designed to seize Tower Hill from behind. This then was his plan, a pincer movement.

The flanking movement would be undertaken by the Hasty Ps. Starting out from *Strada* 121 they would march at night south-eastwards and cross-country with the aim of hitting the Regalbuto-Catenanuova road about a mile south-east of the town at a place where the road passes through a saddle between two hills, Mount Tiglio to the west and Mount San Giorgio to the east. They would still have to cross the ravine but, hopefully, at a place which was not covered by enemy fire. What was not known, however, was whether or not either or both of these hills were currently occupied by the enemy.

The Hasty Ps set off about 22:00 on 1 August and by dawn the next morning had reached and scaled Mount Tiglio which, mercifully, had been abandoned by the Germans. Here they paused to rest and regroup for the next phase which was due to be launched at 16:00. But before zero hour, word was received that a patrol from the 48th Highlanders had entered Regalbuto from the north that morning and found it empty. This caused Simonds to cancel the elaborate fire plan which had been arranged for the final assault on the town and order the Hasty Ps to begin their attack.

Although as they crossed the road and made their way eastwards the battalion did come under some fire from Regalbuto and the southern slopes of Tower Hill, the Hasty Ps discovered that the Germans holding Mount San Giorgio had also abandoned their positions. The attack on Tower Hill, however, would not be as easy and the Hasty Ps' first attempt to cross the valley which separated it from Mount San Giorgio was beaten off by heavy machine-gun and mortar fire. Their second attempt, now supported by on-call artillery fire, proved more successful and Tower Hill was taken by 20:00 that evening.

It was now time for the Allied air forces to wreak havoc on the withdrawing Germans. Later estimates suggest that up to forty vehicles were destroyed by fighter bomber attacks carried out on the Regalbuto-Adrano road that evening.[44] Regalbuto and Centuripe were both captured on 3 August. To the north, Fries and Rodt were still holding the Americans at bay, but on 6 August Rodt would finally have to give up Troina. In the meantime, Hube instructed Conrath to pull his forces back to the Etna Line where, for as long as he retained control of the key town of Adrano, Conrath could still withdraw his forces on either side of Mount Etna. But this would only hold true for as long as Rodt could keep the Americans away from the western highway at Randazzo.

At this stage the Allies were still uncertain as to their enemy's future intentions. On 3 August, Alexander had signalled Cunningham and Tedder noting that he had picked up indications of an intended withdrawal to the Italian mainland. He was expecting to be told of coordinated air and naval plans to deal with this contingency and, ultimately, instructions from Eisenhower as to what part he as the land forces commander should play in the denouement. But AFHQ was far from in agreement as to the current situation. In a signal to the Combined Chiefs of Staff Eisenhower had reported '...no certain indications that enemy already intends [to] withdraw behind Etna, but ability to maintain anticipated line depends mainly on successful defence of Adrano. My present estimate is that a feeling of restrained optimism with regard to Sicily is justified and that the clean up may come sooner than the 30 days estimated by some of our commanders last week.' [45]

It had taken Leese six days to capture the outpost towns of Regalbuto and Centuripe but now the ultimate objective, Adrano, was within sight. On 4 August, Montgomery issued his final instructions to Leese and Dempsey. The evidence that the Germans were pulling back could be both seen and heard. All across Dempsey's front lines, troops were hearing the explosions of demolitions as bridges, culverts and ammunition dumps went up in rapid succession. Dempsey was on notice to continue his long-delayed advance north up the eastern seaboard but, he was told, without incurring heavy casualties, as it was likely that his Corps would spearhead the invasion of the Italian mainland. It was Leese therefore who was to continue doing 'the punching'.

The further north-eastwards 8th Army advanced, the more constrained the battlefield became. Montgomery recognised – and accepted – that if the American 9th Division reached Randazzo before his 8th Army, Messina, like Palermo, would fall to Patton's 7th Army. Meanwhile, it was becoming increasingly difficult for Monty to use all of the divisions currently at his disposal. And so, after the capture of Adrano and Belpasso, the 51st Highland Division, the Canadian 1st Division and the British 5th Division were all told that they would be placed into Army reserve, leaving Evelegh's 78th to bear the brunt of the subsequent fighting. But none of this mattered until Adrano, which controlled the main highway circumventing Mount Etna, was captured.

Shortly before issuing his orders, Leese took Evelegh, Simonds and some of the key corps and divisional staff officers to the top the Centuripe ridge for a grandstand view of the coming battle. Eastwards on the other side of the wide valley of the River Simeto was the objective, Adrano, 12 miles away as the crow flies, the bleached tiled roofs of its houses glinting in the sun on the slopes of Mount Etna. Four hundred metres above the valley floor, Adrano was approachable from the west by two hairpin roads, one to the left leading into the town from the north, and the other, to the right, approaching the town from the south. Below them, between Centuripe and Adrano, was a wide, cultivated plain formed by the junction of the Salso and Simeto rivers. Unlike most of the rivers so far encountered in the campaign, the main course, the Simeto, was still full and fast-flowing as it made its way southwards from the mountains in the north towards the Plain of Catania. In contrast, the River Salso was almost dry as it made its way slowly from west to east. Looking further northwards, the men could see a series of rolling foothills climbing steadily to the peaks of three significant mountain features which filled the northern horizon – Hill 736, Mount Revisotto, and Mount Seggio. To their left was another river, the Troina, which flowed down from the north, passing to the west of Mount Revisotto before joining the Salso at a point where it began its wide meanders. The Simeto came into view to the right behind a long, outlying spur of Mount Seggio on which stood the tiny hamlet of Carcaci, through which the road from Troina descended to its junction with *Strada* 121. The area between the northern peaks and the Salso was full of irrigated plantations of lemon and orange trees but devoid of east-west roads. A single-track railway line the Italians had constructed shortly before the war followed the valley floor westwards towards its terminus, the station at Regalbuto.

Leese intended to attack Adrano on two axes. Setting out from Centuripe, the 78th Division would drop down into the river valley that night (4-5 August) and secure a bridgehead over the Salso River. The following night it would secure a further crossing over the Simeto River just north of its junction with the Salso River. From here it would make the steep climb up the side of Mount Etna on the night 6-7 August with the aim of capturing Adrano before dawn. Meanwhile, the 1st Canadian Division would attack from behind the Troina River and secure both Mount Seggio and an additional bridgehead across the Simeto River (further upstream from the Battleaxe Division) by the night of 5-6 August. Finally, and only if Evelegh's troops had failed to take Adrano as planned, the Canadians were to be prepared to assist the 78th Division in a fresh attack on the night of 7-8 August. The option of using the Canadians this way had been presented by Simonds' earlier decision to task Brigadier Vokes, commanding 2nd Canadian Infantry Brigade (2nd CIB), with sending exploratory patrols into the Salso valley north of Regalbuto. This had occurred on 31 July, whilst the battle for Regalbuto was still raging, and was primarily intended as a precautionary measure in order to establish flank protection from Rodt's forces in the north. But on the following day, Vokes was ordered to follow up the work of these patrols by sending his battalions forward to the line of the Troina River. This would require Vokes to clear any enemy that might be occupying the high ground to the north of the Salso River. Vokes also foresaw a need for his engineers to build a makeshift track through this wilderness so that supplies could be brought forward by trucks as the trails that his patrols had encountered were "dried up stream beds filled with rocks, and going would be difficult even for personnel on mules'.[46]

This movement through the relatively wild Salso valley was an unexpected avenue of approach and one which was to provide dividends when it was later discovered that *Strada* 121 east of Regalbuto was, not unsurprisingly, mined, cratered and generally impassable to traffic. The Germans had had insufficient troops available to protect the entire length of this flank, but they defended one particular feature, Hill 736, in strength, and it would take the Loyal Edmonton Regiment almost two days to shift them. Nevertheless, on 5 August, the 'Eddies' finally took possession of this key feature and this made further progress eastwards along the Salso valley possible, offering Leese the opportunity to attack Adrano from an unexpected quarter - and possibly earlier than planned.

For the first time in the campaign the terrain on the northern side of the Salso valley made it possible for the Canadians to bring forward their tanks in anticipation of a combined infantry-tank assault; but this could only be done after their engineers had strengthened the railway bridge over the Salso River near Regalbuto to get them there. On 5 August, a day after Leese's 'O' Group, Simond's finally launched Vokes's brigade. Simonds had previously placed Lt Col Booth's Three Rivers Regiment and a squadron of the 4th Canadian Reconnaisance Regiment under Vokes's command, and it was Booth's tanks which were now to become the main striking force. In addition to the recce squadron, 'Booth Force' was allocated a battalion of infantry (the Seaforths), a self-propelled battery of artillery, and a couple of troops of anti-tank guns. Booth and Lt-Col Hoffmeister, the CO of the

Seaforth Highlanders, planned the attack together. The tanks and supporting arms were to cross the Salso north of Regalbuto and drive forward along the newly made track to join up with the Seaforths at the Troina crossing point before first light. From this start line, the whole force would then strike eastwards at 06:00 through the vineyards and orchards between the Salso River and the Troina road, swinging north of Carcaci to occupy the spur of high ground on the west bank of the Simeto.

The tanks had had difficulty in crossing the Salso railway bridge and so it was not until 08:00 on 5 August that Booth Force finally set off with the men of the Seaforths carried precariously on top of the advancing Sherman tanks. The Germans, who had seen them coming, held their fire until the last moment in the hope of catching the Seaforths before they disembarked. Fortunately, Hoffmeister had anticipated this eventuality and took the precaution of debussing his men before they came within effective range of German small-arms fire. The battle began at about 10:30 and was watched from the heights of Centuripe by Simonds and Monty, who afterwards agreed that it was a textbook example of how tanks and infantry should support each other in attack.

Although the Germans had positional advantage, they had not expected to see tanks appear from this flank and were therefore without any anti-tank weapons. The Shermans were therefore able to operate with relative impunity using their main armament, firing HE rounds, and machine-guns to clear out identified and suspected enemy positions before the infantry went in. They also used managed to flush the enemy out by using tracer bullets to ignite the tinder-dry grass and brush. Complete success was achieved by mid-afternoon with the enemy withdrawing in some disorder. The Canadians were now in possession of the west bank of the Simeto River. Their next objective would be to secure their northern flank by clearing any enemy which remained on either Mount Revisotto or Mount Seggio. The PPCLI, who were tasked with clearing Mount Seggio, declined the opportunity to attack in battalion strength that night and waited for daylight the next day when they could rely on the support of artillery and heavy mortars; a decision which was later criticised by Vokes. He later remarked that had the Patricias attacked Mount Seggio in battalion strength they might have carried their objective with disastrous results to the enemy withdrawal.[47] Both features were successfully taken, without resistance, on the morning of 6 August.

Having climbed the heights and taken Centuripe from the south the 78th Division now had to get down again in order to proceed with its mission of taking Adrano. This was easier said than done because the Germans had destroyed the road which led northwards down to *Strada* 121. Although it was still passable for infantry on foot, it would take the sappers almost two days to create a track down to the Simeto River which would be capable of taking vehicle traffic.

The Irish Brigade moved out at first light on 4 August and on reaching the valley floor found that the bridge carrying *Strada* 121 over the Salso River had been completely destroyed and, most likely, that would be the case for the bridge over the Simeto River about a mile and a half further on. With the road up to Centuripe repaired and open to traffic, Evelegh's CRA brought all his guns up onto the ridge. As one gunner officer later remarked, 'We had a magnificent view of Etna and, what was more important to us at that moment, a commanding view [from 2000 feet] of the lateral road running along its southern slopes which joined Adrano to Paterno and so on all the way to Catania. We could now dominate this road and the Germans just had to go back.'[48]

The assault across the Salso River took place at 15:00 on 4 August and was led by the London Irish Rifles and the Royal Irish Fusiliers who waded across the river either side of the collapsed bridge. The London Irish, operating on the left, had a relatively easy time of it, but the Fusiliers, operating on the right, faced tough opposition from enemy machine-gun and small arms fire from the bluffs on the far side. However, once again the two battalions were supported by not only their own artillery but also the 25-pdrs of 51st Highland Division and XXX Corps' medium guns. Within two hours, a bridgehead had been secured and handed over to the reserve battalion, the Inniskillings, leaving the two battalions to press on towards the Simeto. It was now up to the engineers to come forward, repair the cratered road, and replace the 100-foot gap in the bridge over the Salso; work which the sappers completed by 05:00 the next day.

As day broke on the 5th, the Fusiliers had managed to seize a precarious foothold on the east bank of the Simeto but were meeting fierce resistance; the Germans were holding the far bank in strength and had good observation and fields of fire. The Simeto at this point was three to four feet deep and fast flowing with precipitous, rocky sides on both banks of the river. Once again, the Germans had made full use of the abundance of caves which existed on the northern slopes to site their machine guns and snipers and there were two stone houses either side of the road, referred to as 'The Casino' and 'The Palace', which had been turned into strongpoints and anchored the German defences. Although Brigadier Russell was confident of success, he left nothing to chance. The attack was to have 'full scale Divisional Artillery support plus 4 Medium Batteries and, in addition, two platoons of 4.2″ mortars were in position'. As he said later, 'Although the issue was never really in doubt, and the action concluded with one third of our infantry in hand, it was slow, hard, bitter fighting.'

H-hour was set for 15:30 and by 21:00 the bridgehead was secure and the sappers were once again able to come forward and begin the work of reinstating the road and bridge. The Casino and the Palace had been the last positions to fall after the London Irish had used a PIAT against the former and the Fusiliers an anti-tank gun against the latter. Whilst it had taken the sappers only twelve hours to construct the first bridge over the Salso, the Simeto was a much bigger task and would take twenty-four hours to complete. Whilst this work was going on, the Canadians operating on their left at Carcaci had made contact and preparations could now be made for the final assault on Adrano. This, however, would be a task for the other two brigades. After four days of continuous fighting and three hard fights (Centuripe, Salso, and Simeto) the Irish Brigade had earned a rest.

The attack on Adrano proved to be something of an anti-climax. The Germans had employed their usual tactics of cratering *Strada* 121 in places where it was impossible to bypass and, by covering these obstacles with mines, booby-traps and stay-behind parties, slowed the momentum of 78th Division's advance from the Simeto bridgehead; but by now Hube had already decided to abandon the Etna Line, so when the East Surreys finally entered the town on 7 August, they found it abandoned by the enemy. Just like Regalbuto, Adrano had suffered badly at the hands of the Allied air forces. One particular raid on the night of 6/7 August had caused massive and probably unnecessary damage, and it had been followed by an artillery barrage that 'seemed to lift the town out of the ground'. Adrano was a mess.

Catania, too, was being abandoned. Intensive air attacks on all approaches to Catania had continued into the first week of August and had virtually isolated the city. On 4 August Dempsey ordered his two divisions to advance. Initially the 50th Division, for so long bottled up in the Primosole bridgehead, found it difficult to proceed, with the Germans using their usual tactics of cratered roads and minefields, covered by snipers, artillery, mortars and machine-gun fire, to slow the Allies down. But by 09:15 on 5 August the men of the Durham Light Infantry were in the city receiving the surrender from the Mayor and being greeted with muted enthusiasm by a cowed and hungry population, who were glad to see the back of the Germans but were now looking to the 8th Army for succour.

21

The End of the Campaign

To Messina and German Evacuation, D-Day Plus 30, Monday 9 August to D-Day Plus 38, Tuesday 17 August

'Hope encourages men to endure and attempt everything: in depriving them of it, or in making it too distant, you deprive them of their very soul.'[1]

On the Eastern Front the Soviets captured Stalingrad on 31 January and quickly capitalised on this victory by reclaiming both Kursk and Kharkov in the weeks that followed. Manstein's counteroffensive, which began at the end of February, retrieved the situation somewhat for the Germans but Guderian's final attack at Kursk, which was taking place at the same time as the Sicily battles were being fought, was to end in failure. Thus, by August 1943, the Germans' final strategic offensive in the Soviet Union was over, leaving the Soviets in the ascendancy. North Africa, of course, had fallen in May and Mussolini had been toppled in July. The morale of German troops, at least in the lower ranks, was becoming fragile and the news they were getting from the home front was no better. The Allied Strategic Air Forces were stepping up their attacks on German cities and this had recently culminated at the end of July, with Operation Gomorrah, the controversial firebombing of Hamburg.

The thing the Germans fighting in Sicily feared most then was the announcement of a Fuhrer order to hold Sicily 'at all costs'. Something similar to that which had condemned Paulus's Sixth Army at Stalingrad and many of their former colleagues fighting in North Africa under von Arnim at 'Tunisgrad'. Surprisingly, this had not been Hitler's initial reaction. Indeed, increasingly concerned about the reliability of his Axis partners, when Mussolini was removed from power by the King, Hitler had been tempted to abandon the Italians to their fate and pull all of his forces out of Sicily immediately.[2] But he was quickly persuaded by Kesselring and Jodl, his chief of operations at *OKW*, to continue to reinforce Sicily – albeit not as rapidly as Hube wanted. Both officers, however, knew that eventually, Sicily would have to be abandoned. This was not a universally held view. Both Rommel and Admiral Doenitz were firmly opposed to any abandonment of Sicily and it was still conceivable that, if their views had held sway with Hitler, a 'fortress order' might yet follow. General Warlimont, Jodl's deputy chief, later claimed that it was Jodl who 'in his calm way succeeded in guiding Hitler to undesirable but necessary decisions'.[3]

Understandably, therefore, both Kesselring and Hube were relieved when, on 26 July, *OKW* gave permission for preliminary planning for the evacuation of Sicily to begin.[4] After a conference with Hube and the principal operations officers of each of his three divisions on 29 July, Kesselring reported back to Berlin that it would be possible to evacuate the island over a period of three nights. Privately, Hube disagreed and, believing that such a hurried departure would result in the loss of much needed equipment, on 2 August he subsequently submitted a revised plan which foresaw an evacuation over five nights. As events transpired, this would be extended to six nights. Kesselring endorsed his plan, but the operational commanders were still hamstrung by Berlin's insistence that no preliminary withdrawals could be undertaken without the express permission of *OKW*; in other words, Hitler.

There was another, equally aggravating stipulation; Hube was forbidden to inform his soldiers that an evacuation was even being planned. This was an order that Hube was not prepared to accept. By 2 August every German soldier fighting in Sicily was aware that salvation was at hand. Although every one of them was expected to do their duty and to fight the Allies to the best of their ability, at least now they knew that their commanders would not condemn them to fighting an unwinnable battle. Hube's disobedience to superior orders went even further when, on 4 August, and again acting on his own initiative, he ordered the evacuation of every non-combat unit that could be spared. Kesselring chose to turn a blind eye to this insubordination. Indeed, many years later, when he came to write his memoirs, the Field Marshal claimed the primary credit for ordering the evacuation without Berlin's prior sanction.[5]

Hube's plan foresaw the withdrawal of *14 Panzer Corps* to Messina and onwards to Calabria, taking place gradually via a series of designated lines of resistance. These would be held for one day each and then abandoned at night. The evacuation would begin as soon as it became obvious that the Etna Line could no longer be held. The first line of resistance was designated as the Tortorici Line but thereafter each subsequent line, and the several intermediate positions between them, were left unnamed. The codename for the whole operation would be *Lehrgang*.

Whilst Hube's own Corps staff planned and executed the withdrawal to Messina, responsibility for the evacuation operation itself was delegated to *Oberst* Ernst-Günther Baade whom Kesselring had appointed as 'Commandant of the Straits of Messina' on 14 July. As the name implies, Baade's authority spanned the Straits and extended to the littoral of Calabria.

Baade had initially been sent to Sicily in the latter part of 1942 to control the flow of reinforcements to Rommel's, and later von Arnim's, troops in North Africa. When Tunis fell, there were already 30,000 German troops still on Sicily and these were hastily incorporated into Baade's command, which, on 14 May, was redesignated as *Division Sizilien*. Baade subsequently relinquished this command to Rodt on 9 June, but he remained on the island and would prove an inspired selection for this new role. Baade was a true eccentric, renowned for wearing a black beret with a tartan ribbon, Highland kilt, and favouring a Scottish claymore as his sidearm in preference to the more orthodox Luger. He was also a talented organiser. The son of a Brandenburg landowner, Baade had volunteered to join the army when war broke out in 1914 and two years later was commissioned into the 6th Dragoon Regiment. He spent the inter-war years running the family estates and breeding horses and latterly both he and his wife had earned a reputation as international show-jumpers. Baade rejoined the army shortly before the outbreak of the Second World War and as a major commanding a cavalry unit, the 17th Reconnaissance Battalion, fought in the Polish campaign. After the fall of France, he transferred to the motorized branch and fought in North Africa where he commanded a Motorized Infantry Regiment within 15th Panzer Division.

As Commandant of the Straits of Messina, Baade ran a truly tri-service organisation. Kesselring had subordinated to him several *Luftwaffe* flak batteries as well as all the Army and Navy anti-aircraft assets. The ferry services, both army and naval, also came under his direct command as well as all the naval assets necessary to protect the entrances to the straits. One of his key subordinates would be Commander Baron Gustav von Liebenstein, the German Naval Officer in Charge of Sea Transport. Prior to the arrival of these two officers, the ferrying situation had been a mess with all three services conducting operations independently of one another. Baade and von Liebenstein brought order to this chaos. In particular, von Liebenstein had introduced what one writer has opined was 'perhaps the first roll-on/roll-off cargo system in military history'; a system which was based around the Siebel ferry.[6] Developed in 1940, primarily for the proposed invasion of Britain, the Siebel ferry was eighty feet long and fifty feet in beam. It could carry about 450 men or ten loaded trucks (sixty tons), make a speed of eight to ten knots, and could mount up to three 88-mm antiaircraft guns. It had a shallow draft, was highly manoeuvrable, and, most importantly, could be loaded and unloaded quickly. No longer were trucks unloaded at the port side and cross-loaded onto ferries (with the process repeated on the far side). With the average time for loading a Siebel ferry reduced to twenty minutes, transit times of the two-mile stretch of water speeded up remarkably, making them less vulnerable to Allied interventions. With this in mind, von Liebenstein also utilised the flexibility of the Siebel ferry to vary both the embarkation and landing places; an innovation which would pay dividends in the coming evacuation. Altogether, Baade and von Liebenstein controlled thirty-three naval barges and L-Boats (barge craft), twelve Siebel ferries, seven MFBs (partially armoured and heavily armed beaching craft with bows that lowered to form a ramp and were capable of taking a hundred tons of cargo), thirteen small landing craft, and seventy-six motorboats; with the Siebel ferry being the key asset within this large armada.

Another measure taken by Baade was the identification and prior allocation of specific areas on the mainland for each of the withdrawing divisions; these would act as rallying points for the disembarking troops. The first to move into these areas were the non-essential, non-combat services, as well as most of the medical establishments, their movements having previously been authorised by Hube. As soon as Operation *Lehrgang* was sanctioned, Baade was reinforced with additional anti-aircraft defences from the 3rd and 22nd *Luftwaffe* Flak Brigades. He also received a large number of additional artillery assets. The US Army estimated that there were perhaps 500 guns guarding the two- to five-mile crossings, of which at least 333 were anti-aircraft guns; defences which those with previous experience cited were more formidable than that currently being experienced over the Ruhr in Germany.

Based on the experience of their previous operations, Baade and von Liebenstein identified a potential network of six evacuation routes, each of which would include several landing places on both shores. From this five were eventually chosen (see map). Routes one to four were all located north of Messina and the fifth, between Pistunina and Gallico, was kept in reserve for emergency use (and in the event was never used except for some supply units which left the island prior to 8 August). Hube then allocated each formation a primary evacuation route: Route 1, Rodt's 15th Panzer Grenadier Division; Route 2, Fries's 29h Panzer Grenadier Division; Route 3, Corps HQ, miscellaneous units, and any potential overflow from the other routes; and finally, Route 4, Conrath's *Hermann Göring Panzer Division*

Hube's orders stipulated that troops were only to cross at night, although Baade was given the discretion to move weapons, equipment and vehicles by both day and by night. These movements were to be carried out in accordance with a strict order of priority: anti-tank weapons, artillery, self-propelled weapons (including tanks and assault guns), trucks, and motor vehicles. All material not transported was to be destroyed. Only once all German troops and their equipment had been successfully evacuated would Hube allow German ferries to be used to evacuate the Italians.

Guzzoni began evacuating Italian troops on 3 August. In fact, he had done so in response to a request from Hube who wanted as many of the Italian units out of the way as possible before he instigated his own evacuation plan. However, unauthorised movements across the Straits had begun immediately the Allies invaded; and it was two-way traffic. Many Italian soldiers used whatever pretext they could find to absent themselves from the island whilst Sicilian soldiers from the mainland began heading westwards, claiming a desire to fight to defend their homeland but secretly intending to desert and join their families when and if the opportunity presented itself.

The troops now most at risk, at least initially, were Conrath's *Hermann Göring Panzer Division*. Whilst they still held Adrano and their sister divisions to their north were successfully keeping the Americans at bay, these troops had two potential escape routes. On Hube's orders, those holding positions on the Etna Line between Adrano and Catania had already begun to thin out to the defensive lines on the eastern side of Mount Etna, using the coastal road from Catania to Messina. But those holding Adrano itself and positions to the north were now forced to use a narrow unpaved road on the western slopes of Mount Etna which led to Randazzo. To make things more difficult, when they got to Randazzo they would themselves be competing for space with Rodt's withdrawing 15th Panzer Grenadier Division. This road was now under attack from the Allied air forces, which made travel during daylight hours difficult, if not impossible.

Whilst Conrath's forces were making their way northwards, Evelegh's immediate concern was getting his troops through Adrano. The enemy may have fled but the damage inflicted by the Allied air forces and his own artillery imposed its own delays. Moreover, the road, or more accurately the track, north of Adrano was not only narrow but also lined on both sides by ancient stone walls. The German engineers had employed their usual tactics. Large craters in the track were liberally surrounded by anti-tank and anti-personnel mines stopping all wheeled traffic until the sappers were able to come forward to lift the mines and begin filling in the craters. And the infantry advancing over the ground on either side were encountering a new and novel problem – lava fields.

The western slopes of Mount Etna are covered with the detritus of centuries of volcanic activity. The 1843 eruption had been particularly spectacular and the flows which emanated from it had produced fields or 'waves' of lava, some 40 to 50 feet high, which now had to be traversed and, in places where it had crossed the track, cut through. Deep fissures in the lava made it a nightmare for the advancing infantry and soldiers, often unable to gain a solid purchase with their boots, stumbled over the sharp, bare surfaces. Falls were common and the ensuing cuts and scratches quickly became infected, which added to the growing number of non-battle casualties, most still from dysentery and malaria. British gunners, vainly trying to find level surfaces for their gun positions, found their picks and shovels were useless in this terrain and had to resort to digging their trenches with 'fourteen-pound sledgehammers and wedges'.[7] The lava fields also introduced another complication – they magnified the effect of the enemy's artillery, mortars and *Nebelwerfers*, producing shards of lava which multiplied the shrapnel effect of the incoming munitions.

Ten miles north of Adrano lay the small settlement of Bronte. For over 140 years this insignificant town on the slopes of Mount Etna had had an obscure connection with England which came about after King Ferdinand III of Sicily granted land and the honorific title of Duke of Bronte to Admiral Lord Nelson in gratitude for England's naval hero having saved the kingdom from conquest by Napoleon's revolutionary forces. Nelson never set foot on his estate in Bronte, but it was still owned by his descendants up until 1940 when the 6th Duke was expelled by Mussolini and the land confiscated. These were facts that were almost certainly unknown to the English soldiers who would now be fighting to wrestle it back.[8] Bronte had been subjected to heavy Allied bombing, although not as badly as Adrano, Regalbuto, or Randazzo, the last raid occurring as the ground forces prepared to enter the town. It had successfully destroyed three tanks in a withdrawing German column. Post-battle analysis later identified that 1,388 bombs had fallen on the town, demolishing or damaging about a quarter of its buildings.[9]

By the morning of 8 August, it was apparent to the 78th Division, now within a mile of Bronte, that the Germans were intent on using the town to further delay progress. Brigadier Edward Cass, whose 11th Brigade was now in the vanguard, planned a full brigade attack. The East Surreys and Lancashire Fusiliers were tasked to capture the heights on either side of the town whilst the Northamptons were to make a frontal assault. The main actions took place around the town's railway station and after some bitter street fighting the Germans successfully withdrew, their work done.

The Division's ultimate objective was the road junction with *Strada* 120 just west of Randazzo. But to get there they would have to take yet another small Sicilian village, Maletto. Six miles away, it straddled the narrow road and the approaches to it were guarded by two prominent hill features. With Brigadier Howlett's 36th Brigade now leading, Maletto was attacked on the morning of 9 August. The Buffs captured the hillside on the left of the village with relative ease, but the Germans holding the right-hand feature, Mount Rivoglio, proved to be more determined. Fighting continued for the rest of the day. Indeed, with mutual support coming from German positions on adjacent hills, it was proving almost impossible to winkle the Germans out of the surrounding terrain. Conrath's men had managed to buy their commander three additional days, for Maletto was not captured until the evening of 13 August. The 11th Brigade now took up the challenge. Joined by men of the Royal Irish Fusiliers from the Irish Brigade, they pushed at the heels of the retreating Germans throughout the night, eventually reaching the outskirts of Randazzo around 09:30 on 14 August where, at the road junction with *Strada* 120, they effected a link up with the US 9th Division.

Hube issued the formal order for evacuation on 10 August, the day on which the British 78th Division was still struggling to capture Maletto, and Baade was instructed to begin the first troop evacuations on the night of 11 August. The Tortorici Line was to be held until 12 August. Conrath had already split his forces and they were now moving on either side of Mount Etna. Those withdrawing along the eastern coast road between Catania and Messina were having a relatively easy time. Having moved into Catania, Dempsey's XIII Corps was finding it difficult to maintain contact with an enemy which had deployed all of its usual delaying tactics. The terrain did not support aggressive manoeuvre and although, initially, Dempsey tried to deploy both of his divisions side by side this proved impossible. It fell to the 50th Division to lead the advance. As their historian explained:

> The country was exceedingly difficult. Immediately north of Catania the plain ceases, and from the lower slopes of Mount Etna proper the ground falls away fairly steeply to the sea. It is intersected at frequent intervals by deep river beds, nearly all dry at this time of year, but none the less complete obstacles to tracks and wheels owing to their steep and often precipitous sides. The Division, advancing along roads near the coast, was always overlooked from the higher ground inland. The whole countryside

> between Mount Etna and the sea is intensely cultivated with vineyards, olive groves and citrus trees, except where it is covered with lava... The terraces are often ten or twelve feet high. Nearly all roads are bordered by...walls varying from four to twelve feet in height. These walls give good cover, but many are unscalable... The country is thickly dotted with villages and farms, all of which have good fields of fire.[10]

To overcome these difficulties, Rear Admiral Rhoderic McGrigor, the senior British naval officer in Sicily, had suggested to Montgomery that he might emulate the American's use of an amphibious hook. Cunningham had already provided him with not only ships to support such an operation but, crucially, sufficient landing craft to make such an operation viable. Writing after the event, Cunningham, no great fan of Montgomery, was circumspect. 'There were doubtless sound military reasons for making no use of this...priceless asset of sea power, and flexibility of manoeuvre; but it is worth considering... whether much time and costly fighting could not have been saved by even minor flank attacks, which must necessarily be unsettling to the enemy. It must always be for the General to decide. The Navy can only provide the means, and advise on the practicability...of the projected operation. It may be that, had I pressed my views more strongly, more could have been done.'[11] And McGrigor had tried to express those views. As he also later wrote, he 'twice had a big Commando force actually embarked, and once even sailed to cut the very vulnerable communications by road and rail along the coast to the north; but each time the Army called it off.'[12] There would be a third attempt, as we shall see later, but by then it was a case of too little, too late.

After the capture of Troina and the breaking of the Etna Line at San Fratello, the Americans posed the greatest threat to Hube's evacuation plans. Although Fries's 29th Panzer Grenadier Division had to rely solely on the northern coastal highway for its salvation, their recent experiences had given them cause for optimism and, the threat of another American amphibious hook notwithstanding, matters here were under control. But Rodt's 15th Panzer Grenadier Division's position was much more precarious. Should either the Americans break through at Cesaro or the British at Maletto and capture Randazzo before the Germans were ready to cede it, it was likely that the whole Division might go into the bag. This explains, in part, the ferocity of the defence that the British were experiencing at Maletto. In this sector the Tortorici Line extended north from Randazzo. Climbing over mountainous terrain before quickly descending to the northern seaboard at Capo d'Orlando, it followed the general line of *Strada* 116 to its junction on the coast road (*Strada* 113) five miles west of Brolo. The north of this road, stretching south from the coast to beyond Naso, was held by elements of Fries's 29th Panzer Grenadier Division whilst the road to the south, centred on the town of Floresta, was defended by parts of Rodt's 15th Panzer Grenadier Division. Forward of this new main battle line, both commanders had deployed strong rearguards designed to delay Truscott's advancing 3rd Division in the north and Eddy's 9th Division, which was now attacking Cesaro.

Eddy had given the task of capturing Randazzo to Colonel Smythe's 47th Infantry Regiment and to assist him he brought all but one battalion of DeRohan's 60th Infantry Regiment down from the mountains north of *Strada* 120. He felt that this would strengthen the main effort and relieve them of the soul-destroying slog through the mountains which had occupied them since 6 August. Cesaro had been captured on 8 August. It is 17 miles from Cesaro to Randazzo along *Strada* 120 and about a third of the way the road crosses the upper reaches of the Simeto River. Smythe had wanted to get his battalions moving forward so that they could be in a position to jump across it at first light, but in this he was frustrated. The movement out of Cesaro did not begin until 06:00 on 9 August and by the time his troops got to the river they were rebuffed by heavy enemy fire. They spent the rest of the day and into the next morning clearing the west bank, even making contact with the British 78th Division to the south, but the Germans successfully prevented every attempt they made to cross the river. The crossing was finally accomplished early on 11 August, mainly because the Germans had, once again, pulled back voluntarily, and Smythe's troops continued what had now become a cautious advance. Despite the almost total lack of opposition, the German mines were taking their toll and by nightfall on 11 August the 9th Division had only progressed a further three and a half miles. Randazzo was tantalisingly close – but still out of reach.

By this time a frustrated Eddy had sent DeRohan's 60th Infantry Regiment back into the mountains north of *Strada* 120. But their presence was to have little effect. By the time DeRohan's 2nd Battalion entered Floresta early on 13 August their quarry had left as, during the previous evening, Rodt had pulled his troops out of Floresta and Randazzo, one group going back through Novara di Sicilia, whilst the rest went north to *Strada* 113.

Hube had released the detailed evacuation plan on the afternoon of 10 August and instructed Baade that the first troops – from Conrath's *Hermann Göring Panzer Division* – should begin embarking for the mainland the following night, 11-12 August. So far things were going better than he could have hoped for. His divisions were holding strong on the Tortorici Line and, despite being the focus of the heaviest of all of the Allied bombing efforts, he would later be able to hold Randazzo until 13 August, thus getting all of Rodt's Division away. It had certainly been grim, and the combination of Allied fighter-bombers patrolling *Strada* 120 and the Allied Tactical Air Force bombing of the town centre itself had earned the area the sobriquet of 'Death Road', but now, once again, the Allied air effort was to prove a double-edged sword. Two bridges which the Allies would need to use to continue the pursuit had been destroyed and it would take time to repair them.[13] This, coupled with the ever-decreasing width of the battlefield, effectively meant the end of the campaign for both Eddy's 9th (US) Division and Evelegh's 78th (Br) Division.

With hindsight, 11 August was to prove the most challenging day of the withdrawal. It was a day when Hube's whole plan could have unravelled, when the event which the German's had most feared – another amphibious landing behind their lines – nearly trapped both Fries's 29th Panzer Grenadier Division and those elements of Rodt's 15th Panzer Grenadier Division that were still in the process of withdrawing north from Floresta. It didn't. Nearly, but not quite.

Having been frustrated by the German's determined defence at Troina and San Fratello, Patton was hell bent on circumventing the northern end of the Tortorici Line by utilising Bernard's battalion for another amphibious 'hook'. Relieved by Sherman's 7th Infantry Regiment, Bernard's diminished force – estimated now to be only about 650 strong – had been pulled out of the line on 8 August, but with a warning that he might be required to make another landing further up the coast almost immediately. The site selected for this second landing was a beach in the small town of Brolo, five miles behind the enemy front line and, significantly, currently out of range of Truscott's artillery batteries.

Truscott and Bradley were now faced with the situation they had most feared; a gung-ho Patton interfering with the tactical battle. Patton was certainly the driving force behind the manoeuvre and although neither Bradley nor Truscott had objections to the operation in principle, both had reservations regarding its timing. Truscott's reservations centred on the practicalities. Once discovered, the Germans were bound to throw everything that they could at Bernard's isolated force. So how could he best support Bernard's troops once they had landed? And how quickly could he break through the Tortorici Line defences at Cape Orlando and along the Naso ridgeline? Struggling to bring his guns forward from behind the Zoppulo River, Truscott desperately wanted more time, and Bradley was willing to give it to him. Patton had wanted Bradley to launch the hook on the morning of the 10th and was only dissuaded from insisting upon it by a *Luftwaffe* attack on the evening of the 9th which sank one of Task Force 88's LSTs. But he would brook no further delay.

Aware of his subordinates' apparent reticence, Patton sent his deputy commander, General Keyes, forward to ginger them up. Arriving at Truscott's headquarters on the evening of 10 August, Keyes discovered that the divisional commander was evidently planning a further twenty-four-hour delay. Truscott's infantry had yet to close on the German positions on the Naso ridge and his engineers were still struggling to repair *Strada* 113, thereby allowing the Division's artillery batteries to move forward into range. Although Keyes tried to impress on him Patton's 'intense feeling' on the subject of the amphibious operation, Truscott was unmoved and picked up the phone to Bradley, who assured him of his continued support. Some time later, Keyes telephoned Patton. During this conversation he evidently gave his commander the impression that Truscott was unwilling to undertake the landing. Truscott, who was present, took the phone from Keyes and tried to explain his reasoning to the Army commander. They were firm friends, but Patton was having none of it. Refusing to listen to Truscott's explanations, he simply shouted 'Dammit, that operation will go on,' and slammed the phone down. Realising that further prevarication would be pointless, Truscott issued orders to Bernard and began to concentrate on the rest of the divisional plan. An hour later, all hell broke out:

> General Patton came storming into my Command Post giving everybody hell from the Military Police at the entrance right on through until he came to me. He was screamingly angry as only he could be. 'Goddammit, Lucian, what's the matter with you? Are you afraid to fight?' I bristled right back: 'General, you know that's ridiculous and insulting. You have ordered the operation and it is now loading. If you don't think I can carry out orders, you can give the Division to anyone you please. But I will tell you one thing, you will not find anyone who can carry out orders which they do not approve as well as I can.' General Patton changed instantly, the anger all gone. Throwing his arm about my shoulder he said: 'Dammit Lucian, I know that. Come on, let's have a drink – of your liquor.' We did. General Patton departed soon after in his usual good spirits. We turned to the problem of getting through to support Bernard.[14]

Bradley's recollection of these events:

> In mounting the first envelopment from the sea at San Fratello, Patton left the delicate problem of timing to II Corps [but when] I asked Patton if we might not delay the manoeuvre until August 12 [because] the amphibious attack means nothing unless we tie in with Truscott's forces by land, he denied my request... I remonstrated but George held fast. When I left his command post that day with his final directive, I was more exasperated than I have ever been. As a subordinate commander of Patton's I had no alternative but to comply with his orders.[15]

Bradley, Keyes, and Truscott all suspected that Patton's intransigence was based, at least partly, on his decision to send a large party of war correspondents to accompany Bernard's force; that, and, of course, his determination to beat Montgomery to Messina. Having already had one postponement, in the words of the official historian, 'Patton would not relish having to tell the writers that the end run had again been delayed. Patton wanted no unfavourable publicity for the Seventh Army.'[16] Subsequent events justified Truscott's concerns.

Bernard's force set sail at 18:00 on 10 August – one LST, two LCIs, and six LCTs – covered by the cruiser *Philadelphia* and six destroyers. Meanwhile, Truscott committed every element of his division to break through the Naso ridge line defences. Forewarned by the earlier amphibious operation on 7 August, Fries had deployed a strong presence all along the coast road behind his front line. Commanded by Colonel Fritz Polack, it consisted mainly of men from the Colonel's own artillery regiment, various anti-aircraft batteries, and elements of the 1st Battalion 71st Panzer Grenadier Regiment. Polack based his headquarters on the north-eastern slopes of Monte Cipolla, a steep hill close to the shoreline just behind the Naso ridge and midway between the Naso and Brolo Rivers. This hill dominated *Strada* 113 and was, coincidentally, the objective which Truscott had ordered Bernard to seize as soon as he made landfall. The base of Monte Cipolla lay about 450 yards inland from the beach and the feature rose sharply to a height of about 750 feet where, on the very top, it divided into two small knolls. Polack's headquarters was sited on the north-eastern one, on the only usable approach from the beach.

The beach itself was not ideal for an amphibious landing. The Palermo-Messina railway line, which paralleled the shoreline here, ran along on a thirteen-foot-high raised embankment less than a hundred yards inland from the foreshore and behind it, three hundred yards further on, lay *Strada* 113. The area between the railway line and the highway was cultivated with lemon trees and featured a multitude of criss-crossing drainage ditches and terraces, the terraces themselves stone-faced. Remarkably, given the assets that Polack had at his disposal, Bernard managed to get his entire force ashore completely undetected. The first wave landed at 02:43 and by 04:00 he had secured both ends of the beach, captured 10 unsuspecting German guards without firing a shot, got both his tank platoon (five tanks) and his four artillery batteries (two self-propelled and two field) ashore, and already had some of his infantry companies climbing the slopes of Monte Cipolla. The only fly in the ointment was proving to be the underpasses beneath the railway embankment, too narrow for either the tanks or the self-propelled artillery to negotiate. A potential solution was found when recce parties returned suggesting that the relatively dry beds of the Brolo and Naso Rivers could be used to exit these tracked vehicles from the beach. It was when these tracked vehicles were about to set off that Bernard's incredible luck ran out.

First, a German motorcycle appeared at speed from Brolo, apparently heading towards Naso. The American soldiers froze and allowed it to pass, hoping to remain undetected. And they might have been, had a German half-track not appeared on the scene a little while later coming from the other direction. Twenty nervous GIs opened fire killing the driver. Moments later another vehicle arrived, and this was dispatched with a well-aimed bazooka, which wounded the driver and killed his passenger, a German officer. Surprise had been lost. Polack's men on the hilltop now observed the American infantry climbing towards them and opened fire. Quickly realising that his headquarters was about to be overrun, Polack gathered his men retreated down the far slope to Brolo, where he telephoned General Fries and alerted him to the danger.

Events now unfolded in very much the way Truscott had feared. Aware that if this threat to his rear was not removed, Fries threw everything he could at Barnard's isolated force. Although Barnard had easily managed to capture Monte Cipolla, the elements of his force still on the low ground below were now fighting for their lives. The tanks could not get off the beach. Three bellied trying to cross ditches and the last two were immobilised trying to knock down stone walls. Unable to manoeuvre, they had effectively been neutralised. The artillery batteries were more fortunate and by daybreak had manage to conceal themselves in the lemon groves. But more and more German troops were rushing to the scene; and they were coming from both directions along *Strada* 113. A third force, consisting of elements of the troops currently holding Ficarra, were approaching Monte Cipolla via a secondary road from the south. The slopes of Monte Cipolla had become a dangerous place to be. All but two of the fifteen mules that Bernard had taken ashore had been killed trying to resupply the men on the top of the hill and further supplies of food and ammunition to these men was becoming increasingly unlikely. By mid-morning, Bernard's force was effectively fighting as two separate and detached elements.

Up until this moment Bernard had been able to call upon naval gunfire support from the *Philadelphia* and her escorting destroyers. They had been firing on pre-arranged targets and on an opportunity basis, but Davidson, believing that his job had now been done, and also aware that Allied air cover could not be guaranteed beyond midday, set sail for Palermo at 10:25. This was, perhaps, understandable. Bernard had not called for any additional naval support and Davidson was acutely aware that the longer he remained relatively stationary offshore, the more he presented a tempting target for the *Luftwaffe*.

Truscott was anxiously monitoring the situation. Having had the foresight to send a liaison officer armed with a powerful radio to sit alongside Barnard, he was well aware of the situation in the beachhead. But, so far, Bernard seemed to be coping and for the present his most pressing concerns were getting the rest of his Division to press home their attacks on the Naso ridge whilst at the same time continuing to urge his engineers to clear the highway of obstacles so that he could get enough of his artillery units forward to support both the beachhead and the main attack. Fries was equally anxious. So far his men were doing a good job of holding the Americans at bay; so well in fact that he was able to pull troops out of the line in order to deal with the threat to his rear. But until, and unless, that threat was removed there was a great danger that at least half of his Division would not escape the trap the Americans had set for him. By making their way cross-country through Ficarra to San Angelo di Brolo, his 15th Panzer Grenadier Regiment defending the Naso ridge still had a protected escape route, but the 71st Panzer Grenadier Regiment, defending the northern end of the Tortorici Line, was entirely dependent on *Strada* 113 for its salvation.

Currently there was no American battalion within ten miles of Bernard's beleaguered troops, but throughout 11 August Truscott continued to impress upon everyone the absolute necessity of breaking through and linking up with the beachhead as quickly as possible. By mid-morning, all of Barnard's long-range radios had failed. The radio which had been taken into the beachhead by Truscott's liaison officer was now the sole source of information from the beachhead. At 11:40 it carried the following message: 'Enemy counter-attack massing east Brolo 1000 yards. Request air mission on that position and 753513 and 729511. Urgent. Also Navy.' With these requests forwarded up the chain of command, another message arrived twenty minutes later: 'Request all possible artillery support on Brolo east 1000 yards.' Although this was at the maximum range of his medium artillery, Truscott issued the orders and the 155mm Long Toms began engaging.

What was going on? How had the situation deteriorated so quickly? And where had the naval support gone? These were the questions that were anxiously being raised in Truscott's command post as yet more messages poured in. 12:30hrs: 'Motor vehicles and M-6 tanks 3000 yards east and in Brolo. Must have everything.' 13:05: 'Navy say they can't fire until 1630. Must have it now. Air not here. Situation critical.' 13:40: Enemy counter-attacking fiercely. Do something.' 14:25: 'Repeat air and navy immediately. Also on Cape. How about other Dogfaces (artillery)? Can Toms reach Cape? Also navy and air. Situation still critical. Must be constant.'[17]

Just as his ships were about to enter Palermo harbour, Barnard's relayed pleas for naval support reached Davidson via his liaison officer in Seventh Army headquarters. Turning about immediately, he arrived off Brolo shortly after 14:00 and began engaging Polack's counter-attacking forces. At almost the same time twelve A-36s began dropping bombs. Thirty minutes later, twelve more A-36 aircraft appeared and continued the attack. The tide had turned, at least for the moment, and the Germans began retreating. It was then that ship-to-shore communications failed. Not wanting to fire on targets without shore control, and thinking that air had the situation under control, at 15:05 Davidson once again pulled his ships out and headed west. The situation was far from under control. As soon as Barnard lost his air and naval support, the Germans returned in force, this time from the west.

Despite facing increasing pressure from the 7th Infantry Regiment to his front, Colonel Krueger, the commander of the 71st Panzer Grenadier Regiment, had nonetheless withdrawn more men from the line and was personally leading a battalion-sized force to attack the bridgehead. Desperate measures were required if his regiment was to reach Messina safely. Truscott, too, wanted to impose his presence, but because of the German mines and cratered roads was finding it difficult to drive out to his forward regiments. Unable to reach Sherman's 7th Infantry Regiment, he stopped at Colonel Roger's command post (30th Infantry Regiment) where he radioed instructions to Sherman to forget about taking the town of Naso, his original objective; both regiments should now concentrate on breaking through to relieve Barnard's bridgehead.

Back at his own command post, more bad news was pouring in from the bridgehead. 16:10: 'Where is reinforcing infantry? Need Doughboys badly. Another counterattack on. Ammo very short. Have little yellow smoke left.' (Yellow smoke was used to direct air attacks.) 17:25: 'Being counter-attacked by battalion from west. Must have navy and air on 702504 immediately or we are lost.' This coordinate was immediately under the western brow of Mount Cipolla. Bernard was calling down fire on his own positions. 18:50: 'Give navy priority and let them...' At this point radio traffic from the bridgehead ceased and was never resumed. Truscott's staff put two and two together and reflected in silence. Their comrades had been overwhelmed.

By ten o'clock that night an even greater gloom descended on Truscott's command post as radio communications with the forward battalions also broke down and now neither of his two regimental command posts had a clear picture of what was happening to their front. As evening approached, cut off from communicating with the outside world and unable to hold back the Germans who were attacking his troops below, Barnard issued orders for every man to make their way as best they could up onto Monte Cipolla. The time had come to make a last-ditch stand.

The *Philadelphia* arrived for the third time just after Bernard had issued his orders. Still unable to communicate with Davidson, one of the shore fire control officers commandeered a DUKW and went out to establish comms. Seeing it depart, three other DUKWs followed suit taking with them the last of the remaining ammunition. A fifth DUKW remained behind and this was hurriedly sent out to sea to retrieve the three errant craft. Now with a clearer understanding of what was required, Davidson began engaging targets on Cape Orlando, Brolo, and the highway east of Brolo. However, fearful of a blue-on-blue, he refrained from firing on targets which were close to Monte Cipolla itself. After about 15 minutes, Davidson unexpectedly became a target himself. Eight German aircraft began engaging his three ships. A thirty-minute duel ensued, but after the arrival of Allied aircraft the attack was beaten off with only one German plane escaping. Still unable to communicate effectively with Bernard's headquarters and fearful of another attack, Davidson once again, and for the final time, set sail for Palermo. By 19:00 the Germans had full control of *Strada* 113 once again. Intent simply on making their escape, Krueger's men paid little heed to the Americans still remaining on the hillside or in the groves near the beach and began evacuating to the east. The reason for their haste soon became clear. By 22:00 the first of Truscott's relieving forces had appeared. The Germans had abandoned the Tortorici Line and, by the skin of their teeth, escaped to fight on.

During the day Bernard had lost nearly a third of his force, killed, wounded or missing. Truscott later claimed that had he been allowed to wait a day, he might well have captured most of the German defenders. Others have disagreed. One historian later wrote: 'The battalion sent to make the landing had been too small for the job.'[18] whilst Admiral Ruge, the German Naval Commander in Italy, commented that he never understood why this type of operation had not been attempted earlier, 'more frequently, and on a much larger scale'.[19] But, as we now know, Hube had not planned to abandon the Tortorici Line until the night of the 12th; so Truscott might well have been correct.

The Patton-inspired amphibious operation at Brolo certainly concerned Fries and Hube and had potentially threatened what, up to then, had been an exemplary withdrawal operation. But ultimately, it neither delayed Hube's general timetable nor caused him to change his plan. The mountainous terrain, especially in the north, continued to favour the defender and the Allies had not yet broken the Tortorici Line south of Floresta. Furthermore, throughout the month-long campaign the Allies had consistently demonstrated an unwillingness – or inability – to deploy its naval assets to exploit the maritime flank by landing forces in sufficient strength and depth to seriously threaten the Axis rear. And time and space for such an operation was rapidly diminishing.

Hube could continue as planned. That's not to say that the Germans were not experiencing problems with the timetable. From the outset, there was only one coastal road on either side of the Straits serving the embarkation and disembarkation points and this meant that strict traffic control measures had to be put in place. Traffic jams were inevitable and posed a serious risk to evacuating troops, who could not risk being caught in the open and stationary as this would leave them vulnerable to attack from both sea and air. One large Allied air raid during the evening of the 11th, in particular, led to delays which meant that most of the ferries leaving that night operated at less than full capacity. Similar problems were experienced the next night; but this time the problem arose from the practicalities of marshalling large numbers of exhausted men in the dark over unfamiliar terrain. Once again, some ferries were leaving almost empty. Matters were compounded that night when the telephone connection across the Straits failed for a number of hours leading to a suspension of activity. When it was restored, a series of allied night bomber attacks added to the mounting delays.

Hube and Baade had planned to evacuate eight to ten thousand men per night, but after the first two nights of the five-day programme these numbers were not being met. The evacuation timetable was getting dangerously behind schedule. In order to get it back on track, Baade and von Liebenstein decided to begin moving troops as well as equipment during daylight hours. For reasons which we will explore shortly, these first daylight movements of troops on 13 August went largely unmolested and by the morning of 14 August, the evacuation was back on track. On the evening of 12 August Hube ordered his divisions to pull back to their next defensive position which, from north to south, followed the general line of Oliveri to Taormina via Novara and Francavilla. At this point the right wing of Montgomery's 8th Army was geographically closer to Messina than Patton's 7th Army. Conrath's *Hermann Göring Panzer Division*, which now had the shortest distances to travel, was under the least pressure and had effectively already broken clean from Dempsey's pursuing XIII Corps. In the centre, Rodt, who had not yet been forced to surrender Randazzo, had managed to buy Hube an extra day and whilst doing so had also begun to thin out his 15th Panzer Grenadier Division. It was only in the north that Fries's 29th Panzer Grenadier Division had been required to deviate from the original plan, and this was on account of Bernard's unwelcome intervention at Brolo. Thus, some of the 71st Panzer Grenadier Regiment were being forced to withdraw along *Strada* 113 earlier than planned and in daylight, making them vulnerable to attack from both air and sea.

The terrain and the weariness of their enemy would come to the aid of the 29th Panzer Grenadier Division. Although Truscott's men had suffered badly in the preceding five days, his 15th Infantry Regiment, crossing the mountains to the south of *Strada* 113, managed to capture the hilltop town of Patti on 13 August and from there they could now drop down to the highway below. But behind them, the rest of the Division was struggling to make progress.

After *Strada* 113 leaves Brolo and crosses the wide estuary of the San Angelo River it meets a rugged headland known as Cape Calava. As the road climbs up from the river valley it first clings perilously close to the sea on overhanging cliffs before dropping down again to a rocky shore line, which it follows for another four miles or so before entering a tunnel under Cape Calava and emerging on the other side some five miles short of Patti. Although the Germans had prepared the tunnel with explosives, in the haste of their withdrawal they had not initiated the demolition. But what they had done was completely remove the road on the other side. One hundred feet above sea level there was now a 150-foot gap which, potentially, would take several days if not weeks to restore or bypass. Thanks to the American war correspondent Ernie Pyle, what Truscott's engineers achieved in the next twenty-four hours became headline news around the world. By noon on 13 August they had created a 'trestle bridge in the sky', capable of taking jeeps. By mid-afternoon Truscott's artillery batteries were crossing, and by midnight his heaviest loads were getting across. Despite this engineering wonder, the delay that had been imposed saved Fries's forces. It would be another day before Truscott would be able to re-establish contact with the German rearguards.

While all this was taking place, General Patton was planning another 'spectacular'. Even before he became aware of Truscott's latest difficulties, the 7th Army commander had instructed his staff to plan a joint amphibious-airborne operation on the north coast well behind the enemy's current lines. This, he felt, was possible because not only had the Navy now promised him more landing craft but Alexander had also authorised the use of a battalion of the 509th Parachute Infantry Regiment, which was currently based in North Africa. This battalion would drop somewhere near Barcellona and hold an important bridge on *Strada* 113 until relieved by a seaborne force consisting of a reinforced regimental combat team from the 45th Infantry Division landing near Bivio Salica. Together these forces would then attack westwards to link up with Truscott's 3rd Division.

In the 8th Army's area of operations the Tortorici Line had been anchored on the town of Riposto and, in advancing towards it, Dempsey had been trying to push two divisions into the narrow coastal strip which separated Mount Etna from the eastern seaboard; he was, however, finding it difficult to maintain contact. The 5th Division, now under the command of Major-General Gerry Bucknell and operating on the left flank of XIII Corps, was restricted to difficult secondary tracks through the cultivated lava fields on the slopes of Mount Etna, whilst below them Kirkman's 50th Division at least had the benefit of the coast road, *Strada* 114, as its main axis.

As Kirkman's Division moved north from Acireale, the restricted terrain and all the usual problems presented by the German engineers was forcing him to echelon his brigades. Two deep-sided rivers, the Mangano and the Leonardello, took time to cross and this, coupled with the other delays imposed by Conrath's rearguards, meant Conrath's Division had effectively broken clean away. From now on, the resistance that Kirkman's forces would face were simply these strong rearguards, something that had yet to be identified by the British intelligence staffs who were now anticipating that the Germans might attempt to hold the line at Riposto for several days.[20]

British forces entered Riposto on 11 August to find that it had already been abandoned. The next day, 5th Division was relieved in place by 51st Highland Division and Montgomery withdrew Dempsey's corps headquarters making Leese's XXX Corps responsible for the operations of the three divisions remaining in action (50th, 51st (HD), and 78th). On 15 August the 51st and 78th Divisions completed the circuit of Mount Etna and joined forces near Linguaglossa and the 50th Division had advanced to Taormina. However, by this time Hube had already ordered the withdrawal to his final phase line just south of Messina and once again, Montgomery's forces found themselves grasping at the coattails of the retreating rearguards.

With his ground forces making disappointingly slow progress, Montgomery had finally decided on making his own amphibious hook. How much of this was in response to Patton's efforts in the north and how much of it was dictated by a feeling that there might still be an outside chance of reaching Messina first, it is hard to tell. Whatever the motives, Operation BLACKCOCK was to prove a damp squib. The plan involved landing a battalion-sized force ten miles south of Messina near Cap d'Ali from where it was to exploit south – to link up with the 50th Division – and north towards Messina. The force, which was to be commanded by Brigadier Currie (4th Armoured Brigade), sailed from Catania on the evening of 15 August and consisted of No 2 Army Commando (Lt-Col John 'Mad Jack' Churchill); a squadron of tanks from the 3rd County of London Yeomanry (CLY); a troop of 105mm self-propelled guns from 56th Field Battery RA; some jeep-drawn 3.7″ howitzers; a troop of 6-pounder anti-tank guns; and the 295th Field Company RE (less one troop). The Commando landed unopposed thirty minutes later than planned at around 03:00 and in the wrong place. The landing had been made five miles further north than intended on a beach by the village of Scalletta. Having arrived on the wrong beach there was now a lengthy delay as engineer recce parties looked for a suitable place to bring ashore the LCTs which were carrying the CLY's tanks. Churchill's commandos fanned out and established roadblocks on *Strada* 114 either side of the village. The southern roadblock proved to be superfluous; Conrath's forces had already passed north. The fighting here would be the final land skirmishes of the Sicily campaign, although it would take another day for this to become known.[21]

Further south, the 50th Division was still struggling to make progress up *Strada* 113. Having reached Taormina, the coastal road was again blocked. But this time responsibility for this lay with the Royal Navy who, in an attempt to hinder the German retreat, had earlier blown away the part of the road which skirted a cliff face. Although German engineers had managed to effect a bypass around this blockage by lifting the rails of the coastal railway line (which, at this point, entered a tunnel below the cliff) and creating a makeshift road, the tunnel had now been blown and it was estimated that it would take the engineers at least a week to restore the gap in the road. Landing craft had had to be brought up and a temporary ferry service put in place.

With Currie's force effectively isolated, plans were made to reinforce him on the night of 16/17 August by sending the 5th East Yorkshire Regiment and miscellaneous supporting elements up the coast in another amphibious lift.[22] But, as events transpired, these plans would be unnecessary. To the north, Bradley and Truscott were now fighting two battles, one of which was internal. On 15 August, having re-established contact with Fries's forces during the previous afternoon, Truscott's 15th Infantry Regiment was approaching Spadafora, which, unbeknownst to the Allies, was the northern anchor point for Hube's final delay line. Hube intended to hold this line for another twenty-four hours. Still wishing to maintain the momentum of his advance, Truscott ordered his forces to continue fighting during the night and he fully expected to be in Messina by the following day, 16 August. Returning to his command post that afternoon, he was astonished to find General Keyes had arrived with news of another unwanted – and this time, unnecessary – amphibious operation. A regimental combat team from the 45th Infantry Division was to land the next morning on beaches east of Cape Milazzo (the airborne operation having been cancelled). Those beaches were behind Truscott's forward troops. What was Army headquarters thinking?

Truscott could easily imagine the carnage that might have taken place if an amphibious force, arriving in his rear and intending to fight their way off the beaches had found themselves witnessing a road full of traffic heading east towards Messina. Apparently, General Keyes lacked that insight. He was reluctant to cancel the operation and so it went ahead shortly after dawn on 16 August. It fell to a party of Truscott's staff officers to greet them as they disembarked and to tell them that the beach was already in friendly hands.[23] Truscott had been wrong in thinking that he would be in Messina on the 16th. That evening the last of Conrath's *Hermann Göring Panzer Division*, together with the paratroopers that had been assigned to him, left the island leaving behind just a single tank detachment which had been assigned to support Fries's rearguards. Once on the mainland, they joined Rodt's 15th Panzer Grenadier Division, which had already completed their crossings, after which both divisions prepared to move north to the Salerno-Naples area. The only Axis troops now remaining on Sicily were the rearguards of Fries's 29th Panzer Grenadier Division.

Shortly after midnight, Fries's last remaining rearguards pulled back from the Casazza crossroads, four miles north west of Messina, and headed for their evacuation ferries. At 05:30 the two one-armed German generals, Hube and Fries, boarded a ferry and left Sicily. They were followed forty-five minutes later by the final ferry carrying the very last of the German rearguards. At 06:35 von Liebenstein reported that Operation *Lehrgang* was completed and Hube was able to report to Kesselring that not a single German soldier, weapon, or vehicle had been left behind.

Epilogue

For some years this short campaign – it only lasted 38 days – was largely ignored by historians. When it came to writing the official histories, the Canadians were first out of the blocks with the appearance of the Canadian Army's account published in 1956. But it was not until 1963, twenty years after the campaign, that the official US history appeared in print; and it would be a further ten years before the British account was published in 1973. In the meantime, there had, of course, been some unofficial accounts, most notably Hugh Pond's *Sicily* published in 1962. But these were few and far between, generic, and largely uncritical in nature. We had to wait until 1988 for the very first detailed analysis of the campaign to be published; *Bitter Victory*, written by the American Carlo D'Este. D'Este was fortunate in being able to interview and gain access to the papers of many of the key players in the campaign. He was also able to benefit from knowledge of ULTRA. The publication of *Bitter Victory* led to a renewed interest in what, up until then, had perhaps been perceived as a mere prelude to an even more flawed campaign on the Italian mainland.

This account of the Sicily Campaign ends not with Patton's 'triumphant' entry into Messina at 10:00 on 17 August 1943 but with the more prosaic departure of the Axis powers earlier that morning. Although lauded at the time as a great victory – and one which ultimately succeeded in removing Italy from the Axis – the Sicily Campaign is now considered by most historians to have been a flawed, if not a Pyrrhic, victory for the Allies. Indeed, this was an assessment made at the time by an internal War Office after-action review, which described the campaign as 'a strategic and tactical failure' and a 'chaotic and a deplorable example of everything that planning should not be.[1]

Winston Churchill is famously attributed with 'Victories are not won by evacuations.' But the British were able to turn the Dunkirk experience to their advantage, and the Germans attempted to do the same regarding their efforts at Messina. On 15 August, two days before the completion of his evacuation, Hube was already drafting some suggestions for Kesselring's final communiqué. In doing so he began by stressing this very point; that, in his opinion, the British had made unjustifiable claims for the success of the 'catastrophe' which was Dunkirk whereas for Germany 'The end of the Sicilian campaign is actually a full success. After the initial fiasco, the fighting as well as the preparation and execution of the evacuation, with all the serviceable material and men (including the wounded) went according to plan... I consider it as especially harmful when, as happens time and again, one encounters communiqués that do not correspond in any manner with the actual situation...and that appear ridiculous to those who were there.'[2]

Of course, Hube could be free with his criticisms of the 'initial fiasco'. He wasn't there. But his points were well made. The statistics, as far as you can rely on statistics in these situations, are telling. In six days, Baade and von Liebenstein ferried out 39,569 German troops (4,444 of whom were wounded), along with 9,605 vehicles, 94 guns (excluding Baade's flak guns), 47 tanks, 1,100 tons of ammunition, 970 tons of fuel, and 15,700 tons of other equipment and supplies. This was in addition to 12,000 Germans, 4,500 vehicles, and nearly 5,000 tons of supplies which had been sent back earlier. The Italians had done equally well, evacuating 62,182 men, 41 guns, 227 vehicles, 1,000 tons of ammunition and fuel, and 14 mules which added to the 7,000 men and sixty guns which had been evacuated during the period 3-10 August.[3] Some German units came out of the campaign with more vehicles than they went in with, having commandeered them from the Italians.

Sicily made and sometimes destroyed reputations. D'Este was generally uncritical of the American leadership which he felt 'at all levels was generally excellent'.[4] He was less complimentary about Alexander and Montgomery. Was he correct in his assessments? By the very nature of his appointment, Eisenhower was generally removed from the day-to-day prosecution of the campaign. Nevertheless, Sicily helped to cement his reputation as a safe pair of hands and an ideal coalition commander. Alexander, however, continues to divide opinions. Churchill believed that Alexander was 'the best [General] we had: better than Monty'. Alanbrooke, Churchill's CIGS, did not necessarily share this high opinion and was particularly frustrated by Alexander's inability to counter Montgomery when the situation warranted it. However, Alex's urbane and unassuming manner certainly endeared him to many – particularly many Americans, who were, perhaps, dazzled by his 'style' – and there can be no doubt about his credentials: he was a proven and physically brave commander who was arguably *the* most experienced field commander then serving in the British Army. But his *laissez-faire* approach to command often infuriated his subordinates. 'Alex' was a man who liked to command with a light touch and by consensus. Whilst this could be seen as a positive in coalition warfare, it proved to be a disadvantage when it came to dealing with strong personalities such as Montgomery and Patton. The British historian James Holland, a great admirer of Alexander, believes that he has had 'an unfair press for Sicily',[5] but it was not Alexander's finest hour. As the land forces component commander, he should have set the agenda for operations on the island. Instead, he allowed Montgomery, and later Patton, to set their own agendas.

Most books about Patton praise his performance in Sicily and seek to minimise or excuse both the infamous 'slapping incidents' and his inability to play nice with his British Allies. His self-assurance led him into frequent and avoidable personality clashes, both up and down the chain of command. Too often his behaviour was explained away at the time and afterwards as being 'Well, that's just George,' but it alienated him even from the very people who wished him nothing but well. Lucian Truscott, who considered him a great friend, found his leadership in Sicily trying and his relationship with Omar Bradley was irreparably harmed by the Sicilian experience. Even Eisenhower, one of his greatest advocates and defenders, was unable to save him from his ability to self-destruct. His desire to assert a degree of independence from 15th Army Group led to the unnecessary and distracting drive on Palermo, which arguably prevented Bradley from exploiting a fleeting opportunity to complete his push to the north coast and exploit eastwards before Fries's 29th Panzer Grenadier Division had fully deployed.

Operation HUSKY is celebrated as being the most significant joint and combined Allied operation of the Second World War prior to Normandy.[6] Arguments still rage about whether or not it was the largest amphibious operation of the war (it all depends on the metrics). But it was not necessarily a good example of either. Collaboration between land, sea and particularly air was patchy if not downright poor. A lot of this can be put down to the fact that the three component headquarters were geographically dispersed. Admiral Cunningham in his post-operational despatch summed up the position:

> Much discussion was devoted to the best location for the combined headquarters from which the three Commanders-in-Chief should conduct the operation. [There was] an undesirable dispersion in that though the navy and army headquarters moved to Malta from Algiers, the Air Officer Commanding-in-Chief [Tedder] found himself unable to move from his existing headquarters at Marsa, where he was in close touch with his main forces... The separation of the Commanders did not in the event have a serious reaction, but was manifestly undesirable and might have proved extremely awkward had things begun to go awry.[7]

The authors of the US Official History were more critical: 'Unlike the naval planners who co-operated closely with Army planners, the Air Forces refused to co-ordinate planning with either Army or Navy.'[8] In part, this can be explained by the relative junior status of the two air arms and the RAF's insistence on being treated as an equal, and more importantly, an *independent* Service. But it can also be explained by the devil which sits on the shoulders of almost all military commanders – ego. Some of the most scathing criticisms – then and now – centre around the inability of the air and naval forces to influence the land battle; and in particular their failure to interdict Baade's operations across the Straits of Messina. In the last chapter we highlighted Admiral Cunningham's frustration at Montgomery's inability to recognise the advantages of an open maritime flank until it was too late. In an earlier part of his despatch Cunningham had this to say about the relationship of the three services in Sicily: 'It cannot be too clearly recognised that a combined operation is but the opening, under particular circumstances, of a primary army battle… It is upon the army tactical plan for the fulfilment of its object that the combined plan must depend.'

Cunningham over-estimated the value of the three 'end runs' Davidson's Task Force 88 executed along the north coast of Sicily. They did not, in his words, save 'days of costly fighting', but they did perhaps demonstrate the flexibility of sea power and, in particular, the speed and flexibility of the naval planners. He also expressed satisfaction with the level and conduct of naval gunfire support to the seaward flank of the 8th Army – 'satisfactory and effective'. Except, that is, at Augusta, where his ships were unable to engage effectively owing to an 'inability to distinguish our own troops'. Tellingly, Cunningham entirely glossed over the evacuation of the Axis forces across the Strait of Messina. It warranted not a single sentence in either his despatch or that of his subordinate, Vice-Admiral Ramsay.

Commentators have excused Cunningham's unwillingness to send naval forces into the Strait of Messina as being a consequence of his earlier experiences in the First World War, in which he served as a naval captain throughout the Gallipoli campaign and where he had witnessed the devastating effect land-based defences could have on naval forces operating in restricted waters. This would certainly explain his refusal to commit his valuable capital ships to such an enterprise. As the naval historian Stephen Roskill explains, 'The concentrated fire which these defences could bring to bear on warships operating only a mile or two off-shore made it suicidal to attempt to keep patrols in the straits for protracted periods.'[9]

What about limited periods? Cunningham had dismissed trying to do anything during daylight hours but was willing to send patrols into the straits at night. The problem he faced was that the light coastal forces at his disposal – MTBs and MGBs – were, in his opinion, unsuitable for offensive operations. According to Roskill:

> From the middle of July the coastal craft were out every night, and after the beginning of August destroyers were regularly sent to support them. But they found very few targets, the light craft frequently came under heavy fire from the enemy's shore guns, and they lost one MGB and three MTBs on these patrols. A number of running fights took place in the glare of the enemy searchlights, but they had little effect on the evacuation traffic.[10]

So, if the navy couldn't stop the evacuation, what about the air forces? Operation HUSKY highlighted, not for the first time in the war, the inability of the air and land forces to work together with a common understanding of the 'correct' application of air power. From the RAF's perspective, this can be demonstrated quite neatly by the tone of the following excerpts from the British Air Ministry's post-operational analysis.

> The American Army expected to find Air Force representatives actually located within the headquarters of each of its formations as part of the staff, and able to enter into Air force commitments, down as low as divisional level. In the circumstances, this was obviously not possible...
>
> The planning of the operation was made more difficult and complicated by the armies concerned who made no attempt to centralise their planning, and expected air forces to break what was an overall air problem requiring careful co-ordination into a number of detailed uncoordinated tasks, each of which were expected to be discussed with minor army formations spread over North Africa and the Middle East.[11]

Tedder saw the air campaign in a much wider perspective than his army and naval counterparts. Initially he was keen to rest his airmen after the conclusion of the Tunisian campaign and leave it to the Strategic Bomber Force to take on 'more distant targets of strategic value and to shipping strikes when such targets were offered'. Only in the week preceding the invasion itself did he want to target *all* German airfields which could mount operations against the armada, not just those on Sicily itself. He also believed that: 'Heavy scale air operations against western Europe...would impose an additional severe strain on the enemy's air resources and make it unlikely that he would be able to reinforce the Mediterranean theatre without weakening himself dangerously elsewhere.'

After the assault had been launched, Tedder's main effort would continue to be 'aimed at denying the air to the enemy's air forces and the primary bombing target would remain the enemy airfields in Sicily'. This is pure air power doctrine. Before we can be in a position to help the land forces directly, our air forces must clear the air of enemy aircraft by achieving air supremacy or, at the very least, air superiority; and by achieving this, Tedder's air forces would also be able to provide protection to Cunningham's ships. 'Throughout HUSKY and particularly on D-Day plus one, the protection of shipping would be a very heavy commitment.'

Whilst he felt unable to commit himself to moving his headquarters to sit alongside Cunningham and Alexander, Tedder was more than willing to require his subordinate commanders to move their headquarters to co-locate with him. Thus, the Commanding General North West African Air Forces (Maj-Gen Carl Spaatz US), the headquarters of the Coastal Air Force (AVM Hugh Lloyd) and the North West African Tactical Air Forces (Air Marshal Sir Arthur 'Mary' Coningham) together with the advanced operational headquarters of the Strategic Air force (Lt-Gen James Doolittle USA) all moved to Marsa. Allied air policy at the time differentiated between the 'Strategic' effort delivered by heavy and medium bombers and 'Tactical' support – the province of light bombers and fighter-bombers, transport aircraft, and fighter aircraft. Tedder laid down strict policy and procedures for both elements, including the location and subsequent movement of headquarters and airfields and detailed command and control arrangements for each phase of the operation. Tedder was very concerned by the potential risk to his aircraft posed by Allied shipping and land forces. He was right to be concerned. Throughout the campaign there were numerous examples of blue-on-blue actions. But it went both ways. There were also numerous occasions when Allied aircraft would strafe and bomb army units on the ground and on more than one occasion army formation headquarters found themselves the unwitting targets of Allied Air.

Tedder blamed a failure of intelligence for his staff's inability to draw up plans for the interception of Baade's operations, claiming that as late as 4 August the Allied Joint Intelligence Committee had written a paper entitled 'Estimate of enemy capabilities to evacuate Sicily' which suggested that 'at the present time there is no sign that the enemy intends an evacuation of Sicily and there is evidence that reinforcements still continue to reach the islands.' Did that really absolve him of all responsibility to begin some form of contingency planning for such an eventuality? That no such planning had taken place is evident by the shock that was felt when Alexander's signal regarding the intelligence he was picking up on the ground arrived. 'It was not until 2210 hours on 14 August that General Alexander...informed Air Chief Marshal Tedder.'

Strikes on the Straits had actually already begun much earlier. On the night of 4/5 August the Strategic Air Force deployed 60 night-flying Wellingtons to attack the Straits at Messina. However, because Allied light naval craft were also operating in the area, they were instructed to confine their attention to the marshalling yards only. Ninety-seven tons of bombs were dropped and after a 4,000 pounder was seen to burst in the marshalling yards, the air crews returned to their bases congratulating themselves on a job well done. The bombers returned on the next night in greater strength – over 100 Wellingtons this time – and their targets were now the barges and ferry traffic. Low cloud and haze prevented effective identification of the targets, and the mission achieved very little. The same applied on the next night when more bad weather meant that just 40 aircraft got airborne, of which only 31 found the target. Night bombing continued for the next seven nights and was considered to be 'extremely effective' – at least in Allied eyes. As we now know, on 13 August the Axis evacuation was in full swing and yet it was on this day that the night bombing effort was diverted to targets on the Italian mainland.

Nowhere in the after-action reports of Allied Air can we detect any elements of real self-reflection or self-criticism. 'Flak in the Messina Strait was encountered only by aircraft undertaking offensive action. This was considered to indicate that the enemy was husbanding his ammunition... By this date [15 August] the Allied Headquarters in Sicily had come to the conclusion that not more than 10,000 Germans were still in the island and that these could easily be evacuated in the next two days... It will be surprising if more than a thousand or so Germans are caught.'[12] The pilots that flew missions into a barrage of flak were undoubtedly incredibly brave, but one comes away thinking that there was a general atmosphere of 'We'll try but really nothing can be done' when it came to a concerted effort to prevent the evacuation. When it came to interdicting the Axis evacuation, Tedder, by and large, left Coningham to his own devices. When the commander of the Tactical Air Force requested the help of the Strategic Air Force, particularly with daylight bombing, it was denied on the basis that they were needed to strike targets further afield.[13]

Many histories are critical of various aspects of the air effort in Sicily and all appear to agree on the abject failure of Air when it comes to the Axis evacuation. For a more balanced and revisionist account, see Alexander Fitzgerald-Black's recently published account of the Allied Air Forces in the Sicilian Campaign, *Eagles over Husky*.

Glossary

Abteilung	roughly battalion or detachment
Aufklärungs Abteilung	Reconnaissance Detachment/Battalion
Bataillon	Battalion
Battaglione	Battalion
Brigata	Brigade
Corpo	Corps
Deutsch-Italienische Panzerarmee	German-Italian Tank Army
EUREKA	British radar homing transmitter used by aircraft to home in on Drop and Landing Zones; paired with a receiver device codenamed REBECCA fitted in the aircraft
Fallschirmjäger	Parachutist or Paratrooper
Fliegerführer Tunesien	Flying/Flight Leader Tunisia
General der Panzertruppe	General of Armoured Troops
Generale di Brigata	Brigade General
Generale di Corpo d'Armata	Army Corps General
Generale di Divisione	Division General
Generalfeldmarschall	General Field Marshal
Generalleutnant	Lieutenant-General
Generalmajor	Major-General
Gruppo Mobili	Mobile Group
Gruppo Tattici	Tactical Group
Heer	Army
Heeresgruppe Afrika	Army Group Africa

Infanterie	infantry
Kampfgruppe	Battle Group
Korps	Corps
LCA	Landing Craft Assault, British landing craft
LCI	Landing Craft Infantry
LCT	Landing Craft Tank
LCVP	Landing Craft Vehicles & Personnel
LSI	Landing Ship Infantry
Leutnant	2nd Lieutenant
LST	Landing Ship Tank
Militärbefehlshaber	Military Commander
MT	Motor Transport
Oberbefehlshaber Süd	Chief Command South
Oberleutnant	1st Lieutenant
Oberst	Colonel
Oberstleutnant	Lieutenant-Colonel
Panzerarmee	Tank Army
Panzer Aufklärungs Abteilung	Armoured Reconnaissance Battalion
Pionier	pioneer; engineer or sapper
Regia Aeronautica	Italian Royal Air Force
Regia Marina	Italian Royal Navy
Reggimento	Regiment
Regio Esercito	Italian Royal Army
Settore Aeronautico Nord	Northern Air Sector (Italian)
Settore Aeronautico Sud	Southern Air Sector (Italian)
Squadra	squadron
Stick	party of paratroopers assigned to a dropping aircraft; the number varied according to the aircraft involved and/or mission

Endnotes

Introduction

1. Quote from John Philip Jones, **Battles of a Gunner Officer** (Barnsley: Pen & Sword, 2014), p. 73
2. See Eric Morris, **Circles of Hell** (London: Hutchinson, 1993), p. 118
3. For 630 gun figure and command arrangements see Brigadier C. J. C. Molony, **The Mediterranean and Middle East, Volume V: The Campaign in Sicily 1943 and the Campaign in Italy 3rd September 1943 to 31st March 1944** (London: HMSO, 1973), p. 235; HAC involvement cited in Jones, **Battles of a Gunner Officer**, p. 73
4. See Molony, **The Campaign in Sicily 1943**, p. 236; for battleship involvement in immediate pre-landing bombardment see Morris, **Circles of Hell**, p. 118
5. For details of the course of planning see for example Lieutenant-Colonel Albert N. Garland & Howard McGaw Smyth, **Sicily and the Surrender of Italy** (Washington DC: Office of the Chief of Military History, Department of the Army, 1993), pp. 16, 23-24, 67-68, 258-260; Gioia is sometimes rendered Gioija
6. See Lieutenant-Colonel G. W. L. Nicholson, **Official History of the Canadian Army in the Second World War, Volume II: The Canadians in Italy 1943-1945** (Ottawa: Edmond Cloutier, 1958), pp. 186-187
7. Quotes from Molony, **The Campaign in Sicily 1943**, p. 223
8. See Nicholson, **The Canadians in Italy 1943-1945**, p. 187
9. See Nicholson, **The Canadians in Italy 1943-1945**, p. 187; Garland & McGraw Smyth, **Sicily and the Surrender of Italy**, p. 260; and Morris, **Circles of Hell**, p. 120
10. See Morris, **Circles of Hell**, p. 121
11. Quotes from Molony, **The Campaign in Sicily 1943**, pp. 222-223
12. See Morris, **Circles of Hell**, p. 120
13. See Molony, **The Campaign in Sicily 1943**, p. 222-223
14. See Molony, **The Campaign in Sicily 1943**, pp. 231-232
15. See Morris, **Circles of Hell**, p. 121
16. See Molony, **The Campaign in Sicily 1943**, p. 228
17. Figures cited in Bryn Evans, **The Decisive Campaigns of the Desert Air Force 1942-1945** (Barnsley: Pen & Sword Aviation, 2014), p. 107
18. See Molony, **The Campaign in Sicily 1943**, pp. 236-238 and Table III 'Sorties flown by Mediterranean Air Command dusk 17th August-dusk 2nd September 1943 (excluding anti-shipping operations and attacks on ports)', p. 254
19. See Nicholson, **The Canadians in Italy 1943-1945**, p. 192

20. See Nicholson, **The Canadians in Italy 1943-1945**, pp. 191-192; and ibid., Map 6 'The Landings in Southern Italy 3-5 September 1943', between pp. 190-191; for artillery piece numbers & details see ibid., p. 204
21. See Molony, **The Campaign in Sicily 1943**, pp. 234-235; the 'Royal Marine Commando' referred to in the Official History was likely Royal Marine A Commando, later rechristened 40 (RM) Commando; see for example James D. Ladd, **Commandos and Rangers of World War II** (London: BCA, 1978), Appendix 7 'Unit Histories', entry for '40 (RM) Commando', p. 261
22. The LCA was a 41-foot twin-engine wooden vessel with a displacement of thirteen tons capable of carrying thirty-five men and 800lb of equipment at a speed of seven knots with a range of fifty to eighty miles; see Ladd, **Commandos and Rangers of World War II**, Appendix 4 'Landing Ships, Craft, Amphibians and Other Vehicles', entry for 'Minor landing craft carrying men etc. from ship to shore', p. 245
23. See Nicholson, **The Canadians in Italy 1943-1945**, pp. 203-206
24. See Molony, **The Campaign in Sicily 1943**, p. 238; and Nicholson, **The Canadians in Italy 1943-1945**, p. 206. The DUKW was an amphibious version of the standard US Army 2.5-ton GMC truck; for details see for example Molony, Appendix: 'The DUKW', p. 147
25. See Molony, **The Campaign in Sicily 1943**, pp. 240-241

Chapter 1

1. See for example Major-General I.S.O. Playfair, **The Mediterranean and Middle East, Volume IV: The Destruction of the Axis Forces in Africa** (London: HMSO, 1966), pp. 1-2; for a more detailed account see Barrie Pitt, **The Crucible of War Volume II: Auchinleck's Command** (London: Cassell, 2001), pp. 292-298
2. See Pitt, **The Crucible of War Volume II**, pp. 337-339; Id., **The Crucible of War Volume III: Montgomery and Alamein**, pp. xi-xiii; and Playfair, **The Destruction of the Axis Forces in Africa**, pp. 1-2, 113
3. For details of the deception effort see for example Playfair, **The Destruction of the Axis Forces in Africa**, pp. 17-19; and Pitt, **The Crucible of War Volume III: Montgomery and Alamein**, pp. 74-76
4. For the LIGHTFOOT plan see Playfair, **The Destruction of the Axis Forces in Africa**, pp. 5, 34-35; and Pitt, **The Crucible of War Volume III: Montgomery and Alamein**, p. 71
5. For the SUPERCHARGE plan see for example Playfair, **The Destruction of the Axis Forces in Africa**, pp. 53, 64-65
6. Cited in Barrie Pitt, **The Crucible of War Volume III: Montgomery and Alamein**, p. 217
7. Sometimes rendered Tel el Aqqakir or Aqqaqir
8. Currently rendered Bwayrat al Hasun
9. For details from the British perspective see for example Playfair, **The Destruction of the Axis Forces in Africa**, pp. 109-112; for the US perspective see George F. Howe, **Northwest Africa: Seizing the Initiative in the West** (Washington DC: Office of the Chief of Military History, Department of the Army, 1993), pp. 10-15
10. See Playfair, **The Destruction of the Axis Forces in Africa**, pp. 112-114; for a table of the HQ structure see Howe, **Northwest Africa: Seizing the Initiative in the West**, 'Chart 1 – AFHQ Organisation, 1 November 1942', p. 34
11. Quote from Howe, **Northwest Africa: Seizing the Initiative in the West**, p. 16; see also Playfair, **The Destruction of the Axis Forces in Africa**, p. 114

12. For details of the Allied ground numbers and Order of Battle see Major-General I.S.O. Playfair, **The Destruction of the Axis Forces in Africa**, pp. 126-127; and George F. Howe, **Northwest Africa: Seizing the Initiative in the West**, pp. 42, 49, 51-53
13. Figures cited in Playfair, **The Destruction of the Axis Forces in Africa**, p. 130
14. For details of the vessels involved see for example Playfair, **The Destruction of the Axis Forces in Africa**, Table 'Operation "Torch" – Maritime Forces Engaged', p. 139; and Howe, **Northwest Africa: Seizing the Initiative in the West**, p. 49
15. See Playfair, **The Destruction of the Axis Forces in Africa**, p. 116
16. For vessel numbers and some warship names see Playfair, **The Destruction of the Axis Forces in Africa**, Table 'Operation "Torch" – Maritime Forces Engaged', p. 139; latter figure (thirty-one) cited in ibid., former figure (twenty-eight) cited in Howe, **Northwest Africa: Seizing the Initiative in the West**, p. 46
17. For units and manpower figures see Howe, **Northwest Africa: Seizing the Initiative in the West**, pp. 42-44
18. Sometimes rendered Fédala, the port was renamed Mohammedia in 1960
19. Combat Loader vessel numbers cited in Playfair, **The Destruction of the Axis Forces in Africa**, Table 'Operation 'Torch' – Maritime Forces Engaged', p. 139; Port Lyautey was renamed Kenitra in 1956, sometimes rendered Quneitra
20. For detailed breakdowns of the composition, strength and equipment of the three Forces see Table 1 – 'Personnel and Vehicles assigned to Force "X" (Blackstone), as of 22 October 1942'; Table 2 – Personnel and Vehicles assigned to Force "Y" (Brushwood), as of 22 October 1942; and Table 3 – Personnel and Vehicles assigned to Force "Z" (Goalpost), as of 22 October 1942 in Howe, **Northwest Africa**, pp. 101, 122 & 151
21. For a detailed account of the French side of the matter including *Général de Division* Béthouart's unsuccessful coup see Howe, **Northwest Africa**, Chapter V 'The French Decide to Fight', pp. 89-96
22. See Howe, **Northwest Africa**, pp. 128-134
23. Mehdia is sometimes rendered Mehdyia
24. For a detailed account of the Mehdia-Port Lyautey landing see Howe, **Northwest Africa**, pp. 147-168
25. For a detailed account of the Safi landing see Howe, **Northwest Africa**, pp. 97-114
26. See Howe, **Northwest Africa**, pp. 121-126
27. See Howe, **Northwest Africa**, pp. 121, 131, 136-137
28. Figures cited in Howe, **Northwest Africa**, p. 144
29. For details se Howe, **Northwest Africa**, pp. 142-145, 171-174
30. Figures cited in Howe, **Northwest Africa**, p. 173
31. See Playfair, **The Destruction of the Axis Forces in Africa**, Table 'Operation "Torch" – Maritime Forces Engaged', p. 139
32. See Playfair, **The Destruction of the Axis Forces in Africa**, pp. 130, 134; and Howe, **Northwest Africa**, p. 185
33. See Playfair, **The Destruction of the Axis Forces in Africa**, pp. 135-136; and Howe, **Northwest Africa**, pp. 185-186
34. Quoted from Howe, **Northwest Africa**, p. 186
35. Quoted from Playfair, **The Destruction of the Axis Forces in Africa**, p. 136
36. Bou Zadjar is sometimes rendered Mersa bou Zedjar, Les Andalouses is currently known as El Anssar and Arzew is sometimes rendered Arzeu
37. For planning details see Howe, **Northwest Africa**, pp. 47-49; and Playfair, **The Destruction of the Axis Forces in Africa**, pp. 146-147. Tafaraoui is sometimes rendered Tafraoui
38. Details from Howe, **Northwest Africa**, pp. 48, 193

39. See Playfair, **The Destruction of the Axis Forces in Africa**, p. 147; 09:45 rendezvous time cited in ibid., Map 'OPERATION "TORCH" The Assault on Oran' pp. 146-147; 09:30 cited in Howe, **Northwest Africa**, p. 193
40. For landing force vessel numbers see Playfair, **The Destruction of the Axis Forces in Africa**, Chart 'Landing Groups and Escorts' between pp. 146-147; for landing force strength figure see Howe, **Northwest Africa**, footnote 5, p. 195; for SS Batory and Bachaquero details see ibid., pp. 195, 196
41. See Howe, **Northwest Africa**, p. 193
42. For a detailed account of the subsidiary landings see Howe, **Northwest Africa**, pp. 193-202
43. For an account of the action see for example James D. Ladd, **Commandos and Rangers of World War II** (London: BCA, 1978), pp. 108-109
44. See Howe, **Northwest Africa**, pp. 210-211
45. For a detailed account of the raid see Christopher Shore and Giovanni Massimello, **A History of the Mediterranean Air War, 1940-1945: Volume 3** (London: Grub Street Press, 2016) pp. 60-63; see also Playfair, **The Destruction of the Axis Forces in Africa**, p. 149; and Howe, **Northwest Africa**, pp. 204-205
46. See Howe, **Northwest Africa**, pp. 211-212; and Playfair, **The Destruction of the Axis Forces in Africa**, p. 150
47. Figures cited in Howe, **Northwest Africa**, p. 202
48. For detailed if slightly contradictory accounts of the action see Howe, **Northwest Africa**, pp. 202-204; and Playfair, **The Destruction of the Axis Forces in Africa**, pp. 147-149
49. Figures cited in Howe, **Northwest Africa**, p. 204
50. For details see for example Lt.-Col. T.B.H. Otway, **Airborne Forces**, pp. 63-70; Karel Margry, 'Tragino 1941: Britain's First Paratroop Raid', **After the Battle Magazine** (No. 81, 1993), pp. 8-29; and George Millar, **The Bruneval Raid: Flashpoint in the Radar War** (London: Bodley Head, 1974)
51. Lieutenant-Colonel Raff's unit is sometimes referred to as being part of the 503rd Parachute Infantry Regiment but it was redesignated as the 2nd Battalion 509th Parachute Infantry Regiment on 2 November 1942, the day before moving to Cornwall for the Oran operation; see for example Gordon Rottman, **US Army Airborne 1940-90** (London: Osprey, 1990), p. 12; and the **National Museum for the United States Army** website, '509th Infantry Regiment History' page at https://armyhistory.org/509th-infantry-regiment/, accessed on 08/10/2019
52. See Gerard M. Devlin, **Paratrooper! The Saga of U.S. Army and Marine Parachute and Glider Combat Troops During World War II** (New York: St. Martin's Press, 1979), pp. 138-145. EUREKA was a British electronic ground transponder beacon weighing twenty-eight pounds complete with collapsible aerial and battery used by Airborne Pathfinder units to mark drop and landing zones; it was paired with the 100-pound, aircraft mounted REBECCA transceiver; for details see for example Otway, **Airborne Forces**, Appendix D 'Radar Homing Devices', pp. 405-406
53. Dates, aircraft & troop numbers & flights, locations and timings cited in Shore & Massimello, **A History of the Mediterranean Air War, 1940-1945: Volume 3**, p. 59; Devlin and Howe cite a total of 556 paratroopers; See Devlin, **Paratrooper!**, p. 151; and Howe, **Northwest Africa**, p. 213
54. For a detailed account see Devlin, **Paratrooper!**, pp. 149-162; see also Howe, **Northwest Africa**, pp. 212-213; and Shore & Massimello, **A History of the Mediterranean Air War**, pp. 58-60
55. see Howe, **Northwest Africa**, pp. 241-244; and Playfair, **The Destruction of the Axis Forces in Africa**, pp. 143-144

56. For details see Playfair, **The Destruction of the Axis Forces in Africa**, Table 'Operation 'Torch' – Maritime Forces Engaged', p. 139
57. See Playfair, **The Destruction of the Axis Forces in Africa**, p. 137; and **Naval-History.Net** website, page for 'HMS Panther (G41) – P Class Destroyer' at http://www.naval-history.net/xGM-Chrono-10DD-49P-Panther.htm, accessed 15/10/2019
58. For details of the evolution of COPPs and an account of their involvement in TORCH see for example Ladd, **Commandos and Rangers of World War II**, pp. 57-67; for details of the various types of canoes employed by COPPs see ibid., pp. 246-247
59. See Bryn Evans, **With the East Surreys in Tunisia, Sicily and Italy 1942-1945** (Barnsley: Pen & Sword Military, 2012), p. 8
60. See Howe, **Northwest Africa**, pp. 234-236, 239-240; and Playfair, **The Destruction of the Axis Forces in Africa**, pp. 142-145. The details vary in some instances between the accounts
61. See Ladd, **Commandos and Rangers of World War II**, pp. 124-126; Howe, **Northwest Africa**, pp. 234-239; and Playfair, **The Destruction of the Axis Forces in Africa**, pp. 142-143, 145
62. See Howe, **Northwest Africa**, pp. 244-249
63. See **Naval-History.Net** website, page for 'HMS Cowdray (L52) – Type II, Hunt-class Escort Destroyer' at http://www.naval-history.net/xGM-Chrono-10DE-Cowdray.htm, accessed 20/10/2019
64. See the **uboat.net** website, page for 'USS Leedstown (AP 73)' at https://uboat.net/allies/merchants/ships/2398.html, accessed 20/10/2019
65. For a detailed account see Howe, **Northwest Africa**, pp. 215-225
66. Figures cited in Howe, **Northwest Africa**, p. 227 and Footnote 32, p. 228
67. For a detailed account see Howe, **Northwest Africa**, pp. 249-252

Chapter 2

1. Bougie is currently known as Béjaëa and Djidjelli as Jijel
2. Ship details from John Grehan & Martin Mace, **Operations in North Africa and the Middle East 1942-1944** (Barnsley: Pen & Sword, 2015), pp.#-#; see also Howe, **Northwest Africa**, p. 278; and Playfair, **The Destruction of the Axis Forces in Africa**, p. 153
3. Maison Blanche is currently known as Houari Boumediene Airport
4. See for example Grehan & Mace, **Operations in North Africa and the Middle East 1942-1944**, pp. ##; and Howe, **Northwest Africa**, p. 278
5. For details see Grehan & Mace, **Operations in North Africa and the Middle East 1942-1944**, pp. ##; Howe, **Northwest Africa**, p. 278; Playfair, **The Destruction of the Axis Forces in Africa**, p. 154; **uboat.net** website, page for 'HMS Tynwald (D 69)' at https://uboat.net/allies/warships/ship/12307.html, accessed 28/10/2019; Clyde Maritime website, page for 'Karanja 1930 HMS –Landing Ship Infantry' at http://forums.clydemaritime.co.uk/viewtopic.php?t=24947, accessed 28/10/2019; ibid., page for 'Cathay 1924 HMS – Armed Merchant Cruiser' at http://forums.clydemaritime.co.uk/viewtopic.php?t=24223, accessed 28/10/2019; and **Naval-History.Net** website, page for 'HMS ROBERTS – Roberts Class 15 in gun Monitor ' at https://www.naval-history.net/xGM-Chrono-03Mon-Roberts.htm, accessed 28/10/2019
6. See Howe, **Northwest Africa**, p. 278
7. Bône is currently known as Annaba
8. See quote from Down, cited in Victor Dover, **The Sky Generals** (London: Cassell, 1981), p. 86

9. See Lt.-Col. T.B.H. Otway, **Airborne Forces**, p. 34; for detailed account of the long and sometimes tortuous process of establishing and initially developing the British Airborne Force see William F. Buckingham, **Paras: The Birth of British Airborne Forces**, especially pp. 168-199
10. See Otway, **Airborne Forces**, pp. 56-57; and Hilary St. John Saunders, **The Red Beret: The Story of the Parachute Regiment at War 1940-1945** (London: Michael Joseph, 1950), pp. 52, 71-73
11. See for example Harry Ward, **The Yorkshire Birdman: Memoirs of a Pioneer Parachutist** (London: Robert Hale, 1990), p. 146
12. See Julian Thompson, **Ready for Anything: The Parachute Regiment at War 940-1982** (London: Weidenfeld & Nicolson, 1989), p. 41; and **The Pegasus Archive** website, Origins Archive, Roll of Honour Section, Table entry for Private Thomas Henry Newton at www.pegasusarchive.org/roll.htm, accessed 01/11/2019. The static-line strop is a length of thick webbing strap connected to the parachute canopy inside the parachute pack. The other end of the strop is connected to a strong point inside the aircraft by the parachutist and automatically pulls the canopy and rigging lines out of the parachute pack as the parachutist drops away from the aircraft
13. For a complete list with dates see for example Otway, **Airborne Forces**, pp. 54-55
14. See Otway, **Airborne Forces**, pp. 61-62, 74
15. See Thompson, **Ready for Anything**, pp. 41-43; the other fatalities were Privates Donald Reid and Leslie Shelley although it is unclear who was involved in what particular mishap and the detached static-line strop may have been the same victim as the Roman Candle; see **The Pegasus Archive** website, Origins Archive, Roll of Honour Section, Table entries for Lieutenant Peter Dennis Hawes Street, Private Donald Jack Reid & Private Leslie Albert George Shelley at www.pegasusarchive.org/roll.htm, accessed 01/11/2019. 'Roman Candle' was the slang term for the appearance of a partly deployed canopy streaming out from the parachute pack. It was caused by the rigging lines emerging from the pack before the parachute canopy was fully deployed, becoming entangled with the canopy and preventing it from developing fully
16. See Maurer Maurer, **Air Force Combat Units World War II** (Washington DC: US Government Printing Office, 1961), pp. 130-131; the British official and semi-official accounts refer to the lift being provided by the 60th Troop Carrier Group and misspell Colonel Dorsett as Dorset; see Otway, **Airborne Forces**, p. 74; and Saunders, **The Red Beret**, pp. 75, 79-80
17. See Saunders, **The Red Beret**, p. 75; embarkation date cited in Major-General John Frost, **A Drop Too Many** (London: Sphere, 1983), p.64
18. See Lt-Col. Howard N. Cole, **On Wings of Healing**, p. 14
19. See Otway, **Airborne Forces**, p. 74; and Saunders, **The Red Beret**, pp. 75-77
20. According to Saunders' semi-official Commando history there were two airfields, at Allerlick and Duzzerville; it is unclear which location the 3rd Parachute Battalion descended upon as most accounts simply refer to Bône airfield; see Hilary St. John Saunders, **The Green Beret: The Commandos at War** (London: Michael Joseph, 1949), p. 133. The location was presumably the current site of Rabah Bitat Airport
21. See Saunders, **The Red Beret**, pp. 79-80
22. See Playfair, **The Destruction of the Axis Forces in Africa**, p. 171
23. See Saunders, the **Red Beret**, pp. 80-81; and Thompson, **Ready for Anything**, p. 44
24. See for example Saunders, **The Green Beret**, p. 133; and Howe, **Northwest Africa**, p. 278
25. I am indebted to Mr Jeremy Stoke for providing career details, documentation and private correspondence regarding his father, Lieutenant Gordon Alexander 'Mick' Stoke MBE DSC RN

26. See Saunders, **The Green Beret**, p. 133
27. See Saunders, **The Green Beret**, p. 133
28. See Saunders, the **Red Beret**, pp. 80-81; and Thompson, **Ready for Anything**, p. 44; 17 November withdrawal date cited in Otway **Airborne Forces**, p. 78
29. Quote and role details cited in letter from then-Sub-Lieutenant Gordon Alexander 'Mick' Stoke DSC RN to his family in the UK, dated 13/01/1943
30. Dates and figures cited in A. D. Divine, **Road to Tunis** (London: Collins, 1944), pp. 239-240. I am again indebted to Mr Jeremy Stoke for bringing this source to my attention
31. Quoted from Divine, **Road to Tunis**, p. 240; for involvement in moving burning vessels and subsequent award of the MBE see letter from then-Sub-Lieutenant Gordon Alexander 'Mick' Stoke DSC RN to his family in the UK, dated 13/01/1943; and **The London Gazette**, No. 36001, Tuesday 4 May 1943, p. 2003
32. The US official history refers to the operation involving thirty-three C-47s but Devlin's account refers to twenty-two, which is supported by his figure of 350 parachutists; see Howe, **Northwest Africa**, p. 279; Devlin, **Paratrooper! The Saga of U.S. Army and Marine Parachute and Glider Combat Troops During World War II** (New York: St. Martin's Press, 1979), pp. 169-171; for presence of British Signals teams see Otway, **Airborne Forces**, p. 76
33. See Howe, **Northwest Africa**, p. 279; for a detailed account see Devlin, **Paratrooper!**, pp. 164-174
34. See Otway **Airborne Forces**, pp. 75-76; and Saunders, **The Red Beret**, p. 81
35. The sources are unclear but the rear party may have been made up of T Company in part or in its entirety
36. See Thompson, **Ready for Anything**, p. 45; 07:00 take-off time cited in Saunders, **The Red Beret**, p. 83, 07:30 take-off time cited in Otway, **Airborne Forces**, p. 76
37. See Thompson, **Ready for Anything**, pp. 45-46
38. See Thompson, **Ready for Anything**, p. 46; 425 figure cited in ibid., p. 47; 16th Parachute Field Ambulance involvement cited in Cole, **On Wings of Healing**, p. 16
39. Quotes from Thompson, **Ready for Anything**, p. 46; and Otway, **Airborne Forces**, pp. 76-77
40. See Saunders, **The Red Beret**, p. 83; 11:00 take-off time cited in Otway, **Airborne Forces**, p. 76
41. See Saunders, **The Red Beret**, p. 86; although usually referred to as a mine the Hawkins device was officially designated the 'Grenade, Hand, Anti-Tank, No. 75'; it was housed in a 150 x 75mm rectangular metal casing equipped with a chemical ignition and could be used as an anti-tank mine or demolition device. The Gammon bomb, officially the No. 82 Grenade, was the invention of Captain R. C. S. Gammon MC from the 1st Parachute Battalion. It consisted of a stockinette bag containing plastic explosive attached to a pull-cord with an instantaneous impact fuse and weighed approximately two and a half pounds
42. See Saunders, **The Red Beret**, pp. 87-88; and testimony from Captain Miles Whitelock, Adjutant, 1st Parachute Battalion; cited in Thompson, **Ready for Anything**, pp. 48-49. The members of the 1st Parachute Squadron RE killed in the incident were Captain Patrick Grattan Geary; Lieutenant John Raymond Holland; Lieutenant George Oscar Napier White; Corporal Reginald Albert Mercer; Lance-Sergeant William Muir; Lance-Sergeant Laurence Dubois Sayer; Lance-Corporal Elgar Frederick Harris; Lance-Corporal Frederick Sydney Hill; Lance-Corporal Francis William Hornsby; Lance-Corporal Norman Thomas Manning; Sapper Albert Arthur Calcott; Sapper Jack David Elvidge; Driver Jack Mason Hillings; Sapper John William Mitchell; Sapper Victor John Mitchell; Sapper Leslie William Moat; Sapper John Albert Rickelton; and Sapper Frank C. Stanmore

43. See Cole, **On Wings of Healing**, pp. 17-19; Both Otway and Saunders give Lieutenant Robb's rank as Captain but Cole consistently refers to him as Lieutenant throughout this period; see Otway, **Airborne Forces**, p. 78; and Saunders, **The Red Beret**, p. 88
44. For details of the action overall see testimony from Captain Miles Whitelock, Adjutant, 1st Parachute Battalion; cited in Thompson, **Ready for Anything**, p. 49; see also Saunders, **The Red Beret**, p. 88; and Otway, **Airborne Forces**, pp. 76-77
45. The 1st Parachute Battalion dead appear to have included Captain John Rattray Chalmers Stewart; Sergeant Desmond Patrick Barnewall; Private Arthur Thomas Cowley; Private Joseph Higgins; Private Robert Stirling; and Private David Agar Watton
46. See Otway, **Airborne Forces**, pp. 77; for a more detailed account of the 1st Parachute Battalion's activities see Saunders, **The Red Beret**, pp. 88-92
47. See Otway, **Airborne Forces**, p. 78; and Frost, **A Drop Too Many**, p. 73
48. See Frost, **A Drop Too Many**, pp.73-74
49. See Frost, **A Drop Too Many**, p. 76
50. See Saunders, **The Red Beret**, p. 93; Cole, **On Wings of Healing**, p. 20; and Otway, **Airborne Forces**, p. 79
51. See Frost, **A Drop Too Many**, p. 76; take off timings cited in Saunders, **The Red Beret**, p. 93; and Otway, **Airborne Forces**, p. 79
52. Roman Candle malfunction cited in Peter Stainforth, **Wings of the Wind**, p.49; jump casualty number cited in Saunders, **The Red Beret**, p. 93
53. see Frost, **A Drop Too Many**, pp. 82-83; Stainforth, **Wings of the Wind**, p.58; Otway, **Airborne Forces**, p. 80; and Saunders, **The Red Beret**, pp. 93-94
54. See Stainforth, **Wings of the Wind**, p.59
55. Frost, **A Drop Too Many**, p. 87; according to Cole the 2nd Parachute Battalion's casualties 'amounted to some 150' and the Commonwealth War Graves Commission (CWGC) records list at least thirty-one dead in the period 29 November – 1 December 1942; see Cole, **On Wings of Healing**, p. 21
56. See Frost, **A Drop Too Many**, p. 84
57. See Otway, **Airborne Forces**, p. 80
58. See Frost, **A Drop Too Many**, pp. 85, 87
59. see Cole, **On Wings of Healing**, p. 21
60. See for example Frost, **A Drop Too Many**, pp. 92-105
61. See Otway, **Airborne Forces**, p. 80; thirty-five dead figure taken from the CWGC records which list at least that number of dead from the 2nd Parachute Battalion between 29 November and 4 December 1942
62. See Otway, **Airborne Forces**, pp. 82-87; for a detailed account of the period see Saunders, **The Red Beret**, pp. 104-118. Bou Farik is sometimes rendered Boufarik
63. 1700 figure cited in Otway, **Airborne Forces**, p. 87; the CWGC records list at least 202 dead from the 1st Parachute Brigade in the period 12/12/1942 to 18/04/1943
64. Quoted from Otway, **Airborne Forces**, p. 89
65. See Playfair, **The Destruction of the Axis Forces in Africa**, pp. 303-304

Chapter 3

1. See for example Playfair, **The Destruction of the Axis Forces in Africa**, p. 170
2. See Playfair, **The Destruction of the Axis Forces in Africa**, pp. 152, 171
3. For German transport aircraft types and numbers see Playfair, **The Destruction of the Axis Forces in Africa**, p. 152; for personnel and supplies lifted figures see ibid., p. 172; and Howe, **Northwest Africa**, p. 257-258

4. See Howe, **Northwest Africa**, pp. 366-367; F.H. Hinsley, **British Intelligence in the Second World War** (Abridged Edition) (London: HMSO, 1994), pp. 289-290; and Ralph Bennett **Ultra and Mediterranean Strategy 1941-45** (London: Hamish Hamilton, 1989), pp. 190-191; cited in David Rolf, **The Bloody Road to Tunis** (London: Frontline Books, 2015), Chapter 2, footnote # 26; final direct quote from Hinsley, p. 290
5. Figures cited in Howe, **Northwest Africa**, p. 258
6. See Howe, **Northwest Africa**, pp. 367-368
7. See Howe, **Northwest Africa**, pp. 365-366; the *Reichsarbeitdienst* (Reich Labour Service) or RAD was a paramilitary labour organisation set up by the Nazi Party initially to offset the impact of unemployment on the German economy during the inter-war period. After the outbreak of war the RAD became an auxiliary support organisation for the *Wehrmacht*, providing logistical and combat support including constructing roads, airfields, fixed and field defences as well as providing gun crews and rear echelon security
8. Figures cited in Howe, **Northwest Africa**, p. 368
9. See Howe, **Northwest Africa**, p. 294
10. Figures cited in Howe, **Northwest Africa**, p. 295; see also Playfair, **The Destruction of the Axis Forces in Africa**, p. 172
11. See for example Howe, **Northwest Africa**, p. 259
12. See Howe, **Northwest Africa**, pp. 261-262, 286
13. See Howe, **Northwest Africa**, p. 286
14. See Playfair, **The Destruction of the Axis Forces in Africa**, p. 173
15. See for example Howe, **Northwest Africa**, pp. 288-289
16. See Howe, **Northwest Africa**, pp. 311, 326; and Playfair, **The Destruction of the Axis Forces in Africa**, p. 183-184
17. See Saunders, **The Red Beret**, pp. 85-86
18. See Howe, **Northwest Africa**, pp. 287-288
19. See Howe, **Northwest Africa**, pp. 289-290, 295
20. Figures cited in Howe, **Northwest Africa**, p. 306
21. See Howe, **Northwest Africa**, pp. 299, 305-306, 308-309; and Hilary St. George Saunders, **The Green Beret**, pp. 136-139
22. For a detailed account see Saunders, **The Green Beret**, pp. 139-141; see also Howe, **Northwest Africa**, p. 309
23. See Howe, **Northwest Africa**, pp. 296, 302-303
24. For full details of BLADE Force's organisation see Howe, **Northwest Africa**, Footnote 12, p. 284
25. El Bathan and Djedeida are currently known as El Bathane and Jedeida
26. See Howe, **Northwest Africa**, pp. 300-302
27. See Playfair, **The Destruction of the Axis Forces in Africa**, pp. 176-177; and Howe, **Northwest Africa**, p. 304
28. For full details of the German plan and forces involved see Howe, **Northwest Africa**, pp. 312-313
29. See Playfair, **The Destruction of the Axis Forces in Africa**, pp. 187-188; for a detailed account see Howe, **Northwest Africa**, pp. 311-320, 326-333
30. See Playfair, **The Destruction of the Axis Forces in Africa**, pp. 220, 222
31. For details see Howe, **Northwest Africa**, pp. 322-326; Axis loss figures cited in Playfair, **The Destruction of the Axis Forces in Africa**, p. 226
32. Figures cited in Howe, **Northwest Africa**, pp. 370-371
33. Figures and details cited in Playfair, **The Destruction of the Axis Forces in Africa**, pp. 272-273
34. Currently rendered Sidi Bouzid and Subaytilah

35. Figures cited in Howe, **Northwest Africa**, pp. 415, 422
36. See Howe, **Northwest Africa**, pp. 505-507, 509
37. See Playfair, **The Destruction of the Axis Forces in Africa**, pp. 325-326; and Howe, **Northwest Africa**, p. 519
38. See Howe, **Northwest Africa**, pp. 365, 512-513; and ibid., Appendix B: Axis Troop and Supply Shipments, Table 9: 'German Supply Shipments Received in North Africa: November 1942 – May 1943', p. 682
39. See for example Bryn Evans, **The Decisive Campaigns of the Desert Air Force 1942-1945**, pp. 83-85; and Howe, **Northwest Africa**, p. 601
40. See Howe, **Northwest Africa**, pp. 367-368; air attack quote from Playfair, **The Destruction of the Axis Forces in Africa**, p. 431
41. See Playfair, **The Destruction of the Axis Forces in Africa**, p. 423
42. See Howe, **Northwest Africa**, Appendix B: Axis Troop and Supply Shipments, Table 10: 'German Losses in Sea Transport to North Africa, November 1942 – May 1943', p. 683
43. See Playfair, **The Destruction of the Axis Forces in Africa**, pp. 423-424
44. See Playfair, **The Destruction of the Axis Forces in Africa**, pp. 431-432
45. Sometimes rendered Operation PUGILIST GALLOP; see for example Howe, **Northwest Africa**, p. 526
46. For a detailed account see Howe, **Northwest Africa**, pp. 526-535; and Playfair, **The Destruction of the Axis Forces in Africa**, pp. 346-347, 369
47. Timing and figures cited in Playfair, **The Destruction of the Axis Forces in Africa**, p. 449
48. See Playfair, **The Destruction of the Axis Forces in Africa**, pp. 452-453; and Howe, **Northwest Africa**, pp. 650, 653
49. Figures cited in Playfair, **The Destruction of the Axis Forces in Africa**, p. 375
50. Figures cited in Playfair, **The Destruction of the Axis Forces in Africa**, p. 454
51. See Howe, **Northwest Africa**, pp. 662-665; and Playfair, **The Destruction of the Axis Forces in Africa**, pp. 453-454, 457-459
52. For dearth of Axis records see Playfair, **The Destruction of the Axis Forces in Africa**, pp. 459-460; figures cited in Rick Atkinson, **An Army at Dawn: The War in North Africa 1942-1943** (London: Abacus, 2004), p. 537
53. US 275,000 figure cited in Howe, **Northwest Africa**, p. 666; remainder cited in Playfair, **The Destruction of the Axis Forces in Africa**, p. 460
54. Figures cited in Playfair, **The Destruction of the Axis Forces in Africa**, p. 460
55. For figures and breakdown of aircraft types see Playfair, **The Destruction of the Axis Forces in Africa**, pp. 460-461
56. Timings and quote cited in Playfair, **The Destruction of the Axis Forces in Africa**, p. 459

Chapter 4

1. See for example Carlo D'Este, **Bitter Victory: The Battle for Sicily July-August 1943**, (London: Collins, 1988) pp. 43-47
2. See Lt. Col. Albert L. Garland & Howard McGaw Smyth, **Sicily and the Surrender of Italy** (Washington DC: Office of the Chief of Military History, Department of the Army, 1993), footnote # 2, p. 2
3. Quote from unpublished manuscript by Dwight D. Eisenhower; cited in D'Este, **Bitter Victory**, footnote #1, p. 51
4. See Garland & Smyth, **Sicily and the Surrender of Italy**, pp. 11-12
5. See D'Este, **Bitter Victory**, p. 39
6. See Garland & Smyth, **Sicily and the Surrender of Italy**, pp. 4-6

7. See D'Este, **Bitter Victory**, p. 40
8. See for example D'Este, **Bitter Victory**, pp. 46-48
9. See D'Este, **Bitter Victory**, p. 36
10. Quote from General Albert C. Wedemeyer, **Wedemeyer Reports!** (New York: Holt, 1958) p. 192; cited in D'Este, **Bitter Victory**, pp. 40-41
11. See for example Garland & Smyth, **Sicily and the Surrender of Italy**, pp. 9-11
12. Quoted from General Sir Ian Jacobs' personal diary of the Casablanca Conference; cited in D'Este, **Bitter Victory**, p. 51
13. See Garland & Smyth, **Sicily and the Surrender of Italy**, p. 11
14. For a detailed account of the pre-TRIDENT discussions and negotiations during the Conference see for example Garland & Smyth, **Sicily and the Surrender of Italy**, pp. 12-22
15. See Garland & Smyth, **Sicily and the Surrender of Italy**, pp. 22-23
16. See for example D'Este, **Bitter Victory**, pp. 142-144; for a detailed précis of the Algiers Conference see the **George C. Marshall Foundation** website, '4-001 Editorial Notes on the Algiers Conference, 1943' at https://www.marshallfoundation.org/library/digital-archive/editorial-note-on-the-algiers-conference/, accessed 26/01/2020
17. See for example Garland & Smyth, **Sicily and the Surrender of Italy**, pp. 53-54; for single Palermo landing see D'Este, **Bitter Victory**, p. 76
18. See D'Este, **Bitter Victory**, pp. 76-77
19. See Garland & Smyth, **Sicily and the Surrender of Italy**, pp. 54-55, 57; and D'Este, **Bitter Victory**, pp. 71-73
20. Quoted from Garland & Smyth, **Sicily and the Surrender of Italy**, p. 55
21. La Bouzaréa is currently rendered Bouzareah
22. See D'Este, **Bitter Victory**, p. 74
23. See Garland & Smyth, **Sicily and the Surrender of Italy**, pp. 56-57; and D'Este, **Bitter Victory**, pp. 74-75
24. See Garland & Smyth, **Sicily and the Surrender of Italy**, p. 58
25. See Bernard Fergusson, **The Watery Maze: The Story of Combined Operations** (London: Collins, 1961), p. 221
26. See Brigadier C. J. C. Molony, **The Mediterranean and Middle East, Volume V: The Campaign in Sicily 1943 and the Campaign in Italy 3rd September 1943 to 31st March 1944** (London: HMSO, 1973), pp. 13, 17-18 & Map 3 'Changes in Plan for Operation "Husky"', p. 16; D'Este, **Bitter Victory**, p. 78; and Clay Blair, **Ridgway's Paratroopers: The American Airborne in World War II** (New York: Quill William Morrow, 1985), p. 64
27. See Garland & Smyth, **Sicily and the Surrender of Italy**, p. 58
28. See Molony, **The Campaign in Sicily 1943**, p. 18; 18 March date cited in D'Este, **Bitter Victory**, p. 79
29. Quote from **WO 214/20**, Sicilian Campaign: Planning and Preparations: Earl Alexander of Tunis, Supreme Allied Commander Mediterranean Theatre: Papers, Cable from Montgomery to Alexander dated 15/03/1943; cited in D'Este, **Bitter Victory**, pp. 79-82. The same quote but with slightly different wording and with no source citation also appears in the British Official History; see Molony, **The Campaign in Sicily 1943**, p. 18
30. Letter from Montgomery to Brooke dated 15/03/1943, Montgomery Papers; cited in D'Este, **Bitter Victory**, p. 82
31. Quote from Fergusson, **The Watery Maze**, p. 222; cited in D'Este, **Bitter Victory**, p. 82
32. See Molony, **The Campaign in Sicily 1943**, p. 19; Garland & Smyth, **Sicily and the Surrender of Italy**, pp. 58-59; and D'Este, **Bitter Victory**, pp. 82-83

33. Quoted from **AIR 23/824** Operation 'Husky': Planning, AFHQ Message No. 2274 dated 07/04/1943; cited in D'Este, **Bitter Victory**, p. 85
34. Quoted from D'Este, **Bitter Victory**, p. 85
35. See **CAB 106/368** Sicily: Diary of Events and Correspondence Relating to the Planning of Operation 'Husky' 1943 Jan.-July, Minute D.72/3 'Most Secret' Churchill to British Chiefs of Staff dated 08/04/1943; the memo is cited in full in D'Este, **Bitter Victory**, p. 86, albeit with an incorrect footnote attributing it to **CAB 120/368**, a Minister of Defence Secretariat file dealing with small-arms ammunition.
36. Quote from **AIR 8/1346** Operation 'Husky', Cable from US Combined Chiefs of Staff to Eisenhower, dated 10/04/1943
37. 10 April 1943 approval date cited in Molony, **The Campaign in Sicily 1943**, p. 20; Eisenhower quote from **AIR 8/1346** Operation 'Husky', Cable from Eisenhower to US Combined Chiefs of Staff, dated 12/04/1943
38. See D'Este, **Bitter Victory**, p. 111
39. Quoted from Garland & Smyth, **Sicily and the Surrender of Italy**, p. 61
40. The signal is reproduced in full in Molony, **The Campaign in Sicily 1943**, pp. 21-22; see also Garland & Smyth, **Sicily and the Surrender of Italy**, p. 61
41. Quoted from Lord Tedder, **With Prejudice: The War Memoirs of Marshal of the Royal Air Force Lord Tedder** (London: Cassell, 1966), p. 431; cited in D'Este, **Bitter Victory**, p. 91
42. See Molony, **The Campaign in Sicily 1943**, pp. 22
43. Quoted from Molony, **The Campaign in Sicily 1943**, p. 24
44. See Garland & Smyth, **Sicily and the Surrender of Italy**, p. 62; Molony, **The Campaign in Sicily 1943**, pp. 22-23; and D'Este, **Bitter Victory**, pp. 115-117
45. Quoted from **Patton Papers**, Manuscript Division, Library of Congress, 'Diary of General George S. Patton', entry for 29/04/1943
46. See Molony, **The Campaign in Sicily 1943**, p. 23
47. See D'Este, **Bitter Victory**, pp. 118-119
48. See Molony, **The Campaign in Sicily 1943**, p. 23; for Montgomery signal see **CAB 106/368** Sicily: Diary of Events and Correspondence Relating to the Planning of Operation "Husky" 1943 Jan.-July, Cable from Alexander to Montgomery, dated 03/05/1943; cited in D'Este, **Bitter Victory**, p. 120
49. See D'Este, **Bitter Victory**, pp. 117, 121, 123
50. See D'Este, **Bitter Victory**, p. 121
51. See Garland & Smyth, **Sicily and the Surrender of Italy**, p. 66; and D'Este, **Bitter Victory**, pp. 142-143
52. Quote from Garland & Smyth, **Sicily and the Surrender of Italy**, pp. 65-66; for 10-14 July window and waxing moon see Molony, **The Campaign in Sicily 1943**, p. 24
53. For approval date see for example D'Este, **Bitter Victory**, p. 144
54. See Garland & Smyth, **Sicily and the Surrender of Italy**, p. 62 and ibid., Footnote # 31
55. For the outline of the plan see for example Molony, **The Campaign in Sicily 1943**, pp. 17-18, 28-29
56. See D'Este, **Bitter Victory**, p. 145
57. See Lieutenant-Colonel G. W. L. Nicholson, **Official History of the Canadian Army in the Second World War, Volume II: The Canadians in Italy 1943-1945** (Ottawa: Edmond Cloutier, 1958), pp. 86-87
58. See F. H. Hinsley, **British Intelligence in the Second World War** (Abridged Edition) (London: HMSO, 1994), p. 341
59. See Michael Howard, **British Intelligence in the Second World War: Volume Five: Strategic Deception** (HMSO: London, 1990), pp. 33-44

60. For a detailed précis see for example D'Este, **Bitter Victory**, pp. 181-191
61. See Hinsley, **British Intelligence in the Second World War** (Abridged Edition), p. 341
62. See D'Este, **Bitter Victory**, p. 191
63. 3,462 figure cited in Molony, **The Campaign in Sicily 1943**, p. 46
64. For squadron totals, aircraft numbers and RCAF Squadron identity see Molony, **The Campaign in Sicily 1943**, p. 46 including Footnote #1 and Appendix 4: 'Orders of Battle Royal Air Force and United States Army Air Forces', pp. 871-877; for US Bombardment Group identities see Maurer Maurer, **Air Force Combat Units of World War II** (Washington DC: Office of Air Force History, 1983), entries for '44th Bombardment Group', '93rd Bombardment Group', '98th Bombardment Group, '376th Bombardment Group' & '389th Bombardment Group', pp. 101-103, 160-162, 168-170, 264-265, 276-277
65. Quote and details cited in Bryn Evans, **The Decisive Campaigns of the Desert Air Force**, pp. 96-97; see also Molony, **The Campaign in Sicily 1943**, Appendix 4: 'Orders of Battle Royal Air Force and United States Army Air Forces', pp. 871-877; for US P-40 presence see Maurer Maurer, **Air Force Combat Units of World War II**, entry for '57th Fighter Group' and '47th Bombardment Group, pp. 104-106, 120-121
66. Twenty days and 670 aircraft figures cited in Garland & Smyth, **Sicily and the Surrender of Italy**, p. 107; seventeen days figure cited in Molony, **The Campaign in Sicily 1943**, p. 46
67. The 2686th Bombardment Wing (Provisional) was reconstituted as the 42nd Bombardment Wing on 31/07/1943 and is sometimes referred to by that title prior to that date.
68. See Garland & Smyth, **Sicily and the Surrender of Italy**, pp. 107-108; and Molony, **The Campaign in Sicily 1943**, Appendix 4: 'Orders of Battle Royal Air Force and United States Army Air Forces', pp. 871-877
69. Quote from personal correspondence from Lord Scarman to Carlo D'Este, dated 02/04/1985; cited in D'Este, **Bitter Victory**, pp. 167-168
70. See D'Este, **Bitter Victory**, pp. 168-169
71. See Garland & Smyth, **Sicily and the Surrender of Italy**, p. 107, Footnote #39; and D'Este, **Bitter Victory**, p. 170. Coningham is incorrectly rendered Cunningham in the Garland & Smyth footnote
72. Quote from Garland & Smyth, **Sicily and the Surrender of Italy**, p. 106
73. Major-General Bull quote cited in Garland & Smyth, **Sicily and the Surrender of Italy**, pp. 106-107, Footnote #37; Patton reaction cited in D'Este, **Bitter Victory**, p. 171
74. Quote from Garland & Smyth, **Sicily and the Surrender of Italy**, p. 107
75. See Molony, **The Campaign in Sicily 1943**, pp. 47-48
76. See Molony, **The Campaign in Sicily 1943**, p. 49
77. See Fergusson, **The Watery Maze**, p. 238; and Evans, **The Decisive Campaigns of the Desert Air Force**, p. 95
78. See Garland & Smyth, **Sicily and the Surrender of Italy**, p. 70. Interestingly, there is no mention of Professor Zuckerman's input in the US official account, which gives the impression that the scientific approach was Eisenhower's idea
79. Quoted from Fergusson, **The Watery Maze**, p. 238
80. For Zuckerman's reasoning and calculations see Fergusson, **The Watery Maze**, pp. 238-239; eight square miles figure cited in Molony, **The Campaign in Sicily 1943**, p. 49, Footnote #1
81. Aircraft types and number cited in Evans, **The Decisive Campaigns of the Desert Air Force**, p. 95; bomb tonnage and sortie figures cited in Molony, **The Campaign in Sicily 1943**, p. 49, Footnote #1

82. See Garland & Smyth, **Sicily and the Surrender of Italy**, p. 71
83. Dates, sortie and bomb tonnage figures cited in Molony, **The Campaign in Sicily 1943**, p. 49
84. See Fergusson, **The Watery Maze**, p. 239
85. See Garland & Smyth, **Sicily and the Surrender of Italy**, pp. 71-72
86. See Molony, **The Campaign in Sicily 1943**, p. 49, Footnote #2; bombing and assault timings cited in Garland & Smyth, **Sicily and the Surrender of Italy**, p. 72
87. See D'Este, **Bitter Victory**, pp. 214-215; Evans, **The Decisive Campaigns of the Desert Air Force**, p. 95; Molony, **The Campaign in Sicily 1943**, p. 49; Fergusson, **The Watery Maze**, p. 239; and Garland & Smyth, **Sicily and the Surrender of Italy**, pp. 72-73
88. Quoted from D'Este, **Bitter Victory**, p. 216
89. Quoted from Garland & Smyth, **Sicily and the Surrender of Italy**, p. 72
90. For presence of Allied aircraft see Garland & Smyth, **Sicily and the Surrender of Italy**, p. 73; for identity of Pantelleria unit see Maurer, **Air Force Combat Units of World War II**, entry for '33rd Fighter Group', pp. 86-87
91. See Molony, **The Campaign in Sicily 1943**, p. 48, Footnote #1
92. See Molony, **The Campaign in Sicily 1943**, pp. 48-49
93. Figures cited in Molony, **The Campaign in Sicily 1943**, pp. 46-47; for Junkers 88 presence see Evans, **The Decisive Campaigns of the Desert Air Force**, p. 100
94. Figures cited in Molony, **The Campaign in Sicily 1943**, p. 48, Footnote #1; for withdrawal to mainland Italy see ibid., p. 49; and Evans, **The Decisive Campaigns of the Desert Air Force**, p. 100
95. See Evans, **The Decisive Campaigns of the Desert Air Force**, p. 100
96. See Hinsley, **British Intelligence in the Second World War** (Abridged Edition), p. 341
97. See Hinsley, **British Intelligence in the Second World War** (Abridged Edition), pp. 341-342

Chapter 5

1. See Brigadier C. J. C. Molony, **The Mediterranean and Middle East, Volume V: The Campaign in Sicily 1943 and the Campaign in Italy 3rd September 1943 to 31st March 1944**, p. 23
2. For 10-14 July window and waxing moon see Molony, **The Campaign in Sicily 1943**, p. 28
3. See Garland & Smyth, **Sicily and the Surrender of Italy**, p. 62 & ibid., Footnote # 31
4. See for example Garland & Smyth, **Sicily and the Surrender of Italy**, pp. 88-96; and Molony, **The Campaign in Sicily 1943**, Tables '8th Army' and '7th United States Army', pp. 26-27
5. 1,700 figure cited in Otway, **Airborne Forces**, p. 87; the CWGC records list at least 202 dead from the 1st Parachute Brigade in the period 12/12/1942 to 18/04/1943; for 2nd Parachute Battalion strength and reinforcement see Saunders, **The Red Beret**, p. 118; 16th Parachute Field Ambulance casualty treatment figure cited in Cole, **On Wings of Healing**, p. 31
6. Figures cited in **WO 175/526** 2nd Parachute Battalion War Diary, entry for 22/04/1943; also cited in Thompson, **Ready for Anything**, pp. 69-70
7. Award figures and quote from Saunders, **The Red Beret**, p. 119
8. For WS29 and KMF13 make up, dates & timings see the **WS Convoy Series** website, 'Military Convoys WS.29 + KMF.13' page at http://www.convoyweb.org.uk/ws/index.html?ws29.php?convoy=29_1~wsmain, accessed 24/05/2020; for presence

of Provost Company and arrival at Oran date see Jack Turnbull & John Hamblett, **The Pegasus Patrol** (Marple, Cheshire: 1994), p. 28; for presence of 9 Field Company RE and 261 Field Park Company RE see Mark Henniker, **An Image of War** (London: Leo Cooper, 1987), p. 113; for Hopkinson's interference, Glider Pilot presence, shipping details and disembarking at Mers el Kébir see Mike Peters, **Glider Pilots in Sicily** (Barnsley: Pen & Sword, 2012), pp. 23-26

9. For a detailed account of Lt.-Col. Henniker's posting, less than straightforward journey to North Africa and presence at Oran docks see Henniker, **An Image of War**, pp. 102-110, 113
10. See Peters, **Glider Pilots in Sicily**, p. 27
11. See for example Peters, **Glider Pilots in Sicily**, p. 27; and Turnbull & Hamblett, **The Pegasus Patrol**, p. 28
12. The date of the downpour and washing out is unclear; Henniker gives the impression it occurred a day or two after the 2nd Parachute Brigade's arrival, whereas Peters' Glider Pilot accounts cites 29 April; see Henniker, **An Image of War**, pp. 114-115; and Peters, **Glider Pilots in Sicily**, p. 28
13. For Provost Company re-billeting & policing details see Turnbull & Hamblett, **The Pegasus Patrol**, p. 29; rough behaviour quote from Henniker, **An Image of War**, p. 116
14. See Otway, **Airborne Forces**, pp. 113-114
15. Quoted from Saunders, **The Red Beret**, p. 122
16. See for example Frost, **A Drop Too Many**, p. 195; for the smoke marker incident see **WO 171/1236**, 1st Parachute Battalion War Diary, Monthly Summary for February 1944, entry for 12/02/1944; for NAAFI burglary see ibid., Monthly Summary for May 1944, entry for 28/05/1944
17. the Battalion commander was Lieutenant-Colonel Eric Yeldham. For medical replacement see Saunders, **The Red Beret**, p. 223; and **WO 171/1238**, 3rd Parachute Battalion War Diary, entry for 03/07/1944; for failing test exercise see Frost, **A Drop Too Many**, p. 195; for exercise details see **WO 171/1238**, 3rd Parachute Battalion War Diary, entries for 26-30/06/1944
18. Quote from Martin Middlebrook, **Arnhem 1944: The Airborne Battle**, p. 25; the commanders were Lieutenant-Colonel Peter Cleasby-Thompson and Lieutenant-Colonel Kenneth Darling, the former was posted to Airborne Forces HQ and the latter to command the 12th Parachute Battalion. For Darling's side of the matter see Thompson, **Ready for Anything**, p. 103; for RSM involvement see **WO 171/1236**, 1st Parachute Battalion War Diary, Monthly Summary for March 1944, entries for 21/02/1944, 29/02/1944 and 02/03/1944
19. See **WO 171/1236**, 1st Parachute Battalion War Diary, Monthly Summary for March 1944, entry for 30/03/1944
20. See Middlebrook, **Arnhem 1944**, p. 25; Thompson, **Ready for Anything**, p. 103; and **WO 171/1236**, 1st Parachute Battalion War Diary, Monthly Summary for April 1944, entries for 01/04/1944, 03/04/1944 & 26/04/1944. Dobie was actually serving as second-in-command of the 12th Parachute Battalion, and his posting was a straight exchange with Darling
21. See Saunders, **The Red Beret**, p. 122
22. See Cole, **On Wings of Healing**, p. 32
23. For WS30 and KMF15 make up, dates & timings see the **WS Convoy Series** website, 'Military Convoys WS.30 + KMF.15' page at http://www.convoyweb.org.uk/ws/index.html?ws30.php?convoy=30_2~wsmain, accessed 28/05/2020; for docking at Oran see Cole, **On Wings of Healing**, p. 33; and Kent, **First In!**, p. 30; for 28 May 1943 date of arrival in Oran see Turnbull & Hamblett, **The Pegasus Patrol**, p. 30

24. Fleurus is currently known as Gdyel
25. See Kent, **First In!**, p. 30; and Cole, **On Wings of Healing**, p. 33
26. See Cole, **On Wings of Healing**, p. 33; for diarrhoea-inducing wine see Kent, **First In!**, p. 30
27. Quote from Kent, **First In!**, p. 31; move date cited in Cole, **On Wings of Healing**, p. 33
28. See Saunders, **The Red Beret**, p. 122
29. Kibrit is often rendered Kabrit in contemporary British accounts
30. See Otway, **Airborne Forces**, pp. 107-110, 114; and Saunders, **The Red Beret**, pp. 139-142
31. Thiersville is currently known as Ghriss and the airfield, which is located three miles south of the town, is still in service as Ghriss Airport; the airfields at Froha and Matemore appear to have been returned to agricultural use
32. See Peters, **Glider Pilots in Sicily**, p. 29.
33. See Victor Miller, **Nothing Is Impossible: A Glider Pilot's Story of Sicily, Arnhem and the Rhine Crossing** (Staplehurst: Spellmount, 1994), p. 21
34. See Otway, **Airborne Forces**, p. 113
35. For Group locations, dates & commanders see Maurer Maurer, **Air Force Combat Units of World War II** (Washington DC: Office of Air Force History, 1961), entries for '60th Troop Carrier Group', '62nd Troop Carrier Group' & '64th Troop Carrier Group', pp. 123-125, 127-129, 130-131
36. See Otway, **Airborne Forces**, p. 113
37. The Airborne Forces Establishment sub-units are sometimes referred to as Squadrons rather than Units; for the Squadron formation dates and location see **AIR 27/1645** No. 296 Squadron Operations Record Book, entry for 25/01/1943; and **AIR 27/1644** No. 295 Squadron Operations Record Book, entry for 03/08/1943
38. See for example Owen Thetford, **Aircraft of the Royal Air Force Since 1918** (London: Putnam, 1979), entry for 'Armstrong Whitworth Albemarle', pp. 34-35
39. For first Albemarle arrival see **AIR 27/1645** No. 296 Squadron Operations Record Book, entry for 27/01/1943; for completion of re-equipping see ibid., addition to entry for 30/04/1943; for operational details see ibid., Appendix Form 541 for February 1943, entries from 09/02/1943 to 28/02/1943
40. See **AIR 27/1645** No. 296 Squadron Operations Record Book, entry for 07/02/1943
41. For unsuitability of the Albemarle for parachuting see for example Saunders, **The Red Beret**, p. 121; for a graphic participant description of the process see Neil Barber, **The Day the Devils Dropped In: The 9th Parachute Battalion in Normandy – D-Day to D+6** (Barnsley: Pen & Sword, 2002), testimony from Major Allen Parry, OC A Company, 9th Parachute Battalion, pp. 43-44, 46-47
42. See **AIR 27/1645** No. 296 Squadron Operations Record Book, entry for 17/05/1943
43. See **AIR 27/1645** No. 296 Squadron Operations Record Book, entries for 23/05/1943 & 03/06/1943
44. See **AIR 27/1645** No. 296 Squadron Operations Record Book, entries for 5, 6, 7, 10 & 11/06/1943; and ibid., Appendix Form 541 for June 1943, entries running from 05/06/1943 to 21/06/1943. Interestingly, the Record Book states that the aircraft movement from the UK was complete by 10 June; see ibid., entry for 03/06/1943
45. See **AIR 27/1645** No. 296 Squadron Operations Record Book, entry for 03/06/1943; for Gibraltar repair see ibid., entry for 07/06/1943; for tyre burst and crash landing see ibid., entry for 11/06/1943
46. See Kent, **First In!**, p. 18; and **AIR 27/1644** No. 295 Squadron Operations Record Book, entry for 11/02/1943

47. See **AIR 27/1645** No. 296 Squadron Operations Record Book, entries for 17/06/1943 & 19/06/1943; and Kent, **First In!**, p. 31
48. See **AIR 27/1645** No. 296 Squadron Operations Record Book, entries for 12/06/1943, 16/06/1943 & 18/06/1943; quote from ibid., entry for 16/06/1943
49. See **AIR 27/1645** No. 296 Squadron Operations Record Book, entries for 11/06/1943 & 17/06/1943
50. Figures and details cited in Otway, **Airborne Forces**, p. 116-117
51. See for example Peters, **Glider Pilots in Sicily**, p. 45
52. See Peters, **Glider Pilots in Sicily**, pp. 38, 43-44
53. Names and arrival dates cited in Peters, **Glider Pilots in Sicily**, pp. 38-39
54. See Brigadier George Chatterton DSO OBE, **The Wings of Pegasus: The Story of the Glider Pilot Regiment** (Nashville: The Battery Press, 1982), p. 40; and Peters, **Glider Pilots in Sicily**, pp. 43-44
55. See Peters, **Glider Pilots in Sicily**, pp. 44-45
56. See Gerard M. Devlin, **Silent Wings: The Story of the Glider Pilots of World War II** (London: W. H. Allen, 1985), p. 81
57. The date of the meeting is unclear. Chatterton refers to it taking place on 1 April, but it must have been at some point after Hopkinson's meeting with Montgomery on 7 May 1943; see Chatterton, **The Wings of Pegasus**, p. 41
58. For quotes and the full exchange, which appears to be the only written account of the meeting, see Chatterton, **The Wings of Pegasus**, pp. 41-42
59. Quoted from Eric Morris, **Circles of Hell: The War in Italy 1943-1945** (London: Hutchinson, 1993), p. 58
60. See Peters, **Glider Pilots in Sicily**, p. 53
61. See for example Thetford, **Aircraft of the Royal Air Force Since 1918**, entry for 'Waco Hadrian', p. 623; and Devlin, **Silent Wings**, pp. 62-63
62. The Gold Coast is now known as Ghana
63. See Peters, **Glider Pilots in Sicily**, p. 48
64. See Devlin, **Silent Wings**, pp. 78-79
65. Numbers cited in Devlin, **Silent Wings**, p. 82
66. See Chatterton, **The Wings of Pegasus**, pp. 42-43; and Peters, **Glider Pilots in Sicily**, p. 52
67. For 60 pilot figure see **WO 169/10341** 1st Battalion Glider Pilot Regiment War Diary, entry for 08/05/1943; for USAAF corporal, instructions and toolkits see testimony from anonymous Sergeant, 1st Battalion GPR; cited in Peters, **Glider Pilots in Sicily**, p. 52; for use of crates as accommodation see for example Chatterton, **The Wings of Pegasus**, pp. 42-43; and testimony from Sergeant Robert Boyce, 2 Squadron, 1st Battalion GPR; cited in Peters, **Glider Pilots in Sicily**, p. 55
68. See **WO 169/10341** 1st Battalion Glider Pilot Regiment War Diary, entry for 12/05/1943
69. Testimony from then Lieutenant-Colonel George Chatterton, Commanding 1st Battalion Glider Pilot Regiment; cited in Peters, **Glider Pilots in Sicily**, p. 56; for night flight details see **WO 169/10341** 1st Battalion Glider Pilot Regiment War Diary, entries for 14/05/1943 & 18/05/1943
70. For lack of luminous instruments and use of torches in lieu see testimony from Sergeant Robert Boyce, 2 Squadron, 1st Battalion Glider Pilot Regiment; cited in Peters, **Glider Pilots in Sicily**, p. 63
71. See testimony from Squadron-Leader Lawrence Wright, HQ RAF No. 38 Wing; and Peters' interview with Staff-Sergeant Michael Hall, 1 Squadron, 1st Battalion Glider Pilot Regiment, dated 24/02/2009; both cited in Peters, **Glider Pilots in Sicily**, pp. 56, 57
72. See Peters, **Glider Pilots in Sicily**, p. 55

73. See testimony from Major John Place, OC 3 Squadron, 1st Battalion Glider Pilot Regiment; cited in Peters, **Glider Pilots in Sicily**, p. 60; Miller, **Nothing is Impossible**, p. 21; and Chatterton, **The Wings of Pegasus**, p. 65
74. Fifty-two figure cited in Peters, **Glider Pilots in Sicily**, Table 'Summary of Glider Pilot Training', p. 104
75. See Peters, **Glider Pilots in Sicily**, p. 60; for despatch of 3 Squadron assembly teams to the coast see testimony from Major John Place, OC 3 Squadron, 1st Battalion Glider Pilot Regiment; cited in ibid., p. 60
76. See **AIR 27/1645** No. 296 Squadron Operations Record Book, entries for 09/06/1943, 20/06/1943 & 21/06/1943; and **WO 169/10182** 1st Battalion The Border Regiment War Diary, entry for 20/06/1943
77. See Peters, **Glider Pilots in Sicily**, pp. 65-67
78. For A Flight re-designation see **AIR 27/1644** No. 295 Squadron Operations Record Book, entry for 22/04/1943; Operation FRESHMAN was launched on 19 November 1942; for a detailed account see for example Otway, **Airborne Forces**, pp. 70-73
79. See **AIR 27/1644** No. 295 Squadron Operations Record Book, entries for 15/05/1943, 19/05/1943, 28/05/1943, 03/06/1943 & 06/06/1943
80. See Peters, **Glider Pilots in Sicily**, pp. 67-68, 73; there is no mention of the despatch of the advance party to North Africa in the No. 295 Squadron Operations Record Book
81. See **AIR 27/1644** No. 295 Squadron Operations Record Book, entries for 16/05/1943, 19/05/1943 & 11/06/1943; and Peters, **Glider Pilots in Sicily**, pp. 69-71
82. See Peters, **Glider Pilots in Sicily**, p. 72
83. See **AIR 27/1644** No. 295 Squadron Operations Record Book, Appendix Form 541 for June 1943, entry for 03/06/1943; for abort due to fog see Peters, **Glider Pilots in Sicily**, p. 73
84. See **AIR 27/1644** No. 295 Squadron Operations Record Book, Appendix Form 541 for June 1943, entry for 03/06/1943; and Peters, **Glider Pilots in Sicily**, pp. 77-78
85. See **AIR 27/1644** No. 295 Squadron Operations Record Book, Appendix Form 541 for June 1943, entries for 03/06/1943; Peters, **Glider Pilots in Sicily**, pp. 76-79; for a detailed account by Staff-Sergeant Jenks see Chatterton, **The Wings of Pegasus**, pp. 44-59
86. See **AIR 27/1644** No. 295 Squadron Operations Record Book, entry for 14/06/1943; ibid., Appendix Form 541 for June 1943, entries for 14/06/1943; Peters, **Glider Pilots in Sicily**, pp. 83-87; for a detailed account by Sergeant Antonopoulos see Chatterton, **The Wings of Pegasus**, pp. 59-63
87. See **AIR 27/1644** No. 295 Squadron Operations Record Book, Appendix Form 541 for June 1943, entries for 26/06/1943 & 27/06/1943; and ibid., Appendix Form 541 for July 1943, entries for 06/07/1943 & 07/07/1943
88. See **AIR 27/1645** No. 296 Squadron Operations Record Book, entries for 19/06/1943 & 21/06/1943
89. Quote from Peters, **Glider Pilots in Sicily**, p. 87; figures totalled from **AIR 27/1644** No. 295 Squadron Operations Record Book, Appendix Forms 541 for June & July 1943, entries between 06/06/1943 & 07/07/1943
90. See Peters, **Glider Pilots in Sicily**, Table 'Summary of Glider Pilot Training', p. 104
91. See **WO 169/10299** 2nd Battalion South Staffordshire Regiment War Diary, entry for 14/06/1943; and Peters, **Glider Pilots in Sicily**, Table 'Summary of Glider Pilot Training', p. 104
92. See Peters, **Glider Pilots in Sicily**, p. 95

93. See **AIR 27/1645** No. 296 Squadron Operations Record Book, entry for 16/06/1943
94. See **WO 169/8666** 1st Airborne Division HQ War Diary, entry for 18/06/1943; and **AIR 27/1645** No. 296 Squadron Operations Record Book, entry for 18/06/1943
95. See Peters, **Glider Pilots in Sicily**, p. 96
96. See **AIR 27/1645** No. 296 Squadron Operations Record Book, entry for 20/06/1943; **WO 169/10299** 2nd Battalion South Staffordshire Regiment War Diary, entry for 20/06/1943; and Peters, **Glider Pilots in Sicily**, pp. 96-97
97. See **WO 169/10299** 2nd Battalion South Staffordshire Regiment War Diary, entry for 01:00, 21/06/1943; and Peters, **Glider Pilots in Sicily**, p. 97; the latter account refers to take off being scheduled for 23:45 on 20 June and the South Staffords 01:00 timing may refer to landing rather than take-off
98. See Peters, **Glider Pilots in Sicily**, p. 97
99. See **AIR 27/1645** No. 296 Squadron Operations Record Book, entry for 24/06/1943
100. See **AIR 27/1645** No. 296 Squadron Operations Record Book, entries between 25/06/1943 & 02/07/1943
101. See **WO 169/8666** 1st Airborne Division HQ War Diary, entries for 26-30/06/1943
102. See **WO 169/10299** 2nd Battalion South Staffordshire Regiment War Diary, entry for 27/06/1943; and testimony from Sergeant Norman Howes, C Company, 2nd Battalion South Staffordshire Regiment; cited in Peters, **Glider Pilots in Sicily**, p. 98. The fifteen dead from the crash included two men from the Glider Pilot Regiment, two from the RAMC and eleven from the 2nd Battalion South Staffordshire Regiment; all are interred in Enfidaville War Cemetery, Tunisia in Plot 4, Row A, Mass Grave 7-21
103. See Peters, **Glider Pilots in Sicily**, pp. 98-100
104. See **WO 175/111** 1st Airlanding Light Regiment RA War Diary, entries for 02/07/1943 & 07/07/1943
105. See Peters, **Glider Pilots in Sicily**, pp. 110-111
106. See **WO 169/10299** 2nd Battalion South Staffordshire Regiment War Diary, entry for 28/06/1943 to 02/07/1943; **WO 169/10182** 1st Battalion The Border Regiment War Diary, entry for 01 & 02/07/1943; **WO 169/10343** 1st Parachute Battalion War Diary, entries for 02, 03, 04 & 05/07/1943; and **WO 169/10344** 2nd Parachute Battalion War Diary, entries for 02, 03, 04 & 05/07/1943
107. See **WO 169/12670** 1st Airlanding Light Aid Detachment REME War Diary, entries for 01/07/1943 & 02/07/1943
108. See **AIR 27/1645** No. 296 Squadron Operations Record Book, entries for 0/07/1943 to 08/07/1943

Chapter 6

1. See Howe, **Northwest Africa**, p. 279; for a detailed account see Devlin, **Paratrooper! The Saga of US Army and Marine Parachute and Glider Combat Troops during World War II** (New York: St. Martin's Press, 1979), pp. 164-174. Sidi Bou Zid is currently rendered Sidi Bouzid
2. El Djem is currently known as El Jem
3. See Devlin, **Paratrooper!**, p. 179
4. For Lt.-Col. Cochran's presence see for example Devlin, **Paratrooper!**, p. 180; Cochran later led the multi-mission 1st Air Commando Group in the China-Burma-India Theatre; for third C-47 and container contents see **509th Parachute Infantry Association** website, 'Third Combat Jump: El Djem Bridge Mission' page at ://w https ww.509thgeronimo.org/combatjumps/jump3.html, accessed 12/07/2020. The latter is a detailed summary of the 509th Parachute Infantry Regiment Field Order 14 which initiated and framed the El Djem mission

5. For detailed accounts see Devlin, **Paratrooper!**, pp. 181-188; and **509th Parachute Infantry Association** website, 'Third Combat Jump: El Djem Bridge Mission' page at https://www.509thgeronimo.org/combatjumps/jump3.html, accessed 12/07/2020; the latter provides a near complete list of the participants
6. For Lieutenant Kunkle's death see for example Devlin, **Paratrooper!**, pp. 159-160
7. See Devlin, **Paratrooper!**, p. 190; for Colonel Raff's secondment to Browning see Guy LoFaro, **The Sword of St. Michael: The 82nd Airborne Division in World War II** (Cambridge, Mass.: Da Capo Press, 2011), p. 70
8. For an overview of these developments see for example Clay Blair, **Ridgway's Paratroopers: The American Airborne in World War II** (New York: William Morrow, 1985), pp. 20-23, 39-44; and LoFaro, **The Sword of St. Michael**, pp. 29-43
9. See Blair, **Ridgway's Paratroopers**, p. 49
10. See LoFaro, **The Sword of St. Michael**, pp. 43-44
11. Different sources cite the move commencing on 17 or 18 April; for the former see Phil Nordyke, **All American All the Way: From Sicily to Normandy: A Combat History of the 82nd Airborne Division in World War II** (Minneapolis: Zenith Press, 2009), p. 25; for the latter see LoFaro, **The Sword of St. Michael**, p. 53
12. See LoFaro, **The Sword of St. Michael**, p. 63; for Convoy UGF.8 details see **Convoy Web: The Website for Merchant Ships during WW2** website, 'Arnold Hague Convoy Database UGF Convoy Series' section, 'Convoy UGF.8' page at http://www.convoyweb.org.uk/index.html, accessed 14/07/2020
13. For dates, timings & convoy division see Nordyke, **All American All the Way**, p. 26
14. For detailed accounts see LoFaro, **The Sword of St. Michael**, pp. 53, 63-64; and Nordyke, **All American All the Way**, pp. 25-29; Marnia is currently rendered Maghnia
15. See Maurer, **Air Force Combat Units of World War II**, entries for '52nd Troop Carrier Wing', 61st, 315th, 314th, 315th & 316th Troop Carrier Groups, pp. 395-396, 125-127, 188-195; for delay in satellite airfields becoming operational see Nordyke, **All American All the Way**, p. 35; Nouvion airfield is currently known as Oujda Angads Airport
16. First quote from LoFaro, **The Sword of St. Michael**, p. 65; Private Tucker quote cited in Nordyke, **All American All the Way**, p. 30
17. Quotes cited in Nordyke, **All American All the Way**, pp. 29-30
18. See LoFaro, **The Sword of St. Michael**, p. 65
19. Testimony from Private Allen Langdon, Company C, 1st Battalion, 505th Parachute Infantry Regiment; cited in LoFaro, **The Sword of St. Michael**, p. 67
20. 1 June 1943 date cited in Nordyke, **All American All the Way**, p. 35
21. See LoFaro, **The Sword of St. Michael**, p. 67
22. See Phil Nordyke, **Four Stars of Valor: The Combat History of the 505th Parachute Infantry Regiment in World War II** (Minneapolis: Zenith Press, 2010), pp. 46-47
23. For Ridgway's edict and ordering Gavin off the C-47 see LoFaro, **The Sword of St. Michael**, p. 66
24. Quote from 'Report of Airborne Operations' by HQ, US Fifth Army Airborne Training Center; cited in LoFaro, **The Sword of St. Michael**, p. 67
25. See Nordyke, **All American All the Way**, pp. 35-36
26. Quoted from Colonel James M. Gavin Personal Diary, entry for 29/05/1943; cited in LoFaro, **The Sword of St. Michael**, p. 67
27. See Nordyke, **Four Stars of Valor**, pp. 47-48
28. Quote from Nordyke, **All American All the Way**, p. 36
29. See Nordyke, **Four Stars of Valor**, p. 48

30. See Nordyke, **Four Stars of Valor**, p. 48; and id., **All American All the Way**, p. 36
31. Quotes from Matthew B. Ridgway & Harold H. Martin, **Soldier: The Memoirs of Matthew B. Ridgway** (New York: Harper & Brothers, 1956), pp. 66-67; cited in LoFaro, **The Sword of St. Michael**, p. 59
32. See Blair, **Ridgway's Paratroopers**, p. 74; and LoFaro, **The Sword of St. Michael**, p. 70
33. See Blair, **Ridgway's Paratroopers**, p. 74; and LoFaro, **The Sword of St. Michael**, p. 70; the honorary membership of British Airborne Forces and award of the British Airborne maroon beret has become a part of the 509th Parachute Infantry Regiment's historical lore; see for example the **509th Parachute Infantry Association** website, 'History of the 509th PIB' section, 'Timeline' page, entry for 6 June 1943 at https://509thgeronimo.org/f509thtimeline, accessed 16/07/2020
34. See Blair, **Ridgway's Paratroopers**, pp. 74-75
35. See for example Devlin, **Paratrooper!**, pp. 215-216
36. See Blair, **Ridgway's Paratroopers**, p. 67; and LoFaro, **The Sword of St. Michael**, p. 70
37. Quotes cited in Blair, **Ridgeway's Paratroopers**, p. 74
38. See Blair, **Ridgway's Paratroopers**, p. 73
39. Glider figures cited in Peters, **Glider Pilots in Sicily**, p. 112
40. See Blair, **Ridgway's Paratroopers**, p. 75; and Nordyke, **All American All the Way**, p.38; RAF aircraft figures cited in Peters, **Glider Pilots in Sicily**, p. 112
41. See LoFaro, **The Sword of St. Michael**, p. 69
42. For details see for example Blair, **Ridgway's Paratroopers**, pp. 50-52
43. Quotes from testimony by then-Lieutenant-Colonel Frank W. Moorman during interview by Clay Blair; cited in Blair, **Ridgway's Paratroopers**, pp. 52-53
44. Quoted from Blair, **Ridgway's Paratroopers**, p. 51
45. See John Cushman Warren, **Airborne Missions in the Mediterranean 1942-1945**, USAF Historical Studies: No. 74 (Maxwell AFB, Alabama: US Air Force Historical Division, Research Studies Institute, 1955: facsimile Ashok Vihar, Delhi, 2015), p. 39
46. See for example Devlin, **Paratrooper!**, pp. 213-214 and endnote 5, p. 680; for D-Day and H-Hour dates and timings see for example Molony, **The Campaign in Sicily 1943**, p. 28 & ibid., Footnote # 1
47. For the 505th Regimental Combat Team's Order of Battle for HUSKY ONE see for example Nordyke, **All American All the Way**, p. 39
48. The River Acate is sometimes known as the River Dirillo
49. See LoFaro, **The Sword of St. Michael**, p. 69; and Nordyke, **Four Stars of Valor**, p. 50
50. See for example Nordyke, **All American All the Way**, pp. 39-41
51. See Nordyke, **All American All the Way**, p. 41; the '57mm Antitank Gun M1' was the US designation for the British 6-Pounder weapon, officially the 'Ordnance, Q.F, 6 pdr'. The gun was adopted by the US Ordnance Board in 1943 as the fighting in North Africa had shown the existing US 37mm Antitank Gun M3 was incapable of dealing with the current generation of German tanks. Weighing 2,471 pounds with a muzzle velocity of 2,700 feet per second capable of penetrating 2.7 inches of armour plate at 1,000 yards, the 57mm M1 became the standard issue towed anti-tank gun used by US infantry divisions during the fighting in north-west Europe. The 82nd and 101st Airborne Divisions were issued with guns from British stocks modified with the Mk. III carriage, which was lightened, shortened and narrowed for Airborne use; it is unclear if the guns issued to the 82nd Airborne for HUSKY were of this modified pattern; see for example Chris Bishop (Ed.), **WWII: The Directory of Weapons** (London: Greenwich Editions, 1998), entry for 'Ordnance, Q.F., 6 pdr', pp. 180-181

52. See Blair, **Ridgway's Paratroopers**, p. 84 and ibid., footnote; for a full breakdown of Ridgway's staff group see Nordyke, **All American All the Way**, p. 41
53. See Nordyke, **All American All the Way**, p. 35; and id., **Four Stars of Valor**, p. 48
54. For Lt.-Col. Gorham departure from Oujda see Nordyke, **Four Stars of Valor**, p. 48
55. See for example Nordyke, **All American All the Way**, pp. 34-35; and Blair, **Ridgway's Paratroopers**, pp. 79-80; for Malta Command Mosquito Squadrons see Molony, **The Campaign in Sicily 1943**, Appendix 4: Orders of Battle Royal Air Force and United States Army Air Forces, Table (a) 'Mediterranean Air Command, 3rd September 1943' pp. 874-875
56. For dates & unit locations see Maurer, **Air Force Combat Units of World War II**, entries for '52nd Troop Carrier Wing', 61st, 314th, 315th & 316th Troop Carrier Groups, pp. 395-396, 125-127, 188-195
57. For Ridgway's order date and transport see for example Nordyke, **All American All the Way**, pp. 36-37; for ten locations see Devlin, **Paratrooper!**, p. 218; for deleterious impact of air shuttle see LoFaro, **The Sword of St. Michael**, pp. 73-74
58. For accommodation and open air showers see Nordyke, **All American All the Way**, pp. 37, 43; and LoFaro, **The Sword of St. Michael**, p. 74; for USO show see Devlin, **Paratrooper!**, pp. 218-219; for 505th Regiment anniversary barbecue see for example Nordyke, **Four Stars of Valour**, p. 52
59. For Moslem cemetery see LoFaro, **The Sword of St. Michael**, p. 74; for supply breakdown see Nordyke, **All American All the Way**, p. 37
60. Quote from Ridgway & Martin, **Soldier: The Memoirs of Matthew B. Ridgway**, p. 66-68; cited in Nordyke, **All American All the Way**, p. 45

Chapter 7

1. See Garland & Smyth, **Sicily and the Surrender of Italy**, p. 62 & ibid., Footnote # 31
2. For 10-14 July window, H-Hour and D-Day timings and date and illumination see for example Molony, **The Campaign in Sicily 1943**, p. 28 and ibid., Footnote # 1
3. See for example Garland & Smyth, **Sicily and the Surrender of Italy**, pp. 88-96; and Molony, **The Campaign in Sicily 1943**, Tables '8th Army' and '7th United States Army', pp. 26-27
4. See for example Bernard Fergusson, **The Watery Maze: The Story of Combined Operations**, pp. 242-243
5. Figures cited in untitled table of ship types and numbers in Molony, **The Campaign in Sicily 1943**, p. 30
6. Names and appointments cited in Garland & Smyth, **Sicily and the Surrender of Italy**, p. 100
7. Following the capture of its founding commander David Stirling in January 1943, the 1st Special Air Service (SAS) Regiment was reorganised in April 1943 into two parts; the Special Raiding Squadron (SRS) commanded by Major Robert 'Paddy' Mayne and the Special Boat Squadron commanded by Major Lord George Jellicoe
8. See Otway, **Airborne Forces**, p. 119; for radio station see Peters, **Glider Pilots in Sicily**, p. 185
9. See Hilary St. George Saunders, **The Green Beret**, pp. 151-152; and Fergusson, **The Watery Maze**, p. 243; for details of the Lamba Doria Battery see the **Invasion of Sicily BlogSpot** website, 'The Fall of the Lamba Doria Coastal Battery' page at http://invasionofsicily.blogspot.com/2016/04/the-fall-of-lamba-doria-coastal-battery.html, accessed 03/08/2020. HMS *Prins Albert* is sometimes rendered *Prince Albert*

10. For ship-to-shore definition see Molony, **The Campaign in Sicily 1943**, p. 25; for landing area code names and formation assignment and missions see ibid., Table '8th Army', p. 26; and Table 'British Landing Areas and Assaulting Troops (North to South)', pp. 69-70
11. For shore-to-shore definition, the 51st Highland Division's landing being of this type and types of landing vessel see Molony, **The Campaign in Sicily 1943**, p. 27 and ibid., Footnote # 1; for landing area code names and formation assignment and missions see ibid., Table '8th Army', p. 26; and Table 'British Landing Areas and Assaulting Troops (North to South)', pp. 69-70
12. See Molony, **The Campaign in Sicily 1943**, p. 60
13. See Lieutenant-Colonel G. W. L. Nicholson, **The Canadians in Italy 1943-1945**, pp. 65-67; and ibid, Map 2 'South-Eastern Sicily 10-12 July 1943 & Inset Map 'Canadian Assaults', between pp. 83-83; see also Molony, **The Campaign in Sicily 1943**, Table '8th Army', p. 26; and Table 'British Landing Areas and Assaulting Troops (North to South)', pp. 69-70
14. See Nicholson, **The Canadians in Italy 1943-1945**, p. 63; and Robin Neillands, **By Sea and Land: The Story of the Royal Marines Commandos** (London: Fontana, 1988), pp. 84-85
15. Quotes from Garland & Smyth, **Sicily and the Surrender of Italy**, p. 91; for Alexander's intent see for example Nicholson, **The Canadians in Italy 1943-1945**, p. 86
16. For details see Garland & Smyth, **Sicily and the Surrender of Italy**, pp. 96-98
17. See Garland & Smyth, **Sicily and the Surrender of Italy**, p. 96
18. For Truscott's overall mission see for example Garland & Smyth, **Sicily and the Surrender of Italy**, p. 98 and Map II 'The Final Landing Plan' & Map III 'The Seventh Army Assault 10 July 1943'; for shore-to-shore landing operation see ibid., p. 100; for a précis of units, beach allocations and immediate missions see Molony, **The Campaign in Sicily 1943**, Table 'American Landing Areas and Assaulting Troops (West to East)', p. 71
19. See Garland & Smyth, **Sicily and the Surrender of Italy**, p. 102
20. For responsibilities and mixed mode of delivery see Garland & Smyth, **Sicily and the Surrender of Italy**, p. 100; for Force X Order of Battle see ibid., Appendix A 'Composition of US Forces on D-DAY, 10 July 1943', p. 555
21. See for example D'Este, **Bitter Victory**, pp. 274-275
22. See Garland & Smyth, **Sicily and the Surrender of Italy**, pp. 99-100 and Map II 'The Final Landing Plan' & Map III 'The Seventh Army Assault 10 July 1943'; for a précis of units, beach allocations and immediate missions see Molony, **The Campaign in Sicily 1943**, Table 'American Landing Areas and Assaulting Troops (West to East)', p. 71
23. See Garland & Smyth, **Sicily and the Surrender of Italy**, p. 102
24. For details of Convoy UGF-9 see Calhoun G. (1999), 'Breaching the Westwall: Hampton Roads' UG Convoys to North Africa', *The Daybook* (Journal of the Hampton Roads Naval Museum), Volume 6, Issue1 Fall 1999, 6-10, 14-15, p. 14; available at https://static.dvidshub.net/media/pubs/pdf_49876.pdf, accessed 10/08/2020
25. See Vice-Admiral H. K. Hewitt, '**Action Report Western Naval Task Force**: The Sicilian Campaign: Operation "HUSKY", July-August 1943', 'Part IV: Execution of the Plan', 'Section VIII: TRANSPORTS Combat Loading', Para. 1, p. 47, at https://www.history.navy.mil/research/library/online-reading-room/title-list-alphabetically/s/the-sicilian-campaign-operation-husky.html, accessed 10/08/2020
26. The River Acate is sometimes known as the River Dirillo

27. See Garland & Smyth, **Sicily and the Surrender of Italy**, p. 100 and Map II 'The Final Landing Plan' & Map III 'The Seventh Army Assault 10 July 1943'; for a précis of units, beach allocations and immediate missions see Molony, **The Campaign in Sicily 1943**, Table 'American Landing Areas and Assaulting Troops (West to East)', p. 71
28. See Garland & Smyth, **Sicily and the Surrender of Italy**, p. 102
29. 3,370 total reached by adding 1,654 figure for British and Other Nations Ships cited in the British Official History and the 1,725 total for US vessels cited in the US Official History; the disparity appears to be due to the British figures undercounting US vessels by almost half. See untitled table of ship types and numbers in Molony, **The Campaign in Sicily 1943**, p. 30; and figures cited in Garland & Smyth, **Sicily and the Surrender of Italy**, p. 100, Footnote # 23
30. See for example Molony, **The Campaign in Sicily 1943**, pp. 29-30, 59
31. See Molony, **The Campaign in Sicily 1943**, p. 29
32. Figures cited in untitled table of ship types & numbers in Molony, **The Campaign in Sicily 1943**, p. 30
33. For details of assignments see the **Naval History** website, various vessel-specific pages accessed from the Home & Contents page at https://www.naval-history.net/xGM-aContents.htm, accessed 16/08/2020
34. See Garland & Smyth, **Sicily and the Surrender of Italy**, p. 106
35. Quoted from Molony, **The Campaign in Sicily 1943**, p. 62
36. See Molony, **The Campaign in Sicily 1943**, pp. 60- 62
37. British 1,042 total from figures cited in Molony, **The Campaign in Sicily 1943**, untitled table of ship types and numbers, p. 30; 1,725 total from figures cited in Garland & Smyth, **Sicily and the Surrender of Italy**, p. 100, Footnote # 23; interestingly, the Molony table gives a lower US total figure of 700 landing craft from an overall total of 945 US vessels
38. See for example Molony, **The Campaign in Sicily 1943**, Appendix 3 'Some Types of Landing Ships and Craft in Use in 1943-44', p. 869; and the **uboat.net** website, 'Allied Warships' section, various vessel-specific entries at 'Landing Ship Infantrys [sic] page at https://uboat.net/allies/warships/types.html?type=Landing+Ship+Infantry, accessed 21/08/2020
39. See Garland & Smyth, **Sicily and the Surrender of Italy**, p. 105
40. See for example Lida Mayo, **The Ordnance Department: On Beachhead and Battlefront** (Washington DC: Center of Military History, United States Army, 1991), p. 156
41. See Mayo, **The Ordnance Department: On Beachhead and Battlefront**, pp. 156-157
42. British 8th Army DUKW figures cited in Molony, **The Campaign in Sicily** 1943, Table: 'Distribution of Beach Groups and DUKWs', p. 141; for despatch of Canadian vehicles from US to the UK see Nicholson, **The Canadians in Italy 1943-1945**, pp. 35-36
43. See Fergusson, **The Watery Maze**, pp. 246-247
44. See Garland & Smyth, **Sicily and the Surrender of Italy**, p. 103
45. See Molony, **The Campaign in Sicily 1943**, p. 56
46. For 45th Infantry Division embarkation date see Garland & Smyth, **Sicily and the Surrender of Italy**, p. 108; for departure date and timings and *Monrovia* presence see US **Naval History and Heritage Command** website, Vice-Admiral H. K. Hewitt, **'Action Report Western Naval Task Force:** The Sicilian Campaign: Operation "HUSKY", July-August 1943', 'Part II: Narrative of Events', entry for 17:00, 06/07/1943, p. 2, at https://www.history.navy.mil/research/library/online-reading-room/title-list-alphabetically/s/the-sicilian-campaign-operation-husky.html, accessed 24/08/2020. The 45th Division/ CENT FORCE convoy

included the attack transports USS *Arcturus*, USS *Bellatrix*, USS *Calvert*, USS *Charles Carroll*, USS *Dorothea L. Dix*, USS *Florence Nightingale*, USS *Frederick Funston*, USS *Leonard Wood*, USS *Neville*, USS *Procyon*, USS *Susan B. Anthony*, USS *Thomas Jefferson* and USS *William P. Biddle*; see **Convoy Web** website, UGF Convoys Section, Convoy UGF-9 Page at www.convoyweb.org.uk/ugf/ugf.php?convoy=9!, accessed 24/08/2020

47. For 1st Division convoy rendezvous timing and location see Hewitt, '**Action Report Western Naval Task Force**, 'Narrative of Events' Section, entry for 13:30, 07/07/1943, p. 2; see also Garland & Smyth, **Sicily and the Surrender of Italy**, p. 108. The 1st Division Algiers convoy included the attack transports USS *Barnett*, USS *Elizabeth C. Stanton*, USS *Joseph P. Dickman*, USS *Lyon* and USS *Thurston*; see the **Convoy Web** website, Shorter Convoy Series Section, Convoy NCF-1 Page at www.convoyweb.org.uk/misc/yyA.php?convoy=NCF.1!, accessed 24/08/2020
48. See Molony, **The Campaign in Sicily 1943**, pp. 52-53; for circumnavigating the Cape of Good Hope see Fergusson, **The Watery Maze**, pp. 242-243
49. See Molony, **The Campaign in Sicily 1943**, p. 60
50. For 3rd Division start points and sailing dates see Molony, **The Campaign in Sicily 1943**, p. 53 and Map 5, 'Invasion of Sicily 10th July 1943: Main Routes of Assault Convoys' between pp. 28-29; for FORCE B/51st Highland Division see ibid.; for Convoy SBF-1 sailing date and vessels see the **Convoy Web** website, Shorter Convoy **Series** Section, Convoy SBF-1 Page at www.convoyweb.org.uk/misc/yyA.php?convoy=SBF.1!, accessed 23/08/2020
51. For a full breakdown with ship names and other details see **Convoy Web** website, KMF Convoy Series Section, Convoy KMF-18 Page at www.convoyweb.org.uk/kmf/kmf.php?convoy=18!, accessed 24/08/2020
52. See Hewitt, '**Action Report Western Naval Task Force**, 'Narrative of Events' Section, entry for 18:00, 07/07/1943, p. 2,
53. See **Convoy Web** website, KMS Convoy Series Section, Convoy KMS-19 Page at www.convoyweb.org.uk/kms/kms.php?convoy=19!, accessed 24/08/2020
54. See Molony, **The Campaign in Sicily 1943**, pp. 53-54
55. Timing cited in Hewitt, '**Action Report Western Naval Task Force**', 'Narrative of Events' Section, entry for 16:30, 09/07/1943, p. 2
56. Quote from Molony, **The Campaign in Sicily 1943**, p. 54
57. See Garland & Smyth, **Sicily and the Surrender of Italy**, p. 108
58. See Molony, **The Campaign in Sicily 1943**, pp. 54-55

Chapter 8

1. See Garland & Smyth, **Sicily and the Surrender of Italy**, p. 76; for Fortress Area details see Molony, **The Campaign in Sicily 1943**, p. 50; and ibid., Footnote #2
2. See Garland & Smyth, **Sicily and the Surrender of Italy**, pp. 75-76
3. See Molony, **The Campaign in Sicily 1943**, p. 41
4. Quoted from Garland & Smyth, **Sicily and the Surrender of Italy**, p. 79
5. 2,000 Italian strength figure cited in Molony, **The Campaign in Sicily 1943**, p. 41; and Garland & Smyth, **Sicily and the Surrender of Italy**, p. 80
6. See Garland & Smyth, **Sicily and the Surrender of Italy**, pp. 80-81; for the Italian Order of Battle with Corps' commanders' names see Molony, **The Campaign in Sicily 1943**, p. 43
7. See Molony, **The Campaign in Sicily 1943**, p. 41; for unit locations see ibid., Map 6: 'General Layout of Axis Forces in Sicily, 9th July 1943', between pp. 42-43; and Garland & Smyth, **Sicily and the Surrender of Italy**, Map I 'The Battleground and the Enemy, 10 July 1943'

8. See Molony, **The Campaign in Sicily 1943**, p. 43
9. See Garland & Smyth, **Sicily and the Surrender of Italy**, pp. 81, 84; for unit locations see ibid., Map I 'The Battleground and the Enemy, 10 July 1943'; and Molony, **The Campaign in Sicily 1943**, Map 6: 'General Layout of Axis Forces in Sicily, 9th July 1943', between pp. 42-43
10. See for example Garland & Smyth, **Sicily and the Surrender of Italy**, pp. 35-36
11. See for example D'Este, **Bitter Victory**, pp. 197-198
12. Quoted from Garland & Smyth, **Sicily and the Surrender of Italy**, p. 73
13. See for example Garland & Smyth, **Sicily and the Surrender of Italy**, p. 51
14. Hube was known as *Der Mensch* (The Man) by his soldiers. A career officer, he was commissioned in 1908 and lost his right arm in the Great War. However, such was his manifest ability that despite being an amputee, he was one of a select officer corps to be retained in the post-war Reichsheer. During the fighting in Russia Hube gained a reputation as a brilliant tactician, an outstanding commander of mobile forces, and an outspoken, although utterly honest, critic of poor planning. A personal favourite of Hitler, Hube had been 'abducted' at gunpoint by members of the Fuhrer's personal bodyguard and taken to Berlin after he had refused an order to leave the Stalingrad 'pocket'.
15. See for example Garland & Smyth, **Sicily and the Surrender of Italy**, pp. 74-75
16. Quoted from Garland & Smyth, **Sicily and the Surrender of Italy**, p. 75
17. See for example Molony, **The Campaign in Sicily 1943**, p. 42; for a breakdown of the units that escaped from Tunisia see the **Axis History** website, 'Division Sizilien' page at https://www.axishistory.com/books/150-germany-heer/heer-divisionen/3042-division-sizilien, accessed 09/09/2020
18. For order of battle details see **Axis History** website, '15. Panzergrenadier-Division' page at https://www.axishistory.com/books/150-germany-heer/heer-divisionen/4115-15-panzergrenadier-division, accessed 09/09/2020; and the **Comando Supremo: Italy in WW2** website, 'Axis Forces in Sicily: July 1943 OOB' page at https://comandosupremo.com/axis-forces-in-sicily/, accessed 09/09/2020; for differing tank numbers see ibid.; and Molony, **The Campaign in Sicily 1943**, p. 42
19. For order of battle details see **Comando Supremo: Italy in WW2** website, 'Axis Forces in Sicily: July 1943 OOB' page at https://comandosupremo.com/axis-forces-in-sicily/, accessed 09/09/2020; and the **Axis History** website, 'Panzer Division Hermann Göring' page at https://www.axishistory.com/list-all-categories/151-germany-luftwaffe/luftwaffe-ground-units/5628-panzer-division-hermann-goering, accessed 10/09/2020. The British Official History cites a total of ninety-nine Panzer III & IVs and thirteen Tiger Is; see Molony, **The Campaign in Sicily 1943**, p. 42; for details of *Panzergrenadier Regiment 382* see Nicholson, **The Canadians in Italy 1943-1945**, p. 154 and Footnote
20. See Garland & Smyth, **Sicily and the Surrender of Italy**, p. 83; Conrath quote cited in D'Este, **Bitter Victory**, p. 207
21. See for example Garland & Smyth, **Sicily and the Surrender of Italy**, pp. 81-82; and Molony, **The Campaign in Sicily 1943**, pp. 40-41. For more detail on von Senger und Etterlin's appointment and background see D'Este, **Bitter Victory**, pp. 199-203
22. See Molony, **The Campaign in Sicily 1943**, p. 42; for the Kesselring-Guzzoni discussion and earlier discussions between Guzzoni and Rodt see Garland & Smyth, **Sicily and the Surrender of Italy**, pp. 83-86
23. See for example Garland & Smyth, **Sicily and the Surrender of Italy**, p. 87; and D'Este, **Bitter Victory**, p. 209

24. See for example Garland & Smyth, **Sicily and the Surrender of Italy**, pp. 86-87; the command and organisation of *Kampfgruppe* Neapel are unclear, see ibid., p. 84, especially Footnote # 53. For the transfer of *Panzer Abteilung 215* to the *Hermann Göring Panzer Division* see D'Este, **Bitter Victory**, pp. 207-208
25. See for example Garland & Smyth, **Sicily and the Surrender of Italy**, pp. 86-87 and Map I 'The Battleground and the Enemy, 10 July 1943'; and Molony, **The Campaign in Sicily 1943**, Map 6: General Layout of Axis Forces in Sicily, 9th July 1943', between pp. 42-43; for order of battle details see for example **Comando Supremo: Italy in WW2** website, 'Axis Forces in Sicily: July 1943 OOB' page at https://comandosupremo.com/axis-forces-in-sicily/, accessed 10/09/2020
26. For a detailed account see Peters, **Glider Pilots in Sicily**, pp. 222-224
27. See Garland & Smyth, **Sicily and the Surrender of Italy**, p. 87
28. Quoted from Garland & Smyth, **Sicily and the Surrender of Italy**, p. 109
29. For timings and other details see D'Este, **Bitter Victory**, p. 223; Molony, **The Campaign in Sicily 1943**, pp. 54-55; and Garland & Smyth, **Sicily and the Surrender of Italy**, pp. 109-111

Chapter 9

1. With the exception of the 1st Airlanding Brigade War Diary, which does not refer to any codename, and the 1st Battalion Glider Pilot Regiment War Diary, which refers to Operation BIGOT-HUSKEY [sic], the War Diaries of all the units involved in the landing refer to the operation as BIGOT; see for example **WO 169/10182** 1st Battalion The Border Regiment War Diary and **WO 169/10299** 2nd Battalion South Staffordshire Regiment War Diary. The more common and popularly recognised Operation LADBROKE is used here to avoid confusion
2. See **WO 169/8666** 1st Airborne Division War Diary, 'Report on the Operations Carried Out by 1st Airborne Division during the Invasion of Sicily (Operation HUSKY): Part 2 – 1st Airlanding Brigade Operations: Section B. 'Ground Operations' 1. Outline Plan (i) Objectives. Hereafter this report is referred to as '1st Airborne Division After Action Report: Part 2'. For codenames and inclusion of the radio station see Peters, **Glider Pilots in Sicily**, pp. 113, 185; for inclusion of the Lamba Doria Battery see Otway, **Airborne Forces**, p. 119
3. For 1st Border strength see **WO 169/10182** 1st Battalion The Border Regiment War Diary, entry for 18:50, 09/07/1943; for 2nd South Staffords strength see **WO 169/8666** 1st Airborne Division War Diary, 1st Airborne Division After Action Report: Part 2 – 1st Airlanding Brigade Operations: Section A. Air Operations, Annexure 5: Figures of Personnel & Equipment taken on Operation at Syracuse
4. For 9th Field Company details see **WO 169/10576** 9th Field Company RE War Diary, entry for 09-15/07/1943. Major Beazley's surname is sometimes rendered Beasley, on occasion both renderings appearing in the same primary source document
5. See **WO 177/775** 181 Airlanding Field Ambulance RAMC War Diary, entry for 17:55, 09/07/1943; and ibid., Appendix 'A': 'Nominal Roll of Personnel Proceeding on Exercise' and 'Report on Medical Aspects of Operation "BIGOT"'
6. See **WO 169/8666** 1st Airborne Division War Diary, 1st Airborne Division After Action Report: Part 2 – 1st Airlanding Brigade Operations: Section B. 'Ground Operations' 1. Outline Plan, Point (ii) Order of Battle
7. See **WO 169/8666** 1st Airborne Division War Diary, 1st Airborne Division After Action Report: Part 2 – 1st Airlanding Brigade Operations: Section A. Air

Operations' Para. 2: 'Availability of A/C'; summarised in Peters, **Glider Pilots in Sicily**, p. 112

8. See **WO 169/8666** 1st Airborne Division War Diary, 1st Airborne Division After Action Report: Part 2 – 1st Airlanding Brigade Operations: Section A. Air Operations, Annexure 5: Figures of Personnel & Equipment taken on Operation at Syracuse and Annexure 6: Summary of Glider Loads Carried on 1 Air Landing Bde Operation
9. Figures cited in Otway, **Airborne Forces**, p. 119
10. See **WO 169/8666** 1st Airborne Division War Diary, 1st Airborne Division After Action Report: Part 2 – 1st Airlanding Brigade Operations: Section B. 1'Ground Operations' 1. Outline Plan, Points (iv) Method and (v) Timings; summarised in Otway, **Airborne Forces**, p. 120
11. For 23:15 timing see **WO 169/8666** 1st Airborne Division War Diary, 1st Airborne Division After Action Report: Part 2 – 1st Airlanding Brigade Operations: Section B. 1'Ground Operations' 1. Outline Plan, Point (v) Timings; for other details see Peters, **Glider Pilots in Sicily**, pp. 114-116; for Sapper inclusion see **WO 169/10576** 9th Field Company RE War Diary, entry for 09-15/07/1943. Peters gives Major Ballinger's forename as Peter, but the Commonwealth War Graves Commission names him as Edwin George and the 2nd South Staffords' War Diary refers to him with the fore initials E.G.
12. Quoted from Otway, **Airborne Forces**, p. 121
13. For Company LZ and mission allocations see **WO 169/10299** 2nd Battalion South Staffordshire Regiment War Diary, entry for 09/07/1943, A & C Company specific entries; for LZ locations see for example Peters, **Glider Pilots in Sicily**, Map 'Vicinity of Landing Zones for LADBROKE Mission, 9-10 July 1943', p. 115
14. 01:15 timing from **WO 169/8845** 1st Airlanding Brigade HQ War Diary, Operation Order No. 1; cited in Peters, **Glider Pilots in Sicily**, p. 116
15. LZ dimensions quoted in testimony from Major John Place, OC 3 Squadron, 1st Battalion The Glider Pilot Regiment; cited in Peters, **Glider Pilots in Sicily**, p. 117; see also ibid., Map 'Vicinity of Landing Zones for LADBROKE Mission, 9-10 July 1943', p. 115
16. For twenty-minute window see **WO 169/10182** 1st Battalion The Border Regiment War Diary, entry for 18:50, 09/07/1943; for 01:15 deadline for reaching the Ponte Grande see **WO 169/8666** 1st Airborne Division War Diary, 1st Airborne Division After Action Report: Part 2 – 1st Airlanding Brigade Operations: Section B. 1'Ground Operations' 1. Outline Plan, Point (v) Timings; for 01:15 main force arrival time see **WO 169/8845** 1st Airlanding Brigade HQ War Diary, Operation Order No. 1; cited in Peters, **Glider Pilots in Sicily**, p. 116
17. For individual Company missions see **WO 169/10299** 2nd Battalion South Staffordshire Regiment War Diary, entry for 09/07/1943, B, D & E Company specific entries; for codenames see Peters, **Glider Pilots in Sicily**, pp. 116-117
18. Timings and quote from **WO 169/10182** 1st Battalion The Border Regiment War Diary, entry for 18:50, 09/07/1943; for objectives and codenames see Peters, **Glider Pilots in Sicily**, p. 113
19. For No. 205 Group involvement see **WO 169/8666** 1st Airborne Division War Diary, Appendix: Part 1: Preparation of 1 Airborne Division for Operation HUSKY, 'Attachment to Appendix 'E': Bombing Attacks in Co-Operation with Airborne Operations', Para. 1 'SYRACUSE 02:15-02:45 hrs 10 July'; and ibid., 1st Airborne Division After Action Report: Part 2 – 1st Airlanding Brigade Operations: Section B. 1'Ground Operations' 1. Outline Plan, Point (v) Timings; quote from Peters, **Glider Pilots in Sicily**, p. 117

20. For Strip F tests see **WO 169/8666** 1st Airborne Division War Diary, entry for 07/07/1943; for German employment in 1940 see for example Cajus Bekker, **The Luftwaffe War Diaries**, (New York: MacDonald, 1966), p. 128
21. See **WO 169/8666** 1st Airborne Division War Diary, Appendix: Part 1: Preparation of 1 Airborne Division for Operation HUSKY, Appendix F: Report on Dropping Dummy Parachutists over Sicily; and Peters, **Glider Pilots in Sicily**, p. 114
22. For distances and release heights see **AIR 27/1646** No. 296 Squadron Operations Record Book: Appendices, Appendix B: 'Operation "LADBROKE", Para. 9 'Route Out' & Para. 13 'Release Heights', dated 08/07/1943
23. For Group-Captain Cooper's command of FRESHMAN and flying as tug co-pilot see for example Otway, **Airborne Forces**, pp. 71-72; for Squadron-Leader Wright's involvement with the glider side of the Central Landing School onward see for example Lawrence Wright, **The Wooden Sword: The Untold Story of the Gliders in World War II** (London: Elek, 1967)
24. Testimony from Group-Captain Thomas Cooper DFC cited in General Sir Anthony Farrar-Hockley, **The Army in the Air: The History of the Army Air Corps** (Stroud: Sutton Publishing, 1994), p. 83; quoted in Peters, **Glider Pilots in Sicily**, pp. 101-102
25. See Peters, **Glider Pilots in Sicily**, pp. 101-102
26. See William F Buckingham, **Arnhem: The Complete Story of Operation MARKET GARDEN, 17-25 September 1944** (Stroud: Amberley Publishing, 2019), pp. 49-51
27. See **WO 169/8666** 1st Airborne Division War Diary, entry for 01/07/1943; and **WO 177/775** 181 Airlanding Field Ambulance RAMC War Diary, entry for 17:00, 02/07/1943
28. See **WO 169/10182** 1st Battalion The Border Regiment War Diary, entry for 03/07/1943; **WO 169/10299** 2nd Battalion South Staffordshire Regiment War Diary, entries for 03/07/1943& 04/07/1943; and **WO 169/10576** 9th Field Company RE War Diary, entry for 03/07/1943
29. See **WO 169/8669** 1st Airborne Division HQ Royal Engineers War Diary, entry for 05/07/1943
30. See **WO 169/10182** 1st Battalion The Border Regiment War Diary, entries for 06 & 07/07/1943; **WO 169/10299** 2nd Battalion South Staffordshire Regiment War Diary, entries for 06 & 07/07/194; **WO 169/10576** 9th Field Company RE War Diary, entries for 06, 07 & 08/07/1943; and **WO 177/775** 181 Airlanding Field Ambulance RAMC War Diary, entry for 07/07/1943
31. Quoted from **WO 169/10182** 1st Battalion The Border Regiment War Diary, entry for 06/07/1943
32. See Peters, **Glider Pilots in Sicily**, pp. 112-114; for a copy of the LADBROKE map see **AIR 27/1646** No. 296 Squadron Operations Record Book: Appendices, Appendix C: 'Report on Operation "LADBROKE" 9th July 1943', n.d.
33. See **WO 169/8666** 1st Airborne Division War Diary, Appendix: Part 1: Preparation of 1 Airborne Division for Operation HUSKY, Appendix A 'Diary of Events', entry for 05/07/1943; and **WO 177/775** 181 Airlanding Field Ambulance RAMC War Diary, entry for 05/07/1943
34. See **WO 169/8666** 1st Airborne Division War Diary, 1st Airborne Division After Action Report: Part 2 – 1st Airlanding Brigade Operations: Section A. Air Operations, Para. 3 'Loading of Gliders; and Peters, **Glider Pilots in Sicily**, p. 122
35. See **WO 169/8674** 1st Airlanding Reconnaissance Squadron War Diary, entry for 14:45, 06/07/1943; **WO 169/10341** 1st Battalion The Glider Pilot Regiment War Diary, entry for 14:00, 06/07/1943; **WO 169/10182** 1st Battalion The Border Regiment War Diary, entry for 07/07/1943; and **WO 177/775** 181 Airlanding

Field Ambulance RAMC War Diary, entry for 06/07/1943; quote and QM details from testimony from Major John Place, OC No. 3 Squadron, 1st Battalion The Glider Pilot Regiment; cited in Peters, **Glider Pilots in Sicily**, pp. 120-121. There is no mention of the incident in the 2nd South Staffords War Diary and the 1st Border War Diary erroneously refers to it occurring on 7 July; the 1st Airlanding Reconnaissance Squadron was subsequently renamed the 1st Airborne Reconnaissance Squadron

36. See **AIR 27/1645** No. 296 Squadron Operations Record Book, entry for 08/07/1943; and testimony from Lieutenant Edward Newport, commanding No. 2 Anti-Tank Platoon, Support Company, 1st Battalion the Border Regiment in Stuart A. Eastwood et al, **When Dragons Flew: An Illustrated History of the 1st Battalion The Border Regiment 1939-45**, p. 64; cited in Peters, **Glider Pilots in Sicily**, p. 133; the latter suggests that the crash took place in the immediate run up to take-off on 9 July but the No. 296 Squadron Record Book entry shows it occurred the previous day
37. See **WO 169/10182** 1st Battalion The Border Regiment War Diary, entry for 08/07/1943; **WO 169/10299** 2nd Battalion South Staffordshire Regiment War Diary, entry for 08/07/194; **WO 169/10576** 9th Field Company RE War Diary, entry for 09/07/1943; **WO 177/775** 181 Airlanding Field Ambulance RAMC War Diary, entry for 08/07/1943; and **WO 169/10341** 1st Battalion The Glider Pilot Regiment War Diary, entry for 08/07/1943. For contemporary film footage of the visit see IWM Film AYY 509/3 'Visit of General Montgomery' at https://film.iwmcollections.org.uk/r/1821, accessed 27/09/2020; the 9th Field Company War Diary erroneously cites the visit taking place on 9 July
38. See **WO 169/10343** 1st Parachute Battalion War Diary, entry for 11:30, 08/07/1943; and **WO 169/10344** 2nd Parachute Battalion War Diary, entry for 10:30, 08/07/1943
39. See **WO 169/10341** 1st Battalion The Glider Pilot Regiment War Diary, entry for 08/07/1943; and Peters, **Glider Pilots in Sicily**, p. 122; 286 figure from **WO 169/8666** 1st Airborne Division War Diary, 1st Airborne Division After Action Report: Part 2 – 1st Airlanding Brigade Operations: Section A. Air Operations, Annexure 4 'Glider Pilot Crews Operation at Syracuse'
40. See **WO 169/8666** 1st Airborne Division War Diary, 1st Airborne Division After Action Report: Part 2 – 1st Airlanding Brigade Operations: Section A. Air Operations, Para. 5 'Marshalling of Glider' [sic]; and **WO 169/10299** 2nd Battalion South Staffordshire Regiment War Diary, entry for 08/07/194; quote & sandwiches from testimony from Lance-Corporal Reginald Brown, 7 Platoon, A Company, 2nd Battalion The South Staffordshire Regiment; cited in Peters, **Glider Pilots in Sicily**, p. 131
41. See Cole, **On The Wings of Healing**, p. 38
42. See **WO 169/8666** 1st Airborne Division War Diary, 1st Airborne Division After Action Report: Part 2 – 1st Airlanding Brigade Operations: Section A. Air Operations, Para. 4 'Move to Airfields'
43. See Peters, **Glider Pilots in Sicily**, pp. 117, 119 & 130
44. See testimony from Major John Place, OC No. 3 Squadron, 1st Battalion The Glider Pilot Regiment; cited in Peters, **Glider Pilots in Sicily**, p. 132
45. See **WO 169/8666** 1st Airborne Division War Diary, 1st Airborne Division After Action Report: Part 2 – 1st Airlanding Brigade Operations: Section A. Air Operations, Para. 6 'Alteration to Height of Release'
46. See testimony from Major John Place, OC No. 3 Squadron, 1st Battalion The Glider Pilot Regiment; cited in Peters, **Glider Pilots in Sicily**, pp. 134-135

47. See **WO 169/8666** 1st Airborne Division War Diary, 1st Airborne Division After Action Report: Part 2 – 1st Airlanding Brigade Operations: Section A. Air Operations, Para. 8 'Take Off' & Para. 9 'Summary of Take-Off'; for glider chalk details see Peters, **Glider Pilots in Sicily**, Appendix 1 'Operation LADBROKE Post Mission Reports', pp. 273-284
48. For Wing-Commander May's involvement see **AIR 27/1646** No. 296 Squadron Operations Record Book: Appendices, Appendix C: 'Report on Operation "LADBROKE" 9th July 1943', n.d.; and Peters, **Glider Pilots in Sicily**, p. 180
49. See **AIR 27/1646** No. 296 Squadron Operations Record Book: Appendices, Appendix B: 'Operation "LADBROKE"', Para. 14 'Speed', dated 08/07/1943
50. See Peters, **Glider Pilots in Sicily**, p. 180; for undercarriage jettisoning see testimony from Lance-Corporal Reginald Brown, 7 Platoon, A Company, 2nd Battalion The South Staffordshire Regiment; cited in ibid., pp. 133-134
51. See **WO 169/8666** 1st Airborne Division War Diary, 1st Airborne Division After Action Report: Part 2 – 1st Airlanding Brigade Operations: Section A. Air Operations, Para. 8 'Take Off'
52. See Peters, **Glider Pilots in Sicily**, p. 181
53. See **AIR 27/1646** No. 296 Squadron Operations Record Book: Appendices, Appendix B: 'Operation "LADBROKE"', Para. 14 'Speed', dated 08/07/1943; and ibid, Appendix C: 'Report on Operation "LADBROKE"' 9th July 1943', n.d.
54. See **WO 169/8666** 1st Airborne Division War Diary, 1st Airborne Division After Action Report: Part 2 – 1st Airlanding Brigade Operations: Section A. Air Operations, Para. 10 'Return of Tug A/C'
55. See Peters, **Glider Pilots in Sicily**, p. 180; and **WO 169/8845** 1st Airlanding Brigade HQ War Diary, Glider No. 128 note in entry for 09/07/1943
56. See **WO 169/8666** 1st Airborne Division War Diary, 1st Airborne Division After Action Report: Part 2 – 1st Airlanding Brigade Operations: Section A. Air Operations, Annexure 3 'Summary of Glider Reports on Operation at Syracuse – 1st Airborne Bde' [sic], entry for Glider No. 129; **WO 169/8845** 1st Airlanding Brigade HQ War Diary, Glider No. 129 note in entry for 09/07/1943; and **WO 169/10299** 2nd Battalion South Staffordshire Regiment War Diary, entry for 09/07/1943
57. See **WO 169/8666** 1st Airborne Division War Diary, 1st Airborne Division After Action Report: Part 2 – 1st Airlanding Brigade Operations: Section A. Air Operations, Annexure 3 'Summary of Glider Reports on Operation at Syracuse – 1st Airborne Bde' [sic], entry for Glider No. 135; **WO 169/10299** 2nd Battalion South Staffordshire Regiment War Diary, entry for 09/07/1943; and Peters, **Glider Pilots in Sicily**, p. 181
58. See **WO 169/8666** 1st Airborne Division War Diary, 1st Airborne Division After Action Report: Part 2 – 1st Airlanding Brigade Operations: Section A. Air Operations', Annexure 3 'Summary of Glider Reports on Operation at Syracuse – 1st Airborne Bde' [sic], entry for Glider No. 134; **WO 169/10299** 2nd Battalion South Staffordshire Regiment War Diary, entry for 09/07/1943; and Peters, **Glider Pilots in Sicily**, pp. 180-181
59. See Peters, **Glider Pilots in Sicily**, pp. 182-183
60. See **WO 169/8666** 1st Airborne Division War Diary, 1st Airborne Division After Action Report: Part 2 – 1st Airlanding Brigade Operations: Section A. Air Operations, Annexure 3 'Summary of Glider Reports on Operation at Syracuse – 1st Airborne Bde' [sic], entry for Glider No. 132; **WO 169/10299** 2nd Battalion South Staffordshire Regiment War Diary, notes on 'No. 17 Platoon' in entry for 09/07/1943; and Peters, **Glider Pilots in Sicily**, pp. 183-184
61. See **WO 169/8666** 1st Airborne Division War Diary, 1st Airborne Division After Action Report: Part 2 – 1st Airlanding Brigade Operations: Section B. 'Ground

Operations' 2. 'Action on Landing', Point (i) 'Capture of PONTE GRANDE'; **WO 169/10299** 2nd Battalion South Staffordshire Regiment War Diary, 'Capture of PONTE GRANDE' in entry for 09/07/1943; for Private Curnock's involvement see Cole, **On The Wings of Healing**, p. 41

62. Quote from **WO 169/10299** 2nd Battalion South Staffordshire Regiment War Diary, 'Capture of PONTE GRANDE' in entry for 09/07/1943; see also Peters, **Glider Pilots in Sicily**, p. 185
63. See **WO 169/8666** 1st Airborne Division War Diary, 1st Airborne Division After Action Report: Part 2 – 1st Airlanding Brigade Operations: Section A. Air Operations, Annexure 3 'Summary of Glider Reports on Operation at Syracuse – 1st Airborne Bde' [sic], glider specific entries; for chalk details see Peters, **Glider Pilots in Sicily**, Appendix 1 'Operation LADBROKE Post Mission Reports', pp. 273-284
64. See testimony from Lt.-Col. George Chatterton, CO 1st Battalion The Glider Pilot Regiment; cited in Peters, **Glider Pilots in Sicily**, p. 160; see also **WO 169/8666** 1st Airborne Division War Diary, 1st Airborne Division After Action Report: Part 2 – 1st Airlanding Brigade Operations: Section A. Air Operations, Annexure 3 'Summary of Glider Reports on Operation at Syracuse – 1st Airborne Bde' [sic], entry for Glider No. 2
65. See **WO 169/8666** 1st Airborne Division War Diary, 1st Airborne Division After Action Report: Part 2 – 1st Airlanding Brigade Operations: Section A. Air Operations, Annexure 2 'Summary of Gliders' Part II, Para 1, Point (a) & Para. 2 Point (a)
66. See **WO 169/8666** 1st Airborne Division War Diary, 1st Airborne Division After Action Report: Part 2 – 1st Airlanding Brigade Operations: Section A. Air Operations, Annexure 3 'Summary of Glider Reports on Operation at Syracuse – 1st Airborne Bde' [sic], entries for Glider Nos. 54, 54a and 111
67. See Peters, **Glider Pilots in Sicily**, p. 158; and **WO 169/8666** 1st Airborne Division War Diary, 1st Airborne Division After Action Report: Part 2 – 1st Airlanding Brigade Operations: Section A. Air Operations, Annexure 3 'Summary of Glider Reports on Operation at Syracuse – 1st Airborne Bde' [sic], entry for Glider No. 112
68. See **WO 169/8666** 1st Airborne Division War Diary, 1st Airborne Division After Action Report: Part 2 – 1st Airlanding Brigade Operations: Section A. Air Operations, Annexure 3 'Summary of Glider Reports on Operation at Syracuse – 1st Airborne Bde' [sic], entries for Glider Nos. 16 and 119
69. See **WO 169/8666** 1st Airborne Division War Diary, 1st Airborne Division After Action Report: Part 2 – 1st Airlanding Brigade Operations: Section A. Air Operations, Para. 13 'General Remarks Regarding Equipment' Point (a); and ibid., Annexure 3 'Summary of Glider Reports on Operation at Syracuse – 1st Airborne Bde' [sic]
70. Testimony from Major John Place, OC No. 3 Squadron, 1st Battalion The Glider Pilot Regiment; cited in Peters, **Glider Pilots in Sicily**, pp. 156-157; see also **WO 169/8666** 1st Airborne Division War Diary, 1st Airborne Division After Action Report: Part 2 – 1st Airlanding Brigade Operations: Section A. Air Operations, Annexure 3 'Summary of Glider Reports on Operation at Syracuse – 1st Airborne Bde' [sic], entry for Glider No. 55
71. See Eastwood et al, **When Dragons Flew**, p. 73; and **WO 169/8666** 1st Airborne Division War Diary, 1st Airborne Division After Action Report: Part 2 – 1st Airlanding Brigade Operations: Section A. Air Operations, Annexure 3 'Summary of Glider Reports on Operation at Syracuse – 1st Airborne Bde' [sic], entries for Glider Nos. 3 and 57; see also **WO 169/10299** 2nd Battalion South

Staffordshire Regiment War Diary, entry for 09/07/1943, Battalion HQ section and Appendix C 'Summary of the Operations on Land'

72. See **WO 169/8666** 1st Airborne Division War Diary, 1st Airborne Division After Action Report: Part 2 – 1st Airlanding Brigade Operations: Section A. Air Operations, Annexure 2 'Summary of Gliders', Part II, Para. 2 Point (a), glider chalk numbers 111-124 from list connected to Strip F & No. 296 Squadron
73. See Kevin Shannon & Stephen Wright, **One Night in June**, pp. 7-8, 22
74. See **WO 169/8666** 1st Airborne Division War Diary, 1st Airborne Division After Action Report: Part 2 – 1st Airlanding Brigade Operations: Section A. Air Operations, Annexure 2 'Summary of Gliders', Part II, Para. 2, Point (b)
75. See Peters, **Glider Pilots in Sicily**, p. 165; and **WO 169/8666** 1st Airborne Division War Diary, 1st Airborne Division After Action Report: Part 2 – 1st Airlanding Brigade Operations: Section A. Air Operations, Annexure 3 'Summary of Glider Reports on Operation at Syracuse – 1st Airborne Bde' [sic], entries for Glider Nos. 24 and 105. The then Staff-Sergeant James Wallwork went on to fly the lead Horsa in the *coup-de-main* attack to secure the Orne Canal Bridge in the very early hours of Tuesday 6 June 1944
76. Quote from testimony from Sergeant Norman Howes, C Company, 2nd Battalion The South Staffordshire Regiment; cited in Peters, **Glider Pilots in Sicily**, pp. 164-165; the load manifest for Glider No. 33 refers to carrying men from B Company; see ibid., Appendix 1 'Operation LADBROKE Post Mission Reports', pp. 273-284; for glider landing location see **WO 169/8666** 1st Airborne Division War Diary, 1st Airborne Division After Action Report: Part 2 – 1st Airlanding Brigade Operations: Section A. Air Operations, Annexure 3 'Summary of Glider Reports on Operation at Syracuse – 1st Airborne Bde' [sic], entry for Glider No. 33
77. Quote from testimony from Staff-Sergeant Jack Barnwell, 1st Battalion The Glider Pilot Regiment; cited in Peters, **Glider Pilots in Sicily**, pp. 164-165; for location and other details see **WO 169/8666** 1st Airborne Division War Diary, 1st Airborne Division After Action Report: Part 2 – 1st Airlanding Brigade Operations: Section A. Air Operations, Annexure 3 'Summary of Glider Reports on Operation at Syracuse – 1st Airborne Bde' [sic], entry for Glider No. 52a
78. See **WO 169/8666** 1st Airborne Division War Diary, 1st Airborne Division After Action Report: Part 2 – 1st Airlanding Brigade Operations: Section A. Air Operations, Annexure 3 'Summary of Glider Reports on Operation at Syracuse – 1st Airborne Bde' [sic], entries for Glider Nos. 8, 35 and 106
79. See Henniker, **An Image of War**, pp. 127-130; for flight and landing location see **WO 169/8666** 1st Airborne Division War Diary, 1st Airborne Division After Action Report: Part 2 – 1st Airlanding Brigade Operations: Section A. Air Operations, Annexure 3 'Summary of Glider Reports on Operation at Syracuse – 1st Airborne Bde' [sic], entry for Glider No. 10
80. See **WO 169/8845** 1st Airlanding Brigade HQ War Diary, Appendix 'Capture of Ponte Grande'
81. See Miller, **Nothing Is Impossible: A Glider Pilot's Story of Sicily, Arnhem and the Rhine Crossing**, pp. 34-40; for flight and landing location see **WO 169/8666** 1st Airborne Division War Diary, 1st Airborne Division After Action Report: Part 2 – 1st Airlanding Brigade Operations: Section A. Air Operations, Annexure 3 'Summary of Glider Reports on Operation at Syracuse – 1st Airborne Bde' [sic], entry for Glider No. 110
82. See **WO 169/10182** 1st Battalion The Border Regiment War Diary, entry for 18:50, 09/07/1943, Para. 3
83. Figure cited in **WO 169/8666** 1st Airborne Division War Diary, 1st Airborne Division After Action Report: Part 2 – 1st Airlanding Brigade Operations: Section

A. Air Operations, Annexure 2 'Summary of Gliders', Part I Para. 5 '[Gliders] Landed on Land', Point (a); and Part II, Para. 1, Point (b) & Para. 2, Point (b); see also Peters, **Glider Pilots in Sicily**, Appendix 1 'Operation LADBROKE Post Mission Reports', pp. 273-284. The War Diary entries give totals of forty-nine and fifty, and none include gliders listed as unaccounted for at the time the reports were compiled or troops who landed in the sea close enough to reach shore

84. Figures cited and calculated from **WO 169/10182** 1st Battalion The Border Regiment War Diary, entry for 8:50, 09/07/1943, Para. 3; and **WO 169/10299** 2nd Battalion South Staffordshire Regiment War Diary, Appendix C: 'Summary of the Operations on Land', 07/1943
85. For number of gliders on assigned LZs see Molony, **The Campaign in Sicily 1943**, p. 80; for five-mile proximity and breadth of scattering see Otway, **Airborne Forces**, p. 121
86. Quoted from **WO 169/10576** 9th Field Company RE War Diary, entry for 9-15/07/1943
87. Glider No. 10 was piloted by Staff-Sergeant Norman Andrews and USAAF Flight-Officer Morris B. Kyle; its chalk included Colonel Osmond Jones, deputy commander 1st Airlanding Brigade; Lieutenant-Colonel Mark Henniker, 1st Airborne Division CRE; Major Raymond Tompkins (sometimes rendered Tomkins), Deputy Assistant Adjutant and Quartermaster General; Captain David Clark, Brigade RASC Officer; Captain R. S. Roberson, Brigade Signals Officer; Brigade Chaplain Captain David Hourigan; several Brigade HQ signallers with radio sets and at least one Bren gunner from the Brigade Defence Platoon; see **WO 169/8666** 1st Airborne Division War Diary, 1st Airborne Division After Action Report: Part 2 – 1st Airlanding Brigade Operations: Section B. 'Ground Operations' 2. Action on Landing, Point (ii) 'Destruction of Enemy Battery at 088238; and Henniker, **An Image of War**, pp. 130-131
88. For detailed accounts see **WO 169/8666** 1st Airborne Division War Diary, 1st Airborne Division After Action Report: Part 2 – 1st Airlanding Brigade Operations: Section B. 'Ground Operations' 2. Action on Landing, Point (ii) 'Destruction of Enemy Battery at 088238; **WO 169/8845** 1st Airlanding Brigade HQ War Diary, Appendix: 'Capture of Ponte Grande'; and **WO 169/10182** 1st Battalion The Border Regiment War Diary, Appendix: Entry for 'Glider No. 123 – No. 2 Sec. Recce Platoon', account by Lt. W. G. Budgen, n.d.; see also Henniker, **An Image of War**, pp. 129-134; and Eastwood et al, **When Dragons Flew**, pp. 81-83
89. See **WO 169/8845** 1st Airlanding Brigade HQ War Diary, Appendix: 'Capture of Ponte Grande'
90. See Peters, **Glider Pilots in Sicily**, p. 187
91. See **WO 169/10576** 9th Field Company RE War Diary, entry for 9-15/07/1943 and Appendix: 'Operations in Sicily', entry 'Aircraft or Glider No. 38'; and **WO 169/8666** 1st Airborne Division War Diary, 1st Airborne Division After Action Report: Part 2 – 1st Airlanding Brigade Operations: Section B. 'Ground Operations' 2. Action on Landing, Point (i) 'Capture of PONTE GRANDE', entry for 05:00
92. For details of some of the elements of the party's journey to the bridge see for example testimony from Lieutenant A. F. Boucher-Giles, OC 9 troop, 3 Squadron, 1st Battalion the Glider Pilot Regiment; cited in Peters, **Glider Pilots in Sicily**, pp186-187, 188; and Miller, **Nothing is Impossible**, pp. 36-46
93. See **WO 169/8666** 1st Airborne Division War Diary, 1st Airborne Division After Action Report: Part 2 – 1st Airlanding Brigade Operations: Section B. 'Ground

Operations' 2. Action on Landing, Point (i) 'Capture of PONTE GRANDE, entry for 05:10

94. See **WO 169/8666** 1st Airborne Division War Diary, 1st Airborne Division After Action Report: Part 2 – 1st Airlanding Brigade Operations: Section B. 'Ground Operations' 2. Action on Landing, Point (i) 'Capture of PONTE GRANDE, entry for 06:30
95. See **WO 169/8845** 1st Airlanding Brigade HQ War Diary, Appendix: 'Capture of Ponte Grande'; and Miller, **Nothing is Impossible**, p. 48
96. For Medical Orderly details see **WO 169/10299** 2nd Battalion South Staffordshire Regiment War Diary, entry for 09/07/1943, Appendix: 'Capture of PONTE GRANDE'
97. See **WO 169/8666** 1st Airborne Division War Diary, 1st Airborne Division After Action Report: Part 2 – 1st Airlanding Brigade Operations: Section B. 'Ground Operations' 2. Action on Landing, Point (i) 'Capture of PONTE GRANDE, entries for 06:30 & 08:00, 10/07/1943; **WO 169/8845** 1st Airlanding Brigade HQ War Diary, Appendix: 'Capture of Ponte Grande'; and Peters, **Glider Pilots in Sicily**, p. 189
98. See **WO 169/8666** 1st Airborne Division War Diary, 1st Airborne Division After Action Report: Part 2 – 1st Airlanding Brigade Operations: Section B. 'Ground Operations' 2. Action on Landing, Point (i) 'Capture of PONTE GRANDE', entries for 09:00, 10:00 and 12:00; and **WO 169/10576** 9th Field Company RE War Diary, entry for 9-15/07/1943; for Italian infantry reinforcement see Peters, **Glider Pilots in Sicily**, p. 191
99. See **WO 169/8666** 1st Airborne Division War Diary, 1st Airborne Division After Action Report: Part 2 – 1st Airlanding Brigade Operations: Section B. 'Ground Operations' 2. Action on Landing, Point (i) 'Capture of PONTE GRANDE', entries for 12:45, 14:00, 14:30, 14:45, 15:15 and 15:30; **WO 169/8845** 1st Airlanding Brigade HQ War Diary, Appendix: 'Capture of Ponte Grande'; and **WO 169/10299** 2nd Battalion South Staffordshire Regiment War Diary, entry for 09/07/1943, Appendix: 'Capture of PONTE GRANDE'; for detailed accounts of the action see for example Miller, **Nothing is Impossible**, pp. 46-63; and Peters, **Glider Pilots in Sicily**, pp. 191-197
100. For Airlanding prisoner numbers and Lt.-Col. Walch's presence see **WO 169/8666** 1st Airborne Division War Diary, 1st Airborne Division After Action Report: Part 2 – 1st Airlanding Brigade Operations: Section B. 'Ground Operations' 2. Action on Landing, Point (i) 'Capture of PONTE GRANDE', entries for 16:15 and 17:00
101. See Peters, **Glider Pilots in Sicily**, pp. 194-195
102. See **WO 169/8666** 1st Airborne Division War Diary, 1st Airborne Division After Action Report: Part 2 – 1st Airlanding Brigade Operations: Section B. 'Ground Operations' 2. Action on Landing, Point (i) 'Capture of PONTE GRANDE', entry for 15:30; **WO 169/8845** 1st Airlanding Brigade HQ War Diary, Appendix: 'Capture of Ponte Grande'; and Peters, **Glider Pilots in Sicily**, p. 194; for Private Charlesworth see **WO 169/10299** 2nd Battalion South Staffordshire Regiment War Diary, entry for 09/07/1943, Appendix: 'Capture of PONTE GRANDE'; for Private Sidebottom from the 1st Border's presence see Eastwood et al, **When Dragons Flew**, pp. 79, 81
103. Figures cited in Otway, **Airborne Forces**, p. 123
104. See **WO 169/10299** 2nd Battalion South Staffordshire Regiment War Diary, Appendix 'C': Summary of the Operations on Land; and **WO 169/10576** 9th Field Company RE War Diary, entry for 9-15/07/1943
105. 101 figure and breakdown cited in Otway, **Airborne Forces**, p. 123; for Missing figures and fluctuations see **WO 169/10341** 1st Battalion The Glider Pilot Regiment War Diary, Appendices dated 17 & 24/07/1943

Chapter 10

1. See for example testimony from Technical-Sergeant William Dunfee, Company I, 3rd Battalion 505th Parachute Infantry Regiment; cited in Nordyke, **Four Stars of Valor**, p. 53
2. See LoFaro, **The Sword of St. Michael**, p. 79
3. See Nordyke, **Four Stars of Valor**, pp. 53-54
4. See testimony from Private First Class Douglas M. Bailey, Battery B, 456th Parachute Field Artillery Battalion; cited in Nordyke, **Four Stars of Valor**, p. 54
5. See testimony from Private W. A. Jones, Mortar Platoon, HQ Company, 2nd Battalion 505th Parachute Infantry Regiment; cited in Nordyke, **Four Stars of Valor**, p. 55; for 64th Troop Carrier Group temporary attachment to the 52nd Troop Carrier Wing see Blair, **Ridgway's Paratroopers**, p. 88
6. See LoFaro, **The Sword of St. Michael**, pp. 77-79; and Nordyke, **Four Stars of Valor**, pp. 54, 57; for honey bucket provision and quote see Blair, **Ridgway's Paratroopers**, p. 86
7. Quotes from testimony by Private Irvin. W. Seelye, Company E, 2nd Battalion 505th Parachute Infantry Regiment and Private Russell McConnell, Company I, 3rd Battalion 505th Parachute Infantry Regiment; cited in Nordyke, **Four Stars of Valor**, pp. 57 and 54 respectively
8. Paratroop and aircraft figures cited in LoFaro, **The Sword of St. Michael**, p. 80; and Nordyke, **Four Stars of Valor**, p. 57. The US Official History refers to 227 C-47s and Devlin to 266, the latter which might be a typing error; see Garland & Smyth, **Sicily and the Surrender of Italy**, p. 101; and Devlin, **Paratrooper!**, p. 223
9. See Nordyke, **Four Stars of Valor**, p. 50; and LoFaro, **The Sword of St. Michael**, pp. 81-83
10. See Blair, **Ridgway's Paratroopers**, pp. 82-83; and LoFaro, **The Sword of St. Michael**, pp. 105-106
11. All distances approximate, based on plotting the route using maps and information in the source material; interestingly, all understate the total distance involved in the HUSKY ONE fly-in, seemingly by omitting the *c*.250 mile return leg, and most place Kairouan and Enfidaville north-west of the forming-up point over Kuriat Island rather than almost exactly due west; see Garland & Smyth, **Sicily and the Surrender of Italy**, p. 101 and Map II 'The Final Landing Plan'; for 355-mile figure see Blair, **Ridgway's Paratroopers**, pp. 82-83; for 415 mile figure see Devlin, **Paratrooper!**, p. 221 and Map 'Planned Flight Route for Husky Number One…', p. 213; LoFaro, **The Sword of St. Michael**, pp. 80-81and Map 'Route of Husky 1 Mission, 9-10 July 1943', p. xv; and Nordyke, **Four Stars of Valor**, Map: 'Planned Air Route of the 505th RCT from Kairouan to Sicily, 9 July 1943', p. 56
12. Testimony from interview with then-Lieutenant-General Matthew B. Ridgway on 05/04/1949; cited in Blair, **Ridgway's Paratroopers**, p. 82; and LoFaro, **The Sword of St. Michael**, p. 81
13. See Garland & Smyth, **Sicily and the Surrender of Italy**, p. 101; Blair, **Ridgway's Paratroopers**, p. 86; and LoFaro, **The Sword of St. Michael**, p. 80
14. Timing and other details cited in John Cushman Warren, **Airborne Missions in the Mediterranean 1942-1945**, USAF Historical Studies: No. 74 (Maxwell AFB, Alabama: US Air Force Historical Division, Research Studies Institute, 1955: facsimile Ashok Vihar, Delhi, 2015), p. 29
15. See Major Edwin M. Sayre, **The Operations of Company A 505th Parachute Infantry (82nd Airborne Division) Airborne Landings in Sicily 9-24 July 1942**, p. 9; cited in Nordyke, **Four Stars of Valor**, p. 57

16. Quote from HQ Fifth Army Airborne Training Center, 'Report of Airborne Operations', p. 6; cited in LoFaro, **The Sword of St. Michael**, p. 79
17. See Garland & Smyth, **Sicily and the Surrender of Italy**, p. 117; Blair, **Ridgway's Paratroopers**, p. 86; and LoFaro, **The Sword of St. Michael**, p. 81
18. Drop timing cited in Warren, **Airborne Missions in the Mediterranean**, p. 34
19. Quote from testimony by Lieutenant Roy M. Hanna, Machine-gun Platoon, HQ Company, 3rd Battalion, 504th Parachute Infantry Regiment; cited in Nordyke, **All American All the Way**, pp. 49-50
20. See Nordyke, **All American All the Way**, pp. 50-51
21. See Blair, **Ridgway's Paratroopers**, p. 87
22. See T. Moffatt Burriss, **Strike and Hold; A Memoir of the 82d Airborne in World War II**, pp. 36-38
23. See Garland & Smyth, **Sicily and the Surrender of Italy**, pp. 101, 117
24. Testimony from Lieutenant Raymond A. Grossman, Battery C, 456th Parachute Field Artillery Battalion; cited in Nordyke, **Four Stars of Valor**, pp. 59-60
25. See Nordyke, **Four Stars of Valor**, pp. 50-52
26. Drop timing cited in Warren, **Airborne Missions in the Mediterranean**, p. 34
27. See Nordyke, **Four Stars of Valor**, pp. 61-62; for Lieutenant Kroener's stick see id., **All American All the Way**, p. 54
28. Drop timing cited in Warren, **Airborne Missions in the Mediterranean**, p. 35
29. See LoFaro, **The Sword of St. Michael**, pp. 81-82; Blair, **Ridgway's Paratroopers**, p. 87; and Nordyke, **Four Stars of Valor**, pp. 63-65
30. See LoFaro, **The Sword of St. Michael**, pp. 88-89; for a detailed account of the fight to clear and secure the Casa di Priolo strongpoint see Nordyke, **Four Stars of Valor**, pp. 69-71; for Italian details see the **Invasion of Sicily BlogSpot** website, 'The Battle of Gela, Part One: The Landing at Gela and the Capture of the Town' page at http://invasionofsicily.blogspot.com/2019/02/, accessed 27/04/2021
31. See Garland & Smyth, **Sicily and the Surrender of Italy**, p. 119; Blair, **Ridgway's Paratroopers**, p. 88; LoFaro, **The Sword of St. Michael**, pp. 82-83, 85-86; and Nordyke, **Four Stars of Valor**, pp. 65-66
32. Drop timing cited in Warren, **Airborne Missions in the Mediterranean**, p. 36
33. For the 2nd Battalion 505th Parachute Infantry Regiment's drop pattern see Garland & Smyth, **Sicily and the Surrender of Italy**, Map III 'The Seventh Army Assault, 10 July 1943'
34. See Nordyke, **All American All the Way**, pp. 55-56, 65-66
35. See LoFaro, **The Sword of St. Michael**, p. 83
36. See Nordyke, **Four Stars of Valor**, pp. 67-69. According to Airborne accounts Major Alexander set up a night perimeter north-west of Marina di Ragusa and moved on to assist elements of the US 45th Infantry Division in securing Santa Croce Camerina in the mid-morning of Sunday 11 July. However, the US Official History clearly refers to the joint securing of Santa Croce Camerina taking place in the early afternoon of D-Day Saturday 10 July; the reason for the anomaly is unclear.
37. Timings and Sfax detachment cited in Warren, **Airborne Missions in the Mediterranean**, p. 34
38. See Warren, **Airborne Missions in the Mediterranean**, p. 34
39. See; Blair, **Ridgway's Paratroopers**, p. 88; and LoFaro, **The Sword of St. Michael**, p. 84
40. Quoted from Garland & Smyth, **Sicily and the Surrender of Italy**, p. 118
41. See LoFaro, **The Sword of St. Michael**, p. 88
42. See LoFaro, **The Sword of St. Michael**, p. 84
43. See Warren, **Airborne Missions in the Mediterranean**, p. 35
44. See William B. Breuer, **Drop Zone Sicily: Allied Airborne Strike, July 1943** (Novato CA: Presidio Press, 1997), pp. 65, 109-110; see also LoFaro, **The Sword of**

St. Michael, p. 85 and Endnote # 41, pp. 580-581. The latter source refers to Captain McGinity holding out on the Ponte Dirillo for two days but the US Official History clearly refers to the Ponte Dirillo being relieved by elements of the 2nd Battalion, 180th RCT shortly after landing on 10 July; see Garland & Smyth, **Sicily and the Surrender of Italy**, p. 143

45. Captured officer quote from D'Este, **Bitter Victory**, p.244; for quote from *OB Süd* report attributed to *76 Panzer Korps* see ibid., footnote, p. 253
46. See Garland & Smyth, **Sicily and the Surrender of Italy**, p. 157

Chapter 11

1. For timing & other details see Vice-Admiral H. K. Hewitt, '**Action Report Western Naval Task Force: The Sicilian Campaign: Operation "HUSKY", July-August 1943**', 'Part II: Narrative of Events', various time-stamped entries 09/07/1943, p. 2, at https://www.history.navy.mil/research/library/online-reading-room/title-list-alphabetically/s/the-sicilian-campaign-operation-husky.html, accessed 27/10/2020, hereafter referred to as Hewitt, '**Action Report Western Naval Task Force**'; and Garland & Smyth, **Sicily and the Surrender of Italy**, p. 123
2. See Hewitt, '**Action Report Western Naval Task Force**', 'Narrative of Events' Section, entries for 11:00 & 22:30 09/07/1943 and 01:00 10/07/1943, pp. 2-3
3. See Hewitt, '**Action Report Western Naval Task Force**', 'Narrative of Events' Section, entries for 00:40, 00:50, 02:39, 02:43 & 02:46, 10/07/1943
4. See Garland & Smyth, **Sicily and the Surrender of Italy**, p. 98 and Map II 'The Final Landing Plan' and Map III 'The Seventh Army Assault 10 July 1943'; for a précis of units, beach allocations and immediate missions see Molony, **The Campaign in Sicily 1943**, Table 'American Landing Areas and Assaulting Troops (West to East)', p. 71
5. See Hewitt, '**Action Report Western Naval Task Force**', 'Narrative of Events' Section, individual timed entries between 19:32 09/07/1943and 00:50, 10/07/1943; for *Bristol* and *Safari* radio contact see ibid., 'Part IV: Execution of the Plan', 'Section IV: BEACON SUBMARINES', Para. 3, p. 37
6. See Hewitt, '**Action Report Western Naval Task Force**', 'Narrative of Events' Section, entry for 23:59, 09/07/1943; 01:35 anchoring time cited in Garland & Smyth, **Sicily and the Surrender of Italy**, p. 124
7. See Hewitt, '**Action Report Western Naval Task Force**', 'Narrative of Events' Section, various timed entries between 01:15 and 02:50, 10/07/1943
8. See Hewitt, '**Action Report Western Naval Task Force**', 'Narrative of Events' Section, entries for 02:04 and 02:15, 10/07/1943
9. See Garland & Smyth, **Sicily and the Surrender of Italy**, p. 125
10. See Hewitt, '**Action Report Western Naval Task Force**', 'Narrative of Events' Section, entries for 02:55 and 03:43, 10/07/1943
11. See Garland & Smyth, **Sicily and the Surrender of Italy**, pp. 125-127; and Hewitt, '**Action Report Western Naval Task Force**', 'Part IV: Execution of the Plan', 'Section V: THE LANDING', Para. 14, p. 41
12. See Hewitt, '**Action Report Western Naval Task Force**', 'Narrative of Events' Section, entries for 04:00, 05:10 and 05:35, 10/07/1943
13. See Hewitt, '**Action Report Western Naval Task Force**', 'Narrative of Events' Section, various timed entries between 04:33 and 06:30, 10/07/1943; mid-morning casualty count cited in Garland & Smyth, **Sicily and the Surrender of Italy**, p. 135
14. For details of Beach assignment and carrying vessels see for example Hewitt, '**Action Report Western Naval Task Force**', 'Part IV: Execution of the Plan', 'Section V: THE LANDING', Para. 2, p. 38

15. See Hewitt, '**Action Report Western Naval Task Force**', 'Part IV: Execution of the Plan', 'Section III: APPROACH', Paras. 10 & 11, pp. 36-37
16. See Hewitt, '**Action Report Western Naval Task Force**', 'Narrative of Events' Section, entries for 23:00 & 23:08, 09/07/1943 and 00:44, 10/07/1943; and Garland & Smyth, **Sicily and the Surrender of Italy**, p. 136
17. See Hewitt, '**Action Report Western Naval Task Force**', 'Narrative of Events' Section, entry for 02:15, 10/07/1943
18. See Garland & Smyth, **Sicily and the Surrender of Italy**, pp. 136-137; and Hewitt, '**Action Report Western Naval Task Force**', 'Narrative of Events' Section, entries between 23:00 09/07/1943 and 04:00,10/07/1943
19. See Garland & Smyth, **Sicily and the Surrender of Italy**, p. 137; Hewitt, '**Action Report Western Naval Task Force**', 'Narrative of Events' Section, entries for 03:00, 03:35 and 04:00,10/07/1943; and ibid., 'Part IV: Execution of the Plan', 'Section V: THE LANDING', Paras. 9 & 14, pp. 40-41
20. For timings see Hewitt, '**Action Report Western Naval Task Force**', 'Narrative of Events' Section, entry for 04:58, 10/07/1943; for survivor and overall casualty figures see D'Este, **Bitter Victory**, p. 276 and Footnote # 2; for missing figure see Hewitt, 'Part VI: MEDICAL', 'Section V: US NAVY CASUALTIES', Para. 2, p. 105; for USS *Intent* involvement see Morison, **Sicily-Salerno-Anzio January 1943 – June 1944**, p. 101
21. For twenty minutes after first light cover timing and USAAF Spitfires see Molony, **The Campaign in Sicily 1943**, p. 65; for identity of USAAF 31st Fighter Group see Maurer, **Air Force Combat Units of World War II**, entry for '31st Fighter Group', pp. 83-85; for CENT fighting and arrival timings see Hewitt, '**Action Report Western Naval Task Force**', 'Narrative of Events' Section, entries for 05:01 & 05:15, 10/07/1943
22. See Hewitt, '**Action Report Western Naval Task Force**', 'Narrative of Events' Section, entries for 05:10, 07:00 and 07:10,10/07/1943; and ibid., 'Part IV: Execution of the Plan', 'Section V: THE LANDING', Para. 14, p. 41
23. For details of Beach assignment and carrying vessels see for example Hewitt, '**Action Report Western Naval Task Force**', 'Part IV: Execution of the Plan', 'Section V: THE LANDING', Para. 3, pp. 38-39; see also Garland & Smyth, **Sicily and the Surrender of Italy**, p. 100 and Map II 'The Final Landing Plan' and Map III 'The Seventh Army Assault 10 July 1943'
24. See Hewitt, '**Action Report Western Naval Task Force**', 'Part IV: Execution of the Plan', 'Section III: APPROACH', Paras. 8-12, pp. 36-37
25. See Hewitt, '**Action Report Western Naval Task Force**', 'Narrative of Events' Section, entries for 22:57 and 23:16, 09/07/1943 and 00:40, 10/07/1943
26. See Hewitt, '**Action Report Western Naval Task Force**', 'Narrative of Events' Section, entries for 02:39 and 02:43,10/07/1943; and ibid., 'Part IV: Execution of the Plan', 'Section V: THE LANDING', Paras. 7 and 10, pp. 36-40
27. See Garland & Smyth, **Sicily and the Surrender of Italy**, pp. 142-144
28. DesRon was the standard US Navy abbreviation of Destroyer Squadron; for details of the destroyers involved see **Destroyer History Foundation Homepage**, 'Benson and Gleaves Classes' Section, 'Squadrons' Page, individual entries for DesRon 15 & DesRon 16 at https://destroyerhistory.org/benson-gleavesclass/squadrons/, accessed 01/11/2020
29. See Hewitt, '**Action Report Western Naval Task Force**', 'Narrative of Events' Section, entry for 03:30,10/07/1943; and ibid 'Part IV: Execution of the Plan', 'Section V: THE LANDING', Para. 13, p. 41 and 'Section XXXII: NAVAL GUNFIRE', paras. 1 and 2, p. 86

30. See Hewitt, '**Action Report Western Naval Task Force**', 'Narrative of Events' Section, entries for 07:10 and 07:42,10/07/1943; and ibid 'Part IV: Execution of the Plan', 'Section XII: SMOKE', Paras. 2-4, p. 62
31. See Garland & Smyth, **Sicily and the Surrender of Italy**, pp. 142-144
32. See Hewitt, '**Action Report Western Naval Task Force**', 'Narrative of Events' Section, entries for 04:48 and 04:55,10/07/1943; for lack of enemy resistance being due to gunfire from DesRon 15 & 16 see ibid., 'Part IV: Execution of the Plan', 'Section XXXII: NAVAL GUNFIRE', Para. 2, p. 86
33. See Hewitt, '**Action Report Western Naval Task Force**', 'Narrative of Events' Section, entries for 04:24, 05:01 and 06:00,10/07/1943
34. For details of the 1st Canadian Division's embarkation and voyage to the Mediterranean see Lieutenant-Colonel G. W. L. Nicholson, **The Canadians in Italy 1943-1945**, pp. 41-49
35. See for example D'Este, **Bitter Victory**, pp. 256-257; for details of the Battery, garrison participant accounts and the Italian perspective see the **Invasion of Sicily BlogSpot** website, 'The Fall of the Lamba Doria Coastal Battery' page at http://invasionofsicily.blogspot.com/2016/04/the-fall-of-lamba-doria-coastal-battery.html, accessed 03/08/2020; for details of where the SRS landed and discussion of its ascent from the beach see the **Operation LADBROKE: Feat of Arms** website, 'SAS Special Raiding Squadron (SRS) – The Cliffs of Cape Porco di Murro' page at http://www.operation-ladbroke.com/sas-special-raiding-squadron-srs-cliffs-cape-murro-di-porco/, accessed 10/10/2020
36. The precise circumstances are unclear, but Lieutenant George Wilfred Holt DSC RNVR was wounded at some point after putting his passengers from No. 3 Commando ashore and subsequently died in a field hospital in Egypt, where he is interred in the Alexandria (Hadra) War Memorial Cemetery. He was awarded the Distinguished Service Cross for his actions in the opening stages of Operation HUSKY; The Commonwealth War Grave Commission gives his date of death as 9 July 1943
37. Quoted from James Ladd, **Commands and Rangers of World War II**, p. 131
38. Quotes from and figures cited in Hilary St. George Saunders, **The Green Beret**, p. 157
39. For details see Ladd, **Commands and Rangers of World War II**, Appendix 3, entry 'Other Weapons', p. 242
40. Quote from Saunders, **The Green Beret**, p. 157
41. Quote from Saunders, **The Green Beret**, p. 158
42. For details see from Saunders, **The Green Beret**, pp. 156-158; and Ladd, **Commands and Rangers of World War II**, pp. 131-132
43. 01:10 departure time cited in Nicholson, **The Canadians in Italy 1943-1945**, p. 68
44. See Saunders, **The Green Beret**, pp. 153-155; and Robin Neillands, **By Sea and Land: The Story of the Royal Marines Commandos**, pp. 84-86
45. Lower RM killed and wounded figures cited in Nicholson, **The Canadians in Italy 1943-1945**, p. 72; higher and Italian figures cited in Saunders, **The Green Beret**, p. 155
46. See Nicholson, **The Canadians in Italy 1943-1945**, pp. 67-68
47. See Molony, **The Campaign in Sicily 1943**, pp. 61-62; and Nicholson, **The Canadians in Italy 1943-1945**, pp. 69-70
48. Quote cited in Molony, **The Campaign in Sicily 1943**, p. 61
49. See Molony, **The Campaign in Sicily 1943**, p. 61; for a detailed account of the 154th Brigade landing see **The 51st Highland Division** website, '154 Brigade – Sicily Landing, Sicily, July 1943' page at https://51hd.co.uk/accounts/154_assault_landing, accessed 08/12/2020

50. For HM Submarine *Unseen* details see the **uboat.net** website, 'Allied Warships' section, 'HMS *Unseen* (P51)' page, 'Notable Events' log, entry for 09/07/1943 at https://uboat.net/allies/warships/ship/3557.html, accessed 08/12/2020; and Molony, **The Campaign in Sicily 1943**, p. 60
51. See **The Royal Hampshire Regiment** website, 'Sicily July-August 1943' page at https://www.royalhampshireregiment.org/about-the-museum/timeline/sicily-july-august-1943/, accessed 08/12/2020
52. See Molony, **The Campaign in Sicily 1943**, pp. 60-61
53. For HM Submarine *Unruffled* locations & timings see and the **uboat.net** website, 'Allied Warships' section, 'HMS *Unruffled* (P46)' page, 'Notable Events' log, entry for 09/07/1943 at https://uboat.net/allies/warships/ship/3554.html, accessed 08/12/2020
54. See Molony, **The Campaign in Sicily 1943**, pp. 59-60

Chapter 12

1. Quoted from Garland & Smyth, **Sicily and the Surrender of Italy**, p. 146
2. Total figure cited in Molony, **The Campaign in Sicily 1943**, Table: 'Sorties flown by Mediterranean Air Command - Dusk 9th to Dusk 10th July', p. 66, Footnote #1
3. Night intruder & patrol sortie figure cited in Molony, **The Campaign in Sicily 1943**, Table: 'Sorties flown by Mediterranean Air Command - Dusk 9th to Dusk 10th July', p. 66, Footnote #1
4. See Molony, **The Campaign in Sicily 1943**, p. 64; for GCI trial in the invasion of Pantelleria see ibid., p. 49, Footnote #2
5. Sortie figure & bomb tonnage figures cited in Molony, **The Campaign in Sicily 1943**, Table: 'Sorties flown by Mediterranean Air Command - Dusk 9th to Dusk 10th July', p. 66, Footnote #1
6. For No. 205 Group missions see for example **WO 169/8666** 1st Airborne Division War Diary, Appendix: Part 1: Preparation of 1 Airborne Division for Operation HUSKY, 'Attachment to Appendix 'E': Bombing Attacks in Co-Operation with Airborne Operations'; for remainder see Molony, **The Campaign in Sicily 1943**, p. 64; for a breakdown of air units and aircraft types deployed see ibid., Appendix 4: 'Orders of Battle Royal Air Force and United States Army Air Forces', Table (A) 'Mediterranean Air Command', pp. 874-875
7. Sortie figure, bomb tonnage and targets cited in Molony, **The Campaign in Sicily 1943**, Table: 'Sorties flown by Mediterranean Air Command - Dusk 9th to Dusk 10th July', p. 66, Footnote #1
8. The North American A36 Apache was an early iteration of the P-51 Mustang using an Allison engine and configured for dive-bombing. It was employed by the USAAF as a fighter-bomber in the Mediterranean Theatre
9. For quote and details see Molony, **The Campaign in Sicily 1943**, p. 65
10. 1,891 fighter sortie figure cited in Molony, **The Campaign in Sicily 1943**, Table: 'Sorties flown by Mediterranean Air Command - Dusk 9th to Dusk 10th July', p. 66, Footnote #1
11. For fighter type allocation and areas see Molony, **The Campaign in Sicily 1943**, p. 65; for Fighter Group identities and base locations see Maurer, **Air Force Combat Units of World War II**, entries for '31st Fighter Group' & '33rd Fighter Group', pp. 83-85, 86-87
12. See Molony, **The Campaign in Sicily 1943**, p. 65
13. For twenty minutes after first light timing see Molony, **The Campaign in Sicily 1943**, p. 65; for US 31st Fighter Group delay see Hewitt, '**Action Report Western**

Naval Task Force', 'Narrative of Events' Section, entries for 04:24, 05:01 and 05:15, 10/07/1943

14. For No. 256 Squadron Mosquito detachment see Evans, **The Decisive Campaigns of the Desert Air Force**, p. 102
15. The RAF Beaufighter night-fighter Squadrons were Nos. 46, 108, 153, 219, 255 and 600 Squadrons; see Molony, **The Campaign in Sicily 1943**, Appendix 4: 'Orders of Battle Royal Air Force and United States Army Air Forces', pp. 871-877; for US 350th Fighter Group equipment details and mission see ibid., p. 64, Footnote #1
16. The *Sentinel* sank at 10:50 on D-Day. See Hewitt, '**Action Report Western Naval Task Force**', 'Narrative of Events' Section, entry for 04:50, 04:58 and 10:50, 10/07/1943; for *Maddox* casualty figures see D'Este, **Bitter Victory**, p. 276 and Footnote # 2; and Hewitt, 'Part VI: MEDICAL', 'Section V: US NAVY CASUALTIES', Para. 2, p. 105
17. See Hewitt, '**Action Report Western Naval Task Force**', 'Narrative of Events' Section, various timed entries between 04:24 and 15:47, 10/07/1943
18. See Hewitt, '**Action Report Western Naval Task Force**', 'Narrative of Events' Section, entries for 18:35 and 19:30, 10/07/1943
19. Quote from Molony, **The Campaign in Sicily 1943**, p. 66
20. See Hewitt, '**Action Report Western Naval Task Force**', 'Narrative of Events' Section, entry for 14:15, 10/07/1943
21. For *c*.08:30 losses see Morison, **Sicily-Salerno-Anzio January 1943 – June 1944**, p. 102; for remainder see Hewitt, '**Action Report Western Naval Task Force**', 'Narrative of Events' Section, entries for 09:45, 13:35, 14:40 and 15:35, 10/07/1943
22. Quote from Molony, **The Campaign in Sicily 1943**, p. 66
23. See Clayton D. Marks, **Combined Operations: The Organization that Planned Allied Raids and Invasions During World War II** (London, Ontario: Andrea Martens, 2016), pp. 83-84; cited in the **1000 Men, 1000 Stories: Canadians in Combined Operations, WW2** website, 'Story re Combined Ops, "Revenge for HMHS Talamba"' page dated 05/02/2016, accessed 16/01/2021
24. See Molony, **The Campaign in Sicily 1943**, p. 66; for location and casualty figures see the **P&O Heritage** website, 'Ship Fact Sheet' section, 'Talamba (1924)' page at https://www.poheritage.com/Upload/Mimsy/Media/factsheet/94661TALAMBA-1924pdf.pdf, accessed 16/01/2021; for a participant account from Junior Engineer Stan Fernando see the **Tyne Area Shipping Club** website, 'Sunk by Enemy Action – SS Talamba' page at https://tyneareasc.org.uk/2012/10/sunk-by-enemy-action-s-s-talamba/, accessed 16/01/2021
25. See Molony, **The Campaign in Sicily 1943**, pp. 65-66; for Malta 1,346 sortie figure see ibid., Table: 'Sorties flown by Mediterranean Air Command - Dusk 9th to Dusk 10th July', p. 66, Footnote #1; for Luftwaffe 300 sortie figure see Andrew Brookes, **Air War over Italy** (London: Ian Allen, 2000), pp. 14-17; cited in Evans, **The Decisive Campaigns of the Desert Air Force**, p. 102
26. See Molony, **The Campaign in Sicily 1943**, p. 48
27. For 300 loss estimate and six loss figure see Nicholson, **The Canadians in Italy 1943-1945**, p. 77; twelve loss figure cited in Evans, **The Decisive Campaigns of the Desert Air Force**, p. 102
28. Quoted from Nicholson, **The Canadians in Italy 1943-1945**, p. 77
29. See Molony, **The Campaign in Sicily 1943**, p. 81
30. See for example **WO 169/8845** 1st Airlanding Brigade HQ War Diary, Appendix: 'Capture of Ponte Grande'
31. See **WO 169/8666** 1st Airborne Division War Diary, 1st Airborne Division After Action Report: Part 2 – 1st Airlanding Brigade Operations: Section B.

'Ground Operations' 2. Action on Landing, Point (i) 'Capture of PONTE GRANDE', entry for 16:15, 10/07/1943; **WO 169/8845** 1st Airlanding Brigade HQ War Diary, entry for 09/07/1943, Section 'Capture of Ponte Grande'; for Lieutenant Welch assisting the 2nd RSF attack see also Peters, **Glider Pilots in Sicily**, p. 196

32. See **WO 169/8845** 1st Airlanding Brigade HQ War Diary, Appendix: 'Capture of Ponte Grande'**WO 169/8666** 1st Airborne Division War Diary, 1st Airborne Division After Action Report: Part 2 – 1st Airlanding Brigade Operations: Section B. 'Ground Operations' 2. Action on Landing, Point (i) 'Capture of PONTE GRANDE', entries for 17:00 and 21:00, 10/07/1943 and 08:00, 11/07/1943; **WO 169/8845** 1st Airlanding Brigade HQ War Diary, entry for 22:00, 10/07/19043
33. See Molony, **The Campaign in Sicily 1943**, pp. 81-82
34. See Molony, **The Campaign in Sicily 1943**, pp. 59-60
35. See Warren, **Airborne Missions in the Mediterranean**, p. 35; and D'Este, **Bitter Victory**, pp.245-246; for common password see ibid., Footnote, p. 246
36. For a detailed account see **The Durham Light Infantry 1920-46** website, 'Sicily 1943' page at https://durhamlightinfantry1920-46.weebly.com/sicily-1943.html, accessed 13/08/2021
37. Urquhart quote from John Baynes, **Urquhart of Arnhem: The Life of Major General R E Urquhart CB, DSO**, (London: Brassey's, 1993), p. 53
38. See Molony, **The Campaign in Sicily 1943**, pp. 60-61; Baynes, **Urquhart of Arnhem**, pp. 52-53; and **The 51st Highland Division** website, 'Vizzini and Francofonte: Sicily, 13th-15th July 1943' page at https://51hd.co.uk/history/sicily_vizzini, accessed 30/01/2021
39. For quote and 07:00 timing see **The 51st Highland Division** website, '154 Brigade – Sicily Landing, Sicily, July 1943' page at https://51hd.co.uk/accounts/154_assault_landing, accessed 31/01/2020
40. See Molony, **The Campaign in Sicily 1943**, p. 61; and **The 51st Highland Division** website, 'The Landing, Op. HUSKEY: (sic) Sicily 10th July 1943' page at https://51hd.co.uk/history/sicily_landing, accessed 03/02/2021
41. See Molony, **The Campaign in Sicily 1943**, pp. 82, 106; and **The 51st Highland Division** website, 'Vizzini and Francofonte: Sicily, 13th-15th July 1943' page at https://51hd.co.uk/history/sicily_vizzini, accessed 05/02/2021
42. For details of the *Luftwaffe* reinforcing effort see Molony, **The Campaign in Sicily 1943**, p. 93; and Peters, **Glider Pilots in Sicily**, pp. 222-224
43. See Molony, **The Campaign in Sicily 1943**, p. 106; and **The 51st Highland Division** website, 'Vizzini and Francofonte: Sicily, 13th-15th July 1943' page at https://51hd.co.uk/history/sicily_vizzini, accessed 05/02/2021
44. The Three Rivers Regiment was also known as the 12th Canadian Armoured Regiment
45. See Nicholson, **The Canadians in Italy 1943-1945**, pp. 70-71
46. See Nicholson, **The Canadians in Italy 1943-1945**, pp. 71-72
47. Ragusa height above sea level and 48,000 population figure cited in Garland & Smyth, **Sicily and the Surrender of Italy**, p. 141 & ibid., Footnote #24
48. See Nicholson, **The Canadians in Italy 1943-1945**, pp. 80-81
49. The transports carrying the 1st Canadian Division's MT as part of Convoy KMS 18B were the SS *City of Venice* and MV *St. Essylt*, sunk on 04/07/1943 by *U-409* and *U-375* respectively, and the MV *Devis* sunk by *U-593* on 05/07/1943; see **The German U-boats of WWII (Kriegsmarine) and WWI (Kaiserliche Marine)** website, 'The U-Boats' section, vessel specific pages at https://uboat.net/boats.htm, accessed 19/02/2021

50. See Garland & Smyth, **Sicily and the Surrender of Italy**, pp. 156, 189
51. See Nicholson, **The Canadians in Italy 1943-1945**, p. 83
52. Quote from Nicholson, **The Canadians in Italy 1943-1945**, p. 79
53. See Nicholson, **The Canadians in Italy 1943-1945**, pp. 82-84; for 'marched well' comment see Molony, **The Campaign in Sicily 1943**, p. 82
54. For 1st Canadian Division vehicle & stores figures see Nicholson, **The Canadians in Italy 1943-1945**, Footnote, p. 84

Chapter 13

1. For details see for example Garland & Smyth, **Sicily and the Surrender of Italy**, pp. 96-98
2. Quotes from Garland & Smyth, **Sicily and the Surrender of Italy**, p. 91
3. See Garland & Smyth, **Sicily and the Surrender of Italy**, pp. 141-146
4. See LoFaro, **The Sword of St. Michael**, pp. 86-87
5. See Garland & Smyth, **Sicily and the Surrender of Italy**, p. 156; and LoFaro, **The Sword of St. Michael**, p. 87
6. See Warren P. Munsell, **The Story of a Regiment, A History of the 179th Regimental Combat Team** (New York: Warren P. Munsell Jr., 1946), p. 11
7. See Garland & Smyth, **Sicily and the Surrender of Italy**, p. 144; and Munsell, **The Story of a Regiment**, p. 12
8. See LoFaro, **The Sword of St. Michael**, p. 87
9. See Garland & Smyth, **Sicily and the Surrender of Italy**, pp. 141, 144, 155-156; and Munsell, **The Story of a Regiment**, p. 12
10. See Munsell, **The Story of a Regiment**, p. 12
11. See Garland & Smyth, **Sicily and the Surrender of Italy**, p. 189; and Munsell, **The Story of a Regiment**, p. 13
12. For details see Garland & Smyth, **Sicily and the Surrender of Italy**, pp. 96-98
13. See Garland & Smyth, **Sicily and the Surrender of Italy**, p. 190; and Munsell, **The Story of a Regiment**, pp. 13-14
14. See Hewitt, **'Action Report Western Naval Task Force'**, 'Narrative of Events' Section, entries for 00:40, 00:50, 02:39, 02:43 and 02:46, 10/07/1943
15. For lack of experienced Coxswains see Samuel E. Morison, **Sicily-Salerno-Anzio January 1943 – June 1944**, p. 130
16. See Garland & Smyth, **Sicily and the Surrender of Italy**, p. 143
17. Quoted from Garland & Smyth, **Sicily and the Surrender of Italy**, p. 161
18. Source unclear: cited in Molony, **The Campaign in Sicily 1943**, p. 62
19. See Garland & Smyth, **Sicily and the Surrender of Italy**, p. 143; for the parachute demolition team see for example LoFaro, **The Sword of St. Michael**, p. 69; for Captain McGinity's presence see for example Garland & Smyth, **Sicily and the Surrender of Italy**, p. 119; and Breuer, **Drop Zone Sicily**, p. 65
20. For Seaman 1st Class Carpenter's involvement and 1st Battalion reorganisation and 06:00 timing see Morison, **Sicily-Salerno-Anzio January 1943 – June 1944**, pp. 131-132; Biscari is currently known as Acate but appears as the former on contemporary maps
21. See Garland & Smyth, **Sicily and the Surrender of Italy**, pp. 148-149, 154-155
22. See Garland & Smyth, **Sicily and the Surrender of Italy**, pp. 163-164
23. See the US **Naval History & Heritage Command** website, 'Beatty I (DD-640)' page at https://www.history.navy.mil/research/histories/ship-histories/danfs/b/beatty-i.html, accessed 19/03/2021
24. Nicknamed 'Cannonball' Major Krause enjoyed a reputation of being 'gung ho' and something of a go-getter in the 505th PIR. Gavin was thus surprised to find

him 'sitting on the side of a foxhole dangling his lower legs into the hole, no equipment, no security out'; when questioned about his lack of application he merely informed a 'dumbfounded' Gavin that '...there were a lot of Germans... toward where the objectives were'; see LoFaro, **The Sword of St. Michael**, p. 95.

25. See LoFaro, **The Sword of St. Michael**, pp. 94-97; and Garland & Smyth, **Sicily and the Surrender of Italy**, pp. 168-169
26. Rendered Biazza in some accounts
27. See LoFaro, **The Sword of St. Michael**, p. 97; the US Official History refers to Krause leading the 3rd Battalion contingent on arrival at Biscari Station and makes no mention of Captain Hagan's role; see Garland & Smyth, **Sicily and the Surrender of Italy**, p. 172
28. Four Tiger figure cited in Garland & Smyth, **Sicily and the Surrender of Italy**, p. 172; six figure cited in LoFaro, **The Sword of St. Michael**, p. 97
29. Testimony from Lieutenant Robert A. Fielder, Communications Officer, HQ Company, 3rd Battalion 505th Parachute Infantry Regiment; cited in Nordyke, **Four Stars of Valor**, p. 82
30. Quotes from Starlyn R. Jorgensen, **History of the 456th Parachute Field Artillery Battalion**, p. 71; cited in LoFaro, **The Sword of St. Michael**, p. 98. For a detailed account of the incident see Nordyke, **Four Stars of Valor**, pp. 85-86
31. See Nordyke, **Four Stars of Valor**, p. 86; LoFaro gives Baldwin's rank as Captain; see LoFaro, **The Sword of St. Michael**, p. 98, Endnote #83, p. 583
32. See Nordyke, **Four Stars of Valor**, pp. 86-87; and LoFaro, **The Sword of St. Michael**, pp. 97-98
33. See Nordyke, **Four Stars of Valor**, p. 84
34. See LoFaro, **The Sword of St. Michael**, p. 99
35. See Nordyke, **Four Stars of Valor**, pp. 84, 87
36. See LoFaro, **The Sword of St. Michael**, p. 99
37. See Garland & Smyth, **Sicily and the Surrender of Italy**, p. 173; and Nordyke, **Four Stars of Valor**, p. 88
38. See LoFaro, **The Sword of St. Michael**, p. 99; and Garland & Smyth, **Sicily and the Surrender of Italy**, p. 173
39. See LoFaro, **The Sword of St. Michael**, p. 100; for details of Lieutenant Swingler's eliminating the Tiger crew and capturing the vehicle see Nordyke, **Four Stars of Valor**, p. 90
40. See Nordyke, **Four Stars of Valor**, p. 89
41. See James M. Gavin, **On To Berlin**, p. 43; cited in LoFaro, **The Sword of St. Michael**, p. 101
42. Figures cited in LoFaro, **The Sword of St. Michael**, p. 100
43. See for example Garland & Smyth, **Sicily and the Surrender of Italy**, pp. 170, 172-173; tank loss cited in LoFaro, **The Sword of St. Michael**, p. 101
44. See Garland & Smyth, **Sicily and the Surrender of Italy**, pp. 205, 217. Passo Pisciaro is currently known as Passopisciaro
45. See Garland & Smyth, **Sicily and the Surrender of Italy**, pp. 189, 206, 208, 220-222
46. Quote from Garland & Smyth, **Sicily and the Surrender of Italy**, p. 222
47. See Garland & Smyth, **Sicily and the Surrender of Italy**, pp. 189-190
48. Quote from the Patton Diary, entry for 15/03/1943; cited in D'Este, **Bitter Victory**, p. 318
49. For an officer eyewitness account of Patton's speech with quotes see D'Este, **Bitter Victory**, p. 317; for date of speech and two increments delivery see ibid., Footnote †, p. 317

50. See D'Este, **Bitter Victory**, pp, 318-320; and Appendix K: The Biscari Incidents, pp.612-613; for a more recent and in-depth discussion see Fred Borch, '*War Crimes in Sicily: Sergeant West, Captain Compton, and the Murder of Prisoners of War in 1943*' **The Army Lawyer** (March 2013) pp. 1-6; available at https://www.loc.gov/rr/frd/Military_Law/pdf/03-2013.pdf, accessed 29/03/2021

Chapter 14

1. Sometimes rendered Rocce; the *Punta due Rocchi* appears to be currently known as Cantigaglione
2. See for example Morison, **Sicily-Salerno-Anzio January 1943 – June 1944**, pp. 75-78
3. See Morison, **Sicily-Salerno-Anzio January 1943 – June 1944**, p. 80
4. For the davit failure see Garland & Smyth, **Sicily and the Surrender of Italy**, p. 125
5. See Morison, **Sicily-Salerno-Anzio January 1943 – June 1944**, pp. 80-81; and Garland & Smyth, **Sicily and the Surrender of Italy**, p. 126; for the locations of the various Italian defensive works see Morison, **Sicily-Salerno-Anzio January 1943 – June 1944**, Map: 'LICATA (JOSS) AREA 10-12 JULY 1943', pp. 76-77
6. See Garland & Smyth, **Sicily and the Surrender of Italy**, pp. 126-127; and Morison, **Sicily-Salerno-Anzio January 1943 – June 1944**, p. 80
7. See Garland & Smyth, **Sicily and the Surrender of Italy**, pp. 127-128
8. See Morison, **Sicily-Salerno-Anzio January 1943 – June 1944**, pp. 81-82; and Garland & Smyth, **Sicily and the Surrender of Italy**, p. 128
9. See Morison, **Sicily-Salerno-Anzio January 1943 – June 1944**, p. 84, footnote # 12
10. Quoted from Morison, **Sicily-Salerno-Anzio January 1943 – June 1944**, p. 83
11. See Garland & Smyth, **Sicily and the Surrender of Italy**, pp. 128-131; and Morison, **Sicily-Salerno-Anzio January 1943 – June 1944**, pp. 82-83
12. See Garland & Smyth, **Sicily and the Surrender of Italy**, p. 128; for unit and objective locations see ibid., Map III: 'The Seventh Army Assault 10 July 1943'
13. See Morison, **Sicily-Salerno-Anzio January 1943 – June 1944**, p. 88
14. See Garland & Smyth, **Sicily and the Surrender of Italy**, pp. 133-134; and Morison, **Sicily-Salerno-Anzio January 1943 – June 1944**, pp. 74, 78, 86, 88-89. According to the latter the 2nd Battalion 30th RCT moved west from BLUE Beach into Licata in the late morning of 10 July, but the US Army Official History clearly refers to the 2nd Battalion occupying the eastern blocking line near Poggio Lungo; see Morison, p. 89; and Garland & Smyth, Map III: 'The Seventh Army Assault 10 July 1943'
15. Formed in August 1942, the Scouts and Raiders were forerunners to the US Navy SEAL Teams established in 1962. Ensign Bucklew was awarded the Navy Cross for his actions at Licata and was involved in Special Warfare operations in Korea and Vietnam until retirement in 1969 with the rank of Captain; Captain Bucklew is sometimes referred to as the 'Father of Naval Special Warfare' and in 1987 the Phil Bucklew Naval Special Warfare Center at the Naval Amphibious Base Coronado, California was named in his honour
16. See Morison, **Sicily-Salerno-Anzio January 1943 – June 1944**, pp. 75, 86-90; and Garland & Smyth, **Sicily and the Surrender of Italy**, p. 133
17. See Garland & Smyth, **Sicily and the Surrender of Italy**, p. 131
18. For locations of strongpoints, gun positions etc. see Morison, **Sicily-Salerno-Anzio January 1943 – June 1944**, Map 'LICATA (JOSS) AREA, 10-12 JULY 1943' pp. 76-77
19. For vehicle landing timing see Morison, **Sicily-Salerno-Anzio January 1943 – June 1944**, p. 85
20. Quoted from Morison, **Sicily-Salerno-Anzio January 1943 – June 1944**, p. 90

21. See Garland & Smyth, **Sicily and the Surrender of Italy**, p. 191
22. See Morison, **Sicily-Salerno-Anzio January 1943 – June 1944**, p. 90; and Garland & Smyth, **Sicily and the Surrender of Italy**, pp. 161
23. Figures cited in Morison, **Sicily-Salerno-Anzio January 1943 – June 1944**, footnote # 26, p. 91
24. See Garland & Smyth, **Sicily and the Surrender of Italy**, pp. 131-133, 135; and Morison, **Sicily-Salerno-Anzio January 1943 – June 1944**, pp. 74-75, 84-86, 89-90
25. Quoted from Morison, **Sicily-Salerno-Anzio January 1943 – June 1944**, p. 91
26. See Garland & Smyth, **Sicily and the Surrender of Italy**, pp. 191-192
27. See Garland & Smyth, **Sicily and the Surrender of Italy**, p. 155; for elements of *15 Panzer Division* approach see ibid., p. 192
28. See for example Garland & Smyth, **Sicily and the Surrender of Italy**, Appendix A: 'Composition of US Forces on D-Day, 10 July 1943', p. 555
29. See Garland & Smyth, **Sicily and the Surrender of Italy**, pp.125, 192-193
30. The T30 Howitzer Motor Carriage (HMC) was an M3 half-track modified to mount an M1 75mm Pack Howitzer. In North Africa and Operation HUSKY the organisation of many US RCTs included an Infantry Cannon Company as an organic artillery support element, equipped with six T30 HMCs and two T19 HMCs mounting M2A1 105mm Howitzers. The self-propelled weapons were subsequently replaced with towed 105mm weapons in infantry divisions and M7 HMCs in armored divisions; the latter were M4 Medium tanks modified with an open-top fighting compartment mounting a M1 105mm Howitzer.
31. See Garland & Smyth, **Sicily and the Surrender of Italy**, pp. 195-196
32. The 39th FA Battalion fired 1,484 rounds and the 39th FA Battalion eighty-six; the reason for the disparity is unclear; see Garland & Smyth, **Sicily and the Surrender of Italy**, footnote # 16, p. 195
33. For Lieutenant Craig's Medal of Honor citation see the **Home of Heroes Medal of Honor & Military History** website, 'World War II Medal of Honor Recipients' section, entry for 2nd Lieutenant Robert Craig at https://homeofheroes.com/medal-of-honor-recipients/world-war-ii/, accessed 17/04/2021; see also Garland & Smyth, **Sicily and the Surrender of Italy**, Footnote # 18, p. 196
34. See Garland & Smyth, **Sicily and the Surrender of Italy**, p. 196
35. See Garland & Smyth, **Sicily and the Surrender of Italy**, pp. 194-195
36. Quoted from Garland & Smyth, **Sicily and the Surrender of Italy**, p. 198
37. See Garland & Smyth, **Sicily and the Surrender of Italy**, pp. 198-200
38. Quoted from Garland & Smyth, **Sicily and the Surrender of Italy**, p. 201
39. See Garland & Smyth, **Sicily and the Surrender of Italy**, p. 209
40. See Garland & Smyth, **Sicily and the Surrender of Italy**, pp. 224-228

Chapter 15

1. See Morison, **Sicily-Salerno-Anzio January 1943 – June 1944**, p. 98; and Garland & Smyth, **Sicily and the Surrender of Italy**, p. 135
2. See Garland & Smyth, **Sicily and the Surrender of Italy**, pp. 99-100 and Map II 'The Final Landing Plan' & Map III 'The Seventh Army Assault 10 July 1943'; for a précis of units, beach allocations and immediate missions see Molony, **The Campaign in Sicily 1943**, Table 'American Landing Areas and Assaulting Troops (West to East)', p. 71
3. For the bonfires see Nordyke, **Four Stars of Valor**, pp. 61-62
4. See Hewitt, **'Action Report Western Naval Task Force'**, 'Narrative of Events' Section, entries for 23:00 & 23:08, 09/07/1943 and 00:44, 10/07/1943; and Garland & Smyth, **Sicily and the Surrender of Italy**, p. 136

5. For vessel names, passengers & assault craft types and numbers see Morison, **Sicily-Salerno-Anzio January 1943 – June 1944**, pp. 95-97; for Col. Darby travelling with the support elements see Ladd, **Commandos and Rangers of World War II**, p. 130
6. 03:15 timing cited in Ladd, **Commandos and Rangers of World War II**, p. 130 and Morison, **Sicily-Salerno-Anzio January 1943 – June 1944**, p. 97; 03:35 timing and reference to almost an hour behind schedule cited in Garland & Smyth, **Sicily and the Surrender of Italy**, p. 137; the difference may be due to the 4th Ranger Battalion coming ashore on GREEN Beach slightly before the 1st Ranger Battalion touched down on RED Beach. Hewitt refers to the landings commencing on schedule at 02:45; see Hewitt, **'Action Report Western Naval Task Force'**, 'Narrative of Events' Section, entry for 02:45, 10/07/1943
7. See Ladd, **Commandos and Rangers of World War II**, p. 130; and the **Invasion of Sicily BlogSpot** website, 'The Battle of Gela, Part One: The Landing at Gela and the Capture of the Town' page at http://invasionofsicily.blogspot.com/2019/02/, accessed 27/04/2021. For Italian civilians mine laying and withdrawing labour see Morison, **Sicily-Salerno-Anzio January 1943 – June 1944**, p. 97
8. For details see Major James B. Lyle, **The Operations of Companies "A" and "B" First Ranger Battalion, at Gela, Sicily 10-11 July 1943**, pp. 12-15
9. See Garland & Smyth, **Sicily and the Surrender of Italy**, pp. 137-139; Morison, **Sicily-Salerno-Anzio January 1943 – June 1944**, p. 97; Ladd, **Commandos and Rangers of World War II**, pp. 130-131; and the **Invasion of Sicily BlogSpot** website, 'The Battle of Gela, Part One: The Landing at Gela and the Capture of the Town' page at http://invasionofsicily.blogspot.com/2019/02/, accessed 27/04/2021
10. For unit & vessel allocations see Morison, **Sicily-Salerno-Anzio January 1943 – June 1944**, p. 98
11. See Hewitt, **'Action Report Western Naval Task Force'**, 'Narrative of Events' Section, entry for 03:35, 10/07/1943
12. See Morison, **Sicily-Salerno-Anzio January 1943 – June 1944**, p. 100
13. See Hewitt, **'Action Report Western Naval Task Force'**, 'Narrative of Events' Section, entries for 09:19 and 12:12, 10/07/1943
14. See Hewitt, **'Action Report Western Naval Task Force'**, 'Part IV: Execution of the Plan', 'Section V: THE LANDING', Paras. 9 & 14, pp. 40-41; Morison, **Sicily-Salerno-Anzio January 1943 – June 1944**, pp. 99-100; and Garland & Smyth, **Sicily and the Surrender of Italy**, p. 139. Hewitt refers to the opposition at YELLOW Beach being 'heavy', RED 2 & GREEN 2 as 'fairly heavy' and the remainder as light, whereas the other sources suggest the opposite
15. See Hewitt, **'Action Report Western Naval Task Force'**, 'Narrative of Events' Section, entries for 09:40, 10:10 and 10:30, 10/07/1943; for closing to 3,000 yards see Morison, **Sicily-Salerno-Anzio January 1943 – June 1944**, p. 104
16. See Morison, **Sicily-Salerno-Anzio January 1943 – June 1944**, pp. 98-99, 102
17. See Garland & Smyth, **Sicily and the Surrender of Italy**, p. 139; for Captain Follmer and Company I's successful drop see for example Nordyke, **Four Stars of Valor**, pp. 61-62
18. See for example Garland & Smyth, **Sicily and the Surrender of Italy**, pp. 110-111; for 01:00 State of Emergency and port demolition see Morison, **Sicily-Salerno-Anzio January 1943 – June 1944**, pp. 69-70
19. For *Gruppo Mobili E* Order of Battle see the **Military Story: Chronicles of War** website, 'The Mobile Groups in Sicily in 1943' page at http://www.militarystory.org/i-gruppi-mobili-in-sicilia-nel-1943/, accessed 02/05/2021; for tank numbers see Morison, **Sicily-Salerno-Anzio January 1943 – June 1944**, p. 103

20. For the *Livorno Divisione* Order of Battle see for example the **Comando Supremo: Italy in WW2** website, 'Axis Forces in Sicily: July 1943 OOB' page at https://comandosupremo.com/axis-forces-in-sicily/, accessed 02/05/2021
21. For the *Hermann Göring Panzer Division* Order of Battle see for example the **Comando Supremo: Italy in WW2** website, 'Axis Forces in Sicily: July 1943 OOB' page at https://comandosupremo.com/axis-forces-in-sicily/, accessed 09/09/2020; and the **Axis History** website, 'Panzer Division Hermann Göring' page at https://www.axishistory.com/list-all-categories/151-germany-luftwaffe/luftwaffe-ground-units/5628-panzer-division-hermann-goering, accessed 10/09/2020.
22. See Garland & Smyth, **Sicily and the Surrender of Italy**, p.147
23. For *OB Süd* involvement see LoFaro, **The Sword of St. Michael**, p. 88; for reconnaissance patrol clashes and Conrath's ignorance of Guzzoni's plan and attachment to *16° Corpo* see for example Garland & Smyth, **Sicily and the Surrender of Italy**, p.148
24. Quote from Garland & Smyth, **Sicily and the Surrender of Italy**, p.148
25. See LoFaro, **The Sword of St. Michael**, p. 90; and Garland & Smyth, **Sicily and the Surrender of Italy**, p.150
26. See Hewitt, **'Action Report Western Naval Task Force'**, 'Narrative of Events' Section, entry for 08:26, 10/07/1943; and Morison, **Sicily-Salerno-Anzio January 1943 – June 1944**, pp. 102-103
27. See LoFaro, **The Sword of St. Michael**, p. 90
28. See Nordyke, **Four Stars of Valor**, p. 72; Sergeant Dyas' account cited refers to the tanks and accompanying infantry being German belonging to the *Hermann Göring Panzer Division*
29. See Morison, **Sicily-Salerno-Anzio January 1943 – June 1944**, p. 103
30. See Garland & Smyth, **Sicily and the Surrender of Italy**, p.151-152
31. See Major Edwin M. Sayre, **The Operations of Company A 505th Parachute Infantry (82nd Airborne Division) Airborne Landings in Sicily 9-24 July 1942**, pp. 13-14; cited in Nordyke, **Four Stars of Valor**, p. 76
32. See Nordyke, **Four Stars of Valor**, pp. 75-76; and Garland & Smyth, **Sicily and the Surrender of Italy**, p. 152. Capt. Sayre's account also consistently refers to the armoured column belonging to the *Hermann Göring Panzer Division* rather than *Gruppo Mobili E*, presumably due to confusion with the action fought in the same location against the former in the afternoon of 10 July
33. See Lyle, **The Operations of Companies "A" and "B" First Ranger Battalion, at Gela, Sicily 10-11 July 1943**, pp. 15-16
34. A Pole Charge consisted of four linked No. 75 Hawkins Grenades attached to the front a rectangular wooden frame with a stout timber attached at an angle to the back to allow the front of the frame to be wedged tightly against the target. It was primarily intended to open holes in walls to allow access to adjoining buildings, a technique referred to as 'mouseholing'; see for example Ladd, **Commandos and Rangers of World War II**, pp. 242-243
35. See the **Comando Supremo: Italy in WW2** website, 'Gela Beachhead Counterattack of 1943: 3rd Battalion, 34th Regiment, "Livorno" Infantry Division in the Gela Beachhead Counterattack: Sicily July 11th-12th 1943' page at https://comandosupremo.com/gela-1943/#:~:text=The%20Division%20was%20at%20nearly,evaporated%20Malta%20amphibious%2Fairborne%20invasion., accessed 04/05/2021
36. See Garland & Smyth, **Sicily and the Surrender of Italy**, pp. 152-153; and Lyle, **The Operations of Companies "A" and "B" First Ranger Battalion, at Gela, Sicily 10-11 July 1943**, p. 16
37. See Garland & Smyth, **Sicily and the Surrender of Italy**, pp. 148-149

38. See Nordyke, **All American All the Way**, p. 51
39. See Hewitt, **'Action Report Western Naval Task Force'**, 'Narrative of Events' Section, entry for 11:40, 10/07/1943; and Morison, **Sicily-Salerno-Anzio January 1943 – June 1944**, p. 104
40. For 57mm gun see Nordyke, **Four Stars of Valor**, p. 76
41. See Garland & Smyth, **Sicily and the Surrender of Italy**, p. 154; and LoFaro, **The Sword of St. Michael**, p. 91
42. See Hewitt, **'Action Report Western Naval Task Force'**, 'Narrative of Events' Section, entry for 19:30, 10/07/1943
43. see LoFaro, **The Sword of St. Michael**, pp. 92-93
44. See Garland & Smyth, **Sicily and the Surrender of Italy**, p. 165
45. See Hewitt, **'Action Report Western Naval Task Force'**, 'Narrative of Events' Section, entries for 09:19, 12:12 & 18:15, 10/07/1943
46. See Morison, **Sicily-Salerno-Anzio January 1943 – June 1944**, pp. 105-108
47. See Garland & Smyth, **Sicily and the Surrender of Italy**, p. 158
48. The order was transmitted through the naval chain of command thirty minutes later; see Hewitt, **'Action Report Western Naval Task Force'**, 'Narrative of Events' Section, entry for 14:30, 10/07/1943
49. See Garland & Smyth, **Sicily and the Surrender of Italy**, p. 158
50. Quote from Morison, **Sicily-Salerno-Anzio January 1943 – June 1944**, p. 108; see also Garland & Smyth, **Sicily and the Surrender of Italy**, pp. 158-159
51. See Garland & Smyth, **Sicily and the Surrender of Italy**, pp. 158-159; sixty-two tank figure cited in Morison, **Sicily-Salerno-Anzio January 1943 – June 1944**, p. 109
52. See Garland & Smyth, **Sicily and the Surrender of Italy**, pp. 165-166
53. See the **Comando Supremo: Italy in WW2** website, 'Gela Beachhead Counterattack of 1943: 3rd Battalion, 34th Regiment, "Livorno" Infantry Division in the Gela Beachhead Counterattack: Sicily July 11th-12th 1943' page at https://comandosupremo.com/gela-1943/#:~:text=The%20Division%20was%20at%20nearly,evaporated%20Malta%20amphibious%2Fairborne%20invasion., accessed 09/05/2021; and Garland & Smyth, **Sicily and the Surrender of Italy**, pp. 164, 166, 170
54. Timings & round figure cited in Morison, **Sicily-Salerno-Anzio January 1943 – June 1944**, Table 'Key to Naval Gunfire Support on Gela Chart, July 1943', p. 113
55. See Lyle, **The Operations of Companies "A" and "B" First Ranger Battalion, at Gela, Sicily 10-11 July 1943**, pp. 17-19; and Garland & Smyth, **Sicily and the Surrender of Italy**, pp. 169-170
56. See the **Warfare History Network** website, 'Bitter Fight at Gela' page at https://warfarehistorynetwork.com/2016/09/27/bitter-fight-at-gela/, accessed 10/05/2021
57. Timings and rounds fired figure cited in Morison, **Sicily-Salerno-Anzio January 1943 – June 1944**, Table 'Key to Naval Gunfire Support on Gela Chart, July 1943', p. 113
58. See Garland & Smyth, **Sicily and the Surrender of Italy**, p. 164
59. See Garland & Smyth, **Sicily and the Surrender of Italy**, pp. 165-166
60. See Morison, **Sicily-Salerno-Anzio January 1943 – June 1944**, p. 110; for timings see ibid., Table 'Key to Naval Gunfire Support on Gela Chart, July 1943', p. 113; for Savannah losing her spotter aircraft see Hewitt, **'Action Report Western Naval Task Force'**, 'Narrative of Events' Section, entry for 08:20, 11/07/1943
61. See Sayre, **The Operations of Company A 505th Parachute Infantry (82nd Airborne Division) Airborne Landings in Sicily 9-24 July 1942**, pp. 15-16; cited in Lo

Faro, pp. 93-94; see also Garland & Smyth, **Sicily and the Surrender of Italy**, pp. 167-168

62. See Hewitt, **'Action Report Western Naval Task Force'**, 'Narrative of Events' Section, entry for 05:00, 11/07/1943; and Morison, **Sicily-Salerno-Anzio January 1943 – June 1944**, pp. 110, 112 and Table 'Key to Naval Gunfire Support on Gela Chart, July 1943', p. 113
63. See Garland & Smyth, **Sicily and the Surrender of Italy**, p. 170
64. See Morison, **Sicily-Salerno-Anzio January 1943 – June 1944**, p. 111
65. For warning to ships of proximity of defenders and attackers see Hewitt, **'Action Report Western Naval Task Force'**, 'Narrative of Events' Section, entry for 15:10, 11/07/1943; for USS *Butler* see Morison, **Sicily-Salerno-Anzio January 1943 – June 1944**, p. 117
66. For ship and timing details see Morison, **Sicily-Salerno-Anzio January 1943 – June 1944**, Table 'Key to Naval Gunfire Support on Gela Chart, July 1943', p. 113; for *Boise* manoeuvring close inshore to make range to Niscemi see ibid., p. 117
67. See Garland & Smyth, **Sicily and the Surrender of Italy**, pp. 172-173
68. For the order translated in full see D'Este, **Bitter Victory**, p. 301
69. Conrath rally message and loss figures cited in Morison, **Sicily-Salerno-Anzio January 1943 – June 1944**, pp. 117-118
70. Quoted from Warren, **Airborne Missions in the Mediterranean**, p. 39
71. See LoFaro, **The Sword of St. Michael**, pp. 103-104
72. Timings and late receipt of operation order cited in Warren, **Airborne Missions in the Mediterranean**, p. 39; for Patton's change of mind and reasoning and Ridgway's code see LoFaro, **The Sword of St. Michael**, p. 104
73. For D-Day warning see Hewitt, **'Action Report Western Naval Task Force'**, 'Narrative of Events' Section, entry for 10:50, 10/07/1943; for receipt of 52nd Troop Carrier Wing signal timing and quote see Morison, **Sicily-Salerno-Anzio January 1943 – June 1944**, p. 120
74. See Garland & Smyth, **Sicily and the Surrender of Italy**, p. 176
75. See LoFaro, **The Sword of St. Michael**, p. 107
76. See Warren, **Airborne Missions in the Mediterranean**, Map 'Route of MACKALL WHITE (HUSKY 2)', p. 38
77. See Warren, **Airborne Missions in the Mediterranean**, p. 39; and LoFaro, **The Sword of St. Michael**, p. 105
78. See Blair, **Ridgway's Paratroopers**, pp. 82-83; and LoFaro, **The Sword of St. Michael**, pp. 105-106
79. See Hewitt, **'Action Report Western Naval Task Force'**, 'Narrative of Events' Section, various time-stamped entries between 05:06 & 22:16, 10/07/1943; and Garland & Smyth, **Sicily and the Surrender of Italy**, p. 177
80. Twenty-three raid figure cited in Warren, **Airborne Missions in the Mediterranean**, p. 40; twenty-four figure cited in LoFaro, **The Sword of St. Michael**, p. 107; aircraft numbers cited in Garland & Smyth, **Sicily and the Surrender of Italy**, p. 177, Footnote #6
81. quote from LoFaro, **The Sword of St. Michael**, p. 107
82. 22:40 drop time cited in Warren, **Airborne Missions in the Mediterranean**, p. 39
83. See Nordyke, **All American All the Way**, p. 83; and Garland & Smyth, **Sicily and the Surrender of Italy**, p. 177
84. For Major Alexander's observation see Nordyke, **All American All the Way**, p. 84
85. Testimony from Captain Delbert A. Kuehl, Regimental Chaplain, 504th RCT; cited in LoFaro, **The Sword of St. Michael**, p. 109
86. See Warren, **Airborne Missions in the Mediterranean**, p. 40
87. See Garland & Smyth, **Sicily and the Surrender of Italy**, p. 181

88. See Garland & Smyth, **Sicily and the Surrender of Italy**, pp. 178-180
89. See Warren, **Airborne Missions in the Mediterranean**, pp. 40-41
90. Testimony from 2nd Lieutenant Charles A. Drew, Company F, 2nd Battalion 504th Parachute Infantry Regiment; cited in Nordyke, **All American All the Way**, pp. 84-85
91. See Garland & Smyth, **Sicily and the Surrender of Italy**, p. 179; for thousand holes see ibid., footnote #16, p. 181
92. See Garland & Smyth, **Sicily and the Surrender of Italy**, p. 183
93. See Warren, **Airborne Missions in the Mediterranean**, p. 40
94. For IFF problems see Warren, **Airborne Missions in the Mediterranean**, p. 40; for US Navy perspective see Morison, **Sicily-Salerno-Anzio January 1943 – June 1944**, p. 120 and especially footnote #49
95. Quoted from Garland & Smyth, **Sicily and the Surrender of Italy**, p. 182-183
96. Quote from Warren, **Airborne Missions in the Mediterranean**, p. 41; for US Army comment on Cunningham's pronouncement see Garland & Smyth, **Sicily and the Surrender of Italy**, Footnote #21, p. 183
97. Figures and timings cited in Garland & Smyth, **Sicily and the Surrender of Italy**, p. 182
98. Figures and timings cited in Warren, **Airborne Missions in the Mediterranean**, p. 41
99. Ridgway quote cited in Garland & Smyth, **Sicily and the Surrender of Italy**, p. 184
100. 08:45 timing and fresh wine cited in Morison, **Sicily-Salerno-Anzio January 1943 – June 1944**, p. 122
101. 16th RCT loss figures cited in Garland & Smyth, **Sicily and the Surrender of Italy**, p. 189; for Colonel Gorham's death see for example Nordyke, **Four Stars of Valor**, pp. 91-92
102. See Garland & Smyth, **Sicily and the Surrender of Italy**, pp. 206, 222

Chapter 16

1. See **WO 169/10346** 4th Parachute Battalion War Diary, entry for 21:00, 10/07/1943; for Private Duncan's George Cross citation see **The Pegasus Archive** website, The 1st Airborne Division in Sicily Archive, Biographies Section, 4th Parachute Battalion page, entry for 'Private Charles Alfred Duncan' at https://www.pegasusarchive.org/sicily/biog_4thBatt.htm [accessed 24/05/2021]
2. See Peters, **Glider Pilots in Sicily**, p. 45; timings cited in Otway, **Airborne Forces**, pp. 124-12. For full details of Operation GLUTTON see **WO 169/8666** 1st Airborne Division HQ War Diary, 1st Airborne Division After Action Report: Part 4: 2 PARA BDE OPERATION
3. See Brigadier J. Durnford-Slater, **Commando**, (first published 1953; Greenhill Books, 2020) pp. 135-136; The Commando Veterans Archive website, No. 3 Commando Section, 'An Account of Ops at Sicily and Malati Bridge' by Lt. John Channon Erskine RE & No. 3 Commando, hereafter referred to as 'Lt. Erskine Account', p. 4, at http://www.commandoveterans.org/JohnErskine3Commando, accessed 29/07/2021; Saunders, The Green Beret, pp. 158-160; and Ladd, Commandos and Rangers of World War II, p. 133
4. See Molony, **The Campaign in Sicily 1943**, p. 94; for distance and Montgomery's stressing the need for haste see Peters, **Glider Pilots in Sicily**, p. 250
5. See Peters, **Glider Pilots in Sicily**, p. 211; and ibid., Map: 'Map of the Assault on the Ponte di Primosole', p. 244; for a participant description of the defences see Peter Stainforth, **Wings of the Wind: Active Service with the 1st Parachute Brigade**, pp. 216-217. The anti-tank bunkers are referred to as housing 40mm weapons,

but the *Regio Esercito* did not field weapons of that calibre in the anti-tank or any other role and the weapons were likely of 37mm or 47mm calibre

6. For details see Peters, **Glider Pilots in Sicily**, pp. 224-225
7. 300 average figure cited in Otway, Airborne Forces, p. 89; 2nd Parachute Battalion figures cited in **WO 175/526** 2nd Parachute Battalion War Diary, entry for 22/04/1943
8. See Otway, **Airborne Forces**, pp. 88-89
9. For 10 May date see Otway, **Airborne Forces**, pp. 113-114; for move to Tunisia date see **WO 169/8666** 1st Airborne Division HQ War Diary, entry for 30/06/1943
10. See **WO 169/8666** 1st Airborne Division HQ War Diary, entry for 18/06/1943; and **AIR 27/1645** No. 296 Squadron Operations Record Book, entry for 18/06/1943; for initial glider allocation see **WO 169/8666** 1st Airborne Division HQ War Diary, 'Report on the Operations Carried Out by 1st Airborne Division during the Invasion of Sicily (Operation HUSKY): Part 3 – 1st Parachute Brigade Operation: Section A. 'Air Operations' Para. 2, 'Availability of A/C'. Hereafter this report is referred to as 1st Airborne Division After Action Report: Part 3'
11. See **WO 169/8666** 1 Airborne Division HQ War Diary, entries for 05 and 06/07/1943
12. See **WO 169/8837** 1 Parachute Brigade HQ War Diary, entry for 02/07/1943; **WO 169/10343** 1 Parachute Regiment War Diary, entry for 20:00, 02/07/1943; **WO 169/10345** 3 Parachute Regiment War Diary, entry for 02/07/1943; and **WO 177/701** 16 Field Ambulance (PARA) RAMC War Diary, entry for 03/07/1943
13. See **WO 169/8837** 1 Parachute Brigade HQ War Diary, entries for 19:00, 07/07/1943 and 09/07/1943; and **WO 169/10344** 2 Parachute Regiment War Diary, entries for 10:00, 07/07/1943, 09:00, 16:00 and 17:00, 10/07/1943, 11:00, 11/07/1943; and 08:30, 12/07/1943
14. See **WO 169/10345** 3 Parachute Regiment War Diary, entries for 09 & 10/07/1943
15. Figures cited in **WO 169/8666** 1st Airborne Division HQ War Diary, 1st Airborne Division After Action Report: Part 3: Section A. 'Air Operations': Annexure E: 1 Parachute Brigade Operation 'FUSTIAN': Summary of Personnel and Containers Part 1: Personnel, Tables A & B
16. For glider allocation and transfer of GLUTTON machines see **WO 169/8666** 1st Airborne Division HQ War Diary, 1st Airborne Division After Action Report: Part 3: Section A. 'Air Operations' Para. 2, 'Availability of A/C'.
17. For aircraft types and numbers and stick details see **WO 169/8666** 1st Airborne Division HQ War Diary, 1st Airborne Division After Action Report: Part 3: Section A. 'Air Operations', Para. 2, 'Availability of A/C'; and ibid., Annexure F: Summary of Loads Carried on 1 Para Bde Operation, Lists A and B
18. USAAF higher command only appears to have become aware of the overloading issue due to C-47s returning to Tunisia with sticks still aboard; for this and the sixteen-man stick optimum see Warren, **Airborne Missions in the Mediterranean**, p. 52; for stick details see **WO 169/8666** 1st Airborne Division HQ War Diary, 1st Airborne Division After Action Report: Part 3: Section A. 'Air Operations', Annexure F: Summary of Loads Carried on 1 Para Bde Operation, List A, Entries 1-25
19. Load details cited in **WO 169/8666** 1st Airborne Division HQ War Diary, 1st Airborne Division After Action Report: Part 3: Section A. 'Air Operations', Annexure F: Summary of Loads Carried on 1 Para Bde Operation, Lists C & D
20. Six-mile distance cited in Warren, **Airborne Missions in the Mediterranean**, p. 48
21. See **WO 169/8666** 1st Airborne Division HQ War Diary, 1st Airborne Division After Action Report: Part 3: Section A 'Air Operations', Para. 9 'General', Point

(a) 'Route'; and Warren, **Airborne Missions in the Mediterranean**, p. 48. For maps of the fly-in and return routes see ibid., Map 8 'Route of FUSTIAN Mission 13-14 July 1943', p. 49; the map is also reproduced in Peters, **Glider Pilots in Sicily**, p. 228

22. See Warren, **Airborne Missions in the Mediterranean**, Map 9 'Vicinity of Drop and Landing Zones for FUSTIAN Mission, 13-14 July 1943', p. 50; the map is also reproduced in Peters, **Glider Pilots in Sicily**, p. 216
23. Ponte Primosole *coup-de-main* stick breakdown cited in Warren, **Airborne Missions in the Mediterranean**, p. 52
24. See **WO 169/8666** 1st Airborne Division HQ War Diary, 1st Airborne Division After Action Report: Part 3: Section B 'Ground Operations', Part 1 'Outline Plan', Para. 2 'Order of Battle', Para. 3 'DZs and LZs', Para. 4 'Method' & Para. 5 'Timings'
25. See Maurice Tugwell, **Airborne to Battle: A History of Airborne Warfare 1918-1971** (London: Kimber, 1971), pp. 163-164
26. Agreed jump height of 500 feet cited in Warren, **Airborne Missions in the Mediterranean**, p. 52
27. See **WO 169/10357** 21 Independent Parachute Company War Diary, entries for 12 and 13/07/1943; for Sergeant Smith flying with the 1st Parachute Battalion CO see Ron Kent, **First In! Parachute Pathfinder Company**, pp. 49-50; for details of the EUREKA homing beacon system see for example Otway, **Airborne Forces**, Appendix D 'Radar Homing Devices', pp. 405-406
28. See Peters, **Glider Pilots in Sicily**, p. 217
29. See **WO 169/8837** 1 Parachute Brigade HQ War Diary, entries for 07:00, 11:00, 18:30 and 22:00, 11/07/1943; and **WO 169/10344** 2 Parachute Regiment War Diary, entries for 10:00 & 11:00, 11/07/1943
30. For airfield unit allocations see **WO 169/8666** 1st Airborne Division HQ War Diary, 1st Airborne Division After Action Report: Part 3: Section A. 'Air Operations': Annexure A: Lay-Out of Aircraft for 1 Para Bde Operation
31. For unit mounting airfields see **WO 169/8666** 1st Airborne Division HQ War Diary, 1st Airborne Division After Action Report: Part 3: Section A. 'Air Operations': Annexure C: Preliminary Report on Success of Drop on Operation FUSTIAN – 1st Parachute Brigade; for 2nd Parachute Battalion detailed breakdown see **WO 169/10344** 2 Parachute Regiment War Diary, Appendix J: 'Administration Instruction to Operation Order "FUSTIAN": Emplaning Order No. 1'
32. For transport arrangements see **WO 169/8666** 1st Airborne Division HQ War Diary, 1st Airborne Division After Action Report: Part 3: Section A. 'Air Operations', Para. 4 'Move to Airfields'; 120 figure for trucks cited in **WO 169/8671** Commander Royal Army Service Corps HQ War Diary, entry for 09:00, 12/07/1943; for departure times see **WO 169/10343** 1 Parachute Regiment War Diary, entry for 13:30, 12/07/1943; **WO 169/10344** 2 Parachute Regiment War Diary, entry for 14:45, 12/07/1943; and **WO 169/8837** 1 Parachute Brigade HQ War Diary, entry for 15:45, 12/07/1943
33. For postponement contingency measures see **WO 169/10343** 1 Parachute Regiment War Diary, Appendix A: 'Transport to Airfields'
34. Quote from **WO 169/10344** 2 Parachute Regiment War Diary, entry for 09:00, 13/07/1943
35. See **WO 169/8837** 1 Parachute Brigade HQ War Diary, entry for 17:00, 12/07/1943; and **WO 169/10343** 1 Parachute Regiment War Diary, Appendix A: 'Transport to Airfields'
36. See **WO 169/8837** 1 Parachute Brigade HQ War Diary, entries for 15:45, 18:00 and 18:30, 13/07/1943. The 1st Parachute Battalion received confirmation at

18:30 and the 3rd Parachute Battalion thirty minutes earlier; see **WO 169/10343** 1 Parachute Regiment War Diary, entry for 18:30, 13/07/1943; and **WO 169/10345** 3 Parachute Regiment War Diary, entry for 18:00, 13/07/1943

37. See **WO 169/10344** 2 Parachute Regiment War Diary, entries for 17:30, 18:15 and 19:10, 13/07/1943
38. See Stainforth, **Wings of the Wind**, pp. 203-204
39. Ten minutes ahead of schedule cited in Warren, **Airborne Missions in the Mediterranean**, p. 48
40. Aircraft and glider totals cited in **WO 169/8666** 1st Airborne Division HQ War Diary, 1st Airborne Division After Action Report: Part 3: Section A. 'Air Operations', Para. G. 'Summary of Take Off'; 1,856 figure cited in ibid., Annexure E: 1 Parachute Brigade Operation 'FUSTIAN': Summary of Personnel and Containers Part 1: Personnel, Table A: Parachute

Chapter 17

1. See Warren, **Airborne Missions in the Mediterranean**, p. 48; timing cited in **WO 169/8837** 1 Parachute Brigade HQ War Diary, entry for 21:40, 13/07/1943
2. Quote from Peters, **Glider Pilots in Sicily**, p. 229; other details cited in Warren, **Airborne Missions in the Mediterranean**, pp. 48-51
3. Fifty-six figure calculated from **WO 169/8666** 1st Airborne Division HQ War Diary, 1st Airborne Division After Action Report: Part 3: Section A. 'Air Operations', Annexure B: Summary of Parachute Aircraft Operating on FUSTIAN – 1 Para Bde; other figures and distances cited in Warren, **Airborne Missions in the Mediterranean**, p. 48
4. For the two C-47s shot down into the sea and stick details see **WO 169/8666** 1st Airborne Division HQ War Diary, 1st Airborne Division After Action Report: Part 3: Section A. 'Air Operations': Annexure C: Preliminary Report on Success of Drop on Operation FUSTIAN – 1st Parachute Brigade, entries for Aircraft Nos. 91 and 104; see also Warren, **Airborne Missions in the Mediterranean**, p. 51; for details of Captain Percival and the RAMC stick rescue see **WO 177/701** 16 Field Ambulance (PARA) RAMC War Diary, Appendix 13: 'Report by Captain A. Percival, RAMC, on the Operation "Fustian"'; and Cole, **On Wings of Healing**, pp. 45-46
5. See Warren, **Airborne Missions in the Mediterranean**, p. 50; for specific aircraft details see **WO 169/8666** 1st Airborne Division HQ War Diary, 1st Airborne Division After Action Report: Part 3: Section A. 'Air Operations': Annexure C: Preliminary Report on Success of Drop on Operation FUSTIAN – 1st Parachute Brigade, entries for Aircraft Nos. 9, 32, 38, 89, 90, 96, 102 & 103
6. See **WO 169/8666** 1st Airborne Division HQ War Diary, 1st Airborne Division After Action Report: Part 3: Section A. 'Air Operations': Annexure C: Preliminary Report on Success of Drop on Operation FUSTIAN – 1st Parachute Brigade, entries for Aircraft Nos. 2, 5, 8 and 9; Warren refers to there being five such instances, see Warren, **Airborne Missions in the Mediterranean**, p. 51
7. See **WO 169/8666** 1st Airborne Division HQ War Diary, 1st Airborne Division After Action Report: Part 3: Section A. 'Air Operations': Annexure C: Preliminary Report on Success of Drop on Operation FUSTIAN – 1st Parachute Brigade, various aircraft-specific entries grouped according to parachute unit and launch airfield. There is some disparity in the figures and totals cited in the British source, and between the latter and the Official US source. In the 1st Airborne Division After Action Report a total of twenty-six aircraft returning with sticks aboard is cited while Warren refers to twenty-five. However, in the former the

Annexure C individual Aircraft entries give a total of twenty-three, and the final Summary table in Annexure B adds up to 124 rather than the 116 aircraft total cited at the end of the overall Summary; see **WO 169/8666** 1st Airborne Division HQ War Diary, 1st Airborne Division After Action Report: Part 3: Section A. 'Air Operations': Annexure B: Summary of Parachute Aircraft Operating on FUSTIAN – 1 Para Bde, Summary paragraph; and Warren, **Airborne Missions in the Mediterranean**, p. 51

8. The 1st Airborne Division After Action Report aircraft entries refer to one stick jumping and two returning with full sticks on board but the 1st Parachute Squadron War Diary clearly states that Captain Trevor Livesey's stick returned as a whole after the pilot and navigator were wounded by flak, Lieutenant Peter Stainforth's stick jumped in its entirety and that twelve of the eighteen in Lieutenant A. E. Houghton's stick jumped; the remainder were unable to access the door after a static line became tangled eight feet back and the pilot refused to go round again; see **WO 169/8666** 1st Airborne Division HQ War Diary, 1st Airborne Division After Action Report: Part 3: Section A. 'Air Operations': Annexure C: Entries for Aircraft Nos. 88, 89 & 90; and **WO 169/10554** 1 Parachute Squadron (RE Para Sqn) War Diary, 'Operation FUSTIAN: Jumpmaster's Report'
9. The US Official account cites eighty-seven while the British After Action Report suggests there were eighty-nine; see Warren, **Airborne Missions in the Mediterranean**, p. 52; and **WO 169/8666** 1st Airborne Division HQ War Diary, 1st Airborne Division After Action Report: Part 3: Section A. 'Air Operations': Annexures B & C
10. For five attempts and aircraft pressing on despite engine problems see **WO 169/8666** 1st Airborne Division HQ War Diary, 1st Airborne Division After Action Report: Part 3: Section A. 'Air Operations': Annexure C: Entries for Aircraft Nos. 34 & 72
11. See testimony from Sergeant Allen, 1st Parachute Brigade to 51st Troop Carrier Wing; cited in Warren, **Airborne Missions in the Mediterranean**, p. 51
12. Testimony from then-Lt.-Col. Alastair Pearson quoted in Max Arthur, **Forgotten Voices of the Second World War**, p. 231; cited in Peters, **Glider Pilots in Sicily**, pp. 229-231; for an unreferenced and slightly different version see Thompson, **Ready for Anything**, p. 78
13. Nine shot down figure cited in Warren, **Airborne Missions in the Mediterranean**, p. 51; and **WO 169/8666** 1st Airborne Division HQ War Diary, 1st Airborne Division After Action Report: Part 3: Section A. 'Air Operations': Annexure B: Summary of Parachute Aircraft Operating on FUSTIAN – 1 Para Bde, Summary section. The latter adds on the two C-47s brought down over the sea by naval anti-aircraft fire for a total of eleven machines shot down
14. See **WO 169/8666** 1st Airborne Division HQ War Diary, 1st Airborne Division After Action Report: Part 3: Section A. 'Air Operations': Annexure C: Entries for Aircraft Nos. 83 and 77 respectively
15. Four ditchings figure cited in Warren, **Airborne Missions in the Mediterranean**, p. 51; aircraft return figures in the British report give a total of six; see **WO 169/8666** 1st Airborne After Action Report: Part 3 – 1st Parachute Brigade Operation: Section A. 'Air Operations' Para. 7 'Report on Return of A/C'
16. Jump injury and fatality figures cited in **WO 169/8666** 1st Airborne Division HQ War Diary, 1st Airborne Division After Action Report: Part 3: Section A. 'Air Operations': Annexure E: Table C 'Casualties Incurred in Air and On Landing'; see also testimony from then-Lt.-Col. Alastair Pearson quoted in Thompson, **Ready for Anything**, p. 78; and Peters, **Glider Pilots in Sicily**, p. 231.

17. Pearson's C-47 was likely from the 62nd Troop Carrier Group which reported a death on landing; two other 1st Parachute Battalion machines, another from the 62nd and one from the 60th or 64th Troop Carrier Group, reported landing injuries and low jump height; see **169/8666** 1st Airborne Division HQ War Diary, 1st Airborne Division After Action Report: Part 3: Section A. 'Air Operations': Annexure C: Entries for Aircraft No. 30 and Nos. 25 & 63
18. Figures cited in **WO 169/8666** 1st Airborne Division After Action Report: Part 3 – 1st Parachute Brigade Operation: Section A. 'Air Operations': Annexure B: Summary of Parachute Aircraft Operating on FUSTIAN – 1 Para Bde, Summary paragraph; and Warren, **Airborne Missions in the Mediterranean**, p. 52
19. For four sticks landing on Mount Etna see Warren, **Airborne Missions in the Mediterranean**, p. 52; one aircraft entry from the 2nd Parachute Battalion specifically mentions despatching near Mount Etna after becoming lost while one aircraft carrying a stick from the 3rd Parachute Battalion refer to dropping twenty five miles wide and another to not dropping on the DZ; see **WO 169/8666** 1st Airborne Division HQ War Diary, 1st Airborne Division After Action Report: Part 3: Section A. 'Air Operations': Annexure C: Entries for Aircraft No. (79)A and Nos. 57 & 82 respectively
20. Timings collated from individual aircraft entries in **WO 169/8666** 1st Airborne Division HQ War Diary, 1st Airborne Division After Action Report: Part 3: Section A. 'Air Operations': Annexure C: Preliminary Report on Success of Drop on Operation FUSTIAN – 1st Parachute Brigade; for late Malta landing see ibid., entry for Aircraft No. 31
21. Timings and figures cited in **WO 169/8666** 1st Airborne Division After Action Report: Part 3 – 1st Parachute Brigade Operation: Section A. 'Air Operations' Para. 7 'Report on Return of A/C
22. See **WO 169/8666** 1st Airborne Division HQ War Diary, 1st Airborne Division After Action Report: Part 3: Section A. 'Air Operations': Annexure C: numerous Aircraft Entries. Warren refers to seventeen aircraft dropping part of their sticks, possibly discounting aircraft where paratroopers remained aboard after being injured or wounded; see Warren, **Airborne Missions in the Mediterranean**, p. 52
23. Casualty figures cited in **WO 169/8666** 1st Airborne Division HQ War Diary, 1st Airborne Division After Action Report: Part 3: Section A. 'Air Operations': Annexure E: 1 Parachute Brigade Operation 'FUSTIAN': Summary of Personnel and Containers Part 1: Personnel, Table C 'Casualties Incurred in Air and On Landing'; three refusals figure cited in Warren, **Airborne Missions in the Mediterranean**, p. 52
24. See **WO 169/8666** 1st Airborne Division HQ War Diary, 1st Airborne Division After Action Report: Part 3: Section A. 'Air Operations': Annexure C: Entries for Aircraft Nos. 95 & 97
25. All figures cited in Warren, **Airborne Missions in the Mediterranean**, p. 51
26. Overall and dropped figures cited in **WO 169/8666** 1st Airborne Division HQ War Diary, 1st Airborne Division After Action Report: Part 3: Section A. 'Air Operations': Annexure E: 1 Parachute Brigade Operation 'FUSTIAN': Summary of Personnel and Containers Part 1: Personnel, Table A: Parachute; for 295 and percentage figures see **WO 169/8837** 1 Parachute Brigade HQ War Diary, figures cited in entry for 07:00, 16/07/1943; and Otway, **Airborne Forces**, p. 127
27. Quote from **WO 169/10345** 3 Parachute Regiment War Diary, entry for 23:05, 13/07/1943
28. Quoted from Saunders, **The Red Beret**, p. 129
29. See **WO 169/10343** 1 Parachute Regiment War Diary, entry for 09:00, 14/07/1943; and **WO 169/10344** 2 Parachute Regiment War Diary, entry for 01:00, 14/07/1943

30. For quote, timings & figures see **WO 169/10345** 3 Parachute Regiment War Diary, entries for 23:20, 23:25 and 24:00, 13/07/1943
31. See **WO 169/10345** 3 Parachute Regiment War Diary, entries for 01:00 and 05:00, 14/07/1943
32. For details see **WO 169/8666** 1st Airborne Division HQ War Diary, 1st Airborne Division After Action Report: Part 3: Section A. 'Air Operations': Annexure C: Bde Headquarters Airfield F Section, Entries for Aircraft Nos. 105-113A
33. See **WO 169/8837** 1 Parachute Brigade HQ War Diary, entry for 23:32, 13/07/1943; **WO 169/8666** 1st Airborne Division HQ War Diary, 1st Airborne Division After Action Report: Part 3: Section B. 'Ground Operations', Para. 2 'Action On Landing'; and Saunders, **The Red Beret**, p. 130
34. See **WO 169/10344** 2 Parachute Regiment War Diary, entry for 02:15, 14/07/1943; and Saunders, **The Red Beret**, p. 130. For birthday greeting see Frost, **A Drop Too Many**, p. 179; see also Peters, **Glider Pilots in Sicily**, p. 242
35. See **WO 169/8838** 1 Parachute Brigade Signals War Diary, '0409 1st Parachute Brigade Signals Section: Story of Operation HUSKY/FUSTIAN', Section G: Personal Description of the Drop by Captain G. Rowland, OC 1 Parachute Brigade Signals, Para. 3; and testimony from Brigadier Gerald Lathbury, CO 1st Parachute Brigade; cited in Peters, **Glider Pilots in Sicily**, p. 242
36. Quote and other details from Saunders, **The Red Beret**, p. 130; for 1st Parachute Squadron RE stick involvement see Stainforth, **Wings of the Wind**, pp. 208-213
37. See **WO 169/8837** 1 Parachute Brigade HQ War Diary, entry for 23:32, 13/07/1943; **WO 169/8666** 1st Airborne Division HQ War Diary, 1st Airborne Division After Action Report: Part 3: Section B. 'Ground Operations', Para. 2 'Action On Landing', Phase I; Section (b) 'The Capture of the Bridge'; **WO 169/8837** 1 Parachute Brigade HQ War Diary, entries for 02:00 and 02:15, 14/07/1943; **WO 169/10343** 1 Parachute Regiment War Diary, entries for 02:14 and 02:30, 14/07/1943; **WO 169/10345** 3 Parachute Regiment War Diary, entries for 01:00, 01:30 and 02:45, 14/07/1943; and Peters, **Glider Pilots in Sicily**, p. 238. The various War Diary entries provide differing and, in some respects, contradictory details; the 3rd Parachute Battalion War Diary claims Lt.-Col. Yeldham despatched Lt. Lasenby's party to scout the north end of the bridge for example
38. See **WO 169/8838** 1 Parachute Brigade Signals War Diary, '0409 1st Parachute Brigade Signals Section: Story of Operation HUSKY/FUSTIAN', Section G: Personal Description of the Drop by Captain G. Rowland, OC 1 Parachute Brigade Signals, Para. 4; **WO 169/10343** 1 Parachute Regiment War Diary, entry for 02:30, 14/07/1943; **WO 169/10345** 3 Parachute Regiment War Diary, entry for 05:00, 14/07/1943; and Stainforth, **Wings of the Wind**, pp. 216-217. The 3rd Parachute Battalion War Diary entry timings are out of synch with the other War Diaries from this point by around two hours
39. See **WO 169/8838** 1 Parachute Brigade Signals War Diary, '0409 1st Parachute Brigade Signals Section: Story of Operation HUSKY/FUSTIAN', Section G: Personal Description of the Drop by Captain G. Rowland, OC 1 Parachute Brigade Signals, Para. 4; see also **WO 169/8837** 1 Parachute Brigade HQ War Diary, entry for 03:15, 14/07/1943; **WO 169/8666** 1st Airborne Division HQ War Diary, 1st Airborne Division After Action Report: Part 3: Section B. 'Ground Operations', Para. 2 'Action On Landing', Phase I; Section (b) 'The Capture of the Bridge'; and **WO 169/10345** 3 Parachute Regiment War Diary, entry for 05:00, 14/07/1943
40. See Stainforth, **Wings of the Wind**, pp. 217-219; and **WO 169/8666** 1st Airborne Division HQ War Diary, 1st Airborne Division After Action Report: Part 3:

Section B. 'Ground Operations', Para. 2 'Action On Landing', Phase I; Section (b) 'The Capture of the Bridge'

41. See for example **WO 169/8837** 1 Parachute Brigade HQ War Diary, entry for 03:30, 14/07/1943; for 30 Italian engineers see **WO 169/10343** 1 Parachute Regiment War Diary, entry for 03:30
42. The use of a permanently attached length of detonator cord called a surcingle charge for removing the rear end of Horsa fuselages in an emergency later became a standard fitting after tests in early 1944; see Otway, **Airborne Forces**, Appendix A: The Glider, Horsa Section Para. 12, p. 392
43. For glider details see **WO 169/8666** 1st Airborne Division HQ War Diary, 1st Airborne Division After Action Report: Part 3: Section A. 'Air Operations': Annexure D: Report on Gliders Operating on 1Para Bde Operation – FUSTIAN; see also Peters, **Glider Pilots in Sicily**, Appendix 2: Operation FUSTIAN Post Mission Reports, pp. 292-294
44. See Peters, **Glider Pilots in Sicily**, p. 243
45. Testimony from Brigadier Gerald Lathbury, CO 1st Parachute Brigade, **British Army Review**, Issue 79, August 1985; cited in Peters, **Glider Pilots in Sicily**, pp. 246-247
46. See **WO 169/8666** 1st Airborne Division HQ War Diary, 1st Airborne Division After Action Report: Part 3: Section A. 'Air Operations': Annexure D: Entry for Glider No. 118C; Sergeant Frederick Highfield Street has No Known Grave and is commemorated on the Cassino Memorial, Panel 12
47. See **WO 169/8666** 1st Airborne Division HQ War Diary, 1st Airborne Division After Action Report: Part 3: Section A. 'Air Operations': Annexure D: Entry for Glider No. 120; and Peters, **Glider Pilots in Sicily**, pp. 234-235
48. See **WO 169/8666** 1st Airborne Division HQ War Diary, 1st Airborne Division After Action Report: Part 3: Section A. 'Air Operations': Annexure D: Entry for Glider No. 128; and Peters, **Glider Pilots in Sicily**, p. 246
49. See **WO 169/8666** 1st Airborne Division HQ War Diary, 1st Airborne Division After Action Report: Part 3: Section A. 'Air Operations': Annexure D: Entry for Glider No. 129; and Peters, **Glider Pilots in Sicily**, p. 247. For Lieutenant Lasenby's involvement see **WO 169/10345** 3 Parachute Regiment War Diary, entry for 02:45, 14/07/1943
50. See **WO 169/8666** 1st Airborne Division HQ War Diary, 1st Airborne Division After Action Report: Part 3: Section A. 'Air Operations': Annexure D: Entry for Glider No. 126; quote from Stainforth, **Wings of the Wind**, pp. 214-216; for a detailed account of the landing including testimony from Staff-Sergeant Protheroe see Peters, **Glider Pilots in Sicily**, pp. 243-246
51. For a detailed account of Lt. Frank's activities immediately post-landing see **The Pegasus Archive** website, The 1st Airborne Division in Sicily Archive, Biographies Section, 2nd Parachute Battalion page, A Company Section, entry for 'Lieutenant Anthony Mutrie Frank' at https://www.pegasusarchive.org/sicily/tony_frank.htm [accessed 03/07/2021]; for the 'actively engaged' stick see **WO 169/10344** 2 Parachute Regiment War Diary, entry for 03:15, 14/07/1943
52. See **WO 169/10344** 2 Parachute Regiment War Diary, entries for 03:15, 04:00, 04:30, 05:00 and 05:30, 14/07/1943; and **WO 169/8666** 1st Airborne Division HQ War Diary, 1st Airborne Division After Action Report: Part 3: Section B. 'Ground Operations', Para. 2 'Action On Landing', Phase I; Section (c) 'The Capture of the high ground in the area 9365'
53. Quote from Saunders, **The Red Beret**, p. 135
54. See **WO 169/10344** 2 Parachute Regiment War Diary, entries for 05:30 and 06:00, 14/07/1943

55. See **WO 169/8666** 1st Airborne Division HQ War Diary, 1st Airborne Division After Action Report: Part 3: Section B. 'Ground Operations', Para. 2 'Action On Landing', Phase I; Section (b) 'The Capture of the Bridge', entry for 04:00; **WO 169/8837** 1 Parachute Brigade HQ War Diary, entry for 05:30, 14/07/1943; and **WO 169/10345** 3 Parachute Regiment War Diary, entry for 05:00, 14/07/1943
56. See **WO 169/8666** 1st Airborne Division HQ War Diary, 1st Airborne Division After Action Report: Part 3: Section B. 'Ground Operations', Para. 2 'Action On Landing', Phase I; Section (b) 'The Capture of the Bridge', entry for 06:30; **WO 169/8837** 1 Parachute Brigade HQ War Diary, entry for 06:15, 14/07/1943; **WO 169/10343** 1 Parachute Regiment War Diary, entry for 05:45, 14/07/1943; and **WO 169/10345** 3 Parachute Regiment War Diary, entries for 05:30 & 06:00, 14/07/1943
57. For radio contact timings see **WO 169/10343** 1 Parachute Regiment War Diary, entries for 06:15, 06:20 & 06:40; for Captain Rowland and the Brigade Signals Section involvement see **WO 169/8838** 1 Parachute Brigade Signals War Diary, '0409 1st Parachute Brigade Signals Section: Story of Operation HUSKY/FUSTIAN', Section G: Personal Description of the Drop by Captain G. Rowland, OC 1 Parachute Brigade Signals, Para. 5. Interestingly, the Brigade HQ War Diary reports that 'no wireless sets were usable' up to 06:15, presumably before Captain Rowland's appropriation of the No. 22 and No. Sets
58. See **WO 169/8838** 1 Parachute Brigade Signals War Diary, '0409 1st Parachute Brigade Signals Section: Story of Operation HUSKY/FUSTIAN', Section G: Personal Description of the Drop by Captain G. Rowland, OC 1 Parachute Brigade Signals, Para. 4
59. See **WO 175/316** 1 Airlanding [Anti-Tank] Battery RA War Diary, 'Report on Operation "FUSTIAN" 13th July to 18th July 1943', Para. 12 'Subsequent Action After Landing' and ibid., Entry (d) 'Individual Actions'.
60. See Stainforth, **Wings of the Wind**, p. 219
61. See **WO 177/701** 16 Field Ambulance (PARA) RAMC War Diary, Appendix 15: 'Report on Operation HUSKY/FUSTIAN, 13/7/43', Section B: 'The Operation', Para. 2 'The Drop' and Para. 5 'Diary of Events', entries for 04:45, 05:30, 05:45, 06:30 and 06:40, 14/07/1943; see also **WO 169/8837** 1 Parachute Brigade HQ War Diary, entry for 07:00, 14/07/1943; and Cole, On Wings of Healing, pp. 46-47
62. Captain Rowland's involvement and quotes from **WO 169/8838** 1 Parachute Brigade Signals War Diary, '0409 1st Parachute Brigade Signals Section: Story of Operation HUSKY/FUSTIAN', Section G: Personal Description of the Drop by Captain G. Rowland, OC 1 Parachute Brigade Signals, Para. 5; timings cited in **WO 169/8837** 1 Parachute Brigade HQ War Diary, entry for 09:30, 14/07/1943
63. See **WO 169/10345** 3 Parachute Regiment War Diary, entry for 03:45, 14/07/1943
64. See **WO 169/10343** 1 Parachute Regiment War Diary, entry for 09:00, 14/07/1943; and **WO 169/8837** 1 Parachute Brigade HQ War Diary, entries for 09:00 and 09:15, 14/07/1943
65. See **WO 169/8837** 1 Parachute Brigade HQ War Diary, entry for 10:00, 14/07/1943; **WO 169/10345** 3 Parachute Regiment War Diary, entry for 10:00, 14/07/1943; **WO 169/10343** 1 Parachute Regiment War Diary, entry for 11:20, 14/07/1943; and Stainforth, **Wings of the Wind**, pp. 221-222. For fighter relay and observing the rearming see Peters, **Glider Pilots in Sicily**, p. 252
66. For Brigade HQ relocation see **WO 169/8838** 1 Parachute Brigade Signals War Diary, '0409 1st Parachute Brigade Signals Section: Story of Operation HUSKY/FUSTIAN', Section G: Personal Description of the Drop by Captain G. Rowland, OC 1 Parachute Brigade Signals, Para. 6

67. See Peters, **Glider Pilots in Sicily**, pp. 249-250
68. See **WO 169/10344** 2 Parachute Regiment War Diary, entries for 06:30, 07:00, 07:30, 08:00, 08:30 and 09:00, 14/07/1943; and Frost, **A Drop Too Many**, pp. 180-181
69. Peters refers to Captain Hodge establishing contact with the cruiser HMS *Mauritius* but the British Official Campaign History and Captain Hodge's obituary refer to the vessel being HMS *Newfoundland* while the British Official and Semi-Official Histories and Frost's account merely refer to an unidentified cruiser; see Peters, **Glider Pilots in Sicily**, p. 251; Molony, **The Campaign in Sicily 1943**, p. 94; **The Daily Telegraph**, Obituary 'Captain Francis Vere Hodge MC, 31 October 1919 – 15 December 2013' published 22/12/2013; Otway, **Airborne Forces**, p. 129; Saunders, **The Red Beret**, p. 135; and Frost, **A Drop Too Many**, p. 181
70. Quoted from Frost, **A Drop Too Many**, p. 181
71. See **WO 169/10344** 2 Parachute Regiment War Diary, entries for 09:00, 10:00 and 10:30, 14/07/1943; for Captain Hodge's presence and activities see also **WO 169/8666** 1st Airborne Division HQ War Diary, 1st Airborne Division After Action Report: Part 3: Section B 'Ground Operations', Annexure 1 'Report on Artillery Aspect of Operation', Section B 'FOO Dets'
72. For Captain Hodge's Military Cross citation see **The Pegasus Archive** website, The 1st Airborne Division in Sicily Archive, Biographies Section, 2nd Parachute Battalion page, entry for 'Captain Francis Vere Hodge' at www.pegasusarchive.org/sicily/francis_vere_hodge.htm [accessed 17/07/2021]
73. See **WO 169/10344** 2 Parachute Regiment War Diary, entry for 11:00, 14/07/1943; for Captain Hodge's presence & activities see also **WO 169/8666** 1st Airborne Division HQ War Diary, 1st Airborne Division After Action Report: Part 3: Section B 'Ground Operations', Annexure 1 'Report on Artillery Aspect of Operation', Section B 'FOO Dets'; and Frost, **A Drop Too Many**, p. 181
74. For Captain Panter's Military Cross citation see **The Pegasus Archive** website, The 1st Airborne Division in Sicily Archive, Biographies Section, 2nd Parachute Battalion page, entry for 'Captain Stanley Charles "Bombs" Panter' at www.pegasusarchive.org/sicily/stanley_charles_panter.htm [accessed 17/07/2021]
75. See **WO 169/10344** 2 Parachute Regiment War Diary, entries for 12:00 and 13:00, 14/07/1943
76. See Peters, **Glider Pilots in Sicily**, p. 252
77. See **WO 169/10343** 1 Parachute Regiment War Diary, entry for 11:20, 14/07/1943; and **WO 169/10345** 3 Parachute Regiment War Diary, entries for 10:00 & 12:10, 14/07/1943
78. See **WO 169/8837** 1 Parachute Brigade HQ War Diary, entries for 13:00, 13:10, 13:20, 13:40, 14:00 & 15:00, 14/07/1943; **WO 169/10345** 3 Parachute Regiment War Diary, entries for 13:00 and 14:30, 14/07/1943; and **WO 169/10343** 1 Parachute Regiment War Diary, entries for 13:50 and 14:10, 14/07/1943
79. See Saunders, **The Red Beret**, p. 132 and Peters, **Glider Pilots in Sicily**, pp. 252-253; for references to fighting north of the bridge see for example **WO 169/8666** 1st Airborne Division HQ War Diary, 1st Airborne Division After Action Report: Part 3: Section B. 'Ground Operations', Para. 2 'Action On Landing', Phase II. 'Subsequent Developments'; Section (b) 'The Fight for and Withdrawal from the Bridge' – the wording here is admittedly ambiguous and could be construed as referring to an attack against the southern perimeter, but this is not supported by the other participant War Diaries or the fact that the northern perimeter force was withdrawn across the Ponte Primosole and the subsequent withdrawal to the JOHNNY I feature was under enemy pressure from the north rather than

elsewhere; see **WO 169/8837** 1 Parachute Brigade HQ War Diary, entries for 14:00, 15:00 & 15:30; **WO 169/10343** 1 Parachute Regiment War Diary, entries for 13:50 & 14:10; and **WO 169/10345** 3 Parachute Regiment War Diary, entry for 15:30, 14/07/1943

80. See **WO 169/10345** 3 Parachute Regiment War Diary, entry for 15:00, 14/07/1943
81. See **WO 169/10344** 2 Parachute Regiment War Diary, entries for 15:00 and 16:00, 14/07/1943; **WO 169/8666** 1st Airborne Division HQ War Diary, 1st Airborne Division After Action Report: Part 3: Section B 'Ground Operations', Annexure 1 'Report on Artillery Aspect of Operation', Section B 'FOO Dets'; and Frost, **A Drop Too Many**, p. 182
82. The 3rd Parachute Battalion War Diary refers to observing the arrival four truckloads, the Brigade HQ War Diary to two; see **WO 169/10345** 3 Parachute Regiment War Diary, entry for 15:00, 14/07/1943; and **WO 169/8837** 1 Parachute Brigade HQ War Diary, entry for 15:00, 14/07/1943
83. See **WO 169/10345** 3 Parachute Regiment War Diary, entries for 15:30, 16:00 and 16:30, 14/07/1943; and **WO 169/8666** 1st Airborne Division HQ War Diary, 1st Airborne Division After Action Report: Part 3: Section B. 'Ground Operations', Para. 2 'Action On Landing', Phase II. 'Subsequent Developments'; Section (b) 'The Fight for and Withdrawal from the Bridge'
84. For Lt. Gardiner and the captured guns and ammunition see **WO 169/8838** 1 Parachute Brigade Signals War Diary, '0409 1st Parachute Brigade Signals Section: Story of Operation HUSKY/FUSTIAN', Section G: Personal Description of the Drop by Captain G. Rowland, OC 1 Parachute Brigade Signals, Para. 6 (Lt. Gardiner's name is incorrectly rendered Gardner); for Driver Reed and Lt. Clapham's involvement see **WO 175/316** 1 Airlanding [Anti-Tank] Battery RA War Diary, 'Report on Operation "FUSTIAN" 13th July to 18th July 1943', Para. 12 'Subsequent Action After Landing', entry (d) 'Individual Actions', individually named entries; for Lt. Clapham's Military Cross citation see **The Pegasus Archive** website, The 1st Airborne Division in Sicily Archive, Biographies Section, 1st Airlanding Anti-Tank Battery RA page, entry for 'Lieutenant Eric Edward Clapham' at https://www.pegasusarchive.org/sicily/edward_eric_clapham.htm [accessed 21/07/2021]
85. See **WO 177/701** 16 Field Ambulance (PARA) RAMC War Diary, Appendix 15: 'Report on Operation HUSKY/FUSTIAN, 13/7/43', Section B: 'The Operation', Para. 4 'The RAPs'
86. For Italian Medical Officer, casualty and operation figures see **WO 177/701** 16 Field Ambulance (PARA) RAMC War Diary, Appendix 15: 'Report on Operation HUSKY/FUSTIAN, 13/7/43', Section B: 'The Operation', Para. 5 'Diary of Events', entries for 10:00, 12:00 & 22:00, 14/07/1943; for details of the work of the MDS, ADS and Battalion RAPs see Cole, **On Wings of Healing**, pp. 47-48
87. See **WO 169/8837** 1 Parachute Brigade HQ War Diary, entries for 16:00 and 17:00, 14/07/1943; for Axis armoured car on road north of the bridge see **WO 169/10345** 3 Parachute Regiment War Diary, entry for 17:00, 14/07/1943
88. For the withdrawal order see **WO 169/8837** 1 Parachute Brigade HQ War Diary, entry for 17:05, 14/07/1943; for 1st Battalion timing, 160 strength figure and lack of casualties see **WO 169/10343** 1 Parachute Regiment War Diary, entry for 17:30; for lack of 3rd Parachute Battalion casualties in the withdrawal see Peters, **Glider Pilots in Sicily**, pp. 253-254. Neither the 3rd Parachute Battalion nor 1st Airlanding Anti-Tank Battery War Diaries mention the withdrawal to the south bank of the River Simeto, although the latter refers to 'All personnel and guns' (plural) being concentrated subsequently; see **WO 175/316** 1 Airlanding

[Anti-Tank] Battery RA War Diary, 'Report on Operation "FUSTIAN" 13th July to 18th July 1943', Para. 12 'Subsequent Action After Landing', entry (b) 'Withdrawal'; for the withdrawal under rather than over the bridge see Stainforth, **Wings of the Wind**, p. 228

89. Quote from Saunders, **The Red Beret**, p. 133
90. See Stainforth, **Wings of the Wind**, p. 229
91. See for example **WO 169/8837** 1 Parachute Brigade HQ War Diary, entries for 18:30, 18:45 and 19:00, 14/07/1943; and **WO 169/10345** 3 Parachute Regiment War Diary, entries for 18:00 & 18:30, 14/07/1943
92. See **WO 169/8666** 1st Airborne Division HQ War Diary, 1st Airborne Division After Action Report: Part 3: Section B. 'Ground Operations', Para. 2 'Action On Landing', Phase II. 'Subsequent Developments'; Section (b) 'The Fight for and Withdrawal from the Bridge'; **WO 169/8837** 1 Parachute Brigade HQ War Diary, entry for 19:15, 14/07/1943; **WO 169/10343** 1 Parachute Regiment War Diary, entry for 18:30, 14/07/1943; and **WO 169/10345** 3 Parachute Regiment War Diary, entry for 19:00, 14/07/1943; for Capt. Talbot quote and Capt. Haggie's involvement see **WO 177/701** 16 Field Ambulance (PARA) RAMC War Diary, Appendix 15: 'Report on Operation HUSKY/FUSTIAN, 13/7/43', Section B: 'The Operation', Para. 5 'Diary of Events', entries for 16:15 & 20:00, 14/07/1943
93. For Major Hunter's visit to JOHNNY I see **WO 169/8837** 1 Parachute Brigade HQ War Diary, entry for 09:20, 14/07/1943
94. See **WO 169/10344** 2 Parachute Regiment War Diary, entry for 18:00, 14/07/1943
95. See **WO 169/10343** 1 Parachute Regiment War Diary, entries for 18:30 and 21:00, 14/07/1943; **WO 169/8838** 1 Parachute Brigade Signals War Diary, '0409 1st Parachute Brigade Signals Section: Story of Operation HUSKY/FUSTIAN', Section G: Personal Description of the Drop by Captain G. Rowland, OC 1 Parachute Brigade Signals, Para. 7; **WO 169/8837** 1 Parachute Brigade HQ War Diary, entry for 06:00, 15/07/1943; and **WO 169/10345** 3 Parachute Regiment War Diary, entries for 19:50 and 20:00, 14/07/1943,
96. See **WO 175/316** 1 Airlanding [Anti-Tank] Battery RA War Diary, 'Report on Operation "FUSTIAN" 13th July to 18th July 1943', Para. 12 'Subsequent Action After Landing', entry (d) 'Individual Actions'; testimony from Staff-Sergeant Protheroe cited in Peters, **Glider Pilots in Sicily**, p. 256
97. See Saunders, **The Red Beret**, p. 134; for MDS capture, liberation, closure and final casualty figures see **WO 177/701** 16 Field Ambulance (PARA) RAMC War Diary, Appendix 15: 'Report on Operation HUSKY/FUSTIAN, 13/7/43', Section B: 'The Operation', Para. 5 'Diary of Events', entries for 05:45, 06:15 and 17:30, 15/07/1943
98. See **WO 177/701** 16 Field Ambulance (PARA) RAMC War Diary, Appendix 15: 'Report on Operation HUSKY/FUSTIAN, 13/7/43', Section B: 'The Operation', Para. 5 'Diary of Events', entry for 21:00, 14/07/1943
99. See **WO 169/8669** 1 Airborne Division: Royal Engineers (RE) HQ War Diary, Appendix B 'Operations in Sicily': Entry for Plane No. 88 signed P. T. Stainforth, Lt. RE, 1st Parachute Squadron RE: for a detailed account see Stainforth, **Wings of the Wind**, pp. 230-236
100. Figures cited in **WO 169/8837** 1 Parachute Brigade HQ War Diary, attached to entry for 07:00, 16/07/1943; for specific 2nd Parachute Battalion figures see **WO 169/10344** 2 Parachute Regiment War Diary, entry for 10:00, 16/07/1943
101. See **WO 169/8668** 1 Airborne Division Royal Artillery (RA) HQ War Diary, entry for *c*.24:00, 13/07/1943
102. For relief date and time and Lt.-Col. Pearson's involvement in the attack on the bridge see **WO 169/8666** 1st Airborne Division HQ War Diary, 1st Airborne

Division After Action Report: Part 3: Section B. 'Ground Operations', Para. 2 'Action On Landing', Phase II. 'Subsequent Developments'; Section (c) 'The Relief'; for Maj. Fitch and Capt. Panter see **WO 169/10344** 2 Parachute Regiment War Diary, entries for 11:00 and 11:30, 15/07/1943. The 1st Airborne Division HQ War Diary refers to the 6th Battalion Durham Light Infantry recapturing the Ponte Primosole in the early morning of 16 July, but the British Official History credits the deed to the 8th Battalion Durham Light Infantry and refers to the 6th Battalion participating in an attack to expand the bridgehead the following day, 17 July, interestingly with no mention of Lt.-Col. Pearson's involvement; see Molony, **The Campaign in Sicily 1943**, p. 103

103. See for example **WO 169/8837** 1 Parachute Brigade HQ War Diary, entries for 07:00 and 16:00, 16/07/1943; and **WO 169/10344** 2 Parachute Regiment War Diary, entry for 10:00 and 15:00, 16/07/1943; for the 1st Battalion's 'refreshing swim' see **WO 169/10343** 1 Parachute Regiment War Diary, entry for 16/07/1943
104. The precise timings of the voyage from Syracuse to Sousse vary slightly between accounts; see for example **WO 169/8837** 1 Parachute Brigade HQ War Diary, entries for 06:00 and 22:00, 17/07/1943, 06:00, 18/07/1943 and 07:00 & 07:30, 19/07/1943; and **WO 169/10344** 2 Parachute Regiment War Diary, entries for 12:00 and 22:00, 17/07/1943, 04:00, 18/07/1943 and 06:30 & 07:30, 19/07/1943

Chapter 18

1. See **WO 169/10344** 2 Parachute Regiment War Diary, entries for 19:30, 19:45, 21:00 and 23:40, 14/07/1943; and **WO 169/8666** 1st Airborne Division HQ War Diary, 1st Airborne Division After Action Report: Part 3: Section B. 'Ground Operations', Para. 2 'Action On Landing', Phase II. 'Subsequent Developments'; Section (c) 'The Relief'
2. See Molony, **The Campaign in Sicily 1943**, p. 94
3. See Molony, **The Campaign in Sicily 1943**, p. 95; Saunders, **The Green Beret**, pp. 160-162; and **The Commando Veterans Archive** website, No. 3 Commando Section, 'Lt. Erskine Account', pp. 5-6, at http://www.commandoveterans.org/JohnErskine3Commando, accessed 29/07/2021
4. See **The Commando Veterans Archive** website, No. 3 Commando Section, 'Lt. Erskine Account', p. 7, at http://www.commandoveterans.org/JohnErskine3Commando, accessed 29/07/2021; and Saunders, **The Green Beret**, p. 162
5. See Saunders, **The Green Beret**, pp. 162-169; and **The Commando Veterans Archive** website, No. 3 Commando Section, 'Lt. Erskine Account', pp. 7-9, at http://www.commandoveterans.org/JohnErskine3Commando, accessed 29/07/2021
6. See Saunders, **The Green Beret**, p. 166
7. Casualty figures cited in Molony, **The Campaign in Sicily 1943**, Footnote #1, p. 95; and Saunders, **The Green Beret**, p. 168
8. See **The Commando Veterans Archive** website, No. 3 Commando Section, 'Lt. Erskine Account', pp. 9-11, at http://www.commandoveterans.org/JohnErskine3Commando, accessed 29/07/2021
9. See Molony, **The Campaign in Sicily 1943**, p. 94
10. See Molony, **The Campaign in Sicily 1943**, p. 103
11. For details and 9th DLI casualty figures see Molony, **The Campaign in Sicily 1943**, p. 103; for relief and timing see **WO 169/8666** 1st Airborne Division HQ War Diary, 1st Airborne Division After Action Report: Part 3: Section B. 'Ground Operations', Para. 2 'Action On Landing, Phase II. Subsequent Developments'; Section (c) 'The Relief'

12. See Molony, **The Campaign in Sicily 1943**, p. 103; quotation cited in Thompson, **Ready for Anything: The Parachute Regiment at War 1940-1982**, p. 83. For Lathbury & Pearson's presence at the 151 Brigade Orders Group (sometimes referred to as the 4th Armoured Brigade) see testimony from then –Lt.-Col. Alastair Pearson, cited in Thompson, **Ready for Anything**, pp. 82-83; and Peters, **Glider Pilots in Sicily**, p. 255-256; for Lathbury arriving at JOHNNY I and being treated at the MDS see **WO 169/8837** 1 Parachute Brigade HQ War Diary, entries for 06:00 & 09:15, 15/07/1943
13. See Molony, **The Campaign in Sicily 1943**, p. 103; for Pearson quote and After Action Report reference to his involvement see Thompson, **Ready for Anything**, pp. 82-83; and **WO 169/8666** 1st Airborne Division HQ War Diary, 1st Airborne Division After Action Report: Part 3: Section B. 'Ground Operations', Para. 2 'Action On Landing, Phase II. Subsequent Developments'; Section (c) 'The Relief'
14. See Molony, **The Campaign in Sicily 1943**, pp. 104-105
15. See Molony, **The Campaign in Sicily 1943**, p. 114
16. ARROW FORCE was made up of 23rd Armoured Brigade HQ; 50th RTR minus two Troops; 2nd Battalion Seaforth Highlanders (attached from 152nd Brigade); 11th Regiment RHA; and 243rd Anti-Tank Battery RA; see Molony, **The Campaign in Sicily 1943**, Footnote #2, p. 115
17. See Molony, **The Campaign in Sicily 1943**, pp. 115-117; for a detailed account of the action by Brigadier Rennie see **The 51st Highland Division** website, 'Battle for Gerbini, Sicily, 18-21 July 1943' page, 'Gerbini Battle, 154 Brigade Commander's Account, Sicily [dated] 14th August 1943' at https://51hd.co.uk/accounts/gerbini_combs, accessed 12/08/2021
18. Figures cited in Molony, **The Campaign in Sicily 1943**, p. 117
19. See Nicholson, **The Canadians in Italy 1943-1945**, pp. 88-94; and Molony, **The Campaign in Sicily 1943**, pp. 117-118
20. Valguarnera is currently known as Valguarnera Caropepe
21. See Molony, **The Campaign in Sicily 1943**, p. 118; for a detailed account see Nicholson, **The Canadians in Italy 1943-1945**, pp. 95-99
22. See Nicholson, **The Canadians in Italy 1943-1945**, pp. 102-110; and Molony, **The Campaign in Sicily 1943**, p. 119
23. Casualty figures cited in Nicholson, **The Canadians in Italy 1943-1945**, p. 110
24. Advance parties of *1 Fallschirmjäger Division* had already been despatched to reinforce *Kampfgruppe* Schmalz at Ponte Primosole but *OKW* remained opposed to sending the whole of *Generalleutnant* Heidrich's *1 Fallschirmjäger Division* to the island on the grounds that there was no requirement for an additional divisional headquarters. This did not please Heidrich who was forced to remain behind and see his elite troops placed under the command of Conrath's *HG Panzer Division*.
25. See for example Garland & Smyth, **Sicily and the Surrender of Italy**, pp. 212-214; and Molony, **The Campaign in Sicily 1943**, pp. 90-91
26. See Garland & Smyth, **Sicily and the Surrender of Italy**, pp. 223-224; and Molony, **The Campaign in Sicily 1943**, pp. 92-94
27. See Molony, **The Campaign in Sicily 1943**, pp. 88-89
28. For Alexander's intent see for example Nicholson, **The Canadians in Italy 1943-1945**, p. 86
29. See Garland & Smyth, **Sicily and the Surrender of Italy**, pp. 91, 206-207; interestingly the British Official History gives the impression that access to the *Strada 124* lay outwith Bradley's competency and that Patton refused him special permission to access it; see Molony, **The Campaign in Sicily 1943**, p. 89
30. See Garland & Smyth, **Sicily and the Surrender of Italy**, pp. 224-226

31. The River Salso is sometimes referred to as the Imera Meridionale (Southern Imera)
32. Quote from Garland & Smyth, **Sicily and the Surrender of Italy**, p. 231; for other details see ibid., pp. 230-233
33. See Molony, **The Campaign in Sicily 1943**, pp.107-109
34. See Garland & Smyth, **Sicily and the Surrender of Italy**, p. 235
35. Quote from Molony, **The Campaign in Sicily 1943**, p. 109
36. 'Lode star' quote from D'Este, **Bitter Victory**, p. 413; 'mad as a wet hen' quote from Garland & Smyth, **Sicily and the Surrender of Italy**, p. 235
37. See Garland & Smyth, **Sicily and the Surrender of Italy**, p. 235
38. See Garland & Smyth, **Sicily and the Surrender of Italy**, pp. 235-236
39. See Garland & Smyth, **Sicily and the Surrender of Italy**, p. 236; for the British view see Molony, **The Campaign in Sicily 1943**, pp. 108-109
40. Entry in Patton's Diary, dated 17/07/1943; cited in D'Este, **Bitter Victory**, p. 415
41. See Bradley, **A Soldier's Story**, p. 140; and id., with Clay Blair, **A General's Life**, p. 193; cited in D'Este, **Bitter Victory**, pp. 426-427
42. See text of interview with US Historian Howard McGaw Smyth, 19/04/1951; cited in D'Este, **Bitter Victory**, p. 427; see also Garland & Smyth, **Sicily and the Surrender of Italy**, p. 200
43. Quote from conversation between Shelford Bidwell and Carlo D'Este, 09/08/1984; cited in D'Este, **Bitter Victory**, p. 427
44. 60,000 Italian troops figure cited in Garland & Smyth, **Sicily and the Surrender of Italy**, p. 238
45. See D'Este, **Bitter Victory**, pp. 414-415. D'Este refers to Lucas flying to Algiers on Thursday 15 July but this was the day before Alexander issued the Directive that spurred Patton's trip to Tunis, and the US Official History refers to Patton discussing the Directive with Lucas and other senior officers in Sicily on receiving the Directive at Midnight on Friday 16 July; see Garland & Smyth, **Sicily and the Surrender of Italy**, p. 235; Midnight receipt timing cited in Molony, **The Campaign in Sicily 1943**, p. 108
46. See Garland & Smyth, **Sicily and the Surrender of Italy**, pp. 244-245; and D'Este, **Bitter Victory**, p. 419
47. For quoted excerpts from the 18 July Directive see for example Molony, **The Campaign in Sicily 1943**, p. 109; and D'Este, **Bitter Victory**, p. 415; both sources imply that Patton was party to the framing and the content of the Directive, which does not appear to have been the case.
48. See Garland & Smyth, **Sicily and the Surrender of Italy**, p. 246 and ibid., Footnote #20; and D'Este, **Bitter Victory**, pp. 425-426
49. Quotes from Omar N. Bradley, **A Soldier's Story of the Allied Campaigns from Tunis to the Elbe** (New York: Henry Holt & Company, 1951), pp. 140, 144; cited in Garland & Smyth, **Sicily and the Surrender of Italy**, p. 246
50. See Garland & Smyth, **Sicily and the Surrender of Italy**, pp. 246-249
51. 05:00 timing cited in Garland & Smyth, **Sicily and the Surrender of Italy**, p. 249; Truscott intentions and toast cited in D'Este, **Bitter Victory**, p. 419
52. See Garland & Smyth, **Sicily and the Surrender of Italy**, pp. 237-238
53. See Molony, **The Campaign in Sicily 1943**, p. 113
54. See Garland & Smyth, **Sicily and the Surrender of Italy**, pp. 238
55. See Molony, **The Campaign in Sicily 1943**, pp. 98-100
56. See Garland & Smyth, **Sicily and the Surrender of Italy**, p. 300; for *29 Panzergrenadier Division's* deployment date to Sicily see ibid., p. 282
57. See D'Este, **Bitter Victory**, pp. 419-423; and Garland & Smyth, **Sicily and the Surrender of Italy**, p. 254

58. Quoted from D'Este, **Bitter Victory**, p. 419
59. See LoFaro, **The Sword of St. Michael**, pp. 111-113; and Garland & Smyth, **Sicily and the Surrender of Italy**, pp. 250-252
60. See D'Este, **Bitter Victory**, p. 422, Footnote †
61. See Garland & Smyth, **Sicily and the Surrender of Italy**, p. 254; and D'Este, **Bitter Victory**, p. 422, Footnotes † & ‡
62. See Garland & Smyth, **Sicily and the Surrender of Italy**, p. 254
63. See D'Este, **Bitter Victory**, p. 423 and ibid., Footnote *
64. The US Official History refers to the River Marsala rather than Sossio; see Garland & Smyth, **Sicily and the Surrender of Italy**, p. 255
65. See LoFaro, **The Sword of St. Michael**, pp. 113-114; and Garland & Smyth, **Sicily and the Surrender of Italy**, p. 255; for Lt.-Col Ireland's involvement as envoy at Trapani see Blair, **Ridgway's Paratroopers**, p. 113
66. See LoFaro, **The Sword of St. Michael**, p. 114
67. Figures cited in LoFaro, **The Sword of St. Michael**, p. 114
68. Figures and duty allocations cited in Garland & Smyth, **Sicily and the Surrender of Italy**, pp. 255-256

Chapter 19

1. See Mitcham, **The Battle of Sicily** p. 219
2. See Mitcham, **The Battle of Sicily** p. 229
3. See Von Senger, **Neither Fear nor Hope** pp. 146-147
4. See Mitcham, **The Battle of Sicily** pp. 275-276
5. Cable from Montgomery to Patton dated 23 July 1943 quoted in D'Este, **Bitter Victory** p. 443
6. Belchem, **All in the Day's March,** p 167, quoted in D'Este, **Bitter Victory,** p. 321
7. See D'Este, **Bitter Victory,** pp. 327-329
8. See Holland, **Sicily '43**, pp. 413-414
9. The story of how Montgomery 'won' his B-17 as the result of a bet is well known. However, accounts vary as to whether Monty's bet was with Smith or with Eisenhower himself.
10. See Follain, **Mussolini's Island,** p 256
11. See Hamilton, **Monty: Master of the Battlefield, 1942-1944**, p. 330
12. Quoted in D'Este, **Bitter Victory,** p 447. Monty was subsequently given a USAAF C-47 to replace the written-off B-17.
13. Most of the reliable sources confirm that Patton was not there to greet Monty at the airfield but one still finds accounts (usually unreferenced) which suggest that he was there to witness the debacle.
14. Quoted in D'Este, **Bitter Victory,** p 449.
15. See Follain, **Mussolini's Island,** p 258; and D'Este, **Bitter Victory,** p 449.
16. Strictly speaking, Operation HARDGATE would be the name that the British attributed to this operation. See Molony p. 149
17. See Garland & Smyth, **Sicily and the Surrender of Italy**, pp.245-257, and pp. 305-306
18. See Garland & Smythe, **Sicily and the Surrender of Italy**, p. 309
19. See Follain, **Mussolini's Island,** p. 263
20. See Garland & Smyth, **Sicily and the Surrender of Italy**, pp. 316-318
21. See Garland & Smythe, **Sicily and the Surrender of Italy**, pp. 301-304
22. See Molony, **The Campaign in Sicily 1943**, p. 92
23. See Garland & Smyth, **Sicily and the Surrender of Italy**, pp. 318-320
24. See Garland & Smythe, **Sicily and the Surrender of Italy**, pp 321-323
25. Quoted in Follain, **Mussolini's Island**, pp. 239-240

26. See Holland, **Sicily '43**, pp 396-397 and pp 407-408; see also Follain, **Mussolini's Island**, pp 239 -242
27. See Follain, **Mussolini's Island,** p. 249
28. See Holland, **Sicily '43**, pp. 408-409
29. Quoted in Granatstein, **The Generals**, p. 152
30. Granatstein, J.L., **The Weight of Command**, pp. 28-29
31. See Graham, **Citizen and Soldier**, p. 134
32. See Graham, **Citizen and Soldier**, pp. 143-144
33. See Graham, **Citizen and Soldier**, p. 163
34. See Nicholson, **The Canadians in Italy 1943-1945**, p. 118
35. See Graham, **Citizen and Soldier**, p. 174
36. See Graham, **Citizen and Soldier**, pp. 174-175
37. See Nicholson, **The Canadians in Italy 1943-1945**, pp. 127-128
38. See Nicholson, **The Canadians in Italy 1943-1945**, 127-130
39. See Nicholson, **The Canadians in Italy 1943-1945**, pp. 137-139
40. See Grehan & Mace, **The War in Italy 1943-1944**, p. 23
41. See Hinsley, **British Intelligence in the Second World War**, pp. 346-347
42. See Kesselring, **The Memoirs of Field-Marshal Kesselring**, p. 165
43. See Bossanyi, **The Sicilian Campaign – An Axis Viewpoint**
44. See Kesselring, **The Memoirs of Field-Marshal Kesselring**, pp. 163-165
45. See Holland, **Sicily '43**, p. 414

Chapter 20

1. The 29th Panzer Grenadier Division had been brought onto the island piecemeal. First to arrive (around 16 July) had been Colonel Max Ulich's 15th Panzer Grenadier Regiment which was in action around Catania before moving north to help stop the US 45th Division's drive along the northern coast road from Palermo. The bulk of the Division, together with its divisional commander, crossed on 18 July with the remainder (less the Armoured Reconnaissance Battalion and Tank Battalion) ordered to follow on four days later. The Reconnaissance and Tank Battalions were retained on the Calabrian mainland for coastal protection duties. See Nicholson, **The Canadians in Italy 1943-1945**, pp. 116-117.
2. Lt-Gen Richard Heidrich, commander of the 1st Parachute Division and a veteran of the Eastern Front, was most unhappy with these arrangements, which would see him and his divisional staff side-lined and kept back on the Italian mainland. See Mitcham, **The Battle of Sicily** p. 142
3. See Garland & Smyth, **Sicily and the Surrender of Italy**, p. 320
4. **Report of Operations of II Corps in the Sicilian Campaign dated 1 Sep 43,** quoted in D'Este, **Bitter Victory,** p 457
5. See D'Este, **Bitter Victory**, p. 463
6. See Garland & Smyth, **Sicily and the Surrender of Italy**, p. 336
7. Carlo D'Este writes at length about the machinations which would lead to Allen's removal from combat duties in Sicily. See D'Este, **Bitter Victory,** pp. 468-475
8. Flint was not without personal bravery. During the battle for Troina he made himself identifiable by walking about the front lines bare-chested with a helmet, black silk scarf (he called it his lucky necktie), rifle in hand, often rolling a cigarette as he went. Deliberately exposing himself to German fire, Flint would contemptuously wave his hand towards their positions and say, 'See, there's nothing to be afraid of. The damn Krauts couldn't hit anything in the last war; they can't hit anything in this war. They can't even hit an old buck like me.' Quoted in D'Este, **Bitter Victory**, p. 460.

9. 1st Division G2 Journal dated 29 July 43, as quoted in Garland & Smyth, **Sicily and the Surrender of Italy**, p. 325
10. See Hulse, Pete and Dean, Don, **91st Cavalry Reconnaissance Squadron and WWII**, pp. 66-67
11. See Garland & Smyth, **Sicily and the Surrender of Italy**, pp. 331-333
12. See Mitcham, **The Battle of Sicily** p. 248
13. See Garland & Smyth, **Sicily and the Surrender of Italy**, p. 337
14. See D'Este, **Bitter Victory**, p. 460
15. See Garland & Smyth, **Sicily and the Surrender of Italy**, p. 340
16. As a result of the fighting on 5 August, 23-year-old Pvt James W Reese, a mortarman, was awarded a posthumous Medal of Honor. His citation reads in part: 'When the enemy launched a counterattack which threatened the position of his company, Pvt. Reese, as the acting squad leader of a 60-mm mortar squad, displayed superior leadership on his own initiative, maneuvered his squad forward to a favorable position from which, by skillfully directing the fire of his weapon, he caused many casualties in the enemy ranks, and aided materially in repulsing the counterattack. When the enemy fire became so severe as to make his position untenable, he ordered the other members of his squad to withdraw to a safer position, but declined to seek safety for himself. So as to bring more effective fire upon the enemy, Pvt. Reese, without assistance, moved his mortar to a new position and attacked an enemy machine-gun nest. He had only three rounds of ammunition but secured a direct hit with his last round, completely destroying the nest and killing the occupants. Ammunition being exhausted, he abandoned the mortar, seized a rifle, and continued to advance, moving into an exposed position overlooking the enemy. Despite a heavy concentration of machine-gun, mortar, and artillery fire, the heaviest experienced by his unit throughout the entire Sicilian campaign, he remained at this position and continued to inflict casualties upon the enemy until he was killed.'
17. On 8 August Kesselring recalled von Senger making Hube officially the senior German officer on the island. See Von Senger, **Neither Fear nor Hope**, p. 147
18. For the moment the withdrawal notice would not apply to Fries's 29th Panzer Grenadier Regiment which was still effectively holding Truscott's 3rd Division at bay on the northern coastal highway.
19. In a battle that was expected to be over in a day but in the end took six days, American casualties were so high that Bradley was appalled. Terry Allen and his assistant divisional commander, Theodore Roosevelt Jr, took most of the blame and were removed from command, albeit 'without prejudice'. But both Bradley and Patton played their part too; Patton by setting the tone of the 'Race to Messina' and Bradley for not anticipating and allocating sufficient resources to Allen when a quick 'win' proved elusive.
20. See Garland & Smyth, **Sicily and the Surrender of Italy**, p. 358
21. See Holland, **Sicily '43**, p. 414
22. See Garland & Smyth, **Sicily and the Surrender of Italy**, p. 320
23. The four possible landing areas were: just east of Sant Agata; west of Brolo; near Patti; and at Barcellona
24. For a detailed blow-by-blow account of the fighting to break the Axis defence on the Etna Line around San Fratello see Garland & Smyth, **Sicily and the Surrender of Italy**, pp. 348-367
25. A report submitted to Kesselring after the 923rd Fortress Battalion had bolted read: 'The battalion fled in the direction of Centuripe in a shameful manner without enemy pressure. The immediate dissolution of the battalion has been ordered.'

In September Field Marshal Keitel instigated a court-martial of the CO and all of his officers. See D'Este, **Bitter Victory**, p. 437.

26. Hugh Pond, **Sicily**, as quoted in Mitcham, **The Battle of Sicily** p. 242
27. Mitcham, **The Battle of Sicily** p. 242
28. Wimberley was not the only senior commander to be relieved at this time. Berney-Ficklin, commander of the 5th Division, was also relieved of his command on 3 August and for much the same reason; both Dempsey, his corps commander, and Monty believing that he was now too old and tired for field command. See Rostron, **The Military Life of General Sir Miles Dempsey**, p.66
29. See D'Este, **Bitter Victory**, pp. 409-410
30. Quoted in Brown, **Scotland on the Frontline**
31. The Division remained on the island for a further three months. On 4 November 1943, and as one of its last acts, it would build and dedicate a monument to the Division's achievements in Sicily. Constructed as a simple stone cairn with an inlaid Celtic cross it marked the start line for the final attack on the Sferro Hills. It still stands today on a ridgeline overlooking the Dittaino River, facing towards Mount Etna and with the battlefield in full view.
32. See Ford, **Battleaxe Division**, p.64
33. Quoted in Ford, **Battleaxe Division**,. p.2
34. See Holland, **Sicily '43**, p. 444
35. See Ford, **Battleaxe Division**, p.65
36. See Ford, **Battleaxe Division**. p.67
37. See D'Este, **Bitter Victory**, p. 504
38. See Mitcham, **The Battle of Sicily** pp. 275-276
39. Quoted in Nicholson, **The Canadians in Italy 1943-1945**, p. 147
40. See Fitzgerald-Black, **Eagles over Husky**, pp, 121-122
41. See Zuehlke, **Operation Husky**, p.377
42. Bowman eventually managed to lead his men northwards through the heart of the town and, miraculously avoiding all of the German positions, reach the safety of the 48th Highlanders lines on Monte Serione. An action for which he was awarded an MC.
43. RCR After Action Report held in the National Archives of Canada, RG24, Volume 10880
44. See Nicholson, **The Canadians in Italy 1943-1945**, p. 152
45. See Molony, **The Campaign in Sicily 1943**, p. 174
46. See Nicholson, **The Canadians in Italy 1943-1945**, p. 154
47. See Nicholson, **The Canadians in Italy 1943-1945**, p. 163
48. Quoted in Ford, **Battleaxe Division**, p.71

Chapter 21

1. Field Marshal Maurice Comte de Saxe (1732) as quoted in The Greenhill Dictionary of Military Quotations ed. Peter G Tsouras (London: Greenhill Books, 2004) p.239
2. See Holland, **Sicily '43**, p. 408 and D'Este, **Bitter Victory**, p. 432
3. See Garland & Smyth, **Sicily and the Surrender of Italy**, p. 375
4. See Mitcham, **The Battle of Sicily** p. 272
5. Kesselring, **Memoirs**, p. 165. However, Jodl also claimed credit for this decision stating that it was he that had ordered Kesselring to begin the evacuation and that he had done it without Hitler's prior knowledge. Indeed Hitler did not order the evacuation until 16 August by which time it was almost complete. See D'Este, **Bitter Victory**, p. 506

6. See Mitcham, **The Battle of Sicily** p. 272
7. See Ford, **Battleaxe Division**, pp.74-75
8. The 6th Duke returned to Bronte after the war and regained possession of his estate. It was eventually sold by his son in 1981. By a quirk of history, the last administrator of the estate, Frank Edward King, had fought in Sicily during the campaign. The family house has now been turned into a museum and tourist attraction.
9. See Fitzgerald-Black, **Eagles over Husky**, p. 128
10. See Clay, **The Path of the 50th**, p. 205
11. Quoted from his Despatch in Roskill, **The War at Sea, 1939-1945**, pp. 142-143.
12. See Roskill, **The War at Sea, 1939-1945**, p. 143
13. See Fitzgerald-Black, **Eagles over Husky**, pp. 129-130
14. See Truscott, **Command Missions**, p. 235
15. See Bradley, **A Soldier's Story**, pp. 157-158
16. See Garland & Smyth, **Sicily and the Surrender of Italy**, p. 390
17. See Truscott, **Command Missions**, p. 238-239
18. Blumenson, **Sicily**, p. 143
19. See Mitcham, **The Battle of Sicily** p. 265
20. See Clay, **The Path of the 50th**, p. 210
21. See Mitcham, **The Battle of Sicily** p. 291
22. See Clay, **The Path of the 50th**, p. 214
23. See Truscott, **Command Missions**, pp. 242-243

Epilogue

1. Combined Operations HQ Bulletin Y/1 dated October 1943 and quoted in Pond, **Sicily**, p. 220
2. Mitcham, **The Battle of Sicily** p. 291
3. These figures are from the OB South papers and are quoted in Mitcham, **The Battle of Sicily** p. 297
4. D'Este, **Bitter Victory**, p. 559
5. Holland, **Sicily '43**, p. 490
6. The definitions of *joint* and *combined* operations have reversed since the Second World War, but in 1943 a joint operation was defined as one which involved the armed forces of more than one nation acting in concert whereas a combined operation was one which involved two or more services of a single nation.
7. See Grehan & Mace, **The War in Italy 1943-1944**, pp. 36-37
8. Garland & Smyth, **Sicily and the Surrender of Italy**, p. 106
9. See Roskill, **The War at Sea, 1939-1945**, p. 146
10. See Roskill, **The War at Sea, 1939-1945**,. p. 147
11. Air Historical Branch Report: The Sicilian Campaign June-August 1943, p. 18
12. These and the previous quotations are all from the Air Historical Branch Report
13. See Fitzgerald-Black, **Eagles over Husky**, p. 146

Bibliography

Primary Sources

UK National Archive Files

AIR 8/1346 Operation 'Husky'

AIR 23/824 Operation 'Husky': Planning

AIR 27/1644 No. 295 Squadron Operations Record Book

AIR 27/1645 No. 296 Squadron Operations Record Book

CAB 106/368 Sicily: Diary of Events and Correspondence Relating to the Planning of Operation 'Husky' 1943 Jan.-July

WO 214/20 Sicilian Campaign: Planning and Preparations: Earl Alexander of Tunis, Supreme Allied Commander Mediterranean Theatre: Papers

WO 169/8666 1 Airborne Division HQ War Diary 01 July 1943 – 31 December 1943

WO 169/8668 1 Airborne Division: Royal Artillery (RA) HQ War Diary 01 July 1943 – 31 December 1943

WO 169/8669 1 Airborne Division: Royal Engineers (RE) HQ War Diary 01 July 1943 – 31 December 1943

WO 169/8671 1 Airborne Division: Commander Royal Army Service Corps (RASC) HQ War Diary 1943 July – Sept.

WO 169/8672 1 Airborne Division: Ordnance Field Park (Ord Fd Pk) 01 April 1943 – 31 December 1943

WO 169/8673 1 Airborne Division: Divisional Workshop REME War Diary 01 July 1943 – 31 December 1943

WO 169/8674 1 Airborne Division: Recce Squadron War Diary July 1943

WO 169/8675 1 Airborne Division: Provost Company CMP War Diary 01 July 1943 – 31 December 1943

WO 169/8837 1 Parachute Brigade HQ War Diary 1943 July, Sept. – Nov.

WO 169/8838 1 Parachute Brigade: Signals War Diary 1943 July

WO 169/8845 1 Airlanding Brigade: HQ War Diary 01 July 1943 – 31 December 1943

WO 169/10182 1 Border Regiment War Diary 1943 July – Sept., Oct., Dec.

WO 169/10299 2 South Staffordshire Regiment War Diary 1943 June – Dec.

WO 169/10341 1 Battalion Glider Pilot Regiment War Diary 1943 July – Dec.

WO 169/10343 1 Parachute Regiment War Diary 01 July 1943 – 31 December 1943

WO 169/10344 2 Parachute Regiment War Diary 01 July 1943 – 31 December 1943

WO 169/10345 3 Parachute Regiment War Diary 1943 July

WO 169/10357 21 Independent Parachute Company War Diary 1943 Jan. – Apr., July, Aug., Nov., Dec.

WO 169/10554 1 Parachute Squadron (RE Para Sqn) War Diary 01 July 1943 – 31 December 1943

WO 169/10576 9 RE Fd Coy (Field Company) War Diary 01 July 1943 – 30 November 1943

WO 169/10677 261 RE Fd Pk Coy (Field Park Company) War Diary 1943 July – Oct.

WO 169/12670 1 Air Landing Light Aid Detachment (REME LAD) War Diary 1943 April – July

WO175/111 1 Airlanding Light Regiment RA War Diary

WO 175/316 1 Air Landing [Anti-Tank] Battery RA War Diary 1942 – 1943

WO 175/526 2 Para. Regt. (2nd Parachute Battalion) War Diary 1942 November – 1943 May

WO177/359 ADMS 1 Airborne Division HQ War Diary 1941 – 1945

WO 177/701 16 Field Ambulance (PARA) RAMC War Diary 01 April 1942 – 30 November 1944

WO 177/775 181 Airlanding Field Ambulance RAMC War Diary 1939 – 1945

US Naval History and Heritage Command Files

File No. A16-3/N31, Serial: 00872 Hewitt, Vice-Admiral H. K. US Navy, 'Action Report Western Naval Task Force: The Sicilian Campaign: Operation HUSKY July-August 1943' accessible at https://www.history.navy.mil/research/library/online-reading-room/title-list-alphabetically/s/the-sicilian-campaign-operation-husky.html

Unpublished Sources

Lyle, Major James B., **The Operations of Companies 'A' and 'B' First Ranger Battalion, at Gela, Sicily 10-11 July 1943 (Personal Experience of a Company Commander)**, (Advanced Infantry Officers Course 1948-1949: The Infantry School General Subjects Section, Fort Benning, Georgia, n.d.)

Sayre, Major Edwin M., **The Operations of Company A, 505th Parachute Infantry (82nd Airborne Division), Airborne Landings in Sicily 9-24 July 1943 (Sicily Campaign) (Personal Experience of a Company Commander)** General Section, Military History Committee, The Infantry School, 10 November 1947

Published Sources

Official Publications

Air Ministry, **The Second World War 1939-1945 Royal Air Force: Air Publication 3231: Airborne Forces** (London: Air Ministry, 1951: facsimile The Naval & Military Press, n.d.)

Boileau, D.W., **Supplies and Transport: Vol 1** (London: War Office, 1954)

Buchanan, AGB, Works Services and Engineer Stores (London: War Office, 1953)

Carter, JAH & Kann, DN, **Maintenance in the Field: Vol 2 – 1943-1945** (London: War Office, 1961)

Garland, Lieutenant-Colonel Albert N. and Howard McGaw Smyth, **Sicily and the Surrender of Italy** (Washington DC: Office of the Chief of Military History, Department of the Army, 1993)

HMSO, **By Air to Battle: The Official Account of the British First and Sixth Airborne Divisions** (London: HMSO, 1945)

Howe, George F., **Northwest Africa: Seizing the Initiative in the West** (Washington DC: Office of the Chief of Military History, Department of the Army, 1993)

Maurer, Maurer (Ed.), **Air Force Combat Units of World War II** (Washington DC: Office of Air Force History, 1983)

Mayo, Lida **The Ordnance Department: On Beachhead and Battlefront** (Washington DC: Center of Military History, United States Army, 1991)

Molony, Brigadier C.J.C. **The Mediterranean and Middle East Volume V: The Campaign in Sicily 1943 and The Campaign in Italy 3rd September 1943 to 31st March 1944** (London: HMSO, 1973)

Morison, Samuel Eliot, **History of United States Naval Operations in World War II, Volume IX: Sicily-Salerno-Anzio January 1943-June 1944** (Boston Mass.: Little, Brown and Company, 1954)

Nicholson, Lieutenant-Colonel G. W. L., **Official History of the Canadian Army in the Second World War, Volume II: The Canadians in Italy 1943-1945** (Ottawa: Edmund Cloutier, 1957)

Otway, Lieutenant-Colonel T.B.H. DSO **The Second World War 1939-1945 Army: Airborne Forces** (London: War Office, 1950: facsimile Imperial War Museum, 1990)

Pakenham-Walsh, Major-General RP, **History of the Corps of Royal Engineers Vol IX** (Chatham: The Institution of Royal Engineers, 1958)

Playfair, Major-General I.S.O., **The Mediterranean and Middle East: Volume IV: The Destruction of the Axis Forces in Africa** (London: HMSO, 1966; facsimile Naval & Military Press, 2004)

Warren, John Cushman, **Airborne Missions in the Mediterranean 1942-1945**, USAF Historical Studies: No. 74 (Maxwell AFB, Alabama: US Air Force Historical Division, Research Studies Institute, 1955: facsimile Ashok Vihar, Delhi, 2015)

Published Works

Alford, Richard, **The memoirs of Field Marshal the Viscount Montgomery of Alamein** (London: Collins, 1958)

Barnes, Barrie S, **The Bloody Road to Catania: A History of XIII Corps in Sicily 1943** (Warwick: Helion & Company, 2021)

Baynes, John, **Urquhart of Arnhem: The Life of Major General R. E. Urquhart CB, DSO** (London: Brassey's, 1993)

Bekker, Cajus, **The Luftwaffe War Diaries** (New York: Elek, 1966)

Belcham, Maj-Gen David, **All in the Day's March** (London, 1978)

Bennett, Ralph, **Ultra and Mediterranean Strategy, 1941-45** (London: Hamish Hamilton, 1989)

Blair, Clay, **Ridgway's Paratroopers: The American Airborne in World War II** (New York: Quill William Morrow, 1985)

Blumenson, Martin, **The Patton Papers, Vol 2, 1940-1945** (New York: Da Capo Press, 1966)

Bradley, Omar N., **A Soldier's Story of the Allied Campaigns from Tunis to the Elbe** (New York: Henry Holt & Company, 1951)

Id. With Clay Blair, **A General's Life: An Autobiography by General of the Army Omar N. Bradley** (New York: Simon & Schuster, 1983)

Breuer, William B., **Drop Zone Sicily: Allied Airborne Strike, July 1943** (Novato CA: Presidio Press, 1983)

Brookes, Andrew, **Air War over Italy** (London: Ian Allen, 2000)

Brooks, Stephen, **Montgomery and the Eighth Army: A selection from the diaries, correspondence and other papers of Field Marshal The Viscount Montgomery of Alamein, August 1942 to December 1943** (London: Bodley Head for the Army Records Society, 1991)

Brown, Chris, **Scotland on the Frontline: A Photo History of Scottish Forces 1939-1945** (Stroud: The History Press, 2012)

Buckingham, William F., **Paras: The Birth of British Airborne Forces from Churchill's Raiders to 1st Parachute Brigade** (Stroud: Tempus Publishing, 2005)

____ **Arnhem: The Complete Story of Operation MARKET GARDEN, 17-25 September 1944** (Stroud: Amberley Publishing, 2019)

Burriss, T. Moffatt, **Strike and Hold: A Memoir of the 82nd Airborne in World War II** (Dulles, Virginia: Brassey's Inc., 2000)

Chalmers, William Scott, **Full Cycle: The autobiography of Admiral Sir Bertram Home Ramsey** (London: Hodder & Stoughton, 1959)

Churchill, Thomas BL, **Command Crusade** (Kimber, 1987)

Cole, David, **Rough road to Rome: a foot soldier in Sicily and Italy 1943-1944** (Kimber, 1983)

Cole, Lieutenant-Colonel Howard N. OBE, **On Wings of Healing: The Story of the Airborne Medical Services 1940-1960** (London: William Blackwood & Sons Ltd., 1963)

D'Este, Carlo, **Bitter Victory: The Battle for Sicily, 1943** (London: Collins, 1988)

D'Este, Carlo, **A Genius for War: A Life of General George S Patton** (London: Harper Collins, 1995)

D'Este, Carlo, **World War II in the Mediterranean 1942-1945** (Algonquin, 1990)

De Guingand, Francis Wilfred, **Operation Victory** (London: Hodder & Stoughton, 1947)

Devlin, Gerard M., **Paratrooper! The Saga of US Army and Marine Parachute and Glider Combat Troops During World War II** (New York: St. Martin's Press, 1979)

____ **Silent Wings: The Story of the Glider Pilots of World War II** (London: W.H. Allen, 1985)

Durnford-Slater, John, **Commando** (Barnsley: Greenhill Books, 2020)

Eastwood, Stuart A., Charles Gray & Alan T. Green, **When Dragons Flew: An Illustrated History of the 1st Battalion The Border Regiment 1939-45** (Kettering: Silver Link Publishing, 1994)

Evans, Bryn, **The Decisive Campaigns of the Desert Air Force 1943-1945** (Barnsley: Pen & Sword, 2014)

Evans, Bryn, **With the East Surreys in Tunisia, Sicily and Italy 1942-1945: Fighting for Every River and Mountain** (Barnsley: Pen & Sword, 2014)

Falvey, Denis, **A well-known excellence: British artillery and artilleryman in World War Two** (London: Brassey's, 2002)

Farrar-Hockley, General Sir Anthony, **The Army in the Air: The History of the Army Air Corps** (Stroud: Sutton Publishing, 1994)

Fergusson, Brigadier Sir Bernard DSO, **Watery Maze: The Story of Combined Operations** (London: Collins, 1961)

Fitzgerald-Black, Alexander, **Eagles over Husky: The Allied Air Forces in the Sicilian Campaign, 14 May to 17 August 1943** (Warwick: Helion & Company, 2017)

Follain, John, **Mussolini's Island: The Invasion of Sicily Through the Eyes of Those Who Witnessed the Campaign** (London: Hodder & Stoughton, 2005)

Ford, Ken, **Battleaxe Division: From Africa to Italy with the 78th Division, 1942-45** (Stroud: Sutton Publishing, 2003)

Ford, Ken, **Assault on Sicily: Monty and Patton at War** (Stroud: Sutton Publishing, 2007)

Frost, Major-General John CB DSO MC **A Drop Too Many** (London: Sphere, 1983)

Gavin, James M., **On to Berlin: Battles of an Airborne Commander, 1943-1946** (London: Leo Cooper, 1979)

Golden, Lewis OBE, **Echoes from Arnhem** (London: Kimber, 1984)

Gooderson, Ian, **Air Power at the Battlefront: Allied Close Air Support in Europe, 1943-45** (London: Frank Cass, 1998)

Graham, Howard, **Citizen and Soldier: The Memoirs of Lieutenant-General Howard Graham** (Toronto: McClelland and Stewart, 1987)

Granatstein, J.L., **The Generals: The Canadian Army's Senior Commanders in the Second World War** (Calgary: University of Calgary Press, 2005)

Granatstein, J.L., **The Weight of Command: Voices of Canada's Second World War Generals and Those that Knew Them** (Vancouver: UBC Press, 2016)

Grehan, John & Martin Mace, **The War in Italy 1943-1944** (Barnsley: Pen & Sword Books Ltd., 2014)

Grehan, John & Martin Mace, **Operations in North Africa and the Middle East 1942-1944** (Barnsley: Pen & Sword Books Ltd., 2015)
Hamilton, Nigel, **Monty: Master of the Battlefield, 1942-1944** [London: Hamish Hamilton, 1983]
Henniker, Mark, **An Image of War** (London: Leo Cooper, 1987)
Hinsley, F.H. **British Intelligence in the Second World War** (Abridged Edition) (London: HMSO, 1994)
Holland, James, **Sicily '43: The First Assault on Fortress Europe** (London: Bantam Press, 2020)
Horrocks, Sir Brian, **Corps Commander** (London: Sidgewick & Jackson, 1977)
Howard, Michael, **British Intelligence in the Second World War: Volume 5: Strategic Deception** (London: HMSO, 1990)
Jones, John Philip, **Battles of a Gunner Officer: Tunisia, Sicily Normandy and the Long Road to Germany: Based on the Unpublished Diary of Major Peter Pettit DSO, TD, HAC** (Barnsley: Praetorian Press, 2014)
Jorgensen, Starlyn R., **History of the 456th Parachute Field Artillery Battalion** (Unpublished: Starlyn R. Jorgensen, 1998)
Kent, Ron, **First In! Parachute Pathfinder Company: A History of the 21st Independent Parachute Company** (London: Batsford, 1979)
Jary, Christopher, **Roy's Boys: The Devons, Hampshires & Dorsets in Sicily & Italy July-September 1943** (Semper Fidelis Publications, 2021)
Kesselring, Field Marshal Albert, **The Memoirs of Field-Marshal Kesselring,** (London: Greenhill Books, 2007)
Ladd, James **Commandos and Rangers of World War II** (London: Book Club Associates by arrangement with McDonald & Jane's Limited, 1978)
LoFaro, Guy, **The Sword of St. Michael: The 82nd Airborne Division in World War II** (Cambridge Mass.: Da Capo Press, 2011)
Marks, Clayton D., **Combined Operations: The Organization that Planned Allied Raids and Invasions During World War II** (London, Ontario: Andrea Martens, 2016)
Millar, George, **The Bruneval Raid: Flashpoint in the Radar War** (London: Bodley Head, 1974)
Miller, Victor, **Nothing is Impossible: A Glider Pilot's Story of Sicily, Arnhem and the Rhine Crossing** (Staplehurst: Spellmount, 1994)
Mitchum Jr, Samuel W & von Stauffenberg, Friedrich, **The Battle of Sicily** (New York: Orion Books, 1991)
Morris, Eric, **Circles of Hell: The War in Italy 1943-1945** (London: Hutchinson, 1993)
Mowat, Farley, **The Regiment** (Toronto: McClelland and Stewart, 1955)
Mowat, Farley, **And No Birds Sang** (Toronto: McClelland and Stewart, 1979)
Munsell, Warren P., **The Story of a Regiment, A History of the 179th Regimental Combat Team** (New York: Warren P. Munsell Jr., 1946)
Nordyke, Phil, **All American All the Way: From Sicily to Normandy: A Combat History of the 82nd Airborne Division in World War II** (Minneapolis MN: Zenith Books, 2009)
____ **Four Stars of Valor: The Combat History of the 505th Parachute Infantry Regiment in World War II** (Minneapolis MN: Zenith Books, 2010)
Otway, Lieutenant-Colonel T.B.H. DSO **Airborne Forces** (London: Imperial War Museum, 1990)
Pack, S.W.C. **Operation HUSKY: The Allied Invasion of Sicily** (London: David & Charles, 1977)
Peters, Mike, **Glider Pilots in Sicily** (Barnsley: Pen & Sword Military, 2012)
Pitt, Barry, **The Crucible of War, Volume II: Auchinleck's Command** (London: Cassell & Co., 2001)
____ **The Crucible of War Volume III: Montgomery and Alamein** (London: Cassell, 2001)

Pond, Hugh, **Sicily** (London: William Kimber, 1962)
Rolf, David, **The Bloody Road to Tunis: Destruction of the Axis Forces in North Africa, November 1942 – May 1943** (London: Frontline Books, 2015)
Rostron, Peter, **The Military Life & Times of General Sir Miles Dempsey: Monty's Army Commander** (Barnsley: Pen & Sword Military, 2010)
Saunders, Hilary St. George, **The Red Beret: The Story of the Parachute Regiment at War 1940-1945** (London: Michael Joseph, 1950)
Id, **The Green Beret: The Story of the Commandos 1940-1945** (London: Michael Joseph, 1949)
Shannon, Kevin and Stephen Wright, **One Night in June** (Shrewsbury: Airlife Publishing, 2000)
Shore, Christopher and Giovanni Massimello, **A History of the Mediterranean Air War, 1940-1945: Volume 3: Tunisia and the End in Africa, November 1942-May 1943** (London: Grub Street, 2016)
Stainforth, Peter, **Wings of the Wind: Active Service with the 1st Parachute Brigade** (London: Grafton Books, 1988)
Steinhoff, Johannes, **Messerschmitts over Sicily: Luftwaffe ace fighting the Allies and Göring** (Barnsley: Pen & Sword Aviation, 2004)
Tedder, Lord, **With Prejudice: The War Memoirs of Marshal of the Royal Air Force Lord Tedder** (London: Cassell, 1966)
Thompson, Julian, **Ready for Anything: The Parachute Regiment at War 1940-1982** (London: Weidenfeld & Nicolson, 1989)
Truesdale, David, **Brotherhood of the Cauldron: Irishmen in the 1st Airborne Division from North Africa to Arnhem** (Newtonard, Co. Down: Redcoat Publishing, 2002)
Truscott, Lt Gen LK Jnr, **Command Missions: A Personal Story** (New York: EP Dutton and Co, 1954)
Tugwell, Maurice **Airborne to Battle: A History of Airborne Warfare 1918-1971** (London: Kimber, 1971)
Turnbull, Jack and John Hamblett, **The Pegasus Patrol** (Marple, Cheshire: 1994)
Von Senger und Etterlin, General Frido, **Neither Fear nor Hope** (London: Macdonald, 1963)
Warner, Philip, **Horrocks: The General Who Led from the Front** (London: Sphere, 1985)
Wedemeyer, General Albert C., **Wedemeyer Reports!** (New York: Holt, 1958)
Whiting, Charles, **Slaughter over Sicily** (Leo Cooper, 1992)
Wright, Lawrence, **The Wooden Sword: The Untold Story of the Gliders in World War II** (London: Elek, 1967)
Zuehlke, Mark, **Operation Husky: The Canadian Invasion of Sicily, July 10 – August 7, 1943** (Vancouver: Douglas & McIntyre, 2010)

Magazine and Periodical Articles

Borch, Fred, '*War Crimes in Sicily: Sergeant West, Captain Compton, and the Murder of Prisoners of War in 1943*', **The Army Lawyer** (March 2013); available at https://www.loc.gov/rr/frd/Military_Law/pdf/03-2013.pdf
Bossanyi, Col. B, '*The Sicilian Campaign – An Axis Viewpoint*', Command and General Staff School (Fort Leavenworth) Review Vol XXIII No. 9 (December 1943)

Websites

Harrison, Gord, **1000 Men, 1000 Stories: Canadians in Combined Operations, WW2** website at http://wavynavy.blogspot.com/, accessed 16/01/2021
Hulse, Pete and Dean, Don, **91st Cavalry Reconnaissance Squadron and WWII**, at https://www.flickr.com/photos/nam_wolfhound/albums/72157626113865926/

Index